ROUTLEDGE HANDE
OF FAMILY LAW AND POLICY

Changes in family structures, demographics, social attitudes and economic policies over the last 60 years have had a large impact on family lives and correspondingly on family law.

The Second Edition of this Handbook draws upon recent developments to provide a comprehensive and up-to-date global perspective on the policy challenges facing family law and policy round the world. The chapters apply legal, sociological, demographic and social work research to explore the most significant issues that have been commanding the attention of family law policymakers in recent years. Featuring contributions from renowned global experts, the book draws on multiple jurisdictions and offers comparative analysis across a range of countries. The book addresses a range of issues, including the role of the state in supporting families and protecting the vulnerable, children's rights and parental authority, sexual orientation, same-sex unions and gender in family law, and the status of marriage and other forms of adult relationships. It also focuses on divorce and separation and their consequences, the relationship between civil law and the law of minority groups, refugees and migrants, and the movement of family members between jurisdictions along with assisted conception, surrogacy and adoption.

This advanced-level reference work will be essential reading for students, researchers and scholars of family law and social policy as well as policymakers in the field.

John Eekelaar is Emeritus Fellow of Pembroke College, Oxford University, UK.

Rob George is Associate Professor of Family Law at University College London, UK and a barrister at Harcourt Chambers, Temple, London.

ROUTLEDGE HANDBOOK OF FAMILY LAW AND POLICY

Second Edition

Edited by John Eekelaar and Rob George

LONDON AND NEW YORK

First published 2021
by Routledge
2 Park Square, Milton Park, Abingdon, Oxon OX14 4RN

and by Routledge
52 Vanderbilt Avenue, New York, NY 10017

Routledge is an imprint of the Taylor & Francis Group, an informa business

First edition published by Routledge 2014

British Library Cataloguing-in-Publication Data
A catalogue record for this book is available from the British Library

Library of Congress Cataloging-in-Publication Data
A catalog record for this book has been requested

ISBN: 978-0-367-19552-6 (hbk)
ISBN: 978-0-367-52821-8 (pbk)
ISBN: 978-1-003-05851-9 (ebk)

Typeset in Bembo
by Apex CoVantage, LLC

CONTENTS

PREFACE TO THE SECOND EDITION

The Covid-19 pandemic began as the book was at its proof stage. It is likely that this could have significant social and economic consequences which could affect issues discussed in this book. Whatever these consequences may be, the discussions in this Handbook will provide an important baseline indicating the state of affairs immediately before whatever new reality began to emerge.

This Handbook is about family law *and* policy. The linkage is crucial and determines the orientation of all the contributions. These do not aim at exposition of sets of legal provisions or even, primarily, at analysis of the differences between the laws of various jurisdictions. Rather, as it was in the First Edition, the purpose has been to focus on the most significant *issues* that have been commanding the attention of family law policymakers (among which we include the courts) in recent years, rather than attempt at an encyclopaedic catalogue of legal provisions. Of course this requires a certain degree of legal exposition. But policy issues may be similar in varying legal contexts, so the legal details are usually of less interest than the overall direction of policy.

For that reason we have sometimes felt able to concentrate on a specific jurisdiction or jurisdictions as exemplars of how they are dealing with policy issues which are also likely to arise in other jurisdictions. Hence the Netherlands and South Africa provide striking cases of possible strategies regarding the recognition of diverse forms of family living (Chapters 1.2 and 1.3); Canada has developed new ways of settling post-divorce financial problems (Chapter 2.7); the UK has pioneered regulation of assisted reproductive technologies (Chapter 3.1) (with Australia providing contrasting approaches between its states: Chapter 3.2) and is struggling with how to respond to domestic abuse (Chapter 5.2) and growing pressures on the child protection system despite economic austerity (Chapter 4.1). The United States provides particularly vivid examples of significant policy debates concerning the role of marriage (Chapter 1.1) and its extension to same-sex couples (Chapter 1.4), as well as policy responses to family migration (Chapter 7.3).

Elsewhere a more comparative approach is adopted. Sometimes this is within chapters, for example, regarding post-divorce property and finances (Chapter 2.6) and inheritance (Chapter 2.8); or between different European regions regarding family support (Chapter 6.1); or more globally concerning divorce law (Chapter 2.1), divorce trends (Chapter 2.2), unmarried cohabitation (Chapters 1.2 and 1.5), issues concerning gender (Chapter 5.1) and access to family justice (Chapter 6.5). At other times, the comparison is found across separate chapters; for example concerning post-divorce parenting (Chapters 3.3–3.5), divorce law (Chapters 2.1, 2.3–2.5), family support (Chapters 6.1–6.2), care of the elderly (Chapters 6.3–6.4) and policies involving the removal of children from their families (Chapters 4.1–4.4).

In some areas a potential (but seldom completely effective) means for achieving a common policy approach is found in international instruments, such as the UN Convention on the Rights of the Child (Chapter 4.6), the African Charter on the Rights and Welfare of the Child (Chapter 4.5), the UN Convention on the Elimination of all Forms of Discrimination against Women (Chapter 5.1), the Hague Conventions on Child Abduction and Intercountry Adoption (Chapter 7.1) and the Hague Convention on Parental Responsibility and Child Protection along with its EU equivalent in the Brussels II Revised Regulation, as well as attempts at the international level to find a common approach to relocation cases (Chapter 7.2). The European Convention on Human Rights has had an important influence on discrete policy areas, for example, with regard to parental rights and some aspects children's rights (Chapters 3.3, 4.1 and 4.6).

Most of the authors in this Second Edition were also contributors to the First Edition. The changes and updates that they have made to their chapters have in many cases been extensive – some more or less starting over again – which reflects the significant developments in law and policy in their respective areas over the six years since the First Edition of this book.

As before, we express our deepest appreciation to all the contributors to this book. They do not hold identical views on all the issues; that would not be expected. But they have presented the policy landscape as they see it, including the rich body of literature that accompanies it. The result should be both informative and enlightening.

John Eekelaar
Rob George
February 2020

CONTRIBUTORS

Waheeda Amien (BA LLB (Cape Town), LLM (Western Cape), LLD (Ghent)) is an associate professor in the Faculty of Law, University of Cape Town. She specializes in family law, religion, culture and human rights with a focus on Muslim personal law and women's rights.

Masha Antokolskaia is Professor of Family Law at the VU University Amsterdam; Head of the Amsterdam Centre of Family Law ACFL; Chair of the Family Law in Europe Academic Community FL-EUR, https://fl-eur.eu/; Member of the Executive Council of the International Society of Family Law (ISFL) and Editor in Chief of the journal *Family & Law*.

Ruth Ballantyne is a lecturer at the University of Canterbury, New Zealand. She teaches family law and has a particular research interest in legal parentage models, identity theory, birth certificates, assisted human reproduction and family violence. She is the author of the *Family Law Student Companion* (2nd edn, 2014).

Fareda Banda is Professor of Law at SOAS University of London where she teaches human rights of women, law and society in Africa and family law.

Jacqueline Bhabha is Professor of the Practice of Health and Human Rights at the Harvard T.H. Chan School of Public Health, the Jeremiah Smith Junior Lecturer in Law at Harvard Law School and an adjunct professor at the Harvard Kennedy School. She is also the director of research at the FXB Center for Health and Human Rights at Harvard.

Karen Broadhurst is Professor of Social Work at Lancaster University, UK, where she Co-Directs the Centre for Child and Family Justice Research. She is an elected fellow of the Academy of Social Sciences, has served on a number of government advisory boards, and led the development of the Nuffield Family Justice Observatory.

Allan Cooke is a barrister specializing in family law in New Zealand. He has a particular interest in the care and protection of children and the intervention of the state in addressing those issues. His PhD (University of Otago, 2014) is entitled 'State Responsibility for Children in Care'.

James G. Dwyer, PhD JD, is the Arthur B. Hanson Professor of Law at the College of William and Mary, USA, where he teaches youth law, family law, trusts and estates, and law and social justice.

John Eekelaar FBA is Emeritus Fellow of Pembroke College, Oxford. He has written and researched extensively in family law and was a founding member of the International Society of Family Law (ISFL), a one-time president of that society, and founding co-editor of the *International Journal of Law, Policy, and the Family*.

Maxine Eichner is the Graham Kenan Distinguished Professor of Law at UNC School of Law. She is the author of *The Free-Market Family: How the Market Crushed the American Dream (and How It Can Be Restored)* (Oxford University Press, 2020) and *The Supportive State: Families, Government, and America's Political Ideals* (Oxford University Press, 2010).

Tony Fahey is Professor Emeritus in the School of Social Policy, Social Work and Social Justice in University College Dublin, Ireland. His research is on family patterns and family policy and a range of other topics in the fields of social policy, demography and housing.

Belinda Fehlberg is Professor of Law in the Melbourne Law School, specializing in family law. Belinda has conducted empirical research over many years on a wide range of family law issues. She is the lead author of *Australian Family Law: The Contemporary Context* (Oxford University Press, 2015).

Marsha Garrison is the 1901 Distinguished Research Professor of Law at Brooklyn Law School and the immediate past president of the International Society of Family Law.

Rob George is Associate Professor of Family Law at University College London and a Barrister at Harcourt Chambers in London, specializing in family law and the international movement of children. He is author of *Relocation Disputes: Law and Practice in England and New Zealand* (2014) and co-author of *Family Law: Text, Cases, and Materials* (2019).

Judith Harwin is Professor in Socio-Legal Studies in the Law School at Lancaster University and co-directs the Centre for Child and Family Justice Research. Her research focuses on child protection; the interrelationship between law, policy and practice; and evaluation of child outcomes for vulnerable children.

Mark Henaghan is Professor of Law at the University of Auckland, New Zealand. Mark has been teaching, researching and writing on family law for over 40 years. He is the editor and lead author of the two major books on New Zealand Family Law – *Family Law in New Zealand* (18th edn, 2019) and *Family Law Policy in New Zealand* (5th edn, 2020).

Jonathan Herring is Professor of Law, Faculty of Law, University of Oxford and DM Wolfe-Clarendon Fellow in Law, Exeter College, Oxford.

Rosemary Hunter is Professor of Law and Socio-Legal Studies at the University of Kent, UK. Her research in family law focuses on domestic abuse and family justice processes. She is the academic member of the Family Justice Council for England and Wales and a regular lecturer on judicial training courses for family judges.

Harumi Ishiwata is Associate Professor (civil law, especially inheritance law and family law) at Tohoku University, Graduate School of Law, Japan, since 2012, and previously Assistant Professor, University of Tokyo Graduate Schools for Law and Politics (2009–2012).

Emily Jackson is Professor of Law at the London School of Economics and Political Science.

Isabel Karpin is Distinguished Professor in the Law Faculty at the University of Technology, Sydney. She specializes in laws regulating the body and, in particular, reproductive technology, biotechnology, genetics and the law, and law and disability.

Sanford N. Katz is the Darald & Juliet Libby Professor of Law Emeritus at Boston College Law School. He has served as President of the International Society of Family Law, Chairman of the American Bar Association Family Law Section and Editor in Chief of the *Family Law Quarterly*. He was a Visiting Fellow at Pemborke College and All Souls College, University of Oxford.

Emiko Kubono is Professor of Law (Civil Law) at Tohoku University Graduate School of Law, Japan, since 2012, and previously Associate Professor, the same school since 2001 after teaching at Faculty of Law of Seikei University since 1997.

Fabiola Lathrop-Gómez, LCJ (Universidad de Chile), PhD (Salamanca), is Professor of Civil Law, University of Chile (Santiago de Chile).

Mavis Maclean, CBE, is Senior Research Fellow of St Hilda's College and member of the Department of Social Policy and Intervention, University of Oxford. She is former President of the RCSL, of the International Sociological Association, and an adviser to the Ministry of Justice. Her recent publications include *After the Act*, with John Eekelaar, and *Digital Family Justice* (ed.) (Bloomsbury 2019).

Ray D. Madoff is Professor at Boston College Law School. She received her JD and LLM in taxation from New York University School of Law. She is the author of *Immortality and the Law: The Rising Power of the American Dead* (New Haven: Yale University Press, 2012) and is the lead author of *Practical Guide to Estate Planning* (Wolters Kluwer, 2020).

Joanna Miles is Reader in Family Law & Policy at the University of Cambridge and a Fellow of Trinity College. She has written extensively on financial remedies on relationship breakdown.

Jenni Millbank is Distinguished Professor and Director of the Law Health Justice Research Centre at University of Technology Sydney (UTS), Faculty of Law. Her research reaches across health, family and reproduction law.

Satoshi Minamikata is Professor Emeritus of Niigata University, Japan. He retired in 2019 after teaching at Ibaraki University, Niigata University and Soka University. He is a member of the International Society of Family Law and his academic interests are mediation, child abuse and elderly issues. His recent publication is *Family and Succession Law in Japan* (Wolters Kluwer, 2019).

Teresa Picontó Novales is Professor of Legal Philosophy and Sociology of Law at the University of Zaragoza, Spain. She specializes in the sociology of family law and rights, welfare and social policies relating to children, gender and family.

Carol Rogerson is Professor of Family Law and Constitutional Law at the University of Toronto. She has written extensively on spousal and child support issues and has worked with federal and provincial governments on issues of family law reform, most recently as co-director of the project to develop a national set of Spousal Support Advisory Guidelines.

Kirsten Scheiwe is Professor of Law at Hildesheim University, Germany, since 1999. She works in the areas of family law, social security and welfare law, legal comparison, law in context and gender studies. Her approach is historical, comparative and interdisciplinary. She was a visiting scholar at Harvard, Oxford and the EUI Florence.

Jens M. Scherpe is Professor of Comparative Law at the University of Cambridge, where he also is the director of the Cambridge Family Law Centre. He also is a Fellow of Gonville and Caius College (Cambridge), Cheng Yu Tung Visiting Professor at the University of Hong Kong and Honorary Professor at the University of Aalborg. He has published several major comparative family law studies.

Wendy Schrama is full Professor of Family Law and Comparative Law at Utrecht, the Netherlands. She is also the director of the Utrecht Centre for European Research into Family Law (UCERF), Utrecht University. Wendy is a part-time family law judge at a Dutch district court. She is editor of several family law journals and commentaries, and she has authored many books on family law issues.

Lei Shi is Associate Professor, Southwest University of Political Science and Law, Chongqing, China. His research focuses on family law and the protection for vulnerable groups such as children, women and the elderly. Email: shilei8311@hotmail.com.

Anna Singer is Professor in Private Law at the Faculty of Law, Uppsala University, Sweden. Her research has focused on the regulation concerning the relationship between children and parents. Questions of particular interest have been the right to become and to be recognized as a parent, the establishment of legal parenthood and children's rights.

Julia Sloth-Nielsen is Professor at the University of the Western Cape in South Africa and she holds a chair of children's rights in the developing world at the University of Leiden, the Netherlands. She has published extensively on children's rights in her own country, but also on children's rights regionally, including Botswana, Mozambique, Tanzania, Namibia, Zanzibar and Kenya. She served a five-year term on the African Committee of Experts on the Rights and Welfare of the Child, and has extensive experience of child law reform processes. Her work focuses mainly on different aspects of children's rights in Africa.

Bruce Smyth is Professor of Family Studies with the Australian National University. In 2018 he received the Stanley Cohen Distinguished Research Award from the AFCC in recognition of outstanding research and research achievements in the field of family and divorce. He has published widely in the area of post-separation parenting.

Mark Strasser is the Trustees Professor of Law at Capital University Law School in Columbus, Ohio, USA. His works include *Free Exercise of Religion and the United States Constitution* (Routledge, 2018), *On Same-Sex Marriage, Civil Unions, and the Rule of Law* (Praeger Publishers/

Greenwood Publishing Group, 2002) and *Legally Wed: Same-Sex Marriage and the Constitution* (Cornell University Press, 1997).

Elaine E. Sutherland is Professor of Child and Family Law at Stirling University Law School, Scotland, and Distinguished Professor of Law Emerita at Lewis & Clark Law School, Portland, Oregon. She has published widely, mainly on domestic, comparative and international child and family law; presents papers at national and international conferences; serves on the Scottish Law Commission's Advisory Group on Family Law and the Law Society of Scotland's Child and Family Law Committee; and is consulted regularly by the Scottish government, the Scottish Parliament and non-governmental organizations.

Liz Trinder is Professor of Socio-Legal Studies at the University of Exeter in the UK. Her research is focused on post-separation parenting and what factors might make that more or less difficult. She has recently conducted empirical studies on litigants in person in private family law cases, on enforcement of courts orders and, most recently, on the grounds for divorce.

PART 1

Marriage and alternative relationships

1.1
THE CHANGING FACE OF MARRIAGE

Marsha Garrison

The decline – and continuing appeal – of marriage

Across the industrialized world, young adults are marrying later and increasing numbers may not marry at all.[1] In the United States, which has long had one of the highest marriage rates among industrialized nations, barely 50 percent of American adults are now married – a record low.[2] This general statistic actually masks some portion of the trend away from marriage as rising male life expectancy has significantly increased the proportion of older Americans who are married.[3] In younger age cohorts, marriage has declined precipitously. In 2018, the proportion of U.S. adults age 18–34 who were married was a mere 28 percent, down from 59 percent in 1972.[4] Although marriage has declined in some regions more than others, the trend away from marriage seems to be universal. One expert has predicted that, by 2035, half of the Japanese population will be single and as many as a third of Japanese men will never have married.[5] (See further Chapter 2.4 of this book.)

The decline of marriage is part of a much broader shift in family life that experts now generally describe as the 'second demographic transition'.[6] This transition has now taken place across most of the industrialized world, bringing with it not only lower marriage rates but also markedly lower fertility and increased non-marital cohabitation, divorce and childbearing outside marriage. In many nations, almost half of marriages now end in divorce, and cohabitation, as a

1 Eurostat, Marriage and Divorce Statistics, 2019. Available at https://ec.europa.eu/eurostat/statistics-explained/index.php/Marriage_and_divorce_statistics.
2 Pew Research Center, *The Decline of Marriage and Rise of New Families*, 2010. Available at http://pewresearch.org/pubs/1802/declline-marriage.
3 W. Wang, 'Marriage Up among Older Americans, Down among Younger', *IFS Blog*, 12 February 2018. Available at https://ifstudies.org/blog/the-state-of-our-unions-marriage-up-among-older-americans-down-among-the-younger.
4 W.B. Wilcox and L. Stone, 'The Happiness Recession', *Atlantic Monthly*, 4 April 2019.
5 'By 2035, Half of Japanese Will Be Single, Predicts Commentator', *Japan Today*, 15 January 2018. Available at https://japantoday.com/category/features/kuchikomi/by-2035-half-of-japanese-will-be-single-predicts-commentator.
6 B. Zaidi and S.P. Morgan, 'The Second Demographic Transition Theory: A Review and Appraisal', *Annual Review Sociology* 43, 2017, 473–92.

precursor or alternative to marriage, has become mainstream. Except in Asia, the proportion of children born outside of marriage has also skyrocketed.[7]

With the decline of marriage has come a shift in its meaning. Traditional, 'institutional' marriage based on fixed, gender-based roles has given way to marriage based on companionship or, more recently, personal fulfilment.[8] Reflecting this new, individualized view of marriage, most adults, particularly young adults, are now neutral or positive toward non-marital and same-sex relationships, with or without children. For example, in recent US surveys, a large majority of respondents expressed positive or neutral views toward a diverse array of family arrangements, including, in one national survey, single women having children without a partner.[9] Surveys in at least 20 other countries exhibit similar patterns.[10] Many individuals also support extending 'spousal' support and a property-division entitlement to at least some heterosexual partners who could have but did not marry,[11] and, in 2011, 39 percent of Americans surveyed said that marriage is becoming obsolete.[12]

While these general trends suggest, at first blush, that marriage is rapidly becoming a moribund legal institution, a closer look reveals both that the trend away from marriage is uneven and that marriage continues to enjoy broad public support. First, the decline in marriage and marital childbearing is concentrated among the least advantaged. In the United States, Russia and many parts of Europe, non-marital birth is associated with lower educational attainment and 'a pattern of disadvantage'.[13] This pattern is particularly striking in the United States, where non-marital birth and marriage behaviour are now highly correlated with race and class. Ninety-six percent of children born to black high school dropouts are born outside of marriage,[14] as compared to about 6 percent of children born to white college graduates.[15] The divorce rate of white college graduates – but not other groups – has also declined.[16] Because of these divergent trends,

7 OECD Family Database, 'Share of Births Outside Marriage', *SF2.4*, 11 November 2018. Available at www.oecd.org/els/family/database.htm.

8 P.R. Amato, 'Institutional, Companionate, and Individualistic Marriages: Change over Time and Implications for Marital Quality', in M. Garrison and E.S. Scott (eds), *Marriage at the Crossroads: The Brave New World of Twenty-First Century Families*, Cambridge: Cambridge University Press, 2012, pp. 107–25.

9 Nat. Survey of Fam. Growth, 2011–15 Table 2, reprinted in S. Stanley, *Cohabitation Is Pervasive*, Inst. Fam. Studies, 2018. Available at https://ifstudies.org/blog/cohabitation-is-pervasive. *See also* Pew Research Center, op. cit., n 2; E. Coast, 'Currently Cohabiting: Relationship Attitudes and Intentions', in J. Stillwell et al. (eds), *Fertility, Living Arrangements, Care, and Mobility*, Dordrecht, NL: Springer, 2009, pp. 105–25, Table 7.1.

10 J. Treas et al., 'Attitudes on Marriage and New Relationships: Cross-National Evidence on the Deinstitutionalization of Marriage', *Demographic Research* 30, 2014, 1495; Z. Gubernskaya, 'Changing Attitudes toward Marriage and Children in Six Countries', *Sociological Perspectives* 30, 2010, 179–200.

11 S. Braver and I. Ellman, *in* M. Garrison and E.S. Scott (eds), op. cit., n 8, pp. 170–98.

12 Twenty-eight percent agreed with this statement in 1978. D.B. Elliott et al., *Historical Marriage Trends from 1890–2010: A Focus on Race Differences*, Population Association of America, SEHSD Working Paper Number 2012-12, 2012, p. 2. Available at www.census.gov/hhes/socdemo/marriage/data/acs/ElliottetalPAA2012paper.pdf.

13 J. Mikolai et al., 'The Role of Education in the Intersection of Partnership Transitions and Motherhood in Europe and the United States', *Demographic Research* 39, 2018, 753–94; B. Perelli-Harris et al., 'The Educational Gradient of Nonmarital Childbearing in Europe', *Population and Development Review* 36, 2010, 775–801.

14 J. Carbone and N. Cahn, 'Red v. Blue Marriage', in Garrison and Scott, op. cit., n 8, pp. 9–29.

15 S. Lundberg et al., 'Family Inequality: Diverging Patterns in Marriage, Cohabitation, and Childbearing', *Journal of Economic Perspectives* 30, 2016, 79–102.

16 W. Wang, 'The Link between a College Education and a Lasting Marriage', *Pew Research Center*, 4 December 2015. Available at www.pewresearch.org/fact-tank/2015/12/04/education-and-marriage/; S. McLanahan and W. Jacobsen, 'Diverging Destinies Revisited', in P.R. Amato et al. (eds), *Families in an Era of Increasing Inequality*, Berlin: Springer, 2015, pp. 3–24.

children of black and poorly educated parents are much more likely to live in a single-parent household. In a recent survey, more than 75 percent of black children whose mothers lacked a high school education lived in a single-parent home, as compared to less than 20 percent of white children whose mothers had at least some college education.[17] Although the data is less robust, single parenthood is also significantly linked to low maternal education in most of Europe[18] and industrialized Asia.[19]

Second, the trend away from marriage masks continuing public enthusiasm for marriage as both a life goal and the prime signifier of a committed relationship. Indeed, the decline of marriage seems to be attributable, at least in part, to the fact that marriage is increasingly idealized as a marker of success.[20] As one young American survey respondent ... put it:

> Marriage is something you earn. ... If [she] graduates and [I] graduate, you can start working and we can afford [a wedding] and that's when you get married. It's not just 'cause we have a child and all of a sudden we need to go out and do it.[21]

Although the 'marriage idealization' phenomenon has been studied most in the United States, there is evidence that marriage continues to be an important lifetime goal in a broad range of nations.[22] The high priority that advocates for gay and lesbian rights have placed on access to civil marriage – and growing public support for such access – also suggests that marriage remains a core social institution that uniquely signifies lifelong relational commitment. In the words of the Lambda Legal Defense Fund: 'Only the word *married* conveys the universally understood meaning applicable to the lifetime commitment many couples make'.[23] In seeming agreement with this sentiment, 61 percent of same-sex couples living together had married within two years after the Supreme Court of the United States declared that same-sex marriage was a constitutional right.[24]

These complex trends pose important policy challenges for policymakers, and neither the experts nor the public has reached consensus on the right response. Some scholars initially welcomed the decline of marriage, arguing that family law has unfairly privileged marriage by granting public and private rights based on marital status; a few went so far as to urge that marriage should be abolished as a legal category.[25] On the other side of the policy fence, more

17 D. Autor and M. Wasserman, *Wayward Sons: The Emerging Gender Gap in Labor Markets and Education 2013*, p. 36, Figure 16. Available at www.thirdway.org/publications/662.

18 J. Härkönen, *Diverging Destinies in International Perspective: Education, Single Motherhood, and Child Poverty*, LIS Working Paper Series 713, 2017. Available at www.econstor.eu/handle/10419/169273.

19 Raymo et al., op. cit., n 5.

20 A. Cherlin, 'The Deinstitutionalization of American Marriage', *Journal of Marriage and Family* 66, 2004, 848–86.

21 M.J. Kefalas et al., 'Marriage Is Something You Earn', *J. Fam. Issues* 32, 2011, 845–75.

22 G. Andersson and D. Philipov, 'Life-Table Representations of Family Dynamics in Sweden, Hungary, and 14 Other FFS Countries: A Project of Descriptions of Demographic Behavior', *Demographic Research* 7, 2002, 67–144; N. Hiekel et al., 'The Meaning of Cohabitation Across Europe'. Available at http://epc2012.princeton.edu/papers/120762.

23 Lambda Legal, *Civil Unions Are Not Enough: Six Key Reasons Why*, 2013. Available at http://data.lambdalegal.org/publications/downloads/fs_civil-unions-are-not-enough.pdf.

24 A. Cherlin, 'Marriage Has Become a Trophy', *Atlantic Monthly*, 12 March 2018 (citing Gallup surveys).

25 M.A. Fineman, 'Why Marriage?', Virginia Journal of Social Policy & the Law 9, 2001, 239–71; N. Polikoff, *Beyond (Straight and Gay) Marriage: Valuing All Families under the Law*, Boston: Beacon Press, 2008; J. Stacey, *Unhitched: Love, Marriage and Family Values from West Hollywood to West China*, New York: NYU Press, 2011.

traditional commentators urged that '[t]he erosion of marriage … lies at the heart of many of the social problems with which the government currently grapples', and 'government policy [thus] should promote … healthy marriage'.[26]

The increasingly successful struggle for same-sex marriage has affected this debate by building consensus that marriage is a core social institution. With high courts in culturally diverse nations – Austria, Ecuador, Taiwan and the United States, among others – concluding that access to marriage is a constitutionally mandated fundamental right, calls for the abolition of legal marriage have largely disappeared (see further Chapters 1.2 and 1.4 of this book).

But there is no emerging consensus, as yet, on the legal relationship between marriage and cohabitation. Some countries, notably Canada and New Zealand, have established conscriptive regimes that impose some or all marital rights and responsibilities on cohabitants based either on a wide-ranging factual inquiry or on a legislatively specified variable such as the duration of cohabitation (see further Chapter 1.5 of this book). Others, notably the United States, have adopted a contractual regime under which cohabitants may enter into agreements to create relational rights and responsibilities. Yet others, notably France, have established registration schemes under which cohabitants may opt into a status that confers some, but not all, marital rights and responsibilities (see further Chapter 1.2 of this book).

In considering the relative merits of these policy responses to current trends, it is important to keep in mind that marital status has long served as the basis for a variety of legislative assumptions about relational expectations and equities. Rules governing spousal inheritance rights, the division of property and support on divorce, and important public benefits and burdens are based on the assumption that a marital household is an integrated economic unit in which sharing is expected and practiced; the law does not make the same assumptions about unmarried cohabitants.[27] Increased family diversity presents the possibility that formal marriage no longer provides an accurate marker of expectations and equity. But before abandoning marriage as a classificatory tool, we need to be confident that another means of accurately and fairly classifying couples, across a wide range of obligations and entitlements, is available.

Marriage is also associated with personal and public benefits. Most significantly, marriage is, everywhere, more stable than cohabitation,[28] and unstable relationships are associated with a serious economic and social risks to children.[29] If marriage plays a *causal* role in promoting stable relationships and reducing child-welfare risks, policymakers should be wary of adopting rules that deter or disadvantage marriage. Of course, family policy must also take account of the fact that many couples will continue to live together and have children outside of marriage. Family law and policy should support autonomous relational choices. They must not discriminate against nontraditional families or ignore their needs and interests.

In sum, the decline of formal marriage poses a number of different challenges to policymakers. Legal rules dealing with both public status and private rights should accurately classify couples to ensure

26 R.E. Rector and M.G. Pardue, *Understanding the President's Healthy Marriage Initiative*, Heritage Foundation Backgrounder #1741, 2004. Available at www.heritage.org/Research/Family/bg1741.cfm. Cf. C.A. Murray, *Coming Apart: The State of White America 1960–2010*, New York: Random House, 2012; J.Q. Wilson, The Marriage Problem: How Our Culture Has Weakened Families, New York: Harper Collins, 2002.

27 E.S. Scott and R.E. Scott, 'Marriage as Relational Contract', *Virginia Law Review* 84, 1998, 1225–332.

28 Z. Žilinčíková, 'Do Children Matter for the Stability of Cohabitation? A Cross-National Comparison', *Population* 72, 2017, 649–70.

29 D. Richter and S. Lemola, 'Growing Up with a Single Mother and Life Satisfaction in Adulthood: A Test of Mediating and Moderating Factors', *PLoS One* 12, 2017, e0179639. https://doi.org/10.1371/journal.pone.0179639.

that relational expectations and equities are met. These rules should not increase risks to children or their parents. They must also support and protect the full spectrum of children and their families.

Does formal marriage still matter?

Marriage as a signal of relational expectations

When a couple marries, each spouse 'agrees to be subject to a complex set of behavioral expectations defining the roles of spouse and parent, expectations that will restrict their freedom and guide their behavior in the relationship'.[30] Marriage vows signal acceptance of these expectations both to one's partner and to the world at large.

The most important behavioural expectations of marriage are sexual fidelity and sharing. Sexual fidelity has long been a core part of the marital bargain, breach of which constitutes, everywhere, grounds for divorce. This expectation has not diminished. Cross-national surveys in fact show *increasing* support for sexual fidelity during marriage.[31] The traditional expectation of marital sharing also persists unabated. When average citizens, married or single, talk about marriage, they typically focus on sharing, and married couples 'speak of sharing – thoughts, feelings, tasks, values, or life goals – as the greatest virtue in a relationship'.[32] Reflecting this sharing ethic, married couples today overwhelmingly report that they share economic resources and that such sharing is a product of love, trust and commitment.[33] Divorce and succession law protect marriage partners who have relied on the sharing norm. They also encourage sharing by assuring spouses that a partner cannot unilaterally end the marital partnership without taking account of the legitimate expectations of the spouse left behind.

Cohabitation is unlike marriage in that there is no event to signal mutual understanding of behavioural expectations. Thus, while some cohabiting couples have sexual-fidelity and sharing expectations like those of a married couple, demographers have identified six or seven different cohabitation 'types', ranging from a substitute for being single to a stage in the marriage process to informal, 'common-law' marriage.[34] The diversity of cohabiting relationships also ensures that cohabiting couples have varied understandings about important aspects of their relationships. Researchers have found that in 20–40 percent of cohabiting relationships partners express different views on whether they plan to marry each other.[35] Surveys also show that substantial percentages of cohabitants disagree about basic issues such as how much time they spend together, the advantages of cohabitation and whether the relationship has produced a high level

30 E.S. Scott, 'Social Norms and the Legal Regulation of Marriage', *Virginia Law Review* 86, 2000, 1901–70; Scott and Scott, op. cit., n 27.

31 Treas et al., op. cit., n 10.

32 R.N. Bellah et al., *Habits of the Heart: Individualism and Commitment in American Life*, New York: Harper & Row, 1985, pp. 90–1.

33 P. Blumstein and P. Schwartz, *American Couples*, New York: Wm. Morrow & Co., 1993, pp. 101, 110; J. Pahl, *Money and Marriage*, New York: St. Martin's Press, 1989, pp. 78, 83, 126–7; J. Stocks et al. (eds), *Modern Couples Sharing Money, Sharing Life,* Houndsmill Basingstroke, UK: Palgrave Macmillan, 2007, pp. 11, 16–17, 49.

34 P. Heuveline and J.M. Timberlake, 'The Role of Cohabitation in Family Formation: The United States in Comparative Perspective', *Journal of Marriage & Family* 66, 2004, 1214–30; K. Kiernan, 'The Rise of Cohabitation and Childbearing Outside Marriage in Western Europe', *Int'l Journal of Law, Policy, & Family* 15, 2001, 1–21.

35 S.L. Brown, 'Union Transitions among Cohabiters: The Significance of Relationship Assessment and Expectations', *Journal of Marriage & Family* 62, 2000, 833–46; S. Sassler and J. McNally, 'Cohabiting Couple's Economic Circumstances and Union Transitions: A Re-Examination Using Multiple Imputation Techniques', Social Science Research 32, 2004, 553–78.

of happiness.[36] Cohabitation thus differs dramatically from marriage in its capacity to reveal a couple's mutual understanding of their relationship.

The available evidence strongly suggests that cohabitants do not *typically* embrace marital norms, however. Cohabitants are much less likely to express commitment toward or support for their partners.[37] They are less likely to adopt a joint lifestyle.[38] They are more likely to split expenses instead of pooling their resources.[39] Indeed, surveyed cohabitants often describe the advantages of cohabitation as a function of non-commitment.[40] Highlighting the distinction between cohabitation and marriage, survey data suggest that many cohabitants plan to marry at some point.[41] Even in Sweden and Norway, where cohabitation is a widely accepted alternative to marriage, most cohabitants do go on to marry a current or future partner.[42]

Neither relational duration nor the birth of a child appears to alter the commitment level of cohabiting couples. Even in Scandinavia, the birth of a child is not significantly correlated with the seriousness of a cohabiting relationship,[43] and cohabiting couples are significantly less likely than married couples to pool resources even after the duration of the relationship, the presence of children and other socio-economic variables are taken into account.[44] In sum, policymakers cannot assume that cohabitation (or even some types of cohabitation) and marriage are substitutes, with similar expectations of commitment and sharing.

The marital advantage: correlation or causation?

Formal marriage has long been associated with a range of health, wealth and happiness benefits to marriage partners.[45] Recent evidence suggests that, when compared to cohabitation, these adult benefits may have declined and, in some nations, disappeared entirely.[46]

36 Brown, op. cit., n 35; Coast, op. cit., n 9.

37 S. Nock, 'A Comparison of Marriages and Cohabiting Relationships', *Journal of Family Issues* 16, 1995, 53–76; S.M. Stanley et al., 'Interpersonal Commitment and Premarital or Nonmarital Cohabitation', Journal of Family Issues 25, 2004, 496–519.

38 K. van Houdt and A.-R. Poortman, 'Joint Lifestyles and the Risk of Union Dissolution: Differences between Marriage and Cohabitation', *Demographic Research* 15, 2018, 431–58.

39 D. Hamplová et al., 'Is the Cohabitation Marriage Gap in Money Pooling Universal?', *Journal of Marriage and Family* 76, 2014, 983–97; N. Hiekel, *The Different Meanings of Cohabitation across Europe: How Cohabiters View Their Unions and Differ in Their Plans and Behaviors*, PhD thesis, Amsterdam University, Amsterdam, 2014; K. Knudsen and K. Waerness, 'Shared or Separate? Money Management and Changing Norms of Gender Equality among Norwegian Couples', *Community, Work and Family* 12, 2009, 39–55.

40 Coast, op. cit., n 8; S. MacRae, *Cohabiting Mothers*, London: Policy Studies Institute, 1993.

41 N. Hiekel et al., 'The Meaning of Cohabitation and Marriage across European Societies', Princeton University, 2011. Available at http://paa2011.princeton.edu/papers/110661.

42 T. Lappegård and T. Noack, 'The Link between Parenthood and Partnership in Contemporary Norway', *32 Demographic Research* 32, 2018, art. 9; K.A. Wiik et al., 'A Study of Commitment and Relationship Quality in Sweden and Norway', *Journal of Marriage and Family* 72, 2009, 465–77.

43 Wiik et al., op. cit., n 42.

44 T.H. Lyngstad et al., 'Pooling of Economic Resources: A Comparison of Norwegian Married and Cohabiting Couples', *European Sociological Review* 27, 2011, 624–35.

45 C.M. Wilson and A.J. Oswald, *How Does Marriage Affect Physical and Psychological Health? A Survey of the Longitudinal Evidence*, IZA Bonn Discussion Paper No. 1619, 2005; D.T. Ellwood and C. Jencks, 'The Uneven Spread of Single-Parent Families: What Do We Know? Where Do We Look for the Answers', in K.M. Neckerman (ed.), *Social Inequality*, New York: Russell Sage Foundation, 2004.

46 M. Mikucka, 'The Life Satisfaction Advantage of Being Married and Gender Specialization', *Journal of Marriage and Family* 78, 2016, 759–79; B. Perelli-Harris et al., 'Mind the "Happiness" Gap: The Relationship between Cohabitation, Marriage, and Subjective Well-Being in the United Kingdom,

Marriage is also associated with advantages for children. As we have seen, marriage is, everywhere, significantly more stable than cohabitation,[47] and relational instability is associated with serious financial, physical and educational risks during childhood that extend into adulthood.[48] There is also evidence that the advantages conferred by marital childbearing and rearing extend beyond the specific benefits associated with residential and economic stability: married fathers appear to be more involved and spend more time with their children than unmarried fathers; if parental separation occurs, they see their children more often and pay child support more regularly.[49] Growing up in a single-parent household is negatively, and significantly, correlated with adult income, health, emotional stability, marital discord and divorce.[50] Because of these various advantages of marital parenting, in the United States, marriage is now an important determinant not only of childhood poverty but also of growing adult income inequality.[51] This pattern of 'diverging destinies' based on parents' marital status is also evident in a number of other nations.[52]

A stable marital relationship does not invariably confer benefits on children, of course. The continuation of a high-conflict marriage is *negatively* associated with health and happiness for both children and spouses.[53] Nor does remarriage appear to confer the same advantage as a first marriage. Children living in step-families, for example, tend to score lower on tests of emotional and social well-being than children living with both parents in intact families.[54]

A large portion of the marital advantage in both stability and associated benefits is also explained by 'selection effects'. Married couples tend to be older, better educated and better off

---

Australia, Germany, and Norway', *Demography* 56, 2019, 1219–46; J.L. Kohn and S.L. Averett, 'Can't We Just Live Together? New Evidence on the Effect of Relationship Status on Health', *Journal of Family & Economic Issues* 35, 2014, 295–312.

47 L. DeRose et al., *The Cohabitation-Go-Round: Cohabitation and Family Instability across the Globe*, Table 1, Social Trends Institute, 2017; J. Dronkers, *Cohabitation, Marriage, and Union Stability in Europe*, Figure 3, Institute for Family Studies, 2016. Available at https://ifstudies.org/blog/cohabitation-marriage-and-union-instability-in-europe/; K. Musick and K. Michelmore, 'Cross-National Comparisons of Union Stability in Cohabiting and Married Families with Children', Paper presented at Population Association of America Annual Meeting, 2016.

48 A.J. Cherlin, *The Marriage-Go-Round: The State of Marriage and the Family Today*, New York: Alfred A. Knopf, 2009; S. McLanahan and A.N. Beck, 'Parental Relationships in Fragile Families', *Fragile Families* 20, 2010, 17–37.

49 S.L. Brown, 'Family Structure and Child Well-Being', *Journal of Marriage and Family* 66, 2004, 351–67; M. Carlson et al., *Unmarried But Not Absent: Fathers' Involvement with Children after a Nonmarital Birth*, CRCW Working Paper 2005–07, 2007; S.L. Hofferth and K.G. Anderson, 'Are All Dads Equal? Biology versus Marriage as a Basis for Paternal Investment', *Journal of Marriage and Family* 65, 2003, 213–32.

50 P.R. Amato, 'The Impact of Family Formation Change in the Cognitive, Social, and Emotional Well-Being of the Next Generation', *Future of Children* 15, 2005, 75–96; P.R. Amato and J. Cheadle, 'The Long Reach of Divorce: Divorce and Child Well-Being across Three Generations', *Journal of Marriage and Family* 67, 2005, 192–3; W. Sigle-Rushton and S. McLanahan, 'Father Absence and Child Well-Being: A Critical Review', in D.M. Moynihan et al. (eds), *The Future of the Family*, New York: Russell Sage Foundation, 2004, pp. 126–30.

51 D. Bloom, 'Childhood Family Structure and Intergenerational Income Mobility in the United States', *Demography* 54, 2017, 541–69; McLanahan and Jacobsen, op. cit., n 16.

52 Härkönen, op. cit., n 18; B. Perelli-Harris and M. Lyons-Amos, 'Partnership Patterns in the United States and across Europe: The Role of Education and Country Context', *Social Forces*, 95, 2016, 251–82; J.M. Raymo and M. Iwasawa, *Diverging Destinies: The Japanese Case*, Singapore: Springer, 2017.

53 P.R. Amato and A. Booth, *A Generation at Risk: Growing Up in an Era of Family Upheaval*, Cambridge, MA: Harvard University Press, 1997, pp. 106–17; R.E. Emery, *Marriage, Divorce, and Children's Adjustment*, Thousand Oaks, CA: Sage Publications, 1999.

54 Brown, op. cit., n 49; S.L. Hofferth, 'Residential Father Family Type and Child Well-Being: Investment versus Selection, *Demography* 43, 2006, 53–77.

than cohabiting couples.[55] At least in the United States, cohabiting couples also have more physical, emotional and substance-abuse problems than married couples.[56] Much of the marital advantage can thus be explained by partner characteristics that precede family formation.[57] Separating advantages produced by marriage from selection effects is difficult, but the more that researchers are able to control for other explanatory variables, the more the marital advantage diminishes.[58] Indeed, when researchers are able to control for a wide range of socio-economic, educational and life-history factors, the marital advantage tends to decline precipitously, or even to disappear entirely.[59]

The bottom line is that we still do not fully understand just how the marital advantage has been produced or to what extent cohabitation can provide the economic and health benefits associated with marriage. It is logical to suppose that entry into a public legal status that confers binding obligations and mandates formal exit procedures represents a different, more carefully considered, and more secure experience than entry into an informal relationship; certainly, any number of theorists has supposed – across a broad range of legal categories – that this is so.[60] Many unmarried mothers also suggest that the ceremonial aspects of marriage are important and meaningful to them.[61] Cohabitation offers no equivalent 'marker' event to support commitment and stability; indeed, it is often difficult to determine just when – or even if – cohabitation has begun.[62] But we lack the data to prove that formal marital obligations alter individual experience, and many logical suppositions about the sources of greater health and happiness ultimately prove to be unfounded.

Even after controlling for a wide range of variables, marital relationships do appear to be more stable than non-marital cohabitation for children.[63] In Scandinavia, which has the longest experience with cohabitation as a mainstream family form, demographers continue to find that marital childbearing is associated with greater childhood stability,[64] and that single

55 C. Acs, 'Can We Promote Child Well-Being by Promoting Marriage?', *Journal of Marriage and Family* 69, 2007, 1326–44; C. Crawford et al., 'Cohabitation, Marriage and Child Outcomes: An Empirical Analysis of the Relationship between Marital Status and Child Outcomes in the UK Using the Millennium Cohort Study', *Child and Family Law Quarterly* 4, 2012, 176–98; A. Goodman and E. Greaves, *Cohabitation, Marriage and Child Outcomes*, London: Institute of Fiscal Studies, 2010. Available at www.ifs.org.uk/comms/comm114.pdf.

56 M. DeKlyen et al., 'The Mental Health of Parents with Infants: Do Marriage, Cohabitation, and Romantic Status Matter?', *American Journal of Public Health* 96, 2006, 1836–41; McLanahan and Jacobsen, op. cit., n 16.

57 McLanahan and Jacobsen, op. cit., n 16; B. Perelli-Harris & M. Styrc, 'Mental Well-Being Differences in Cohabitation and Marriage: The Role of Childhood Selection', *Journal of Marriage and Family* 80, 2018, 239–55; J.H. Su et al., 'Better for Baby? The Retreat from Mid-Pregnancy Marriage and Implications for Parenting and Child Well-Being', *Demography 52*, 2015, 1167–94.

58 Acs, op. cit., n 55; Crawford, op. cit., n 55; R.E. Emery et al., 'Marriage and Improved Weil-Being: Using Twins to Parse the Correlation, Asking How Marriage Helps, and Wondering Why More People Don't Buy a Bargain', in Garrison and Scott, op. cit., n 4, pp. 126–41.

59 Goodman and Greaves, op. cit., n 55.

60 C.R. Sunstein, 'On the Expressive Function of Law', *University of Pennsylvania Law Review* 144, 1996, 2021–53; Symposium, 'The Legal Construction of Norms', *Virginia Law Review* 86, 2000, 1577–839.

61 K. Edin and M. Kefalas, *Promises I Can Keep: Why Poor Women Put Motherhood before Marriage*, Berkeley, CA: University of California Press, 2005; K. Edin et al., 'A Peek Inside the Black Box: What Marriage Means for Poor Unmarried Parents', *Journal of Marriage and Family* 66, 2004, 1007–14.

62 J. Knaab, *Cohabitation: Sharpening a Fuzzy Concept*, Princeton, NJ: Princeton Center for Research on Child Wellbeing Working Paper #04–05FF, 2005.

63 Dronkers, op. cit., n 47; Musick and Michaelmore, op. cit., n 47.

64 K. Kiernan, 'European Perspectives on Union Formation', in L. Waite (ed.), *The Ties That Bind*, New York: Aldine de Gruyter, 2000.

parenthood is a risk factor for children even when controlling for a wide range of demographic variables.[65]

However, we have very limited data comparing outcomes for couples who marry with those who formally enter an alternate status that confers more limited rights and benefits. Virtually all of the data we do have relate to the French *pacte civil de solidarité* (*pacs*), a purely French institution offering a legal status between being single and being married (see further Chapters 1.2, 1.5 and 2.1 of this book). The *pacs* was originally aimed at same-sex couples but has been, from the beginning, open to opposite-sex couples as well. The *pacs* has achieved real popularity; in 2016, four French couples chose to *se pacser* for every five who married.[66] Thus far, *pacs* relationships are less stable than marriage. But 40 percent of *pacs* that dissolve do so to make way for marriage between the *pacsé* couple.[67] *Pacsé* couples are also far more likely to cite instrumental reasons for entering into a *pacs* as compared to those who marry, and they are dramatically less likely to hold a public celebration.[68] These data suggest that many, perhaps most, *pacsé* couples do not see the *pacs* as a marriage alternative but, instead, as a way station between unregistered cohabitation and formal marriage.

The behavioural divide between marriage and cohabitation may also be waning. In a recent US bank survey, only 70 percent of Millennial couples waited until marriage to start a joint account, vs. 88 percent of couples 55 and older. Twenty-six percent of Millennials opened their first account when they were living with their partner (vs. 9 percent of 55 and older) and 19 percent merged finances after being engaged (vs. 6 percent of 55 and older).[69]

In sum, although the health, wealth and happiness advantages traditionally correlated with marriage appear to be waning, marriage remains significantly more stable than cohabitation even when compared with a formal status like the French *pacs*. Marital stability is likely promoted by marital commitment and sharing. But much of the stability and other advantages associated with marriage are explicable by pre-existing characteristics of those who elect marriage. It is also possible, given current trends, that the marital advantage will eventually disappear.

The policy challenges

So, how should policymakers respond to the decline – and continuing appeal – of marriage?

65 K. Breivik and D. Olweus, 'Children of Divorce in a Scandinavian Welfare State: Are They Less Affected than U.S. Children?', *Scandinavian Journal of Psychiatry* 47, 2006, 61–74; I. Storksen et al., 'Marriages and Psychological Distress among Adult Offspring of Divorce: A Norwegian Study', *Scandinavian Journal of Psychiatry* 48, 2007, 467–76; G.R. Weitoft et al., 'Mortality, Severe Morbidity, and Injury in Children Living with Single Parents in Sweden: A Population-Based Study', *Lancet* 361, 2003, 289–95.

66 W. Rault, 'Is the Civil Solidarity Pact the Future of Marriage? The Several Meanings of the French Civil Union', *Int'l J. L. Policy and Family* 33, 2019, 139–59; S. Sayare and M. De La Baume, 'In France, Civil Unions Gain Favor Over Marriage', *New York Times*, 15 December, 2010.

67 G. Ferrari and L. Toulemon, 'Is the French PACS Similar to Cohabitation or Marriage? Recently Merged Census and Tax Data on Partnership Situations and Transitions', Paper presented at Population Association of America, 2018. Fifty-seven percent of pacsé partners report that they eventually intend to marry. *See* Rault, op. cit., n 66.

68 Rault, op. cit., n 66.

69 P.R. Newswire, 'TD Bank Survey Finds Many Couples Maintain Separate Bank Accounts', 24 March 2014. Available at www.prnewswire.com/news-releases/td-bank-survey-finds-many-couples-maintain-separate-bank-accounts-251917121.html.

Should the law continue to rely on marriage as a marker of relational expectations and equities?

Hostility to marriage is typically grounded in claims that all families should be treated equally and that a 'special' status for marriage is harmful to other families. This critique stems, in part, from the long-standing exclusion of same-sex couples from marriage. It also has roots in traditional family law's harsh treatment of non-marital families. Until the 1960s, non-marital children were ineligible for inheritance rights and other benefits available to children whose parents were married. During this era, contracts between cohabitants were also, in many jurisdictions, treated as thinly veiled prostitution agreements and thus unenforceable.

Certainly, differences in the legal treatment of marital and non-marital families require careful scrutiny and justification. But the evidence does not support the claim that preserving marriage as a marker of relational expectations and equities is discriminatory. First, constitutional and statutory reforms have abolished overtly discriminatory policies toward non-marital children and relationships;[70] remaining differences in the law's treatment of marital and non-marital relationships are grounded, rationally, in the different understandings, expectations and behaviours of married and unmarried couples. This differential treatment produces penalties as well as benefits for married couples.[71]

Second, formal marriage continues to serve an important signaling function. Given the range of cohabiting relationships, factually distinguishing marriage-like informal unions from casual affiliations that do not warrant special legal treatment is rife with difficulty; indeed, differences in the wording of questions have been shown to affect self-reports of cohabitation status among cohabiting couples, couples with non-marital children and even classification by researchers.[72] 'Common-law' marriage – which relied on a private marital agreement and public 'holding out' as a married couple instead of a marriage ceremony – has been abolished in most jurisdictions precisely because of the difficulty of separating spurious from genuine marital claims. It is thus desirable for committed couples to formally marry so that their agreement and expectations can be recognized without expensive, time-consuming and potentially inaccurate fact finding.[73]

Third, differential treatment of marriage and cohabitation supports personal autonomy and choice. Many cohabiting couples choose not to marry precisely to avoid marital obligations. Current law also permits intimate partners to designate one another as will beneficiaries, enter into contracts, take joint title to property and otherwise individualize their relational expectations.

These various reasons for retaining differential treatment of marriage and cohabitation suggest that lawmakers should not adopt conscriptive rules that retrospectively treat some cohabiting couples as if they were married based on either an open-ended inquiry into the relationship or specified criteria such as having a common child and relational duration. The imposition of marital status based on relationship duration or parenthood creates serious risks of misclassification given that neither of these variables is significantly correlated with marital understandings or behaviours; the frequency with which cohabiting couples disagree about important aspects of their relationships reinforces these risks. Conscriptive rules needlessly reduce personal

70 *Levy v Louisiana*, 391 U.S. 68 (1968); *Marckx v Belgium* [1979] 2 EHHR 330.

71 D.J. Besharov and N. Gilbert, 'Marriage Penalties in the Modern Social Welfare State', *R Street Policy Study No. 40*, 2015. Available at www.welfareacademy.org/pubs/family/Marriage_Penalties_in_the_Modern_Social-Welfare_State.pdf; S. Bach, 'Taxation of Married Couples in the U.K. and Germany: One-Earner Couples Maker the Difference', *International Journal of Microstimulation*, 6, 2013, 3–24.

72 Knaab, op. cit., n 62.

73 M. Garrison, 'Is Consent Necessary? An Evaluation of the Emerging Law of Cohabitant Obligation', *UCLA Law Review* 52, 2005, 815–97.

autonomy. They reintroduce – and expand – all of the evidentiary problems created by the common law marriage doctrine. Given that targeted legislation focused directly on remedying relationship-induced disadvantage can prevent unjust enrichment, there is no reason to risk such negative effects.[74] (For further discussion, see Chapters 1.2 and 1.5 of this book.)

Conversely, however, the arguments in favour of maintaining differential treatment of marriage and cohabitation strongly support opening marriage to same-sex couples. If marriage continues to be a unique signal of relational commitment, then nondiscrimination and support for individual autonomy demand rules that make such a commitment available to all.[75] Gender roles within marriage, and the law's treatment of these roles, have evolved in response to changing social conditions and values. The extension of marriage to same-sex couples represents a similar adaptation to ensure that marriage, as a legal status, is consistent with evolving social values and personal goals for intimate and family life.

At this point, the evidence is insufficient to tell us whether registration schemes that create an intermediate status between marriage and singlehood are desirable. Most of the current registration options were created to provide an alternate status for same-sex couples; if marriage is made available to same-sex couples, such a status is unnecessary. The popularity of the French *pacs* is also unusual. In the handful of other nations that have experimented with registration options, registration has not attracted significant public interest once marriage becomes available to same-sex couples.[76] (For further discussion, see Chapter 1.2 of this book.)

Should government promote formal marriage?

In recent years, marriage advocates, particularly in the United States, have urged a diverse array of marriage-promotion initiatives, including divorce reform, the elimination of marriage 'penalties', and various initiatives to reduce marital conflict.[77] By and large, these initiatives are not supported by the evidence. Because only low-conflict, enduring relationships offer significant benefits to adult partners and their children, reforms aimed at deterring divorce or broadly promoting marriage may do more harm than good by promoting the continuation of high-conflict relationships. This problem is particularly acute if incentives are targeted at the poor, who have the lowest marriage rate. Low-income unmarried mothers often report that they have not married their children's fathers because of serious problems such as violence, addiction, criminal misbehaviour and chronic conflict,[78] all of which are strongly associated with both relationship failure and poor outcomes for children.[79] There is no reason to promote marriage in such relationships. To the contrary, for high-conflict relationships, the data suggest that government policy should aim to discourage marriage and facilitate divorce.[80]

74 Garrison, op. cit., n 73; M. Garrison, 'The Decline of Formal Marriage: Inevitable or Reversible?', *Family Law Quarterly* 41, 2007, 491–520; M. Garrison, 'Nonmarital Cohabitation: Social Revolution and Legal Regulation', *Family Law Quarterly* 42, 2008, 309–31.

75 M. Garrison and E.S. Scott, 'Legal Regulation of Twenty-First Century Families', in Garrison and Scott, op. cit., n 8, pp. 303–26.

76 Sayare and De La Baume, op. cit., n 66.

77 D. Blankenhorn, *The Future of Marriage*, New York: Encounter Books, 2007; L.J. Waite and M. Gallagher, *The Case for Marriage: Why Married People Are Happier, Healthier, and Better Off Financially*, New York: Broadway Publishers, 2000.

78 Edin and Kefalas, op. cit., n 61.

79 Sigle-Rushton and McLanahan, op. cit., n 50.

80 Amato and Booth, op. cit., n 53; Emery, op. cit., n 41.

Instead of promoting marriage, government policy should focus on ameliorating the disadvantages that promote relational difficulties and failure. The underlying stresses that promote relational dysfunction and instability also contribute to other, arguably far more serious, deficits in family functioning. Single and adolescent parenting, substance abuse, mental health problems, adult family violence, child maltreatment, lack of social support and low socio-economic status are all highly correlated.[81] While the magnitude of the marriage 'premium' is controversial, it is entirely clear that marriage, by itself, cannot cure either pre-existing problems in family functioning or the stresses that promote such problems. It is also clear that these functional stresses are far more important predictors of outcomes for children than marital status.[82] Government policies aimed at ensuring that families can adequately provide for their children, educationally, emotionally and economically, are thus best calculated to promote family stability and child well-being in a range of dimensions.

81 M. Garrison, 'Reviving Marriage: Could We? Should We?', *Journal of Law and Family Studies* 10, 2008, 279–35; Garrison and Scott, op. cit., n 75.

82 Acs et al., op. cit., n 55.

1.2

MARRIAGE AND ALTERNATIVE STATUS RELATIONSHIPS IN THE NETHERLANDS

Wendy Schrama

Introduction

Over the last 20 years the trend set by the Netherlands (following Denmark, Norway and Sweden) in 1998 with the introduction of registered partnership and in 2001, with the opening up of marriage for same-sex couples, has been followed by a growing number of jurisdictions.[1] Meanwhile the status of marriage not only altered as a result of the movement towards equal rights for same-sex couples but also by the growing number of non-marital cohabitants. As a result of these changes, the position of marriage has been profoundly changed. The Netherlands therefore provides a good case study of a jurisdiction which has moved to a strongly diversified system of models for interpersonal relationships.[2]

In this contribution the legal developments in relation to marriage in the Netherlands over the past decades will be discussed. The central thesis is that the law dealing with intimate relationships evolved over the last two decades from a model based exclusively on marriage as the only relationship provided for and protected by the law to a more fluid relationship model. Next, attention will be paid to the challenges for the future. The first challenge is how to balance the trend of further individualization in marriage law with the fact that people still tend to make certain decisions which ask for a higher level of protection. Secondly, non-marital cohabitation,[3] which is a blind spot in the Dutch Civil Code where it concerns inter-partner relationships, will put pressure on the system.

The term 'relationship law' is used to identify the law regulating intimate relationships and in particular relationships between partners. Relationship law includes marriage law,[4] registered partnership law and the law in relation to non-marital cohabitation, which in the Netherlands is mostly case law.

1 See the developments described J. Scherpe, 'The Past, Present and Future of Registered Partnerships', in J. Scherpe and A. Hayward (eds), *The Future of Registered Partnerships*, Cambridge: Intersentia, 2017, and J. Scherpe, *The Present and Future of European Family Law*, Cheltenham: Edward Elgar Publishing Limited, 2016.

2 J. Miles, 'Unmarried Cohabitation in European Perspective', in J.M. Scherpe (ed.), *European Family Law*, vol. 111, Cheltenham: Edward Elgar, 2016, Ch. 3.

3 Different concepts are used for non-marital cohabitation such as unmarried cohabitation, informal cohabitation, de facto union, informal couples relationship, informal relationship. Here mostly the term non-marital cohabitation will be used.

4 Marriage law in the Netherlands only deals with civil marriage. Religious marriages are only allowed after a civil marriage has been concluded.

Legal change affecting the status of marriage

Three major themes, all centring around equality, have profoundly influenced relationship law. Equality is the driving force that influenced the relationship between men and women, between parents and children and between opposite-sex partners and same-sex partners.[5] In this section the legal changes which affected the status of marriage and which are the result of rapid social change are dealt with.

Equality and gender in relationship law

The legal position of men and women has been subject to substantial change over the last four decades. Many social developments initiated or triggered this legal reform.[6] (For further discussion of gender issues, see Chapter 5.1 of this book.) In the early 1970s marriage was the preferred and prescribed model for families. The Dutch system was, albeit implicitly, based on a marriage model in which the man's duty was to provide for the family and the woman's was to take care of the children and household. This was based on supposed differences between men and women.[7] Both spouses were important but contributed to the marriage in their own ways. Marriage law did not treat men and women alike.[8]

During the last three decades the legal position of women has improved. In 1974 gender equality was put on the government's agenda.[9] The policy changed from a separate but equal concept towards a marriage model in which men and women should be treated alike. Secularization accelerated the process. The traditional division of a full-time job for the male and no (paid) job for the female partner altered to a combination of a full-time job for men and a part-time job for women.[10] As a result of the legal changes in the Civil Code, marriage law is now gender neutral, at least in the books.[11] Society and the law no longer prescribe an exclusive type of marriage based on a gender-specific role division. Individuals have more freedom how to arrange their married lives.

Equality and children

Not only did the position of men and women change but so did the relationship between parents and children.[12] The explicit legal differences resulting in an inferior position for chil-

5 W.M. Schrama, 'Ontwikkelingen in het familierecht, Een blik in het verleden en op de toekomst van Boek 1 BW', *Ars Aequi* 2, 2012, 144–50.

6 For instance the general availability of contraceptives, individualization, secularization, increased welfare, economic growth and increasing labour participation of women.

7 See also E. Beck-Gernsheim, 'From Rights and Obligations to Contested Rights and Obligations: Individualization, Globalization, and Family Law', *Theoretical Inquiries in Law* 13, 2012, 1–14.

8 For instance, under the Civil Code until 1970 the man was the head of the family. Since 1957 women no longer lose their legal capacity when they marry. Asser-De Boer, *Mr. C. Asser's Handleiding tot de beoefening van het Nederlands Burgerlijk recht, Personen- en familierecht*, Deventer: Kluwer, 2010, No. 182.

9 F. Bucx, 'Gezinnen en gezinsbeleid, Een introductie', in F. Buck (ed.), *Gezinsrapport 2011, Een portret van het gezinsleven in Nederland*, The Hague: Sociaal en Cultureel Planbureau, 2011, p. 22.

10 J. van Thor, W. Portegijs and B. Hermans, *Gaan vrouwen steeds meer werken?, Emancipatiemonitor*, Den Haag: SCP/CBS, 2018.

11 Not in its operation. For example, maintenance law is in itself gender neutral, but in reality the overwhelming majority of creditors are women.

12 As a result of a number of social trends, including individualization and secularization, the law's approach towards children changed to a more individualized approach. See for instance: J. Noordman and H. van

dren born to unmarried mothers have been gradually abolished.[13] However, whereas a married father is a child's parent as a matter of law and shares parental responsibilities with the mother automatically, unmarried fathers still have to formally recognize the child no matter how long they cohabit with the child's mother and take formal steps to obtain parental responsibilities with the mother.[14] Recently, a more child-centred divorce law developed which also improved fathers' rights after a divorce.[15] By stressing the equality of parents after divorce, not only is the child's right to have a relationship with both parents reinforced but so are the father's rights (for further discussion, see Chapters 3.3–3.5 of this book). The position of children and fathers in informal relationships has been the topic of debate. It has been argued that family law should take societal trends into account.[16] The number of children born out of wedlock is still increasing.[17] Some Members of Parliament introduced a bill proposing to automatically grant joint parental responsibilities at the time the child is recognized by the father or second mother. Since then three years passed in which not much happened, which makes it rather unlikely that a concrete new act will be the result.[18]

Equality and same-sex couples

The most recent influence of equality on the law concerns the legal position of same-sex partners compared to that of opposite-sex partners (for further discussion, see Chapters 1.3–1.5 of this book). In 1991, in its report *Leefvormen* (Lifestyles), the Kortmann Committee recommended the creation of two types of registration for opposite-sex and same-sex partners. The first would be with the local municipal administration and would mainly have public law effects.[19] The second would be in the civil status register and would bring about the same effects as marriage. This was meant as an alternative to marriage for all couples, regardless of their sex. In 1993 the government agreed with the view of the committee that different lifestyles should be taken into account in the legislation, but rejected the proposed municipal registration.[20] The government adopted the form of registration in the civil status register, but excluded partners of the opposite sex. The subsequent government, however, changed the

---

Setten, *De ontwikkelingen van de ouder/kind-verhouding in het gezin*, in H. Peeters e.a., *Vijf eeuwen gezinsleven*, Nijmegen: SUN, 1988, pp. 140–62.

13 Asser-De Boer op. cit., n 6, nos 689–91a.

14 W.M. Schrama, 'Family Function over Family Form in the Law on Parentage?', *Utrecht Law Review* 4, 2008, 83–98. Available at www.utrechtlawreview.org.

15 Wet van 27 november 2008, Stb. 2008, 500;. Wet van 9 oktober 2008, Stb. 2008, 410.

16 W.M. Schrama, 'Over vaders, seks en afstamming: het afstammingsrecht voor verwekkers kritische beschouwd', *Ars Aequi*, maart 2016, 212–18; W.M. Schrama, *Aanpassing afstammings- en gezagsrecht gewenst voor ongehuwd samenwonende ouders*, Justitiële Verkenningen 2016, nr. 4, Den Haag: Boom Juridische Uitgevers 2016, pp. 30–44; M. Vonk, Niet samen zijn, NTM/NJCM-bull. 2013/40.

17 Central Statistics the Netherlands. Available at https://opendata.cbs.nl/statline/#/CBS/nl/dataset/82056NED /table?ts=1572515292622 (accessed 31 October 2019). In 2018 93.500 children were born out of married parents, and 55.800 out of unmarried parents. It is not exactly known how many of these parents cohabit.

18 Parliamentary Papers II, 2016–2017, No. 34605, *Voorstel van wet van de leden Bergkamp en Van Wijngaarden tot wijziging van Boek 1 van het Burgerlijk Wetboek in verband met directe koppeling van erkenning en gezamenlijk gezag voor ongehuwde en niet-geregistreerde partners*. Available at www.eerstekamer.nl/behandeling/20161115/voorstel_van_wet/document3/f=/vk97n9jt1fzh.pdf (accessed 31 October 2019).

19 For instance in the field of social security law. With regard to private law effects the partners would be obliged to maintain each other during the registration and for a short period thereafter.

20 It would be too expensive while the aim (prevention of fraud) would not be met.

proposals. It extended the possibility of registration to couples of the opposite sex, but excluded it for the small group of people who are not permitted to marry by reason of being too closely related by blood.

Making marriage available to same-sex partners was not seriously considered at the initial stage, but later during the debates in Parliament the question arose whether it would still constitute discrimination if same-sex partners were allowed only to register their relationship, but not to marry. The second Kortmann Committee was appointed to report on this subject and on relationships with children in these types of relationship. Meanwhile, the bill on registered partnership continued its way through the legislative process. In October 1997, by a majority of five to three, the committee recommended that marriage should be opened up to same-sex couples, because only in this way could discrimination be removed. The committee however unanimously concluded that registration of a partnership should have no such effects on parentage. Protection of the legal position of children should be achieved through shared custody and guardianship, but not by making the partners legal parents.

In February 1998 the government initially expressed the view that it was opposed to giving same-sex couples the right to marry, but a majority in Parliament did not agree. Following the general election in May 1998 the new coalition government agreed to prepare a bill to make marriage available to same-sex couples. In December 1998 the bill was presented to the Council of State.[21] Then in 2001 marriage was opened up to same-sex couples as the first jurisdiction in the world to do so.[22] Between 2011 and 2017, 11,420 male and 12,722 female couples have married.[23]

The next stage in the equal rights development relates to parenting rights and duties for same-sex couples. First, the social mother was allowed to adopt her partner's child.[24] Furthermore, the same act allowed intercountry adoption for married same-sex couples, from which they were previously excluded.[25] In addition, the option to obtain joint parental responsibilities was extended to social parents, although a court order was necessary.[26] Next, the system of joint parental responsibilities was changed so that the mother and the social mother obtained joint parental responsibilities as a matter law if they were married or registered partners.[27] This was regardless whether the spouses were the legal parents of the children.[28] Part of the package to improve the legal position of parents and children in this situation was a change in the law concerning names as a result of which children could acquire the surname of the social parent. Subsequently, the adoption conditions for internal Dutch adoptions have been relaxed for mothers. The social mother can apply to the court for an adoption order even before the child's birth.[29] The conditions which normally apply in case of adoption are exempted, which makes it easier, faster and less risky to become a parent.

21 An advisory body.

22 Wet van 21 december 2000 tot wijziging van Boek 1 van het Burgerlijk Wetboek in verband met de openstelling van het huwelijk voor personen van hetzelfde geslacht (Wet openstelling huwelijk), Stb. 2001, 9.

23 Central Statistics, Statline database (http://statline.cbs.nl). See table: 'Huwen; huwelijkssluitingen en huwende personen naar diverse kenmerken' (accessed 31 October 2019).

24 Wet van 24 december 1997; Wet van 21 december 2000.

25 Wet van 24 oktober 2008, Stb. 2008, 425.

26 Wet van 30 oktober 1997.

27 On condition that the child does not have another parent. Wet van 4 oktober 2001.

28 Art. 1:253sa Civil Code.

29 Wet van 24 oktober 2008, Stb. 2008, 425. in force since 1 January 2009.

In the meantime the Kalsbeek Committee[30] advised the government in 2007 to introduce statutory provisions to the effect that the social mother was allowed to legally acknowledge the child born within the relationship thus establishing a legal parental relationship with the child.[31] A study was commissioned by the Ministry of Justice[32] concerning the position of a donor and what this might imply for the child's right to know its father. This culminated in a bill regarding the parentage of the social mother, which was accepted by the Second Chamber of Parliament in 2013. To summarize, a social mother who is married to the biological mother of a child who is conceived with an unknown[33] donor, is as a matter of law its legal parent. If a known donor is used or if the child is born outside marriage, the social mother may acknowledge the child. A known donor who shares 'family life' with the child (that is, who has close personal ties with the child) may also acknowledge the child. In some cases, the court will have to decide on competing claims on parenthood if both the social mother and the donor with family life apply for replacing consent to acknowledge the child because a child can only have two parents. These changes fundamentally alter the biological concept of the law on descent, since in most heterosexual relationships both parents are the biological parents, whereas in homosexual relationships they never both are. In the Second Chamber a large majority supported the bill, but in the First Chamber a critical approach seems to prevail, so it remains to be seen what will be the outcome (for further discussion, see Chapters 3.1–3.2 of this book).

Although the law has been profoundly altered, these changes hardly raised any protest. No mass demonstrations occurred, such as happened in France when marriage was opened up to same-sex couples and there is hardly any debate in relation to the plans to change the law of descent.[34] In only 20 years family law fundamentally changed, mostly on a step by step basis.

In 2016 a government appointed committee (*Staatscommissie Herijking Ouderschap/Government Committee Reassessment Legal Parentage*) published its report.[35] It had *inter alia* to take up the legal rethinking of parentage, parenthood and parental responsibilities in the light of the rise and lobbying of multi-parent families for a better legal position for children and parents. Would it be wise to adopt a new act on multi-parentage and parental responsibilities for more than two parents? This is particularly relevant for same-sex couples, for example a two-father family which will conceive and raise a child with a two-mother family. The far-reaching advice of the

30 Appointed as a result of a motion in the Second Chamber of Parliament: Parliamentary Papers II 2006/07, 30 800 VI, No. 60. Commissie lesbisch ouderschap en interlandelijke adoptie, *Rapport lesbisch ouderschap*, The Hague, October 2007 and *Rapport interlandelijke adoptie, Alles van waarde is weerloos*, The Hague 29 May 2008.

31 Parliamentary Papers II, 2007–2008, Letter of the Minister of Justice of 12 August 2008 to the Second Chamber.

32 C. Forder, *Erkenning door de vrouwelijke partner van de moeder*, The Hague, 2 February 2009. Available at www.tweedekamer.nl/images/305510024bijlage01_118-188576.pdf.

33 Unknown is relative: insemination will only take place with sperm of registered donors and information about the donor is at different stages available to the parents and the child.

34 In the literature some critical remarks have been made, for instance: A.J.M. Nuytinck, 'Lesbisch ouderschap. Bespreking van het rapport van de Commissie lesbisch ouderschap en interlandelijke adoptie', *commissie-Kalsbeek*. Available at http://repub.eur.nl/res/pub/11421/Lesbisch%20ouderschap.pdf; M.J.A. van Mourik, *Interview with the Volkskrant*. Available at www.volkskrant.nl/vk/nl/2844/Archief/archief/article/detail/446407/1996/04/18/Met-homohuwelijk-schaf-je-in-wezen-het-huwelijk-af-Echtverbintenis-verwordt-volgens-notaris-en-hoogleraar-Van-Mourik-tot-een-organisatiemodel.dhtml.

35 Staatscommissie Herijking Ouderschap, Kind en Ouders in de 21ste eeuw, The Hague, 2016. English summary of the report is available at www.government.nl/documents/reports/2016/12/07/childand-parent-in-the-21ste-century.

Committee was to give legal recognition to these new types of family, both in parentage law and in terms of parental responsibilities.[36] A maximum of four adults is foreseen, who live in at most two households. They could make a preconception agreement on various issues regarding the child: division of care, main residence of the child, financial obligations of all the parents, the surname to be given to the child, and how intended parents plan to address possible disputes and changes to the agreement. The family court would then have to test this agreement in light of the best interest of the child (which is, at this point, not even conceived yet). If the judge grants the order, all parents will become a legal parent from the child's birth with all of them having full parental responsibilities.

Objections were raised in particular regarding parental responsibilities, because three or four parents with full parental responsibilities would substantially raise the potential for conflicts if the parents separate or are no longer be able to cooperate together.[37] The government then commissioned research: into the implications of deviating from the classical two-parent family in other areas of law. Inheritance and succession law, tax law, social security law and immigration law are not as easily adapted as family law could be to more than two legal parents. In July 2019 the government's reaction was published to these reports. Given the far-reaching nature of the advice, the policy of the government is rather restricted. The step forward is the plan to introduce shared parental responsibilities for a maximum of four adults. Only two of the adults would have full parental responsibilities; the other two would have a far more limited type of parental responsibility (in Dutch: *deelgezag*, translated as partial parental responsibilities) which does not exist under the current law. It would basically only give a right to take simple everyday decisions and actions, such as being present at a parent-teacher meeting, which are not very problematic anyway. But adults with partial parental responsibility would have a right to veto a substantial change in the allocation of care, which the parents with full parental responsibilities could only overcome with the consent of the family court. So the government did not follow the advice to introduce a multi-parent legal framework, nor did it introduce full parental responsibilities for more than two parents.[38] It refers to the higher level of conflicts which is expected to occur if that were to be introduced. This is striking, since the debate in the legal doctrine focused mostly on problems resulting from shared parental responsibilities and not in respect of parentage.

Another argument put forward by the government for its decision is that multi-parentage is really exceptional worldwide, so there is hardly any experience of it and it is not clear whether more conflicts are a serious threat to the child's development. Finally, perhaps the most important reason, even if not explicit, is that introduction of multi-parentage and parental responsibilities for more than two adults would require large-scale adaptation of other areas of law (tax law, social security, etc.) as well a complete revision of the civil and population registry. This would be costly and complex.[39] Taking the experiences from the past as a crystal ball for future developments, I expect that it is a matter of time, just as it was with registered partnership and the opening of marriage for same-sex couples, before further steps will be announced. In the meantime the government is buying time to come up with adequately prepared legislation.[40]

36 I. Boone, 'Co-Parenting before Conception: The Low Countries' Approach to Intentional Multi-Parent Families', *Family & Law*, February 2018. DOI: 10.5553/FenR/.000034.

37 See Boone, n 36, in the Conclusions.

38 Parliamentary Papers II, 2018–2019, 33863, No. 45.

39 Ibid., at pp. 10–11.

40 For further discussion of these issues, see G. Kessler, 'The Parentage Disruption: A Comparative Approach', *Int. J. Law, Policy & Fam.* 33(3), 2019, 316–36.

The status of marriage

The changing status of marriage is marked by changes in relationship behaviour. As a result of individualization, secularization and the emancipation of women, the popularity of marriage has diminished.[41] (See Chapter 1.1 of this book.) The marriage rate decreased, whereas the divorce rate rose.[42] (See Chapter 2.2 of this book.) Furthermore, the number of single-person households rose,[43] as did the number of relationships without children.[44] Lifestyles different from traditional marriage became more prominent, including serial monogamy and stepfamilies.[45] Registered partnership, which, from a legal perspective, is very similar to marriage, became more popular than expected.[46] About 10,000 couples (both opposite and same-sex) register their partnerships every year compared to 69,000 to 75,000 couples who marry every year. There has been an increase in couples who opt for registered partnership. In 2018, 20,000 registered a partnership, which is twice the number in 2014.[47] The number of cohabiting couples is estimated at one million.[48] Some data indicate that non-marital cohabitation as a permanent alternative to marriage is increasing,[49] including a growing proportion of second and third children who are born to non-marital cohabitants.[50] New data show that of all couples who started to cohabit in 2000, 53 percent were still together after 15 years. Of the couples still together, almost all had children and 80 percent had married. Another 8 percent had children and were still cohabiting.[51] Obviously marriage is no longer perceived as the only acceptable relationship in which to have children. The percentage of children born out of wedlock rose from 2 percent in the 1970s to 42 percent in 2012, but dropped to 38 percent in 2018.[52] Thus, the exclusive link between procreation and marriage has been broken.[53]

Nevertheless, marriage remains the prevailing type of relationship, out of a number of possible relationship types people may choose, but both registered partnership and unmarried cohabitation are on the rise.[54]

41 Bucx, op. cit., n 9, p. 20.
42 Ibid., p. 14: one in four marriages are estimated to end in a divorce.
43 The average number of children dropped from 2,6 in 1970 to 1,66 in 2018: Central Statistics: http://statline.cbs.nl, in the table: 'Geboorte; kerncijfers vruchtbaarheid, leeftijd moeder, regio' (accessed 31 October 2019).
44 A. De Graaf, 'Gezinnen in cijfers', in F. Buck (ed.), *Gezinsrapport 2011, Een portret van het gezinsleven in Nederland*, The Hague: Sociaal en Cultureel Planbureau, 2011, pp. 36–7.
45 Ibid., p. 35; Bucx, op. cit., n 9, p. 20.
46 K. Boele-Woelki, I. Curry-Sumner, M. Jansen and W.M. Schrama, *Huwelijk of Geregistreerd Partnerschap?*, Deventer: Kluwer, 2007.
47 S. te Riele and K. Stückradt, *Ruim twintig jaar geregistreerd partnerschap*, The Hague: CBS, 2019. Available at www.cbs.nl/nl-nl/achtergrond/2019/25/ruim-twintig-jaar-geregistreerd-partnerschap (accessed 31 October 2019).
48 Central Statistics. Available at https://opendata.cbs.nl/#/CBS/nl/dataset/82905NED/table?ts=1572593196398.
49 J. Latten, *De schone schijn van de burgerlijke staat*, CBS, Bevolkingstrends, 4e kwartaal 2004, pp. 46–60. A. de Graaf, *Gezinnen in cijfers, Gezinsrapport*, The Hague: SCP, 2011, pp. 45–6.
50 Central Statistics. Available at http://statline.cbs.nl.
51 Central Statistics. Available at www.cbs.nl/nl-nl/nieuws/2019/06/helft-eerste-samenwoners-na-15-jaar-nog-samen.
52 Central Statistics. Available at https://opendata.cbs.nl/#/CBS/nl/dataset/82055NED/table?ts=1572592694019.
53 Compare G.F. Douglas, 'Marriage, Cohabitation, and Parenthood: From Contract to Status?', in S. Katz, J. Eekelaar and M. Maclean (eds), *Cross Currents: Family Law and Policy in the US and England*, Oxford: Oxford University Press, 2000, pp. 211–33 at p. 212.
54 See also Beck-Gernsheim, op. cit., n 7.

Current policy challenges

Policy goals of relationship law

From a policy perspective it is clear that in recent decades the government has not encouraged people to choose marriage over non-marital cohabitation. Rather, one of the most important policy goals has been to promote equality and to give people the opportunity to choose their own type of relationship. The right to self-determination and tolerance towards different family forms are predominant; the liberal orientation of the state includes an open-minded approach in which the state does not prescribe what type of relationship people should live in.[55] Have we attained this goal?

Important questions have been left unanswered, which may be partially due to the focus on equality. The first is: what is the role of the state in relation to intimate relationships, other than realizing fundamental rights, like equality? Twenty-five years ago, some Dutch and Belgian legal scholars were of the opinion that it would be best to abolish marriage.[56] The state could leave it to the parties to agree on the legal effects of their relationship. If partners wished to celebrate marriage, they could go to church. Those ideas are faintly echoed today,[57] but the large majority of legal scholars are of the opinion that the state does have a role in the field of relationship law. But what that role is or should be is often unclear.

In order to answer that question, we will have to disentangle what the policy goals of relationship law are. Remarkably, little is to be found in the Dutch legal literature on this subject. More inspiration is to be derived from the Anglo-Saxon debate on what family law is and what it is for. Ferguson and Brake recently argued that family law 'can serve as crucial state endorsement to individuals' relationships through permitting individuals to enter into a formal legal 'status' such as marriage or parenthood; it can serve as a mechanism for the enforcement of rights and obligations between and against 'family' members, as well as signalling the justifiability of such enforcement; and it can serve as a mechanism for privileging 'familial' above 'nonfamilial' relationships (…), as well as suggesting the justifiability of such privileging'.[58] Diduck concludes that family law should deal with defining (and thus creating) responsibilities both in the relation of partners, but also in relation to the state.[59] Eekelaar puts the role of family law over time in perspective and comes to the conclusion that, while in earlier times its primary purpose was to uphold existing power structures, this had declined through the development of countervailing rights to protect the interests of individuals against the way power is exercised and that, while it still has a role in constructing supportive frameworks (whether marriage or equivalent

55 See also Beck-Gernsheim, op. cit., n 7, who sees a general trend that legislators do not prescribe particular forms of family life.

56 For instance: A. Heyvaert, 'Het wezen van de instituten afstamming en huwelijk', *Rechtskundig Weekblad* 1979–1980, 737; H. Willekens, 'De werking van grondrechten in de verhouding tussen samenwonende sexuele partners', in K. Rimanque (ed.), *De toepasselijkheid van grondrechten in private verhoudingen*, Antwerpen: Kluwer 1982, p. 341; J. Hes, 'Dereguleren en bezuinigen: schaf het huwelijk af', *Nederlands Juristenblad* 1984, 233; H. van Maarseveen, 'Het *huwelijk* privatiseren', *Tijdschrift voor Familie- en Jeugdrecht* 1985, 37–9; W.M. Schrama, *De niet-huwelijkse samenleving in het Nederlandse en Duitse recht*, Deventer: Kluwer 2004, p. 566; F. Swennen, *Het huwelijk afschaffen?*, Antwerpen: Intersentia, 2004.

57 F. Schonewille, *Partijautonomie in het relatievermogensrecht*, Apeldoorn: Maklu, 2012. For a US discussion see A. Bernstein (ed.), *Marriage Proposals: Questioning a Legal Status*, New York and London: New York University Press, 2006.

58 R.J.S. Schwitters, *Recht en samenleving in verandering: inleiding in de rechtssociologie*, Deventer: Kluwer 2008, p. 27; W.M. Schrama, 'Een redelijk en billijk relatierecht', *Tijdschrift voor Privaatrecht* (4), 2010.

59 A. Diduck, 'What Is Family Law For?', *Current Legal Problems* 64, 2011, 288.

institutions) the emphasis has, according to him, shifted to dealing with the consequences of casualties of damaged personal relationships.[60] Leckey writes: 'The general idea is that the state benefits from the stability and caregiving produced when individuals invest in long-term relationships'.[61]

Although there seems to be some differences between the various authors on what the role of family law actually is, these views accord with a socio-legal point of view, expressed in the Netherlands, where at least four policy goals of relationship law have been discerned. The first is to regulate the effects of living together and sharing a life on the basis of an intimate relationship. If there was no relationship law, the interpersonal effects of the relationship would be governed by general property and contract law. These are not particularly suited to deal with these types of relationship. A second, closely related, function is to prevent or minimize conflicts between the partners. By regulating intimate relationships, the potential conflict level between the ex-partners will probably be lower, since the terms and conditions of the relationship are clear. In this way, the law can indirectly contribute to relationship stability, although (perhaps remarkably), this is not the explicit policy of the government.[62] The third function is to protect weaker spouses and indirectly the children by imposing a certain minimum level of mandatory partner solidarity, in particular after a relationship breakdown. The community of property system,[63] the spousal maintenance system[64] and the effects of marriage on pensions,[65] are typical examples of this protection. This seems to be most closely related to Eekelaar's dealing with the consequences of damaged relationships. A fourth function is to promote rights of individuals, such as equality for same-sex couples and men and women; this reflects the power structure inherent in family law and its exclusive character which not only affects partners and children, but also the relation vis-à-vis the state.

These policy aims are presumably not only in the interest of individual partners, but they also serve a public policy goal. If the law could to some extent prevent poverty in families after a divorce or separation in low-income families or if it could indirectly promote relationship stability and distribute the risks of a relationship (and the division of roles between spouses), it would serve a general interest. There are clear indications from research of Dutch sociologists that lower-educated families in particular opt more often for informal relationships, and have at the same time a higher risk of separation. Almost 33 percent of unmarried couples with a lower educational level who have a child are separated after 15 years as opposed to 12 percent of higher-educated couples with children. This higher risk of a relationship breakdown has potential high financial risks for women and for children who usually reside with their mothers after separation.[66]

60 J. Eekelaar, 'Family Law and Legal Theory', in E. Brake and L. Ferguson (eds), *Philosophical Foundations of Children's and Family Law*, Oxford: Oxford University Press, 2018, pp. 41–58.

61 R. Leckey, 'Cohabitants, Choice and the Public Interest', in E. Brake and L. Ferguson (eds), ibid., pp. 121–2.

62 As in some other jurisdictions has been considered to be an important goal, eg Douglas op. cit., n 53. In the Netherlands an explanation might be that tolerance and self-determination is perceived as so important that it is the role of the state is to facilitate these choices.

63 It includes all assets of both spouses regardless whether they are acquired before or after the marriage celebration and includes donations or inheritance; art. 1:94 CC.

64 In principle a maximum of twelve years under the old law and 5 under the new law (having effect from 1 January 2020), related to the financial position of the spouses during marriage, art. 1:157 CC.

65 In principle spouses are both entitled to the old age pension one of them acquired during the marriage: art. 1:153 CC.

66 R. van Gaalen, K. van Houdt and A.-R. Poortman, 'Trouwen, kinderen krijgen en (echt)scheiden naar opleidingsniveau, Demografische beslissingen binnen huishoudens aan het begin van de 21e eeuw', in *Statistische trends*, Den Haag: CBS, 2019, p. 14.

One of the difficulties in identifying policy challenges is that in order to assess the effectiveness of the current policy, empirical insight is necessary. However, in the Netherlands hardly any empirical legal studies in this field have been carried out, which makes it difficult to develop evidence-based policy.[67] Evidence-based research is necessary in order to see what is going on in the real world and to assess the effects of family law and family policy.[68] Both economic research and sociological knowledge helps to underpin family law with a solid base in reality.[69] In the absence of empirical data, in the next sections some thoughts concerning future challenges will be presented.

A first challenge: individualized or care-based relationship law

One challenge relates to the ongoing individualization, which will probably increasingly affect relationship law.[70] A more individualized relationship law would reduce the legal effects of the relationship; each partner would only be responsible for his or her acts and there would be little room for a common perspective and little place for taking into account acts which serve a common interest, such as taking care of the children. One could argue that in the light of the diminishing differences in role division between working men and caretaking women, the need for protection by way of state intervention will be reduced (for further discussion, see Chapters 6.1–6.2 of this book). In some respects, the loosening of the post-relationship ties has already begun in relation to maintenance. In 1994, the lifelong duty to maintain a needy ex-spouse was reduced in principle to 12 years.[71] On January 2020, a new act entered into force in the Netherlands, introducing a shorter duration of spousal maintenance rights and duties.[72] The reduction is substantial, from 12 years to five years with some exceptions for older spouses and couples with young children. In January 2018 new legislation was introduced on the scope of the community of property system. Previously, the Dutch community of property had a universal nature, absorbing almost all assets, regardless how they were acquired by the spouses. Now the Netherlands finally has a system in line with most other countries, which have a matrimonial property regime whereby premarital assets are excluded from the community of property, as are

67 One example is the study which addresses the issue whether a high level of legal commitment (e.g. marriage versus non-marital cohabitation) results in more investment by the partners in the relationship in the Netherlands, which turned out not to be the case. A.-R. Poortman and M. Mills, 'Investments in Marriage and Cohabitation: The Role of Legal and Interpersonal Commitment', *Journal of Marriage and the Family* 74, 2012, 357–76.

68 For instance: K. Bogenschneider, H. Normandin, E. Onaga, S. Bowman and S.M. MacDermid, 'Generating Evidence on Disseminating Evidence to Policymakers', in K. Bogenschneider and T. Corbett (eds), *Evidence-Based Policymaking: Insights from Policy-Minded Researchers and Research Minded Policymaker*, New York: Taylor & Francis, 2010, pp. 253–90; Bogenschneider, K. and T.J. Corbett, 'Family Policy: Becoming a Field of Inquiry and Subfield of Social Policy', *Journal of Marriage and Family* 72, 2010, 783–803.

69 M.J. Brien, L.A. Lillard and S. Sterni, 'Cohabitation, Marriage, and Divorce in a Model of Match Quality', *International Economic Review* 47, 2006, 451–94; M. Brinig (ed.), *Economics of Family Law*, Northampton: Edgar Elgar Publishing, 2007; C. Vogler, 'Cohabiting Couples: Rethinking Money in the Household at the Beginning of the Twenty First Century', *The Sociological Review* 53, 2005, 1–29; J. Pahl, 'Individualisation in Couple Finances: Who Pays for the Children?', *Social Policy and Society* 4, 2005, 381–91.

70 See also Beck-Gernsheim, op. cit., n 7.

71 Wet Limitering alimentatie van 28 April 1994, Staatsblad 324.

72 Wet van 18 juni 2019 tot wijziging van Boek 1 van het Burgerlijk Wetboek en van enige andere wetten in verband met de herziening van het stelsel van partneralimentatie (Wet herziening partneralimentatie), Staatsblad 2019, 283.

gifts and assets inherited during marriage. On the one hand, this change makes perfect sense, since the extent of solidarity under a universal community of property appears out of line with social norms of more individuality. On the other hand, almost all married couples have lived together as a couple before entering into marriage. Many unmarried couples have children. That implies that imbalances between partners arise long before marriage but are no longer compensated for, whereas under the old system the premarital assets became part of the community property. Basically, there is more individualism at the cost of a more relational concept of choices made during the lifespan of the relationship – whether that is married or unmarried. A more individualistic approach comes at a price, since there is a clear gender dimension in this respect.[73] (For further discussion, see Chapter 2.6 of this book.)

On the other hand one could argue that, although the former gender-specific role division has been changed, differences between men and women as regards social roles and social norms are still substantial, in particular in the Netherlands with a strong mother culture[74] and where a one-and-a half-earner model is dominant for couples with children.[75] The presence of children and the related loss of earning capacity justify a higher level of protection in order to balance the risks of an unequal, gender-based division of work and caretaking. In this respect more evidence-based knowledge would be welcome. Does maintenance after divorce actually make a difference? How many children in one-parent divorced families headed by the mother are facing financial difficulties? What are the effects of the community of property system? With more evidence about actual practice, it would be possible to design a more effective policy. This type of research could also explore the arguments in favour and against a care-based model.

A second challenge: non-marital cohabitation

The second challenge concerns non-marital cohabitation (for further discussion, see Chapters 1.1, 1.3 and 1.5 of this book). This topic has received attention in large comparative family law projects. The first is the Empowering European Families project,[76] carried out by principal investigators Christiane Wendehorst and Wendy Schrama (author of this chapter) together with a working group consisting of both academics and legal professionals from various countries in Europe.[77] On the basis of a questionnaire 27 reporters explained their legal system as regards informal couple relationships. Particular attention was given to the level of party autonomy for couples to arrange their own legal affairs. On the basis of these reports a toolkit for legal professionals has been developed when they deal with cross-border informal couples, published

73 A.J.M. Nuytinck, *Van huwelijksvermogensrecht naar samenlevingsvermogensrecht?*, Ars Notariatus LXX, Deventer: Kluwer, 1996.

74 A culture in which mothers are deemed to be the best carers for children: W. Portegijs, S. Alejandro Perez and M. van den Brakel, 'Wie zorgt er voor de kinderen?', in *Emancipatiemonitor*, The Hague: SCP/CBS, 2018.

75 Ibid. In 2017, men worked on average 39 hours, and women 28. Women spend more hours on family care, for children but also other relatives (older parents). Part of the couples aims for a more equal division, but only 20 percent actually manages.

76 See the website: www.europeanlawinstitute.eu/projects-publications/completed-projects/completed-projects-sync/empowering-european-families/. Country reports will be published at a later date.

77 The Working group consisted of Anne Barlow (professor, United Kingdom), Kerstin Bartsch (mediator, Germany), Margareta Brattström (professor, Sweden), Pedro Carrión García de Parada (Notary, Spain), Mark Harper (solicitor, United Kingdom); Maarit Jänterä-Jareborg (professor, Sweden), Matthias Neumayr (Judge, Austria), Eve Põtter (notary, Estonia), François Trémosa (notary, France).

on the website. The second large comparative law project was carried out by the Commission on European Family Law (CEFL), chaired by Katharina Boele-Woelki. The country reports[78] on *de facto* unions (as they are called within the CEFL context) were used for the development of European Principles of Family Law on this topic.[79] Both projects show an increasing number of jurisdictions where specific laws have been introduced for non-marital cohabitation, providing both legal certainty as to the applicable rules, as well as protection.[80] The contents of these laws differ considerably, ranging from an (almost) equal-to-marriage-model to a more ad hoc approach, dealing with some legal aspects of the relationship, but not all. The Netherlands is, however, one of the many countries which has still not adopted a policy in this respect. The approach of the Dutch system is 'schizophrenic', a term used by Barlow in the context of English law[81] but equally suitable for the Dutch approach.[82] In most areas of law, non-marital cohabitation is legally recognized, for instance in tax law, social security law, criminal law, but not in family and inheritance law where non-marital cohabitation is unrecognized in the Civil Code. Instead of specific relationship law, general contract and property law apply in the relation between the partners, which often result in unpredictable and unfair outcomes.[83] The conflict level is high and many partners go to court to resolve their financial and property issues. One might think that party autonomy is the key to the solution, since the partners can make their own relationship model. The percentage of couples with a cohabitation contract drawn up by a notary is relatively high, at about 50 percent,[84] which is the highest in Europe. However, we know little about their characteristics, for example whether or not they later marry. But even with a contract, the problems are not resolved. Explorative empirical research indicates that the contents of the contract seem to be more determined by the notary than by the actual situation of the couple.[85] Another essential problem is that life is dynamic, while cohabitation contracts are static. This creates problems, since cohabitants rarely return to the notary to update their contract. Besides, partners seem not to contract with an eye to an eventual separation, since they simply do not imagine they will ever separate.[86] Under present conditions, cohabitation contracts are no real solution for the absence of specific provisions in the Civil Code.

Given the very low level of protection, the lack of certainty and the high conflict potential, one would expect some government policy on the matter. But the Dutch government is slow in its actions, and instituted research only some years ago. The researchers have concluded that

78 See the CEFL's website: https://ceflonline.net/ (accessed 31 October 2019).

79 K. Boele-Woelki, F. Ferrand, C. González-Beilfuss, M. Jänterä-Jareborg, N. Lowe, D. Martiny and V. Todorova, *Principles of European Family Law Regarding Property, Maintenance and Succession Rights of Couples in de facto Unions*, Antwerp: Intersentia, 2019.

80 In Europe: Finland, Hungary, Italy, Ireland, Malta, Portugal, Scotland, Slovenia, Spain, Sweden and Serbia (not included in both projects). Outside Europe Canada, Norway, Russia, Ukraine, different states in Australia and the US, New-Zealand.

81 A. Barlow, 'Regulation of Cohabitation, Changing Family Policies and Social Attitudes: A Discussion of Britain Within Europe', *Law & Policy* 26, 2004, 57–86.

82 W.M. Schrama, 'The Dutch Approach to Informal Lifestyles: Family Function over Family Form?', *International Journal of Law, Policy and the Family* 22, 2008, 311–32. See also W.M. Schrama, Dutch country report CEFL, See the CEFL's website: https://ceflonline.net/ (accessed 31 October 2019).

83 See also G. Douglas, J. Pearce and H. Woodward, *A Failure of Trust: Resolving Property Disputes on Cohabitation Breakdown*, Report of a Research Study funded by the ESRC, Cardiff, 2007, p. 140.

84 A. de Graaf, *CBS, Webmagazine*, 10 February 2010. Available at www.cbs.nl.

85 Research by P. Kuik, W. Schrama and L. Verstappen, *Publication Aimed in: Familie & Recht*. Available at www.familienrecht.nl.

86 Schrama, op. cite., n 56, p. 588.

a small proportion of partners in a non-marital relationship encountered severe problems,[87] and that a number of specific legal instruments[88] could be introduced to overcome them. However, in 2012 the government declined to follow the recommendations.[89] It argued that the suggested legal instruments were not necessary, since contract and property law were sufficient. Although this might be true in theory, practice for over 20 years shows that lawyers and courts deal with these provisions quite differently. Moreover, some problems cannot be resolved within the legal system, even theoretically.[90] It is a missed opportunity. During the debates in Parliament on the shortening of spousal maintenance for married couples, questions regarding maintenance rights for informal couples were raised. The government is still not in favour, but promised an empirical legal study on this topic, expected in 2021. The existing pension splitting system for married couples has recently been evaluated. One issue was whether pension rights should be extended to unmarried cohabitants. The researchers concluded that it would be better not to do so. Reference is made to 'facts' that unmarried cohabitants themselves would not feel a need for sharing each other's pension rights, that unmarried cohabitants are more often financially independent than married couples and that these couples would be fully legally aware in opting for less solidarity. These claims are not based on any facts or research. It is more likely that a second set of arguments in the report had been decisive, namely, that it would be difficult and more costly for pension funds to work with unmarried couples. The Minister of Justice agreed with the report and decided to leave things as they stand now.[91]

It should not be the form of the relationship that is decisive, but its function.[92] If non-marital cohabitation is functionally equivalent to marriage, the law should also take non-marital couples into account in family law and inheritance law.[93] Care within families is crucial, not only in terms of parents for minor children but, increasingly, given the ageing of society, by adult children (-in law) for parents (-in law). This issue should definitely be considered by the state, because it is likely that informal couples will take care of older parents. In a marriage partners are to some extent protected against the negative effects. If the same support is provided during an informal relationship, this is seen as an individual choice. To my mind that is not wise.

87 M.V. Antokolskaia, B. Breederveld, J.E. Hulst, W.D. Kolkman, F.R. Salomons and L.C.A. Verstappen, *Koude uitsluiting, Materiële problemen en onbillijkheden na scheiding van in koude uitsluiting gehuwde echtgenoten en na scheiding van ongehuwd samenlevende partners, alsmede instrumenten voor de overheid om deze tegen te gaan*, The Hague: WODC, 2011. As a very rough estimation, about 20,000 women with children suffer serious financial difficulties after a relationship breakdown. The number of couples who experience an unfair dissolution of their non-marital relationship could not be estimated.

88 Including a maintenance right after separation based on a discretionary power of the court. The government at first seemed to opt for this solution, but after consultation of the judiciary, solicitors and notaries, decided against it, since it would not be practicable. Parliamentary Papers II 2011–12, 28 678 No. 29.

89 Parliamentary Papers II 2011–12, 28 867 No. 23.

90 In particular investments in the relationship by taking care for children are not in any way successfully to be redressed under the current provisions.

91 Letter of the Minister of Justice 8 March 2018, reference number 2018-0000025158, Evaluatie Wet verevening pensioenrechten bij scheiding.

92 Schrama, op. cit., n 82.

93 See A.-R. Poortman and M. Mills, 'Investments in Marriage and Cohabitation: The Role of Legal and Interpersonal Commitment', *Journal of Marriage and the Family* 74, 2012, 357–76. See for England: J. Eekelaar and M. Maclean, 'Marriage and the Moral Bases of Personal Relationships', *Journal of Law and Society* 31, 2004, 510–38.

Conclusion

Marriage law has been reformed in just a few decades to an unanticipated extent. The Dutch policy with respect to relationships and families has been primarily aimed at realizing equality and facilitating individual life choices. As a result of the social and legal changes, the law dealing with intimate relationships evolved from a model based exclusively on heterosexual marriage with children as the only relationship provided for and protected by the law to a more fluid relationship model in which a greater variety of choices is possible. A minimum level of prescribed solidarity is intact and protection of vulnerable spouses is seen as a task of the state.

The fast and fundamental changes present new challenges. It is up to the government to develop an up-to-date long-term perspective on relationship law. Relationship law will presumably become more individualized. It will be a real challenge to find a balance between party autonomy and protection. For those couples who, married or not, raise children, the state should intervene by imposing a higher protection level. Party autonomy is important, but it is up to the state to intervene when general interests are at stake. The persistent differences between men and women in relation to work and care which is typical for the Netherlands will require future attention.

It is inevitable that non-marital cohabitation will put the existing rigid boundaries between formal and informal relationships in family law and inheritance law under increasing pressure. The lack of any regulation, conflict prevention and protection for non-marital cohabitants results in conflicts, injustice and legal uncertainty. A functional approach could be helpful, in which not the legal form but the real function of the relationship is taken as a point of departure. Whether relationship law is the most suitable instrument to deal with these two challenges is a matter which needs further investigation on an empirical basis. Research could be very valuable in this respect in order to develop evidence-based policy and evidence-based law.

Despite the fundamental changes, marriage still holds a strong position. Furthermore, while equality has almost done its job, it is likely that non-marital cohabitation will become the newest branch of relationship law, in one way or another. Policy will also have to deal with families consisting of more than two parents. Introducing only partial parental responsibilities will probably not be a sustainable solution. Family law is, after all, always on the move.

1.3

THE RECOGNITION OF RELIGIOUS AND CUSTOMARY MARRIAGES AND NON-MARITAL DOMESTIC PARTNERSHIPS IN SOUTH AFRICA

Waheeda Amien

Introduction

The question regarding what forms of marriage should be recognized for legal purposes is a significant one in a world of increasing cultural and religious diversity. For some countries, this is a relatively recent phenomenon. Other countries have long been made up of a variety of religious and cultural populations and have approached the issue in different ways. This chapter addresses the developments and challenges relating to the recognition of customary and religious marriages, and domestic partnerships in South Africa. South Africa provides a good example of development of policies in this area because, like most countries that were colonized by Britain and Europe, it inherited a colonial legacy that was heavily influenced by a Christian understanding of marriage, which is characterized mainly by monogamy and heterosexuality. The colonial Christian underpinnings for marriage were eventually adopted by the South African apartheid state, where marriage was defined as 'the union of one man and one woman to the exclusion while it lasts of all others'.[1] However, since the advent of democracy in South Africa in 1994, family law policy had to recognize the vast religious and ethnic diversity of the country. This chapter considers how this has been done.

The Christian understanding of marriage was incorporated into the institution of civil marriage, which is regulated by the Marriage Act 25 of 1961.[2] To enjoy the patrimonial benefits of a civil marriage, including reciprocal spousal maintenance obligations, equal parental rights and responsibilities regarding minor children born of a marriage, and each spouse being compensated for contributions to the other's estate, heterosexual and monogamous unions must be

1 *Seedat's Executors v The Master (Natal)* 1917 A.D. 302 at 309. *Kader v Kader* 1972 (3) SA 203 (R., A.D.) at 206H. *Ismail v Ismail* 1983 (1) SA 1006 (AD) at 1019H.

2 As former British colonies, India and Canada similarly enacted legislation, which reflect the Christian ethos of monogamy and heterosexuality. For example, see the Indian Special Marriage Act 43 of 1954. In Canada, provincial laws govern civil marriages. For instance, the Ontario Marriage Act R.S.O. 1990, c. M.3 governs civil marriages in Ontario.

registered under the Marriage Act. Therefore, unmarried heterosexual cohabitants in domestic partnerships who live together 'monogamously' are outside the ambit of the Marriage Act. The heterosexual and monogamous understanding of marriage also excludes potentially polygynous and same-sex marriages from being treated as lawful marriages. Under the colonial and apartheid eras, potentially polygynous marriages were specifically denied recognition as lawful marriages on the basis that they were contrary to public policy.[3] This meant that potentially polygynous marriages, including customary marriages and religious marriages such as Muslim, Hindu and Jewish marriages, were not afforded full legal recognition.

Due to racial divisions imposed by the apartheid government, customary marriages were only recognized in certain parts of the former Natal province (now called KwaZulu-Natal)[4] and the former 'independent' homeland of Transkei (which now forms part of the Eastern Cape).[5] Muslim, Hindu and Jewish marriages also received partial recognition in limited circumstances, but usually in a way that did not benefit spouses of those marriages. For example, the apartheid-era Insolvency Act 24 of 1936 included spouses in religious marriages in its definition of spouse.[6] That meant that if a spouse in a religious marriage was sequestrated, her spouse was divested of her estate, which along with the sequestrated spouse's estate, vested in the Master of the High Court and thereafter the trustee of the estate.[7]

In stark contrast to the pre-1994 period, post-1994 South Africa is characterized by a constitutional democracy that heralds an undertaking for all South Africans to reject the monolithic and racist approach of the colonial and apartheid orders, and to replace it with one that is tolerant of plurality. The uniqueness of the 1996 South African Constitution lies in the fact that it not only incorporates western liberal understandings of human rights such as non-discrimination, it also recognizes that a diversity of laws operates within the country that are equally deserving of recognition, including customary and religious laws. For instance, section 15(3)(a) of the Constitution, which forms part of the freedom of religion clause, permits government to enact legislation that recognizes religious and traditional personal or family law systems, or religious and traditional marriages. Section 31(1) further enables persons belonging to, among others, religious and cultural communities to establish, become members of and maintain religious and cultural associations and to enjoy their culture and practice their religion in association with other members of their cultural and religious communities. Yet, the Constitution also attempts to balance respect for diversity with protection of individual human rights. So, section 31(2) of the Constitution requires the associational right entrenched in section 31(1) to be exercised in a manner that is not inconsistent with other provisions of the Constitution, including gender equality. Similarly, section 15(3)(b) requires that legislation recognizing religious and traditional personal or family law systems, or religious and traditional marriages must be consistent with other provisions of the Constitution such as gender equality. The latter is protected in section 9(3) of the Constitution, which prohibits unfair discrimination on the basis of *inter alia*, sex and gender.

In light of the aforementioned constitutional provisions, South Africa has taken, and continues to take, steps to recognize the diversity of unions that exist within the country. Two key examples of personal relationships that are otherwise excluded from recognition under the Marriage Act, but have been afforded recognition under parallel legislation, are same-sex unions and customary marriages.

3 *Ismail* op. cit., n 1, 1024D-F.
4 KwaZulu Act on the Code of Zulu Law 16 of 1985.
5 Transkei Marriage Act 21 of 1978.
6 Section 21(13).
7 Section 21(1).

In common with many western jurisdictions (see Chapters 1.2 and 1.4 of this book), South Africa legislated to allow monogamous same-sex couples to register civil unions through the Civil Union Act 17 of 2006. Monogamous heterosexual couples may also register a civil union under the Civil Union Act if they do not wish to be married under the Marriage Act. Civil unions for same-sex and heterosexual partners are regulated in the same way as civil marriages for opposite-sex spouses and bear the same consequences. Still, for legal purposes, the two unions (civil unions and civil marriages) are treated as distinct. The main challenge presented by intimate heterosexual partnerships relates to the definition of marriage and the extent to which the definition is capable of including unions that do not involve the type of public ceremony that is commonly associated with marriage. Therefore, heterosexual spouses who choose to register a civil union under the CUA may not simultaneously register a civil marriage under the Marriage Act.[8]

South Africa also legislated to recognize customary marriages through the Recognition of Customary Marriages Act 120 of 1998 (RCMA). The regulation of customary marriages presents a policy challenge for a particularly western understanding of family law, given their distinct features that are not common to the western concept of marriage. For example, customary relationships are often polygynous. Similar policy challenges are presented for the recognition of religious marriages that are potentially polygynous such as Muslim marriages. Recognition of some features of customary and religious marriages therefore presents a challenge to individual human rights such as gender equality, which South Africa is committed to protect and promote.

To address the policy challenges associated with the recognition of a variety of marriages, this chapter provides a brief exposition of the RCMA, followed by a consideration of the limited legal options that exist for spouses in religious marriages and domestic partners. While there appear to be moves afoot to afford full legal recognition to religious marriages and possibly also domestic partnerships, legislation has not yet been enacted to achieve such recognition. The legal interventions to address the non-recognition of religious marriages and domestic partnerships that have been proposed since 1994 are therefore also reflected upon, namely, the Muslim Marriages Bill, the Recognition of Religious Marriages Bill, the Domestic Partnerships Bill and the more recently proposed Single Marriage Statute.

Recognition of customary marriages

Given the lack of respect that was accorded to customary marriages by the colonial and apartheid dispensations, it was a welcome intervention when the RCMA was passed in 1998. The RCMA provides full legal recognition to customary marriages and places them on an equal footing vis-à-vis civil marriages. This does not mean that customary marriages are regarded as civil marriages. In the same way that civil unions under the CUA are treated as distinct from civil marriages under the Marriage Act, customary marriages are distinguished from civil marriages and civil unions, and spouses may not simultaneously enter into a civil marriage or civil union while having registered a customary marriage.[9]

At the same time, the way in which customary marriages are regulated is surprisingly similar to the way in which civil marriages are regulated. The RCMA reflects an attempt to assimilate customary marriages into the civil form of marriage.[10] Except for the recognition of a few fea-

8 Civil Union Act 17 of 2006, section 8(2).
9 RCMA, section 3(2); Civil Union Act 17 of 2006, section 8(2).
10 C. Himonga, 'The Advancement of African Women's Rights in the First Decade of Democracy in South Africa: The Reform of the Customary Law of Marriage and Succession', *Acta Juridica* 85, 2005, 82–107.

tures particular to customary marriages – namely, *lobolo* (transfer of property by the husband or head of his family to the head of the wife's family) and polygyny,[11] and the fact that the RCMA defines a customary marriage as one that is 'concluded in accordance with customary law'[12] – every aspect of the RCMA mimics the requirements of the Marriage Act for the conclusion of a civil marriage. This might suggest that the constitutional respect for diversity of marriages has not translated into full respect for diversity within marriages.

Of significance is the fact that features of a civil marriage that are alien to customary marriages are incorporated into the RCMA. For instance, although customary marriages are traditionally entered into over an extended period of time, the RCMA requires that they be entered into immediately.[13] Another example relates to the notion of a matrimonial property regime, which is foreign to customary law. Under traditional customary law, property was managed for the benefit of the family. Yet, through section 7(2), the RCMA introduced community of property as the default regime for monogamous customary marriages entered into after the commencement of the RCMA. The community of property matrimonial property system is the default regime that applies to civil marriages in the absence of an ante-nuptial contract.[14] Furthermore, section 8(2) of the RCMA regulates customary divorces in the same way as civil divorces, even though traditional customary law expects separation between spouses to be negotiated between their families.[15] So, the RCMA effectively converts the nature of customary marriages signifying a connection between families[16] into one that focuses on individual spouses, which is typical of a western-type marriage.[17]

The legislature's intention to draw parity between civil and customary marriages may have been to ensure equality between spouses within customary marriages. In fact, certain provisions of the RCMA were raised for adjudication and the courts attempted to infuse equality into the interpretation of those provisions. For instance, in *Gumede (born Shange) v President of the Republic of South Africa and Others*,[18] the Constitutional Court confirmed that section 7(1) of the RCMA was unconstitutional because it unfairly discriminated against spouses in monogamous customary marriages entered into prior to the enactment of the RCMA on the basis of among others, gender.[19] Unlike section 7(2), which, as mentioned previously, creates a community of property regime for monogamous customary marriages entered into after the commencement of the RCMA, section 7(1) required customary marriages entered into before the commencement of the RMCA to continue being governed by customary law. As a result of the *Gumede* judgment, the matrimonial property regimes of monogamous customary unions entered into before and after the commencement of the RCMA are now in community of property.

11 Section 1.

12 Section 1. The RCMA defines 'customary law' as 'the customs and usages traditionally observed among the indigenous African peoples of South Africa and which form part of the culture of those peoples'.

13 E. Curran and E. Bonthuys, 'Customary Law and Domestic Violence in Rural South African Communities', *South African Journal of Human Rights* 21, 2005, 607–35, 615.

14 Community of property involves a joint estate that comprises assets and liabilities of both spouses, which they each acquire before entering marriage and during the marriage. Each spouse has a 50 percent share in the joint estate. Matrimonial Property Act, Chapter III.

15 Himonga, op. cit., n 10, 89.

16 *Gumede (born Shange) v President of the Republic of South Africa and Others* 2009 (3) SA 152 (CC) at para 18; Curran and Bonthuys, op. cit., n 13.

17 W. Amien, 'Reflections on the Recognition of African Customary Marriages in South Africa: Seeking Insights for the Recognition of Muslim Marriages', in A. Claassens and D. Smythe (eds), *Marriage, Land and Custom*, Cape Town: Juta & Co Ltd, 2014, Ch. 17.

18 2009 (3) SA 152 (CC).

19 Paras 58–9.

Following *Gumede*, the constitutional validity of section 7(1) was again challenged in the case of *Ramuhovhi and Others v President of the Republic of South Africa and Others*,[20] but this time in the context of polygynous customary marriages entered into before the commencement of the RCMA. In *Ramuhovhi*, Venda customary law was at issue, in terms of which no rights of ownership or control over marital property vests in wives.[21] The Constitutional Court confirmed that section 7(1) of the RCMA unfairly discriminated on the basis of among others, gender and marital status in as far as it precluded wives in polygynous customary marriages entered into prior to the commencement of the RCMA from owning and controlling marital property vis-à-vis wives in monogamous customary marriages and wives in polygynous customary marriages entered into after the commencement of the RCMA. In respect of the latter, section 7(6) of the RCMA requires a husband in a customary marriage who wishes to enter into a polygynous customary marriage to apply to court for the approval of a written contract governing the matrimonial property system of his subsequent marriage. The Court interpreted section 7(6) as providing wives in polygynous customary marriages entered into after the commencement of the RCMA equal capacity to acquire and dispose of assets.[22] This interpretation is reinforced by section 6 of the RCMA, which confers equal status and capacity on spouses in customary marriages to among others, acquire and dispose of assets.[23]

In response to the *Ramuhovhi* judgment, a Recognition of Customary Marriages Amendment Bill was drafted, which incorporates the Constitutional Court's findings in the *Gumede* and *Ramuhovhi* judgments regarding the matrimonial property regimes of monogamous and polygynous customary marriages.[24] Clause 2(2) of the bill proposes that the default regime of all monogamous customary marriages should be in community of property. Clause 2(1) of the bill recommends a more complex regime for polygynous customary marriages entered into before the commencement of the RCMA in what appears to be an attempt by the legislature to balance customary law imperatives and equality. The bill proposes that spouses in polygynous customary marriages should have joint and equal ownership, management and control over marital property, which includes house property and family property. House property accrues to a particular family unit comprising the husband and a particular wife. Family property accrues to all the houses of the husband and his wives. The husband and wives are required to exercise their rights in the family property in the best interests of all the houses of the husband's customary marriages whereas rights relating to house property must be exercised in the best interests of a particular family unit. In contrast, the bill exempts personal property belonging to the husband and each wife from joint ownership so that each spouse retains exclusive rights over their personal property. The bill further proposes that each category of property will derive their meaning from customary law. What constitutes family property, house property and personal property will depend on the meaning that a particular ethnic group ascribes to each type of property.

The Constitutional Court further interpreted aspects of customary law on which the RCMA is silent. For instance, in *Mayelane v Ngwenyama and Another*,[25] the Constitutional Court developed Xitsonga customary law to require the consent of the first wife should her husband wish to enter into a valid polygynous customary marriage with another woman.[26] In *Mabena v*

20 2018 (2) SA 1 (CC).
21 Paras 1, 9.
22 Para 35.
23 Ibid.
24 Available at www.justice.gov.za/legislation/bills/2019-RCMA-Bill.pdf (accessed 9 December 2019).
25 2013 (4) SA 415 (CC).
26 Paras 87, 89.

Letsoalo,[27] the Transvaal Provincial Division (as it then was) held that the mother of the bride could participate in the *lobolo* negotiations and consent to the *lobolo* agreement. The finding of the Court in the *Mabena* case gave effect to living customary law and developed customary law in accordance with the 'spirit, purport and objects' of the Bill of Rights.[28] Therefore, the validity of a customary marriage is no longer dependent on only the male guardian of the bride providing his consent to the *lobolo* agreement.

To some extent, the RCMA along with judicial interpretation of aspects of customary law succeeded in achieving at least formal equality between customary law spouses. For instance, wives in customary marriages have equal rights to divorce and are assured of equal division of property upon termination of the marriage. In other respects, failure to consider the lived realities of indigenous African communities causes certain safeguards that are incorporated into the RCMA to prove unworkable. For example, the RCMA requires a husband to obtain court approval for polygynous marriages and that existing wives be joined in the application, presumably to afford them an opportunity to provide their opinion on the proposed subsequent marriage.[29] Not only is seeking court intervention for the purpose of concluding polygynous marriages unknown to traditional customary law, it requires wives in rural areas to travel great distances to attend court. Given that the rural parts of South Africa comprise the most poverty-ridden areas in the country, wives in those areas are unable to afford the costs involved in travelling to court and legal costs that might be incurred in joining the application.[30] Consequently, many polygynous marriages are entered into without court intervention despite the RCMA requirement that they must.[31]

Limited recognition of religious marriages and domestic partnerships

Under the Marriage Act, parties married by Muslim, Hindu and Jewish rites are able to access benefits of secular legislation if they enter into civil marriages. Spouses in religious marriages are also able to benefit from specific pieces of legislation that were enacted under apartheid but amended post-1994, some as a result of judicial intervention and others without judicial intervention. Other pieces of legislation were newly enacted to afford protection in specific circumstances to spouses in religious marriages and/or cohabitants in domestic partnerships. The aforementioned options are discussed next.

Options for civil marriage available to religious communities

Section 3 of the Marriage Act enables a person who solemnizes 'marriages according to Christian, Jewish or Mohammedan rites or the rites of any Indian religion' to be designated as a marriage officer. Muslims, Hindus and Jews can therefore either enter into a separate civil marriage before or after concluding their religious marriage, or have their religious marriage solemnized by a person who is designated as a marriage officer under the Marriage Act. When the marriage officer performs the designated religious marriage, he could simultaneously register the marriage as a civil marriage. In this way, spouses entering into the designated

27 1998 (2) SA 1068 (T).
28 At 1074–5.
29 Section 7(6).
30 Himonga, op. cit., n 10, 106.
31 Ibid.

religious marriage can access the patrimonial benefits attached to civil marriages.[32] As spouses in a civil marriage, they are also able to enjoy all the benefits accruing to civil law spouses that emanate from secular legislation. While section 3 includes the major faith religions in South Africa, it potentially excludes other faiths. The section could therefore be constitutionally challenged by other faith adherents on the basis that it unfairly discriminates on the ground of religion.[33]

Anecdotal evidence suggests that most South African Jewish and Hindu couples enter into civil marriages while many South African Muslims do not. It appears that many Jewish *rabbis* and Hindu *pandits* who officiate religious marriages within their communities are marriage officers authorized to perform civil marriages. Until 2014 hardly any Muslim *imāms* who officiate Muslim marriages were registered as marriage officers under the Marriage Act. In 2014 the Department of Home Affairs initiated an '*Imām* Project' where they succeeded in getting more than 100 *imāms* across South Africa to be registered as marriage officers.[34] However, very few of those *imāms* actually perform civil marriages today. Of those who do, they usually require a Muslim couple to enter into an ante-nuptial contract that precludes community of property on the basis that traditional Islamic law requires the estates of married persons to be kept separate. In the South African context, this places many Muslim wives in a financially disadvantaged position, especially when the marriage terminates through death or divorce because the wives are left financially destitute.

For those spouses who enter into religious and civil marriages and can therefore access benefits that secular legislation makes available to lawful spouses, the civil marriage still does not assist them in being able to enforce all the features of their religious marriage. For instance, a Muslim wife who wishes to obtain a Muslim divorce but is unable to acquire one from her husband or the '*ulamā* (Muslim clergy) and a Jewish wife who wants to obtain a Jewish divorce from her husband but is unable to obtain his consent, are not able to seek relief in a secular court. While they might be able to obtain dissolution of their civil marriage, failure to obtain a religious divorce has a disparate effect on women who wish to exit their religious marriage. They are placed in the position of not being able to move on with their lives and enter into a religious marriage with someone else even though their husbands may be able to do so, due to the potentially polygynous nature of their marriages.

To a limited extent, section 5A of the Divorce Act 70 of 1979 attempts to provide an incentive for parties to obtain a religious divorce before obtaining a civil divorce.[35] If a spouse applies for a divorce order to dissolve her or his civil marriage and the other spouse is preventing a religious divorce, the court has discretion to, among others, not grant the civil divorce until the religious divorce is granted. As mentioned previously, a wife in a religious marriage such as a Muslim and Jewish marriage needs a religious divorce to marry someone else by religious rites whereas her husband may not be similarly constrained. So, while an application of section 5A could work in the wife's favour if the party applying for the divorce is the husband, it is of no assistance to the wife if she seeks a civil and religious divorce because the court cannot compel the recalcitrant husband to grant her a religious divorce.

32 Similar provisions exist in other jurisdictions. For example, Marriage Act R.S.O. 1990, c. M.3, section 20(2) (Ontario); Marriage Act 1949, sections 53–7 (UK).

33 Constitution of South Africa 1996, section 9(3).

34 South African Government News Agency, *Imams Graduate as Marriage Officers*, 1 May 2014. Available at www.sanews.gov.za/south-africa/imams-graduate-marriage-officers (accessed 9 December 2019).

35 Canadian Divorce Act R.S.O., 1985, c. 3 (2nd Supp.), section 21(1)(3) contains a similar provision. See also Divorce (Religious Marriages) Act 2002 (UK).

Limited recognition of spouses in religious marriages and cohabitants in domestic partnerships through legislation

Some apartheid-era legislation was amended during South Africa's democratic order to enable spouses in religious marriages and cohabitants in domestic partnerships to benefit from legislation that they were previously excluded from. For example, an amendment to the Income Tax Act 58 of 1962 recognizes the aforementioned parties as spouses for the purpose of being exempt from paying tax for donations made by one spouse or unmarried cohabitant to the other.[36]

Other legislation that extends protection to spouses in religious marriages and/or unmarried cohabitants was newly introduced after 1994 such as the Compensation for Occupational Injuries and Diseases Act 130 of 1993, Demobilisation Act 99 of 1996, Special Pensions Act 69 of 1996, Domestic Violence Act 116 of 1998 and Children's Act 38 of 2005.

Limited recognition of religious marriages through case law

There are also apartheid era laws that were amended after 1994 as a result of case law to include spouses of religious marriages that were not formalized under the Marriage Act, within the ambit of the legislation. This followed the groundbreaking approach adopted in the case of *Ryland v Edros*.[37] *Ryland* was the first case in the post-apartheid constitutional dispensation to afford relief to a Muslim wife who instituted claims based on her Muslim marriage. The Cape Provincial Division (as it then was) accepted the Muslim marriage as a contract and was willing to enforce proven terms and customs arising from that contract.[38] The Court justified its decision on the basis that public policy in South Africa is informed by the constitutional values of equality and tolerance of diversity.[39] Thus, the Court upheld the Muslim wife's claims for *nafaqah* (maintenance) until the end of her *iddah* (waiting period following divorce) and her claim for *mut'ah* (Islamic law compensation permitted to her when the husband unjustifiably terminates the marriage).[40]

The *Ryland* case laid the basis for later courts to recognize rights and obligations arising from Muslim and Hindu marriages within the ambit of specific legislation. For instance, in the case of *Amod v Multilateral Motor Vehicle Accidents Fund*,[41] the Supreme Court of Appeal found that a Muslim husband's unilateral duty of spousal support arising from the Muslim marriage is worthy of legal recognition for the purpose of the Multilateral Motor Vehicle Accidents Fund Act 93 of 1989 (now the Road Accident Fund Act 56 of 1996).[42] The Act incorporates the common law dependant's action, which enables a surviving spouse to be compensated for loss of support in circumstances where the deceased had a legal duty of support and was unlawfully killed in a motor vehicle accident as a result of the negligent driving of a third party.[43] One of the overriding considerations that informed the Court's decision was its finding that the *boni mores* of South African society encapsulates the constitutional values of 'tolerance, pluralism and

36 Section 1: definition of 'spouse'.
37 1997 (2) SA 690 (C).
38 *Ryland v Edros* 1997 (2) SA 690 (C) at 707E-H.
39 Ibid., 708J.
40 Ibid., 718I-J.
41 1999 (4) SA 1319 (SCA).
42 Paras 14–15, 20, 25.
43 Paras 1, 3, 10.

religious freedom'.[44] Thus, the Court extended the ambit of the act to include surviving spouses in monogamous Muslim marriages.

Thereafter, in the cases of *Daniels v Campbell*,[45] *Hassam v Jacobs*[46] and *Govender v Ragavayah*,[47] the South African judiciary recognized monogamous and polygynous Muslim spouses as well as monogamous Hindu spouses as 'surviving spouses' for the purpose of the Intestate Succession Act 81 of 1987, and a monogamous Muslim spouse as a 'spouse' for the purpose of the Maintenance of Surviving Spouses Act 27 of 1990.

More recently, in the case of *Moosa NO and Others v Minister of Justice and Correctional Services and Others*,[48] the Constitutional Court further recognized a spouse in a Muslim marriage as a 'surviving spouse' for the purpose of section 2C(1) of the Wills Act 7 of 1953. In terms of section 2C(1), if a deceased person leaves a will and makes testamentary provision for a descendant and the surviving spouse of the deceased to benefit from the deceased's estate but the descendant renounces her right to receive the benefit, the benefit then vests in the surviving spouse. To the extent that the impugned provision excluded spouses in a Muslim marriage from being recognized as a 'surviving spouse', the Constitutional Court confirmed the court *a quo's*[49] order of constitutional invalidity on the basis that section 2C(1) violated the constitutional rights of Muslim spouses to equality and dignity.[50] To remedy the constitutional defect, the Constitutional Court read into section 2C(1) words that enable a spouse in a monogamous and polygynous Muslim marriage to be included in the definition of 'surviving spouse' for the purpose of section 2C(1).[51]

The judiciary further recognized Muslim and Hindu husbands' duties of spousal support arising respectively from their monogamous Muslim and Hindu marriages for the purpose of maintenance claims and specifically in the context of the Maintenance Act 99 of 1998. In *Cassim v Cassim*[52] and *Laxmi Prag v Daya Prag*,[53] the Transvaal Provincial Division (as it then was) and the Wynberg Magistrate's Court respectively granted the Muslim wife's claim and the Hindu wife's claim for spousal maintenance under the Maintenance Act. Furthermore, the Court in *Khan v Khan*[54] extended the application of the Maintenance Act to Muslim wives in polygynous marriages by bringing them too within the ambit of the Maintenance Act.

In fact, Muslim wives who institute matrimonial actions against their husbands may also be awarded maintenance *pendente lite* in terms of Rule 43 of the Uniform Rules of Court. The latter enables a spouse to claim *inter alia*, interim maintenance pending the finalization of a matrimonial action. In the cases of *AM v RM*[55] and *Hoosain v Dangor*,[56] the Muslim wives in the respective cases instituted divorce actions against their husbands. In the two cases, the wives

44 Para 20.
45 2004 (5) SA 331 (CC).
46 2009 (5) SA 572 (CC).
47 2009 (3) SA 178 (D).
48 2018 (5) SA 13 (CC). For a more detailed analysis of the case, see W. Amien, 'A Discussion of Moosa No and Others v Harnaker and Others Illustrating the Need for Legal Recognition of Muslim Marriages in South Africa', *Journal of Comparative Law in Africa* 6(1), 2019, 115–30.
49 *Moosa NO and Others v Harneker and Others* 2017 (6) SA 425 (WCC). For a more detailed analysis of the case, see Amien, ibid.
50 Paras 11–16.
51 Para 21.
52 (Part A) (TPD) (Unreported 15 December 2006, Case No: 3954/06).
53 Wynberg Magistrates' Court (2 November 2009).
54 2005 (2) SA 272 (T).
55 2010 (2) SA 223 (ECP). Also published as *Mahomed v Mahomed* [2009] JOL 23733 (ECP).
56 Case No: 18141/09, Judgment delivered 18 November 2009 (WCC).

respectively asked the Eastern Cape and Western Cape High Courts to apply the provisions of the Divorce Act 70 of 1979 to the dissolution of their Muslim marriages and that the Courts declare their Muslim marriages valid under the Marriage Act. In each case, the Court granted the wives' requests for maintenance *pendente lite*.[57]

The parties in the preceding cases reached out-of-court settlements. So, the courts were not afforded an opportunity to pronounce on the merits of the wives' claims for an order declaring the validity of their Muslim marriages and that their divorces be governed by the Divorce Act. Had the cases been pursued to their natural conclusion, it is most likely that the judiciary may neither have found the Muslim marriages to be valid under the Marriage Act nor that the Divorce Act applies to the dissolution of Muslim marriages. The main reason for this assertion is that the judiciary has up to now been reluctant to provide general recognition to Muslim marriages. In the *Amod* case, the Supreme Court of Appeal clearly indicated that it views such recognition to be best addressed by the legislature.[58]

It seems that the judiciary is more likely to grant claims arising from religious marriages if the bases of the claims are compatible with secular law. For instance, the Court in *Ryland* applied the principles of South African contract law because it was satisfied that a Muslim marriage could be treated as a contract.[59] Similarly, the husband's duty of support arising from a Muslim or Hindu marriage could easily be accommodated in secular legislation. However, expecting a secular court to apply the provisions of the Marriage and Divorce Acts to religious marriages and divorces may not be tenable, especially when the rules of secular legislation may be incompatible with religious rules. For instance, many Muslims treat the notion of community of property as incompatible with Islamic law. If a Muslim marriage is regarded as valid under the Marriage Act, this might entail a conversion of the matrimonial property system of Muslim marriages from one that traditionally treats the estates of spouses as separate to one that is in community of property. It is therefore important that the process of affording legal recognition to religious marriages entails consultations with religious communities. The judiciary's recommendation that full legal recognition of religious marriages should be the responsibility of the legislature is most likely a wise one since the legislature is best placed to conduct the necessary consultations with the relevant stakeholders within those communities.

Given the protracted delay on the part of the South African state to enact legislation to recognize Muslim marriages, an application was brought in the case of *Women's Legal Centre Trust v President of South Africa and Others, Faro v Bingham N.O. and Others, Esau v Esau and Others*[60] to compel the state to enact legislation to recognize and regulate Muslim marriages. The application resulted in a groundbreaking judgment delivered by a full bench of the Western Cape High Court in 2018. The Court found that continued non-recognition of Muslim marriages violates several constitutional rights, including equality, access to justice, the best interests of the child, and freedom of religion and dignity.[61] The Court further found that failure by the state to provide legislative recognition for Muslim marriages, which resulted in a violation of the aforementioned

57 *Hoosain*, op. cit., n 65, para 31; *AM*, op. cit., n 63, para 14.

58 *Amod*, op. cit., n 46, para 28.

59 A similar approach was adopted by the British Columbia Supreme Court of Appeal, which was willing to treat a *mahr* agreement as a valid and enforceable marriage agreement under the British Columbia Family Relations Act R.S.B.C. 1996, c. 128. In particular, the Court found that the *mahr* agreements conformed to the provisions of the Act. *Nathoo v Nathoo* [1996] B.C.J. No. 2720 (S.C.) [Q.L.]; *Amlani v Hirani* [2000] B.C.J. No. 2357 (S.C.) [Q.L]; *N.M.M. v N.S.M.* [2004] B.C.J. No. 642 (S.C.) [Q.L.].

60 2018 (6) SA 598 (WCC). For a detailed analysis of the case, see W. Amien, 'Islamic Family Law Reform in Non-Muslim Majority Countries: The Case of South Africa', *Journal of Islamic Law* 1, 2019.

61 Paras 57, 179.

rights, constitutes an abdication of its section 7(2) and section 237 constitutional obligations.[62] Section 7(2) obliges the state to 'respect, protect, promote and fulfil the rights in the Bill of Rights'. Section 237 requires '[a]ll constitutional obligations [to] be performed diligently and without delay'. The Court thus ordered the state to enact legislation within 24 months of the date of judgment to recognize and regulate the consequences of Muslim marriages.[63]

Until legislation is enacted, Muslim marriages remain without legal recognition and parties to those marriages are left without legal protection. The same goes for all other religious marriages. So, whenever spouses in religious marriages seek recognition, they need to convince a court to include them within the ambit of a specific piece of legislation. For instance, the *Govender* case only extended the sphere of the Intestate Succession Act to spouses in monogamous Hindu marriages. Spouses in polygynous Hindu marriages still need to institute a separate claim to be afforded protection under the Intestate Succession Act. This involves a cumbersome and costly process. Furthermore, if parties wish to assert claims that arise from the Muslim marriage contract such as *mahr*, they need to institute a specific claim for that. This too can prove costly and time-consuming and would most likely require legal representation.

General non-recognition of religious marriages also means that spouses in a religious marriage cannot rely on a secular court to amend religious rules that are harmful to them. This is particularly due to the judiciary's reluctance to become involved with issues relating to religious doctrine.[64] For example, in the case of *Singh v Ramparsad*,[65] the Durban High Court refused to recognize a civil divorce in favour of the wife in circumstances where the parties had not registered a civil marriage under the Marriage Act, and had only entered into a Hindu marriage according to the Sanathan or Vedic tradition, which does not permit religious divorce. The Court was not prepared to meddle in theological issues and grant a divorce in circumstances where the religion regulating the parties' marriage did not recognize divorce.[66]

For the aforementioned reasons, full legal recognition of religious marriages is important. Attempts were made over the past two decades to afford recognition to a specific type of religious marriage, all religious marriages, domestic partnerships and/or all forms of intimate unions. In about 2005, the Commission for Gender Equality and the Department of Justice and Constitutional Development drafted a Recognition of Religious Marriages Bill.[67] During 2010, a Muslim Marriages Bill was approved for parliamentary consideration by the South African Cabinet.[68] In 2008, the Department of Home Affairs published a Domestic Partnerships Bill for public comment.[69] More recently, the South African Law Reform Commission and the Department of Home Affairs are conducting parallel consultation processes, in which they seek input for the drafting of legislation to afford recognition to all forms of marriages.[70]

62 Para 252.

63 Ibid.

64 This is referred to as the doctrine of religious entanglement, which was confirmed in *Taylor v Kurtstag NO and Others* 2005 (1) SA 362 (W). In *Taylor*, the Witwatersrand Local Division of the High Court dismissed an application to restrain the *Beth Din* (Jewish Ecclesiastical Court) from issuing, publishing or disseminating a *cherem* to excommunicate the applicant from the Jewish faith (paras 39, 61, 65).

65 2007 (3) SA 445 (D).

66 Paras 50–1.

67 A copy of the bill is on file with the author.

68 Ibid.

69 Available at www.gov.za/sites/default/files/gcis_document/201409/30663b.pdf (accessed 9 December 2019).

70 South African Law Reform Commission, Project 144 *Single Marriage Statute* Issue Paper 35 (2019). Available at www.justice.gov.za/salrc/ipapers/ip35_prj144_SingleMarriageStatute.pdf (accessed 9 December 2019). Department of Home Affairs, *The Consultative Stakeholder Engagements for*

Each of the aforementioned pieces of proposed legislation is discussed in greater detail in the following sections.

Recognition of Religious Marriages Bill

The Recognition of Religious Marriages Bill (RRMB) proposes full legal recognition for all religious marriages in South Africa. It recommends that religious communities should regulate their religious marriages but that dissolution of religious marriages should mimic the approach espoused in the Divorce Act.[71] So, the RRMB tries to accommodate the interests of religious communities by allowing them to manage their own marriages while assimilating the way in which those marriages are dissolved to enable conformity with civil divorces.

The approach reflected in the RRMB presents two main challenges. First, the RRMB leaves the regulation of religious marriages for determination by religious communities. It particularly does not seek to regulate practices that are potentially harmful to women, such as polygyny and denying women the right to exit unwanted religious marriages. Religious interpretations and practices adopted by religious communities that are harmful to women could therefore potentially persist.[72] Secondly, like the RCMA, the RRMB's expectation that religious divorces should follow the same process as civil divorces is an attempt to ensure an equal right of divorce for women and men.[73] However, this assimilation approach is subject to the same limitation faced by the RCMA, namely, it fails to take sufficient cognizance of the lived experiences of members of religious communities where spouses feel compelled to obtain religious divorces. While the RRMB proposes the incorporation of a clause similar to section 5A of the Divorce Act,[74] the net effect will be the same as described in the previous section: if the uncooperative spouse is the husband and the wife is seeking a divorce, a court will not be able to compel the husband to grant her a religious divorce.

The RRMB did not undergo widespread consultations with religious communities and civil society. It also did not appear to elicit much support from those sectors and consequently appears to have been shelved.

Muslim Marriages Bill

In contrast, the Muslim Marriages Bill (MMB), which was drafted by the South African Law Reform Commission (SALRC) in 2003,[75] underwent extensive consultations with the South African Muslim community and human rights organizations and garnered general consensus among them for its enactment. The MMB recommends comprehensive regulation of the features of Muslim marriages and divorces, which includes *inter alia, mahr*, marriage by proxy, the husband's unilateral duty of support toward his wife and children, polygyny, a wife's claim for compensation within the marriage, mediation, arbitration and different forms of Muslim divorce.

---

the Development of the Marriages Policy, September 2019. Available at www.dha.gov.za/index.php/notices/1286-the-consultative-stakeholder-engagements-for-the-development-of-the-marriages-policy (accessed 9 December 2019).

71 Clause 10(1)-(2) RRMB. See also Divorce Act 70 of 1979, section 3(a).

72 See further W. Amien, 'A South African Case Study for the Recognition and Regulation of Muslim Family Law in a Minority Muslim Secular Context', *International Journal of Law, Policy and the Family* 24(3), 2010, 361–96, 369.

73 Clause 10(1)-(2) RRMB.

74 Clause 10(3) RRMB.

75 A detailed analysis of the 2003 MMB is available in Amien, op. cit., n 88, 370.

Since non-recognition of Muslim marriages impacts particularly negatively on the more marginalized spouse within the marriage, namely, the wife,[76] gender activists advocate for the legal recognition and regulation of Muslim marriages through legislation such as the MMB.[77]

As mentioned earlier in this chapter, apart from being unable to access all the civil law benefits that are available to their civil law counterparts, Muslim wives must endure the '*ulamā*'s interpretations of Muslim family law that do not always weigh in their favour. Regulation of Muslim marriages will thus enable Muslim women to have increased access to their Islamic law rights and benefits including divorce options that Islamic law makes available to them, such as those included in the MMB.

Currently, Muslim women are also unable to challenge decisions emanating from '*ulamā* bodies. Gender activists push for Muslim family law to be adjudicated in secular courts to increase the chances of gendered reform of Muslim family law.[78] If the features of a Muslim marriage are regulated by legislation, the judiciary will have a basis for engaging with the doctrines of Islamic law where necessary and particularly in those instances where the legislation is vague. This will put the current judicial doctrine of religious non-entanglement to the test. To prevent the judiciary from having to engage with religious doctrine, it is important that legislation provide as much certainty as possible.

In 2009, the Department of Justice and Constitutional Development (DoJCD) amended the MMB, which received Cabinet approval in the following year. The amendments were affected without consulting the relevant stakeholders including the '*ulamā*. Two amendments in particular appeared to be of concern to the '*ulamā*, which caused them to withdraw their support of the amended MMB.[79] First, the amended MMB enables any judge from within the secular court system to adjudicate disputes arising from the MMB,[80] whereas the 2003 MMB required a Muslim judge to preside with Islamic law specialists as assessors.[81] The '*ulamā* are of the view that any issue of an Islamic nature should be decided upon by a Muslim judge. Secondly, the 2003 MMB required a process of compulsory mediation to precede the finalization of the divorce.[82] This is consistent with the '*ulamā*'s view that mediation/arbitration of Muslim family law disputes is compulsory under Islamic law. In contrast, the amended MMB converts the compulsory feature of the mediation/arbitration process that was recommended in the 2003 MMB into a voluntary one.[83]

Currently, arbitration is not permitted in South Africa for family matters. It is only permitted for commercial matters.[84] This approach is being revisited by the SALRC, which is considering draft legislation, namely, a Family Dispute Resolution Bill to regulate alternative dispute resolution in family matters.[85] The proposal involves a 'mandatory mediation model' and 'voluntary family arbitration'. The SALRC recommends that 'family disputes affecting the welfare of chil-

76 For a description of the negative impacts of non-recognition of Muslim marriages on women, see Amien, op. cit., n 88, 363 and Amien, op. cit., n 74.

77 W. Amien and R. Shabodien, *Comments to the Minister of Justice and Constitutional Development on the Muslim Marriages Bill*. Compiled on behalf of the Recognition of Muslim Marriages Forum, 23 May 2011.

78 Ibid.

79 W. Amien, 'Politics of Religious Freedom in South Africa', *The Immanent Frame: Secularism, Religion and the Public Sphere*, SSRC, 2012. Available at http://blogs.ssrc.org/tif/2012/07/24/politics-of-religious-freedom-in-south-africa/ (accessed 9 December 2019).

80 See clause 1: definition of 'court'.

81 Clause 15 (1) (a)-(b).

82 Clause 13 (1).

83 Clause 12 (1).

84 Arbitration Act 42 of 1965, section 2.

85 South African Law Reform Commission Discussion Paper 148 Project 100D, *Alternative Dispute Resolution in Family Matters*, 2019. Available at www.justice.gov.za/salrc/dpapers/dp148-prj100D-ADR-FamilyMatters-Nov2019.pdf (accessed 9 December 2019).

dren' should be dealt with by the Family Dispute Resolution Bill and any awards that are made 'affecting the rights and interests of children' must be confirmed by a High Court.[86] In contrast, the SALRC proposes 'that family disputes not affecting the rights and interests of children' should be regulated by the Arbitration Act 42 of 1965.[87] Although not entirely clear, it appears that the SALRC may intend for all disputes involving minor children to be subject to judicial oversight including financial awards made in favour of either parent that could potentially affect the rights and interests of the children.[88] Therefore, family arbitration awards that do not affect the rights and interests of children will most likely not be appealable; only the processes resulting in those awards will be capable of being reviewed.

Presently, the *'ulamā* conduct arbitration and mediation of family disputes within the South African Muslim community. In doing so, many invoke Islamic law interpretations and practices that militate against women. For example, many members of the *'ulamā* do not grant *faskhs* to wives even where clear Islamic law grounds exist. Instead, they often advise women to return to their marriages and attempt reconciliation, including in instances where husbands are abusive. Where *faskhs* are granted, it is usually on the occasion that husbands fail to appear at the *faskh* hearings. Should mediation and/or arbitration awards by *'ulamā* who adopt and apply gender-discriminatory Muslim family law rules and practices be made enforceable through the aforementioned proposed law reforms, the rights of Muslim women could be detrimentally affected, particularly in the absence of judicial oversight. In fact, even if their mediation and arbitration awards were made subject to appeal, the financial and emotional cost implications involved in the appeals process may discourage women from pursuing appeal claims. The aforementioned concerns are equally applicable to mediations and arbitrations that are conducted in other faith-based communities in South Africa, in which awards are informed by gender-discriminatory rules and practices.

Since the proposed family dispute resolution mechanisms would enable the *'ulamā* to maintain authority over the Muslim family law realm, it may be why notwithstanding the *'ulamā*'s concerns about the amended MMB, the United Ulama Council of South Africa (UUCSA), which represents the majority of *'ulamā* bodies in South Africa appears to have reversed its decision about the MMB and now expresses its support for the MMB.[89]

Both the 2003 and amended versions of the MMB attempt to balance religious rights with the constitutional imperative to promote gender equality. This is why I have argued elsewhere that the MMB adopts an integration approach, as opposed to a strictly accommodation approach.[90] The MMB tries to do this by incorporating benefits that are traditionally afforded to women under Islamic law, even though they may not be practiced within the community. For example, it provides for a default out of community of property regime to ensure that the spouses' estates are kept separate. To balance this, it includes a wife's right to be compensated for her direct contributions during the marriage. I have also argued that the MMB does not go far enough to include the gender-friendliest interpretations of Islamic law, which is a component of the approach that I advocate for the drafting of legislation that deals with religious family laws, namely, a Gender-Nuanced Integration approach.[91] For instance, the MMB does not make provision for a wife to be compensated for her intangible contributions to the marriage. Nevertheless, in trying to achieve the balance between religious/customary rights and gender equality, the

86 Ibid., 8.
87 Ibid.
88 Ibid., 243.
89 *Women's Legal Centre Trust*, op. cit., n 60 at para 100.
90 Amien, op. cit., n 72, 373.
91 Ibid., 381.

MMB seems to have been more successful than the RCMA and RRMB. Yet, regardless of the benefits that the MMB potentially offers to South African Muslims, especially Muslim women and the fact that the MMB is supported by most of the religious authorities within the South African Muslim community, it still has not been submitted for parliamentary consideration.

Domestic Partnerships Bill

Apart from draft legislation proposing the recognition of Muslim marriages, the legislature also took steps in 2008 to recommend legal recognition for domestic partnerships in South Africa. This resulted in the drafting of a Domestic Partnerships Bill, which is the next subject of discussion.

Although the issue of unmarried cohabitants is dealt with elsewhere in this book (see especially Chapters 1.2 and 1.5), it bears some consideration in this chapter since the South African context adds a dimension to the discussion that is not found in many westernized jurisdictions. That dimension relates to one of the more pernicious effects of colonialism and apartheid that resulted in the disintegration of the extended African family and its replacement with a nuclear type family.[92] The fragmentation of the extended African family emanated directly from the colonial and apartheid legacies of the migrant labour system and land dispossession.[93] In particular, the migrant labour system required black (indigenous) African men to migrate from rural areas to urban areas where they provided a cheap source of labour for white mine owners.[94] As mine workers, they were forced to live in the mine compounds without their families. This resulted in the formation of numerous domestic partnerships between indigenous African men and women in the urban areas while their wives remained in the rural areas and became responsible for the maintenance of the rural-based family.[95] These days, domestic partnerships are also entered into within other population groups, including the coloured, Indian and white communities, but still to a lesser extent than those found in indigenous African communities.[96]

While the post-1994 judiciary is inclined to bring spouses in religious marriages within the ambit of specified legislation, it adopts a less generous stance toward unmarried cohabitants. The main reason appears to be the judiciary's understanding that, unlike religious marriages, the words 'marriage', 'spouse' and 'surviving spouse' as they appear in legislation do not include domestic partnerships and unmarried cohabitants.[97]

92 *Green Paper on Families: Promoting Family Life and Strengthening Families in South Africa*, Government Gazette No. 34657, General Notice 756, 3 October 2011, pp. 24–5, 6. Available at www.info.gov.za/view/DownloadFileAction?id=152939 (accessed 26 June 2013).

93 Ibid., 6. Land dispossession was codified in the Native Land Act 27 of 1913 and Group Areas Act 41 of 1950. The Native Land Act dispossessed indigenous Africans from 87 percent of their arable land and allowed them to own up to only 13 percent of arid land. This forced many indigenous Africans to move to urban areas in search of work.

94 *Green Paper on Families*, op. cit., n 92, 6.

95 Ibid., 17.

96 Apartheid classifications, namely, black, coloured and Indian, are retained in South Africa only for the purposes of implementing affirmative action measures to protect and promote members of historically racially disadvantaged groups. Under the Employment Equity Act 55 of 1998, black Africans, coloureds and Indians are generically referred to as black. *Green Paper on Families*, op. cit., n 116, 16–17. Indigenous Africans comprise the majority of South Africa. They account for 79.2 percent of a total population of 51,770,560. Coloureds and whites each make up 8.9 percent of the total population, while Indians comprise 2.5 percent of the total population. Statistics South Africa, *Census 2011: Census in Brief*, 18, 21, Statistics South Africa, 2012. Available at www.statssa.gov.za/Census2011/Products/Census_2011_Census_in_brief.pdf (accessed 27 June 2013).

97 *Volks v Robinson* [2005] ZACC 2.

To address the preceding lacuna, the Department of Home Affairs drafted a Domestic Partnerships Bill (DPB) in 2008. The DPB makes provision for the legal recognition of registered domestic partnerships,[98] the legal status of domestic partners[99] and enforcement of the legal consequences of domestic partnerships.[100] The DPB adopts a 'functional' approach[101] to domestic partnerships by recommending that a 'spouse' for the purpose of *inter alia*, the Maintenance of Surviving Spouses Act, must be construed to include a registered domestic partner.[102] Along the same vein, the DPB recommends that registered domestic partners be brought within the definition of 'spouse' in the Intestate Succession Act.[103] The DPB further proposes that partners in a registered domestic partnership have a reciprocal duty of support.[104] Thus, it could further potentially bring registered domestic partners within the protection of the Maintenance Act.

At the same time, the DPB confirms that a domestic partnership is not equivalent to a marriage to the extent that it does not require registration of a domestic partnership to be witnessed.[105] Thus, domestic partnerships would not entail the public characteristic that typifies marriage. Termination of domestic partnerships is also distinguished from civil divorces in that the DPB recommends that the latter require court intervention while the former should simply involve registration of a termination agreement.[106] The only time that judicial oversight of a termination agreement is proposed is when minor children are involved.[107] The latter requirement is to ensure that the paramount principle of the best interests of the child is upheld, which is constitutionally required and legislatively protected in the Children's Act.[108]

To assist in the determination of property division, the DPB makes provision for the consideration of financial and non-financial contributions that are made directly or indirectly to the maintenance or growth of the partners' joint property or each of their separate property.[109] It also recognizes non-financial contributions made by a homemaker or parent for the welfare of the other partner and/or child of the domestic partners.[110] In other words, the DPB specifically recommends giving legal recognition to the value of unpaid labour in the home in the context of a registered domestic partnership. The latter recommendation is made in view of the DPB's proposal that the default matrimonial property regime for domestic partnerships should entail separate estates, unless the registered domestic partnership agreement stipulates otherwise.[111] Since secular legislation does not make specific provision for unpaid labour in the home to be valued in the context of civil marriages and civil unions,[112] a registered domestic partnership may potentially provide more protection for non-financial contributions in the home. In relation to

98 Preamble, clause 6.
99 Clause 2(a).
100 Preamble.
101 *Volks*, op. cit., n 97 at para 172.
102 Clause 19.
103 Clause 20.
104 Clause 9.
105 Preamble, clause 6.
106 Clause 13.
107 Clause 15(1).
108 Constitution of South Africa 1996, section 28(2); Children's Act 38 of 2005, section 9.
109 Clause 1.
110 Ibid. This provision incorporates the Supreme Court of Appeal's finding that a domestic partnership may be inclusive of family life therefore non-financial contributions such as unpaid labour in the home could form part of a partnership agreement. *Butters v Mncora* 2012 (4) SA 1 (SCA) at para 23.
111 Clauses 7(1) and 7(3).
112 Marriage Act, Civil Union Act, Matrimonial Property Act.

registered domestic partners, this might raise the question of equal treatment for spouses in civil marriages or partners in civil unions who are married out of community of property but are not as easily able to be compensated for their direct and indirect contributions within marriage.

Finally, although the DPB mimics the civil law expectation of marriage that only one legal domestic partnership may be registered at a time,[113] it is simultaneously attentive to the customary law practice of polygyny among indigenous Africans. Where there may be competing claims for maintenance by an unregistered surviving domestic partner and a surviving customary spouse, the DPB recommends that the court make an order that it deems just and equitable in relation to all the parties.[114] It is unclear why the DPB does not make a similar recommendation in the context of Muslim spouses since polygyny is also practiced within the South African Muslim community.[115]

In spite of the huge amounts of time, labour and taxpayers' money that was expended to produce draft legislation for the legal recognition of domestic partnerships as well as religious marriages, none of the draft legislation discussed in the preceding sections were enacted. Instead, the South African state now appears to want to produce a consolidated piece of legislation that will afford recognition to all forms of marriages and domestic partnerships. Two parallel consultative processes are being engaged for the drafting of the consolidated legislation; one by the South African Law Reform Commission (SALRC) and another by the Department of Home Affairs (DHA). At this stage, it is unclear if the two processes are working in tandem with each other to produce one draft legislation or if two pieces of draft legislation will emanate from the parallel consultative processes.

In 2019 the SALRC published an Issue Paper,[116] which sought input from the public for the drafting of the aforementioned consolidated legislation. Shortly thereafter, the DHA published a concept paper,[117] which contains a programme for ministerial dialogues with relevant stakeholders for the drafting of a marriage policy preceding a new marriage statute. It seems that one of the objectives underpinning the drive to draft new marriage legislation is to ensure equality for all persons engaged in intimate forms of relationships.[118] Both the SALRC and the DHA are investigating the formulation of either a single marriage act or omnibus legislation. While the DHA has not provided any detailed information regarding the proposed consolidated legislation, the SALRC's Issue Paper provides some discussion about the proposed legislation, which it calls the 'Single Marriage Statute'. In the next section, the SALRC's proposed single marriage statute is briefly considered.[119]

Single marriage statute

As mentioned previously, the SALRC recommends that the single marriage statute should comprise either a single marriage act or an omnibus legislation.[120]

113 Clauses 1, 4(1).
114 Clause 29(3)(c).
115 The recommendation may not be pertinent for the South African Hindu community. Although polygyny is permissible in Hindu marriages, monogamy appears to be the norm among South African Hindu marriages. D.S.P. Cronje and J. Heaton (eds), *South African Family Law*, 3rd edition, South Africa: LexisNexis, 2010, p. 237.
116 Op. cit., n 70.
117 Department of Home Affairs, op. cit., n 70.
118 South African Law Reform Commission, op. cit., n 70, 14. Department of Home Affairs, ibid.
119 For a more detailed analysis of the proposed single marriage statute, see Amien, op. cit., n 60.
120 South African Law Reform Commission, op. cit., n 70, 22.

A single marriage act would involve 'a unified set of requirements (and possibly consequences)' for all marriages while an omnibus legislation would comprise 'different chapters which reflect the current diverse set of legal requirements for and consequences of civil marriages, civil unions, customary marriages, Muslim and possibly other religious marriages'.[121]

By expecting one standard of requirements and consequences to apply to all types of marriages and partnerships, the first option, namely, a single marriage act, involves a form of assimilation of one kind of marriage or partnership into another. It is unclear which standards will be used as the baseline by which all marriages and partnerships will be expected to conform. Given the diverse nature, requirements and consequences of marriages within South Africa, a single set of requirements and consequences is not capable of regulating all the specific features of the different types of marriages and partnerships in the country. This is already evident in the existing Marriage Act, which as highlighted earlier in this chapter, contains specific Judeo-Christian expectations of marriage to which religious marriages such as Muslim marriages must conform for parties to access matrimonial-related benefits. This leaves certain features of religious marriages unregulated such as religious divorce. A single marriage act that requires all marriages and partnerships to comply with the same requirements and consequences will most likely have the same effect as the Marriage Act – that certain features will be left unregulated. Where those features militate against women, the latter will be left unprotected. For example, unless each type of religious divorce is recognized and regulated, women will continue to experience difficulty in accessing the types of religious divorces mentioned earlier in this chapter. So, even though a single marriage act appears to offer the potential for formal equality among married and unmarried intimate partners, it cannot enable substantive equality because it is not capable of responding to all the lived realities of people within South Africa.

Depending on which form the second option, namely, omnibus legislation, takes, it has the potential to recognize and regulate specific features of different types of marriages and partnerships. This will only be possible if the omnibus legislation contains different chapters, in which each chapter regulates the requirements, features and consequences of a specific type of marriage and partnership. Some types of marriages may require more or less regulation. This can only be determined in consultation with communities that are affected directly by the regulation of their marriages. Since the Muslim Marriages Bill (MMB) has already undergone extensive consultations with the South African Muslim community and gender activists, it may make sense to incorporate the MMB into the omnibus legislation as a chapter recognizing and regulating Muslim marriages.

The omnibus option also presents an opportunity for existing marriage legislation and draft legislation such as the Domestic Partnerships Bill to be revisited, amended where needed and incorporated into the omnibus legislation as separate chapters. Should the omnibus legislation take a similar form to that of the Recognition of Religious Marriages Bill (RRMB) where recognition is afforded to different marriages and partnerships without regulation of the specific features of those marriages, the same concerns raised earlier regarding the RRMB will be equally applicable to the omnibus legislation.

Conclusion

Great strides in relation to the recognition of religious marriages and domestic partnerships were made in the past 26 years since the advent of democracy in South Africa. Tremendous efforts

121 Ibid., 15.

were made on an ad-hoc legislative basis to include spouses in religious marriages and unmarried cohabitants in domestic partnerships within the ambit of specified legislation. Although the judiciary is disappointing in its treatment of domestic partnerships, it provided as much relief as possible to spouses in religious marriages who were adversely affected by the non-recognition of their marriages and will most likely continue to do so on an ad-hoc basis. This change in approach to religious marriages from the racist, exclusivist paradigm of the apartheid regime is a direct result of the injection of constitutional values into the public policy and *boni mores* of post-apartheid South Africa, which embraces freedom of religion, equality, human dignity, diversity, pluralities and inclusivity.

Despite the significant steps that were taken to enable spouses in religious marriages and unmarried cohabitants in domestic partnerships to reclaim their dignity as contributing members within family structures, a great deal more is still required. Limited recognition of religious marriages and domestic partnerships that is afforded in an ad-hoc manner and in specific circumstances has proven to be insufficient. Unlike spouses in religious marriages who can rely on the judiciary to provide relief to them in the absence of legislation affording full legal recognition to religious marriages, unmarried cohabitants in domestic partnerships may not be as fortunate. This might suggest that legislative intervention to afford full legal recognition to domestic partnerships may be more urgent than in respect of religious marriages.

Nevertheless, spouses in religious marriages and unmarried cohabitants will only be able to operate on equal terms with civil, same-sex and African customary law spouses when their unions too receive legal recognition. That is not to say that the solution is as simple as enacting legislation to simply afford recognition to religious marriages or to ensure uniformity among the different types of marriages. Such an approach may further disadvantage the more marginalized members of the community. Instead, legislation recognizing religious marriages must comprehensively address the full range of features that are characteristic of those unions and be cognizant of the needs of the community it aims to serve, particularly the more marginalized members of the community, including women.

1.4
FAMILY, SAME-SEX UNIONS AND THE LAW

Mark Strasser

Introduction

Courts and legislatures in various parts of the world are examining the issues implicated in affording or refusing to afford legal recognition to gay and lesbian couples and their families. Sometimes, the focus is on the relationship between the adults, whereas at other times the focus is on the children whom they may be raising. As a general matter, the individuals themselves, their immediate families and society as a whole are benefited when lesbian and gay relationships are legally recognized, although the particular benefits sometimes differ depending upon other aspects of domestic relations law prevailing in the jurisdiction.

Jurisdictions face at least two kinds of questions with respect to families headed by same-sex couples – one involves whether or how the jurisdiction recognizes the relationship between the adults and another involves whether or how the jurisdiction recognizes the relationship between the adults and children in the family. Many of the reasons supporting a state's recognizing the relationship between the adults also support recognizing the relationships between the adults and children.[1]

Adult relationships

The benefits of marriage

Jurisdictions deciding whether to afford legal recognition to same-sex, adult relationships must answer at least two questions: (1) whether to afford legal recognition to such relationships at all; and if so (2), what kind of legal recognition to afford.[2] Some nation states, for example, give legal recognition to same-sex adult relationships through forms of civil or registered partnership,[3]

1 For a discussion of some of the different kinds of families recognized, see generally F. Banda and J. Eekelaar, 'International Conceptions of the Family', *International and Comparative Law Quarterly* 66, 2017, 833–62.

2 See, for example, 'Taiwan legalizes same-sex marriage in historic first for Asia': www.cnn.com/2019/05/17/asia/taiwan-same-sex-marriage-intl/index.html.

3 See, for example, 'Chile's couples celebrate same-sex unions: "History changes today"': www.theguardian.com/world/2015/oct/22/chiles-same-sex-couples-celebrate-civil-unions.

with some, many, or almost all of the legal consequences of marriage,[4] and in some cases this status is open also to different-sex couples.[5] In the US, same-sex adults may marry in all of the states, assuming the absence of other conditions that would preclude their marrying, e.g. being too closely related by reason of consanguinity or affinity. A few states continue to recognize domestic partnerships or civil unions,[6] sometimes permitting individuals of the same sex or of different sexes to enter into these relationships (see further Chapters 1.2, 1.3, and 1.5 of this book). Any analysis of whether states should legally recognize different statuses requires an examination of the purposes served by recognizing adult relationships more generally and whether those purposes are served by permitting individuals to opt for an alternative status. For example, some states permit individuals to enter into a domestic partnership if one of the parties is 62 years old, because that way the person can enter into a recognized relationship without marrying and possibly losing pension or social security benefits.[7]

Marriage is associated with a variety of benefits. For example, married individuals tend to live longer and happier lives,[8] although commentators debate whether marriage causes or is merely correlated with these desirable effects (see further Chapter 1.1 of this book). Some of the benefits of marriage are established by statute. In the US, many state and federal benefits are tied to marital status, for example, an individual might not be able to have his or her adult partner protected under an insurance policy unless the latter individual is a marital partner. For those families choosing to have one of the adult members concentrate his or her work efforts within the home and the other concentrate his or her efforts outside the home, it may well be quite important for the individual working within the home to be covered under a partner's health insurance policy – that way, the individual taking care of children or elderly parents will not be at risk should health care be needed. Other kinds of benefits are also afforded to a spouse, for example, a privilege not to testify against one's marital partner.[9] This privilege promotes fuller and more honest communications between the partners, which as a general matter will promote the health and duration of the relationship. Another kind of benefit accorded to married couples

4 See C. Hall, 'Sound the Shofar in Luxembourg: Cross-Border Recognition of Same-Sex Spouses in the European Union and Israel's *Ben Ari v. Director of Population Administration*', *Indiana International & Comparative Law Review* 28, 2008, 197–220, 202 ('[T]he European Union has a mixed record amongst its Member States with regard to recognizing same-sex marriage, civil partnerships, and other legally designated same-sex relationships').

5 J. Kim, S. Oliver and M. Ryznar, 'The Rise of PACs: A New Type of Commitment from the City of Love', *Washburn Law Journal* 56, 2017, 69–92, 81. See also *R. (Steinfeld and Keidan) v Secretary of State for International Development* [2018] UKSC 32 (holding that precluding a different-sex couple from entering into a civil partnership was incompatible with art. 14 read in conjunction with art. 8 of the ECHR).

6 See L. Dennis, N. Elrafei, A. Gwozdecky, C. Jamieson and C. de Montaigu, 'Marriage and Divorce', *Georgetown Journal of Gender & Law* 19, 2018, 397–454, 412 (those states include Colorado, Hawaii, Illinois, New Jersey, California, the District of Columbia, Hawaii, Maine, Nevada, Oregon, Washington, and Wisconsin).

7 See Washington Revised Code Annotated § 26.60.010

> While these couples are entitled to marry under the state's marriage statutes, some social security and pension laws nevertheless make it impractical for these couples to marry. For this reason, chapter 156, Laws of 2007 specifically allows couples to enter into a state registered domestic partnership if one of the persons is at least sixty-two years of age, the age at which many people choose to retire and are eligible to begin collecting social security and pension benefits.

8 M. Garrison, 'Nonmarital Cohabitation: Social Revolution and Legal Regulation', *Family Law Quarterly* 42, 2008, 309–32, 326.

9 See e.g. Alabama Code 1975 § 12–21–227.

is the presumption that a child born into the marriage is a child of the parties.[10] This presumption protects the family from external challenge absent a desire of one of the members of the couple to challenge the other's parental status.[11] This, too, is thought to promote the stability and duration of the marriage.[12] These benefits might but need not be afforded to those who have opted for a different status. For example, Hawaii's reciprocal beneficiary status affords certain rights and benefits[13] but is not intended to confer all of the benefits of marriage,[14] whereas Nevada affords almost all of the rights of spouses to domestic partners.[15] The federal statute precluding the federal government from recognizing same-sex marriages for federal purposes has been struck down by the US Supreme Court.[16] However, the Court did not hold that the federal government must recognize civil unions or domestic partnerships for federal purposes.[17]

The federal government's refusal to recognize civil unions or domestic partnerships for federal purposes might be viewed in a somewhat different light now that all of the states must recognize same-sex marriage. Both same-sex and different-sex couples can obtain the relevant federal benefits through marriage, so it is not as if the refusal to recognize those unions precludes same-sex couples from having access to the benefits at issue. That said, it might nonetheless be wise to permit[18] both same-sex and different sex couples in civil unions and domestic partnerships to receive federal benefits because some of the purposes served by recognizing marriages, e.g. providing a safety net for partners or children, might also be served by recognizing these relationships too.

10 See e.g. Colorado Revised Statutes Annotated § 19–4–105 (1) (a).

11 See e.g. *Michael H. v Gerald D.*, 491 U.S. 110 (1989).

12 See ibid., pp. 135–6 (Stevens, J., concurring in the judgment) (agreeing that the presumed biological parent does not have a constitutionally guaranteed right to visitation at least in part because the couple's marriage had 'developed a stability that now provides Victoria [the child] with a loving and harmonious family home').

13 See, for example, Hawaii Revised Statutes Annotated § 323–2 ('A reciprocal beneficiary, as defined in chapter 572C, of a patient shall have the same rights as a spouse with respect to visitation and making health care decisions for the patient').

14 See Hawaii Revised Statutes Annotated § 572C-6 ('Unless otherwise expressly provided by law, reciprocal beneficiaries shall not have the same rights and obligations under the law that are conferred through marriage').

15 See Nevada Revised Statutes Annotated § 122A.200 (a)

> (Domestic partners have the same rights, protections and benefits, and are subject to the same responsibilities, obligations and duties under law, whether derived from statutes, administrative regulations, court rules, government policies, common law or any other provisions or sources of law, as are granted to and imposed upon spouses.).

But see Nevada Revised Statutes Annotated § 122A.210 (1) ('The provisions of this chapter do not require a public or private employer in this State to provide health care benefits to or for the domestic partner of an officer or employee').

16 See *United States v Windsor*, 133 S. Ct. 2675 (2013).

17 M. Barnhardt, J. Lillesand and D. Lettau, 'A Holistic Approach to Planning for the Aging Same-Sex Couple: Special Considerations in Light of the U.S. v. Windsor Decision', *Saint Thomas Law Review* 26, 2013, 1–36, 4 ('The Supreme Court ruling in *United States v. Windsor* does not change the landscape of rights created under domestic partnerships'); D. Widiss, 'Non-Marital Families and (or After?) Marriage Equality', *Florida: State University Law Review* 42, 2015, 547–72, 564 (discussing the 'federal government's refusal to recognize civil unions and domestic partnerships that offer full spousal benefits and obligations under state law').

18 Arguably, couples in such unions might be permitted but not required to receive the relevant benefits if only because some couples might choose civil unions or domestic partnerships over marriage precisely because they do not wish to sacrifice other federal benefits that would be lost were the federal government to afford official recognition to the status. See supra n 5 and accompanying text.

Those arguing that marriage causes these beneficial effects suggest that married individuals tend to invest more in their relationships,[19] perhaps because of the increased legal and emotional security afforded by the official recognition of their unions. Thus, married individuals may feel more comfortable about making sacrifices or, perhaps, taking reasonable risks that will inure to their own and their family's benefit. Such risks might include getting further education or relocating for career advancement. Further, married individuals might be more likely to reallocate family responsibilities, for example, allowing one individual to take on more duties at home while another individual takes on more duties outside the home, thereby yielding a better outcome for the family as a whole than would have been possible had there been no reallocation of responsibilities (see further Chapter 1.2 of this book).

Marriage can have religious or emotional symbolic value for the parties themselves,[20] and the public statement of commitment might itself further cement the relationship, which may be especially important during difficult economic times.[21] Individuals who are in satisfying long-term relationships may not only live healthier, happier lives than those who are not but also may be more productive, which not only benefits the individuals themselves but society as a whole. It is simply unclear whether civil unions or domestic partnerships afford the same emotional benefits.

Policy considerations related to extending benefits of marriage to same-sex relationships

The policy issue here is whether the state should be affording to same-sex couples an opportunity already enjoyed by different-sex couples. The kinds of benefits that can be accrued through marriage will redound regardless of the composition of the couple – same-sex couples, like different-sex couples, can benefit from the security and stability afforded by marriage. Thus, same-sex couples and society as a whole can benefit where the law provides security so that partners can divvy up their responsibilities or, perhaps, so that they can take reasonable risks to enhance long-term prospects for the family as a whole, e.g. by changing jurisdictions to avail themselves of economic opportunities.

Thus far, the discussion has focused on benefits to the adult members of the couple. But an important element of marriage for some families involves the benefits that the relationship can bring for children who are being raised within that family.[22] This is yet another policy reason in

19 See M. Wald, 'Same-Sex Couple Marriage: A Family Policy Perspective', *Virginia Journal of Social Policy & Law* 9, 2001, 291–344, 304.

20 See *Turner v Safley*, 482 U.S. 78, 95–6 (1982).

21 A comparison of the dissolution rate of (different-sex) marriages and (same-sex) civil partnerships from 2005 to 2008 in the UK showed the rate of dissolution of marriages to be higher. However, a longer time-run is necessary to allow firm conclusions to be drawn: H. Ross, K. Gask and A. Berrington, 'Civil Partnerships Five Years on', *Population Trends* 145, 2011, 1–31, 16 (UK Office for National Statistics).

22 Regrettably, some justices on the United States Supreme Court refuse to recognize that recognition of same-sex marriage can provide benefits for children, see *Obergefell v Hodges*, 135 S. Ct. 2584, 2641 (2015) (Justice Alito, with whom Justice Scalia and Justice Thomas join, dissenting) ('This understanding of marriage, … focuses almost entirely on the happiness of persons who choose to marry'), even where other members of the Court have expressly noted that recognizing same-sex marriage will help children. See ibid. at 2600 ('A third basis for protecting the right to marry is that it safeguards children and families').

favour of recognizing same-sex marriage – the stability afforded by marriage will benefit children being raised within that setting.[23]

Prior to the US Supreme Court's issuance of *Obergefell v Hodges*[24] in which the Court held that same-sex marriage bans violate constitutional guarantees, US courts refusing to recognize that same-sex marriage is constitutionally protected sometimes suggested that states have a special interest in promoting marriages between different-sex individuals because accidentally conceived children will then be more likely to be born within a marital setting.[25] Such an analysis is mistaken for several reasons. First, it assumes that the state must choose between granting marriage licenses to same-sex couples on the one hand and different-sex couples on the other. But that is incorrect. The state can recognize both same-sex marriages and different-sex marriages,[26] and the state goal of making it more likely that accidentally conceived children will be born into an existing marriage will not be at all hindered by recognizing same-sex marriages, too. As Lady Hale stated in the United Kingdom Supreme Court:[27]

> No one has yet explained how failing to recognise the relationships of people whose sexual orientation means that they are unable or strongly unwilling to marry [where 'marriage' is defined as being restricted to heterosexual unions] is necessary for the purpose of protecting or encouraging the marriage of people who are quite capable of marrying of they wish to do so.

Second, the emphasis on increasing the likelihood that accidentally conceived children will be raised in a marital home should not be permitted to decrease the likelihood that *intentionally* conceived children will be raised in a marital home. Same-sex couples who plan to raise a child conceived through the use of assisted reproductive technologies[28] or, perhaps, adopted by one or both of them, should also be permitted to provide that child with a stable home where the child might thrive.[29] Children who are intentionally brought into families should also be given the opportunity to enjoy the benefits that marriage can bring, and the state's desire to promote the interests of accidentally conceived children should not be permitted to undermine the interests of intentionally conceived children, especially when undermining the interests of the latter does nothing to promote the interests of the former.

Third, the courts seem inordinately focused on the conditions in which the child is brought into the world. But couples who intentionally rather than accidentally bring children into the world will nonetheless face a variety of stressors in their relationships as they raise their children, so it is important to consider the health of the adults' relationship even after the child has been

23 *Obergefell v Hodges*, 135 S. Ct. 2584, 2600-01 (2015) ('The marriage laws at issue here [precluding same-sex marriage] thus harm and humiliate the children of same-sex couples').

24 135 S.Ct. 2584 (2015).

25 See *Hernandez v Robles*, 855 N.E.2d 1, 7 (N.Y. 2006) abrogated by *Obergefell v Hodges*, 135 S. Ct. 2584 (2015); *Andersen v King County*, 138 P. 3d 963, 982 (Wash. 2006), abrogated by *Obergefell v Hodges*, 135 S. Ct. 2584 (2015).

26 See *Hernandez*, 855 N.E.2d at 30 (Kaye, C.J., dissenting) ('There are enough marriage licenses to go around for everyone').

27 *Secretary of State for Work and Pensions v M* [2006] UKHL 11, [2006] 2 FLR 56, para 113.

28 For a discussion of differing ART policies within Scandinavian countries, see M. Jantera-Jareborg, 'Parenthood for Same-Sex Couples: Scandinavian Developments', in K. Boele-Woelki and A. Fuchs (eds), *Legal Recognition of Same-Sex Relationship in Europe: National, Cross-Border and European Perspectives*, Cambridge, UK: Intersentia, 2012, pp. 91, 106–16.

29 See A. Wax, 'Traditionalism, Pluralism, and Same-Sex Marriage', *Rutgers Law Review* 59, 2007, 377–412, 408.

brought into the home. Cohabiting couples who have children together end their relationships at a higher rate than do married couples.[30] But if married couples are more likely than cohabiting couples to stay together, and if the marriages themselves contribute to that greater longevity, then same-sex couples (with or without children) should be afforded the opportunity to marry, both for their own sakes and for the sake of any child that they are or might be raising.

Marriage or civil (registered) partnership?

The preceding policy considerations speak to offering legal recognition of same-sex couples, although a different question is whether to recognize same-sex marriage or, instead, a separate status like a domestic partnership, civil partnership or a *pacte civil de solidarité* (see further Chapters 1.1, 1.2, and 2.1 of this book). Numerous factors might be considered when deciding as a matter of public policy which option makes more sense. If marriage is not available, then an alternative arrangement will still afford same-sex couples, their families and society as a whole, some of the benefits that would be accorded were same-sex marriages recognized. However, setting up an alternative institution, perhaps with the same benefits as marriage or perhaps with fewer benefits, also has costs, especially if this alternative is not simply one of the options that couples have as a general matter but is offered instead because same-sex couples are somehow deemed unworthy of marriage. The costs of setting up the alternative arrangement, whether administrative or symbolic, must also be considered when analyzing which approach makes the most sense from a public policy perspective. Many European countries, however, have already established such institutions, so their policy decision is whether to add same-sex marriage to the available options or, instead, to replace the other options with same-sex marriage.

Various commentators argue that same-sex marriage somehow threatens the institution of marriage,[31] some of whom believe that recognizing civil unions or domestic partnerships would also somehow threaten marriage.[32] When assessing such arguments from a policy perspective, it is important to establish what counts as harm. Suppose that the test for harm is simply whether the proposed institution would somehow result in a decrease in the number of people who marry or remain married. It might be thought that a new institution reserved for same-sex couples would not affect the rate at which different-sex couples marry, because the latter couples could not enter into those civil unions or partnerships.[33] But that would not end the analysis, because it is possible that some individuals would refuse to marry their different-sex partners because the state was now affording recognition to same-sex unions.[34] By the same token,

30 H. Alvaré, 'Beyond the Sex-Ed Wars: Addressing Disadvantaged Single Mothers' Search for Community', *Akron Law Review* 44, 2011, 167–220, 181 ('Two years from a baby's birth, 30% of cohabiting pairs have dissolved as compared to only 6% of married parents, and half of cohabiting households disintegrate by the time a child is nine').

31 See L. Wardle, 'The Attack on Marriage as the Union of a Man and a Woman', *North Dakota Law Review* 83, 2007, 1365–91.

32 See K. Spaht, 'State Constitutional Amendments Prohibiting Same-Sex Unions: Winning the "Dual Object" Argument', *Florida Coastal Law Review* 7, 2005, 339–64, 361.

33 See P. Busch, 'Is Same-Sex Marriage a Threat to Traditional Marriages?: How Courts Struggle with the Question', *Washington University Global Studies Law Review* 10, 2011, 143–65, 157 (suggesting that the German Federal Constitutional Court reasoned that civil partnerships did not threaten marriage because the partnerships were only open to same-sex couples).

34 But see *Dragovich v U.S. Dep't of Treasury*, 2012 WL 1909603, 13 (N.D. Cal. 2012) ('There is no reasonable basis to believe that heterosexual couples are more inclined to marry and have children or to enter into a marriage after accidentally conceiving a child, due to this limiting federal definition enacted in 1996').

however, it is also possible that some different-sex couples would be willing to marry precisely because the state was now affording recognition to same-sex couples as well.

Suppose that the test of harm is whether the number of individuals entering into marriage has been reduced because of the introduction of the new institution, and the new institution is open to both same-sex and different-sex couples. One could not simply assume that because some different-sex couples had registered for the civil union that it was therefore clear that marriage had been harmed.[35] One would want to know in addition whether the different-sex couples who had registered for the civil union would instead have married had there been no civil union option. Marriage rates have been dropping in many countries that have not introduced any alternative.[36] One would also want to know how many had been dissuaded from or induced into marrying because the state had adopted this alternate relationship. To make the analysis even more difficult, it is not clear that a different-sex couple having chosen a civil union rather than a marriage would establish that the couple had rejected marriage. Instead, such a couple might be choosing the civil union option as a kind of trial marriage, just as some might choose cohabitation as a precursor to marriage.[37]

Does recognizing same-sex marriage threaten traditional marriage?

Consider the claim that recognizing same-sex marriage somehow threatens traditional marriage. If the way to establish harm is to show a reduction in different-sex marriages, then there is no evidence that the recognition of same-sex unions harms traditional marriage.[38] Of course, a separate question is whether the appropriate test for determining whether one group should be allowed to marry is whether another group would thereby be deterred from marrying or remaining married. Suppose that empirical data established that by permitting interracial or intergenerational or interreligious couples to marry, intra-racial or intra-generational or intra-religious couples would be less likely to marry. Would that justify a state precluding the former from marrying?

Sometimes, the alleged harm of same-sex marriage is that it undermines the purpose of marriage, namely, 'the need to provide a biological father and mother committed to each other, hopefully for life, for the purpose of rearing healthy children'.[39] But this is incorrect, at least in part, because there is no single purpose for marriage. Individuals who will not or cannot procreate are not (and should not be) precluded from marrying on that account,[40] which suggests that the state recognizes that marriage serves a variety of purposes,[41] only one of which is that it provides a setting in which children might thrive. Same-sex couples fulfil many of the purposes of marriage, including providing a place where the young can be nurtured, and this provides a

35 See Busch, op. cit., n 34, 158 (noting that the German Federal Constitutional Court

also acknowledged that the civil partnerships law was restricted to couples who could not legally marry, suggesting that it might find a constitutional violation if there were a parallel institution to marriage that was an alternative for those who could legally marry).

36 B. Atwood. 'Marital Contracts and the Meaning of Marriage', *Arizona Law Review* 54, 2012, 11–42, 41 (noting that in 'Europe … a steeper decline in marriage rates than in the United States has occurred').

37 See E. Diederich, 'Cause Breaking Up Is Hard to Do: The Need for Uniform Enforcement of Cohabitation Agreements in West Virginia', *West Virginia Law Review* 113, 2011, 1073–98, 1095.

38 M. Neely, 'Indiana Proposed Defense of Marriage Amendment: What Will It Do and Why Is It Needed', *Indiana Law Review* 41, 2008, 245–72.

39 See Spaht, op. cit., n 33, 361.

40 See L. Green, 'Sex-Neutral Marriage', *Current Legal Problems* 64, 2011, 1–21, 12.

41 For empirical evidence from the UK on the reasons why people marry, see J. Eekelaar, 'Why People Marry: The Many Faces of an institution', *Family Law Quarterly* 41, 2007, 413–31.

strong policy reason why they should have their relationships recognized. In cases in which the relationship must be dissolved, the state has interests implicated in assuring an orderly dissolution of the relationship, including an equitable distribution of property, the provision of support in appropriate cases, and visitation and custody awards where children are involved.[42] The state's interests in assuring an orderly breakdown of long-term relationships are implicated whether the couple is composed of individuals of the same sex or of different sexes.

Even if one excludes the issue of same-sex marriage from consideration, state policies do not support the claim that *the* purpose of marriage is to induce adults (able and willing to have children together) to marry and raise a family. The state encourages adults to marry whether or not they will have or raise children. A different issue is raised if one of the parties induces the other party to marry by falsely claiming to want to have children,[43] but the reason that such a misrepresentation can be the basis for annulling the marriage is not simply because the individual wants to be childless but, rather, because it is a misrepresentation about a very important subject. A New Jersey court annulled a marriage because the husband had induced his wife to marry him by falsely claiming that he did *not* want to have children.[44] If the sole purpose of marriage were to produce children, then the court would have been unlikely to grant the wife an annulment because the husband had lied when saying that he did not want to have children.

States within the US differ about whether first cousins are allowed to marry. Some states prohibit such marriages,[45] some states prohibit the celebration of such marriages within the state but will recognize them if validly celebrated elsewhere,[46] and some states permit them to be celebrated locally.[47] What is interesting for purposes here is that some states prohibit first cousin marriages unless the couple *cannot* have children through their union.[48] A state that permits a marriage only if the parties cannot have a child through their union obviously does not believe that the only purpose of marriage is to encourage individuals to have children through their union.

There are additional reasons to believe that the state does not privilege biology in the way some commentators claim – the state encourages adults to raise children who are not biologically related to each of them, whether through adoption policies generally[49] or step-parent adoption policies in particular.[50] State encouragement of adoption sends a much stronger message that it is unnecessary for parents to be biologically related to the children whom they are raising than does recognizing same-sex marriage. The point here is not to undermine the wisdom of promoting adoption – on the contrary, adoption can provide a child with opportunities and a setting in which he or she can thrive that simply would not have been available absent the adoption.

Consider step-parent adoption, where a child is adopted by the partner of the child's biological or adoptive parent. The state promotes step-parent adoption, where no other adult's parental

42 See *Baker v State*, 170 Vt. 194, 243, 744 A.2d 864, 898–99 (1999) (Johnson, J., concurring in part and dissenting in part) ('The State's interest in licensing marriages is regulatory in nature. ... The regulatory purpose of the licensing scheme is to create public records for the orderly allocation of benefits, imposition of obligations, and distribution of property through inheritance').
43 See *Montenegro v Avila*, 365 S.W.3d 822 (Tex. App. 2012).
44 See *V.J.S. v M.J.B.*, 592 A.2d 328 (N.J. Super. Ch. 1991).
45 See eg Kentucky Revised Statutes § 402.010 (1).
46 See *Mazzolini v Mazzolini*, 155 N.E.2d 206 (Ohio 1958).
47 See *Mason v Mason*, 775 N.E.2d 706, 709 (Ind. App. 2002).
48 See eg Indiana Code § 31–11–1–2; Wisconsin Statutes Annotated § 765.03 (1).
49 See eg Alabama Code 1975 § 26–10A-5 (a).
50 See eg Indiana Code § 31–19–15–2 (a) and Indiana Code § 31–19–15–2 (b).

rights are implicated, because permitting the non-biologically related partner to adopt the child will further cement the family in a variety of ways that will likely inure to the child's benefit. By promoting step-parent adoption, the state sends the message that its priority is promoting the interests of the child, and that those interests can be promoted even by individuals who are not biologically related to the child. Recognition of same-sex marriage does not undermine the state's messages regarding family and children but, instead, reinforces them.

Equality issues

Some jurisdictions, such as Canada[51] and South Africa,[52] have instituted same-sex marriage as a result of judicial interpretation of equality provisions in constitutional instruments. The relevant policy arguments in those cases have been shaped by constitutional discourse. In other cases, the debate has occurred primarily in the political arena. The European Court of Human Rights has held that the European Convention on Human Rights does not provide a right to enter a same-sex marriage,[53] so the policy debate assumes a more overtly political flavour.

When the US Supreme Court struck down Virginia's interracial marriage ban in *Loving v Virginia*,[54] the Court reasoned that the prohibition was 'designed to maintain White Supremacy'[55] and as such was 'invidious racial discrimination'[56] that had no legitimate independent purpose. The Court would presumably also have rejected a 'separate but equal' status as stigmatizing and hence unconstitutional.[57] One must wonder what legitimate, independent purpose is served by refusing to permit same-sex couples to marry.[58] The point here is not to undermine the desirability of same-sex couples having a legal status for their relationships even if it is a civil partnership rather than a marriage, because even a separate status would afford many of the emotional, religious and tangible benefits afforded by marriage. Those are important and are not to be taken lightly. Nonetheless, by creating a separate status, the state sends additional messages, e.g. that it does not want the institution of marriage to be tainted by permitting those with a same-sex orientation to have access to it.[59] Yet, that is presumably exactly the kind of message that the state should not be sending insofar as it wishes to promote respect for all persons. By the same token, when the state makes marriage a restricted institution only open to certain individuals even though those denied access would both benefit from and serve the purposes of the institution, the state sends additional messages, e.g. that marriage itself is simply yet another pawn to be used in the culture wars. But sending such a message does more to demean the

51 See W.K. Wright, 'The Tide in Favour of Equality: Same-Sex Marriage in Canada and England and Wales', *International Journal of Law, Policy and the Family* 20, 2006, 249–85.

52 *Minister of Home Affairs and Another v Fourie and Another; Lesbian and Gay Equality Project and Others v Minister of Home Affairs and Others*, 2006 *(1) SA 524 (CC), 2006 (3) BCLR 355 (CC)*. However same-sex marriages take place under a new statutory framework (the Civil Union Act) which operates alongside the traditional Marriage Act: see B.S. Smith and J.A. Robinson, 'The South African Civil Union Act 2006: Progressive Legislation with Regressive Implications?', *International Journal of Law, Policy & the Family* 22, 2008, 356–92. See also Chapter 1.3 of this book.

53 *Schalk and Kopf v Austria*, Application 30141/04: judgment finalised 24 June 2010; *Gas and Dubois v France*, Requête 25951/07 (15 June 2012). See J. Eekelaar, 'Perceptions of Equality: The Road to Same-Sex Marriage in England', *International Journal of Law, Policy and the Family* 28, 2014, 1–25.

54 388 U.S. 1 (1967).

55 Ibid. at 11.

56 Ibid.

57 See *Brown v Board of Education*, 347 U.S. 483, 495 (1954).

58 See *Goodridge v Department of Public Health*, 798 N.E.2d 941, 961 (Mass. 2003).

59 See *Perry v Schwarzenegger*, 704 F.Supp.2d 921, 1002 (N.D. Cal., 2010): ('Proposition 8 was premised on the belief that same-sex couples simply are not as good as opposite-sex couples').

institution in the eyes of many than permitting same-sex couples and their families to enter the fold ever could.[60]

While all states in the US must permit same-sex couples to marry, a separate question is whether states are permitted to distinguish among marriages affording some more rights and responsibilities than others. The US Supreme Court has held that states cannot treat same-sex and different-sex marriages differently by reserving some rights for the latter unions.[61] That said, states may permit couples to opt into marriages that include more severe limitations on the conditions under which divorces will be granted.[62]

Perhaps it would be thought that recognizing same-sex marriage somehow sends a message of disapproval to those who oppose such unions. But it is of course true that individuals who oppose same-sex unions are not being told that they cannot marry. So, too, individuals who believe that it is important for individuals to marry within their faith are not somehow being denigrated when the state permits individuals of different faiths or of no faith to marry. The recognition of same-sex marriages does not imply that different-sex marriages are not valuable, just as the recognition of interracial, interreligious or intergenerational marriages does not imply that intra-racial, intra-religious or intra-generational marriages are not valuable.

Same-sex marriage and religious institutions

Various religious institutions have offered their own views regarding whether same-sex unions should be recognized. Some suggest that such unions should be afforded no recognition,[63] whereas others have suggested that such unions should receive recognition but not as marriages.[64] In the UK, the Quakers have supported same-sex marriage.[65]

A few issues should be clarified when discussing how religious institutions are impacted by the recognition of same-sex unions. Even where the state recognizes same-sex unions (whether as partnerships or as marriages), it is seldom proposed that the churches should be required to celebrate such unions if doing so contradicts their religious beliefs or practices – on the contrary, the religious institutions are permitted to celebrate or not celebrate such unions as their doctrines dictate. In England and Wales, for example, religious organizations must expressly agree

60 There might be two different ways in which this might occur. In one, those opposing same-sex marriage might be viewed as simply trying to promote traditional marriage with its gender roles and power imbalances. See J. Feinberg, 'Exposing the Traditional Marriage Agenda', *Northwestern Journal of Law and Social Policy* 7, 2012, 301–51. Or, those opposing same-sex marriage might be thought to be doing so out of hostility, which might itself taint the institution. See T. Wilson, 'Changed Embraces, Changes Embraced? Renouncing the Heterosexist Majority in Favor of a Return to Traditional Two-Spirit Culture', *American Indian Law Review* 36, 2012, 161–88.

61 See *Pavan v Smith*, 137 S. Ct. 2075, 2078 (2017) ('[A] State may not "exclude same-sex couples from civil marriage on the same terms and conditions as opposite-sex couples."') (citing *Obergefell v Hodges*, 135 S. Ct. 2584, 2605 (2015).

62 See Louisiana Statutes Annotated § 9:307 (specifying the limited conditions under which those in a covenant marriage may divorce).

63 See Congregation for the Doctrine of the Faith, *Considerations regarding proposals to give legal recognition to unions between homosexual persons*. Available at www.vatican.va/roman_curia/congregations/cfaith/documents/rc_con_cfaith_doc_20030731_homosexual-unions_en.html.

64 See www.churchofengland.org/our-views/marriage,-family-and-sexuality-issues/same-sex-marriage.aspx

65 Quakers in Britain, *Quakers and Same-Sex Marriage*. Available at www.quaker.org.uk/about-quakers/our-history/marriage-equality (accessed 4 February 2019).

to 'opt-in' to the power to formalize same-sex marriages.[66] As a general matter, then, jurisdictions weighing whether to recognize same-sex unions are not trying to decide whether to force religious institutions to celebrate such unions, religious doctrine notwithstanding. On the contrary, the state is debating whether to offer a non-religious venue in which such unions can be celebrated or, instead, whether to refrain from recognizing same-sex marriages in particular or same-sex unions more generally, at least in part, because the recognition of such unions is not in accord with the beliefs of particular religious groups.

When analyzing whether states should recognize same-sex unions and, if so, how, one should not frame the debate in terms of whether the state is changing the fundamental definition of marriage.[67] Various jurisdictions already recognize same-sex marriage in particular or same-sex unions more generally, so it is difficult to see how a particular jurisdiction's decision to afford recognition to same-sex relationships is going to effect a radical change in anything. An analogous point might be made with respect to religious traditions. Some religious traditions recognize same-sex unions[68] while others do not. To suggest that the recognition of such a union involves a fundamental redefinition of the institution of marriage is simply to reject the religious beliefs of those who celebrate same-sex unions.

It is of course both permissible and expected that faith traditions will have differing views about a number of matters – no faith tradition has a monopoly on truth. But part of the persuasiveness of the claim that recognition of same-sex marriage radically changes the definition of marriage lies in its allegedly representing a universal truth, i.e. a truth to which all or almost all individuals ascribe. But such a claim is false whether measured by the beliefs of varying religious traditions or the practices of various jurisdictions. While religious groups are of course entitled to say that the recognition of same-sex unions is not in accord with their religious tradition, state policy could hardly concede to them the power to override other traditions holding contrary views. Consider a state's willingness to permit divorce. Faith traditions have differing views about the conditions, if any, under which divorces can be granted. That the state cannot help but adopt a policy not in accord with some religious beliefs and practices does not mean that the state should do nothing – instead, the state should examine the public policy implications of recognizing or not recognizing the practices at issue and make a decision in light of those cost-benefit analyses. It should also be remembered that for centuries western law reflected the hierarchical structure of the marital dyad found in St Paul, which positions the husband as 'head' of the family to whom the wife is under an obligation of obedience.[69] Yet western laws have moved away from that structure, in some cases quite recently. Since state law has already modified the fundamental obligations of marriage as long understood within some religious traditions, the objection to a different modification that does not affect those obligations could be said to have little weight.

66 Marriage (Same Sex Couples) Act 2013, ss. 2–4. However, the Church of England is not given this power, since this would imply Parliament was attempting to override canon law, so same-sex marriages cannot be formalized according to the rites of that church. See Eekelaar, op. cit., n 54.

67 See L. Wardle, 'The Boundaries of Belonging: Allegiance, Purpose and the Definition of Marriage', *Brigham Young University Journal of Public Law* 25, 2011, 287–312.

68 See M. Isaak, '"What's in a Name?": Civil Unions and the Constitutional Significance of "Marriage"', *University of Pennsylvania Journal of Constitutional Law* 10, 2008, 607–43, 637 ('Same-sex marriages are performed and recognized by Jewish denominations including Reform, Reconstructionist, and Conservative; some Episcopalians and other mainline Christian denominations, such as the United Church of Christ; as well as other religious groups, including Unitarians and some Buddhists').

69 Ephesians: 5: 22–5.

The point here is not to claim that same-sex marriage should be recognized because some religious traditions recognize them. Were no religious traditions to recognize interfaith marriages that would not be a reason for the state to refuse to recognize such marriages. By the same token, merely because a religious tradition recognizes certain marriages does not mean that the state should do so as well. For example, the state might refuse to recognize marriages involving very young children even if those unions were recognized by a particular religious group. States can and should impose some limitations on marriage. If there are public policy reasons that justify refusing to recognize same-sex unions that outweigh the public policy reasons for recognizing such unions, then states might be able to justify their restrictions barring other kinds of claims, e.g. respect for human rights, constitutional guarantees, etc. But it is simply too late in the day to offer the radical redefinition argument as if it should have independent weight.

Religious groups should not be forced to surrender their beliefs merely because those beliefs do not coincide with those of others. But no one is requiring religious groups to surrender their beliefs. However, some difficulties may remain even once it is understood that religious groups are not being forced to modify their beliefs. Suppose that a particular religious organization refuses to recognize certain marriages and an individual working for that institution marries someone civilly, religious prohibition notwithstanding. Suppose further that the individual wishes to have his or her marriage recognized by the religious institution or, perhaps, wishes to retain his or her job notwithstanding having celebrated such a marriage. It is not entirely clear how such a case should be handled. Religious institutions themselves may not react to those circumstances in the same ways – some will find ways to accommodate individuals who marry contrary to the church's teachings and others will not. Further, states themselves may adopt differing approaches depending upon the particular facts and circumstances presented and on the state's constitutional or other laws regarding discriminatory practices. This might raise a specific problem in England and Wales. Marriages conducted in accordance with the rites of the Church of England, and the practices of Quakers and Jews, are accorded automatic legal recognition. Other religious forms of marriage are recognized under certain conditions. Same-sex marriages can only be effected through a religious procedure if the organization has opted-in (and that opportunity is not available to the Church of England). It is arguable that this strategy could be challenged under anti-discrimination and human rights legislation. (See further Chapter 6.5 of this book.) The policy choice between enforcing equality principles and respecting religious practice may therefore eventually be debated in the courts.

In the US, some individuals refuse to provide goods or services to same-sex couples, claiming that the promotion of same-sex unions is contrary to faith. The US Supreme Court heard a case challenging the imposition of a fine for refusing to provide baked goods to a same-sex couple in violation of a public accommodations law.[70] The Court vacated the fine, believing that commission members imposing the fine had been motivated by anti-religious bias. In future, the Court will have to decide whether an individual's sincerely held convictions will require that he or she be exempted from public accommodation laws. Given the diversity of sincerely held religious beliefs in the US, such an exemption, if recognized, will go a long way in gutting public accommodation law that seek to prevent discrimination on the basis of race, religion, gender, sexual orientation, etc. Needless to say, the Court might have approached this issue differently.

70 *Masterpiece Cakeshop Ltd. v Colorado Civil Rights Commission*, 138 S. Ct. 1719 (2018). In *Lee v Ashers Baking Co. Ltd*, [2018] UKSC 49, the UK Supreme Court considered whether a baker refusing to bake a cake containing a message supporting same-sex unions was thereby discriminating inter alia on the basis of sexual orientation. The Court held that the baker was not, distinguishing *Masterpiece Cakeshop* by noting that in the latter case no particular message was at issue.

On children

Jurisdictions vary with respect to their treatment of gay and lesbian parenting. Historically, an individual might lose custody or visitation privileges because of his or her relationship with someone of the same sex. Currently, lesbians or gays can as individuals adopt children in almost all of the states in the United States.[71] Two people of the same sex have been able to adopt a child jointly in England and Wales since 2002,[72] and this is the position in a number of European countries.[73] (See further Chapter 4.3 of this book.)

Two issues should be distinguished: (1) whether a lesbian or gay man can as an individual adopt a child and (2) whether the members of a lesbian or gay married couple will be treated in the same way that different-sex married couples are treated. Consider the state of Utah, which permits a lesbian or a gay man to adopt a child. However, the state precludes adoption by any adult who is in a cohabiting relationship with another adult.[74] Thus, a gay man or a lesbian not in a committed relationship will be permitted to adopt a child, but a gay man or a lesbian who had found a life-partner with whom to share his or her life would be precluded from adopting unless the parties had married,[75] notwithstanding the benefits that might accrue to the child from being raised by two loving parents rather than one. This contrasts with the position in England and Wales which permits joint adoption by same-sex couples if they are living as partners 'in an enduring family relationship'.[76]

Utah law also precludes members of different-sex, non-marital couples from adopting,[77] so it is not as if the state's prohibiting non-marital couples from adopting discriminates against same-sex couples in particular. However, there is another part of the law that seems to disfavour same-sex married couples. Basically, Utah law allows married couples to adopt.[78] However, there is another provision that seems to give a preference to different-sex married couples.[79] No

71 Some states have attempted to bar adoptions by gay or lesbian parents by statute, although such statutes have not fared well in the courts. See, for example, *Fla. Dep't of Children & Families v Adoption of X.X.G.*, 45 So. 3d 79, 81 (Fla. Dist. Ct. App. 2010) (striking down such a statute as not having a rational relationship to a legitimate state interest). See also *Stewart v Heineman*, 892 N.W.2d 542 (Neb. 2017) (upholding lower court precluding use of a policy that would have prevented gay men and lesbians from being foster or adoptive parents).

72 Adoption and Children Act 2002, s. 144 (4).

73 See B. Verschraegen, 'The Right to Private and Family Life, the Right to Marry and to Found a Family, and the Prohibition on Discrimination', in K. Boeli-Woelki and A. Fuchs (eds), *Legal Recognition of Same-Sex Relationships in Europe*, Cambridge, UK: Intersentia, 2012, p. 258.

74 See Utah Code Annotated § 78B-6–117 (4).

> (To provide a child who is in the custody of the division with the most beneficial family structure, when a child in the custody of the division is placed for adoption, the division or child-placing agency shall place the child with a man and a woman who are married to each other.)

75 See Utah Code Annotated § 78B-6–117 (3) ('A child may not be adopted by a person who is cohabiting in a relationship that is not a legally valid and binding marriage under the laws of this state').

76 Adoption and Children Act 2002, s. 144(4).

77 See Utah Code Annotated § 78B-6–117 (3) ('A child may not be adopted by a person who is cohabiting in a relationship that is not a legally valid and binding marriage under the laws of this state').

78 Utah Code Annotated § 78B-6–117(2)(a) (2) ('A child may be adopted by adults who are legally married to each other in accordance with the laws of this state, including adoption by a stepparent').

79 Utah Code Annotated § 78B-6–117 (4)

> (To provide a child who is in the custody of the division with the most beneficial family structure, when a child in the custody of the division is placed for adoption, the division or child-placing agency shall place the child with a man and a woman who are married to each other).

appellate court has construed this provision since *Obergefell* was decided – it is unclear whether the provision will be interpreted to be privileging marital couples over single individuals unless certain conditions obtain[80] or whether the law will be construed to be privileging different-sex married couples over same-sex married couples and single adults. Courts have struck down statutes precluding gay or lesbian adults from adopting, because children can thrive whether with same-sex or different-sex parents.[81]

Realizing that children are better off being adopted and allowed to thrive in a stable home even if the cohabiting couple is unwilling or unable to marry, most states do not preclude adoption merely because the would-be adoptive adult is in a committed, non-marital relationship. That said, however, some states preclude each member of a cohabiting couple from having a legally recognized relationship with a child.[82] Thus, only one member of the couple will be recognized as the child's parent, and the other individual raising the child may be considered a legal stranger to that child. In contrast, in other states, members of non-marital couples can each establish a legal relationship with the same child. States permitting each of the two adults raising a child to have a legally recognized relationship with that child help the parents and the child in both practical and symbolic ways. Consider an individual who is living with a same-sex partner and that partner's biological child.[83] If the non-biologically related individual is allowed to adopt the child, that adult may then be legally recognized as having the authority to make educational or medical decisions for the child. Further, that now-recognized parent might then have the ability to cover the child under an insurance policy, and the child might then be entitled to receive government benefits should the now-legally recognized parent die.[84] Or, suppose that the biological parent dies. If the state only afforded legal recognition to the adult and child who were biologically related, then the adult who had been helping to raise the child might simply be viewed as a legal stranger to the child, which in effect might mean that the child had lost both parents when the biological parent died.

A different issue sometimes arises where a same-sex couple is raising a child but only one of the adults is recognized as the child's legal parent. Suppose that the adults' relationship comes to an end. Were the relationship between the child and the non-biologically related adult recognized, then a court could order custody or visitation in light of what would best promote the child's best interests. However, if the only legally recognized relationship was between the biological parent and child, then the continuation of the relationship between the child and one of the adults raising that child would be left up to the discretion of a possibly estranged former partner. While one might hope that a parent would put his or her child's best interests ahead of bruised feelings, it would be unsurprising for the biological parent in such a scenario to bar or severely limit visitation with the former partner, child's best interests to the contrary notwithstanding.[85] (See further Chapters 3.3–3.5 and 4.6 of this book.)

80 See Utah Code Annotated § 78B-6-117(4)(b-d).
81 See *Stewart v Heineman*, 892 N.W.2d 542, 551 (Neb. 2017).
82 See *In re Adoption of Luke*, 640 N.W.2d 374 (Neb. 2002) (holding that Nebraska law does not permit the non-marital partner of a parent to adopt the parent's child so that each adult would be legally recognized as a parent of that child).
83 The points here would have equal force if the partner is living with an adoptive parent and that parent's child.
84 See *Adoption of Tammy*, 619 N.E.2d 315, 320 (Mass. 1993).
85 Some but not all states have equitable remedies whereby an individual who is functioning as a parent to the child will be recognized as a parent for certain purposes should the relationship between the adults end. See *V.C. v M.J.B.*, 725 A.2d 13, 22 (N.J. Super. App. Div. 1999).

The preceding scenarios speak to why it might be in a child's best interests to have a legally recognized relationship with a parent's partner in case the adults' relationship ends because of death or dissolution. But there are benefits to affording legal recognition to the relationship between the child and the non-biological parent even when the adults' relationship is ongoing. Suppose, then, that the members of a same-sex couple are living together and raising the biological child of one of the partners. Suppose, further, that there is no other recognized legal parent of that child and that all parties are in favour of the adoption. Affording legal recognition to the relationship between the child and the non-biologically related adult helping to raise that child would afford that adult increased confidence that the parent-child relationship would continue even if the adults' relationship ended. This would create more of an incentive for that adult to invest emotionally and financially in the child, increasing the likelihood that deep bonding would occur, which would benefit all concerned parties. It is worth mentioning that research on children's well-being has not shown that being brought up by a same-sex couple has any detrimental effects compared to being brought up by a different sex couple.[86]

As a general matter, adoptions will only be granted when the adoption will promote the best interests of the child. In some cases, an individual should not be allowed to adopt a child because his or her doing so would undermine rather than promote the child's interests. That might be true whether the adult had a same-sex or a different-sex orientation. The point here is merely that orientation should not be a bar to an individual being an adoptive parent where the adoption would promote the best interests of the child. Precluding a lesbian or gay individual from adopting a child might mean that the child would instead be adopted by no one, which as a general matter would not promote the child's interests, the would-be adoptive adult's interest, or the interests of society as a whole. Further, whether or not the state recognizes the adults' relationship, the state should recognize the relationship between the parent's partner and the child (assuming that no one else has parental rights, the parties consent and the adoption would promote the best interests of the child), because doing so would benefit the parties themselves and society as a whole.

While gay men and lesbians sometimes adopt children, they also become parents in other ways, e.g. by making use of assisted reproductive technologies. Thus, gay men might use a surrogate, and lesbians might make use of either artificial insemination or in vitro fertilization (they, too, might use a surrogate). The complications that can arise in these kinds of cases are analogous to the kinds of complications that can arise when different-sex couples make use of assisted reproductive technologies. Thus, different-sex couples sometimes must rely on others to donate gametes and different-sex couples must also sometimes use surrogates to carry a child to term. In these kinds of cases, it is important to make clear at the outset who will have legal rights and responsibilities with respect to any child born through the use of these technologies. This means that the original agreement must be both clear and comprehensive, so that none of the parties is surprised to discover after the birth that he or she is or is not a parent after all. Further, whether the means chosen by which the child is created involves donated gametes, surrogacy, or both, it is important that an individual not be accorded rights or responsibilities contrary to the understanding reached. Couples, whether composed of individuals of the same sex or of different sexes, make use of assisted reproductive technologies to create their families, and many would not do so but for the assurance

86 G.J. Gates, 'Marriage and Family: LGBT Individuals and Same-Sex Couples', *The Future of Children* 25, 2015, 67–87; S. Golombok, *Modern Families: Parents and Children in New Family Forms*, Cambridge: Cambridge University Press, 2015.

that they would be able to raise the child thereby created (see further Chapters 3.1–3.2 and 4.3 of this book).

As a general matter, society and the individuals themselves benefit when the state affords legal recognition to the relationships between same-sex adults and to the relationships between such adults and the children whom they are raising. The failure to afford that recognition cannot be justified as matter of public policy or of individual rights.

1.5
UNMARRIED COHABITATION

Elaine E. Sutherland

Introduction

As more couples live together without formalizing their relationship many legal systems around the world have been re-examining what, if any, legal consequences should attach to intimate, non-marital cohabitation. The issue is often brought into sharp focus when the relationship ends, either through separation or the death of one of the parties, but it may also be significant while the parties are together, particularly for matters like domestic abuse protection, state benefits and taxation. The diversity of couples who cohabit and their reasons for doing so present a particular challenge to legal systems and divergent responses are found around the world.[1] That divergence is prompted by very different views about the role of the legal system in regulating intimate relationships and the debate often juxtaposes party autonomy and protecting the vulnerable.

Prevalence and profile

In most developed, western countries, the incidence of cohabitation has undoubtedly increased in recent decades, albeit it is notoriously difficult to produce wholly accurate statistics and international comparisons are problematic.[2] The OECD statistics give a general impression of the prevalence of cohabitation, with some 20 percent of relationships in Estonia, Iceland and

1 See further, K. Boele-Woelki, C. Mol and E. van Gelder (eds), *European Family Law in Action*, vol. 5, Informal Relationships, Cambridge: Intersentia, 2015; J. Miles, 'Unmarried Cohabitation in European Perspective', in J.M. Scherpe (ed.), *European Family Law*, Vol. 3, Cheltenham: Edward Elgar, 2016; C. Mol, 'Reasons for Regulating Informal Relationships: A Comparison of Nine European Jurisdictions', *Utrecht Law Review* 12(2), 2016, 98–113; A. Stepień-Sporek and M. Ryznar, 'The Consequences of Cohabitation', *University of San Francisco Law Review* 50(1), 2016, 75–102 (US and Europe); New Zealand Law Commission, Report on the Review of the Property (Relationships) Act 1976 (New Zealand Law Commission Report No. 143, 2019), Chapter 6 (primarily New Zealand, but reviewing comparative provisions in a range of, largely common law, jurisdictions).

2 P. Heuveline and J.M. Timberlake, 'The Role of Cohabitation in Family Formation: The United States in Comparative Perspective', *Journal of Marriage and Family* 66(5), 2004, 1214–30; T. Sobotka and L. Toulemon, 'Changing Family and Partnership Behaviour: Common Trends and Persistent Diversity across Europe', *Demographic Research* 19(6), 2008, 85–138.

Sweden being described as between 'domestic partners'.[3] Thereafter, the other Nordic countries tend to show a higher incidence of cohabitation (> 10 percent) than those in northern Europe and Canada, with the lowest incidence being reported in southern Europe, Asia, Israel and the United States.[4] The increased prevalence of cohabitation corresponds to it being more socially acceptable and, indeed, there is probably something of a symbiotic relationship between the two.[5] As cohabitation becomes more widespread, more children are born outside marriage[6] and more children live with a parent's cohabitant.

In framing the debate over whether legal consequences should flow from cohabitation, it may be helpful to know why couples cohabit, rather than marrying, and how they live their lives together.[7] Some couples undoubtedly choose cohabitation because they reject marriage quite expressly, sometimes due to its religious or patriarchal associations. For others, it is the package of consequences that accompanies marriage that may not suit their needs.[8] Yet others are engaged (pun intended) in a form of 'trial marriage' and are unwilling to commit to matrimony until they test how they get along together.[9]

Choice, however, is not a luxury given to the many couples to whom marriage is simply not available, as remains the case for same-sex couples who live in jurisdictions that do not permit same-sex marriage and it was their exclusion that explains, at least in part, why marriage-like consequences were sometimes extended to cohabitants. In New Zealand, for example, it was some 12 years after marriage-like consequences were attached to cohabitation that marriage was extended to same-sex couples.[10] Where absence of choice is due to the fact that one of the parties is not free to marry (or neither is), their disability is likely to be temporary given the ease of divorce in most jurisdictions.

Choice is only a meaningful marker when it is based on full information and there is an abundance of evidence that many people are very ill-informed about the legal consequences of marriage and cohabitation, sometimes sharing common misconceptions.[11] They may believe that the legal consequences of cohabitation are greater than they are; that they qualify as 'common

3 OECD, 'Family', in *Society at a Glance 2011: OECD Social Indicators*, OECD Publishing, 2011. http://dx.doi.org/10.1787/soc_glance-2011-9-en, p. 49, table GE4.1. In the United Kingdom, 'The Number of Cohabiting Couple Families Continues to Grow Faster Than Married Couple and Lone Parent Families, with an Increase of 25.8% over the Decade 2008 to 2018', in *Families and Households: 2018*, London: Office of National Statistics, 2019, p. 2.

4 More recent statistics from the United States reflect an increase in non-marital cohabitation overall of 29 percent between 2007 and 2016, with a rise of 75 percent amongst those aged 50 and over: R. Stepler, 'Number of U.S. Adults Cohabiting with a Partner Continues to Rise, Especially among Those 50 and Older', *News in the Numbers*, Pew Research Centre, 6 April 2017.

5 E. Harrison and R. Fitzgerald, 'A Chorus of Disapproval? European Attitudes to Non-Traditional Family Patterns', in *National Centre for Social Research, British Social Attitudes Survey: 26th Report*, London: Sage Publications, 2010; J. Horowitz, N. Graf and G. Livingston, *Marriage and Cohabitation in the U.S.*, Washington, DC: Pew Research Center, 2019. Available at www.pewsocialtrends.org/2019/11/06/marriage-and-cohabitation-in-the-u-s/

6 OECD, op. cit., n 3; Sobotka and Toulemon, op. cit., n 2.

7 R. Probert, 'Cohabitation: Current Legal Solutions', Current Legal Problems 62(1), 2009, 316–45, 321–2; A. Barlow, S. Duncan, G. James and A. Park, *Cohabitation, Marriage and the Law: Social Change and Legal Reform in the 21st Century*, Oxford: Hart Publishing, 2005.

8 S.L. Brown, J.R. Bulanda and G.R. Lee, 'Transitions into and Out of Cohabitation in Later Life', *Journal of Marriage and Family* 74(4), 2012, 774–93.

9 Heuveline and Timberlake, op. cit., n 2, pp. 1216–17.

10 Marriage (Definition of Marriage) Amendment Act 2013.

11 Barlow et al., op. cit., n 7, pp. 27–47; P. Pleasence and N.J. Balmer, 'Ignorance Is Bliss: Modelling Knowledge of Rights in Marriage and Cohabitation', *Law and Society Review* 46(2), 2012, 297–333, 321–2.

law' spouses when they do not; or that their legal system recognizes common law marriage when it does not. Added to the mix are asymmetrical couples where one partner is well-informed and the other is ignorant of, or misinformed about, the law.

In all of this, there is no denying the fact that many couples are not making an active choice at all. They simply start living together and life goes on without either of them giving any thought to the law. It is not until something goes wrong – that is, when the relationship breaks down or one of the parties dies – that the legal consequences of their actions become apparent to them.

The debate

Opposition to putting cohabitation on a par with marriage comes, perhaps unsurprisingly, from those who wish to protect the privileged position of marriage (sometimes only different-sex marriage) in the legal system. Numerous academic authors argue that marriage is functionally different from cohabitation, that it reflects greater commitment by the parties and that it leads to better outcomes for society in terms of family stability.[12] Some lay most of the ills of society at the door of increased cohabitation,[13] with Duncan going as far as to contrast the 'social good' of marriage with the 'social evil' of cohabitation.[14] Others confine themselves to claims that marriage produces greater 'health, wealth and happiness' for spouses and their children,[15] a theme taken up in more populist literature.[16] (See further discussion in Chapters 1.1 and 1.4 of this book.)

This thinking resonates in some quarters in England and Lewis found that a 'central concern about the fate of the traditional family in the face of profound change' was 'linked to much greater caution regarding the legal recognition of new family forms'.[17] Baker went as far as to assert that 'any ostensible and direct challenge to the institution or "sanctity" of marriage is still regarded as political suicide',[18] which may explain why the, thus far unsuccessful, attempts at legislative reform in England and Wales have been initiated by (unelected) members of the House of Lords.[19] This can be contrasted with the prevailing view in much of the rest of the western world. Thus, the range of legally recognized relationships in the Netherlands is explained by Schrama as being due to the fact that 'policy making has not been influenced at all by the fear that the status of marriage would be negatively affected by recognizing non-marital cohabitation'.[20] (See further Chapter 1.2 of this book.)

12 E. Scott, 'Marriage, Cohabitation and Collective Responsibility for Dependency', *University of Chicago Legal Forum* 2004, 225–64, 237.
13 M.F. Brinig and S.L. Nock, 'Marry Me, Bill: Should Cohabitation Be the (Legal) Default Option?', *Louisiana Law Review* 64(3), 2003–2004, 403–42; W.C. Duncan, 'The Social Good of Marriage and Legal Responses to Non-Marital Cohabitation', *Oregon Law Review* 82(4), 2003, 1001–31; M. Garrison, 'Non-marital Cohabitation: Social Revolution and Legal Regulation', *Family Law Quarterly* 42(3), 2008–2009, 309–31; L.D. Wardle, 'Is Marriage Obsolete?', *Michigan Journal of Gender & Law* 10(1), 2003, 189–235.
14 Duncan, op. cit., n 13, 1030.
15 Garrison, op. cit., n 13, 325–6 and Scott, op. cit., n 12, 240.
16 L.J. Waite and M. Gallagher, *The Case for Marriage: Why Married People Are Happier, Healthier and Better Off Financially*, New York, NY: Doubleday, 2000.
17 J. Lewis, 'Debates and Issues Regarding Marriage and Cohabitation in the British and American Literature', *International Journal of Law, Policy and the Family* 15(1), 2001, 159–84, 160.
18 H. Baker, 'Family Law Down under: Can the Old World Learn from the New?', *International Family Law* 23(2), 2009, 165–73, 173.
19 The most recent is the Cohabitation Rights Bill, HL Bill 97 of 2019–20, introduced by Lord Marks of Henley-on-Thames who has introduced similar bills every session since 2013–4.
20 W.M. Schrama, 'The Dutch Approach to Informal Lifestyles: Family Function over Family Form', *International Journal of Law Policy and the Family* 22(3), 2008, 311–32, 328.

But how true are the claims surrounding the benefits of marriage? Does marriage really reflect a greater level of commitment than cohabitation? In their empirical study of cohabitants in England at the beginning of this century, Barlow et al. found that, while they may have different reasons for cohabiting, 'Cohabitants show just as much commitment to their partnership when compared like with like, as married people. Some cohabitants are less committed than others, but the same goes for married people'.[21]

Research by Eekelaar and Maclean led to a similar conclusion.[22] What of health, wealth and happiness? Again, the empirical evidence is far less clear than the marriage proponents would have one believe. In Britain, Kohn and Averett found no statistical difference between marriage and cohabitation in terms of health,[23] while, in the US, Musick and Bumpass concluded that 'the married fared better in health than cohabitors, but the opposite was true of happiness and self-esteem'.[24] Even if it could be established that marriage has quality of life dividends when compared to cohabitation, is that a reason to deny legal recognition to cohabitation? The thinking here is that, by refusing to offer cohabitants legal protection similar to that attaching to marriage, they will be encouraged to marry rather than simply living together. This presupposes, of course, that people understand the legal and social consequences and make lifestyle choices on the basis of them; and, as we have seen, neither is true for whole sections of the population. Even where the parties do have a firm grasp of the law, the failure to attach marriage-like consequences to cohabitation may make matrimony more attractive to an economically vulnerable partner, but the opposite may be true for a self-interested, wealthy partner.

It is sometimes suggested that there is no need to accord legal recognition to cohabitation because other, more general legal remedies (contract, trusts, unjust enrichment and so forth) can accommodate their needs, possibly with a little modification.[25] While these avenues have been pursued successfully on occasion,[26] there is ample evidence that the ordinary, mainstream legal remedies are not meeting the needs of the majority of cohabitants.[27] In most jurisdictions, cohabitation contracts are no longer struck down by the courts on public policy grounds, but concluding the contract in the first place requires that the cohabitants are well-informed and free from the 'new relationship optimism' that prevents most couples, whether marrying or simply moving in together, from taking that step.[28]

21 Barlow et al., op. cit., n 7, p. 74.

22 J. Eekelaar and M. Maclean, 'Marriage and the Moral Bases of Personal Relationships', *Journal of Law and Society* 31(4), 2004, 510–38, 538.

23 J.L. Kohn and S.L. Averett, 'Can't We Just Live Together? New Evidence on the Effect of Relationship Status on Health', 2010, Working Paper. Available at http://papers.ssrn.com/sol3/papers.cfm?abstract_id=1539783, p. 2.

24 K. Musick and L. Bumpass, 'Reexamining the Case for Marriage: Union Formation and Changes in Well-Being', *Journal of Marriage and Family* 74(1), 2012, 1–18, 12–13.

25 Scott, op. cit., n 12, 229; Garrison, op. cit., n 13, 310–11.

26 The Supreme Court of California accepted that implied and express contract, constructive and resulting trusts and *quantum meruit* could be used by cohabitants: *Marvin v Marvin*, 18 Cal. Rptr. 815 (1976). Trusts doctrines have been employed extensively in England and Wales.

27 Probert, op. cit., n 7, 317–18; A. Sanders, 'Cohabitants in Private Law: Trust, Frustration and Unjust Enrichment in England, Germany and Canada', *International & Comparative Law Quarterly* 62(3), 2013, 628–55.

28 R.M. Panades, R. Corney, C. Ayles, J. Reynolds and F.M. Panades, *Informing Unmarried Parents about Their Legal Rights at Birth Registration*, London: One Plus One, 2007, p. 32; H. Mahar, *Why Are There So Few Prenuptial Agreements?*, Cambridge, MA: John M. Olin Center for Law, Economics, and Business, Discussion Paper 09/2003. Available at www.law.harvard.edu/programs/olin_center/papers/436_mahar.php.

In the past, the concept of common law marriage was sometimes helpful to former cohabitants if their relationship broke down or one of them died. Establishing a common law marriage was premised on the fact that the couple held themselves out as married and, thus, did not challenge the social norms of the society in which they lived. Its use by cohabitants was limited by the fact many make no secret of their unmarried state and there is something of a moral deficit when legal systems reward deception while punishing honesty. The trend has been for legislatures to abolish common law marriage[29] and it has been argued that attaching marriage-like consequences to cohabitation amounts to its resurrection.[30] That the concepts are distinct was demonstrated by the Scottish Parliament when it (all but) abolished common law marriage and expanded the legal consequences of cohabitation in the same statute.[31]

Perhaps the most morally and intellectually persuasive of all the arguments against attaching legal consequences to cohabitation is respect for the autonomy of the parties. If they have rejected the concept of marriage or its trappings, it can be argued that to foist the very consequences they sought to avoid upon them is to deny them freedom of choice.[32] The issue of choice lay at the heart of the decisions of courts in two federal systems. The Supreme Court of Canada found no violation of the Canadian Charter of Rights and Freedoms in treating unmarried cohabitants differently to their married counterparts since they had chosen not to marry.[33] Following that decision, a number of provinces and territories extended the rights of cohabitants by statute. The autonomous regions in Spain had done just that only to have the legislation declared unconstitutional and, thus, void since the rights and obligations applied without the express agreement of the parties and, as such, infringed their fundamental right to the free development of personality.[34]

While the operative ignorance of many cohabitants renders the notion of choice somewhat illusory, what of couples who made thoroughly well-informed decisions? One option, adopted in many jurisdictions where cohabitation has significant legal consequences, is to permit the parties to contract out of most or all of them, just as spouses may often contract out of the default package of remedies attaching to marriage. This puts the onus on the parties to take that step, but those who are aware that their lifestyle choice has legal consequences are arguably in the best position to do so. The price, of course, is less protection of the vulnerable but, by contracting, at least they may be alerted to the fact that they are sacrificing something.

Those who support attaching some or all of the marriage-like consequences to cohabitation rely on a combination of functionalism and the legal system's obligation to protect the vulnerable. Many cohabitants behave just like married couples, combining their efforts, making sacrifices for the relationship, developing the same levels of dependence and, sometimes, having or adopting children together.[35] In these circumstances, legal systems offer protection to

29 The concept lingers in a small number of US states, but was recently abolished in South Carolina: *Stone v Thompson*, Supreme Court of South Carolina, July 24, 2019; 2019 WL 3310480.

30 This reasoning was accepted by the Supreme Court of Illinois in *Hewitt v Hewitt*, 77 Ill. 2d 49 (1979), when it denied a remedy to a woman who had lived with her partner for 15 years, raising their three children.

31 Family Law (Scotland) Act 2006.

32 R.L. Deech, 'The Case Against Legal Recognition of Cohabitation', *International & Comparative Law Quarterly* 29, 1980, 480–97; Garrison, op. cit., n 13, 324; M.M. Mahoney, 'Forces Shaping the Law of Cohabitation for Opposite Sex Couples', *Journal of Law and Family Studies* 7(1), 2005, 135–204, 200.

33 *Nova Scotia (Attorney General) v Walsh* [2002] 4 SCR 325.

34 See, L. Marquez, 'Regulating Cohabitation in Spain: The Unconstitutionality of Current Legislation', *International Family Law* 2014 (March), 44–7, 46, commenting on judgment 93/2013, 23 April.

35 Baker, op. cit., n 18; Barlow et al., op. cit., n 7; J.H. DiFonzo, 'How Marriage Became Optional: Cohabitation, Gender, and the Emerging Functional Norms', *Rutgers Journal of Law & Public Policy* 8(3), 2011, 521–66; E. Hess, 'The Rights of Cohabitants: When and How Will the Law Be Reformed?',

spouses – and particularly to the economically vulnerable spouse – when the marriage breaks down by conducting what often amounts to an end-of-relationship reckoning that can result in orders for the transfer of property, the payment of money and so forth. If similar protection is not offered to cohabitants, then the legal system is simply abandoning them to their fate. If a valid function of the legal system is, indeed, to protect the vulnerable then the case is made for it to intervene (see further Chapter 1.2 of this book).

Millbank put this case to the Australian Senate Committee considering the matter in the following terms:

> It makes absolute sense to put *de facto* and married couples in the same property regime. It does not remove people's choice; it protects the vulnerable party in an economic and emotional relationship ... economic interdependence and dependence happens and should be recognised.[36]

Much the same case can be made in respect of inheritance. Most legal systems accord spouses a special position when a partner dies intestate, while many others go as far as to protect the surviving spouse against disinheritance by the deceased in his or her will (see Chapter 2.8 of this book). Again, if a surviving cohabitant is not afforded protection in similar circumstances, then he or she may face hardship.

How legal systems have responded

Legal systems around the world have responded very differently to non-marital cohabitation. Where extra-marital sex remains criminal, cohabitation may attract penalties,[37] but that is no longer the case in developed, western countries. Thus, the British Columbia Supreme Court was careful to restrict its decision upholding the criminalization of polygamy to marriage-like relationships, excluding cohabitation and multi-partner relationships that do not seek to mirror marriage from its scope.[38] While an ever-shrinking number of US states still have fornication provisions on the statute books,[39] it is widely accepted that they are unconstitutional as a result of the US Supreme Court decisions in *Lawrence v Texas*[40] and *Obergefell v Hodges*.[41]

Lest it be assumed that recognition of non-marital cohabitation by the legal system is always beneficial to at least one of the parties, it is worth noting what Aloni characterizes as 'deprivative recognition': that is, 'when neither partner will benefit from recognition and yet the state still recognizes the relationship, a recognition that results in deprivation'.[42] At its worst, this can

---

Family Law 39, 2009, 405–11; J.M. Scherpe, 'Protection of Partners in Informal Long-Term Relationships', *International Law Forum du droit international* 7(3), 2005, 206–12.

36 Senate Standing Committee on Legal and Constitutional Affairs (Australia) (2008), para 3.50.

37 Z. Livio, 'Decriminalising Consensual Heterosexual Conduct Outside Marriage: The Women's Case under International Human Rights Law', *Netherlands Quarterly of Human Rights* 20(3), 2002, 299–314. Recent plans to reform the criminal code in Indonesian include provisions that would criminalize extra-marital sex: K. Lamb, 'Indonesia's Criminal Code: What Is It, Why Does It Matter, and Will It Be Passed?', *The Guardian*, 26 September 2019.

38 *Reference re: Section 293 of the Criminal Code of Canada* 2011 BCSC 1588, paras 1037–41.

39 The trend is to repeal these provisions as was done in Florida, in 2016 (removal of reference to cohabitation in Florida Statutes Ann. § 798.02), and in Utah, in 2019 (Utah Code Ann, § 76–7–104, repealed by Laws 2019, c. 420, § 10).

40 539 U.S. 558 (2003).

41 576 U.S. ___; 135 S.Ct. 2584 (2015).

42 E. Aloni, 'Deprivative Recognition', *UCLA Law Review* 61(5), 2014, 1276–345, 1281.

result in a legal system engaging in deprivative recognition in order to deny access to state benefits, while refusing to acknowledge the relationship for purposes that are advantageous to one or both of the parties.

Many jurisdictions that are not overtly hostile to cohabitation extend specific protections, like those addressing domestic abuse, to cohabitants. More broadly, some cohabitants may gain redress by using existing legal concepts, like trusts and contracts. Marriage-alternatives (registered or civil partnerships or unions) can offer a more comprehensive solution where they attract most or all of the legal consequences of marriage and are available to all couples.[43] However, since they require the couple to register their relationship, they fail to meet the needs of the uninformed, the misinformed and those who simply do not think about the legal consequences of their actions. A similar objection applies to other 'opt-in' systems, like the French *pacte civil de solidarité*[44] and the Belgian *cohabitation légale*,[45] both of which apply to a broader range of relationships than simply the conjugal, since they require the parties to conclude a contract (see Chapters 1.1–1.2 and 2.1 of this book).

In the attempt to offer protection more widely, an increasing number of jurisdictions have attached marriage-like legal consequences to cohabitation automatically. This is sometimes described as 'marriage by ascription' or, particularly by opponents, as 'conscriptive'.[46] While 'Croatia, Hungary, Slovenia and Sweden have regulated informal relationships since the 1970s',[47] developments elsewhere in Europe are of more recent vintage. Two distinct models have been adopted in different jurisdictions around the world. One aims at compromise and cohabitants receive some, but not all, of the marriage package, while the other model seeks to create parity between cohabitation and marriage.

The compromise approach is found in Scotland where cohabitants who qualify under the statutory definition may seek a capital sum, designed to balance advantages gained and losses sustained as a result of the relationship and/or to effect the sharing of future childcare costs.[48] They may also apply to the court for a discretionary award out of a deceased partner's intestate estate. This falls well short of the comprehensive package of remedies available to a spouse on divorce or the death of a partner and the law there is currently under review.[49] A similar approach is taken in Ireland[50] and by the European Commission on Family Law in its model *Principles*.[51] In the US, where family law is, of course, a matter for the individual states, the American Law

43 In the United Kingdom, civil partnership, which has the same legal consequences as marriage, was initially available only to same sex couples. It has been extended to different sex couples in England and Wales (Civil Partnerships, Marriages and Deaths (Registration Etc.) Act 2019) and soon will be so extended in Scotland (Civil Partnership (Scotland) Bill 2019).

44 French Civil Code, art. 515. See further, J. Godard, 'Pacs Seven Years On: Is It Moving Towards Marriage?', *International Journal of Law, Policy and the Family* 21(3), 2007, 310–21.

45 Belgian Civil Code, arts 1475–9.

46 Garrison, op. cit., n 13, 325.

47 Mol, op. cit., n 1, p. 99.

48 Family Law (Scotland) Act 2006, ss. 25–9. See further, E.E. Sutherland, 'From "Bidie-In" to "Cohabitant" in Scotland: The Perils of Legislative Compromise', *International Journal of Law, Policy and the Family* 27(2), 2013, 1–33.

49 At the time of writing, the Scottish Law Commission is reviewing the law on cohabitation: see Scottish Law Commission, *Discussion Paper on Cohabitation* (Scot Law Com Discussion Paper No 170, 2020).

50 Civil Partnership and Certain Rights and Obligations of Cohabitants Act 2010, Part 15. See further, J. Mee, 'Cohabitation Law Reform in Ireland', *Child and Family Law Quarterly* 23(3), 2011, 323–43.

51 K. Boele-Woelki, F. Ferrand, C. González-Beilfuss, M. Jänterä-Jareborg, N. Lowe, D. Martiny and V. Todorova, *Principles of European Family Law Regarding Property, Maintenance and Succession Rights of Couples in de facto Unions*, Cambridge: Intersentia, 2019 (CEFL *Principles*).

Institute devised a scheme designed to deal with disputes over children and property in the event of cohabitation breakdown, but not addressing inheritance.[52] The difficulty with these various solutions is, perhaps, the fate of many compromises. In seeking to please everyone they are destined to please no one. But they present more fundamental problems for legal systems. Since they often take only parts of the comprehensive marriage package, they lose coherence and there is the danger of further confusing already ill-informed members of the public and creating a false sense of security.

Undoubtedly, the most radical solution is to attach all of the legal consequences of marriage to cohabitation automatically – during the relationship, when it breaks down or when one of the parties dies. A particularly clear example of this approach is found in New Zealand,[53] where it was endorsed recently by the New Zealand Law Commission.[54] A number of Canadian provinces and territories have passed legislation extending the rights of cohabitants, with them being put on a par with spouses in Saskatchewan and British Columbia.[55] In Israel, legislation dating back to the 1950s began the process of giving rights to 'reputed spouses' and subsequent legislation and decisions of the Israeli Supreme Court have advanced the process to the point that cohabitants are now virtually indistinguishable from spouses in terms of legal consequences.[56]

Unlike marriage, cohabitation does not come in a neat package, with starting and termination dates, and, if legal consequences are to flow from cohabitation, the relationships that qualify must be identified. A small number of jurisdictions define qualifying relationships by reference to marriage, with the Scottish statute using the test of 'living together as spouses',[57] while its counterpart in British Columbia talks of a 'marriage-like relationship'.[58] It has been argued that this can have the effect of the claimant's relationship being judged on the basis of 'classed and gendered understandings of a good companionate marriage'.[59]

Other jurisdictions simply provide a definition of the protected relationship, often accompanied by a non-exclusive list of factors to be considered in determining which qualify, with the Antipodean lists being the most expansive.[60] Some definitions explicitly exclude couples who are so closely related that they would not be permitted to marry[61] or where one of the

52 American Law Institute, *Principles of the Law of Family Dissolution: Analysis and Recommendations*, Newark, NJ: Matthew Bender/LexisNexis, 2002, chs 2, 3 and 6.

53 Property (Relationships) Amendment) Act 2001. See further, B. Atkin, 'The Rights of Married and Unmarried Couples in New Zealand: Radical New Laws on Property and Succession', *Child and Family Law Quarterly* 15(2), 2003, 173–84 and M. Briggs, 'Which Relationships Should Be Included in a Property Sharing Scheme?', in J. Palmer, N. Peart, M. Briggs and M. Henaghan (eds), *Law and Policy in Modern Family Finance: Property Division in the 21st Century*, Cambridge: Internsentia, 2017.

54 New Zealand Law Commission, op. cit., n 1.

55 Family Property Act, SS 1997 and Family Law Act, SBC 2011. See, A. Leckey, 'Cohabitation, Law Reform and the Litigants', *International Journal of Law, Policy and the Family* 31(2), 2017, 131–46, 134–5.

56 R. Schuz and A. Blecher-Prigat, 'Israel: Dynamism and Schizophrenia', E.E. Sutherland, *The Future of Child and Family Law: International Predictions*, Cambridge: Cambridge University Press, 2012, paras 6.60–6.61.

57 Family Law (Scotland) Act 2006, s.25(1) when read with the Marriage and Civil Partnership (Scotland) Act 2014, s.4.

58 Family Law Act 2011, s.3(1)(b).

59 R. Leckey, 'Judging in Marriage's Shadow', *Feminist Legal Studies* 26(1), 2018, 25–45, 44.

60 Family Law Act 1975, s.4AA(2) (Australian) and the Property Relationships Act 1976, s.2D(2) (New Zealand).

61 Family Law Act 1995, s.4AA(1)(b) (Australian) and the Civil Partnership and Certain Rights and Obligations of Cohabitants Act 2010, s.172(3) (Ireland).

cohabitants is in a formal relationship with a third party.[62] The definition may specify a minimum duration of cohabitation, with the period often being shorter for couples with children than those without. In Ireland, for example, the minimum cohabitation period is two years for couples with a child in common and five years for those with no children.[63] In New Zealand, it is three years,[64] subject to the court having discretion to make an order for the division of property following a shorter cohabitation where there is a child of the relationship or one party has made a substantial contribution and serious injustice would otherwise result.[65] The American Law Institute scheme anticipates different periods of time depending on the presence or absence of children, but leaves it to states to determine their precise duration.[66] A shared household may be required, as in Sweden,[67] or that may be one of the factors to be considered in evaluating whether the relationship qualifies under the statute. However, a court in Israel found that a couple qualified as 'reputed spouses' despite their being registered as living at different addresses,[68] and a similar view has been taken in Australia.[69] How protected non-marital cohabitation is defined may result in the exclusion of some relationships, like those of couples who are 'living apart together'[70] and polyamorists,[71] and those of siblings and close friends who cohabit on an inter-dependent, non-intimate basis.

Conclusion

The response of legal systems around the world to non-marital cohabitation spans the spectrum from criminalisation to treating qualifying cohabiting couples in the same way as spouses. Where legal recognition is accorded to cohabitants, the challenge lies the balancing two rightly respected values: autonomy and protection. Autonomy requires that individuals have the opportunity to make choices and meaningful choice implies selecting from options that differ in some significant respect. The most effective way for a legal system to distinguish between relationships is by attaching different consequences to them. Yet that will result in less protection being afforded to parties in one kind of relationship than to those in another, something that is of particular concern where the parties are not in positions of equality.

62 Civil Partnership and Certain Rights and Obligations of Cohabitants Act 2010, s.172(6) (Ireland) and the Property Relationships Act 1976, s.2D(1)(c) (New Zealand). The CEFL *Principles*, op. cit., n 51, provide expressly that their application is not excluded by the fact that one of the partners is in a formal relationship with a third party: Principle 5:3.

63 Civil Partnership and Certain Rights and Obligations of Cohabitants Act 2010, s.172(5).

64 Property Relationships Act 1976, s.1C(2)(b and s. 14A(3).

65 1976 Act, s.14A(2).

66 *Principles of the Law of Family Dissolution*, op. cit., n 52, §6.03.

67 Cohabitation Act 2003, s.1.

68 *Plonit v Plonit*, FLA 3497/09, Nevo (4 May 2009).

69 *Clarence & Crisp* [2016] FamCAFC 157.

70 See I. Levin, 'Living Apart Together: A New Family Form', *Current Sociology* 52(2), 2004, 223–42, 226–7 and C.G. Bowman, 'How Should the Law Treat Couples Who Live Apart Together?', *Child and Family Law Quarterly* 29(3), 2017, 335–58.

71 See E.F. Emens, 'Monogamy's Law: Compulsory Monogamy and Polyamorous Existence', *North Texas University Review of Law and Social Change* 29, 2004, 277–376, 283.

PART 2

Dissolution of status, death and their consequences

2.1
DISSOLUTION OF MARRIAGE IN WESTERNIZED COUNTRIES

Masha Antokolskaia

Introduction

Ever since the French Revolution, Europe, North America and other westernized countries[1] have been split into two camps: a progressive one, inspired by the ideology of the Enlightenment, and a conservative one which aspires to preserve or restore traditional family forms and values.[2] Over the last two centuries, divorce law has represented the main family law policy challenge for both European and North American proponents of these conflicting ideologies. Since the turn of the millennium, divorce has definitely lost its position as the major policy challenge, having been replaced by the issue of recognition of same-sex relationships (see Chapters 1.1–1.2 and 1.4 of this book). However, this does not mean that divorce has completely lost its controversial character. As we are entering the third decade of the twenty-first century, the main policy challenge seemed to have shifted from grounds of divorce[3] to the role of the state in dealing with uncontested divorce – e.g. the choice between judicial and administrative procedure, private or summary procedure;[4] and with contested divorce with minor children – e.g. preventing escalation of conflict between the parents by introducing mediation and other ADR-schemes.

In this chapter I illustrate that in the jurisdictions with relatively restrictive divorce laws, such as England and Wales (at least in theory) France, Italy and where liberalization of divorce used to be a big issue, have suddenly introduced sweeping liberation, by providing for private or administrative procedures for uncontested cases. Meanwhile several jurisdictions with

1 This term is used to cover the jurisdictions which general follow the patterns of European history and whose ideas on marriage and divorce are profoundly influenced by the Enlightenment: Eastern and Western Europe, Canada and the United States, as well as Australia and New Zealand. This chapter covers only the European and North American jurisdictions.
2 For more details, see M. Antokolskaia, *Harmonisation of Family Law in Europe: A Historical Perspective: A Tale of Two Millenia*, Antwerp: Intersentia, 2006.
3 H. Krause, 'Comparative Family Law', in M. Reimann and R. Zimmermann (eds), *The Oxford Handbook of Comparative Law*, Oxford: Oxford University Press, 2006, p. 1113.
4 For more background information history and development of administrative divorce in Europe, see M. Antokolskaia, 'Divorce Law From a European Perspective', in J. Scherpe (ed.), *Research Handbook on European Family Law*, Cheltenham: Edward Elgar Publishing, 2013.

long-standing traditions with long-standing liberal divorce, like Denmark and the Netherlands,[5] have focused their attention on the prevention and resolution of parental conflicts and minimizing negative effects of divorce for children, through diminishing the adversarial nature of the divorce procedure by promoting agreements, and employing mediation and collaborative divorce. Denmark did not shy away from making a small backward step in the liberalization of divorce law for the sake of protecting children from divorce-related conflicts. Since 2005 all divorces in Denmark start as an administrative divorce, and parents who agree to divorce may divorce directly, whereas parents who do not agree must await a six-month separation period. A new law that came into force on 1 April 2019 introduced a mandatory waiting period of three months for spouses with minor children. Prior to this change these parents could divorce directly. The purpose of this reform is to provide parents with time for learning about the effects of the break-up on the children and how to best support the child during and after the divorce.[6]

The regulation of the consequences of divorce: parental responsibilities and child residence, child support, spouses' maintenance and the division/reallocation of property, however, falls outside the ambit of this chapter (see Chapters 2.6–2.7 and 3.3–3.5 of this book). Also mediation relates chiefly to the adjudication of the ancillary matters and not to the obtaining of a divorce as such (see Chapter 6.5 of this book).

This chapter focuses on the ideological, political and socio-economic context of the policy challenges surrounding the recent divorce reforms in Europe and North America rather than on the positive law on divorce.[7] Issues and data concerning measurement of rates of divorce are dealt with in Chapter 2.2.

Historical preface

Conflicting ideologies

The policy challenge surrounding the transformations taking place in current divorce law in the westernized world cannot be understood without having a brief look at its ideological roots in the period of the Enlightenment. From the eleventh to the sixteenth centuries, marriage and divorce law were governed exclusively by the canon law of the Roman Catholic and Eastern Orthodox Churches. From the sixteenth century Protestant teachings on divorce also came into play. Until the Enlightenment, marriage and divorce laws were discussed solely in religious terms and marriage was seen as a social and religious duty. Divorce was impossible in Catholic

5 In the Netherlands a reshaping divorce procedure in a less adversarial matter is currently under consideration. See: M. Antokolskaia et al., *Naleving van contact-/omgangsafspraken na scheiding: een rechtsvergelijkend en sociaalwetenschappelijk perspectief*, The Hague: WODC, 2019.

6 *Lov om ændring af forældreansvarsloven, lov om ægteskabs indgåelse og opløsning og forskellige andre love,* Wet nr. 1711 van 27.12.2018. See: C.G. Jeppesen de Boer, in M. Antokolskaia et al., op. cit., p. 268.

7 For an overview of the positive divorce laws in Europe (although a bit out of date), see the CEFL National Reports for 22 jurisdictions http://ceflonline.net/country-reports-by-jurisdiction/ and K. Boele-Woelki, B. Braat and I. Sumner (eds), *European Family Law in Action*, vol. 1: *Grounds for Divorce*, Antwerp: Intersentia, 2003, a synopsis by D. Martiny, 'Divorce and Maintenance between Former Spouses: Initial Results of the Commission on European Family Law', in K. Boele-Woelki (ed.), *Perspectives for the Unification and Harmonisation of Family Law in Europe*, Antwerp: Intersentia, 2003, pp. 529–51. For a recent overview, see Antokolskaia, op. cit., n 4. For a worldwide overview, see: B. Verschraegen, 'Divorce', in A. Chloros et al. (eds), *International Encyclopaedia of Comparative Law, Persons and Family*, vol. 4, Tübingen: Mohr Siebeck, 2004/2007, Ch. 5.

countries or restrictively admitted as a punishment for a matrimonial offence in Orthodox and Protestant jurisdictions.

This perception was first challenged by the precursors of the Enlightenment, John Milton[8] and John Locke,[9] and then by the Enlightenment philosophers. The French philosophers saw marriage as a union based on the sentiment of love,[10] rather than as a conventional social and economic relationship.[11] The right to dissolve an unhappy marriage was the logical result of a vision of marriage as 'one of the avenues open to man in his pursuit of happiness'.[12] From this point of view, the 'state had no right to prevent its citizens from pursuing such happiness' or 'to make impossible or cumbersome the exercise of the natural right of divorce'.[13] From the Enlightenment perspective, divorce was no longer seen as a punishment for a matrimonial offence but rather as a remedy for marital breakdown.[14]

The Enlightenment ideas inspired a whole wave of family law reforms from sources as disparate as the codifications of enlightened monarchs,[15] French Revolutionary legislation and – to a lesser extent – Napoleon's *Code Civil*, which influenced the law of Netherlands, Belgium, Luxembourg, Sweden, Italy and large parts of Germany, Louisiana and Québec. Since the eighteenth century, Europe, followed later by other westernized countries, has been split into two camps: the proponents of the progressive Enlightenment ideology and its conservative opponents. The ideas of the Enlightenment were, from the outset, violently opposed by the conservative camp. Divorce was irredeemably associated with the secularism and libertarianism of the French Revolution.[16] The conservative wave of the Restoration wiped away divorce in France, Italy and (temporarily) in Austria and made divorce more restrictive in the Netherlands. In the course of the century, restrictive divorce was (re)introduced in France, Austria and Hungary.

By the end of the nineteenth century, the vast majority of European and North American jurisdictions only permitted fault-based divorce and it was only in the Nordic countries that no-fault grounds and fault grounds co-existed.[17] Marriage remained indissoluble in several Catholic jurisdictions such as Spain, Italy, Malta and Portugal, and in several states of the USA. The beginning of the twentieth century witnessed several radical reforms of divorce law which resulted in the introduction of liberal divorce law in Portugal after the revolution of 1910, in Russia after the revolution of 1917 and in the Nordic region in the beginning of the twentieth century. However, in the majority of the European and North American jurisdictions, divorce laws in the books remained restrictive and fault-based until the family revolution of the 1960s and 1970s.

8 J. Milton, 'The Doctrine and Discipline of Divorce, Restored to the Good of Both Sexes, from the Bondage of Canon Law (1644)', in *Complete Prose Works of John Milton*, vol. 2, New Haven: Yale University Press, 1959.
9 J. Locke, *Two Treatises of Government*, 1689.
10 J. Traer, *Marriage and the Family in the Eighteenth-Century France*, Ithaca: Cornell University Press, 1980, pp. 70–1.
11 Ibid., p. 49.
12 M. Rheinstein, *Marriage Stability, Divorce, and the Law*, Chicago: Chicago University Press, 1972, p. 25.
13 Ibid., p. 196.
14 R. Phillips, *Putting Asunder: A History of Divorcé in Western Society*, Cambridge: Cambridge University Press, 1988, p. 172.
15 For instance, the 1794 *Allgemeines Landrecht für die Preussischen Staaten* (ALP).
16 A. Dicey, *Lectures on* **the** *Relations between Law and Public Opinion in England during the Nineteenth Century*, 2nd edition, London: Macmillan, 1963, pp. 123–4.
17 T. Schmidt, 'The Scandinavian Law of Procedure in Matrimonial Causes', in J. Eekelaar and S.N. Katz (eds), *The Resolution of Family Conflicts*, Toronto: Butterworths, 1984, p. 81.

A new policy challenge: mass divorce by collusion

From the end of the nineteenth century, divorce practices in reality started to deviate from the patterns prescribed by the restrictive divorce law in the books. Industrialization and the profound social and cultural and demographic changes, the latter known as the first demographic transition, led to a rapid increase in divorce during the *belle époque* and even more so after the First World War, as unhappy spouses started to find resort in the consensual divorce by collusion and, in the US, also in migratory divorce to a state with the most lenient law. The patterns of this change varied slightly from one jurisdiction to the other, but the result was the same everywhere. A false allegation of adultery presented the easiest way for a couple to divorce by collusion. As a result, couples could obtain a divorce 'as easily as a motor licence and rather more easily than a passport'.[18] Max Rheinstein called this situation a 'democratic compromise',[19] as it postponed the necessity of facing the challenge of modernization that divorce law brought with it. For the time being the conservatives were content with the restrictive laws in the books and the liberals with the permissive law in action.[20] However, in the long term, the situation created a new challenge for the legislator and continued to feed progressive/conservative discord. The conservatives called for a ban on the collusion/migratory divorce by making substantive and procedural divorce law more restrictive and/or by limiting the recognition of migratory divorce. The progressive camp aspired to bringing the restrictive law in the books in line with the lenient law in action. This was the policy background against which the current divorce laws were shaped when the second demographic transition of the 1960s and 1970s took place.

The birth of current divorce law: the banning of compromise

The law on divorce was deeply affected by the sex and gender revolutions which occurred in the 1960s and 1970s. The second demographic transition, the economic, social and legal emancipation of women and the emergence of the welfare state,[21] combined to create the socio-economic conditions that made implementation of the Enlightenment ideas on marriage and divorce finally possible. The generally progressive climate of the 1960s and 1970s allowed the advocates of liberalization or the (re)introduction of divorce to gain the upper hand. Divorce lost its social stigma and was no longer seen as 'a deviant act but rather as part and parcel of a new concept of marriage and the family'.[22] Countries, traditionally adhering to the Catholic doctrine of indissolubility of marriage, – Spain, Italy, Ireland[23] and Malta[24] – have introduced divorce after furious controversies, often involving several referendums. Remarkably, Spain and Italy have later reformed their, initially rather restrictive, divorce laws so radically, that they now can be attributed to the forerunners camp.

18 A. Herbert, 'Holy Deadlock' (1934), cited in S. Cretney, *Divorce Reform in England: Humbug and Hypocrisy or a Smooth Transition*? in M. Freeman (ed.), *Divorce: Where next?*, Dartmouth: Aldershot, 1996, p. 41.

19 Rheinstein, op. cit., n 12, pp. 247 ff.

20 J. Gorecki, 'Moral Premises of Contemporary Divorce Laws: Western and Eastern Europe and the United States', in J. Eekelaar and J. Katz (eds), *Marriage and Cohabitation in Contemporary Society*, Toronto: Butterworths, 1980, p. 125.

21 Krause, op. cit., n 3, pp. 1112–13.

22 J. Commaille, 'Towards a New Definition of Divorce', in J. Trost (ed.), *Family in Change*, Västerås: International Library, 1980, p. 108.

23 Family Law (Divorce) Act, 1996, Part II.

24 See art. 66B Civil Code of Malta.

Despite the fact that after the 1960s, the advocates of the progressive modernization of divorce law were leading the way, non-compromise divorce reforms – like those in Sweden in 1973, or in Spain in 2005 – remained rather infrequent. In most jurisdictions the main policy challenge was to find a compromise between the two opposing paradigms. The first was the liberal belief in the right of the spouses to decide for themselves whether, and when, their marriage had to come to an end. The second was the belief that divorce should not to be made too easy, as the primary purpose of divorce law was to buttress the institution of marriage. As the balance of political power of conservative and progressive forces differed significantly from one jurisdiction to another, these compromises and, consequently, the national divorce laws, appeared to be rather dissimilar. The following close-up will present a selection of the various types of divorce law reform based on various kinds of compromises.

Non-compromise reforms: introducing permissive divorce law in California, Sweden and Russia

California and the Uniform Marriage and Divorce Act: setting an example for the United States

The divorce rate in the US has always been higher than in Europe. Divorce law was traditionally the subject of the jurisdiction of individual states with considerable diversity as a result.[25] Unhappy spouses from the states with restrictive divorce laws were attracted by the possibility of obtaining a divorce in the states with more lenient divorce laws.[26] In the late nineteenth and early twentieth centuries, the increasing use of migratory divorce prompted conservative proponents of marital stability to various attempts to put an end to forum shopping. One of these attempts was a failed endeavour to unify the divorce law of the US and make divorce the subject of federal jurisdiction;[27] another was to make the recognition of migratory divorce more difficult.[28]

The conservative/progressive discord and the resulting policy challenges surrounding the divorce reforms were very similar in the US to those that occurred in Europe on the eve of the family revolution of the 1960s and 1970s.[29] The pre-reform struggle for the liberalization of divorce united liberals[30] and liberal feminists, cutting 'across class and interest lines'.[31] It is interesting to note that, at the time, there was very little polarization on dominant moral issues (which included the accessibility of divorce) across the lines of religion, church attendance or party allegiance.[32] The claims for reform were voiced in terms of individual rights, autonomy and equality.[33] Glendon suggested that a clear difference from Europe was the US's heavier

25 See N.M. Blake, *The Road to Reno: A History of Divorce in the United States*, New York: Macmillan, 1962.
26 Ibid., pp. 152–72.
27 A.L. Estin, 'Divorce and Federalism: Balancing State Interests and Individual Rights', in L. Wardle and C. Willams (eds), *Family Law: Balancing Interest and Pursuing Priorities*, Buffalo, NY: William A. Hein, 2007, p. 543.
28 See Estin, op. cit., n 27, pp. 544–6.
29 W.L. O'Neill, *Divorce in the Progressive Era*, New York: New Viewpoints, 1973, pp. ix–x.
30 In both the classic (those who favour minimal government), and contemporary (those who favour greater progressive government intervention) meanings of this term.
31 O'Neill, op. cit., n 29, pp. 266–7.
32 N. Cahn and J. Carbone, *Red Families v Blue Families: Legal Polarisation and the Creation of Culture*, Oxford: Oxford University Press, 2010, p. 5.
33 M. Grossberg, 'Balancing Acts: Crisis, Change, and Continuity in American Family Law', *Indiana Law Revview* 28, 2012, 273–328.

accent on individual rights.[34] This was the setting in which the radical no-fault reform in California took place in 1969. Before this reform, the divorce rate in California was already almost twice the rate of the American average.[35] This was partly caused by migratory divorce and partly by the broader interpretation of 'cruelty', allowing psychological distress to be enough.

In order to tackle this 'festering problem', in 1966 the Californian governor appointed the Governor's Commission on Family Law. The initial mandate of the Commission was not to bring the restrictive law in the books in accord with the lenient law in action but rather to 'launch a concerted assault on the high incidence of divorce'.[36] Instead the Commission proposed[37] abandoning the fault grounds and shortening and simplifying divorce proceedings by abolishing the interlocutory degree[38] and, to this effect, introduced the 1969 Family Law Act which replaced the fault grounds with two no-fault grounds: irreconcilable differences that had caused irretrievable breakdown of marriage as well as incurable insanity.[39] Fault was completely eradicated; even providing evidence of fault in divorce procedure was explicitly forbidden by law.[40] A mere statement that irreconcilable differences that have caused irretrievable breakdown of marriage, if uncontested, made in an application for divorce by one or both spouses constituted sufficient proof of the breakdown. Initially the conservatives succeeded in preserving the interlocutory decree which made divorce procedure a bit lengthier,[41] but it was abolished already in the 1980s. This heralded the start of the 'no-fault revolution' and introduced the most permissive divorce law among the westernized jurisdictions of that day. Present-day Californian divorce law also provides for an easy summary procedure, allowing consenting spouses married for fewer than five years and having neither minor children or substantial property, an easy, automatic divorce within six months after completing the required form and sending it to court.[42]

The second step in the liberalization of American divorce law was taken when the Uniform Marriage and Divorce Act (UMDA) was approved by the National Conference of Commissioners on Uniform State Law in 1970. The Commission, influenced by the Californian reform,[43] proposed a divorce law based on irretrievable breakdown 'pure and simple'.[44] For non-contested divorces no proof of the breakdown of the marriage was initially required, which amounted to the introduction of consensual divorce. However, such a liberal proposal met strong opposition from the American Bar Association (ABA) which managed to amend the Act and make it more conservative. In the text that was finally approved by the ABA in 1994 the breakdown of the marriage had to be proven by either a de facto separation for 180 days or serious marital discord, and divorces were not to be granted until all the ancillary matters were settled.[45]

34 M.-A. Glendon, *Abortion and Divorce in Western Law*, Cambridge, MA: Harvard University Press, 1987, p. 131.
35 Rheinstein, op. cit., n 12, p. 373.
36 Phillips, op. cit., n 14, p. 568.
37 The Commission also proposed a family court system with counselling and divorce prevention measures, but this part of the proposal has never been implemented.
38 Rheinstein, op. cit., n 12, p. 376.
39 Sec. 4506 of the California Civil Code.
40 Sec. 2335 of the California Civil Code.
41 Rheinstein, op. cit., n 12, p. 378.
42 Sec. 2320 sq. of the California Civil Code.
43 According to the H. Hill Kay, 'An Appraisal of California's No-Fault Divorce Law', *California Law Review* 75, 1987, 291–302. Cited in M.A. Glendon, *The Transformation of Family Law*, Chicago: Chicago University Press, 1989, p. 188.
44 Rheinstein, op. cit., n 12, p. 47.
45 Phillips, op. cit., n 14, p. 570.

Both the Californian example and the UMDA profoundly influenced the other American states. Although only eight states actually adopted the UMDA, many others have used it as model.[46] Several states abolished fault altogether, and most added no-fault grounds to the existing fault ones.[47] With the introduction of a unilateral no-fault divorce in New York in 2010 the no-fault revolution was complete. Seventeen states have purely no-fault divorce procedures and the rest combine fault and no-fault grounds. Most of the states require a period of separation in one form or another before divorce is granted.[48] Like California, many states have various forms of easy and quick summary procedures for uncontested cases.

So far, the history of the liberalization of divorce in the US was very similar to that of Europe. But the US no-fault movement was not the end of the story. After no-fault divorce became an option in the US, the policy challenges surrounding divorce reform moved from the grounds for and accessibility of divorce to the regulation of its consequences. However, while the consequences of divorce are not the subject of this chapter, a few words have to be said as this matter relates closely to the issue of divorce grounds and the accessibility of divorce. As soon as the liberal feminists discovered the 'unexpected social and economic consequence' it had for ex-wives,[49] they immediately started another 'political and ideological battle'[50] for a divorce law which would take into account 'women's disadvantaged position in the society'.[51] They sought to promote equal, gender-neutral divorce laws that included gender-neutral rules on adjudication of the consequences of divorce. They maintained that the first round of no-fault laws deprived the economically dependent wife of the bargaining power that had formerly enabled her to negotiate her consent to a divorce in exchange for a favourable financial settlement. Abolishing the principle of 'maternal preference' and the growth of shared parenting threatened the privileged position of the mother after divorce.[52] The urgency of this problem in the US, Glendon explains, was caused by its slowness to follow other western jurisdictions in ensuring a fair adjudication of the economic consequences of divorce.[53] This made the US 'unique among Western countries in its relative carelessness about assuring either public or private responsibility for economic casualties of divorce'.[54] As a result of this re-evaluation, the political will to abolish the remaining role of fault in divorce has waned and fault grounds remained alongside the no-fault grounds in the majority of the states. Moreover, in many states access to no-fault ground remains restricted by various requirements, varying from waiting periods to a requirement of full agreement on ancillary matters.[55] At the beginning of the new century several scholars 'across the spectrum' came to doubt the merits of the total eradication of fault.[56]

46 Verschraegen, op. cit., n 7, p. 4.
47 For more details see H. Jacob, *Silent Revolution: The Transformation of Divorce Law in the United States*, Chicago: Chicago University Press, 1988, pp. 80–103.
48 L.D. Elrod and R.G. Spector, 'A Review of the Year in Family Law', Chart 4, Grounds for Divorce and Residency Requirements, *Family Law Quarterly* 45, 2012, 500–3.
49 See L. Weitzman, *The Divorce Revolution: The Unexpected Social and Economic Consequences for Women and Children in America*, New York: Free Press, 1985.
50 M.A. Fineman, *The Illusion of Equality: The Rhetoric of Equality of Divorce Reform*, Chicago: Chicago University Press, 1991, p. 27.
51 Ibid., p. 35.
52 Ibid., pp. 32–3.
53 Glendon, op. cit., n 34, p. 105.
54 Ibid., p. 64.
55 On restricting access to fault ground see, for instance: E. Wright, 'Agree to Disagree: Moving Tennessee toward Pure No-Fault Divorce', *Lincoln Memorial University Law Review* 4(2), 2017, 86–117.
56 K. Silbaugh, 'Money as Emotion in the Distribution of Wealth at Divorce', in R.F. Wilson (ed.), *Reconceiving the Family: Critique on the American Law Institute's Principles of the Law of Family Dissolution*, Cambridge: Cambridge University Press, 2006, p. 234.

Another notable difference between the US and Europe and Canada is that the period of relative uniformity of the 1960s and 1970s, during which the proliferation of no-fault divorce occurred, was followed by a period of 'Great Divergence'.[57] While Western European and Canadian society remained fairly homogenous,[58] economic, cultural and political disparity was continuing to grow in the US.[59] As Naomi Cahn and June Carbone explain in *Red Families v Blue Families*, during this period the old conservative/progressive divide between the proponents of liberal and conservative family values started to coincide with the political divide between the two main US political parties: the Republicans ('red') and the Democrats ('blue').[60] This change is associated with the transition from an industrial to a post-industrial, information economy. In the US, with its relatively weak welfare state, this transition produced a sharp shift in well-paid jobs, favouring the college-educated members of the middle-class, males as well as females,[61] which resulted not only in a growing economic disparity between two-breadwinner middle-class (blue) families and the more traditional working-class (red) families, but also in the distinctly different family patterns and opposing ideological responses to family change.[62] Blue families are characterized by late marriages, the first-career-then-children attitude, equal parenting, greater reliance on contraception and low birth rates. This so-called middle-class strategy leads to a lower divorce rate. Red élites, who tend to be more religious, find this strategy anathema because it involves non-marital sex, unmarried cohabitation and birth control. Red families in general are typified by more children, higher marriage rates and earlier marriages (sometimes triggered by unplanned pregnancy); but working-class and poor red families are characterized by declining marriages and high divorce rates.[63] This conflates the class divide produced by a changing economy and the ideological divide that responds to it. In the field of divorce, this diversity manifested itself in the opposing trends of the divorce rates. Divorce rates rose rapidly for both red and blue families following the no-fault reforms. However, in the first decade of the twenty-first century, the divorce rate for college-educated individuals has steadily decreased to the level of the mid-1960s (before the sexual revolution and no-fault reform). In contrast, the divorce rate for non-college educated couples, married in the early 1990s, has remained high after a brief levelling-off period.[64] Since 2010 there is a strong general persistent decline of overall divorce rate, albeit higher education, Caucasian or Hispanic ethnicity and economic security are still relevant predictors of lower chance for divorce.[65] The decline is being connected to several factors: diminishing demographic influence of Baby Boomers, responsible for a high divorce rate; as well as marriage becoming increasingly selective, rarer

57 T. Noach, 'The United States of Inequality: Introducing the Great Divergence', *Slate.com.*, 3 September 2010. Cited in J. Carbone and N. Cahn, 'Red v. Blue Marriage', in M. Garrison and E. Scott (eds), *Marriage at the Crossroads: Law, Policy, and the Brave New World of Twenty-First-Century Families*, Cambridge, 2012, p. 4 of the electronic copy. Available at http://ssrn.com/abstract=1995822.

58 In Western Europe and Canada, according to the Gini coefficient (after taxes and transfers), income inequality between the 1970s-80s and late 2000s has decreased in Belgium, Greece, France, Ireland and Portugal and increased only slightly in Canada and the rest of Western Europe. In contrast, in the US and the UK, the same period witnessed a significant increase in income inequality. *Income distribution – Inequality* – OECD Staistics.

59 Carbone and Cahn op. cit., n 57, p. 5.

60 Ibid.

61 Ibid., p. 1.

62 Ibid., p. 6.

63 Ibid., pp. 7–8.

64 Ibid., p. 7.

65 V.J. Schweizer, 'Marriage to Divorce Ratio in the U.S.: Demographic Variation, 2018', *National Center for Family and Marriage Research Family Profiles Sociology*, 2019 FP-19–27.

and more stable – a more elite status – than it was in the past,[66] and thus merely reserved for the blue families. The persistent decline in the divorce rate is in stark contrast with the simultaneous trend toward more cohabitation and less stability within cohabiting couples,[67] overrepresented among red families. Ideologically,[68] the difference between the red and the blue families has reached the point of 'cultural war' for establishing 'dominant forms of family life and the meaning of marriage within it'.[69] The presidency of Donald Trump has only exacerbated this. Most of this war is being waged around the recognition of same-sex relationships, abortion and contraception, but divorce still remains an important battlefield.

One of the prominent responses of the 'red' camp to the growing permissiveness of divorce law is the covenant marriage. Three states, Louisiana (1991), Arizona (1999) and Arkansas (2001), adopted legislation allowing prospective spouses to sign a covenant promising to voluntarily restrict the grounds upon which they would seek divorce to the fault grounds and/or agreeing to seek divorce only after a stated period of separation.[70] The 'blue' attitude to divorce can be found in the 2002 ALI Principles of the Family Dissolution[71] approach to fault which recommended that fault should be totally eradicated from both the grounds of divorce and the adjudication of the consequences of divorce.[72] The Principles even suggested that any agreement made between the spouses that fault should influence their divorce should be unenforceable.[73] Both covenant marriages, seeking to turn back the tide by using private ordering, and the ALI Principles, which argue for an uncompromising step to be made forwards, have a more symbolic than practical impact. The ALI Principles have had – for the first eight years at least – almost no direct effect on the states' legislation,[74] presumably because they 'may be ahead of our time',[75] and covenant marriages never attracted more than 2 percent of couples and didn't take off in other states.[76]

Sweden: most permissive present-day divorce

Sweden was the first Western European country to radically liberalize its divorce law. Even before the reform of 1973, Swedish divorce law was one of the most permissive in Europe. Preparing the reform, the radical socialist government[77] announced in its 1969 Guidelines[78] that

66 P.N. Cohan, 'The Coming Divorce Decline', *Socius: Sociological Research for a Dynamic World* 5, 1–6.
67 Ibid.
68 Ideological divide is greater at the élite level, but the working-class families are more likely to marry, divorce and remarry in red states and more likely to cohabit in blue states.
69 Carbone and Cahn, op. cit., n 57, p. 3.
70 N. Maxwell, 'Unification and Harmonisation of Family Law Principles: The US Experience', in K. Boele-Woelki (ed.), *Perspectives for the Unification and Harmonisation of Family Law in Europe*, Antwerp: Intersentia, 2003, p. 263.
71 *Principles of the Family Dissolution: Analysis and Recommendations published* by the American Law Institute (ALI) in 2002 after 11 years of work and designated as a model law on divorce and its consequences.
72 Principle § 1, topic 2. See also Wilson, op. cit., n 56, p. 34.
73 Principle § 7.08(1). See also Wilson, op. cit., n 56, p. 34.
74 See R.F. Wilson and M. Clisham, 'American Law Institute's Principles of the Law of Family Dissolution, Eight Years after Adoption: Guiding Principles or Obligatory Footnote?', *Family Law Quarterly* 42, 2008, 573–618.
75 Krause, op. cit., n 3, p. 1107.
76 Carbone and Cahn, op. cit., n 57, p. 125.
77 For more details on the Swedish 'New Radicalism' see L. Gyllensten, 'Swedish Radicalism in the 1960s: An Experiment in Political and Cultural Debate', in D. Hancock and G. Sjoberg (eds), *Politics in the Post-Welfare State: Responses to the New Individualism*, New York: Columbia University Press, 1972.
78 Guidelines outlined by the Swedish Minister of Justice for The Committee on Family Law – the group of experts appointed to prepare the new law on marriage and divorce. Official Reports Series of

one of the main policy challenges was that the 'legislation should not under any circumstances force a person to continue to live under a marriage from which he wishes to free himself'.[79] The concept of fault disappeared entirely from Swedish divorce law just as it had done in California, but Sweden went even further and introduced divorce on demand.[80]

The law introduced in 1973[81] reduced the state's intervention to a minimum, and an autonomous decision of the spouse(s) became the effective ground for divorce.[82] This choice signified the rejection of the traditional model of marriage dissolution, based on the idea that divorce law could and should influence the social practice of divorce in order to buttress the stability of marriage.[83] If both spouses agreed upon divorce and no minor children were involved, the divorce was required to be granted immediately upon their demand.[84] If a divorce was requested by only one of the spouses, or the spouses had minor children, the divorce was to be automatically granted if the demand for divorce was renewed after a six-month period of reflection.[85] Hence, partly due to ideological reasons and partly due to pragmatic reasons, Swedish law openly left the concept of the irretrievable breakdown of marriage behind and started, instead, to consider divorce in terms of entitlements and rights.[86] Divorce on demand still remains the most permissive divorce form among westernized jurisdictions. Finland and Spain followed the Swedish example in 1987 and 2005 respectively.

Russia: building on revolutionarily heritage and setting a model for much of Eastern Europe

Before the last divorce reform of 1995, Russia already had a long-standing tradition of libertarian divorce. The Bolshevik revolution of 1917 led to a profound modernization of divorce law. Fault divorce was abolished and administrative divorce was introduced for non-contested cases. In 1926, with the legal consequences of formal and informal marriage being made equal, formal divorce lost its constitutive role in terminating the marriage. Marriage was dissolved by an autonomous decision taken by both spouses or one of them acting alone. The registration of divorce became a mere formality; an administrative procedure without any inquiry into divorce

---

Swedish Legislative and Investigative Commission, 1972, No. 41 *Family and Marriage*. For an English translation see: *Abstract of protocol in justice department matters*, 15 August 1969.

79 Abstract of protocol in justice department matters, 15 August 1969.

80 Divorce on demand is not entirely new in European history. It closely resembles the unilateral divorce of *repudium* in the Classical Roman law and was temporarily reintroduced into Europe by the Russian post-revolutionary law.

81 Entered into force on 1 January 1974. In 1987 the rules on divorce were incorporated in the new Marriage Code.

82 A. Agell, 'Should and Can Family Law Influence Social Behaviour?', in J. Eekelaar and T. Nhlapo (eds), *The Changing Family: International Perspectives on the Family and Family Law*, Oxford: Hart Publishing, 1998, p. 128.

83 J. Sundberg, 'Marriage or No Marriage: The Directives for the Revision of Swedish Family Law', *International and Comparative Law Quarterly* 20, 1971, 223–38, 234.

84 A. Lögdber, 'The Reform of Family Law in the Scandinavian Countries', in A. Chloros (ed.), *The Reform of Family Law in Europe*, Boston: Kluwer, 1978, p. 206.

85 M. Jänterä-Jareborg, *CEFL National Report for Sweden: Grounds for Divorce*, 2003. Available at http://ceflonline.net/wp-content/uploads/Sweden-Divorce.pdf, p. 4.

86 D. Bradley, *Family Law and Political Culture: Scandinavian Laws in Comparative Perspective*, London: Sweet & Maxwell, 1996, pp. 71–2.

grounds was extended to all divorce cases. Many scholars were puzzled. How could such a liberal divorce be introduced by a dictatorial regime that was neither liberal nor permissive?[87] The explanation of this paradox[88] lies in the fact that Soviet divorce reform was not primarily based on the Bolsheviks' or even the socialists' ideas on marriage and divorce, but rather the most profound implementation of the Enlightenment ideas on marriage and divorce into law.[89] In Stalin's time Russian divorce law took a temporary step backwards, partly retrieved by the 1969 Family Code.

The current Family Code of 1995[90] is built on the heritage of the liberal divorce law of the 1920s. The main policy challenge for the drafters[91] was to diminish the role of the State in divorce proceedings and to ensure better protection of the spouses' privacy. Several steps were taken to achieve this. First, the law explicitly stated that spouses are not required to disclose the reasons for a non-contested divorce. Second, the administrative procedure was extended to cover non-contested cases in which spouses had disputes on ancillary matters, separating the granting of the divorce from the adjudication of the ancillary matters which could then be dealt with in a different court procedure at a later date. Third, while the consensual divorce of the spouses with minor children still required a court procedure, the judge was bound to grant consensual divorce automatically, without any inquiry into the divorce grounds. Thus, the court acted in the same manner as the administrative authority did. The only reason for retaining the court procedure for consensual divorce with minor children was to ensure that agreements concerning children did not escape judicial scrutiny.

The formal ground of contested divorce remains the irretrievable breakdown of marriage. However, the judge has to grant divorce order if attempts to reconcile the spouses have failed and one of the spouses continues to insist on divorce. An attempt at reconciliation can entail no more than postponing the divorce by up to three months. If the petitioner renews the demand after three months, the court has no other option but to grant a divorce order.[92] This provision met with opposition from the Russian Supreme Court which attempted to mitigate it by strengthening procedural requirements.[93] However, current Russian divorce law provides for at least uncontested divorce on demand and remains one of the most liberal in Europe. After the fall of the Soviet Union, the provisions of the Russian 1995 law served as a model for the divorce laws of the Ukraine, Moldova, Belorussia and several Post-Soviet Middle Asian states.

87 See for instance: Rheinstein, op. cit., n 12, pp. 231–43.

88 For a more extensive account see Antokolskaia, op. cit., n 2, pp. 246–8.

89 Phillips acknowledges this:

> Soviet family policy [...] found support – qualified and unqualified – across the liberal and socialist spectrum in Europe and America. It responded to liberal and socialist hostility to the oppressive character of bourgeois marriage, and complemented the socialist feminist critiques of Western family institutions and practices. In this sense the Soviet experiments [...] reinforced the individualistic tendencies of the Lefts' analysis of the family.
>
> *(Phillips, op. cit., n 14, p. 538)*

90 Russian Family Code of 8 December 1995, in force 1 March 1996.

91 The author of this chapter was a member of the team of six drafters who were commissioned to draft the Code by the Committee of the State Duma of the RF on the Women, Youth and Family Affairs.

92 M. Antokolskaia, *CEFL* National Report for Russia: *Grounds for Divorce*, 2003, 9. Available at http://ceflonline.net/wp-content/uploads/Russia-Divorce.pdf, pp. 7–10.

93 Ibid.

Compromise solutions: England and Wales, Canada, Germany, France and Italy

England and Wales: a conservative compromise

Two divorce reforms, one in England and Wales in 1969 and the other attempted there in 1996, respectively, provide one of the best illustrations of the compromising nature of most divorce reforms in Europe. In both reforms, the main policy challenge was to strike a balance between the wishes of the conservatives to uphold State control upon marriage dissolution and the wishes of the proponents of liberalization to promote the autonomy of the spouses.[94] In both cases, uneasy compromises were reached.

On the eve of the 1969 reform, an intolerable situation with mass divorce by collusion[95] was acknowledged by both the conservatives and their progressive opponents; their approaches to resolving the problem were, however, in opposition. The solution put forward by the proponents of liberalization in the Law Commission Report, *Reform of the Grounds of Divorce: the Field of Choice*[96] was to derive evidence of an irretrievable breakdown from a stated period of separation and absence of evidence to the contrary.[97] The conservatives, whose views were stated in the Report of the Group of the Archbishop of Canterbury, *Putting Asunder,*[98] advocated that a full investigation/inquest be conducted in order to make consensual divorce by collusion practically impossible. These two conflicting approaches have largely determined the contradictory character of the compromise in which the 1969 Divorce Reform Act 1969[99] was grounded. According to this law, the irretrievable breakdown of the marriage should be established without a full inquest, but only upon proof of the existence of five 'facts' listed in the law.[100] Three of these 'facts' were 'the same old matrimonial faults':[101] adultery, desertion and cruelty, which was now called 'unreasonable behaviour'.[102] In addition, two new no-fault 'circumstances' were added: a two-year separation followed by an application for divorce by mutual consent, and a five-year separation, followed by a unilateral application, contested by the other spouse.

In 1973, the government, unable to cope with the growing number of divorce petitions,[103] introduced a provision to cover a range of non-contested cases,[104] a so-called special procedure.[105]

94 According to Cretney, the main concern of the proponents of the modernization of divorce law was the 'recognition that the decision whether or not a marriage should be dissolved was one for the parties which the state was not in a position to question': S. Cretney, *Family Law in the Twentieth Century: A History*, Oxford: Oxford University Press, 2003, p. 391.

95 See S. Jenkinson, 'The Co-Respondent's Role in Divorce Reform after 1923', in R. Probert and C. Barton (eds), *Fifty Years in Family Law: Essays for Stephen Cretney*, Antwerp: Intersentia, 2012, pp. 201–2.

96 The Law Commission, *Reform of the Grounds of Divorce: The Field of Choice*, London: HMSO, 1966.

97 Ibid., p. 53.

98 *Putting Asunder: A Divorce Law for Contemporary Society*, London: S.P.C.K., 1966. According to this report admission of purely consensual divorce 'would virtually repudiate the community's interest in the stability of marriage, because a judge (the community representative) would take no effectual part in the proceedings'.

99 In force from 1 January 1971, incorporated into the Matrimonial Causes Act 1973 and still in force.

100 B.H. Lee, *Divorce Reform in England*, London: Peter Owen, 1974, p. 73.

101 L. Stone, *Road to Divorce: England 1530–1987*, Oxford: Oxford University Press, 1990, p. 307.

102 Ibid.

103 B. Hale, 'The Family Law Act 1996: The Death of Marriage?', in C. Bridge (ed.), *Family Law towards the Millennium: Essays for P. M. Bromley*, London: Butterworths, 1997, p. 6.

104 Namely for certain cases where no minor children of the family were involved. Cretney, op. cit., n 86, p. 382.

105 For a description of the special procedure, see J. Herring, *Family Law*, 5th edition, Harlow: Pearson, 2011, pp. 109–10.

In 1977 this procedure was extended to cover all non-contested cases. As almost all divorce petitions were actually non-contested, in practice the special procedure became the ordinary divorce procedure.[106] It was now possible, with the special procedure, to obtain a divorce without requiring a court hearing or legal aid. State control of divorce thus became very much a fiction. As a result, the time span (from petition to decree) of a typical non-contested fault divorce case under the special procedure became fewer than four months.[107] This was in sharp contrast to the law in the books which did not allow a no-fault divorce by mutual consent to be obtained any earlier than after two years of de-facto separation. It is no wonder that most consenting couples opted for the shorter and cheaper fault divorce by collusion, rather than waiting for two years.[108] The emerging gap between the law in the books and the law in action once more accentuated the 'unsatisfactory nature of the compromise between offence-based facts and the breakdown principle'.[109]

Dissatisfaction with this situation[110] made new reform inevitable. The attempted 1996 reform shows that accessibility of divorce and divorce grounds still remained a primary policy challenge in England and Wales. But this time there was agreement, albeit not unanimous, that irretrievable breakdown should truly become the sole ground for divorce.[111] However the 1996 Family Law Act showed that a no-fault divorce did not automatically mean an easily accessible one. The no-fault divorce under the act became more lengthy and difficult than the fault-based divorce ever was. Under the 1996 Act, fault disappeared, but a non-contested divorce for couples without minor children could be obtained only after a one-year period of reflection. The reflection period for contested divorces, and for all the divorces of couples with minor children, was set at 16 months.[112] In effect, however, getting a divorce could have taken even longer because all the ancillary matters would now have had to be adjudicated within the same divorce procedure. However, introduction of these reforms was delayed while the government piloted proposals requiring people proposing to divorce to attend information meetings intended to assist people to reflect whether they really wished to divorce and, if they did, to encourage them to use mediation rather than legal services. The results suggested that the meetings were failing to achieve these objectives, and the reforms were abandoned. So, the 1996 Family Law Act was repealed in 2001 before its main provisions entered into force. As result, divorce in England and Wales is still governed by the 1969 provisions.

The 1996 fiasco was followed by a long period of political reluctance to deal with divorce reform,[113] until the 2017 Supreme Court decision in *Owens v Owens*[114] shook both public and

106 Ibid.

107 *Fourth Annual Report* of the Advisory Board in Family Law, 2000/2001, para 3.5.

108 The Law Commission referred to 73 percent of divorce petitions being based on fault grounds. Law Commission, *Family Law: The Grounds for Divorce*, Law Com. No. 192, London: HMSO, 1990, para 2.3.

109 Cretney, op. cit., n 18, p. 42.

110 For an overview, see N. Lowe and G. Douglas, *Bromley's Family Law*, 10th edition, London: Butterworths, 2007, pp. 288 ff.

111 Cretney, op. cit., n 18, p. 42.

112 Family Law Act 1996, section 7.

113 In 2011 it has been proposed that the process for initiating divorce should begin with an application on line and dealt with entirely administratively, unless the divorce is contested (*Family Justice Review, Final Report*, London: Ministry of Justice, 2011, p. 178). The government has accepted this recommendation, but did not implemented it. *The Government Response to the Family Justice Review: A System with Children and Families at Its Heart*, London: Ministry of Justice and Department for Education, 2012, p. 81.

114 [2018] UKSC 41.

politicians awake. This rare defended divorce case, which the husband successfully defended against his wife, who petitioned on the ground of 'behaviour', exposed the hypocrisy of the current system that allowed for immediate unilateral divorce on demand in undefended 'behaviour' cases but was 'masked by an often painful, and sometimes destructive, legal ritual with no obvious benefits for the parties or the state'.[115] The case gave rise to 'fundamental questions about the state of divorce law and, in particular, about whether it should be possible for parties to be compelled by the state to remain in an unhappy marriage'.[116] In 2017–2019 a group of academics, headed by law professor Liz Trinder, involved in a large-scale Finding Fault Project,[117] published a range of reports, including a seminal report *Finding Fault*.[118] Those reports provided a theoretical, empirical and comparative framework for the legislative reform.

In July 2018 a short-lived private Divorce Law Review Bill[119] was introduced into the House of Lords. The bill required the Lord Chancellor to review the law relating to divorce, including consideration of whether the law should be changed so that irretrievable breakdown would be proven solely by a system of application and notification.[120] In September 2018, the government launched a public consultation following proposals to reform divorce law involving replacing the five facts currently required for establishing breakdown of marriage with a notification process whereby one or both parties notify the court of the irretrievable breakdown of their marriage; and the removal of the possibility to defend the divorce.[121] The outcome of the consultation reinforced the government's assessment that the existing requirement to make allegations about behaviour of the other spouse 'can introduce or worsen ongoing conflict and be harmful to any children', and thus a genuinely no-fault divorce was urgently needed.[122]

On 12 June 2019 the government introduced the Divorce, Dissolution and Separation Bill in the House of Commons. Due to cross-party support the bill was progressing smoothly but fell as a result of the dissolution of Parliament in December 2019, to be reintroduced in the House of Lords in January 2020. The reform proposed in the bill[123] closely follows the suggestions of the *Finding Fault* report and a comparative-law inquiry,[124] based upon the most liberal European examples. According to the government the purpose of the bill is to 'remove issues that create conflict' in the divorce process, to 'minimize' the impact of divorce on children[125] and to ensure that separating couples should not be put through legal requirements which do not serve their or

115 L. Trinder et al., *Finding Fault?: Divorce Law and Practice in England and Wales*, Summary Report, London: Nuffield Foundation, 2017, p. 3.

116 S. Trotter, 'The State of Divorce Law', *The Cambridge Law Journal* 2019, 38.

117 Nuffield Foundation Project, *Finding Fault?: Divorce Law and Practice in England and Wales*, October 2015–2015. Results are available at www.nuffieldfoundation.org/project/finding-fault-divorce-law-in-practice-in-england-and-wales/.

118 L. Trinder et al., op. cit., n 115. See also: L. Trinder and M. Sefton, *No Contest: Defended Divorce in England and Wales*, London: Nuffield Foundation, 2018, and other reports.

119 Divorce (etc.) Law Review Bill [HL]. Introduced by Baroness Butler-Sloss.

120 Explanatory Notes to the Divorce (etc.) Law Review Bill [HL].

121 Ministry of Justice, *Reducing Family Conflict: Reform of the Legal Requirements for Divorce*.

122 Divorce, Dissolution and Separation Bill [HL] Explanatory Notes, p. 4. Available at https://publications.parliament.uk/pa/bills/lbill/2019-2019/0003/20003en.pdf.

123 Divorce, Dissolution and Separation Bill [HL] (HL Bill 2). Available at https://publications.parliament.uk/pa/bills/lbill/58-01/002/5801002_en_1.html.

124 J. Scherpe and L. Trinder, *No Fault Divorce Proposal Is Consistent with International Trends*, London: Nuffield Foundation, 2019.

125 Divorce, Dissolution and Separation Bill [HL]: Briefing for Lords Stage.

the state's interests and which can lead to ongoing conflict and poorer outcomes for children.[126] At the same time the legislation should ensure the decision to divorce is a 'considered one'.[127]

The proposed reform is truly revolutionary by English standards and notably simple. Fault grounds are completely eradicated. The ground for divorce remains irretrievable breakdown by name, but it can be conclusively proved by joint or unilateral statement of the spouse(s) that their marriage has broken down. As a defence against a unilateral statement of breakdown is not admitted, the situation will closely resemble the Finnish, Swedish and Spanish divorce on demand. Unlike in Spain and in some cases in Sweden, the bill does not allow for an immediate divorce. The initial application needs to be confirmed after 20 weeks, and only then will a 'conditional order' (current decree nisi) be made. Another six weeks have to pass before the conditional order can be automatically converted into the final order (current decree absolute). That amounts to an overall mandatory delay of six months that will allow spouses to cool off, reconsider their decision and deal with the ancillary matters. Although the smooth passage of the bill so far allows optimistic expectations, learning from the past warns us that no one can really predict the outcome until the very end.[128]

Canada: from a conservative to a more progressive compromise

In contrast with the US, the power in Canada to legislate on divorce belonged to the federal government, but remained unused until 1968. Before 1968, divorce was regulated at the level of the provinces and the accessibility of divorce in Canada lagged behind most other westernized jurisdictions.[129] In Catholic Quebec and the predominantly Catholic Newfoundland, marriage dissolution was only possible by a private Act of Parliament and other provinces only allowed divorce on the ground of adultery. In Nova Scotia, divorce grounds included cruelty.[130]

The liberalization of divorce through federal law became possible when the Canadian Catholic Conference[131] stated that, in line with the spirit of the Second Vatican Council,[132] Catholics were no longer obliged to oppose the introduction of divorce.[133] These major compromises by the Catholic Church cleared the way for divorce to be introduced at the federal level, but left many questions about the content of the new law open. The main policy choice was between breakdown 'Californian style' and the traditional divorce grounds including fault. Influenced to a certain extent by the recently published English report *Putting Asunder*, the traditional grounds won.[134] Canadian divorce law resembled the English rather closely. There were three fault grounds, which included adultery and cruelty, and several failure grounds such as three years separation and five years separation if the separation was caused by the petitioner's desertion of the respondent.[135] However, in Canada, fault and breakdown were two separate grounds, whereas in England and Wales fault was regarded as one of the circumstances required for proving the breakdown.

126 Divorce, Dissolution and Separation Bill [HL] Explanatory Notes, p. 4.
127 Divorce, Dissolution and Separation Bill [HL]: Briefing for Lords Stage.
128 The Progress of the Bill Could Be Followed. Available at www.gov.uk/government/publications/divorce-dissolution-and-separation-bill.
129 See B. Bodenheimer, 'The New Canadian Divorce Law', *Family Law Quarterly* 2, 1968, 213–27, 214.
130 Ibid., 214.
131 The national organization of the Catholics Bishops of Canada.
132 Council of the Roman Catholic Church held in 1962–1965.
133 Bodenheimer, op. cit., n 129, 217.
134 Bodenheimer, op. cit., n 107, 218.
135 Divorce Act, 1968, ss. 3 and 4.

Following this rather conservative compromise, pressure for liberalization soon built. In the early 1980s, the liberal government unsuccessfully tried to replace the existing grounds with the single breakdown ground.[136] Eventually the Divorce Act 1985 introduced the breakdown of marriage as the sole ground. This could be proven by a one year's separation, adultery, or cruelty committed by the respondent.[137] Thus Canadian divorce law became rather permissive by western standards. A faultless contested divorce can be obtained upon joint or sole petition after just one-year separation – a considerably shorter period than in England and Wales, France and Germany. Adultery and cruelty came to serve as a kind of 'hardship clause' allowing an aggrieved spouse to liberate her/himself from the offender without a waiting period.[138] After several unsuccessful attempts the Canadian Divorce Act has been modernized in 2019 by the Bill C-78.[139] This bill represents the first major change to Canada's federal divorce law over the last 20 years. The bill does not introduce much change into the ground of divorce or accessibility of divorce. The most noteworthy change in that regard is the abolition of the previously existing obligation of the court to ascertain that reconciliation of the spouses is not possible. Instead, it introduces a new section 7.7(1), reaffirming current legal responsibly of the legal advisers to discuss the possibility of reconciliation with their clients.[140] The main focus on the bill is not on the spousal relationships but rather on the parent-child relationship.[141] It introduces modern child-centred terminology and promotes, when appropriate, alternative dispute resolution, parental plans and other child-focused instruments. This broadly endorsed Canadian reform is symptomatic of the current emphasis on prevention and resolution of parental conflicts and minimizing the negative effects of divorce for children.

Germany: a pragmatic compromise

The German 1976 divorce reform had a better starting position than those in England and France, as the 1938 *Ehegesetz* already provided for divorce on the ground of the irretrievable breakdown of marriage. However, this required three years of separation and was a much more lengthy and difficult process than divorce on the ground of fault. Germany also wrestled with the problem of divorce by collusion.[142] The main policy challenge during the reform was how to prove the breakdown of marriage, and especially, whether mutual consent should be regarded as such proof. All the proposals to introduce an easily accessible consensual divorce in order to put an end to divorce by collusion were rejected. The conservatives claimed that recognition of divorce by consent would 'reduce marriage to the level of [an] ordinary contractual obligation which can be disposed of freely'.[143] Instead two modes of proof of the breakdown of marriage

136 B. Ziff, 'Recent Developments in Canadian Law: Marriage and Divorce', *Ottawa Law Review* 18, 1986, 121–210, 138.

137 Divorce Act, 1985, s. 4. subs 8(1), (1).

138 See the explanation by the Canadian Minister of Justice cited in Ziff, op. cit., n 115, 138, n 102.

139 Bill C-78, *An Act to amend the Divorce Act, the Family Orders and Agreements Enforcement Assistance Act and the Garnishment, Attachment and Pension Diversion Act and to make consequential amendments to another Act*, received Royal Assent on June 21, 2019.

140 K. Azoulay, A. Smith and N. Sweeney, 'Legislative Summary of the Bill C-78', *An Act to Amend the Divorce Act, the Family Orders and Agreements Enforcement Assistance Act and the Garnishment, Attachment and Pension Diversion Act and to Make Consequential Amendments to Another Act, Legal and Social Affairs Division, Parliamentary Information and Research Service, Publication No. 42–1-C78-E, 5 October 2018, Revised 19 April 2019, p. 2.*

141 Op. cit., p. 8.

142 D. Giesen, 'Divorce Reform in Germany', *Family Law Quarterly* 7, 1973, 351–80.

143 Ibid., 359.

were considered: the subjective mode, based on an inquiry that must convince the judge that the marriage had broken down, and the objective mode, based on a stated period of separation. As in England and France, the new German law was doomed to become a compromise.[144]

Finally, the general rule came to be that marriage could be dissolved if a court was convinced that the marriage had failed. However, if the spouses had not been living apart for at least one year, marriage could only be dissolved in exceptional circumstances: the petitioner should attest that the continuation of the marriage would create unreasonable hardship for him or her from causes attributable to the other spouse.[145] If the spouses had been living apart for one year and both spouses apply for divorce,[146] the breakdown was irrebuttably presumed.[147] If the spouses had been living apart for three years, this also constituted an irrebuttable presumption of breakdown, even if only one spouse had applied for the divorce.[148] These two presumptions exemplify an objective proof of breakdown, although, even if the breakdown of marriage is presumed, divorce is not granted automatically. State control over divorce is further safeguarded by maintaining a hardship clause.[149]

France: divorce à la carte, including private divorce

On the eve of the reforms of the 1970s, divorce in France had already had a long and difficult history of political controversy. In the 1970s, French public opinion was as deeply split on divorce as it had been throughout the preceding two centuries. The legal situation largely resembled the English one; while the law in the books allowed only for fault-based divorce, in practice a quarter of divorces were estimated to be collusive.[150] Both liberals and conservatives called for reform,[151] but while the former advocated the abolition of fault-based divorce, the latter opposed this, and the general public was hopelessly divided.[152] The solution found by the chief architect of the divorce law of 1975,[153] Jean Carbonnier, came to be known as *divorce à la carte*.[154] This system accommodated fault and no fault grounds alongside each other,

144 To the surprise of many people, the reform was finally achieved by a series of 'ingenious' compromises in a vexed parliamentary situation. By these compromises, the legislature remarkably succeeded in avoiding clear and definite positions on many problems. It thus followed the time-honoured pattern of evading politically sensitive issues by adopting meaningless rules which serve to neutralize rival claims.

(W. Müller-Freienfels, 'The Marriage Law Reform of 1976 in the Federal Republic of Germany', *International and Comparative Law Quarterly* 28, 1979, 184–210, 186)

145 N. Dethloff, *Familienrecht*, 30th edition, Munich: Beck, 2012, p. 78.

146 § 630 Code of Civil Procedure.

147 Para 1566 I BGB. See: D. Martiny, 'Family Law', in I. Zekoll and M. Reimann (eds), *Introduction to German Law*, 2nd edition, Deventer: Kluwer 2005, p. 259.

148 Para 1566 III BGB.

149 Dethloff, op. cit., n 145, p. 179.

150 J. Foyer, 'The Reform of Family Law in France', in A. Chloros (ed.), *The Reform of Family Law in Europe*, Deventer: Kluwer, 1978, p. 106.

151 According to an opinion poll conducted in the early 1970s, the majority of the respondents supported the divorce reform: C. Dadomo, 'The Current Reform of French Law of Divorce', *International Family Law* 2004, 220.

152 M-A. Glendon, 'The French Divorce Reform Law of 1976', *The American Journal of Comparative Law* 24, 1976, 199–228, 201.

153 Law of 11 July 1975, in force on 1 January 1976.

154 J. Carbonnier, *Droit civil: La famille, l'enfant, le couple*, 21st edition, Paris: Press Universitaires de France, 2002, p. 541.

reflecting the plurality of the ideas about divorce held in the French society.[155] The new law provided for several routes to divorce: a fault-based divorce-sanction, two forms of consensual divorce and a unilateral divorce-remedy on the ground of the irretrievable breakdown of marriage.[156]

The main achievement of the French law, compared to the English, was in allowing divorce by mutual consent without a waiting period. With this the French legislature managed to solve the problem of collusive divorce. However, the 'oppressive formality'[157] of consensual divorce rather diminished its attractiveness.[158] The long period of separation which was required for a non-consensual divorce meant that a spouse who fell in love with someone else became 'a prisoner of the conjugal bond'[159] for at least six years. The still very popular[160] fault-based divorce appeared to aggravate conflict and trauma for the divorcing spouses.[161] In the late 1990s, these concerns prompted the left-wing government to commission several reports and studies, the two most important of which were by the sociologist Irène Théry[162] and the Professor of Law Françoise Dekeuwer-Défossez.[163]

It soon became apparent that, yet again, no consensus could be reached.[164] Because of this, in 2001–02 two private bills[165] aimed at introducing no-fault divorce were unsuccessfully submitted to the French Parliament. The political momentum for the introduction of no-fault divorce stalled as the Left lost its majority in parliament in June 2002. Following this, in October 2002, the government announced a new reform[166] resulting in the law of the 26 May 2004.[167] This was a modified version of the existing *divorce à la carte*. Fault was retained because of the conviction that it still 'meets the needs of the majority of French people'.[168] But both forms of consensual divorce became less formal and complicated and the period of separation required for unilateral divorce upon irretrievable breakdown of marriage was shortened from six to two years.

What happened next was completely unexpected. Although administrative divorce had been proposed[169] already during the preparation of the 2004 reform, and again in 2007 and in

155 G. Cornu, *Droit civil, La famille*, 8th edition, Paris: Montchrestien, 2003, No 312.

156 A. Bénabent, *Droit civil: La famille*, 10th edition, LexisNexis: Litec, 2001, No 228.

157 H. Fulchiron, S. Ferré-André and A. Gouttenoire, 'A Pause in the Reform of French Family Law', in A. Bainham (ed.), *The International Survey of Family Law*, Bristol: Jordan Publishing, 2004, p. 184.

158 Only 41 percent of divorcing couples used this form of divorce: Fulchiron, Ferré-André and Gouttenoire, op. cit., n 128, p. 184.

159 Bénabent, op. cit., n 156, No. 230.

160 On the eve of 2004 reforms, fault grounds accounted for 42 percent of all divorce proceedings: Fulchiron, Ferré-André and Gouttenoire, op. cit., n 157, p. 185.

161 Ibid., p. 186.

162 I. Théry, *Couple, filiation et parenté aujourd'hui: le droit face aux mutations de la famille et de la vie privée: rapport remis au Ministre de l'emploi et de la solidarité et au Garde des sceaux Ministre de la justice*, Paris: Odile Jacob, 1998.

163 F. Dekeuwer-Défossez, *Rénover, le droit de la famille: Propositions pour un droit adapté aux réalités et aux aspirations de notre temps: Rapport au Garde des Sceaux, Ministre de la justice*, Paris: La Documentation française, 1999.

164 B. Bastard, 'Administrative Divorce in France: A Controversy over a Reform That Never Reached the Statute Book', in M. MacLean (ed.), *Making Law for Families*, Oxford: Hart Publishing, 2000, p. 79.

165 Proposition de loi relative à la réforme du divorce, N° 3189, 26 Juin 2001 and Proposition de loi visant à remplacer la procédure de divorce pour faute par une procédure de divorce pour cause objective, N° 12, 10 Octobre 2001.

166 Dadomo, op. cit., n 151, p. 223.

167 Law 2004–439 of 16 May 2004, in force on 1 January 2005.

168 Fulchiron, Ferré-André, Gouttenoire, op. cit., n 157, p. 184.

169 One of the most influential proponents of administrative divorce has been Irène Théry: see n 162.

2013 it was every time heavily criticized and rejected as 'degrading marital status to the state of concubinage',[170] undermining protection of children and the weaker party,[171] and primarily aimed at decreasing the workload of judges.[172] However, administrative divorce, expelled through the front door, managed to get through the back door in the form of private notarial divorce. It was introduced in 2015 as a last-minute government amendment to the Bill on the Justice in the Twenty-First Century. The reform took place in a hurry.[173] The enactment of the new law was surrounded by much controversy: the amended bill was adopted by the *Assemblée nationale*, rejected by the *Sénat*, but became the law on 12 October 2016 after the decision of the *Sénat* has been overruled by the *Assemblée nationale*.[174] The new law survived the challenge before the *Conseil constitutionnel* and came into force on 1 January 2017.[175] Under the new law, uncontested divorce has been changed quite dramatically. The wording suggests that for spouses divorcing by mutual consent, there is now only one – private – road to divorce.[176] The private divorce entails two steps: (1) making an agreement on divorce and all ancillary matters called 'convention', signed by the spouse after 15 days of mandatory reflection and countersigned by two private legal advisers, representing the interests of each of the spouses; (2) after a merely formal test by public notary, registering and depositing the convention in the notarial files.[177] Once registered and deposited with a public notary, the convention acquires executive force. Judicial divorce is now reserved for spouses who cannot reach agreement upon divorce and ancillary matters, as well as for the spouses who have reached such consent, one of whom has been placed under an adult protection measures, or if a minor child of the spouses wishes to be heard by the judge. This last rule has been justly criticized for putting a heavy responsibility on children's shoulders by making them responsible for the route to divorce their parents have to take.[178]

The ideological background of this law is twofold. One the one hand, it is the increasing emphasis on the contractual nature of marriage and growing reluctance to assign to the state any role in its dissolution.[179] On the other hand, it is pure pragmatism, aimed at diminishing the burden upon an overloaded judicial system.[180] The reform as a whole is appraised by several renowned scholars as a 'huge and ill-thought-out step towards privatisation of divorce'.[181] The criticism points at legal uncertainty related to the possibility of annulment of the divorce convention using general rules of private law on nullity of civil contract; removing the scrutiny of child-related arrangements by a state competent authority, and its doubtful effect on saving costs.[182] Also recognition of this private divorce abroad remains highly uncertain.

170 Bastard, op. cit., n 164, p. 79.

171 S. Guinchard, *L' ambition raisonnée d'une justice apaisée, Rapport au garde des Sceaux*, Paris: La Documentation française, 2008.

172 F. Ferrand, 'Non-Judicial Divorce in France: Progress or a Mess?', in G. Douglas, M. Murch and V. Stephens (eds), *International and National Perspectives on Child and Family Law. Essays in Honour of Nigel Lowe*, Cambridge: Intersentia, pp. 193–4.

173 C. Bidaut-Garon and H. Fulchiron et al., 'A Chronicle of French Family Law', in M. Brining (ed.), *The International Survey of Family Law*, Bristol: LexisNexis, 2017, p. 99.

174 Law No. 2016–1547 of 18 November 2016 *de modernisation de la justice du XXIe siècle.*

175 Ferrand, op. sit., n 172, p. 194.

176 Ibid., p. 197.

177 Art. 229–1, French CC, Bidaut-Garon and Fulchiron, op. cit., n 173, p. 99.

178 Ferrand, op. cit., n 172, p. 203.

179 Ibid., p. 195.

180 Bidaut-Garon and Fulchiron, op. cit., n 173, p. 99.

181 Ferrand, op. cit., n 172, p. 204 and in more moderated words Bidaut-Garon and Fulchiron, op. cit., n 173, p. 99.

182 Ferrand, Ibid., pp. 201–4.

Italy: from indissolubility to administrative divorce

At the time of the family revolution of the 1960s and 1970s, marriage in Italy was still indissoluble and the introduction of civil divorce became 'a national issue of prime importance'.[183] The nation was split into two camps – the *dovorzisti* and the *anti-divorzisti*.[184] The parties to the left of the Christian Democrats supported divorce, so the Communists[185] found themselves in an unusual alliance with the Liberal party.[186] The Christian Democrats, together with the Extreme Right, opposed divorce.[187] At a certain point, as Pocar and Ronfani note, the divorce debate in Italy 'lost its original legal character and acquired a political or moral tone, with strong emotional and irrational implications'.[188] The arguments put forward in this debate were 'liberty' and 'progress' versus the 'defence of sacred family values'.[189] A political breakthrough was achieved, in 1962, when a coalition government that included the Socialists but not the Christian-Democrats was formed[190] and, in 1970, civil divorce became a legal possibility.[191]

The law provided for both fault and no-fault divorce, but was heavily weighted towards fault[192] and required a long period of separation.[193] The constitutionality of divorce (its compatibility with the Concordat) was unsuccessfully challenged before the Constitutional Court and the opponents of divorce launched a campaign for a referendum on the abrogation of the law on divorce.[194] This referendum was held on 12 May 1974.[195] At the very last moment public opinion shifted in favour of the divorce law and the *anti-divorzisti* quite unexpectedly lost.[196] In 1987, divorce law was liberalized a little by the introduction of divorce by joint application and the reducing to three years of the period of separation, required in case of joint application.[197] However, even after that, Italian divorce law remained rather restrictive by European standards.

A significant change came in 2014 and in 2015[198] and suddenly placed Italy into the European vanguard. Divorce grounds formally remained the same. Several fault and no-fault facts,

183 Rheinstein, op. cit., n 12, p. 189.

184 Ibid.

185 The communists supported divorce quite reluctantly as the surrounding commotion threatened the co-operation with the Christian Democrats which they were eager to establish. See T. Abse, 'Italy: A New Agenda', in P. Anderson and P. Camiller (eds), *Mapping the West European Left*, London: Verso, 1994, pp. 201–3.

186 G. Sgritta and P. Tufari, 'Italy', in P. Chester (ed.), *Divorce in Europe*, Leiden: Nijhoff, 1977, p. 261.

187 Ibid.

188 V. Pocar and P. Ronfani, 'Family Law in Italy: Legislative Innovations and Social Change', *Law and Society Review* 12, 1977–8, 607–44, 612.

189 Ibid.

190 Rheinstein, op. cit., n 12, p. 189.

191 Law No. 898, of 1 December 1970, in force on 18 December 1970.

192 Phillips noticed that 'the principle of fault lay at the core of the 1970 legislation': Phillips, op. cit., n 14, p. 574.

193 The law required a judicial separation. De facto separation starting at least two years before the new law came into force, only sufficed for divorce during the transitional period. Sgritta and Tufari, op. cit., n 149, p. 259.

194 V. Librando, 'The Reform of Family Law in Italy', in A. Chloros (ed.), *The Reform of Family Law in Europe*, Deventer: Kluwer, 1978, p. 170.

195 Pocar and Ronfani, op. cit., n 188, p. 612.

196 41 percent voted for abrogating the divorce law and 59 percent voted in favour of maintaining it: Sgritta and Tufari, op. cit., n 186, pp. 260–1.

197 S. Patti, *CEFL* National Report for Italy: *Grounds for Divorce* (2003) 4. Available at http://ceflonline.net/wp-content/uploads/Italy-Divorce.pdf, p. 44.

198 Decree of 12 September 2014 No 132, converted into Law of 10 November 2014 No 162 and Law of 6 May 2015 No 55.

resulting in irretrievable breakdown – although almost never used in practice – have been preserved. The most used grounds – formal separation, has been reduced in 2015 to six months for consensual separation and to one year for separation upon unilateral application. Divorce procedure still entails two steps: formal separation and divorce itself.[199] However, the procedural rules on how divorce and separation can be obtained have been changed dramatically. Separation and subsequent divorce upon unilateral application always requires judicial procedure. Consensual separation and divorce can – since 2014 – be obtained either through a court procedure or through an administrative procedure.

Judicial separation can be granted upon request of one or both spouses. In case of unilateral application, judicial separation includes two steps: a conciliation attempt – formally required but not applied in practice – and judicial inquiry. Irretrievable breakdown, at least in theory, still has to be proven. Although separation is considered to be a no-fault ground, spouse(s) could require allocation of responsibly for the breakdown of relationship. Such allocation is of significant influence for ancillary matters inter spouses (e.g. inheritance and maintenance).[200] Twelve months later a divorce degree can be obtained.

Spouses who agree to separate can jointly apply to court for a separation by presenting to court their agreement on separation and ancillary matters. The court scrutinizes the agreement and grants the separation order. The whole procedure consists of one single hearing.[201] Six months later a divorce decree can be granted.

The most far-reaching innovation introduced in 2014 was two forms of administrative procedures allowing spouses to separate and subsequently divorce without going to court. The first form – consensual separation by a so-called *negotiation agreement* – is open for all couples. A *negotiation agreement* can be drafted by spouses, assisted by two lawyers, which then has to be scrutinized by the public prosecutor. If the spouses have minor or dependent children, such scrutiny is substantial; in other cases it is just a formality. This way state control regarding the best interest of the children has been safeguarded.[202] If the scrutiny is successful the agreement can be registered in the public register and has the same effect as a court order.[203] The second form is reserved for couples without minor or dependent children and has some restrictions as to the division of matrimonial property. In this case spouses do not need to be represented by lawyers or have their agreement scrutinized by a public prosecutor. They can just present their self-made agreement on separation or dissolution of their marriage and ancillary matters to the registrar (or a deputy) for registration, who registers the agreement after a formal check.[204] This reduces state control upon dissolution of marriage to a minimum. In contrast to France, the Italian reform has met a more balanced response. As in France, one of the main drivers behind the reform was decreasing the caseload of the judiciary as well as cost-saving.[205] Another objective was creating a less adversarial procedure and empowering spouses to arrange their separation with the help of legal counsel.[206] Unlike in France, protection of the interests of the children has been safeguarded through scrutiny of agreements by the public prosecutor.

199 C. Valente, 'An Overview on Italian Panorama: Family Law Daces Social, Changes', in B. Atkin (ed.), *The International Survey of Family Law*, Bristol: LexisNexis, 2016, p. 290.
200 Sections 548 and 585 Italian CC.
201 Valente, op. cit., n 199, p. 291.
202 Ibid., pp. 292–3.
203 Sections 2 and 6 ICC.
204 Section 12 ICC. Valente, op. cit., p. 293.
205 Valente, op. cit., n 199, pp. 292–3.
206 Ibid.

Dissolution of registered partnerships

It is not easy to summarize the rules on the dissolution of registered partnerships in westernized jurisdictions as they differ significantly. Moreover, these differences are often grounded in dissimilar policy choices rather than in the mere use of different legislative techniques. The policy choices have been made in the context of legislative responses to the main contemporary family law policy challenge, the legal recognition of same-sex relationships. The conservative/progressive divide influenced the way various jurisdictions dealt with this challenge in manner very similar to the way the liberalization of divorce was dealt with.

In the last decade of the twentieth century the Nordic European countries and several North American states were the first to respond to this challenge by adopting various forms of registered partnerships. Three patterns can be distinguished: (1) total equalization by the introduction of same-sex marriage; (2) separate but equal – the strong form of registered partnership 'Nordic' style or civil unions; and (3) separate and unequal – the weak form of registered partnership or domestic partnership.[207]

Dissolution of a same-sex marriage does not differ from the dissolution of a heterosexual marriage and therefore requires no specific attention in this paragraph.

Dissolution of strong forms of registered partnerships

Strong forms of registered partnerships were introduced in the jurisdictions which were sufficiently prepared to grant same-sex couples almost all the benefits of marriage, but as yet not prepared to grant their union the name of marriage.[208] The model of registered partnership 'Nordic style' was first introduced in Denmark in 1989 and, in the following decade, spread rapidly over the whole Nordic region and many other Western European jurisdictions. In 1998, the Netherlands introduced the same model with one significant difference: the partnership was open to both same-sex and different-sex couples. In 2001, Germany generally followed the Nordic example too, but, initially,[209] because of political and constitutional constraints, went significantly less far in equalizing registered partnership and marriage.[210] In North America strong forms of registered partnerships (civil unions) have been introduced in several US states and in the Canadian province of Québec. One difference is notable: while in Europe only the Netherlands has a gender-neutral strong form of registered partnership, it is common in the North American jurisdictions: e.g. Hawaii, Illinois, Québec, Colorado and California.[211] Strong forms of registered

207 For similar classifications, see: M. Sáez, 'Same-Sex Marriage, Same-Sex Cohabitation, and Same-Sex Families around the World: Why "Same" Is So Different'. Available at www.wcl.american.edu/journal/genderlaw/19/19.1.Saez.JCI.pdf; F. Swennen and S. Eggermont, 'Same-Sex Couples in Central Europe: Hop, Step and Jump', in K. Boele-Woelki and A. Fuchs (eds), *Legal Recognition of Same-Sex Relationships in Europe: National, Cross-Border and European Perspective*, Antwerp: Intersentia, 2012, p. 19.

208 A. Agell, 'Family Forms and Legal Policies: A Comparative View from a Swedish Observer', *Scandinavian Studies in Law* 38, 1999, 197–216, 208.

209 In December 2004, the Act on Amending the Life Partnerships was upgraded *eingetragene Lebenspartnerchaft* to the level of a registered partnership 'Nordic' style. The law of 15 December 2004, passed by the *Bundesrat* on the 26 November 2004, came into force on 1 January 2005.

210 *Law on Termination of the Discrimination against Same Sex-Communities; Life Partnerships* of 16 February 2001. Came into force on 1 August 2001.

211 In California it is open to opposite-sex couples only if one of the partners has reached the age of 62.

partnerships generally resemble marriage in all its features with, initially,[212] the exception of the presumption of paternity of the partner of the mother of the child and the possibility of adoption.

In the majority of jurisdictions, the rules on the dissolution of marriage apply *mutatis mutandis* to the strong forms of the registered partnerships. In several jurisdictions the differences are insignificant,[213] but, in a small number of jurisdictions, these are fairly important. Thus, in the Netherlands, a childless registered partnership can be dissolved administratively, provided both partners reach an agreement on the dissolution and the ancillary matters. In contrast married couples can only resort to juridical divorce. Also, in California, a childless civil union can be terminated administratively if several conditions are met.[214]

The introduction of same-sex marriage makes strong forms of registered partnerships, open only to same-sex couples, no longer necessary. Thus, the introduction of same-sex marriage was followed by the repeal of registered partnership and civil union acts in Nordic states and some American states. In contrast, in jurisdictions with gender-neutral strong forms of registered partnerships, the partnership remains in existence alongside the same-sex marriage as a sort of 'marriage lite'.

Dissolution of weak forms of registered partnerships

Weak forms of registered partnerships were introduced in the jurisdictions that were not prepared, at that time, to grant same-sex relationships extensive legal protection. Some domestic partnerships in North America and various forms of weak partnerships in Europe (the French *Pacte civil de solidarité* (PACS), the Belgian *cohabitation légale* and the stable unions in the Spanish autonomies, etc.) have been deliberately constructed to be as different from marriage as possible. In most countries this approach was the product of uneasy political compromises and self-imposed constraints. In France and Belgium it was considered preferable to 'mask the issue of the same-sex relationships behind the façade of cohabitation'.[215] Weak forms of registered partnership legislation have been introduced in several states of the US, in three Canadian provinces and in several European countries.[216]

These unions often give partners only very limited protection and in all jurisdictions except the Czech Republic and Slovenia,[217] are open to both same-sex and opposite-sex couples. Moreover, in several jurisdictions, e.g. Belgium, some US states and Canadian provinces they are even open to any persons who share the same household, disregarding the nature of their relationships. A good example of this is the Belgian *cohabitation légale*. Under pressure from the Christian Democrats,[218] the rules of statutory cohabitation were made applicable upon registra-

212 Most jurisdictions later renounced one or both of these exceptions.

213 For details, see Swennen and Eggermont, op. cit., n 207, p. 29.

214 California Family Code, para 299(a).

215 E. Steiner, 'The Spirit of the New French Registered Partnership Law: Promoting Autonomy and Pluralism or Weakening Marriage', *Child and Family Law Quarterly* 10, 2000, 13–17.

216 See C. González Beilfuss, 'All or Nothing: The Dilemma of Southern Jurisdictions', in K. Boele-Woelki and A. Fuchs (eds), *Legal recognition of Same-Sex Relationships in Europe: National, Cross-Border and European Perspective*, Antwerp: Intersentia, 2012, pp. 45–9.

217 For more details on registered partnerships in Eastern Europe, see M. Jagielska, 'Eastern European Countries: From Penalisation to Cohabitation or Further?', in K. Boele-Woelki and A. Fuchs (eds), *Legal Recognition of Same-Sex Relationships in Europe: National, Cross-Border and European Perspective*, Antwerp: Intersentia, 2012, pp. 55–69.

218 In this way, the Christian-Democrats wished to provide minimal protection to any family members living in the same household: P. Senaeve, 'De Belgische "wettelijke samenwoning" en het Franse "Pacte civil de solidarité"', in A. Verbeke et al. (eds), *Facetten van ondernemingsrecht. Liber Amicorum Professor Frans Bouckaert*, Leuven: Leuven University Press, 2000, p. 442.

tion to any two unmarried persons living together, irrespective of their gender, familial, sexual or affective bond. Thus, statutory cohabitation came to cover as wide a range of relationships as same-sex and opposite-sex couples, a mother and her adult daughter, and even 'a priest and his maid'.[219]

The dissolution of weak forms of registered partnerships is, as a rule, much easier than that of a marriage, thus stressing its inferiority to marriage. In most jurisdictions, the marriage of one of the partners does not require the prior dissolution of their partnership, but automatically terminates it. In France, Belgium, the Spanish autonomies, Slovenia, Luxembourg, Nova Scotia and several American states[220] a partnership can be dissolved administratively by making a joint or unilateral declaration.[221] In many jurisdictions, weak forms of registered partnership also appeared to be the first step towards total equalization through same-sex marriage. However, as weak partnerships are so different from marriage, making marriage gender-neutral does not usually lead to their abolition. In Belgium, the Canadian provinces, the Spanish autonomies and France they continue to exist in addition to gender-neutral marriage.[222]

Conclusion

This sketch of the political background of recent divorce reforms in the westernized world suggests that Harry Krause is only partly right in calling the controversies surrounding divorce 'yesterday's "great debates"'.[223] The recent reforms in France (2016), Italy (2014–2015) and the reform currently underway in England and Wales show that the liberalization of divorce still remains a major policy challenge and continues to stand high on the political agenda.

Developments in divorce law over the last two centuries show a clear trend towards more liberal and permissive forms of divorce. All the westernized jurisdictions are following this same trend, but the pace and the profundity of the liberalization differs significantly between jurisdictions. For example, compare the Swedish immediate divorce on demand with the Maltese divorce which requires four years of separation before a divorce petition can be lodged. Considering this range of differences and the political sensitivities involved, it can be concluded that no common regime of marriage dissolution currently exists in westernized countries or is likely to be established in the foreseeable future. This same political sensitivity probably explains why the ALI Principles on Marriage Dissolution in the US and their less distinguished European

219 Parliamentary Proceedings. *Senaat* 15 July 1998, 1–109 (Senator Raes).

220 I. Curry-Sumner and S. Curry-Sumner, 'Is the Union Civil? Same-Sex Marriages, Civil Unions, Domestic Partnerships and Reciprocal Benefits in the USA', *Utrecht Law Review* 4, 2008, 249–55. Available at www.utrechtlawreview.org/index.php/ulr/article/view/77/0.

221 Code Civil, arts 515–7 (3 and 4) l. J.-J. Lemouland, 'Pacte civil de solidarité (PACS). Formation et la dissolution de Pacte Civil de Solidarité', *JCP La Semaine Juridique, Edition Notariale et Immobilière* 9, 2000, 409.

222 For a recent overview, see I. Curry-Sumner, 'A Patchwork of Partnerships: Comparative Overview of Registrations Schemes in Europe', in K. Boele-Woelki and A. Fuchs (eds), *Legal Recognition of Same-Sex Relationships in Europe: National, Cross-Border and European Perspective*, Antwerp: Intersentia, 2012, pp. 71, 49, 87.

223 Krause, op. cit., n 3, p. 1113.

counterpart, the CEFL[224] Principles of European Family Law Regarding Divorce,[225] have had less profound practical influence that it might have been expected.[226]

The whole picture is constantly in motion and divorce law in the westernized world is far from being settled. Current reform underway in England and Wales shows that grounds of divorce still have an important symbolic meaning and their modification keeps involving controversy. In the recent years two major reforms, e.g. in France and Italy, took place without much preparation and ideological debate, under the disguise of the pragmatic argument of diminishing the caseload of the judiciary. In others liberalization has occurred indirectly by way of some 'hypocritical' compromise which meant any relaxation of law affected only the way the law worked in action, while the rigid law in the books was left untouched. In still other jurisdictions, like in Poland, liberalization of any kind has not occurred yet.

Although divorce laws are currently evolving in the same direction and in a framework of a rather similar process, it would be a fallacy to suggest that there is some kind of teleological model with, as its final point, the ultimate liberalization of divorce that all jurisdictions would sooner or later achieve.[227] The de-institutionalization of marriage is an open-ended process and one whose future development we cannot possibly know. The only reasonable prediction is that reforming divorce law is likely to remain a policy challenge well into the future.

224 The Commission on European Family Law is an academic initiative established in 2001 to elaborate *The Principles of European Family Law*, which could provide a model for the voluntary bottom-up harmonisation of family law in Europe. See http://ceflonline.net/.

225 K. Boele-Woelki et al., *Principles of European Family Law Regarding Divorce and Maintenance between Former Spouses*, Antwerp: Intersentia, 2004.

226 So far, the CEFL Principles have directly influenced 2008 divorce reform in Portugal (G. de Oliveira, 'Recent Developments in Portuguese Family Law', *Famrz* 15, 2009, 1559–61) and in Czech Republic (Z. Králíčková, 'New Family Law in the Czech Republic: Back to Traditions and towards Modern Trends', in B. Atkin (ed.), *He International Survey of Family Law*, Bristol: Jordan Publishing, 2014, pp. 80–2.

227 See M. Antokolskaia, 'Convergence and Divergence of Divorce Laws in Europe', *Child and Family Law Quarterly* 18, 2006, 307.

2.2
DIVORCE TRENDS AND PATTERNS
An overview

Tony Fahey

Introduction

The main aim of this chapter is to provide a general overview of trends and patterns in divorce in the developed world, focusing especially on the interaction between legal and behavioural aspects of union dissolution. The chapter also recognizes, however, that the advent of new forms and routes of entry to sexual coupledom represented by the growth of cohabitation and same-sex partnerships has changed the context in which marriage and divorce occur and has altered their social significance. When marriage was the standard method of union formation, divorce could and for a time did become the standard method of exit, though as we will see in this chapter its dominance in that regard was often incomplete. However, as routes of entry expanded and forms of union became more diverse, routes of exit also diversified and reduced the centrality of divorce. These processes are often linked to ideas about the 'de-institutionalization of marriage'[1] but at the same time, not all trends point unambiguously in the same de-institutionalizing direction. The idea of same-sex marriage, for example, scarcely existed anywhere in the world at the end of the twentieth century but as the twenty-first century dawned, that idea took large parts of the globe by storm. By late 2019, 30 countries around the world recognized same-sex marriage.[2] The pace of this change has astonished many observers,[3] but it is also notable that the liberal *avant garde* who led it should have held the institution of marriage in such high regard as to clamour for a place within it for same-sex couples. The expansion of the boundaries of marriage in this way could thus be thought of either as an affirmation of its continuing significance and a counter to de-institutionalisation or – the opposite – as yet another sign of the growing porosity and loosening boundaries of marriage that confirmed its institutional decline.

In any event, the advent of same-sex marriage has been followed by the advent of same-sex divorce. It has thereby added to the field we are mainly concerned with here, though same-sex

1 H. Willekens, 'Is Contemporary Family Law Historically Unique?', *Journal of Family History* 28(1), 2003, 70–107.

2 Pew Research Center, 'Same Sex Marriage around the World', *Fact Sheet*, 28 October 2019.

3 N.G. Bennett, 'A Reflection on the Changing Dynamics of Union Formation and Dissolution', *Demographic Research* 36, 2017, art. 12, 371–90.

divorce is still too recent and small in extent to have developed stable patterns.[4] On top of that is the step-change in diversity of couple arrangements that has accompanied the advent of same-sex unions: there are now three types of gender-union rather than one (male-male and female-female in addition to male-female) and two broad institutional categories of union (cohabitation and marriage, not to speak of possible sub-categories of cohabitation). Divorce is no longer adequate as a catch-all label for exits from these many types of union, and one question that arises for us here is exactly what its continuing role in this new era of union diversity might be.

The account of these issues presented in this chapter is written from a sociological rather than a legal perspective. Its purpose is to give background and context for other chapters in this book rather than directly to address the legal regulation of couple breakup. It first provides a brief outline of trends in divorce rates in industrialized countries over the past half-century, highlighting both the overall upward shift which occurred and the varied timing, pace and extent of that shift between countries. That is followed by some reflections on the interpretation of these trends, focusing on features of the data that raise questions about what they really tell us. The chapter then turns to the growth of cohabitation and its implications for the status of marriage and divorce and the challenges it poses for legal regulation. A final section concludes.

Trends in divorce

The liberalization (to a greater or lesser extent) of divorce and a surge in divorce rates are now widely pointed to as more or less universal developments in the industrialized world in the final third of the twentieth century. While this perception, with many qualifications, is generally valid, countries differed in how soon, how fast and how far their divorce rates rose. The extent of variation is evident from looking at crude divorce rates (divorces per 1,000 population) across countries from the 1960s to the present in the industrialized world (Figures 2.2.1a–2.2.1d). Much of Northern and Central Europe, the Baltic region and the non-European Anglophone states most closely conform to the general shape of what we now often think of as the standard evolution: divorce rates were low until the mid-1960s but then, over a period of one to two decades, they increased two- to threefold. That was followed by a period of two to three decades to the present when they either fluctuated around an overall flat trend or showed some signs of decline.

Although the general shape of the divorce curve is common to many countries, its amplitude differs across countries. Latvia (in Figure 2.2.1c) and the United States (in Figure 2.2.1d) make an unexpected pairing in this regard in that their upsurge in divorce started early (that is, in the mid to late 1960s), quickly reached great heights (they both peaked in the early to mid-1980s at above five divorces per 1,000 population) but then subsided over a long period up to the present (though see following on questions about the validity of this picture for the United States). Estonia and Russia are the only two other countries of those included in Figure 2.2.1 which have had divorce rates above four per 1,000 population for sustained periods.[5] Lithuania briefly joined the club of high-divorce societies with a rate above 3.5 per 1,000 population for a time in the 1990s. Otherwise, around the industrialised world, the divorce surge was more muted, with most countries in Figure 2.2.1 consistently remaining below the threshold of three divorces per 1,000 population.

4 See, for example, E. Ketcham and N.G. Bennett, 'Comparative Couple Stability: Same-Sex and Male-Female Unions in the United States', *Socius: Sociological Research for a Dynamic World* 5, 2019, 1–15.

5 A. Adveev and A. Monnier, 'Marriage in Russia: A Complex Phenomenon Poorly Understood', *Population: An English Selection* 12, 2000, 7–50.

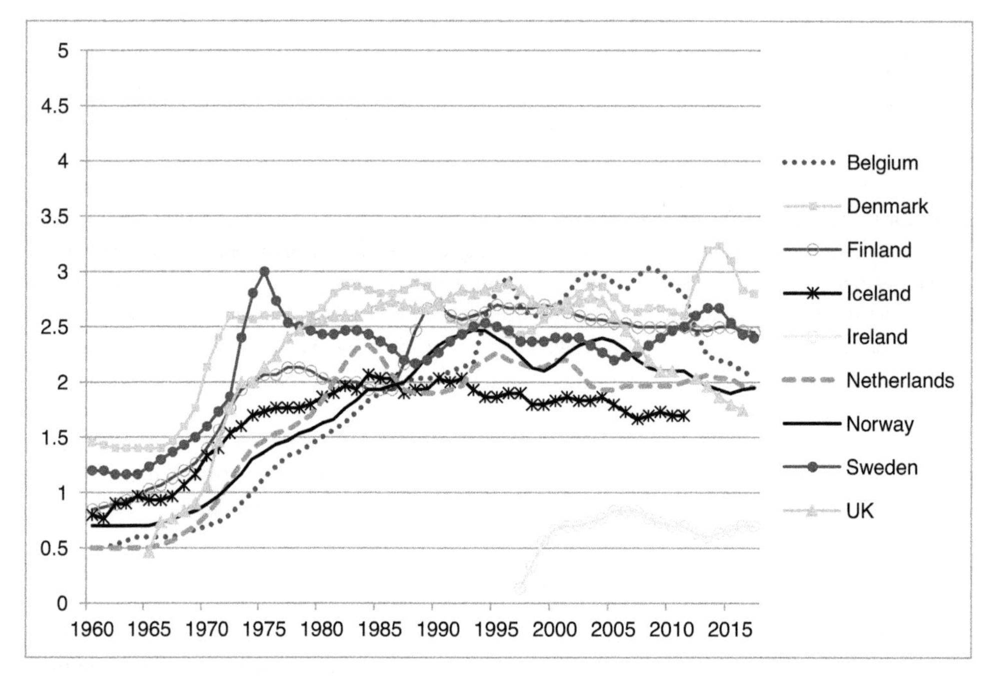

2.2.1a Northern Europe

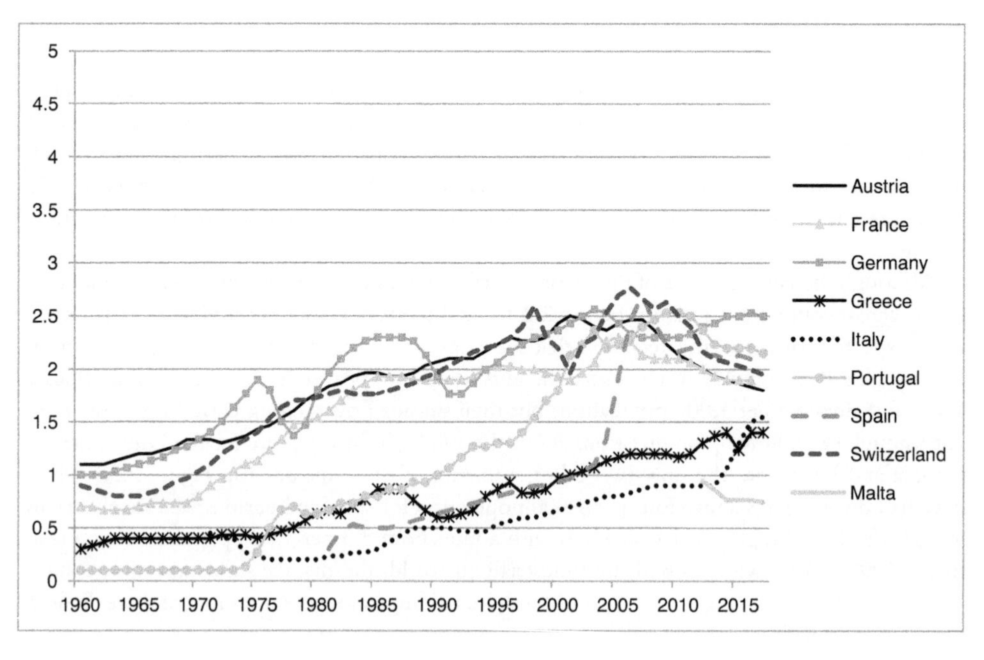

2.2.1b Central and southern Europe

Figure 2.2.1 Crude divorce rates in industrialized countries, 1960–2017 (three-year moving averages)

Sources: European countries – Eurostat database Divorce indicators [demo_ndivind]. Other countries: OECD Family Database.

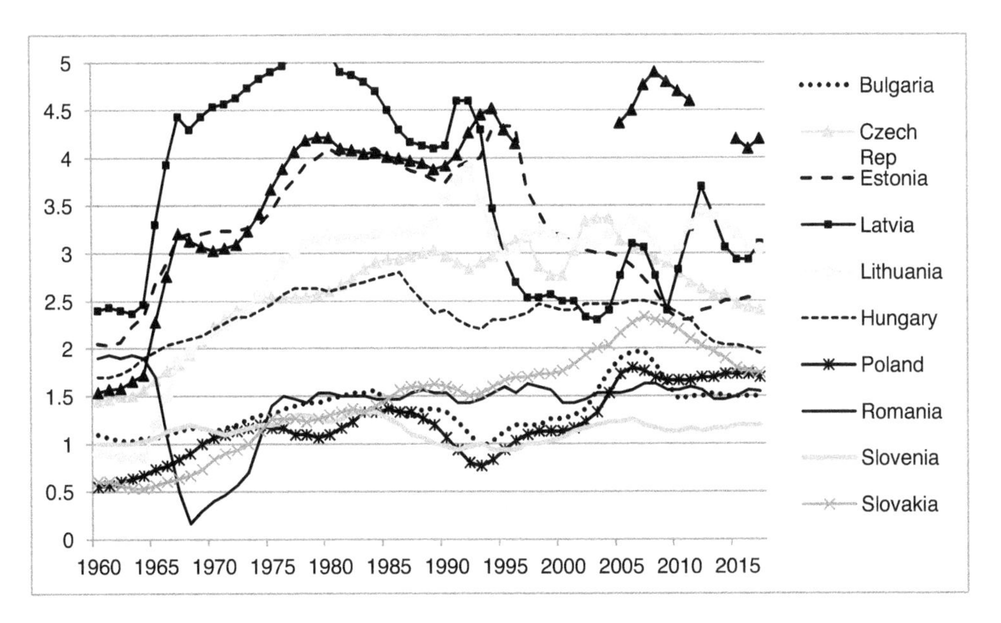

2.2.1c Eastern Europe

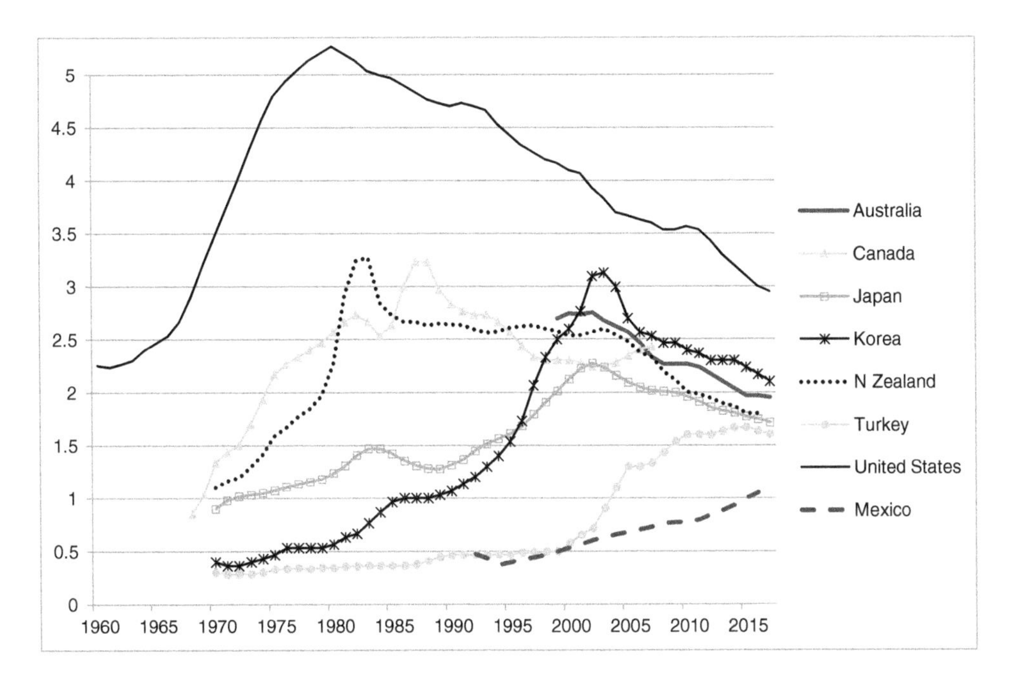

2.2.1d Other industrialised countries

Figure 2.2.1 (Continued)

Denmark is an example where the upswing in divorce was reasonably early and rapid but plateaued from the 1970s onwards at a level below three divorces per 1,000 population. It thus never rose very high nor experienced any period of sustained decline. Belgium, on the other hand, rose more slowly but, following an easing of divorce law in 1995,[6] experienced a surge after that point and matched Danish levels for the first decade of the present century. It has since fallen back to the level of the pre-1995 liberalization. Ireland is a clear outlier in Northern Europe: it had no provision for divorce until 1997 but even after divorce was introduced take-up was limited and by the early 2000s the divorce rate flattened out at an exceptionally low level (below 0.8 per 1,000). Part of the explanation for the unusual Irish trend is the late and restrictive nature of the divorce law that was introduced and the effect that had in diverting Irish couples into other exit routes from marriage (see further Chapter 2.1 in this book). This is an issue I will return to later when considering how the data on divorce trends should be interpreted.

The southern European region of Portugal, Spain, Italy, Malta and Greece was somewhat slow to introduce divorce and initially went for more restrictive legislation. This meant that for a time this region seemed to be set on a trajectory of low divorce (well below one per 1,000) that set it off from countries further north. In Portugal, however, legislation to allow divorce by consent with only limited restrictions was introduced in 1975. This was followed by a long steady climb in divorce rates which by the early 2000s brought Portugal into the same range as central and northern Europe. Divorce laws adopted in Italy in 1970 and Spain in 1981 were less liberal in that they required a period of legal separation (usually two to three years) prior to divorce.[7] The result was a two-step process of exit from marriage where many of those taking the first step into legal separation were deterred from taking the second step into divorce by the cost and slowness of the procedures involved and possibly also by the limited interest in the right to remarry which is the main focus of the second step. The picture changed suddenly in Spain in 2005 when the new socialist government introduced a one-step 'express' divorce law.[8] The incidence of divorce leaped in response, going from 52,000 divorces in 2004 to 141,000 in 2007, with the numbers settling back to around 100,000 per year by the end of the decade. The divorce law introduced in Malta in 2011 echoed the provisions of the Irish divorce legislation of 1997 in that it required a four-year period of separation before divorce could be granted.[9] Like Ireland, its divorce rate has remained extremely low even by the moderate standards common in Europe but here too, as in Ireland, other exit routes from marriage have to be considered to get a full picture of the level of marital disruption.

Moving directly eastwards from these southern European states, we find a further large belt of relatively low divorce in some southerly ex-communist states, particularly Bulgaria, Romania and Slovenia, as well as the more northerly Poland. Waves of high divorce along the lines of Latvia referred to earlier may have come and gone elsewhere in Eastern Europe in the early years of communist rule but, as William Goode long ago pointed out, the true picture is obscured by the poor data and ideological rhetoric of that era.[10] The low level of divorce in Turkey until 2000

6 T. Vanhove and K. Matthijs, *The Socio-Demographic Evolution of Divorce and Remarriage in Belgium*, Working Paper, Centre of Population and Family Research, Department of Sociology, University of Leuwen, 2002.

7 G.E. Glos, 'The Spanish Divorce Law 1981', *The International and Comparative Law Quarterly* 32, 1983, 667–88.

8 F. Bernardi and J.-I. Martínez-Pastor, 'Divorce Risk Factors and Their Variation over Time in Spain', *Demographic Research,* 2001, 24, art. 31, 771–800.

9 R. Pace, 'Growing Secularisation in a Catholic Society: The Divorce Referendum of 28 May 2011 in Malta', *South European Society and Politics* 17:4, 2012, 573–89.

10 W.J. Goode, *World Changes in Divorce Patterns,* New Haven and London: Yale University Press, 1993, pp. 110–35.

and its upward movement since then reflect the tension between modernizers and traditionalists that still feature in Turkish politics and social debate, not least in regard to family life.[11]

The crude divorce rates just looked at are the most widely used measure of the instability of marriage but they have the limitation that they express divorce rates with reference to the entire population, including children and single adults, rather than concentrating on the population at risk, namely the currently married. When we use a better-focused measure that quantifies divorce per 1,000 married people (which is possible only for countries where up-to-date data on the marital status of the population are available), the picture of cross-national differences in divorce rates alters but not dramatically. This is shown in Figure 2.2.2 which presents the two indicators side by side for 34 counties in or around 2017. The similarity of the patterns revealed by these two indicators is indicated by the strong statistical correlation between them (with a Pearson correlation coefficient of 0.93). But there some differences, especially for the Nordic countries where non-marital cohabitation is distinctively high and the population of married people is correspondingly small. The divorce rate calculated per 1,000 married people in these countries is higher than what is suggested by the crude divorce rate. This is so, for example, for Sweden, where the divorce rate measured on a population-wide basis is considerably below that of the United States but rises above the US rate when it is measured per 1,000 married people.

Interpreting the data

Some general features of the data reviewed in the previous section complicate their meaning and make it difficult to decipher their real import. Technical measurement issues constitute one general source of difficulty. Underreporting of divorce has been identified as a feature of official data in the United States and is a concern especially because it seems to have increased over recent decades, thus distorting the picture of trends over time.[12] It is unknown whether similar problems of underreporting occur in other countries. A more general issue arises from the effect of the shifting age-composition of the population which may cause divorce rates to rise or fall because of the changing size of the age-groups most prone to divorce rather than because of changed behaviour across age-groups. Age-standardization is the technical solution to this problem but is rarely applied to divorce data, in part because in many cases sufficient detail on the age-structure of population at risk of divorce – the currently married – is not available. In any event, the impact of shifting age-composition may mean that real behavioural change in the recourse to divorce might differ from what is suggested by recorded divorce data.

The combined effect of undercounts of divorce and age-effects on divorce rates is uncertain but has been shown to be large at least in the significant case represented by the United States. A study by Sheela Kennedy and Steven Ruggles found that, once these features were corrected for, the divorce rate in the US rose rather than fell from 1990 to 2008 and is now at an all-time high rather than a new low.[13] This is quite different picture from that of steady decline in the divorce over this period suggested in Figure 2.2.1. It also calls into question the substantial American

11 G. Therborn, *Between Sex and Power: Family in the World, 1900–2000*, Abingdon: Routledge, 2004, pp. 87–9.

12 S. Kennedy and S. Ruggles, 'Breaking Up Is Hard to Count: The Rise of Divorce in the United States, 1980–2010', *Demography* 51, 2014, 587–98. See also R. Stepler, 'Led by Baby Boomers, Divorce Rates Climb for America's 50+ Population', *Pew Research Center FactTank News in Numbers*, 9 March 2017.

13 Kennedy and Ruggles, ibid.

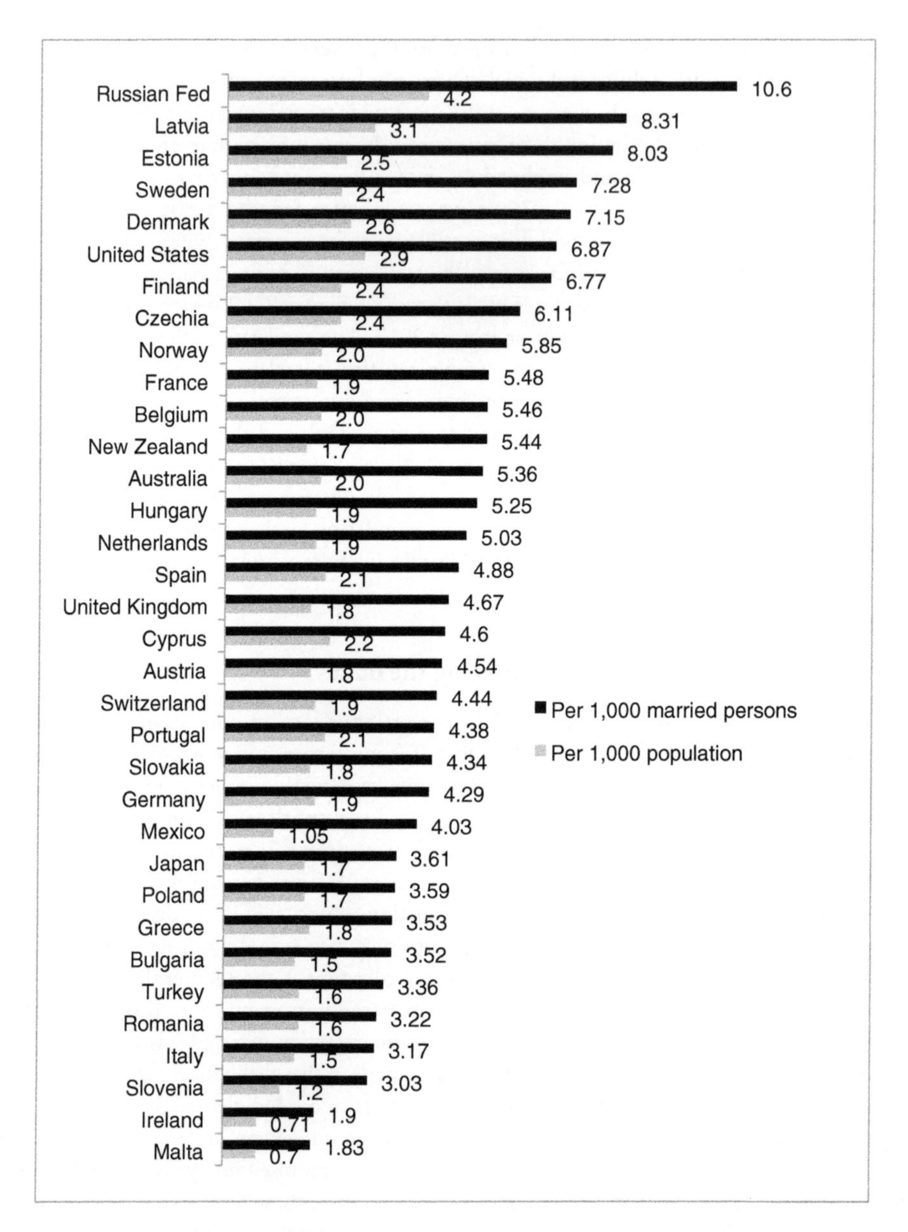

Figure 2.2.2 Two measures of divorce in 34 countries in 2017 or nearest available year.

Note: Data are for 2017 except: Australia, Ireland and Mexico (2016); New Zealand (2013).

Sources: Crude divorce rates – as Figure 2.2.1. Divorce rates per 1,000 married population – author's calculations using marital status data from Eurostat Database, UN World Marriage Report 2017 and Statista. Data for the United States exclude five states not reporting divorce data, amounting to 16 percent of the married population.

literature that has grown up around attempts to explain a decline in marital disruption that may not have actually occurred.[14]

Aside from methodological problems in measuring the incidence of divorce, a more fundamental issue is that divorce rates, evenly if perfectly measured, are only a partial indicator of the extent of marital dissolution and are easily misinterpreted if their limitations in that regard are overlooked. Other exit routes from marriage exist, some covered in official data but many not, and these have to be taken into account to get a full picture. In some jurisdictions, legal separation is available as a distinct type of formal exit from marriage. This is especially so in jurisdictions with a Catholic heritage, given the long-standing distinction drawn in Catholic moral teaching between legal separation, which does not allow remarriage, and divorce, which does. In those countries, legal separation and divorce viewed together give a better picture of marital disruption than divorce on its own. In Spain, for example, with the separation-followed-by-divorce process introduced in 1981 mentioned previously, separations typically outnumbered divorces by about 50 percent each year and showed a slowly rising trend over time. When the one-step 'express divorce' law was introduced in 2005, that dualism ended. Divorce quickly took over as the dominant exit route from marriage and legal separations largely dropped out of the picture.[15] Thus the divorce surge for Spain reported for the period around 2005 in Figure 2.2.1 is to a great extent an artefact of the displacement of legal separation by divorce as an exit route from marriage. The real underlying trend in marital disruption is best measured by the rate of legal separation up to 2005 and by the divorce rate plus a small incidence of legal separation thereafter.

It is likely that the same holds for Italy, where the divorce law of 1970 created a two-step process of legal exit from marriage similar to that of Spain and yielded a similar numerical dominance of legal separation over divorce. Through the 1990s and early 2000s, annual legal separations in Italy exceeded annual divorces by 80–95 percent, an even wider margin than in Spain, though by 2009 the excess had narrowed to 53 percent.[16] Taking account of a possible element of *de facto* separation on top of legal separation and some 'divorce tourism',[17] it is probably safe to say that the rate of marital breakdown in Italy had long been close to double the divorce rate, which would leave it around 2010 with a marital breakdown rate close to two per 1,000 population per year rather than circa one per 1,000 as shown in Figure 2.2.1b. The sharp uptick in measured divorce shown for Italy in Figure 2.2.1b coincided with a reform in 2015 which speeded up the divorce process,[18] but the divorce rate still may have some way to go before it catches up with the rate of marital disruption.

Ireland and Malta are further instances of the same pattern but the Irish case differs somewhat in that the distinction between legal separation and divorce does not capture either the full diversity in the legal provisions relating to marital breakdown nor the main divide that

14 See, for example, T.B. Heaton, 'Factors Contributing to the Increase in Marital Instability in the United States', *Journal of Family Issues* 23(3), 2002, 392–409; B. Stevenson and J. Wolfers, 'Marriage and Divorce: Changes and Their Driving Forces', *Journal of Economic Perspectives* 21(2), 2007, 27–52.

15 There were 89,000 more divorces in Spain in 2006 than in 2004 but 68,000 fewer legal separations (Table 2 in Instituto Nacional de Estadística *Social Statistics*, 2011 edition). Thus, divorces rose more than separations fell but this may have been due to the clearing of the backlog of separations that had accumulated prior to the reform of the law in 2005 rather than to an underlying increase in marital breakdown.

16 ISTAT, *Separations and Divorces in Italy 2010*, typescript pdf, 2 July 2012.

17 According to a report in the *New York Times* (14 August, 2011), Romania's flexible residency requirements and simple divorce procedures had made it a favourite destination for Italian divorce tourism in this period.

18 *The Economist*, 'Divorce in Italy', 2 May 2015.

arises in the system. Legal separation and divorce overlap a great deal as legal procedures in Ireland (divorce simply adds the right to remarry to separation settlements) and both procedures lie within the jurisdiction of the mid-level courts where division of property can be dealt with. In addition, a range of piecemeal measures are available in the lower courts which do not have jurisdiction over property settlements but deal with a range of other aspects of the marriage-exit process (maintenance, guardianship of children, custody of and access to children and – what is remarkably common in Irish practice – barring orders in domestic violence cases which evict the offending partner, usually the man, from the family home).[19] Even before Ireland legalized divorce in 1997, it had developed a diverse range of these formal, semi-formal and informal exits from marriage and these continued to play a largely undiminished role after divorce arrived.

The less-than-complete role of divorce in regulating marriage exit is not confined to countries that highlight a legal distinction between separation and divorce. The United States is one such jurisdiction where the historical and continuing extent of other routes of exit is relatively well documented. For the decades prior to the liberalization of divorce law in the 1960s, census-based measures suggest that the incidence of marital dissolution in the US was high but was only partly captured in divorce data. Tomas Cvrcek reports, for example, that of marriages occurring in the early 1930s, of the order of 30 percent broke up within 20 years, with about half ending through divorce and the rest through informal separation or desertion.[20] Looking at married persons aged under 40, Steven Ruggles points to a rising incidence of marital disruption throughout the twentieth century coupled with a gradual shift in the mode of dissolution from informal separation to divorce.[21] He broadly echoes Cvrcek's conclusion that divorce data in the pre-liberalization era captured only around half of marital dissolutions. He further shows, first, that while an increase in divorce did occur in the 1960s and 1970s, it did not fully displace informal separation, and second, that these trends differed strongly by race, with a higher risk of both overall disruption and informal separation rather than divorce among blacks compared to whites. Today, as Neil Bennett reports, what he calls the 'state of permanent limbo' represented by separation still persists and is still racially differentiated: after ten years of separation, 5 percent of white separated couples in the United States have yet to divorce compared to 23 percent of black separated couples.[22]

Cohabitation

In the previous section, we have seen that even at times and in places when marriage held an institutional near-monopoly over sustained sexual coupledom, divorce did not quite have the same degree of monopoly as a route of exit. Various forms of legal and informal separation and desertion also widely occurred and, as cases as diverse as the United States, Ireland and Italy show, have persisted into the present. Undoubtedly, however, by the turn of the present century the major development in the social context of couple relationships was the widespread emergence and acceptance of cohabitation. This new category of co-residential sexual partnerships

19 The account of the Irish case here is based on T. Fahey, 'Small bang? The Impact of Divorce Legislation on Marital Breakdown in Ireland', *International Journal of Law, Policy and the Family* 26(2), 2012, 242–58.

20 T. Cvrcek, 'U.S. Marital Disruptions and Their Economic and Social Correlates, 1860–1948', *Journal of Family History* 36(2), 2011, 142–58.

21 S. Ruggles, 'The Rise of Divorce and Separation in the United States, 1880–1990', *Demography* 34(4), 1997, 455–66.

22 Bennett, op. cit., n 3, 376.

has evolved new conventions of entry and exit and new options for serial couple arrangements that by-pass conventional divorce. Demographers now routinely acknowledge this novel development by using new terms to refer to processes of entry into and exit from couple relationships: they speak of unions rather than marriages, of union dissolution rather than divorce and of re-partnering rather than re-marriage.[23]

Table 2.2.1 gives an indication of the place now occupied by cohabitation across 35 countries in or around the year 2011. Sweden is often pointed to as an historical pioneer in the social acceptance of cohabitation[24] and its continued standing as a leader in that regard is confirmed in Table 2.2.1, with Estonia as the only other country with a similar incidence of cohabitation. In both Sweden and Estonia, over 30 percent of all couples and over 60 percent of young-adult couples (those aged 20–34 years) are cohabiting. Most countries, however, are well below these levels: the average for the 28 OECD countries in Table 2.2.1 is 17 percent of all couples and 42 percent of young-adult couples in cohabitation rather than marriage. The United States is an example of a country where cohabitation has attracted much comment but its incidence is relatively low, with only 12 percent of all couples and 29 percent of young-adult couples in cohabitation. Another band of countries has lower levels still: Croatia, Greece, Malta and Poland are at or below 5 percent of couples in cohabitation. These proportions suggest that, for all its expansion of recent years, cohabitation is still far from being on a par with marriage in crude quantitative terms, even in those countries where it is most prevalent. Outside the young-adult population, then, marriage is still the dominant form of sexual partnership and that lends divorce a continued significance as a dominant route of exit.

One factor that keeps the count of cohabiting couples down is the transience of much cohabitation: high inflow is sufficiently counterbalanced by high outflow to keep the stock of people in cohabitation low at any given time.[25] However, cohabitation is quite diverse in that it spreads across a continuum of durability and stability, ranging from the fleeting to the long-lasting. It has been suggested, in fact, that insofar as there is a critical divide along the stability continuum, it lies not between cohabitation and marriage but between tentative cohabitation where people are trialling their relationship on the one hand versus, on the other hand, both marriage and longer term cohabitation.[26] In that context, the comparison reported in the third and fourth columns in Table 2.2.1 is notable. It suggests that where cohabiting couples do exist, that most family-like characteristic – the presence of children – is surprisingly common. On average across 28 OECD countries, 47 percent of cohabiting couples have children and that proportion is as high in cohabitation-averse Poland (50 percent) as it is in cohabitation-friendly Sweden (also 50 percent). In general also, according to the data in the table, cohabiting couples are as likely to have children as married couples, which would suggest that even when it is quantitatively in a secondary role to marriage, there is a large sub-category of cohabiting relationships that have marriage-like characteristics. However, differences in age-composition between the married and cohabiting populations would need to be taken into account before drawing too many conclusions from this similarity.

23 Bennett, ibid. See also A.J. Cherlin, 'Introduction to Special Collection on Separation, Divorce, Repartnering and Remarriage around the World', *Demographic Research* 37, 2017, art. 38, 1275–96.

24 J. Kok and D. Leinarte, 'Cohabitation in Europe: A Revenge of History?', *The History of the Family* 20, 2015, 489–514.

25 J. Dronkers, 'Cohabitation, Marriage and Union Instability in Europe', *Institute for Family Studies Release*, 7 April 2016.

26 See, e.g. E.A. Wiik, E. Bernhardt and T. Noack, 'A Study of Commitment and Relationship Quality in Sweden and Norway', *Journal of Marriage and the Family* 71, 2009, 465–77.

Table 2.2.1 Cohabitation in 35 countries in 2011

	Cohabiting couples as % of all couples		*% of couples with children in household*	
	20+ year olds	*20- to 34-year-olds*	*Married couples*	*Cohabiting couples*
Australia	16	38		
Austria	16	43	47	43
Belgium	14	35	47	47
Bulgaria	16	44	42	62
Canada	19	39	48	44
Croatia	5	12	53	42
Cyprus	7	22	55	24
Czech Republic	11	31	46	46
Denmark	22	57	45	42
Estonia	31	61	44	57
Finland			43	37
France	23	57	45	53
Germany	14	44	41	32
Greece	3	12	49	14
Hungary	18	44	47	53
Iceland	21	53	56	81
Ireland	15	43	60	41
Italy	9	24	49	50
Latvia	19	37	50	54
Lithuania	11	22	53	50
Luxembourg	9	25	55	51
Malta	4	12	54	41
Netherlands	21	54	47	40
New Zealand	24	51		
Norway	24	55	50	60
OECD-28 average	17	42	49	47
Poland	4	9	55	50
Portugal	13	36	48	54
Romania	7	14	50	48
Slovak Republic	8	19	56	57
Slovenia	14	40	47	75
Spain	14	41	52	43
Sweden	31	63	45	50
Switzerland	17	40	49	23
United Kingdom	20	50	44	43
United States	12	29	47	39

Source: OECD Family Database

Implications for legal regulation

For many years after the wave of liberalization in divorce law occurred in western countries in the final third of the twentieth century, social science research devoted much attention to the question whether divorce law itself was an influence on the behaviour it was trying to regulate. Did 'easy' divorce help cause the rise in divorce rates of that period or was the change in the law itself merely a consequence of wider forces that impelled both law and behaviour to move in the same direction? Studies of this question initially focused on comparisons of states within the United States, taking advantage of the different dates at which divorce was liberalized across states and the different trajectories of accompanying divorce rates. It then extended to comparisons of European states and included some single-country studies.[27] A tentative consensus emerged from this research to suggest that easier divorce law did tend to raise divorce rates but only by a modest amount and for a limited time.[28]

The new diversity in human coupling that has emerged in the present century has rendered this old set of questions largely redundant given that new currents of behaviour have burst the banks of existing convention and created new channels of entry into and exit from sexual partnerships. The regulatory impact of divorce is reduced if any blocking action it takes causes behaviour simply to flow around it and find new channels of movement. One consequence is that cohabitation may cause a reduction in divorce rates by shifting the site of partnership instability away from marriage towards informal unions. The mechanism most likely to produce this effect is a possible self-selection of couples with less secure or promising relationships away from marriage and towards cohabitation or unpartnered childbearing. One in-depth qualitative study in the United States, for example, suggests that poor American women who are keen to have children often opt for informal unions and unmarried motherhood, not because they have no regard for marriage, but because they view it as an ideal which is beyond their reach or which they could not hope to sustain even if they did manage to enter it in the first place.[29] Middle-class and professional women, by contrast, are more likely to delay motherhood until they complete their education, establish careers and find a partner who is likely to stay the course. The result is that higher status couples preserve much of the structure and stability of traditional marriage (though with more egalitarian gender roles) and are more successful in avoiding both divorce and unstable cohabitation. Lower status couples and their children are more likely to experience the disruption and insecurity that Sarah McLanahan has captured in the concept of the 'fragile family' and the 'diverging destinies' between children in poorer and better-off families.[30]

Class differences in these patterns are usually thought to be less extreme in Europe but nevertheless are widely found and typically incline in the same direction as in the United States. Cohabitation is more common lower down the social scale and those who commence their childbearing as cohabiting couples have on average poorer relationship quality and are more likely to split up than their married counterparts.[31] Here too, then, we have evidence of

27 Contributions to this literature include L. Friedberg, 'Did Unilateral Divorce Raise Divorce Rates? Evidence from Panel Data', *American Economic Review* 88, 1998, 608–27; J.M. Binner and A.W. Dnes, 'Marriage, Divorce, and Legal Change: New Evidence from England and Wales', *Economic Inquiry* 39(2), 2001, 298–306; J. Wolfers, 'Did Unilateral Divorce Laws Raise Divorce Rates? A Reconciliation and New Results', *American Economic Review* 96, 2006, 1802–20; T. Kneip and G. Bauer, 'Did Unilateral Divorce Laws Raise Divorce Rates in Western Europe?', *Journal of Marriage and the Family* 71, 2009, 592–607.

28 One overview concluded that easing of divorce law raised the divorce rate by about 10 percent for about ten years, an almost trivial impact in light of the doubling and trebling of divorce rates which were common in western countries during the era of reform. See D.W. Allen and M. Gallagher, 'Does Divorce Law Affect the Divorce Rate? A Review of Empirical Research', *iMAPP Research Brief* 1, 1995–2006. 1 July 2007. See also Wolfers, op. cit., n 27; Kneip and Bauer, op. cit., n 27.

29 K. Edin and M. Kefalas, *Promises I Can Keep: Why Poor Women Put Motherhood Before Marriage*, Berkeley: University of California Press, 2005, p. 9. See also C.M. Gibson-Davis, K. Edin and S. McLanahan, 'High Hopes But Even Higher Expectations: The Retreat from Marriage among Low-Income Couples', *Journal of Marriage and the Family* 67, 2005, 1301–12.

30 S. McLanahan, 'Diverging Destinies. How Children Are Faring under the Second Demographic Transition', *Demography* 41(4), 2004, 607–27; S. McLanahan and C. Percheski, 'Family Structure and the Reproduction of Inequalities', *Annual Review of Sociology* 34, 2008, 257–76; Stevenson and Wolfers, op. cit., n 14.

31 B. Perelli-Harris, W. Sigle-Rushton, M. Kreyenfeld, T. Lappegård, R. Keizer and C. Berghammer, 'The Educational Gradient of Childbearing within Cohabitation in Europe', *Population and Development*

divergence between the married and cohabiting route to family formation such that manifestations of instability tend to concentrate on the cohabiting side of the divide.

This is not to say that we can easily establish correlations between rising rates of cohabitation and falling rates of divorce, as might be expected if the former were to attract a growing share of the union instability that might otherwise attach to marriage. It may be the case that trialling relationships through periods of cohabitation in early adulthood may help reduce the incidence of divorce in later life. Yet there is no strong indication that differing levels of cohabitation can be linked to different rates of divorce across countries. As we have seen earlier, for example, Sweden has twice the incidence of cohabitation as the United States yet that does not protect it from having a divorce rate that, if anything, is somewhat higher than in the United States (see Figure 2.2.2).

Whatever its effect on marital stability, the growth of cohabitation as a family form has implications for family law in that it raises the question whether there should be state regulation of union dissolution extending beyond the break-up of marriage and encompassing exits from a wide range of non-marital unions. This in turn gives rise to challenges in defining when such unions make the transition from transient arrangements that have no legal significance to ongoing unions with family-like features. Having children is one transition that is often regarded as crucial in this respect, and indeed the regulatory challenges posed by children of informal unions are nothing new.[32] In particular, family law in western countries has long grappled with the question of whether and how the obligation to support non-marital children should be imposed on their fathers (see further Chapter 2.7 in this book).

Historically, that desire was constrained by a countervailing interest in protecting the institution of marriage, which required that non-marital children and their mothers by denied the same rights as married mothers and their children and even that they suffer social disgrace in order to avoid the moral hazard that might arise from equal treatment of extra-marital partnership and parenthood. Today, the core objective is to avoid discrimination between children based on the marital status of their parents and to avoid disadvantage for women because they are mothers, irrespective of the circumstances of their motherhood. Responding to that challenge not only requires a downgrade to the legal status of marriage but also a shift away from divorce as the centrepiece of the legal response to union instability. It could, in fact, be said to entail a reversion to the concerns which previously dominated the law on legal separation – namely, the issues of maintenance, access and custody of children, division of family property, inheritance and succession rights – with a lesser emphasis on the right of separated spouses to enter a new marriage, which is the distinctive focus of divorce.

This brings us to the second implication of this development, which has to do the role of social policy – the public provision of income supports and services for families – as the other major dimension of the state's response to union instability. Socializing the caring functions of the family through state provision of child and elder care and individualizing the welfare entitlements of adults irrespective of spousal or partnership relations have been powerful currents in western welfare states in recent decades, especially in Europe.[33] These currents have sought to

---

Review 36(4), 2010, 775–801; A.C. Liefbroer and E. Dourleijn, 'Unmarried Cohabitation and Union Stability: Testing the Role of Diffusion Using Data from 16 European Countries', *Demography* 43, 2006, 203–22.

32 R. Nygren, 'Interpreting Legitimacy', *Journal of Family History* 28(1), 2003, 149–60.

33 J. Lewis, 'Gender and the Development of Welfare Regimes', *Journal of European Social Policy* 2(3), 1992, 159–73; M. Daly, 'Changing Conceptions of Family and Gender Relations in European Welfare States and the Third Way', in J. Lewis and R. Surender (eds), *Welfare State Change towards a Third Way*, Oxford: Oxford University Press, 2004, pp. 135–54.

protect individuals from the insecurities of family life as well as of market forces. In the case of those in couple relationships, particularly those who have dependent children, it has sought to guarantee their basic living standards and access to necessary services even when their partners fail to deliver. States differ in how far they have gone in these directions and much comparative analysis now seeks to categorize state welfare systems according to how extensively they have either de-marketized or de-familized economic support systems for individuals and family units.[34] Legal scholars now recognize the regulatory aspects of such systems for family behaviour and accept in consequence that family law is now less distinct and separate as a regulatory system than it used to be but has to be viewed as a part of much larger welfare regimes[35] (see further Chapters 6.1–6.5 of this book). Here too, however, social class differences within states matter, since outside of the universalistic welfare states of the Nordic countries, social policy is a greater concern for those lower down the social scale than it is for the middle and upper classes, while conversely family law may continue to be the dominant regulatory framework for better-off couples.

Conclusion

The period immediately after the Second World War is sometimes called the 'golden age of marriage' in the western world – what Therborn calls the era of the 'western honeymoon' of the institution of marriage.[36] This was the era when the love-based union of working husband and stay-at-home wife became more widespread and more revered than ever before – more people married, they did so at younger ages, they were somewhat more likely than their parents to have children and to do so within marriage, and they were just as expectant as previous generations that only death would them part. Yet by the time those who rushed into youthful and hopeful marriage in the late 1940s and 1950s had reached middle age, the ideal of love for life was fraying at the edges, the cracks in the male breadwinner model of the family were beginning to appear, and the gender and sexual revolutions were on the horizon. The children born to couples of that era turned against much of the family model that had produced them as they entered adulthood in the 1960s and 1970s and instead espoused sexual liberation, the release of women from the home, much lower fertility and much less stability in couple relationships.

The rise in divorce of the latter period was a part of that development. The outline of that development presented in this chapter has indicated some of its variations across countries not only in regard to pace and timing but also in regard to what divorce meant and how it related to underlying trends in marital breakdown. In addition, it has suggested that the rise of divorce was itself surrounded by wider currents which in some ways reduced its significance. A parallel world of cohabitation arose alongside and partially overlapped with marriage. Because unions in that world were generally less stable than marriage, it gave rise to new levels and types of union instability. Divorce itself adapted and became more flexible as the flood of marriage failures mounted, even though the role of divorce became less central as cohabitation diverted less secure relationships into alternative arrangements. In any event, what often mattered more for families in this era was

34 See especially G. Esping-Andersen, *Social Foundations of Postindustrial Economies*, Oxford: Oxford University Press, 1999.

35 J. Eekelaar, 'The End of an Era', *Journal of Family History* 28(3), 2003, 108–22; K. Scheiwe, 'Caring and Paying for Children and Gender Inequalities: Institutional Configurations in Comparative Perspective', *Journal of Family History* 28(3), 2003, 182–98.

36 Therborn, op. cit., n 11, pp. 162–70; S. Coontz, *Marriage, a History: How Love Conquered Marriage*, London: Penguin, 2005, pp. 228–44.

not the rules of family formation and dissolution prescribed by family law but the rules of entitlement and obligation embedded in welfare provisions and the manner in which these facilitated new kinds of family behaviour. Part of the diversity in the practical meaning of family law across western countries arises from differences in how far and how fast their welfare regimes transformed the material bases of family life. Diversity also arises within countries since marital instability and new kinds of family formation are socially stratified, which means that the precise mix of family law and social provision that impinges on families differs as we move up and down the social scale.

2.3

DIVORCE PROCEDURE REFORM IN CHINA

Lei Shi

Introduction

The Marriage Law of China[1] Amendment 2001 (MLA 2001) added new provisions such as defining when spousal affection can be held no longer to exist, visitation rights of parents after divorce and compensation for contributions to homemaking,[2] thus responding to people's expectations in the new century. However, rapid social and economic development has brought significant changes in attitudes to marriage and families and the crude divorce rate is rising steadily. (For further discussion of divorce trends, see Chapter 2.2 of this book.) In 2016 China decided to compile a civil code. The legislature planned first to draft the General Rules of the Civil Law and then those of particular areas of civil law. The General Rules took effect on 1 October 2017. The final Civil Code is expected to pass in 2020. This chapter presents the divorce system in China, the proposed reform in the Civil Code draft and the other progress of reform in family justice.

Divorce statistics

The crude divorce rate in China has risen since 2003. In 2003 1,331,000 couples divorced, 154,000 more than in 2002. Of these, 691,000 registered their divorces, up by 118,000 from 2002; 640,000 obtained their divorce orders from courts, 36,000 more than in the previous year. The crude divorce rate rose from 1.05‰ in 2003 to 3.2‰ in 2017, when 4,374,000 couples divorced, of whom 3,704,000 registered the divorce and 669,000 obtained the divorce in the people's court. (See Figure 2.3.1.)

China's divorce system

Under the MLA 2001, couples can divorce by registration or litigation.

1 For the purposes of the research referred to in this chapter, 'China' refers to the Mainland of China, not including Hong Kong, Macao, and Taiwan.

2 See W. Chen (ed.), *Marriage, Family and Succession Law (hunyin jiating jicheng faxue)*, Beijing: Mass Press (qunzhong chubanshe), 2012, p. 27.

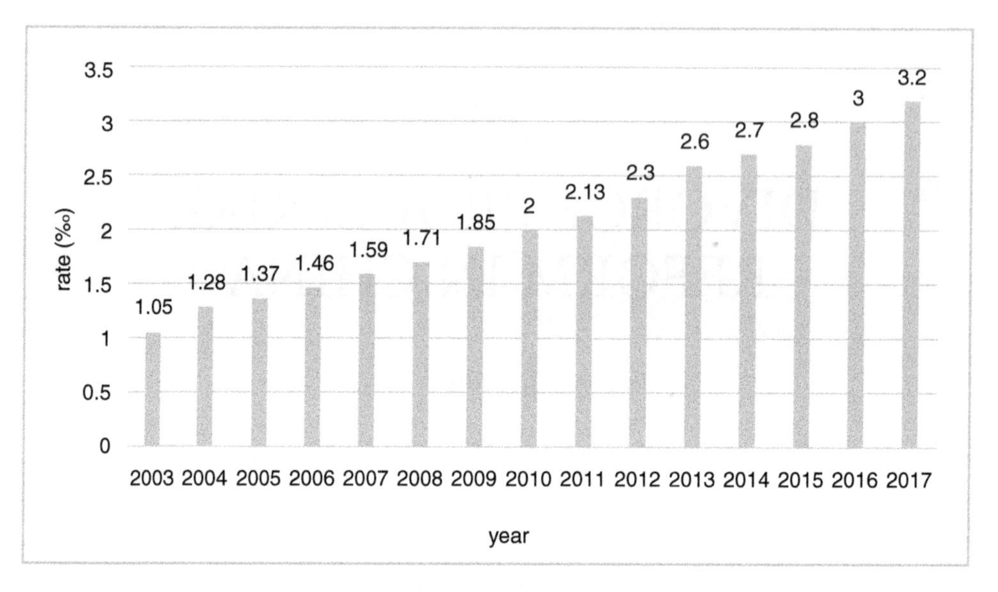

Figure 2.3.1 China's crude divorce rate, 2003–2017

Divorce registration

The traditional divorce registration system was simplified by the Marriage Registration Regulations 2013 (MRR 2013). By this procedure, the couple jointly file an application for divorce in a registration office. The registrar examines the application and registers the divorce if it complies with the MLA 2001 and the MRR 2013.

The following are the requirements to obtain a divorce certificate:

1 The parties must be validly married. Cohabitants' applications will be rejected.
2 Applicants must be fully capable and file the application themselves. Both must be present before the registrar when applying. Persons lacking competence or with limited competence cannot register their divorces.
3 The parties must have agreed to divorce voluntarily without any fraud or coercion.
4 The parties must have reached a written post-divorce agreement including child support, property and obligations. The child support agreement covers with whom the children should live after divorce and visitation issues, and whether the non-residential party pays child support, and if so, how much and in what way. Both should agree on the division of joint property and repayment of obligations. If a spouse will be in financial difficulty after divorce, the other with the ability to pay should provide some financial assistance, so the divorce agreement should specify the amount of this money, the period of financial assistance, and method of payment.

The marriage registration office will reject applications without a written agreement, where a party has no or limited juristic competence, and if the marriage is not registered in China's Mainland or an embassy of China.[3]

3 See art. 12 in the Marriage Registration Regulations. People married in the Embassy of the PRC in a foreign country can get a registered divorce there.

Applicants should submit certain materials to the marriage registration office in a civil affairs branch in the county-level government or an administration in a village or a town.[4] The materials include one's family book, identity card, marriage certificate and a divorce agreement written in triplicate.[5] Four stages of the procedure follow:[6]

First examination: a registrar will examine the application to confirm whether they have jurisdiction,[7] whether the required materials are all submitted, whether there are any counterfeit certificates and whether the divorce agreement is complete.

1 Acceptance: for those qualified, the office will issue declaration forms which the parties must complete and sign in the presence of the registrar.
2 Examination: the registrar will inquire about each item in the divorce agreement to check whether both agree freely.
3 Registration: after informing both parties of the divorce consequences including child support duties and visitation rights, the registrar will let them sign the examination form and then issue divorce certificates.

For failed applications, the registrar will issue a rejection notice if requested.[8] Applicants may resort to the higher-level office for review. It is impossible for an ex-spouse to obtain revocation or nullification of a registration. However, with regard to a property division clause in the divorce agreement, art. 9 in the Interpretations of the Supreme People's Court on Several Problems Concerning the Application of the 'Marriage Law of the PRC' (II) stipulates that if there is any fraud or coercion, the applicant can petition for modification or cancellation of the agreement regarding partitioning of property within one year after both registered their divorce.

Divorce by litigation

Divorce by litigation refers to cases where one spouse seeks divorce or both agree to divorce but cannot agree on post-divorce arrangements. In this way, the applicant petitions in a court where a judge hears the case in accordance with the legal procedures.

The law also sets the statutory requirements for this divorce.

The parties must be validly married. They either have a marriage certificate or comply with the requirements of a de facto marriage, that is, legally cohabiting without registration before 1 February 1994 when the Regulations on the Administration of Marriage Registration took effect.[9]

1 The claim should be filed by a spouse, although, in accordance with art. 8 in the Interpretations of the Supreme People's Court on Several Problems Concerning the Application of the 'Marriage Law of the PRC' (III), in exceptional situations, a guardian may petition

4 See art. 2 in the Marriage Registration Regulations.
5 See art. 11 in the Marriage Registration Regulations.
6 See regulations in Chapter 6 of the Interim Regulations on Marriage Registration (hunyin dengji gongzuo zanxing guifan) promulgated by the Ministry of Civil Affairs on 1 October 2003.
7 Both parties should go to the office in the district where one spouse has registered residence.
8 Art. 61 in the Regulations of Marriage and Divorce Registration 2016.
9 This means that the cohabitants meet the marriageable requirements. See art. 5 in the Interpretations of the Supreme People's Court on Several Problems Concerning the Application of the 'Marriage Law of the PRC' (I).

for divorce as an agent for a person without juristic competence in order to safeguard this person's interests.

2 The court has jurisdiction. The Civil Procedure Law of PRC (amended in 2012) provides that the petitioner should file in the court within a jurisdiction where the respondent is domiciled. If the respondent's domicile is different from his habitual residence, the case should be heard by the court within a jurisdiction where the respondent's habitual residence is.

There are three stages to the process:

1 Filing and acceptance: the petitioner should file a divorce petition in duplicate to the court.[10] The court will send the duplicate to the respondent requiring a written defence statement within 15 days. The respondent's failure to do so would not stop the court from hearing the case.
2 Mediation: art. 145 of the Opinions of the Supreme People's Court on Some Issues Concerning the Application of the Civil Procedure Law of the PRC 2015 prescribes that the court shall conduct mediation when hearing divorce cases, but must reach a decision. Therefore judicial mediation in the hearing, also called in-court mediation, is a requirement in divorce cases.[11] The presiding judge will conduct the mediation. If necessary, the relevant work units of both parties or the people's mediation committee[12] will be invited to participate. The court's mediation decision is legally binding. After mediation, the following three possibilities arise: (1) The parties may be reconciled. The judge will record this and the parties and other litigants will sign it. The hearing is over.[13] (2) The parties may agree to divorce and reach an agreement over child support and property. Then the court will give a decision of mediated divorce. Once both sign their names after receiving the decision, it will be effective.[14] (3) Mediation fails. The judge will then make an order after hearing the case.
3 Hearing and decision: divorce shall be granted if mediation fails and the parties' mutual affection no longer exists. A party has the right to file an appeal against the decision to the court at the next higher level within 15 days from the date of service of the judgment. The decision of the appellate court is final.[15]

10 Illiterate petitioners may file an oral petition. The People's Court will write it down and inform the respondent.
11 Attention should be given to mediation outside of courts. Art. 32 section 1 in the Marriage Law stipulates that, if one party alone desires a divorce, the organization concerned may carry out mediation or the party may file a petition in a People's Court. 'Mediation' here, i.e. mediation outside of courts, refers to mediation conducted before filing a divorce petition in a court. It is also called mediation where it occurs in hearings before the working units where the parties work or conducted by the villages committee or residence committee for those without work. But this is not a necessary procedure for courts hearing divorce cases.
12 People's mediation committees are public organizations established according to relevant laws with a view to providing mediation for disputes.
13 These cases will be dismissed if the plaintiff files a petition again within 6 months after the first hearing without any new evidence and new grounds. But if the respondent files a divorce petition, the restriction is not applied.
14 A mediated divorce decision has the same effect as a divorce order and divorce certificate issued by the marriage registration office.
15 Art. 202 in the Civil Procedure Law (amended 2012) specifies that a party shall not file a petition for retrial against an effective judgment or mediation decision which dissolves a marital relationship. If both are willing to resume their spousal relation, they may register again in relevant offices.

There are two exceptions. Art. 33 in the MLA 2001 stipulates that a soldier's spouse must obtain his or her consent before divorce petition unless the soldier has committed grave wrongs. Art. 34 requires that a husband cannot petition for a divorce when his wife is pregnant, or within one year after the birth of the child, or within six months after the termination of her gestation. This restriction does not apply where the wife herself petitions for divorce, or where the court deems it necessary to accept the divorce petition from the husband.

Policy challenges confronting China's divorce system

Problems with divorce registration

The MRR 2003 changed the divorce registration requirements. The previous requirements to submit introduction letters from one's work unit, the village committee or the residence committee and an examination period lasting one-month were abolished.[16] Introduction letters had been required as proof that the couple were married, and were known in the unit, which could even have effective power to sanction their divorce.[17] This infringes the parties' privacy. On the other hand, in some rural or less-developed areas the examination period had been used to delay the divorce registration. Therefore, the MRR 2003 repealed the old provisions to promote private autonomy and safeguard privacy and divorce freedom.[18]

Registered divorces are steadily increasing (see Figure 2.3.2) and becoming dominant. The percentage of registered divorces per year has been going up, reaching 84.7 percent in 2017. However, this divorce model is facing challenges.

Lightning divorce[19] and remarriage to ex-spouse

The new policies have had a great impact on the traditional views of marriage, i.e. lifelong fidelity.[20] Now, 'lightning' marriage and divorce are not rare.[21] Some of the divorced regret their decision and want to have their spouse back. According to the Chongqing Civil Affairs Bureau, a quarter of couples divorcing in 2010 had been married under a year.[22] On the other hand, statistics in 2017 from the National Statistics Bureau indicate that 398,500 couples remarried, more than eight times compared with the Figure 20 years ago. In Hangzhou in 2017

16 The present divorce registration procedure can be completed in a day.

17 C. Wu and Y. Xia, 'The Evolution of China's Marriage Legislation During the 30 Years after the Opening and Reform Policy (gaige kaifang sanshi nian zhongguo hunyin lifa zhi shanbian)', in W. Chen (ed.), *Review and Prospect: On Marriage, Family and Succession Law during the 30 Years after the Opening and Reform Policy (gaige kaifang sanshi nian hunyin jiating jicheng fa yanjiu zhi huigu yu zhanwang)*, Beijing: China University of Political Science and Law Press (zhongguo zhengfa daxue chubanshe), 2010, pp. 3–15.

18 Y. Xia, 'Comments and Rethinking: China's Divorce Registration System (dui zhongguo dengji lihun zhidu de pingjia yu fansi)', *Law Science Magazine (faxue zazhi)* 2, 2008, 13–17.

19 This refers to a divorce after a short marriage lasting just a few days.

20 See K. Wang, 'Love: Free, Puzzled and Returning', *Beijing Times*, 16 December 2008, 17.

21 People born after 1990 have been instituting more 'lightning' divorces than those born after 1980 and before 1990. See Y. Ji, 'Young Couple Divorced after 5 Days of Marriage Just Because of 100,000 Gifts for Their Marriage', *Today Morning Express*, 20 October 2012, 3.

22 K. Tao, '293,000 Couples Married, 105,000 Couples Divorced Last Year', *Chongqing Times*, 10 January 2013, 8.

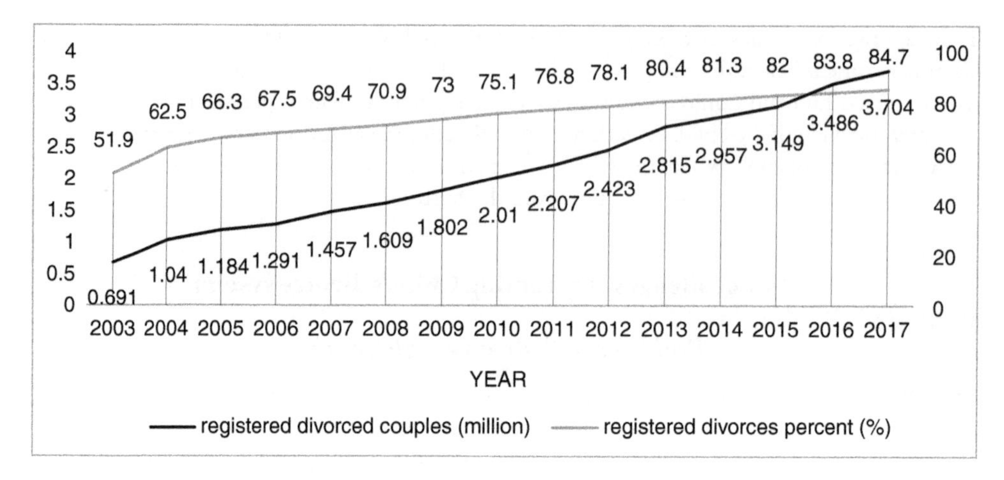

Figure 2.3.2 China's registered divorces, 2003–2017

remarried couples increased by 1017 (21.9 percent) in the last four years.[23] This shows that although the present divorce registration system safeguards divorce freedom, it fails to inhibit reckless divorces.

'Cheating' divorce[24] and 'fake' divorce[25]

Without enough technical support and with a substantial workload, registrars find it difficult to detect 'cheating' and 'fake' divorces, especially involving persons without full capacity or those seeking divorce for financial benefits. How should such cases be dealt with?

Registrars can only ascertain the parties' intentions through their written agreement, as they do regarding child support and visitation agreements. This is only a formality. In their words, they have no compulsory powers to check whether the agreement is genuine or in the child's best interest, thus risking infringement of women and children's legitimate rights and interests in post-divorce disputes. Between 2007 and 2010, 94.5 percent of cases concerning post-divorce property disputes heard in Jiading District court in Shanghai related to disputes arising after divorce registration.[26] The Third Intermediate Court in Beijing dealt with 97 post-divorce disputes in 2014, 103 in 2015 and 121 in 2016, showing an upward trend too.[27]

23 H. Sun, 'Fresh Love News: The Remarriage Rate Increases Sharply! What's Your Opinion', *China Youth Online*, 6 April 2018. Available at http://m.cyol.com/content/2018-04/16/content_17104395.htm.

24 This refers to when a spouse tricks the other spouse into registering their divorce.

25 This indicates that both parties cheat the marriage registration office and obtain a divorce in order to acquire financial advantage. Some will remarry each other again after they receive their benefits.

26 G. Xudong, 'The Third Intermediate People's Court in Beijing: The Post-Divorce Cases Go Steadily Up', *Long Peace in China Net*. Available at www.chinapeace.gov.cn/chinapeace/c53712/2017-05/05/content_11666548.shtml.

27 S. Gao, Z. Xu and Z. Wang, '6 Factors Lead to a Rise of Divorce Property Disputes', *Beijing Suburbs Daily*, 8 January 2010, 2.

Problems with divorce by litigation

According to the MLA 2001, the statutory ground for a divorce order is that mutual affection no longer exists. It is based on a theory that a marriage is grounded in and maintained by love. However, most marriages in China are based on mixed elements including economic and affectional factors.[28] Furthermore, judges have found it difficult to confirm the statutory ground. Therefore, in 1989 the Supreme People's Court promulgated a judicial interpretation listing 14 situations where the ground can be confirmed. It greatly helps the judges, but not all the situations in the list are proof that 'mutual affection no longer exists'. Some are cases where the marriage should be declared void, including that a party has a disease making them unfit for marriage, or that a party's mental illness was concealed before marriage and the illness cannot be cured after a long treatment during the marriage, or that a party obtained a marriage certificate by fraud. Some marriages are without spousal affection from the beginning, such as marriages arranged by a third party, or a mercenary marriage, or where both parties cohabit for many years without affection.

The MLA 2001 also tried to resolve the problem. Art. 32 adds four instances that can confirm that natural affection no longer existed.[29] In one of the following cases, divorce shall be granted if mediation fails: (1) bigamy or cohabiting with another person of the opposite sex;[30] (2) domestic violence and abuse or desertion of the family; (3) being an incorrigible gambler or drug addict and refusing to reform after numerous help; (4) being separated for two years from lack of mutual affection. Then there is added a catch-all clause: (5) other cases leading to the shattering of spousal affection. Additionally, where one party is declared to be missing and the other party starts divorce proceedings, divorce shall be granted. In practice, some judges hold that the aforementioned illustrations are not necessarily proof of loss of spousal affection.[31] We maintain that not all divorces are the result of loss of spousal affection, for example, a spouse bedridden after a serious accident may seek divorce out of consideration for the other's happiness, although mutual affection still exists.

Reforms in progress

The Civil Code compilation opens a new era for marriage and family law. The importance of this marriage and family part in the Civil Code is self-evident. In its second draft published in June 2019, the reform of divorce articles in the first draft is kept intact.

At the same time, the Supreme People's Court is carrying out family justice reform. The number of family disputes heard by courts at all levels exceeded 1.5 million a few years ago. From 2013 to 2015, family cases increased steadily. In 2015, there were 1.7 million family cases dealt with in the People's Court, an increase of 7.04 percent over the previous year. Family cases accounted for more than three-tenths of civil cases heard by courts.[32] Additionally, there is an

28 See W. Chen, *On Legislation of Marriage and Family Law in China (Zhongguo hunyin jiating fa lifa yanjiu)*, Beijing: Mass Press (qunzhong chubanshe), 2000, p. 261.

29 In November 1989, the Supreme People's Court promulgated a judicial interpretation listing 14 situations where the ground can be confirmed. Among them, Sections 7, 9, 10, 12 and 13 set a basis for the addition of statutory situations where that affection no longer exists.

30 This was the interpretation given in art. 2 of the Interpretations of the Supreme People's Court on Several Problems Concerning the Application of the 'Marriage Law of the PRC' (I).

31 L. Wang, 'Forward or Backward: Comments on Exemplary Legislative Model of China's Divorce Ground (shi jinbu haishi daotui ping woguo lihun biaozhun zhong de lishi zhuyi lifa moshi)', *Journal of Law Application (falv shiyong)* 12, 2005, 35–40.

32 Q. Zhou, *Annual Report of the Supreme People's Court 2018*, 9 March 2018.

insufficient number of judges. There is a glaring contradiction between the small number of judges and the huge number of cases waiting to be heard.[33] The traditional trial mode used in general civil cases has disadvantages when applied in family cases hearings. Against this background, the Supreme People's Court issued 'The Supreme People's Court's Opinions on the Pilot Reform of Family Justice and Its Working Mechanism' in April 2016 (The Pilot Opinions 2016). Since 1 June 2016, more than 100 pilot courts have carried out relevant reforms of family justice and its working mechanisms. The pilot period lasted two years.[34] Regarding the grassroots reforms carried out by the 118 pilot courts, the judge in charge concluded the following lessons: first, a diversified dispute resolution mechanism should be quickly constructed. Second, judges and court teams should be helped to specialize. Third, relevant regulations of family justice should be promulgated. Fourth, relevant facilities and equipment such as family reconciliation rooms, sand table analysis rooms, one-sided mirror observation rooms and psychological counselling rooms etc. should be set up. Fifth, the working mechanism of family justice should be innovated. Some pilot courts have established and improved the relevant systems such as psychological counselling and intervention in family cases, family investigation, marital cooling-off period, pre-litigation reconciliation and post-litigation feedback collection.[35] Shortly after the end of this pilot period, based on the pilot courts' experiences, the Supreme People's Court promulgated the 'Opinions on Further Deepening the Reform of Family Justice and Its Working Mechanisms' (hereinafter referred to as 'The New Opinions') on 18 July 2018.

Divorce registration reform proposal

The second Draft added a new system called 'the divorce cooling-off period' to deal with hasty divorce. Art. 854 stipulates that

> Within one month after the marriage registration authority receives the divorce application, if either party does not want to divorce, he or she may withdraw the divorce application from the marriage registration authority. Within one month after the expiration of the period specified in the preceding paragraph, both parties shall apply in person to the marriage registration authority for the issuance of a divorce certificate. If no application is made, the application for divorce registration shall be deemed to be withdrawn.

Divorce litigation reform proposal

At the legislative level, the second draft added a small change in divorce grounds at art. 856 that if the couple has been living apart for another year after the divorce rejection judgment and a party re-petitions for divorce, the court should grant the divorce.

33 The statistics in QJ court situated in East Chongqing shows that this court closed 12708 cases in 2016, 163 cases per judge. 15509 cases were closed in 2017, 207 cases per judge. In 2018, judges closed 16702 cases, each finishing 355 cases. See further, X. Wang, 'Local Experiences in Multiple Resolutions of Family Disputes', Proceedings of the Family Justice Reform and Revision of Family Law Symposium, May 2019, pp. 49–58.

34 The Supreme People's Court, *The Supreme People's Court's Opinions on the Pilot Reform of Family Justice and Its Working Mechanism*, 21 April 2020.

35 W. Du, 'Carrying Forward the Core Values and Promoting Family Tradition Construction (hongyang shehui jiazhi guan, cujin jiafeng jiating jianshe)', *Journal of Southwest University of Political Science and Law* (xinan zhengfa daxue xuebao) 20(1), 2018, 17–23.

Since some couples also faced embarrassment when having to prove their divorce in commercial transactions, the new draft at art. 857 also clears away obstacles for divorced couples to live their own lives by emphasizing the marriage ends once the divorce is registered or the divorce judgment or the divorce mediation agreement[36] becomes effective.

At the judicial level, the New Opinions 2018 gave much more information. Compared with the Pilot Opinions 2016, the New Opinions 2018 stick to three guidelines advocated in the Pilot Opinions 2016. First, as regards the ideology of family justice reform, they emphasize humanizing the procedure in family justice, giving full play to family justice's role of diagnosis, repair and treatment of marriage and family relations. Second, the New Opinions 2018 adhere to professionalization of the organizations and judges in family justice. For example, art. 5 specifically urges that attention be given to the admission, training and performance evaluation of family judges. Third, the New Opinions 2018 still put emphasis on the diversified dispute resolution mechanism. A family dispute can be dealt with in a judicial way as well as in an administrative way and even with other social avenues. Among these stipulations, the New Opinions 2018 also add detailed stipulations on judicial assistance in divorce procedures, especially in the following three layers, that is, family reconciliation, family investigation and psychological counselling.

Regarding family mediation, two important articles are provided. Art. 6 in the New Opinions 2018 stipulates that the people's court shall conduct mediation throughout the whole process of the family justice – from case registration to final judgment, except where mediation is not suitable according to the case's nature such as those involving validity of a marriage, the confirmation of parentage and domestic violence. Furthermore, art. 9 stipulates that, before case registration, the people's court may commission a specific organization or a mediator to carry out mediation with the consent of the parties or if it deems necessary where the parties have not submitted a mediation application. These provisions highlight the significance of mediation as the first step in hearing common family disputes unless the exceptions apply.

In respect of family investigation, the New Opinions 2018 first specify in detail the qualifications and selection of family investigators.[37] These investigators will be recommended by the judicial or educational department, women's federations, communities or other grassroots public organizations. The people's court will then appoint those qualified to be family investigators. Regarding the qualification of an investigator, the New Opinions 2018 set requirements such as competent communication skills, rich experiences in social work etc. Those working in a grassroots unit or achieving a degree relevant to dealing with family disputes will be prioritized. In minority ethnic groups, the court usually appoints those with ethnic language skills and who understand local traditions and customs as well as their religions. Second, it also sets out the investigation procedures.[38] The New Opinions 2018 require that, for fairness, an investigation should be carried out by two family investigators.

The people's court will notify the party concerned within three days after choosing a family investigator. The parties have the right to apply for disqualification of an investigator for justified reasons[39] and request the court to appoint or jointly select other investigators. Thirdly,

36 For those couples who make agreement with the help of the judge, the court will issue a formal and written divorce mediation agreement to them. It is effective once both parties sign the document. Such an agreement cannot be appealed. It is legally binding and any party can petition for the enforcement of such a document based on their agreement. See art. 97 in the Civil Procedure Law of PRC amended in 2017.

37 Arts 17 and 18.

38 Arts 19 and 20.

39 For instance, the investigator is a close relative to the party or his or her agent; There is a conflict of interests; Or the investigator has other relationship with the party or his or her agent which might have adverse influence on the investigation.

the investigator's terms of reference are decided by the people's court,[40] including (1) the personal experience, personality, education level, physical and mental status of the parties, family situation, marital relationship, living environment and work performance; (2) their roles in raising the children, the children's psychological state and their studies at school; (3) support for the elderly; (4) other necessary matters. Fourth, the work should be finished within the statutory 15-day period, starting from the day of accepting this commission. If necessary, the work time could be extended to a maximum of 30 days.[41] The investigation report may serve as a reference for the court to make a judgment.

As regards psychological counselling, the New Opinions 2018 also provide detailed stipulations.[42] There are two ways to start counselling service, either by the people's court or the parties' application. In the following five situations, the people's court can recommend the parties or minors to obtain psychological counselling: (1) where one party agrees to divorce, the other party disagrees with divorce and is emotionally agitated; (2) in parent-child relationship disputes such as visitation disputes, custody disputes and others, the parties' emotions fluctuate greatly; (3) where domestic violence has a significant impact on the physical and mental health of the parties; (4) where the minor involved in the case has emotional reactions or abnormal behaviour which call for counselling; (5) other situations. The counselling would cease if expressly rejected. For those finishing this counselling service, the relevant cooperative organization will issue a counselling report to the people's court, which may serve as a reference for the judge in reaching a decision such as who the child will live with. All materials of psychological counselling shall be attached to the case file and shall not be made public.

Other important reforms include (1) where both parties cannot agree on child raising and refuse to deal with this problem before the court, the court can give a no-divorce judgment (art. 39); (2) if agreed by both parties, the court can set up a cooling off period of fewer than three months, and the court can carry out mediation, family investigation and send counsellors to them (art. 40); and (3) the people's court may issue a divorce certificate to the litigants if they apply. With respect to divorce disputes involving the division of property, the people's court shall serve a Property Declaration Form when serving notice of acceptance of the case and notice of response to the action to the parties concerned (art. 44).

Notably, the New Opinions 2018, like the former, is not a judicial interpretation which has a binding effect on the lower courts, but is a guidance document for the family justice reform. However, it also indicates where the judicial reform is going.

Conclusion

The present reform of divorce procedure in China reflects the changes in society. To face the tide of individualism in private life, the state seems to try to embrace welfarism by setting up more measures directed at the stabilization of families and protection of the vulnerable.[43] Regarding the final result of the reform and its effect on the society, we will wait and see.

40 Arts 21 and 22.

41 Art. 23.

42 Arts 28, 31, 32 and 34.

43 Further see J. Eekelaar, *Family Law and Personal Life*, Oxford: Oxford University Press, 2007, p. 11.

2.4
DISSOLUTION OF MARRIAGE IN JAPAN

Satoshi Minamikata

Introduction

This chapter outlines the legal issues concerning dissolution of marriage and discusses developments in the law and social trends in contemporary Japan based primarily on the latest statistical data. It mainly focuses on matters arising after 1990 as the breakdown of the bubble economy and subprime mortgage crisis in 2008 brought about serious family problems. The main issues examined here are the grounds for divorce, financial protection after divorce, treatment of a child after divorce and divorce procedure.

Trends affecting the family and family law

In 1996 the Civil Code Division of the Law Reform Committee published proposals for revised provisions on family matters including divorce. They considered whether the existing provisions of the 1947 Civil Code reflected the principle of 'respecting individual dignity and achieving the essential equality of the sexes' stated in art. 24 of the Constitution. However, the revision failed due to opposition from conservatives. Meanwhile, various family-related social changes began to occur, such as a decrease in marriages,[1] a trend towards late marriage,[2] an increase in divorces (see Figure 2.4.1), declining birth rates,[3] an upsurge of the ageing population,[4] an increase in reported

1 The unmarried rate at age 50 was 1.70 percent for males and 3.33 percent for females in 1970, 5.57 and 4.33 in 1990, 12.57 and 5.82 in 2000, 20.14 and 10.61 in 2010 and 23.37 and 14.06 in 2015, respectively (National Institute of Population and Social Security, *Population Statistics 2019*. Available at www.ipss.go.jp/syoushika/tohkei/Popular/Popular2019.asp?chap=0, Figure 6–23). A major reason for young people hesitating to enter into, or giving up on the idea of, marriage is a lack of sufficient income or financial instability (Cabinet Office, *A 2019 Declining Birthrate White Paper*. Available at www8.cao.go.jp/shoushi/shoushika/whitepaper/measures/w-2019/r01webhonpen/index.html, Figures 1–1–15, 1–1–17 to 1–1–19).

2 The average year of first marriage was 27.8 for a husband and 25.2 for a wife in 1980 but 31.1 and 29.4 respectively in 2017 (Cabinet Office, op. cit., Figure 1–1–11).

3 The total fertility rate changed from 2.14 in 1973, 1.57 in 1989, 1.26 in 2005 and 1.43 in 2017 (Cabinet Office, op. cit., Figure 1–1–3).

4 Population aged 65 and over out of all population shows 14.6 percent in 1995 to 27.7 percent in 2017 (Cabinet Office, *White Paper on Ageing Society 2018*. Available at www8.cao.go.jp/kourei/whitepaper/w-2018/html/zenbun/index.html, Figure 1–1–2).

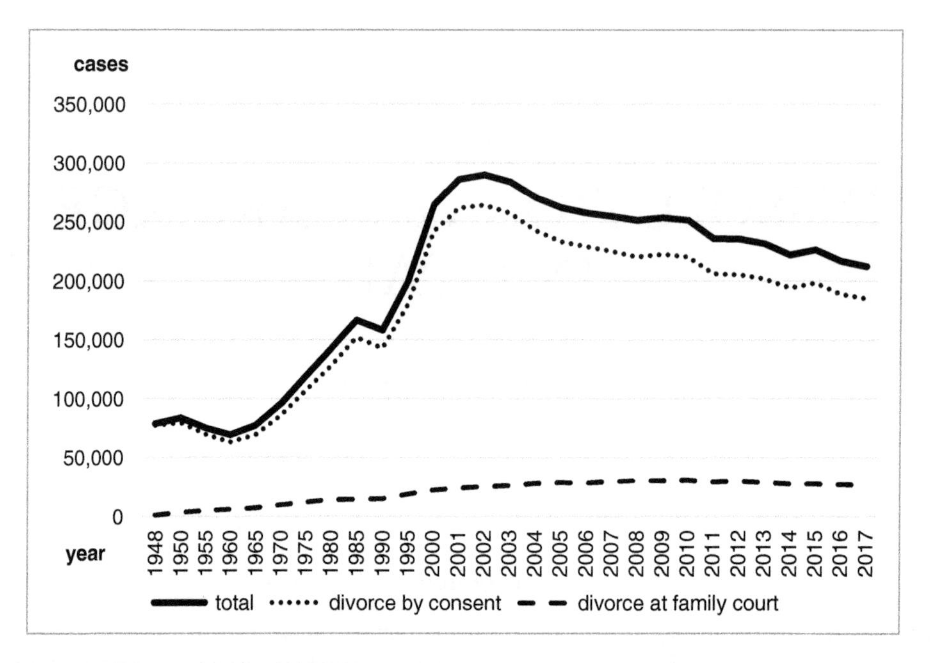

Figure 2.4.1 Divorces by type 1948–2017

cases of the unattended death of single people,[5] the voice for recognition and fair treatment of as regards SOGI (Sexual Orientation and Gender Identity)[6] and the impoverishment of families.[7] The conservative government introduced policies emphasizing the independence of individuals and advocating individual responsibility based on a competitive ideology. However, the result was the loosening of close relationships amongst family and relatives which had functioned as an

5 Single households out of all households with a person aged 65 and over increased from 6.0 percent in 1970 to 17.7 percent in 2015 (National Institute of Population and Social Security, op. cit., Figure 7–21) and the number of reported unattended death cases increased from 1,451 in 2003 to 3,179 in 2016 (only in Tokyo area) (Cabinet Office, *White Paper on Ageing Society 2018*. Available at www8.cao.go.jp/kourei/whitepaper/w-2018/html/zenbun/index.html, Figure 1–2–4–16).

6 For instance, the Moka Branch of Utsunomiya District Court recognized a same-sex couple as a de facto marriage stating the phrase 'both sexes' in art. 24 of the Constitution (Marriage shall be based only on the mutual consent of both sexes) does not mean to deny same-sex couples since there was no assumption that same-sex couples would get married when the Constitution was enacted (The Asahi Shimbun (Digital), 19 September 2019. Available at www.asahi.com/ajw/articles/AJ201909190050.html).

7 UNICEF (2016) Innocenti Report Card 13, Fairness for Children A league table of inequality in child well-being in rich countries, UNICEF, pp. 4–5. Poverty became an invisible social problem in Japan. Relative poverty rate, which is calculated based on the standard set by OEC, shows 12.8 percent in 1985, 13.7 percent in 1994, 15.3 percent in 2000, 16.1 percent in 2012 and 15.7 percent in 2015 and relative poverty rate for children 10.9 percent, 12.6 percent, 14.5 percent, 16.2 percent and 13.9 percent, respectively. In the case of single adult household with at least one child (usually a single parent family), relative poverty rate for children shows 54.5 percent, 53.2 percent, 58.2 percent, 54.6 percent and 50.8 percent during the abovementioned period, while in the case of a two or more adult household with at least one child, 9.9 percent, 10.2 percent, 11.5 percent, 12.4 percent and 10. Percent, respectively (Ministry of Health, Labour and Welfare, *Overview of Comprehensive Survey of Living Conditions 2016*. Available at www.mhlw.go.jp/toukei/saikin/hw/k-tyosa/k-tyosa16/, Figure 10). Those figures indicate that a single parent family is obviously in financial difficulties.

invisible network of support and integration, and finally the impoverishment of all households whose average annual income fell from ¥6.6 million in 1994 to ¥5.6 million in 2016.[8]

New legislation and major precedents relating to family matters

In 1999 the government commenced a radical revision of the judicial system in order to establish one which would protect citizens' interests by operating within clear legal rules, applying the principles of self-determination and self-responsibility, providing citizens with easier access to the judiciary, encouraging all parties to participate in the process of dispute resolution and providing a fairer treatment of the parties through strengthening the functions of the family court. By revision of the Civil Code in 2018, the age of marriage was set at 18 from 2022 compared to 18 years for males and 16 years for females under the current section 731; the age of majority will be lowered from 20 to 18. As a result, no parental consent will be required for marriage.

Grounds for divorce – the five years separation clause

The types of divorce obtainable are divorce by mutual consent, divorce by *Chotei* (family court mediation), divorce by family court determination and divorce by decree (see Figure 2.4.1). In the case of divorce litigation, section 770 of the Civil Code based on the no-fault principle[9] applies. One of the major issues of divorce law is deciding what objective criteria to use to determine the breakdown of a marital relationship. The Supreme Court held that one of the factors was the length of separation[10] and accordingly the Law Reform Committee proposed a clause of five years separation as a divorce ground in the draft revision of section 770 in 1996. Some lawyers claimed that a five-year period of separation would benefit a spouse who wished to obtain a divorce but the other party opposed it unreasonably. In such a case, particularly one of domestic violence, the former spouse could divorce after five years separation without any other additional grounds. Other lawyers emphasized that even a guilty spouse leaving his or her family would be granted a divorce merely due to the passage of time, which would be unfair on the innocent party. Because of the failure of the revision in 1996, in practice courts grant divorce if a couple have been separated for considerable number of years throughout their marital life, amounting in many cases to around ten years.[11]

Revision and implementation of the new divorce procedure

Under the old procedure, a divorcing couple needed to institute divorce proceedings in a district court after failure of *Chotei* in a family court.[12] This process placed a heavy burden on divorcing parties and any agreement made during divorce litigation was regarded as lacking binding force, and parties could not abandon the litigation by agreeing a settlement since divorce litigation was considered to be a public matter. In this respect, the old divorce procedure was not regarded as

8 Ministry of Health, Welfare and Labour, *Overview of Comprehensive Survey of Living Conditions 2017*. Available at www.mhlw.go.jp/toukei/saikin/hw/k-tyosa/k-tyosa17/, Figure 8.

9 Adultery, willful neglect, incurable mental disease and irretrievable breakdown of marriage are stipulated in the subsection (1).

10 SD 2 September 1987 Minshu 41–6–1423.

11 Cf. Tokyo HD 26 June 2002 Hanji 1801–80 and SD 8 Nov. 1990 Hanji 1370–55.

12 *Chotei* procedure has some similarities to a court-based mediation in other countries but it has major differences in its structure and administration.

user-friendly. The Personal Affairs Litigation Act 2003 gave family courts jurisdiction in divorce litigation so that divorcing parties could apply to a family court if they failed to settle a divorce dispute. In addition, the parties were allowed to withdraw from the litigation under certain conditions.[13] These changes reflect the principle of recent law reform moves such as respecting the will of an individual, providing parties with a variety of options for dispute resolution and encouraging parties towards self-determination. In addition to the respect for self-determination, the public have become aware of the importance of securing the safety of divorcing parties during the divorce process since a divorcing wife was killed by her husband when she appeared at the court premises for attending a divorce *Chotei* in 2019.[14]

Implementation of the Family Affairs Proceedings Act 2011

The Family Affairs Proceedings Act 2011[15] aims at providing easy access to the procedure for all parties, more respect for and protection of legal status of both parties and other interested persons involved in family disputes. For instance, an interested person as well as the parties is eligible to participate in a determination case (FAPA section 42(2)), a written application by an applicant will be sent to a respondent as a rule (FAPA section 67(1)) and any interested person is entitled to have access to information relating to him or her with the approval by a family court (FAPA section 47(1)). A minor (usually 15 years of age and over) will be given an opportunity to express his or her wishes where their interests will be affected by a family court determination (FAPA section 65 and 152(2)). The new procedure has relieved the parties from cumbersome court procedures, but most divorces end in agreement at court (see Figure 2.4.2).

Property and financial settlement

Despite the separate property system (Civ section 762), a court may divide and allocate matrimonial property to divorcing spouses in order to achieve substantial equality by considering all circumstances notwithstanding to which spouse the property belongs (see Civ section 768). In many cases, courts take the view that the matrimonial property should be basically divided equally between the spouses. In addition, courts have decided that a retirement payment[16] and pension[17] that would be realized in the near future could be included as matrimonial property and be divided between the spouses, though with some conditions. However, one difficult issue in the division of matrimonial property is finding and confirming what property and other financial resources a divorcing couple has at the time of divorce. A party has few efficient measures to force the other party to disclose the fact of his/her really possessing property, making it difficult to settle disputes.

It is clear that financial support for a vulnerable spouse after divorce, especially a housewife with minors, should be ensured especially as the age of divorcing couples has risen for nearly three decades (see Figure 2.4.3). As for the right to a pension, a housewife can obtain additional payments as the wife of the contributor husband as long as their marriage continues, but

13 Section 89 of the Civil Proceedings Act 1996 and section 37 of the PALA 2003.

14 The Asahi Shimbun (Digital), 20 March 2019. Available at www.asahi.com/articles/ASM3N56RKM3NUTIL03T.html.

15 The 2011 Act will apply to *Chotei* and determination and the PALA 2003 will apply to litigation relating to family matters.

16 Tokyo FO 23 June 2010 Kagetsu 63–2–159.

17 Nagoya HD 20 December 2000 Hanta 1095–233.

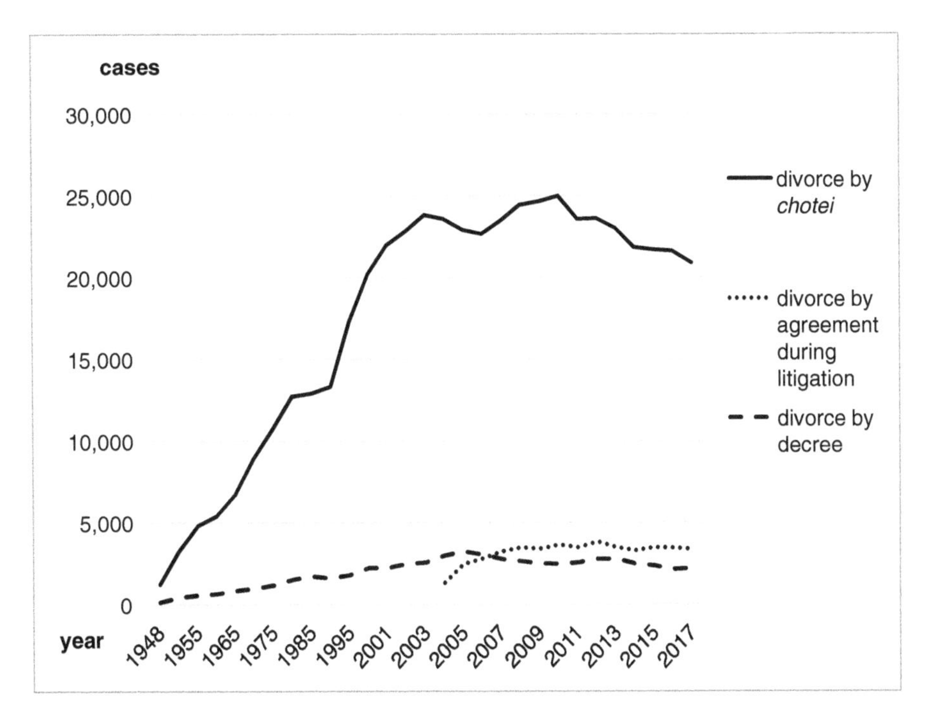

Figure 2.4.2 Divorce at court 1948–2017 (Vital Statistics)

Source: Figure 2.4.2 does not include the cases of divorce by determination and acceptation of divorce during litigation because of small numbers.

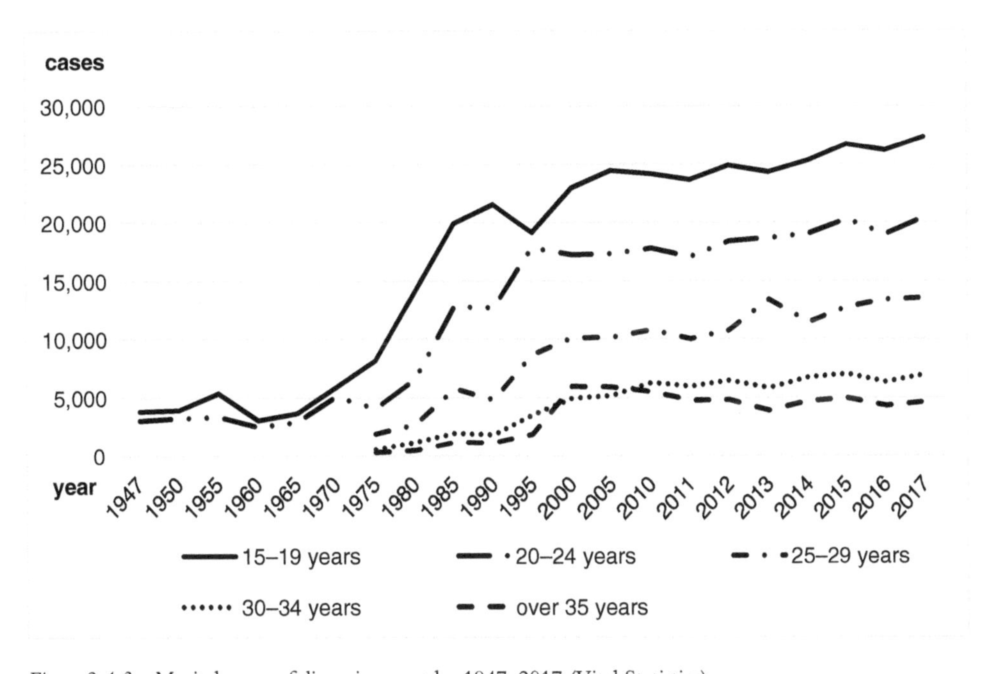

Figure 2.4.3 Marital years of divorcing couples 1947–2017 (Vital Statistics)

she loses that right after divorce and consequently must survive only on her own basic pension. In order to achieve fairness between an employed husband and a housewife, the court, in one case, ordered a husband to make a regular payment of 30 percent of his retirement pension to his divorced wife until the time of her death.[18] Meanwhile, the pension scheme was completely revised in 2004 and a divorcing couple can reach an agreement on dividing a payment of the retirement pension up to a half of the payment at the time of divorce and after.[19] Furthermore, a party can claim a half of the payment as a statutory right after 2008 (section 78–13 of the Employee Pension Insurance Act 1954). Consequently, in addition to his/her own basic pension, a spouse is eligible to claim his/her portion of the other spouse's additional pension when he/she reaches pension age, perhaps some years after the actual divorce and the amount of portion shall be calculated according to the period of marriage.[20]

Moreover, a court has made a new interpretation in order to protect a vulnerable spouse. A husband, in one case, had transferred most of the property registered in his name to a third party in order to escape the obligation of dividing matrimonial property, so there was insufficient property left to provide for the wife at the time of divorce. The court declared that the wife was entitled to have the transaction set aside provided that the husband and the third party were aware that a divorce would be completed in the very near future or the third party knew the true intention of the transaction.[21]

Such changes in law and legal interpretations suggest that financial matters are regarded as serious for divorcing parties and to be dealt with by various measures in court. For instance, a single-parent family could be in financial difficulty after divorce. Usually, a divorced mother holds the parental rights and duties and takes care of the child after divorce (see Figure 2.4.4). Most are middle-age women with two young children. It is likely to be difficult for a housewife to find a regular job to obtain sufficient income, and even an employed mother has to cope with financial problems since the income of women is in many cases lower than that of men. The annual income of a divorced single mother-household was merely ¥3.5 million compared with ¥7.1 million for a household with minors in 2015.[22] In 2016, 41.8 percent of divorced single mothers complained that they were only able to deposit less than half million yen[23] and pointed to financial issues as the one of the main difficulties in everyday life.[24] In such situations, it is understandable that divorcing mothers often fight to gain property or financial support from husbands[25] and tend to resist reaching agreement in the divorce process.

18 Sendai DD 22 March 2001 Hanji 1829–119.

19 Tokyo FO 12 May 2008 TKC data 25471165.

20 See sections 78–2, 78–13 and 78–14 of the Employee Pension Insurance Act 1954. For instance, in the case of a housewife with no history of employment, a husband made a contribution to the basic pension and additional pension scheme for a 20-year marital period. They divorced when they were 50 years old, the wife shall be eligible to claim her half portion of the husband's additional pension for the 20-year period (period of marriage). When she reaches 65 years of age, she shall be entitled to claim her own basic pension and half of the 20 years portion of her ex-husband's additional pension if he is already retired.

21 Kyoto DD 19 June 1992 Hanta 813–237.

22 Ministry of Health, Welfare and Labour, *Results of the Survey on Single Parent Households, etc. in FY 2016*. Available at www.mhlw.go.jp/file/04-Houdouhappyou-11923000-Kodomokateikyoku-Katei fukishika/0000190325.pdf, p. 38.

23 Ibid., p. 47.

24 Ibid., p. 87.

25 Single fathers also often face difficulties which are different in nature from those of single mothers (see Ministry of Health, Welfare and Labour, *Results of the Survey on Single Parent Households, etc. in FY 2016*, op. cit., p. 86).

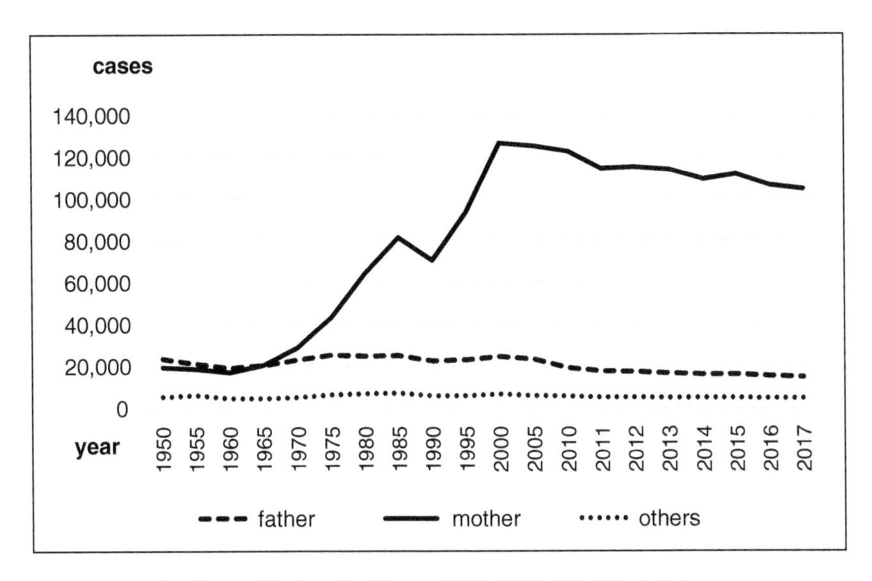

Figure 2.4.4 Parental rights and duties after divorce 1950–2017 (Vital Statistics)

If a couple have few financial resources, then it is usually a case of 'nothing comes from nothing' or 'an empty bag cannot stand upright'. Legal measures providing financial protection for divorcing couples have improved over two decades, but under the current economic conditions, sufficient financial protection of divorced parties is inadequate.[26] In particular, the case of a divorced single-mother household reveals the discrepancy between law and economic reality in Japanese society.

In addition to division of the matrimonial property, a spouse is entitled to claim compensation from the other spouse for distress caused by the divorce (Civ section 768 and 709).[27] The reason that the compensation is available is to financially protect the vulnerable party since, as mentioned previously, a simple division of matrimonial property often fails to provide sufficient financial support after the divorce. Under section 709, a spouse is entitled to claim compensation from a third person who has wrongfully contributed to the marital breakdown in addition to the other spouse. For instance, where a husband has committed adultery leading to divorce the wife can take proceedings in tort against her husband and his mistress as joint tortfeasors. However, the Supreme Court held in 2019 that a spouse shall not be entitled to claim compensation for

26 The average annual income of all households in Japan was ¥5.6 million and households with a minor child ¥7.4 million in 2016 (Ministry of Health, Labour and Welfare, *Overview of Comprehensive Survey of Living Conditions 2017*, op. cit., Figure 7), while the Ministry of Health, Welfare and Labour reveals that an annual income of a divorced single-mother is only ¥3.5 million (*Results of the Survey on Single Parent Households, etc. in FY 2016*, op. cit., Figure 16-(1)-3.

27 Section 709 of the Civil Code stipulates that a person who has intentionally or negligently infringed any right of others, or legally protected interest of others, shall be liable to compensate any damages resulting in consequence. Section 710 stipulates that persons liable for damages under the provisions of the preceding section must also compensate for damages other than those to property, regardless of whether the body, liberty or reputation of others have been infringed, or property rights of others have been infringed.

divorce from the third person who had an affair with his/her spouse unless there exist special circumstances.[28]

Divorce and the child[29]

In Japan, joint custody, joint parental obligations or joint parental rights and duties after divorce are not available but only sole parental rights and duties,[30] as set out the Civil Code[31] (see Figure 2.4.4). Under the current Civil Code, divorcing parents do not need to decide on contact and maintenance as a requirement of divorce. Furthermore, an agreement made by parents on contact cannot be enforced effectively unless they make it in a notarized public document. However, contact between a child and a non-resident parent is regarded as important for a child's life and in practice contact has been dealt with as a key issue relating to childcare (Civ section 766). In 2010, section 766 was revised in order to improve the welfare of the child, meet the demands of a non-resident parent and provide clear criteria for disputes by clarifying the wording of the section (see Figure 2.4.5). Furthermore, in one case a court ordered a resident parent to make payment because of failure to comply with obligations relating to contact.[32]

However, in 2016, contact agreements were made in only 24.1 percent of cases where children were living with their mother and in only 27.3 percent where the child was living solely with the father. In the case of divorce by mutual consent, 20.5 percent of the former and 21.5 percent of the latter families reached agreement on contact while in the case of settlement at family court the figures were 49.4 percent and 58 percent respectively.[33] In reality, a child and a non-resident parent will have difficulty in establishing the opportunity of contact after divorce despite revision of the law.[34] (See further Chapters 3.3–3.5 of this book.)

Child abduction between divorcing parents

The Family Affairs Proceedings Act and the Habeas Corpus Act will be chiefly applied to abduction cases and a court can issue a determination or a writ to take back and place the

28 SD 19 January 2019 Court Website.

29 See A. Harada, 'Family Reorganization in the Japanese Family Conciliation System: Resolving Divorce Disputes Involving Minor Children', *Int. Jo. Law, Policy & Fam* 33, 2019, 75–103.

30 The current system of sole parental rights and duties after divorce has been criticized as causing unnecessary disputes between divorcing parents. However, the Minister of Justice has argued that joint parental rights and duties after divorce might harm the interests of children, and the matter required careful consideration. Meanwhile, the Ministry of Foreign Affairs is conducting comparative research on the post-divorce parental rights and duties in 24 countries at the request of MOJ (Ministry of Justice, 17 May 2019. Available at www.moj.go.jp/hisho/kouhou/hisho08_01128.html).

31 Sections 766 and 819 of the Civil Code.

32 SK 6 August 2003 Kagetsu 56–2–160.

33 Ministry of Health, Labour and Welfare, *Results of the Survey on Single Parent Households, etc. in FY 2016*, op. cit., Figures 18-(2)-5 to 18-(2)-8.

34 Family Problems Information Centre (public interest incorporated foundation) was established in 1993 in order to support and encourage the parents with respect to executing contact activity in several large cities. In addition to FPIC, several organizations are operated to support divorcing parents involved in disputes, but such services are not always available to all divorcing parents since the services are, for instance by FPIC, not free.

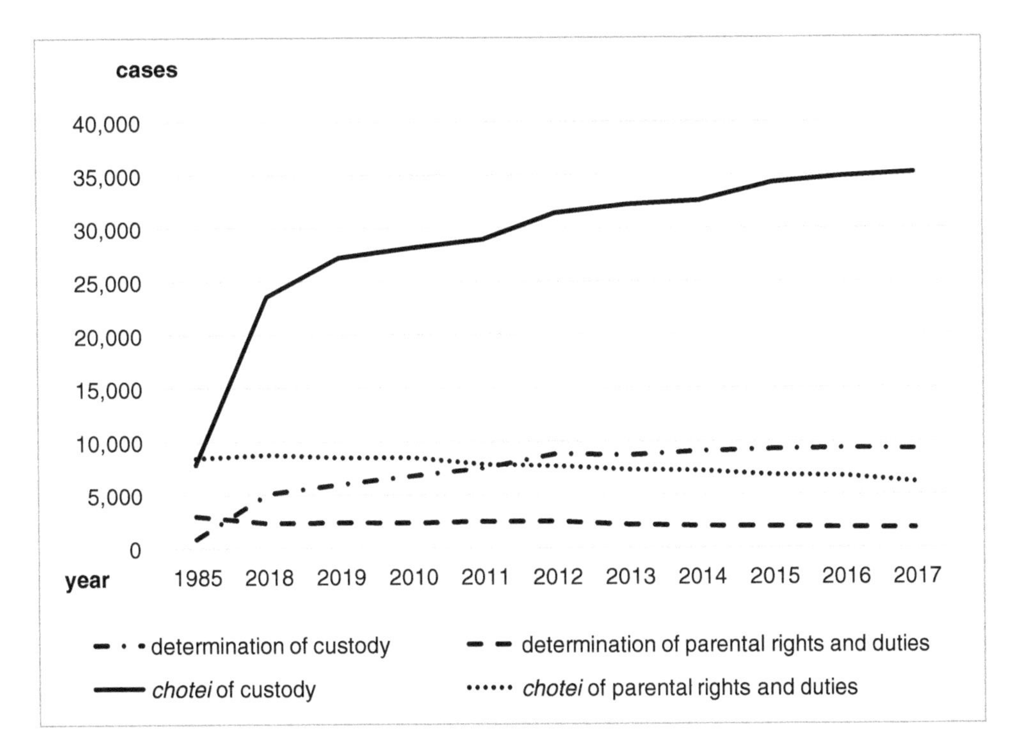

Figure 2.4.5 Application to family court 1985 to 2017 (Judicial Statistics)

Note: In this Figure 'custody' means the cases of access, maintenance and disputes over abduction between parents (breakdown of the data is not available).

child in the care of a resident parent.[35] However, in many cases it is difficult to return the child to a resident parent from a non-resident parent due to ineffective measures for enforcing the determination or writ under current law. As a result, in some cases parents cannot resist the temptation to take or recover the child by force rather than taking legal action. In an extreme case, a non-resident parent of foreign nationality who intended to take the child abroad with him was prosecuted and found guilty of the kidnapping of a minor (Cri section 224).[36] The issue relating to enforcement in abduction disputes remains but in one case, the Supreme Court held that the detention of a child of 13 years of age was obviously wrong and he should be freed since the mother did not obey the court decision ordering her to return him to his habitual residence and she continued to keep him under her control.[37] In 2019 the Civil Execution Act was revised in order to ensure more effective enforcement procedure relating abduction disputes (see sections 174 and 175 of the Civil Execution Act for domestic cases and sections 136 and 140 of the Implementation of the Convention on the Civil Aspects of International Child Abduction Act 2013).

35 SD 19 October 1993 Minshu 47–8–5099.
36 See SD 6 December 2005 Keishu 59–10–1901. Section 224 stipulates that a person who kidnaps a minor by force or enticement shall be punished by imprisonment for not fewer than 3 months but not more than 7 years.
37 SD 15 March 2018 Minshu 72–1–17.

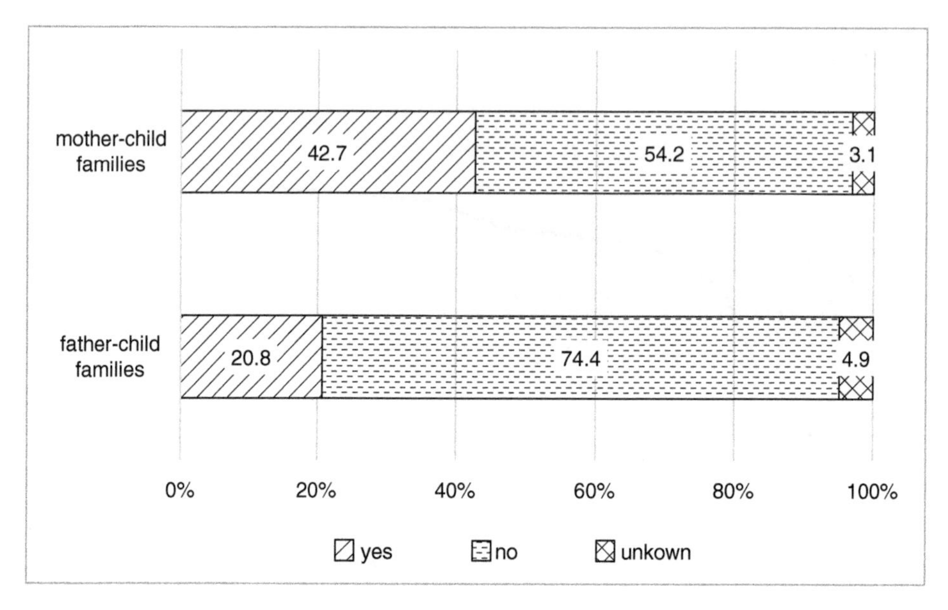

Figure 2.4.6 Agreement of maintenance in 2016 (Results of the survey on single parent households, etc. in FY 2016)

Maintenance of a child after divorce

It is widely accepted that parents are obliged to maintain a minor even after divorce, but they are not legally required to make an agreement on maintenance at the time of divorce. As a result, in 2016 the majority of parents made no agreement on child maintenance subsequent to divorce (see Figure 2.4.6).[38] The relevant survey shows the major reasons behind the lack of agreements are that the claiming parent is aware of the other's poor financial situation so that negotiation on maintenance would be useless (20.8 percent of mothers and 22.3 percent of fathers), that they do not want to meet or make contact with the other (31.4 percent of mothers and 20.5 percent of fathers), and that they can afford to survive on their own financial resources (2.8 percent of mothers, 17.5 percent of fathers).[39] (See further Chapter 2.7 of this book.)

As for calculating the amount of payment, a group of specialists privately published a calculation table in 2003[40] that a family court often uses as a basic reference for deciding on the amount of child maintenance. The parties often claim the amount calculated on the basis of the table. As regards making the payments, the survey in 2016 shows that only 24.3 percent of mother-child families receive continuous payment from a non-resident father.[41] Meanwhile,

38 Ministry of Health, Labour and Welfare, *Results of the Survey on Single Parent Households, etc. in FY 2016*, op. cit., Figures 17-(2)-7 and 17-(2)-8.

39 Ibid., Figures 17-(2)-11-1 and 17-(2)-11-2. In once case, Yokohama Family Court made a determination with indirect compulsory execution relating to maintenance (Yokohama FK 3 September 2007 Kagetsu 60–4–90). Yokohama Family Court made a determination with indirect compulsory execution).

40 Hanta 1111–291.

41 Ministry of Health, Labour and Welfare, *Results of the Survey on Single Parent Households, etc. in FY 2016*, op. cit., Figure 17-(3)-1.

under the current procedure of enforcing payments by a non-resident parent, a parent-claimant is eligible to apply to a family court to issue a determination ordering the obligor to make payment where there is no prior agreement on maintenance. The parent can request a family court to recommend an obligor parent to perform his or her obligation of payment or to make a determination ordering him or her to perform the obligation if they have already made a maintenance agreement, and can apply to a court for compulsory execution of the payment if they made an agreement in a notarized public document (FAPA sections 289 and 290). Furthermore, by revision of section 152(3) of the Civil Execution Act 2003, the provisions regarding seizure were altered so that payment of maintenance was given priority, and by sections 151–2 and 167–16, execution against a maintenance claim may be commenced even with respect to the portion of the claim for periodic payments for which the fixed due date has yet to arrive if any part of such claim is in default. By section 167–15 a court can order the obligor parent to pay a reasonable amount of money to the parent-claimant in order to secure performance of the payment of maintenance. In 2019 the Civil Execution Act was revised in order to ensure more effective enforcement procedure relating to matters on disclosure and acquisition of information of the obligator's property (see sections 197, 205 to 207 of the Civil Execution Act). Such legal changes gave parent-claimants more effective means to secure child maintenance payments.

The child as an individual in the divorce process

After implementation of the Convention on the Rights of the Child in 1989,[42] the view that a child should be regarded as a subject in the process of their parents' divorce began to be asserted. Some claimed that a scheme of independent representation of a child should be introduced into Japanese law, but nothing has yet changed. In the meantime, a child over 15 years of age will be given the opportunity to express their wishes regarding matters relating to their interests and a court should consider their wishes in making a decision in the divorce process (FAPA sections 65 and 152(2)) (see Chapter 4.4 of this book).

Conclusion

Recent legislation and court cases reveal characteristics that reflect the changes in family structure and life since 1990. First, parties should be respected as independent persons who can resolve their disputes by themselves and accordingly their intentions and wishes should be valued in the process of divorce. Secondly, substantial equality and remedies should be achieved between the parties with respect to financial matters and human relations such as contact. Thirdly, clear criteria, such as the five years separation for divorce ground, should be applied in the court procedure. Fourthly, access to court and user-friendly procedures should be improved. And finally, contact with and the maintenance of a child after divorce should be given primary consideration in divorce processes. However, problems arising from divorce remain because of income disparity between the sexes, poverty encroaching on family life and the slow development of supporting schemes for families in trouble.

42 The Japanese government finally ratified in 1994.

Abbreviations

Civ	Civil Code
Cri	Criminal Code
FAPA	Family Affairs Proceedings Act
FK	Family Court Order
FO	Family Court Determination
Hanji	*Hanreijiho* (law journal)
Hanta	*Hanreitaimuzu* (law journal)
HD	High Court Decree
Kagetsu	Law Reports on Family Cases
Keishu	Law Reports on Criminal Cases at Supreme Court
Minshu	Law Reports on Civil Cases at Supreme Court
PALA	Personal Affairs Litigation Act
SD	Supreme Court Decree
SK	Supreme Court Order

2.5
RELAXATION AND DISSOLUTION OF MARRIAGE IN LATIN AMERICA

Fabiola Lathrop-Gómez

Introduction

In the light of statistics and as in other regions of the world, the traditional model of the family in Latin America has experienced several changes.[1] While some authors see the steady increase in divorce rates as a factor of crisis of this model,[2] available socio-legal studies have pointed out that the transformation of the traditional family model in the region has multiple causes, and that the spread of divorce is far from being the main one.[3]

The wider variety of family forms in Latin America is expressed in a variety of constitutional conceptions of this social institution. Among these conceptions we find those that are *restrictive*[4] (where only 'natural' men and women are recognized as having the right to marry or enter into de facto civil partnerships); *intermediate*[5] (where the Constitution provides protection for all forms of family, but only recognizes marriage between a man and a woman); and *wide*[6] (where the Constitution establishes a wide mandate for the 'integral protection of the family', leaving space for all forms of family, marriage or civil partnerships).[7] Accordingly, Latin American family law seems to be situated in a hybrid space. On the one hand, secular law remains affected by the influence exerted by the Catholic Church on the codification process and the prevailing

1 D. Davison, *Separación y Divorcio*, Buenos Aires: Editorial Universidad, 2006, pp. 21–3 and C. Caldani and M. Ángel, 'Bases para la armonización del Derecho de Familia en el Mercosur', in *Hacia una armonización del Derecho de Familia en el Mercosur y países asociados*, Buenos Aires: LexisNexis, 2007, p. 19.

2 H. Corral, *Ley de divorcio: las razones de un no*, Colección de Estudios de Derecho Actual, Editorial Santiago de Chile: Universidad de Los Andes, 2001, pp. 15 and 168 and R. Navarro, 'Matrimonio y Derecho', AA.VV., *El matrimonio: ¿contrato basura o bien social?*, Pamplona: Thomson Aranzadi, 2008, pp. 55–71.

3 C. Grosman and I. Martínez, *Familias ensambladas*, Buenos Aires: Editorial Universidad, 2000, p. 29 and M. Cerrutti and G. Binstock, 'Cambios en las familias latinoamericanas y demandas para la acción pública', CEPAL, *Las familias interrogadas. Hacia la articulación del diagnóstico, la legislación y las políticas*, Santiago de Chile: Serie Seminarios y conferencias, N° 61, 2011, pp. 44–52.

4 Art. 112° of the Constitution of Honduras.

5 Art. 226° of the Constitution of Brazil and art. 67° of the Constitution of Ecuador.

6 Art. 14° *bis* of the Constitution of Argentina.

7 M. Herrera, 'La Familia en la Constitución 2020, ¿Qué Familia?', in R. Gargarella (coord.), *La Constitución en 2020: 48 propuestas para una sociedad igualitaria*, Buenos Aires: Siglo Veintiuno Editores, 2011, pp. 85–94.

recognition of Canon Law, which did not allow divorce.[8] On the other hand, family law in Latin America is progressively recognizing the autonomy of partners and regulating new forms of family, a process that leads to the existence of a trilogy of institutions that end, dissolve or relax the marriage (see further Chapters 1.2 and 2.1 of this book).

Typology of divorce and separation

In Latin America it is possible to recognize a double (or parallel) system of marriage breakdown. On the one hand, there is *judicial separation*, which does not dissolve the marriage but suspends certain rights and obligations emanating from the marriage (hence it is called a 'relaxation' of the marital link). On the other hand, there is *divorce* itself ('dissolution of marriage').[9]

Judicial separation exists in most Latin American legislation.[10] This institution may be invoked in two cases: (1) where one of the spouses has violated his/her marital obligations (fault separation) or (2) when one or both spouses want to legally recognize the separation of bodies, yet are not fully convinced that the marital link should be broken (agreed separation).[11] While this institution played a particular role mainly for the Catholic population – allowing only a physical separation and the suspension of specific marital rights and obligations – judicial separation is in retreat, as divorce has gained ground.[12]

As for the institution of divorce, the generality of Latin American laws recognizes the so-called subjective divorce or fault divorce (*divorcio por culpa*) and objective divorce or remedy divorce (*divorcio remedio*). In the case of fault divorce, one of the spouses has to prove culpable conduct by the other party (e.g. infidelity, violence, drug abuse, etc.). In remedy divorce, one or both spouses must prove the effective non-existence of the common marital life; that is, the cessation of *affectio maritalis*.[13]

Grounds and conditions for judicial separation and divorce

As we have seen, certain types of conduct by the spouses are considered as grounds for both judicial separation and divorce. Among these actions, we can identify conduct that is contrary to the duties of cohabitation, fidelity and assistance, all of which may lead to a declaration of fault separation or fault divorce. As an example, Chilean law states that a spouse may seek legal separation should a serious violation of the duties and obligations towards the other spouse or their children make the familial co-existence intolerable. In turn, Chilean law considers as legal

8 Dominican Republic and Cuba are early exceptions to this trend, recognizing legal divorce in 1897 and 1918, respectively. Bolivia established divorce in 1932, while Colombia, Peru and Chile did not have full divorce until 1976, 1977 and 2004, correspondingly. In countries where full legal divorce was not recognized, spouses used to utilize frauds like annulments based on the incompetence of public officers (Chile) or fictitious allegations of guilt between couples (Argentina).

9 In some American countries, there has also been a tendency to regulate what could be called a third way for spouses to obtain a divorce, which consists of processing the divorce outside of the judicial context, before a Notary Public. Cuba, Colombia, Ecuador, Brazil, Peru, Bolivia and Nicaragua have made progress in this regard. See M.M. Culaciati, *El divorcio contemporáneo: pasado presente y perspectivas de futuro*, Santiago: Ediciones Olejnik, 2018, pp. 333–42.

10 Argentina, Brazil, Chile, Colombia, Ecuador, Paraguay, Peru, Uruguay, Venezuela, among others.

11 Some laws have a 'time for reflexion' between spouses after which they may decide to fill in a divorce petition. See art. 127 Civil Code of Uruguay and art. 27 of the Civil Marriage Statute of Chile.

12 As an example, in Chile there are around 200 legal separations per year, while in the same period there are more than 58,000 divorces.

13 The Civil Code of Argentina is an exception to this rule, considering separate grounds for the determination of *maritalis affectio* for these purposes.

grounds for divorce an attempt on the life of or serious ill-treatment against physical or psychological integrity of a spouse or any children, serious and repeated transgressions of the duties of cohabitation, support and fidelity, homosexual behaviour, alcoholism or drug addiction.[14]

In the case of remedy divorce, legislation presumes that continuous physical separation (separation of bodies) implies the absence of *affectio maritalis*.[15] Consequently, once the absence of common marital life has been verified by a court of law, it is possible to declare the divorce.[16] As for the period of cessation of cohabitation required for declaring judicial separation or remedy divorce, Latin American law varies from country to country. In the case of unilateral petitions for separation or divorce, legislation requires no fewer than two years of continuous physical separation.[17] When the petition for separation or divorce has been presented by both spouses, legislation requires no less than one year of physical separation.[18]

The periods of cessation of cohabitation required have been the focus of some constitutional debates. For example, in 2006, the Constitutional Court of Argentina declared, as 'excessive and even nonsensical', the three-year requirement in the case of divorce.[19] In contrast, the Constitutional Court of Chile decided in 2013 that the time-requirement established by law (even in the case of remedy divorce) did not constitute a restriction on the right to seek a divorce.[20]

Finally, some recent legislation in Latin America does not require the cessation of the *affectio maritalis* as a condition to seek separation or divorce, but only that one or two years should have passed since the celebration of marriage.[21] Alternatively, some legislation has removed all time-frame prerequisites, requiring only the consent of the spouses to the divorce (determined in a court of law).[22]

Rules of procedure

As a general rule, Latin American laws require judicial (non-administrative) proceedings for spouses who want to separate or divorce from their partners.[23] Nevertheless, and despite the

14 Arts 26 and 54 of Civil Marriage Statute of Chile. In similar vein, arts 202 and 214 n 1 of the Civil Code of Argentina; art. 333 n 1–10 of the Civil Code of Peru; arts 267 n I-III-IV-V-VI-XIII-XV and 270 of Federal Civil Code of Mexico; and art. 130 of Family Code of Bolivia.

15 Chilean legislation is particularly strict in terms of the document-based evidence required for establishing the exact dates of the cessation of cohabitation. See arts 22, 23 and 25 of the Civil Marriage Statute. In contrast, Brazilian Law allows parties to provide different forms of evidence (art. 1580.2 Civil Code of Brazil). See T. Vainsencher, 'El divorcio en el Derecho brasileño', in A.A. Penco and L.P. Gallardo (cords), *El divorcio en el Derecho Iberoamericano*, Zaragoza: Temis-Ubijus-Reus-Zavalia, 2009, p. 128.

16 Argentinean Law also recognizes the right of spouses to fill in a claim of divorce, merely based on serious causes, which, in turn, make life in common morally impossible and after three years since the marriage was celebrated; art. 215 of the Civil Code of Argentina.

17 Two years: art. 267 n XVIII of Federal Civil Code of Mexico; arts 339 and 333 n 2 of Civil Code of Peru; art. 1580.2 of Civil Code of Brazil; art. 131 of Family Code of Bolivia; art. 154 n 8 of Civil Code of Colombia. Three years: art. 110.2 of Civil Code of Ecuador; art. 55.3 of Civil Marriage Statute of Chile; arts 148.9 and 187.3 of Civil Code of Uruguay. As an exception, art. 4° Law N° 45/91 of Paraguay (which requires one year of separation without the intention of resuming cohabitation).

18 Art. 55.1 of Civil Marriage Statute of Chile; art. 1580.2 of Civil Code of Brazil; art. 333.12 of Civil Code of Peru.

19 Family Court Referee, N° 5, Rosario, M., D.G.C.G., F.A., 14 November, 2006.

20 Rol N° 2207-12-INA, p. 27.

21 Art. 154 Civil Code of Guatemala; art. 274 of Federal Civil Code of Mexico; and art. 212 n 10 of Family Code of Panama.

22 Arts 107–108 of Civil Code of Ecuador; arts 175–179 of Civil Code of Nicaragua; art. 154.9 of Civil Code of Colombia, and art. 651 Civil Procedural Code of Colombia.

23 See Argentina, Bolivia, Costa Rica, Chile, Panamá and Puerto Rico, among others.

predominance of generally expeditious judicial procedures, especially if both spouses request the court's intervention, there is a growing tendency towards non-judicial proceedings, such as public certifications.[24] This tendency towards non-judicial proceedings in divorce matters is generally restricted when there are children involved. In these cases, legislation tends to require judicial proceedings, even when there is a mutual agreement between spouses, for example, as in Brazil,[25] Mexico[26] and Peru.[27] Finally, in some states, regardless of the common intention of both spouses to divorce, legislation requires the judge to initiate a compulsory process of judicial conciliation.[28]

Emerging debates

Divorce, morality and intimacy

The use of fault grounds for separation or divorce seems open to criticism. Among other reasons, there seems to be a lack of justification for interfering in the intimate sphere of spouses on grounds of their conjugal performances and without the existence of concrete damage to the other party's basic rights.[29] At the same time there is a straightforward difficulty in condemning the (single) fault of one of the spouses for the violation of certain conjugal (relational) duties, particularly in the case fidelity. Additionally, fault divorce may intensify the conflicts within the family unit in these kinds of divorce.[30]

In any case, it should be noted that Latin American laws are gradually moving towards the elimination of fault divorce.[31] This is the case regarding Brazilian legislation, which only recognizes remedy divorce, without requiring an express reason to be given by spouses, but only the effluxion of a certain period of time before seeking divorce. In Brazil, direct divorce, that is, not dependent on a previously legal separation, may be obtained by one or both spouses if de facto separation exceeds two years. In the case of indirect divorce, one year of prior judicial separation is required.[32]

Agreements in anticipation of rupture

There is an incipient discussion at a doctrinal and jurisprudential level on agreements in anticipation of matrimonial rupture. In Argentina, in particular, there is a debate on the validity of agreements entered into with a view to divorce, before the cause for dissolution arises. Observers have noted that such accords would be null and void if they involve a waiving of alimony and their validity is debated when they define the partition and liquidation of assets. For some

24 For example, in Cuba since Decreto-Ley n 154/1994 and Colombia since 2005 art. 34 ley 962 de 2005, in Ecuador since Ley n 2006–62 de 2006.

25 Art. 1124-A of Civil Procedural Code of Brazil.

26 Art. 272 of Federal Civil Code of Mexico.

27 Art. 4 a) Law N° 29.227 of 2008.

28 See art. 236° of the Civil Code (Argentina); art. 67° of the Civil Marriage Statute of Chile (Chile) and art. 5° Law N° 45/91 (Ley de Divorcio vincular, Paraguay).

29 J. Eekelaar, *Family Law and Personal Life*, Oxford: Oxford University Press, 2017, pp. 118–21.

30 M. Herrera, 'Una mirada crítica y actual sobre el divorcio vincular en el Mercosur y países asociados a la luz de los Derechos Humanos', in *Revista de Derecho Privado*, Mexico City: Instituto de Investigaciones Jurídicas UNAM, edición especial 2012, pp. F215–20.

31 Cuba being the first in only considering remedy divorce in 1975.

32 Art. 1580° of the Civil Code of Brazil.

authors, since the marital property regime is imperatively imposed by law, it is appropriate to view such agreements as invalid, and some jurisprudence maintains this same thesis even if the spouses are de facto separated. However, Argentine jurisprudence has recognized the validity of agreements entered into on the occasion of divorce by joint presentation accepted prior to the judgment, even though they are subject to a double condition: the dissolution of the marriage and judicial approval. This solution is the one that best suits the family interest, as it tends to avoid incidents and litigious issues that will have a negative impact on future relations between former spouses, with pernicious effects on the children.[33]

In Chile, where these agreements are not legally recognized, a comparative study shows that the main objection raised in the past against these pacts – that is, being contrary to public order insofar as they attack the idea of an indissoluble, or at least stable and permanent, marriage – has been overcome by the social phenomenon of the existence and application of divorce; and that it is possible to argue in favour of their validity in countries such as Chile.[34]

Damages and family relationships

For some decades now, suits based on civil liability for damages arising from family relationships, such as lack of timely recognition of filiation, domestic violence, obstruction of contact between parent and child and, especially, failure to comply with conjugal obligations have been on the rise.

While marriage law provides for certain penalties, for example, in cases of breaches of the obligation of fidelity (such as divorce, as discussed previously), no special form of compensation for damages is set forth. Moreover, the Argentinean Civil and Commercial Code, dispelling doubts about the nature of the duty of fidelity, attempts to clarify that there is, in fact, no legal sanction but rather only a moral one in the event of infringement.[35]

Jurisprudence, in turn, has admitted this type of compensation aimed at repairing damages to certain rights, but not the mere breach of a marital duty. In Chile, for example, there are no second instance court rulings that have accepted the thesis of the extensive and general application of torts in family law.[36]

Among the arguments put forward by the minority doctrinal thesis that accepts the application of compensation for damages in cases of breach of conjugal duties we find: defence of the principle that no damage within the family should go without reparation; that conjugal duties are obligations of full legal value, with legal and not merely moral sanctions; that the field of family law, and the specific sanctions and effects it describes, does not impede the supplementary application of the rules of tort; that the reparatory function of civil liability and the principle of comprehensive reparation of damages should lead to compensation for such damages; that the very application of civil liability between the domestic partners would make it possible, by means of its preventive function, to deter lax conduct; that, within the family, there is a greater need for diligent behaviour given the risk of harm that may be caused to other persons within

33 A. Kemelmajer, 'La autonomía de la voluntad en el derecho de familia argentino', in Sistema Argentino de Información Jurídica (SAIJ) (ed.), *Derecho de las Familias, Infancia y Adolescencia. Una mirada crítica y contemporánea*, Buenos Aires: Sistema Argentino de Información Jurídica (SAIJ), 2014, pp. 30–1.

34 E. Aldunate and C. Riveros, 'Acuerdos pre y posmatrimoniales. Conceptos y modelos de regulación', *Revista de Derecho* 29(2), 2016, 153.

35 Art. 431: Support. The spouses undertake to work together on a common life plan based on sharing, cooperation and the moral duty of fidelity. They must provide each other with reciprocal assistance.

36 M. Tapia, *Divorcio y Responsabilidad civil*, Santiago de Chile: Rubicon, 2018, p. 29.

the family unit; and, lastly, that compensation for damages for breach of conjugal duties would restore value to the – in principle indissoluble – commitment acquired by marriage.[37]

The arguments of the opposite and majority doctrine are: families are constituted by bonds of cooperation and solidarity that would be weakened if the door were opened to compensation claims; family law follows its own principles, where there is no room for these economic concepts; family law has established specific sanctions for non-compliance with its duties, so that burdening relatives with compensation would involve a double penalty; if family obligations are not, by nature, susceptible to forced compliance, they cannot be subject to compensation for damages; and, lastly, that the general origin of such compensations in family law would discourage marriage, since future couples could be at risk of not only divorce but also to compensatory actions.[38]

In my opinion, if the breach of certain duties in marriage causes damage to people's rights, compensation is appropriate, provided that the requirements of private law are met. As has been said, compensation should not be paid for the typical and immediate consequences derived from the breach of the duty of fidelity, such as deception or deceit; but would be appropriate in the event of damage that exceeds a certain magnitude, such as infidelity of a highly public nature, concealment of paternity or the transmission of a sexually transmitted disease.[39] In such a situation, what the compensation seeks to mitigate is the harm caused to an individual's rights, not the breach of a family duty per se; this breach may have a specific penalty in family law that seeks to attain a separate objective (not to repair such harm). The rules of family law are not sufficient to remedy such damages in and of themselves.

The growing priority of the best interests of the child

Family law in the Region is in the process of distinguishing between the effects of divorce and separation on the spouses and those affecting their children. Accordingly, the legislation seems to regulate/limit more intensively the autonomy of parents on matters that may have an impact on their children after the separation. This tendency may be observed in the wider margin of judicial discretion and competence granted to judges in order to review the terms of divorce agreements in relation to children. By contrast, spouses have more freedom to arrange issues that affect themselves only, such as the distribution of the marital property or the awarding of the family home.[40]

I believe that the growing concern for the best interests of the child in both separation and divorce proceedings is a positive one, fully in line with arts 3.1. and 18.1. of the United

37 See: G. Medina, 'Daños en el Derecho de Familia en el Código Civil y Comercial unificado de Argentina', *Actualidad Jurídica Iberoamericana* (3), agosto 2015, 23–9. See further also J.E. Hasday, *Intimate Lies and the Law*, New York: Oxford University Press, 2019.

38 Tapia, op. cit., n 36, p. 70.

39 G. Hernández, 'Responsabilidad por incumplimiento del deber conyugal de fidelidad', in C. Domínguez (coord.), *Estudios de Derecho de Familia III*, Santiago de Chile: Thomson Reuters, 2018, pp. 195 and 204. The author highlights the restricted juridicity of the duty of fidelity, and the practically insurmountable difficulties in verifying compliance with the requirements of civil liability, especially damage and causality, on the one hand, and guilt, on the other.

40 This liberty in the regulation of the consequences of divorce between spouses is also limited in some countries by the principle of protecting the economically weaker spouse (usually, the wife). For example, art. 3, para 1, Civil Marriage Statute of Chile, where both the interest of the child and of the weaker spouse are considered as leading principles for the interpretation of the Law.

Nations Convention on the Rights of the Child.[41] (See further Chapters 4.4 and 4.6 of this book.) Such concern manifests itself in two exemplary regulations. On the one hand, the legal obligation imposed on divorcing spouses to submit before the court a full regulatory agreement on the future economic and personal life of their children, reviewed by the tribunal.[42] On the other hand, this increasing concern for the best interests of the child is seen in the growing recognition and regulation of parental co-responsibility, allowing shared custody of the child and more flexible regimes for parental visiting (e.g. shared or alternate residence).[43] (See further Chapters 3.3–3.5 of this book.)

41 Art. 3.1: In all actions concerning children, whether undertaken by public or private social welfare institutions, courts of law, administrative authorities or legislative bodies, the best interests of the child shall be a primary consideration; art. 18.1: States Parties shall use their best efforts to ensure recognition of the principle that both parents have common responsibilities for the upbringing and development of the child. Parents or, as the case may be, legal guardians, have the primary responsibility for the upbringing and development of the child. The best interests of the child will be their basic concern.

42 See arts 21°, 27° and 55° of the Civil Marriage Statute of Chile and art. 236° of the Civil Code of Argentina. In other countries, the law determines the legal impacts of divorce on children, while regulating remedy divorce. See arts 340°-342° of the Civil Code of Peru.

43 See arts 1583° and 1584° of the Civil Code of Brazil, as reformed in 2008 and the current debate on the Chilean Congress for recognizing shared custody of the child on the Civil Code. See A. Kemelmajer de Carlucci, 'La guarda compartida. Una visión comparativa', in *Revista de Derecho Privado*, Mexico City: Instituto de Investigaciones Jurídicas UNAM, edición especial 2012, pp. 281–6.

2.6

THE LEGAL CONSEQUENCES OF DISSOLUTION

Property and financial support between spouses

Joanna Miles and Jens M. Scherpe

Introduction

The international rise in divorce in western jurisdictions over the last half-century (see Chapter 2.2 of this book) has brought with it the challenge of determining how best to deal with the economic consequences of matrimonial breakdown, both procedurally and substantively. That significant demographic change has been accompanied in many jurisdictions by substantial socio-economic changes which might also have a bearing on economic justice on divorce, not least the increased number of women and mothers engaged at least part-time in paid employment.[1] However, empirical data counsel caution in relying on the labour market to avoid economic hardship to women (and, by extension, children)[2] following divorce or in assuming that a 'clean break' package of remedies will suffice in many cases. In the absence of extensive public welfare provision or re-partnering, the impact of past and ongoing child-care obligations on the primary carer's (and in practice still mostly women's) lifetime earnings and pension savings may not be ameliorated without significant economic redistribution between the spouses following divorce.[3] But in evaluating different jurisdictions' view of economic justice between the spouses on divorce, it is essential to bear in mind that diversity in demographic, socio-economic, housing market, social security provision and other factors may have a bearing both on what financial solutions on divorce are practicable in any given jurisdiction and on perceptions of

1 See for example data reported in J. Miles and E. Hitchings, 'Financial Remedy Outcomes on Divorce in England and Wales: Not a "Meal Ticket for Life"', *Australian Journal of Family Law* 32, 2018, 43–80 and E. Hitchings and J. Miles, 'Rules versus Discretion in Financial Remedies on Divorce', *Int. J. Law, Policy and the Family* 33(1), 2019, 24–50.

2 This chapter does not address child support, but that will commonly be an important income-based component of the overall financial settlement following divorce (see Chapter 2.7 of this book).

3 See generally D. Price, 'Pension Accumulation and Gendered Household Structures: What Are the Implications of Changes in Family Formation for Future Financial Inequality', in J. Miles and R. Probert (eds), *Sharing Lives, Dividing Assets: An Interdisciplinary Study*, Oxford: Hart, 2009; H. Fisher and H. Low, 'Divorce Early or Divorce Late? The Long-Term Financial Consequences', *Australian Journal of Family Law* 32, 2018, 6–27; J. Eekelaar, 'The Financial Consequences of Divorce: Law and Reality', *Australian Journal of Family Law* 32, 2018, 28–42.

what economic 'justice' – or 'fairness' – on divorce requires by way of redistribution between the parties.[4]

While they arise only at the point of dissolution, the nature, basis, intensity and duration of the financial and property rights and remedies that arise on divorce are fundamentally important to an understanding of marriage itself. They tell us something about each jurisdiction's conception of the marital relationship and the obligations to which it gives rise: whether marriage is viewed as a partnership in which gains and losses must be shared, as a relationship of dependency or inter-dependency, as a relationship of mutual insurance, or a combination of these, and whether fault should potentially limit or enhance the financial settlement made in favour of the 'guilty' or 'innocent' party respectively.[5] They tell us something about each jurisdiction's view about whether the marital relationship should have enduring consequences beyond divorce or end with a clean economic break freeing each party to move on to new relationships unencumbered by the first. These issues have been explored in an extensive corpus of normative academic literature exploring different accounts of 'fairness' on divorce and elaborating different subsidiary principles which give content to that (by itself, meaningless) 'principle'.[6] Various law reform commissions and other working parties have also been active in this area, and their working papers and reports provide further useful expositions of the principles in play.[7]

Is marriage a status-based relationship whose content is determined by the state or a contractual relationship negotiable by the parties?[8] In truth, it is better viewed as a combination of

4 J. Miles and J.M. Scherpe, 'The Future of Family Property in Europe', in K. Boele-Woelki, J. Miles and J.M. Scherpe (eds), *The Future of Family Property in Europe*, Cambridge/Antwerp: Intersentia, 2011, pp. 423–32.

5 We do not explore that issue in this chapter. For an overview of European jurisdictions' treatment of fault in divorce settlements, see K. Boele-Woelki et al., *Principles of European Family Law Regarding Divorce and Maintenance between Former Spouses*, Antwerp: Intersentia, 2004, pp. 100–3.

6 See, for example, A. Diduck, 'Ancillary Relief: Complicating the Search for Principle', *Journal of Law and Society* 38, 2011, 272–300; J. Eekelaar, *Regulating Divorce*, Oxford: Clarendon, 1991, Ch. 4; J. Eekelaar and M. Maclean, 'Property Adjustment after Divorce', in K. Hawkins (ed.), *The Human Face of Law*, Oxford: Clarendon, 1997, pp. 223–43; I. Ellman, 'The Theory of Alimony', *California Law Review* 77, 1989, 1–82; K. Gray, *Reallocation of Property on Divorce*, Abingdon: Professional Books, 1977; P. Parkinson, 'Reforming the Law of Family Property', *Australian Journal of Family Law*, 13, 1999, 117–39; C. Rogerson, 'Spousal Support after *Moge*', *Canadian Family Law Quarterly* 14, 1997, 281 and 'Spousal Support after *Bracklow*', *Canadian Family Law Quarterly*, 19, 2001, 185; T. Sverdrup, 'Compensating Gain and Loss in Marriage: A Scandinavian Comment on the ALI Principles', in R.F. Wilson (ed.), *Reconceiving the Family: Critique on the American Law Institute's Principles of the Law of Family Dissolution*, Cambridge: Cambridge University Press, 2006; articles in the special issue of *International Journal of Law, Policy and the Family*, 19, 2005, issue 2 and in the special issue of *Australian Journal of Family Law*, 32, 2018, issues 1 and 2; and J. Miles, 'Property Division on Relationship Breakdown: A Theoretical Analysis of the New Zealand Legislation', *New Zealand Universities Law Review* 21, 2004, 268–308, which draws on much of the foregoing literature, amongst other works.

7 See, for example, Scottish Law Commission, *Report on Aliment and Financial Provision*, Scots Law Com 67, Edinburgh: HMSO, 1981; Law Commission for England and Wales, *Matrimonial Property, Needs and Agreements*, Law Com CP 208, 2012 and Law Com No 343, 2014; American Law Institute, *Principles of the Law of Family Dissolution*, Philadelphia: ALI, 2003; and the work of Prof C. Rogerson and Prof R. Thompson on the Canadian Spousal Support Advisory Guidelines. Available at www.justice.gc.ca/eng/fl-df/spousal-epoux/ssag-ldfpae.html (accessed 22 October 2019); Law Commission for New Zealand, *Review of the Property (Relationships) Act 1976*. Available at www.lawcom.govt.nz/our-projects/review-property-relationships-act-1976 (accessed 12 October 2019).

8 See I. Schwenzer, *Vom Status zur Realbeziehung*, Baden-Baden: Nomos, 1987 and C. Sörgjerd, *Reconstructing Marriage: The Legal Status of Relationships in a Changing Society*, Cambridge/Antwerp: Intersentia, 2012.

both. As we explore later, whilst spouses commonly enjoy some freedom to determine through contract the extent of any property sharing or financial responsibility, that freedom is also commonly limited in some respects on grounds of public policy, enabling us to identify what might be called an 'irreducible'[9] core of matrimonial obligation which necessarily and inalienably arises on marriage.

A note on unmarried cohabitation

This chapter is principally concerned with the dissolution of marriage (and functionally equivalent same-sex institutions), and so does not deal directly with the financial consequences of the breakdown of non-marital relationships, in particular cohabitation – but some brief notes are offered here (see further Chapters 1.1–1.2 and 1.5 of this book). As marriage rates in many jurisdictions decline, rates of cohabitation and non-marital fertility have increased, in some jurisdictions dramatically. Increasing numbers of jurisdictions provide statutory financial and property remedies on the separation of unmarried cohabitants,[10] though high rates of cohabitation are not universally accompanied by such legislative responses, as the example of Québec strikingly illustrates.[11] Where the legislator has intervened, in some jurisdictions eligibility for financial remedies or property division depends on parties having institutionalized their relationship in some form of registered partnership or contract, whilst in others eligibility is determined on a de facto basis, some requiring the relationship to have endured for a minimum period or for the parties to have a joint child. There is huge variety internationally in this area, some jurisdictions assimilating the position of cohabitants with that of spouses, others providing deliberately less extensive remedies, but many others (the majority) leaving cohabitants to resolve their financial disputes under the general law (of property, trusts, contract, unjust enrichment and so on).[12] There are distinctive – often locally controversial – policy decisions to be made here: whether to legislate at all and whether, in principle, it is thought appropriate to assimilate cohabitants' position with spouses (though the answer to that may depend on the nature of the matrimonial laws in each jurisdictions and their perceived suitability – normatively and functionally – for cohabitants). But, those crucial decisions aside, the range of legislative options are no different from those available between spouses, and so the discussion which follows is relevant to cohabitants.

Methodological routes to 'fair' outcomes

It is commonly said that the objective of financial remedies and property division on divorce is to achieve a 'fair' outcome. While the particular routes to achieving fairness differ substantially

9 See Baroness Hale, *Radmacher v Granatino* [2010] UKSC 42, para 132; see also the findings of comparative projects such as the work of the Commission for European Family Law (K. Boele-Woelki et al., op. cit., n 5) and J.M. Scherpe (ed.), *Marital Agreements and Private Autonomy in Comparative Perspective*, Oxford: Hart, 2012.

10 For comparative overviews, see J. Miles, 'Unmarried Cohabitation in European Perspective', in J.M. Scherpe (ed.), *European Family Law Vol. III: Family Law in a European Perspecive*, London: Elgar, 2016, pp. 82–115; and J.M. Scherpe and N. Yassari (eds), *Die Rechtsstellung nichtehelicher Lebensgemeinschaften / the Legal Status of Cohabitants*, Tübingen: Mohr Siebeck, 2005, and especially J.M. Scherpe, 'Rechtsvergleichende Gesamtwürdigung und Empfehlungen zur Rechtsstellung nichtehelicher Lebensgemeinschaften', pp. 571–605.

11 *Attorney General of Quebec v A and B* [2013] SCC 5 (Supreme Court of Canada).

12 See generally Miles, op. cit., n 10 and Scherpe and Yassari, op. cit., n 10.

internationally, there is in fact more common ground and convergence amongst ostensibly different jurisdictions than might at first glance be appreciated: the routes may be different, but the destinations similar.[13] In this section, we explore some basic methodological questions concerning the route to fair outcomes: pillar systems versus equitable redistribution systems; and the use of rules, principles, guidelines and discretion. In the next section, we then explore four key substantive components of 'fairness' which are evident internationally, albeit presented and implemented differently.

Pillar systems versus equitable redistribution systems

The law of many jurisdictions, notably the civil law jurisdictions of continental Europe, is based on what may be called a 'pillar system' in which the package of financial remedies for a spouse on divorce is constructed on a number of discrete elements (or pillars) each of which addresses a different issue: the division of property according to the rules of the applicable matrimonial property regime, sharing of retirement pension funds or income, regular maintenance (alimony/spousal support) payments, compensatory capital adjustment and allocation of the use of the former matrimonial home.[14] The basis on which each pillar operates – for example, the range of property to be shared, the bases upon which maintenance might be payable – varies between jurisdictions, but the pillar structure is a shared feature. Meanwhile, equitable redistribution systems, prevalent amongst common law jurisdictions, take a more flexible and holistic, less compartmentalized approach. They equip the courts with an extensive 'tool box' of remedies which empowers them to do all the sorts of things which the continental European pillars achieve, but leave it to the courts to determine what combination of remedies to deploy in any given case in pursuit of an overall result which is judged to be fair.

Rules, principles, guidelines and discretion

The equitable redistribution jurisdictions' emphasis on discretion and explicit pursuit of overall fairness can give rise to the perception that the pillar jurisdictions ignore fairness, attending in a rule-driven, mechanical way to each pillar regardless of the overall picture. However, whilst there is clearly significant distance between jurisdictions such as Ireland which continue to assert a strong judicial discretion to achieve 'proper provision' on divorce and jurisdictions with apparently more rule-based approaches, comparative analysis reveals a more complex but shared picture. Whilst jurisdictions such as France and Germany take a strictly rule-based approach to property division,[15] discretion is exercised in relation to other pillars, notably maintenance; some other jurisdictions, such as the Nordic Countries and Austria,[16] even have an element of discretion within their property sharing pillar. So whilst the approaches may be very different, the underlying principles are not. Discretion concerning the financial consequences of divorce is not wholly alien to the pillar jurisdictions, and within the equitable redistribution jurisdictions' holistic approach one can increasingly see distinct principles in operation which correspond closely with the concerns of civil lawyers' pillars.[17]

13 See J.M. Scherpe, 'Marital Agreements and Private Autonomy in Comparative Perspective', in Scherpe op. cit., n 9, pp. 443–518 and esp. 446–82.

14 Ibid.

15 See the chapters by A. Dutta and W. Pintens in Scherpe, op. cit., n 9, pp. 158–99 and 68–98.

16 See the chapters by M. Jänterä-Jareborg and S. Ferrari in Scherpe, op. cit., n 9, pp. 370–402 and 51–67.

17 Scherpe, op. cit., n 13.

Another key methodological issue here is the growing interest in the adoption of guidelines or formulae in preference to strong, unpredictable exercises of judicial discretion as a means of providing greater certainty, particularly regarding the quantum and duration of spousal support/alimony payments (see further Chapter 2.7 of this book). Whilst discretion has the advantage of enabling outcomes to be tailored precisely to the circumstances of individual cases, it is costly to operate and assumes that the parties have access to a judge, or at least to a lawyer who can provide expert advice as to the likely range of adjudicated outcome in order to provide the parameters for negotiation. At a time when budgets for the delivery of family justice and provision of legal aid are coming under considerable pressure worldwide and there is also significant policy interest in moving private family cases out of court into alternative dispute resolution, there is increasing need for the law to provide more predictable outcomes – a more distinctive shadow in which parties can bargain out of court,[18] quite possibly without expert legal guidance or indeed without any professional assistance at all.[19] As Carol Rogerson has said in the context of Canada's Spousal Support Advisory Guidelines, 'average justice' delivered with the aid of more formulaic legal models potentially offers systemic advantages over 'individualised justice' that may be judged to be worth the (largely theoretical?) sacrifice of more nuanced, 'Rolls Royce' service offered by strong judicial discretion.[20]

Substantive ingredients of 'fairness'

Financial and property orders on divorce are – from the perspective of the general law – expropriatory: they deviate from the general law, either by reflecting distinctive matrimonial property rights or by creating entitlements and enforcing financial obligations which exist only because of the parties' (now defunct) marital relationship (the significance of this for marital agreements is discussed later). Matrimonial law is therefore an important source of legal obligation founded on its own rubric of fairness. What is regarded as fair between (ex) spouses is a matter for debate and for change over time as social attitudes towards marriage, divorce and spouses alter. 'Traditional' justifications for husbands' maintenance obligations, for limitations on wives' contractual (in)capacity or for denial of relief to the 'guilty' spouse a century ago may have no resonance today, and so new accounts of fairness need to be found for contemporary circumstances. This section explores four key ingredients of fairness which are evident internationally today, picking up on methodological issues in the course of that discussion: (1) sharing of property pursuant to a principle of matrimonial partnership; (2) the alleviation of need pursuant to a principle of matrimonial obligation; (3) compensation for relationship-generated losses; and (4) respect for couple autonomy.

Sharing of property

The marital union has always been perceived as one of shared lives, but sharing of assets is a more recent phenomenon, certainly in England and Wales. There it was only established in *White v*

18 R. Mnookin and L. Kornhauser, 'Bargaining in the Shadow of the Law: The Case of Divorce', *Yale Law Journal* 88, 1979, 950–97.

19 For recent discussion of these issues in the English context, see Law Commission for England and Wales, CP 208, 2012, Part 5, and J. Miles, 'Should the Property Regime Be Discretionary or Rules-Based?', in J. Palmer et al. (eds), *Law and Policy in Modern Family Finance*, Cambridge: Intersentia, 2017, pp. 261–92.

20 See C. Rogerson, 'Developing Spousal Support Guidelines in Canada: Beginning the Discussion', *Ottawa: Department of Justice*, 2002. Available at www.justice.gc.ca/eng/rp-pr/fl-lf/spousal-epoux/ss-pae/pdf/ss-pae.pdf (accessed 22 October 2019), at p. 6.

White[21] that, subject to a variety of circumstances, marriage may lead to an equal sharing of assets in case of divorce (at least in the absence of a marital agreement, on which see later). The move away from awards made for the financially weaker spouse solely on the basis of his/her 'reasonable needs' was revolutionary and completely changed the nature of financial relief for that jurisdiction – and presumably also the meaning and nature of marriage. This understanding of marriage as a partnership of equals, with husband and wife[22] in principle being seen as equal contributors irrespective of their roles in the relationship and thus entitled to an equal share,[23] came about much earlier in the civil law jurisdictions and indeed many other common law jurisdictions.

But a basic starting point of 'equal sharing' in itself does not mean very much unless it is clear what exactly is to be shared. In the civil law jurisdictions with their matrimonial property regimes, the sharing pool is (more or less) certain, but the approaches of the various regimes to sharing at least at first glance seem to be fairly disparate.

Matrimonial property regimes can be broadly categorized into two groups: those based on a separation of property and those based on a community of property between the spouses. In the former we find, for example, the German community of accrued gains where the sharing is limited to a monetary claim[24] for half of the share of the gains accrued by both spouses during the marriage, excluding inheritances and gifts (but including, for example, capital gains and value increases of premarital property). Another approach is taken by the Nordic countries, where the default regimes are all a type of deferred community of property. Here the spouses' property, irrespective of when and how acquired, remains separate during the marriage but upon divorce in principle all property of the spouses becomes part of the sharing pool. However, there is – to a certain extent – judicial discretion to exempt certain assets from the sharing exercise, and (oversimplifying) this discretion is most often used in case of short marriage and/or in connection with premarital assets and gifts and inheritances.[25]

Amongst the community of property jurisdictions in Europe, the Netherlands until the end of 2017 was the only one where a *universal* community of property was created upon marriage, meaning that in principle all property was to be shared equally; it is hardly surprising therefore that prenuptial agreements (on which see later) were very common in the Netherlands (see Chapter 1.2 of this book). By far the most prevalent approach in Europe (since 2018 also including the Netherlands) and South America is the community of acquests. Here the spouses both retain their premarital assets (and inheritances and individual gifts received after the wedding) as

21 [2001] 1 AC 596. This approach was then later confirmed and refined in *Miller v Miller; McFarlane v McFarlane* [2006] UKHL 24 with Baroness Hale and Lord Nicholls between them referring to the 'fruits' of the marriage/matrimonial partnership/the couple's labours nine times (in paras [17], [19], [20], [21], [85], [141], [149] and twice [154]) and the 'joint/common endeavours' of the spouses three times (in paras [22], [91] and [143)].

22 Or now also husband and husband or wife and wife in many jurisdictions.

23 Except for Greece where the (rebuttable) presumption is that each spouses only contributed 1/3 to the other's assets; see E. Zervogianni, 'The Changing Concept of "Family" and Challenges for Family Law in Greece', in J.M. Scherpe (ed.), *European Family Law Vol. II: The Changing Concept of 'Family' and Challenges for Domestic Family Law*, London: Elgar, 2016, pp. 86–106.

24 Hence there never is any form of community of property, despite the somewhat misleading name of the regime.

25 A. Agell, *Nordisk äktenskapsrätt*, Copenhagen: Nordiska Ministerrådet, 2003, pp. 373 et seq.; J.M. Scherpe, 'Privatautonomie im Familienrecht der nordischen Länder', in S. Hofer, D. Schwab and D. Henrich (eds), *From Status to Contract? – Die Bedeutung des Vertrages im europäischen Familienrecht*, Bielefeld: Gieseking, 2005, pp. 212–19; J.M. Scherpe, 'Matrimonial Causes for Concern? A Comparative Analysis of *Miller v Miller; McFarlane v McFarlane*', *King's Law Journal* 18, 2007, 348–60.

separate property, but all assets acquired during the marriage immediately become part of the common property from which each spouse is entitled to half a share, not only in case of divorce but already during the marriage. By providing the financially dependent spouse with immediate property rights, it has been argued that this puts them in a stronger position in comparison to those whose property rights only materialize on divorce (or death of the other spouse).[26]

But irrespective of the difference of approach, a comparative analysis quite clearly shows agreement between these jurisdictions about what property should be shared: only assets acquired or accrued during the marriage as 'fruits of joint labour', thus excluding inherited and gifted assets. Interestingly, this is not only the approach that Scotland as a mixed jurisdiction has always taken,[27] but is also becoming increasingly common in common law jurisdictions. Thus for example Singapore defines matrimonial assets in a similar way,[28] as does New Zealand with 'relationship property'.[29] However, unlike the formulaic approaches in the civil law jurisdictions, these jurisdictions often allow for certain separate assets to become matrimonial/relationship assets over time; if, for example, they were used by the family, in particular the family home. It appears that England and Wales has embarked on a similar path,[30] but unlike other common law jurisdictions has done so through judicial development rather than legislation, at least for the time being.[31] This of course brings with it a greater flexibility to deal with individual cases at the expense of legal certainty.

So in summary one can argue with some confidence that the law regarding the sharing of property in most jurisdictions has followed social developments in that marriage is perceived as a partnership of equals. This means that the spouses' contributions to the family, whatever their nature, in principle lead to an equal share of the 'marital' assets or their value and that those marital assets are in principle confined to those actually generated during the marriage by spouses. Hence premarital assets as well as assets received as inheritance or gift are either not part of the sharing pool at all or, in some jurisdictions, only if they have become part of the marital assets by being 'maritalized'.

Responsibility for needs

In many jurisdictions, the relief of need retains a central place in the matrimonial remedies provided on divorce. But not in all. The broader socio-economic context matters immensely, with different jurisdictions taking different views about the relative responsibility of private actors and public agencies to assist indigent citizens. Jurisdictions which have extensive social provision (in terms of social security, housing, high quality child-care, gender neutral parental leave entitlements) provide a very different playing field for spouses, both during marriage and following separation, from that in jurisdictions with more modest public provision (see

26 For a discussion of this aspect see Scherpe, op. cit., n 13, p. 474.

27 Family Law (Scotland) Act 1985, s. 10(4). K. McK Norrie, 'Marital Agreements and Private Autonomy in Scotland', in Scherpe op. cit., n 9, pp. 289–310.

28 Women's Charter s. 112(10).

29 Property (Relationships) Act 1976, s. 8.

30 J.M. Scherpe, 'Towards a Matrimonial Property Regime for England and Wales?', in R. Probert and C. Barton (eds), *Fifty Years in Family Law: Essays for Stephen Cretney*, Cambridge/Antwerp: Intersentia, 2012, pp. 129–42 and Scherpe, op. cit., n 13, pp. 481–3; J.M. Scherpe, 'A Comparative Overview of the Treatment of Non-Matrimonial Assets, Indexation and Value Increases', *Child and Family Law Quarterly* 25, 2013, 61–79. But compare the impact of decisions such as *Hart v Hart* [2017] EWCA Civ 1306 and *Sharp v Sharp* [2017] EWCA Civ 408.

31 For potential legislative reforms see Law Commission for England and Wales, op. cit., n 7.

further Chapters 6.1–6.2 of this book). So in Sweden, for example, whilst maintenance on divorce is theoretically available, it is almost never awarded in practice; the spouses will both be adequately provided for by their share in matrimonial property and, where needed, by the state welfare system.[32] Elsewhere, and particularly in jurisdictions where wives continue to play a more traditional role (often induced to do so by local fiscal, social security and labour market arrangements, as well as cultural expectations), need looms large as a justification for resource allocation on divorce.

But the way in which need is satisfied varies. In 'pillar jurisdictions', the property allocated to a spouse upon divorce through the matrimonial property regime will not always be sufficient to cover the needs of a spouse, and therefore need will often be attended to explicitly through the provision of maintenance (or related remedies) and the allocation of use of the former matrimonial home. Equitable redistribution jurisdictions will take a more broad-brush view of needs that may extend to capital provision. This is particularly notable in England and Wales, where high property prices and a limited rental accommodation market in many parts of the country mean that the division of capital is considered vital to meeting the parties' needs.

This different understanding of how 'need' should be met can lead to inter-jurisdictional confusion, highlighted in the private international law context by the characterization of financial orders on divorce for the purposes of the European Union Maintenance Regulation:[33] what an English family lawyer regards as needs-based and so a matter of 'maintenance' will not correspond with a German family lawyer's view of the same case.[34] While the German lawyer will be able to point to two distinct parts of a German divorce package – participation in gains (property sharing) and maintenance payments – the English lawyer's holistic perspective will not permit so neat a division. In the vast majority of English cases, the award will be regarded for domestic purposes as 'needs-based' even if, within that provision, one might identify a theoretical property sharing component departed from in order to produce unequal shares in view of the parties' differing needs.[35] Should the UK remain subject to EU private international law rules, the discipline required by the Maintenance Regulation may push English law towards a more explicitly principled/pillared approach.

But identifying the role of need within the overall package is only part of the problem. The greater problem, which has received extensive academic and law reform attention in recent decades, is what is meant by 'need' at all. For which, if any, of my needs might my now-ex-spouse be liable and to what extent? Is any distinction to be drawn for these purposes according to the source of my needs, as originating in my caring obligations undertaking for the benefit of our children or other family members, in my old age, illness or disability, or in my unemployment? Does it matter whether the source of my need pre-dates the marriage, arose during it, or arose following separation? How are the needs for which the obligor spouse is liable to be measured (by reference to the standard of living during the marriage or by some other, more objective measure?),[36] and for how long after the marriage has ended ought the obligor's liability

32 See chapters by M. Jänterä-Jareborg and J.M. Scherpe in Scherpe (ed.), op. cit., n 9.

33 Council Regulation (EC) 4/2009, which governs conflict of law issues and the recognition and enforcement of decisions regarding spousal and child maintenance. See further Chapter 7.2 of this book.

34 A. Dutta and J.M. Scherpe, 'Cross-Border Enforcement of English Ancillary Relief Orders: Fog in the Channel: Europe Cut Off?', *Family Law* 40, 2010, 386–91.

35 For a recent attempt to disentangle these aspects of English awards, see Law Commission for England and Wales, CP 208, 2012, paras 4.93–4.94, with particular reference to the family home.

36 For the various positions of European jurisdictions on this issue, see Boele-Woelki et al., op. cit., n 5, pp. 89–90.

to last?[37] The answer to that last question might be used as a basis for calculating an appropriate clean break capital award, rather than an ongoing spousal support liability.[38]

Different courts, law reform bodies and legislators have given more or less close attention to these questions. Some jurisdictions – such as England and Wales and Canada – have offered relatively little clear guidance. The English statute hints only very loosely (in the course of its unranked, statutory checklist for the court to consider in exercising its wide discretion) to the possibility of needs-based provision on grounds such as illness and disability;[39] few English cases have had to confront the issues directly, but the Law Commission has recently provided an extensive and rigorous analysis of the issues.[40] The leading Canadian decision, whilst making clear that liability may arise for needs not connected with the claimant spouse's contributions to the marriage, gave little guidance on how far that liability might extend, creating significant uncertainty and so prompting developments addressed in the next section.[41]

By contrast, German law identifies specific grounds upon which maintenance may be claimed,[42] which have even been prioritized by the court for the purposes of determining when, if at all, those obligations might be ousted by party agreement.[43] Need arising from marriage-related disadvantage (in particular, from childcare obligations) was placed at the core of the legal rules regulating the financial consequences of divorce, followed by need arising from old age and (if arising during the marriage) from illness, leaving need arising from factors such unemployment on the periphery.[44] The closer to the core the less likely it is that an agreement ruling out such maintenance claims will be upheld in a German court.

Analyses such as that provided by German law reflect a policy view that whilst some needs are properly seen as a matter of joint obligation, others may properly be left for the individual concerned to deal with: the ex-spouse is not an insurer for all losses. In articulating that position, German law highlights a perceived problem with imposing liability based on 'need' per se on the ex-spouse (rather than on some other family member or the state): the lack of clear justification for that liability. This argument has been made most cogently in the seminal work of Ira Ellman,[45] who would become the Chief Reporter on the American Law Institute's project on the *Principles of the Law of Family Dissolution*.[46] Ellman argued that neither contract nor partnership theories afforded an adequate explanation of the ex-spouse's liability, the contract being too vague, adjudicating its breach too problematic and the partnership being over. Instead, Ellman

37 For the variety on that issue within Europe, ibid., pp. 112–15.

38 Indeed, in some jurisdictions, the award may always be capitalized (if payable by instalments), e.g. the French *prestation compensatoire*.

39 Matrimonial Causes Act, 1973, s 25(2)(e).

40 See *North v North* [2007] EWCA Civ 760, *Seaton v Seaton* [1986] 2 FLR 398, and remarks of Mostyn J in *SS v NS* [2014] EWHC 4183, [31] and Lord Wilson in *Wyatt v Vince* [2015] UKSC 14, [33]; Law Commission for England and Wales, *The Financial Consequences of Divorce: The Basic Policy*, Law Com No 103, London: HSMO, 1980 and *The Financial Consequences of Divorce*, Law Com No 112, London: HMSO, 1981; cf. Law Commission for England and Wales, op. cit., n 7.

41 *Moge v Moge* [1992] 3 SCR 813, *Bracklow v Bracklow* [1999] 1 SCR 420, and commentaries by Rogerson, op. cit., n 6.

42 See §§ 1569–1576 BGB (Bürgerliches Gesetzbuch, the German Civil Code) Ref to BGB provisions and Dutta, op. cit., n 15, esp. pp. 164–5.

43 See esp. the seminal decision by the Bundesgerichtshof (Federal Court of Justice) of 11 February 2004 (XII ZR 265/02), BGHZ 158, 81 = FamRZ 2004, 601 = NJW 2004, 930.

44 See chapter on German law by A. Dutta in Scherpe (ed.), op. cit., n 9, and for other jurisdictions see Boele-Woelki et al., op. cit., n 5, from pp. 87ff.

45 I. Ellman, 'The Theory of Alimony', *California Law Review* 77, 1989, 1–82.

46 American Law Institute, op. cit., n 7.

argued that the strongest justification for requiring the obligor spouse to pay following divorce arose when the needs for which payment is sought arose from the parties' contributions to the marriage, in particular the economic sacrifice made by the party who undertook childcare obligations in lieu of paid employment. This justification takes us away from 'need' and towards alternative bases for financial provision which rest on some sort of compensatory argument and in more formulaic methodologies for calculating this component of awards on divorce.

Compensation for relationship-generated losses

Increased interest in compensatory bases for spousal support originates not just in the theoretical deficiencies of needs-based support but also in the influence of empirical data which demonstrate the full extent of losses incurred over the lifetime by wives in consequence of discharging their domestic roles and the failure of existing remedies to achieve substantive economic equality for wives following divorce.[47] Such data – or at least awareness of the issues they highlight – have to some extent influenced both judicial[48] and legislative[49] developments which have introduced a compensatory element into the financial package on divorce.

Financial relief based on compensatory ideas seeks to elevate the claimant spouse from the position of 'needy supplicant' and to capture (more fully than needs-based relief can do) the true impact on her economic position of sacrifices made by her for the benefit of the relationship, impact to which she is exposed by the dissolution of the marital partnership: however 'need' is measured, it has a ceiling which may be lower than that of an award based on compensatory ideas. It may take the form of an adjustment of the parties' shares in property (as in New Zealand,[50] Scotland,[51] and Spain,[52] for example), underpin the award of spousal support (as in Canada),[53] or simply feed into the holistic analysis (as in England and Wales).[54]

The central issue with compensatory relief is to determine what loss is being compensated (or shared). In some jurisdictions, compensatory relief might be regarded – or certainly operate in practice[55] – as a more focused needs-based concept, providing relief specifically for needs arising from the division of roles in the marriage and following divorce. The principal

47 See for example data cited to the Canadian Supreme Court in *Moge v Moge* [1992] 3 SCR 813, discussed by A. Diduck and H. Orton, 'Equality and Support for Spouses', *Modern Law Review* 57, 1994, 681–702.

48 Note in particular the judgment of Justice L'Heureux-Dubé in *Moge*, ibid.

49 For example, New Zealand, where concerns about substantive economic inequality post-divorce underpinned the new economic disparity provision in the Property (Relationships) Act 1976, introduced in 2002: see Report of the Royal Commission on Social Policy (1988), summarised by B. Atkin and W. Parker, *Relationship Property in New Zealand*, Wellington: Butterworths, 2001, ch 1.7; and contributions to parliamentary debates, such as Hon Margaret Wilson, *Hansard NZ*, vol, 591, col 8625–8626 (29 March 2001). But see the more recent work of the Law Commission of New Zealand on this issue, n 7.

50 Property (Relationships) Act 1976, s. 15.

51 Family Law (Scotland) Act 1985, s. 9(1)(b): economic advantage/disadvantage principle.

52 See J. Ferrer-Riba, 'Marital Agreements and Private Autonomy in Spain', in Scherpe op. cit., n 9, pp. 350–69, esp. pp. 356–7. However, the Spanish *prestación compensatoria (like its French counterpart, the prestation compensatoire; see Pintens, op. cit., n 15)* also has a strong maintenance function.

53 Under the Divorce Act 1985, s. 15.2, *Moge v Moge* [1992] 3 SCR 813, calculated by reference to the Spousal Support Advisory Guidelines.

54 See *Miller, McFarlane* [2006] UKHL 24; for discussion of how the compensation principle appears to be operating in practice, see Law Commission for England and Wales, *Marital Property Agreements*, Law Com CP 198, paras 2.55–2.58.

55 As it perhaps does in England and Wales: see Law Commission, ibid.

difficulties here then lie in evidencing and measuring those losses to the extent that they are based on claimed earning capacity loss. Some commentators object that this approach raises impossible 'what if … ' questions: how is one to determine what earning capacity the claimant spouse would have enjoyed had not been for the role division in the parties' marriage? And with which hypothetical alternative future of the claimant spouse is that spouse's current situation to be contrasted? It might be objected that if she had not married this husband and divorced him, she would instead not have climbed the professional heights but have married someone else and made the same sacrifices, in which case compensation for the lost professional career may be too generous.[56]

How, too, is the law to deal with the fact that the 'loss' sustained by the claimant is one for which she must bear some responsibility as the product of what will commonly have been a joint decision of the parties? Does that suggest that the obligor should only have to pay half the loss, and then only up to a point which brings the parties to economic parity, or should relief simply be payable up to the point of parity even if that means the obligor spouse pays off the loss in full?[57] What mitigation activities can the claimant spouse be expected to undertake? Indeed, what if giving up paid employment was entirely the choice of the claimant spouse?[58] More fundamentally, do all of these questions (and the fact that we are here discussing private law remedies) wrongly presuppose that the value of care-giving is measurable only in terms of losses associated with its performance, distracting attention from what Martha Fineman has eloquently argued is its immense positive public value?[59]

Rather than struggle to base compensation directly on actual, individualized (but very hard to measure) losses sustained, a compensatory remedy might instead adopt a rather different measure of loss and/or a more formulaic means of measuring the compensatory relief due. These alternative measures do not focus on the claimant as an individual worker disadvantaged in her pursuit of paid employment, instead focusing on the economic effect on each party of the unravelling of the marital partnership on which each of them has, in different ways, depended, their lives having become merged over time.[60] Compensatory relief may therefore aim at the point of divorce to 'smooth out' the loss of marital living standard, the loss of inter-dependence, by measuring spousal support (or an equivalent capitalized award) by reference to the disparity in the parties' incomes following divorce and the duration of the marriage. The longer the marriage, the greater the claimant spouse's accrued entitlement to continue following divorce to participate in the obligor spouse's standard of living via income-sharing and the longer the transitional period permitted before full financial independence from the obligor must be attained.

Measuring relief by reference to income disparity rather than earning losses sustained avoids the formidable evidential problems that loss-based compensation schemes encounter. Indeed,

56 See J. Eekelaar, 'Property and Financial Settlements on Divorce: Sharing and Compensating', *Family Law* 36, 2006, 754–8.

57 In the New Zealand context, see J. Miles, 'Dealing with Economic Disparity: An Analysis of Section 15 Property (Relationships) Act 1976', *New Zealand Law Review* 2003, 535–68.

58 See discussion of issues arising from New Zealand case *X v X (Economic Disparity)* [2006] NZFLR 361 in J. Miles, 'Responsibility in Family Finance and Property Law', in J. Bridgeman et al. (eds), *Regulating Family Responsibilities*, Farnham: Ashgate, 2011, at pp. 108–9.

59 See M. Fineman, *The Autonomy Myth: A Theory of Dependency*, New York: The New Press, 2004, discussed in Miles, op. cit., n 58.

60 See S. Sugarman, 'Dividing Financial Interests on Divorce', in S. Sugarman and H. Kay (eds), *Divorce Reform at the Crossroads*, New Haven: Yale University Press, 1990, Ch. 5, discussed by Law Commission for England and Wales, op. cit., n 7, from para 4.52. J. Eekelaar, *Family Law and Personal Life*, Oxford: Oxford University Press, 2017, pp. 109–111.

schemes based on (income disparity x duration of marriage) may also provide a satisfactory alternative to the difficulties entailed in operating any sort of needs-based relief, providing remedies that will in practice cover needs howsoever arising, without needing to inquire whether those particular needs are ones which ought in principle to be met by the former spouse. Unsurprisingly, the development of these ideas has occurred in tandem with the formulation of guidelines and other tools for calculating spousal support, which adopt proxy measures of loss and averaged notions of justice in lieu of any attempt at more individualized decision-making. Leading examples of these approaches are provided by the Canadian Spousal Support Advisory Guidelines (SSAG), which have unique status as non-legislated, research-generated guidelines with appellate court approval and are now widely used across Canada,[61] and the recommendations of the American Law Institute.[62] (See further Chapter 2.7 of this book.) Nor are such approaches the preserve of common law jurisdictions: it has been suggested that the calculation of both the French *prestation compensatoire* (effectively capitalized maintenance) and German maintenance awards (by reference to formulae developed by regional courts) reflect similar income-sharing principles.[63]

These approaches to the quantification of spousal support (whether viewed as needs-based or compensatory in nature) offer a very useful tool for parties seeking to settle their cases out of court. Moreover, whilst they may, in their more sophisticated formats (as in the case of the Canadian SSAG), ideally depend for their proper operation upon the availability professional legal advice, formulaic approaches have a self-evident appeal within a resource-limited family justice system.

Respect for autonomy

Marital agreements have been the subject of much recent attention in several jurisdictions,[64] whether in the form of pre-/ante-nuptial, post-nuptial or separation agreements regarding the division of assets and other post-marital financial obligations, particularly maintenance/alimony.

The fact that each jurisdiction has a default set of rules to govern the financial consequences of divorce instead of the general law means that it is generally accepted that the general law is inappropriate to deal with this social situation (see the preceding discussion about the displacement of the general law of property by matrimonial rights and remedies). It is therefore somewhat surprising that in most jurisdictions it is possible for the spouses to opt out of this protective default system, at least in part.

However, in those jurisdictions where a more or less rigid system of matrimonial property is imposed on the spouses, it was quite apparent (once divorce was an accepted fact) that that system might not be suited to every marriage and that there should therefore be scope for the spouses themselves to decide on their property relations. This particularly applies to community of property jurisdictions where the regime of immediate sharing of some (or all) assets might be inappropriate for tax or estate planning reasons or because of the financial risks one spouse incurs in professional or commercial activities. In jurisdictions such as England and Wales, Ireland and Australia where no matrimonial property regime exists, the justification for allowing

61 See Rogerson and Thompson, op. cit., n 7, and the discussion of this material by the Law Commission for England and Wales, CP 208, 2012, in Part 4.

62 Op. cit., n 7.

63 See Law Commission, CP 208, 2012, paras 4.59–4.60, and other European jurisdictions discussed in Boele-Woelki et al., op. cit., n 5, p. 82.

64 Particularly in England and Wales and Germany, where the law changed quite dramatically through decisions of the highest courts (see *Radmacher v Granatino* [2010] UKSC 42 and Bundesgerichtshof, op. cit., n 43), as well as in Australia and New Zealand where legislation on marital agreements was implemented (Part VIIIA Family Law Act 197 (Cth) and Part 6 Property (Relationships) Act 1976).

such agreements could be to allow the parties to achieve certainty with regard to their financial relations in case of divorce. The fundamental difference between the two has been aptly described by Lord Wilson as replacing one certain outcome with another certain outcome in jurisdictions with matrimonial property regimes, but replacing a (deliberately) undefined outcome with an outcome defined by the parties in those without such a regime.[65]

But irrespective of the default position that applies in the absence of an agreement (which of course is crucial for understanding each jurisdiction's rules on marital agreements), the fundamental challenge remains the same in all jurisdictions: to what extent should the spouses be free to opt out of the default regime? Or, in other words, how much autonomy is each jurisdiction willing to allow the parties in determining their financial relations? Given that the default system was set up to protect the financially weaker spouse, the ultimate question is therefore to what extent a spouse will be allowed to forfeit the default protection by private agreement.

Unsurprisingly, with the exception of Scotland,[66] no jurisdiction[67] appears to allow the spouse(s) to forfeit *all* protection by the default rules; but at the same time all jurisdictions will allow *some* of the protection to be forfeited. While there of course remain significant differences between the approaches in the various jurisdictions, they appear to have in common that the validity of an agreement opting out of the default rules is looked at in two stages.[68]

The first stage looks at the circumstances of the conclusion of the agreement in general: it can be called the stage of protection *of* autonomy. Here the question is whether both spouses actually were in a position to take an autonomous decision, taking into account not only the general law but also the specific situation of the (pre-)marital relationship.

The second stage, for cases where both spouses acted autonomously in concluding the agreement, is that of protection *from* autonomy: here the subject of scrutiny is the outcome of the agreement in the situation prevailing when that agreement comes to be relied on. This is where each jurisdiction draws a line which must be not crossed, regardless of how deliberate, informed and autonomous was the original the agreement.

The UK Supreme Court's decision in the English case of *Radmacher v Granatino* nicely exemplifies this two-stage approach:

> The court should give effect to a nuptial agreement that is freely entered into by each party with a full appreciation of its implications unless in the circumstances prevailing it would not be fair to hold the parties to their agreement.[69]

65 The Rt Hon Lord Wilson of Culworth, 'Foreword', in Scherpe op. cit., n 9, p. vii.

66 See K. McK Norrie, 'Marital Agreements and Private Autonomy in Scotland', in Scherpe op. cit., n 9, pp. 289–310.

67 Even Australia has now retracted from its original position after introducing legislation on prenuptial agreements, see e.g. O. Jessep, '*Marital Agreements and Private Autonomy in Australia*', in Scherpe op. cit., n 9, pp. 17–50.

68 J.M. Scherpe, 'Fairness, Freedom and Foreign Elements: Marital Agreements in England and Wales after Radmacher v. Granatino', *Child and Family Law Quarterly* 23, 2011, 513–27 and Scherpe, op. cit., n 13, pp. 514–18.

69 *Radmacher v Granatino* [2010] UKSC 42, para 75. Interestingly, even the test suggested by Lady Hale, who was in the minority in this case, in para 170 in principle follows this approach (although it reverses the burden of proof):

> Did each party freely enter into an agreement, intending it to have legal effect and with a full appreciation of its implications? If so, in the circumstances as they now are, would it be fair to hold them to their agreement?

The second stage of this test tends to be the more important and difficult one, where the policies underpinning the law and what is perceived to be a fair outcome in a given jurisdiction emerge most clearly: the jurisdictions 'draw the line' in very different ways. But while initial comparisons appear to reveal vastly disparate attitudes towards what is 'fair', a closer analysis actually reveals striking similarity in principle between jurisdictions: allowing the spouses to opt out of the sharing element of the default regime seems to be acceptable and the spouses' decision not to share their assets generally is respected; but when it comes to the compensatory or needs elements of the remedies available, jurisdictions greatly or even fully restrict the freedom of the spouses to opt out of the protective default rules.[70]

So if we assume that what the spouses cannot opt out of by marital agreement represents the 'irreducible core' of the matrimonial obligations, then it appears that there is an international consensus that compensating for relationship generated disadvantages and covering the needs of the other spouse even after divorce, at least to a certain extent, is this core. However, as already mentioned, what is perceived to be need or a relationship-generated disadvantage (and how these are to be covered) differs greatly from jurisdiction to jurisdiction.

Concluding remarks

In western jurisdictions today, very few legal rules regulate how a marriage should be lived. This broadly reflects the modern understanding that is primarily for the spouses to decide how to live their lives and that the state should not interfere unduly. Most of the policy objectives the law still pursues therefore are realized through the (generally very limited) requirements that must be satisfied in order to be eligible to enter into a marriage and then, should it come to this, the requirements to end a marriage and the consequences of doing so. The way marriage is perceived has changed considerably over the last century. In most jurisdictions, legislative reform has reflected those social changes. However, in some jurisdictions (including England and Wales), the courts, in the absence of legislative intervention, have been the driving force behind such changes.

When looking at the financial consequences of divorce, a clear development is evident in all jurisdictions: that marriage today (at least nominally) is considered to be a partnership of equals. This transpires most clearly from the almost universal understanding that certain assets should be shared equally on divorce. While there are considerable differences regarding *which* assets are to be shared, there seems to be a clear trend towards sharing only those assets that are the 'fruits of joint labour', i.e. were generated during and by the marriage; so premarital assets, gifts and inheritances are often excluded.[71]

But these assets are not necessarily totally excluded, and this arguably is where the other policy objectives of need and compensation come into play. In many jurisdictions, assets can become family assets (and consequently are shared) by the way they are used (the family home, for example); in others, there is a discretion to redistribute non-matrimonial property in case of divorce if that is needed to achieve the overall policy objectives. Finally, in some jurisdictions while these assets may be exempt from any form of property redistribution as such, other remedies safeguard the policy objectives (particularly through maintenance obligations).

70 Scherpe, op. cit., n 13, pp. 501–11 (again, with the exception of Scotland, see McK Norrie, op. cit., n 66). But see remarks in *Brack v Brack* [2018] EWCA Civ 2862, [102]-[103].

71 See e.g .the work of Law Commission of New Zealand on this issue, n 7 above.

A further interesting development in many jurisdictions, also in line with a more modern and liberal understanding of marriage, is the growing importance of marital agreements,[72] emphasizing the spouses' autonomy to regulate their own affairs and thus continuing the move away from regulating marriage and the withdrawal of the state from the private sphere. However, autonomy can cut both ways: while it empowers the spouses to regulate their lives and thus encourages independence, it can lead to the stronger spouse taking advantage of the weaker one. Since full equality between the spouses (between men and women, in particular) is not yet a social reality, it is unsurprising that the state has not completely withdrawn from regulating the spousal relationship. Hence spouses are generally not given complete freedom to abrogate the default rules. Certain policy objectives of these default rules – the covering of needs and compensation for relationship-generated disadvantages (however understood in each jurisdiction) – are mostly deemed to be matters of public interest which individual couples cannot limit fully (or even partially) by contracting out of the remedies that are meant to cover these. And so, to a certain degree, substantive fairness is ensured. So even in the twenty-first century and despite concerns by some to the contrary, marriage still counts for something and will continue to do so.

72 Although actually in some jurisdictions the freedom to contract out of the default rules recently has been more restricted, for example in Germany (see n 43).

2.7

CHILD SUPPORT, SPOUSAL SUPPORT AND THE TURN TO GUIDELINES

Carol Rogerson

Introduction

In Chapter 2.6, Miles and Scherpe introduced the policy challenges facing western jurisdictions, in the wake of the no fault divorce revolution, of how to best deal with the financial consequences of matrimonial breakdown. The challenges were described as both substantive and procedural in nature. That chapter dealt with the financial obligations that arise between spouses, specifically the remedies of sharing of property and spousal support and their interrelationship. It referred to the use of 'guidelines' based on mathematical formulas as one methodological route to 'fair outcomes' in the case of spousal support. One of the purposes of this chapter is to provide a more detailed look at the concept behind and practical development of such guidelines. The primary focus will be on Canada as their Spousal Support Advisory Guidelines[1] are regarded as a pioneering project, at least in the common law world.

However, the use of guidelines, or formulae, had been developed earlier in the context of child support, an obligation that has taken on increased significance since the 1980s. In 1997, following the path taken by the United States, England, Australia and New Zealand, Canada legislated a scheme of child support guidelines under which child support is assessed as a specified percentage of parental income rather than on the basis of individual budgets.[2] While many common law jurisdictions have adopted child support guidelines, Canada has gone further in extending that methodology of income-sharing guidelines to the much more contentious and complex area of spousal support. Because the Canadian spousal support guidelines were developed against the backdrop both of the new priority given to child support and a successful experience with 'income-sharing' child support guidelines, this chapter will first examine the basis of the child support obligation, its relationship to spousal support and the development of a scheme of child support guidelines in Canada.

1 C. Rogerson and R. Thompson, *Spousal Support Advisory Guidelines*, Department of Justice Canada, July 2008. All documents relating to the guidelines can be found at http://library.law.utoronto.ca/spousal-support-advisory-guidelines.

2 Federal Child Support Guidelines, SOR/97–175 as amended, enacted as regulations pursuant to the *Divorce Act*, R.S.C. 1985, c. 3 (2nd Supp.).

The increasing reliance on support guidelines, as illustrated by the Canadian experience, reflects what Dewar has identified as one of the characteristics of modern family law systems: a retreat from discretionary standards and an increasing reliance on more rule-like provisions, driven in large part by concerns about efficient dispute resolution.[3] The advantages of rules must, of course, be balanced against their disadvantages – the sacrifice of fine-tuned individual justice, undue rigidity and arbitrary and unfair results. Ironically, it is at the very time that family law has come to recognize the diversity of family forms that the need for rules and standardization has increased.[4] However, as a practical matter, there are many points on the spectrum between rules and discretion from which policymakers can choose. The search for the appropriate balance between rules and discretion in family law may be influenced, in part, by the legal culture in a particular jurisdiction. With respect to its law of financial remedies, Canada has been described as very 'rule-friendly' as compared to other common law jurisdictions.[5]

The development of support guidelines, as one example of the process of reforming substantive law in a more-rule like direction, is a complex mixture of theory and practice, substance and process. Debates over normative principles merge into the technical exercise of developing somewhat crude proxy measures that can be effectively administered. The introduction of more rule-based provisions may be part of a bold process of law reform or it may simply involve clarifying norms that have evolved from practice under an existing discretionary regime. Rules, presumptions or guidelines can be generated by various legal actors – not only by legislatures but also by courts, lawyers and even academics. Support guidelines can be developed and structured in many ways: they can be formal or informal; mandatory or advisory; and more or less complex both with respect to the structure of the basic formulas and the openings for discretion and deviation. In Canada the child support guidelines are legislated, mandatory and fairly rigid, whereas the spousal support guidelines, dealing as they do with a much more complex and normatively contested area of law, are informal, advisory guidelines based on norms that have evolved through practice and that allow greater scope for discretion and deviation.

The adoption and construction of child support guidelines

Over the past several decades child support has come to be viewed as an important part of the response both to the economic disadvantage experienced by children in single-parent families and to the growing costs of state support to such families[6] (for the economic affect of child support, see Chapter 6.1 of this book). Across western jurisdictions significant state efforts have been directed at increasing levels of child support and developing effective and efficient mechanisms for its assessment and enforcement. The discretionary determination of child support by courts through application of the vague concept of 'need' has been identified as contributing to the problem of historically low and inadequate levels of child support. New child support policies have increasingly emphasized standardization and transparency, including the development

3 J. Dewar, 'Family Law and Its Discontents', *Int. J. Law, Policy and the Family* 14, 2000, 59–85. For an excellent review of the policy choice between rules and discretion see E. Hitchings and J. Miles, 'Rules Versus Discretion in Financial Remedies on Divorce', *Int. J. Law, Policy and the Family* 33, 2019, 24–50.

4 K. Baker, 'Homogenous Rules for Heterogeneous Families: The Standardization of Family Law When There Is No Standard Family', *University of Illinois Law Review* 2012, 319–71.

5 J. Miles, 'Should the Regime Be Discretionary or Rules-Based?', in J. Palmer et al. (eds), *Law and Policy in Modern Family Finance*, Cambridge: Intersentia, 2017, pp. 261–91.

6 On whether these policy goals have been achieved see M. Hakovirta and M. Jokela, 'Contribution of Child Maintenance on Lone Mothers' Income in Five Welfare States', *J. of European Social Policy* 29, 2019, 257–72.

of formulas and guidelines for determining the amount of child support.[7] In the common law world, the American states were the pioneers in developing child support guidelines as a result of federal requirements imposed in 1988.[8] Australia,[9] England,[10] New Zealand[11] and Canada[12] followed suit. In each of these jurisdictions the guidelines were formally legislated[13] and the terminology of 'guidelines' is in fact misleading, for these are mandatory schemes[14] that generate precise amounts of child support. In England, Australia and New Zealand, the adoption of child support guidelines was part of a larger reform of child support law which involved the removal of child support matters from the courts and the creation of an administrative agency to both assess and enforce child support. In Canada, as in the US, child support determinations, using the guidelines, continue to be made by courts, although one of the clear objectives of the guidelines is to encourage out of court settlement.

The guideline models developed in the American context have to a large extent provided the framework and starting point for the development of child support guidelines in other common law jurisdictions.[15] Those models shift the basic approach in determining child support from one of *cost*-sharing to one of *income*-sharing, with basic child support amounts determined as a percentage of parental income.[16] The process of assessing of children's 'needs' on the basis of individual budgets has thus been abandoned. The significant policy question is how the percentages of income utilized by the guidelines are to be determined. This in turn requires clarification of the substantive principles that structure the child support obligation. What do parents owe their children financially? What are the costs of raising children? Because children require caregivers and share a household standard of living with them, challenges arise in delineating the boundary between child support and spousal remedies; between the obligations attached to parenthood

7 P. Parkinson, *Family Law and the Indissolubility of Parenthood*, Cambridge: Cambridge University Press, 2011. For cross-jurisdictional overviews of child support see OECD Family Database, 'PF1.5, Child Support'. Available at www.oecd.org/els/family/41920285.pdf and C. Skinner and J. Davidson, 'Recent Trends in Child Maintenance Schemes in 14 Countries', *Int. J. Law, Policy and the Family* 23, 2009, 25–52.

8 The Family Support Act of 1988 (now found in scattered sections of 42 U.S.C.) required states to implement mandatory child support guidelines as a condition for receipt of federal funding of their welfare programs.

9 Child Support Assessment Act 1989, significantly amended in 2008 by the Child Support Legislation Amendment Act 2006, with further modest amendments by the Family Assistance and Child Support Legislation Amendment (Protecting Children) Act 2018.

10 Child Support Act 1991, which has undergone successive major reforms, see C. Skinner, 'Child Maintenance in the United Kingdom', *European J. of Social Security* 14, 2012, 231–51 and B. Fehlberg and M. MacLean, 'Child Support Policy in Australia and the United Kingdom: Changing Priorities but a Similar Tough Deal for Children?', *Int. J. Law, Policy and the Family* 23, 2009, 1–24.

11 Child Support Act 1991. Significant amendments modelled on those in Australia in 2008 were introduced by the Child Support Amendment Bill 2011 (passed April 2013).

12 See n 2. The federal CSG apply to determinations of child support under the federal Divorce Act. All of the provinces subsequently introduced guidelines applicable to child support determinations in contexts not involving divorce, with all but one scheme identical to the federal guidelines.

13 Prior to their enactment there were examples of courts creating their own informal guidelines. Informal guidelines for the determination of child support have also been created by judges in Germany (the *Duesseldorfer Tabelle*) and the Netherlands (the TREMA guidelines).

14 England's most recent reforms (see below) have reduced the mandatory element by placing the primary emphasis on private ordering.

15 These models are reviewed in L. Harris, 'The New ALI Child Support Proposal', *Williamette Law Rev.* 35, 1999, 717–60.

16 Guidelines can be constructed in different ways. In Germany and Sweden, for example, standardized amounts of child support are based on the 'average' costs of supporting children.

and the obligations attached to the spousal relationship. Most child support guidelines have addressed this challenge through adoption of what has been called a 'marginal cost' approach, whereby child support is based on the costs of adding a child to an already existing household. This approach clearly separates the claims and needs of children, which are to be met by child support, from those of their caregivers, which are to be met by property division and spousal support (where it is available).

For the purposes of developing formulaic guidelines, aggregate economic data has been used to determine average or proxy measures of these costs. The evidence used to construct child support guidelines has typically been household expenditure surveys from which it is possible to determine the additional costs to households at different income levels when children are added. From this aggregate data economists calculate what percentages of parental income are spent as additional children are added to the household and these percentages are used in turn to construct the formulas on which the child support guidelines are based.[17] The goal of the guidelines is typically stated as ensuring that children continue to have access after divorce to the same percentage of parental income that they did before the divorce – the 'continuity of expenditure' principle.

The methodology used to create child support guidelines in the common law world is not without its problems. Critics point to the flawed assumptions that underlie the guidelines – the marginal cost approach, the use of economic data from intact families to determine costs where parents live apart, the failure to take into account base income disparities between the parents – as well as to contentious interpretations of the economic data.[18] Several academic proposals have contemplated restructuring the child support obligation around principles that focus on fair allocations of household or family income, thereby incorporating elements of caregiver support within the child support obligation. Included here would be the equalization of household income model[19] and the more modest proposal of the American Law Institute to add a formulaic supplement to basic child support amounts calculated on a marginal cost basis to reduce gross disparities in household standard of living between non-resident parents and children.[20] These remain live issues in what is often an ongoing process of revision and reform of child support guidelines. Despite the aura of mathematical precision that attaches to child support guidelines, they are based on very crude economic data and their adoption is governed as much by politics as technical expertise.[21] They are acceptable because they generate numbers that appear overall to be reasonable while offering the advantages of certainty and predictability, and they acquire legitimacy through their consistent application.[22] Models aimed at reducing household income

17 See I. Ellman, 'Fudging Failure: The Economic Analysis Used to Construct Child Support Guidelines', *U. Chicago Legal Forum* 2004, 162–224 and Harris, op. cit., n 15. In Canada, attempts to use household expenditure data proved unsuccessful and instead Statistics Canada 40/30 household equivalency scales were used to construct the formula; see Federal/Provincial/Territorial Family Law Committee, *Summary Report and Recommendations on Child Support*, Ottawa: Department of Justice, Communications and Consultation Branch, January 1995.

18 See Ellman, op. cit., n 17 and D. Allen and M. Brinig, 'Child Support Guidelines: The Good, the Bad, the Ugly', *Family Law Quarterly* 45, 2011, 135–56.

19 Discussed in M. Garrison, 'Autonomy or Community? An Evaluation of Two Models of Parental Obligation', *Cal. L. Rev.* 86, 1998, 41–117.

20 American Law Institute, *Principles of the Law of Family Dissolution: Analysis and Recommendation*, St Paul, MN: American Law Institute Publishers, 2002, Ch. 3. The ALI proposal is reviewed in Harris, op. cit., n 15.

21 See E.S. Perry, 'Evidence-Based and Politics-Driven: Comparing Child Support Evaluations Across Welfare-State Models', in C. Rogerson et al. (eds), *Family Law and Family Realities*, The Hague: Eleven Publishing, 2019, pp. 285–301.

22 See Baker, op. cit., n 4.

disparity have had little political traction. Undue complexity of some of the proposed models may be one reason; another may be resistance to paying spousal support in the guise of child support.[23]

Within the framework of this general methodology for constructing child support guidelines, there is much room for variation in the particular schemes adopted in each jurisdiction.[24] The percentages of income used in the child support formula vary, reflecting not only different data sources and methods of analysis but also different political and legal contexts, including the availability of other financial remedies within the family law system and government benefits. The percentages in Canada, for example, are roughly 11 percent of gross income for one child, 18 percent for two children and 23 percent for three children.[25] From a comparative perspective, these percentages are in the middle of the range that exists in common law jurisdictions. In Wisconsin in the US the comparable percentages are 17, 25 and 29.[26] In Australia and New Zealand, following the recent reforms, the basic percentages for one, two and three or more children respectively are 17, 24 and 27;[27] and in England 12, 16 and 19.[28]

The specific formulas vary in their degree of complexity, involving trade-offs between simplicity and efficiency, on the one hand, and more finely tuned justice on the other. The simplest guidelines take into account only the income of the payor (the 'percentage of payor income' model) whereas others look to the incomes of both parents (the 'income shares' model). Canada's guidelines, like those in England and a minority of American states, are based on the former model. However, as shown in the recent overhauls of the child support guidelines in Australia and New Zealand, there is increasing attraction to models that rely upon the incomes of both parents, in part for their symbolic representation of dual parental responsibility. In the more complex schemes, the income percentages vary with the income level of the parents and also, in some, with the ages of the children, reflecting respectively that lower percentages of overall income are spent on children at higher income levels and that teenagers are more expensive than younger children.

The degree to which the formula is calibrated to take into account variations in the amount of time each parent spends with the child also varies. Although many first generation formulas, like the Canadian formula, provide for no adjustment until arrangements come close to equal time sharing,[29] increasing politicization around the issue of shared custody has resulted in new guideline models in Australia, New Zealand and England that incorporate more complex sliding scale approaches in which child support amounts are proportionately reduced as time spent with

23 In some jurisdictions, such as Canada, spousal support may be available to supplement child support and reduce household income disparity.

24 See J.T. Oldham, 'Lessons from the New English and Australian Child Support Systems', *Vanderbilt Journal of Transnational Law* 29, 1996, 691–732.

25 Because the Canadian formula is based upon the 40/30 household equivalency scales and works on net incomes there are no explicit percentages of gross income set out; these percentages are extrapolated and will vary somewhat with income level. A discretionary approach is allowed for incomes over $150,000, but Canadian courts have largely ignored that 'ceiling' and have continued to apply the formula to extraordinarily high income levels.

26 These are the percentages for incomes under $84,000. For the portion of income between $84,000 and $150,000 the respective percentages are: 14, 20 and 23 and for the portion of income over $150,000: 10, 15 and 17.

27 In both Australia and New Zealand the basic percentages increase for older children (i.e. teenagers), but decrease for incomes above a certain level. As well, there are significant reductions for shared care, beginning with one night per week in Australia and two nights per week in New Zealand.

28 The percentages decrease for incomes above a certain level and there are also shared care reductions.

29 Section 9 of the CSG establishes a 40 percent time threshold for any adjustment for shared care.

the child increases.[30] In England and Australia these adjustments begin at quite modest levels of direct care: one overnight per week.

Finally, there are differences in the degree to which the schemes provide for deviations from or exceptions to the formula based on individual circumstances. In general those jurisdictions like Canada and the US where child support determinations remain within the purview of the courts provide more opportunities for deviation than those schemes that rely on administrative processes. Some degree of discretion would seem to be required for successful operation of any scheme of child support guidelines.[31]

The experience with child support guidelines in the common law world has admittedly been more positive in some jurisdictions than in others. In England the scheme originally introduced in 1991 was plagued by monumental administrative shortcomings combined with a complicated formula, the potential for unreasonably high awards and no discretion to depart from the formula. The scheme has been the subject of successive reforms, the most significant being those in 2012 which focused on simplifying the formula and the administration of the scheme, with an emphasis on encouraging private settlement.[32] (In Australia, heated gender-based politics around post-divorce parenting have had a strong influence on child support policy, leading to changes in the direction of increased complexity and reduction of child support amounts.)[33]

In Canada, on the other hand, the experience with child support guidelines has been very positive. They are widely supported by family lawyers, judges, mediators and parents and they have not been significantly reformed since their introduction in 1997.[34] Under the CSG child support continues to be dealt with by courts.[35] although in the vast majority of cases parents are able to work out the appropriate levels of child support on their own. One of the main virtues of the Canadian scheme is its relative simplicity. In a standard case the calculation of child support is relatively easy. The basic amount of child support is determined by easily accessible child support tables based on two factors: the payor's income and the number of children. The amount of support can be increased above the table amount, on a discretionary, individual basis to take account of certain special or extraordinary expenses and can be reduced in cases of undue hardship. Additional provisions create exceptions for shared care (with a very high threshold of each parent having care of the child for at least 40 percent of the time), children over the age of majority, high incomes and step-parent support, allowing for a more discretionary approach. In many cases Canadian judges have preferred to constrain rather than expand their discretion under the CSG, reflecting a strong Canadian preference for the efficiency and structure provided by rules-oriented schemes of financial relief. In cases where there is additional ability to pay, spousal support awarded on a compensatory basis to recognize the opportunity costs of

30 More generally see E. Claessens and D. Mortelmans, 'Challenges for Child Support Schemes: Accounting for Shared Care and Complex Families', *J. of European Social Policy* 28, 2018, 211–23.

31 See Oldham, op. cit., n 25.

32 Discussed by Miles, op. cit., n 5, who argues that the negative experience with the child support guidelines in England and Wales has created hostility to rule-based schemes for financial relief.

33 See also B. Fehlberg et al., 'The Perils and Pitfalls of Formal Equality in Australian Family Law Reform', *Federal Law Review* 46, 2018, 367–96.

34 In its review of the CSG five years after they were introduced the federal government concluded that they were working well in meeting their goals of fair, predictable and consistent awards: see 'Children Come First: A Report to Parliament Reviewing the Provisions and Operation of the *Federal Child Support Guidelines*' (Minister of Justice and Attorney General for Canada, April 2002).

35 Responding to access to justice concerns, one province (Ontario) has recently introduced the possibility, in uncomplicated cases, of online child support orders issued by an agency rather than a court.

ongoing child-care responsibilities is available to supplement child support and reduce disparities in household standard of living.

Although from an academic perspective the CSG do not deal particularly well with shared parenting or complex post-divorce families,[36] these concerns have not generated sufficient political pressure to create a more complex, second-generation formula. During the recent process of Divorce Act reform,[37] the primary focus was on post-divorce parenting arrangements and dispute resolution processes; the modest reforms to child support were directed at other important components of an effective child support policy – administrative recalculation and enforcement – and not the guidelines.

Spousal support guidelines and the Canadian SSAG

While child support guidelines have become a familiar feature of the family law landscape in the common law world since the late 1980s and early 1990s, spousal support guidelines are rarer, although of increasing interest. In jurisdictions where spousal support has become an extremely limited remedy and where financial relief is accomplished almost exclusively through property division[38] there is no pressing need for spousal support guidelines, unless as part of a major reform to radically reshape the law.[39] In such jurisdictions guidelines, if they exist at all, focus on strict durational time limits.[40] More complex schemes of spousal support guidelines that deal with amount and duration will only be of interest in jurisdictions where spousal support, as a distinct spousal remedy that attaches to post-divorce (or more accurately post-separation) incomes, remains a significant, litigated and contentious issue. The multiplicity of competing objectives and factors and the lack of a clear theoretical or political consensus in this area of law (in contrast to child support) have tended to lead to the conclusion that it was not amenable to guidelines. However, pragmatic concerns with the lack of certainty, predictability and consistency in this area of law, hindering efforts to settle and creating perceptions of unfairness, have begun to trump the absence of theoretical consensus. This is evidenced by a growing interest in spousal support guidelines in the common law world, specifically the US and Canada.[41] The focus here will be on the Canadian Spousal Support Advisory Guidelines (SSAG), the most ambitious and comprehensive scheme of spousal support guidelines to have been implemented to date in the common law world.[42] Here we see a different, more flexible

36 See n 31.

37 An Act to Amend the Divorce Act, S.C. 2019, c. 16.

38 For example, Australia: see B. Fehlberg, 'Spousal Maintenance in Australia', *Int. J. of Law, Policy and the Family* 18, 2004, 1–37.

39 See the proposal of the New Zealand Law Commission to create a new financial remedy for future income sharing (FIFA): Law Commission, *Review of the Property (Relationships Act) 1976 Act: Preferred Approach*, Wellington, NZ, November 2018, Ch. 5.

40 Found in several American states and in Scotland's 3-year cut-off under the Family Law Act (Scotland) 1985. In England and Wales, a proposed Divorce (Financial Provision) Bill (2017–19), later abandoned, had a 5-year cut-off.

41 For a brief overview of the use of spousal maintenance guidelines in European jurisdictions see K. Boele-Woelki, et al., *Principles of European Family Law Regarding Divorce and Maintenance between Former Spouses*, European Family Law Series No. 7, Antwerp: Intersentia, 2004, p. 82.

42 See n 1. For a more extensive discussion of the SSAG see C. Rogerson and R. Thompson, 'The Canadian Experiment with Spousal Support Guidelines', *Family Law Quarterly* 45, 2011, 241–70 and R. Thompson, 'Canada's Spousal Support Advisory Guidelines: A Half-way House between Rules and Discretion', *International Family Law* 2010, 106–16.

form of guidelines, a 'halfway house between rules and discretion',[43] reflecting the more complex nature of this area of law.

The SSAG are a set of informal, advisory guidelines with national scope intended to assist in the determination of the amount and duration of spousal support under the federal Divorce Act.[44] A final version of the guidelines was released in 2008, the culmination of a seven year project directed by two law professors and supported by the federal Department of Justice. Unlike the child support guidelines, the Canadian spousal support guidelines are not legislated and their application is not mandatory. They are informal, advisory guidelines developed through consultation with family lawyers and judges and intended to reflect current practice under the existing legislation rather than to change the law. Their development was a practical rather than a theoretical exercise. Although only advisory, they have received the endorsement of appellate courts across the country and are now widely used across the country by lawyers, mediators and judges. While there continue to be some concerns surrounding the use of the guidelines, they have been viewed as a largely successful policy initiative.

Background factors

What were the backdrop conditions that generated this successful experiment with spousal support guidelines? The first was a very expansive basis for entitlement to spousal support. Unlike in many jurisdictions, spousal support is a significant issue in Canada. In a series of major decisions in the 1990s interpreting the spousal support provisions of the Divorce Act, the Supreme Court of Canada rejected a 'clean break' approach that prioritized spousal self-sufficiency after divorce, emphasizing both the important compensatory role of spousal support, particularly with respect to gender-based economic disadvantage,[45] as well as its continuing role in meeting post-divorce need and more generally in recognizing the reliance and expectations generated by the merger of lives over time (what Canadians call non-compensatory support).[46] However, as the basis for spousal support expanded, the law became more discretionary and uncertain as judges and lawyers struggled with implementing the broad and vague concepts of compensation and need and with balancing the range of factors and objectives to be taken into account. Lawyers increasingly expressed their frustration with this area of family law practice.

Second, Canada's family law culture had already become fairly rule-oriented. Provincial matrimonial property regimes adopted in the 1970s and 1980s all incorporated a presumption of equal division of matrimonial assets. This was followed, as discussed previously, by the successful introduction of child support guidelines in 1997 which had accustomed judges and lawyers to the use of income-sharing formulas to determine support. Indeed, some lawyers and judges had begun to develop their own income-sharing formulas for spousal support, attempting to carry this new methodology over to spousal support.

Third, some concrete models for developing spousal support guidelines had emerged in the US over the course of the previous decade. Several American states had successfully experimented with spousal support guidelines.[47] Many of these were informal guidelines created

43 Thompson, op. cit., n 44.

44 See n 2. Spousal support is dealt with in s. 15.2.

45 *Moge v Moge*, [1992] 3 S.C.R. 813.

46 *Bracklow v Bracklow*, [1999] 1 S.C.R. 420.

47 For a review of the early American guidelines, see T. Larkin, 'Guidelines for Alimony: The New Mexico Experiment', *Family Law Quarterly* 38, 2004, 29–66. Many of these guidelines only dealt with interim or temporary support.

by local bar associations. Building on these experiences, the American Law Institute (ALI) had developed a much more sophisticated formulaic approach to spousal support that formed part of its blueprint for a substantive reconceptualization of the law of alimony around the concept of compensation.[48] Two major compensable losses were recognized; a basic claim in all marriages of significant duration for loss of the marital standard of living (which some would argue relates more to need and non-compensatory support than to compensation) and, in cases where there had been children, an additional claim based on loss of earning capacity because of disproportionate responsibility for childcare. Two formulas were proposed for adoption by state legislatures that would quantify such losses using proxy measures of income disparity and length of marriage/child rearing period.[49] Although differences in substantive law meant that the ALI guidelines were not completely transferrable to the Canadian context, they provided suggestive models for constructing formulas that could take into account some degree of diversity in length and types of marriages while remaining cognizant of the need to rely upon somewhat crude proxy measures in order to create guidelines that could be administered in a practical and efficient way, for example the decision to use income disparity (and hence the income of the higher earning spouse) as a measure for loss of earning capacity of the lower-earning spouse.

Construction of the SSAG

The Canadian spousal support guidelines were developed through an intensive consultative process with judges and lawyers. The academic directors of the project worked with an advisory group of lawyers and judges. Much of the work in developing the guidelines involved identifying the dominant patterns of outcomes across a range of *typical* cases, relying both on reported case law and on the practical experience of the advisory working group. The premise under the guidelines project was that despite the uncertainty and unpredictability in this area of law, there were some dominant patterns emerging in typical cases that required clearer identification. Mathematical formulas were then developed to capture these patterns in the law, both with respect to amount and duration. The results obtained suggested two basic formulas, reflecting strong distinctions between cases with and without dependent children. Because results clustered rather than converging on precise outcomes, the formulas were constructed to generate ranges rather than precise numbers for both amount and duration. The guidelines went on to identify a list of circumstances or 'exceptions' that would justify departure from the formula outcomes.[50] A draft version of guidelines was produced and released in January 2005. Then, after an extensive process of consultation with the family law bar and judiciary across the country, a final version was released in July of 2008.

At the heart of the SSAG are a set of formulas to be applied after entitlement has been established. These formulas generate ranges for both amount and duration of support based upon factors such as the parties' incomes, the length of their relationship, their ages, the

48 American Law Institute, op. cit., n 20, Ch. 5 (draft version published in 1997).

49 Under each formula the amount of support would be a specified percentage of the income disparity that would increase incrementally with the length of the marriage/child rearing period and the duration would be based on a durational factor which would similarly increase with the length of the marriage/child rearing period.

50 Including compelling financial circumstances in interim period, debt payments, prior support obligations, illness and disability, disproportionate losses or gains in short marriages, high and low incomes and second families.

presence of dependent children, the ages of the children and the allocation of custodial responsibility. There are two basic formulas, distinguished by the presence or absence of minor children and hence a concurrent child support obligation. The 'without child support' formula relies upon two main factors – the length of the marriage and the income difference between the parties with both amount and duration increasing incrementally with the length of the marriage. The formula is described as reflecting the concept of 'merger over time' which encompasses elements of both compensatory and non-compensatory support. In simplified form, the amount generated under this formula is 1.5 to 2 percent of the income difference for each year of marriage (capping at 50 percent) and duration is one-half to one year of support for each year of marriage, with no specified time limit after a martial duration of 20 years or more. In the case of a 15-year marriage without children the guidelines would suggest an amount in the range of 22.5 to 30 percent of the income difference between the spouses for a period of between 7 and 15 years. In the case of a 27-year marriage where the children are now adults the amount would be 37.5 to 50 percent of the income difference and there would be no time limit set.

The 'with child support' formula is more complex as it must take into account both the priority given to child support as the first claim on income under Canadian law and also adjust for differences in tax treatments of child and spousal support, requiring computer based calculations. The formula works with net parental incomes after removal of amounts dedicated to child support and allocates this remaining income so that the lower income spouse with primary care of the children is left with between 40 to 46 percent of this income. Thus under this formula amount does not vary with the length of the marriage. As well, the ranges for duration are sensitive not only to the length of the marriage but also, in shorter marriages, to the ages of the children and thus the length of the post-divorce child-rearing period. This formula represents distinctive patterns found in Canadian law in cases involving minor children captured by the concept of 'parental partnership'. It provides a formulaic measure for what Canadian law recognizes as strong compensatory spousal claims based on past and ongoing responsibility for childcare. In cases where child support does not exhaust ability to pay, spousal support determined under this formula can constitute a significant supplement to household income and reduce disparities in household standard of living. In a typical case with two dependent children in the custody of the mother, the amounts of spousal support generated by the guidelines would, when combined with child support, leave the custodial parent with between 52 to 57 percent of the parties' net combined incomes.

Responses and assessment

Initial reactions to the SSAG were mixed. Concerns were voiced both about their illegitimacy[51] and about applying 'cookie cutter' justice to complex, fact-specific issues. Often these initial reactions were based on mistaken assumptions about the actual nature of scheme and assumed a more rigid scheme than the one that was actually developed. Some of the criticisms also reflected disagreement with the broad basis for spousal support recognized in the Canadian law. The guidelines made the dominant patterns more explicit and exposed substantive disagreement and outliers. Over time the response has become largely positive.

51 For a defence of the legitimacy of the SSAG see J. Lazare, 'The Spousal Support Advisory Guidelines, Soft Law, and the Procedural Rule of Law', *Canadian J. of Women and the Law* 31(2), 2019, 317–45.

The guidelines, which have now been in existence for over ten years, have become widely accepted and are used both by lawyers and judges across the country. The result has been greater consistency and predictability of outcomes and reduced conflict.[52] The SSAG have received strong endorsement from appellate courts across the country, which have identified them as a useful tool and have treated their legal status as analogous to a compilation of precedent.[53] While emphasizing that the SSAG do not eliminate the need for an individualized analysis, appellate courts have recognized that they provide a useful starting point or litmus test. The use of the SSAG has been facilitated by the development of computer software to perform the calculations under the formulas and by a series of 'User's Guides' that review ongoing developments and the growing body of judicial decisions. Lawyers find the guidelines very useful in shaping client expectations and providing a structure for negotiation. Typical cases are resolved much more easily. The guidelines also provide some assistance to spouses attempting to settle spousal support on their own without lawyers.[54] Within the judicial arena, the SSAG have provided a clearer structure for analyzing spousal support cases, making the basis for discretionary decisions more transparent and constraining outlier decisions.

The SSAG are undoubtedly complex and have not provided formulaic answers to all of the difficult issues that arise in spousal support. The main problem that has been identified is that of unsophisticated use – a tendency among lawyers and judges to turn the SSAG into default rules, to ignore the exceptions and choose the midpoint of the ranges by default. In part this reflects lack of knowledge of or misunderstandings of the guidelines and is a problem that will diminish time with increased use and education. It also reflects, however, the strong attraction of rules and easy solutions in an overburdened family justice system.

Conclusion

The Canadian experience with the Spousal Support Advisory Guidelines offers some useful lessons to other jurisdictions; it shows that spousal support can be amenable to a guidelines regime provided the guidelines are sufficiently flexible and sophisticated; that guidelines can accommodate multiple support objectives in a practical way; that they can resolve large numbers of typical cases and offer a structure that can inform resolution of more difficult cases; and that legislative reform is not the only way that guidelines may be introduced. Since the Canadian initiative, interest in formulaic spousal support guidelines based on income-sharing has continued to grow, although it is not surprising that these schemes reflect substantive norms of spousal support different from, and often less generous than, those in Canada.

In the United States, although the ALI proposals have had little direct take-up,[55] in part because of the theoretical debates they unleashed about the substantive basis for the spousal

52 Confirmed by a 2012 formal evaluation: Prairie Research Associates, *Assessing the Impact of the Spousal Support Advisory Guidelines (SSAG)*, 30 January 2012, prepared for the Department of Justice Canada [on file with author].

53 For two early examples see *Yemchuk v Yemchuk*, 2005 BCCA 406 and *Fisher v Fisher* 2008 ONCA 11. The notable exception to the widespread use and judicial endorsement of the SSAG is the province of Quebec, which has a distinctive legal culture shaped by its civil law system; see J. Lazare, 'Spousal Support in Quebec: Resisting the Spousal Support Advisory Guidelines', *Les Cahiers de Droit* 59, 2018, 929–72.

54 Assisted by a free, simplified version of the software called 'My Support Calculator' available online.

55 A modified version of the ALI formulas was the basis for informal guidelines introduced in Maricopa County, Arizona.

support, this has not stopped the desire for practical solutions to the excessively discretionary nature of spousal support. As well, in many American states alimony reform is currently being driven by a desire to eliminate or restrict permanent alimony and guidelines, particularly for duration, are seen as an instrument for achieving this goal. A major development in the US has been the 2008 guidelines proposed by the American Association of Matrimonial Lawyers based on outcomes in practice.[56] In England and Wales, as part of its project on ways to clarify the law of 'financial needs' on divorce, the Law Commission drew on the Canadian experience with the SSAG in recommending further exploration of the possibility of developing advisory guidelines as an aid to calculation,[57] although the negative experience with child support guidelines there suggests that any such development will not come quickly.[58] The New Zealand Law Commission has also drawn on the Canadian experience with the SSAG in developing its recommendation for a new financial remedy for future income sharing, albeit recognizing that the different substantive norms in that country would not support the expansive basis for spousal support that exists under Canadian law.[59]

56 See M. Kisthardt, 'Re-Thinking Alimony: The AAML's Considerations for Calculating Alimony, Spousal Support or Maintenance', *J. of the American Academy of Matrimonial Lawyers* 21, 2008, 61. These guidelines were the basis for subsequent legislative reforms in New York, Massachusetts and Illinois, and for proposed reforms in Connecticut and Ohio.

57 Law Commission, *Matrimonial Property, Needs and Agreements*, Law Com No. 343, February 2014 at 3.121 ff.

58 Discussed in Miles, op. cit., n 5.

59 See n 41.

2.8
INHERITANCE AND DEATH
Legal strategies in the United States and England

Ray D. Madoff

Introduction

Family relationships that are not otherwise terminated during life are eventually terminated by death. What happens to a decedent's property can have a significant impact on the well-being of the surviving family members. This chapter considers at current policy challenges regarding how family members are, and are not, provided for upon death in a variety of jurisdictions.

This chapter consists of two parts. The first provides an overview of the rules governing the distribution of property at death in both common law and civil law countries. The second focuses on current policy issues in succession law in two common law countries, the United States and England (which for these purposes includes Wales).

Overview

Common law countries view property as being owned by individuals and not families. This individualistic notion of property is expressed in their law in a variety of ways. First, in most common law jurisdictions, marriage has no effect on property ownership. If one spouse earns $1 million over the course of the marriage, and the other spouse earns nothing, the non-wage earning spouse generally has no ownership interest in the wage-earning spouse's property.[1] If the non-wage earning spouse dies first, she has no control over the property acquired by the wage-earning spouse. If the wage-earning spouse dies first, some common law jurisdictions (including most states in the US) provide some limited protection against disinheritance in the form of elective share statutes, which give a surviving spouse the ability to claim a portion of the decedent spouse's estate. However, there is wide variation in the amount of protection afforded to surviving spouses.

Second, common law jurisdictions start with the premise of freedom of testation, the ability of an individual to control the disposition of his or her property at death. In the US, this means that children are generally not protected against disinheritance. However, most other common law countries provide protections for family members through the adoption of family

1 R. Madoff, C. Tenney, M. Hall and L. Mingolla, *Practical Guide to Estate Planning*, Chicago: CCH, 2013, Section 6.02[C].

maintenance statutes. These statutes do not provide fixed shares for family members as a matter of right (like forced succession statutes found in civil law countries), but rather give individuals the ability to appeal to a court for a reasonable financial provision.[2]

Civil law countries view property as being owned by a family unit as opposed to an individual.[3] This notion of property belonging to the family is expressed in the laws of civil law countries in multiple ways. Most civil law countries have adopted marital property rules whereby property earned by either spouse during a marriage is community property, over which both spouses have ownership interest (property earned before the marriage or received during the marriage by gift or inheritance is treated as separate property and is controlled by the individual). Upon death, each spouse is entitled to control all of his separate property and 50 percent of the couples' community property.[4]

Civil law countries also reflect the family nature of property by requiring that a significant portion of a person's estate be given to family members. These statutes, referred to generically as forced succession statutes, are found in civil codes throughout continental Europe, South America and in Japan. (For Japan, see Chapter 6.4 of this book.) They generally provide protection against disinheritance for the decedent's children (and if they are not living, grandchildren and other issue). Some statutes also provide protection for the decedent's spouse, parents and/or more distant blood relatives as well. These protections designate a set share for family of between 50 percent and 80 percent of the decedent's estate, leaving the decedent with freedom to control as little as 20 percent of his or her estate.[5]

The United States and England

Current issues in succession law in the US and England include:

- Who counts as a spouse
- Who counts as a child
- How is property allocated among family members when a person dies without a will
- To what extent is a spouse or other person allowed to claim a share of the decedent's estate despite freedom of testation.

Classification of individuals: spouses and children

Succession laws extend their protections to individuals based on status. In recent years, some of the most significant policy debates in succession law have concerned issues of taxonomy: in particular, 'who counts as a spouse?' and 'who counts as a child?' The rules of intestacy, spousal elective share statutes and family maintenance statutes all depend on this ability to categorize individuals. But seemingly simple questions like, who counts as a spouse, quickly get more complicated when considering a host of related questions such as how are same-sex couples treated? What about other cohabitating, but unmarried adults? What about married couples who are living apart, but

2 R. Kerridge and D.H. Parry, *Parry and Kerridge: The Law of Succession*, 12th edition, London: Sweet & Maxwell/Thomson Reuters, 2009.

3 T.G. Watkin, *An Historical Introduction to Modern Civil Law*, Hampshire, UK: Ashgate, 1999, pp. 192–218.

4 Madoff et al., op. cit., n 1, Section 6.02[B].

5 M. Reimann and R. Zimmermann, *The Oxford Handbook of Comparative Law*, New York: Oxford University Press, 2007, p. 1085; D.J. Hayton, *European Succession Laws*, European Practice Library, London: Chancery Law Publishing, 1991.

have not been formally divorced? The questions involving 'who counts as a child?' are even more varied and complex, concerning issues such as what is the effect of adoption on a child's relationship to the adopting and biological family? How, if at all, does the marital status of the parents affect the status of the child? What if any is the effect of a child being born or conceived after the death of the parent? Jurisdictions have struggled with these questions in recent years.

Who counts as a spouse?

Civil unions

No single question in family law has attracted such debate in recent years as who should count as a spouse (see Chapters 1.1–1.5 of this book). For centuries, the question was simply whether there was a lawful marital union between a man and a woman. However, beginning in the late twentieth century, there was a growing acceptance of same-sex relationships, and with it, an awareness of the limitations of inheritance systems that failed to take these relationships into account.

In the US, this was first addressed in 1999 as a number of states began adopting statutes which provided mechanisms for non-married couples to register their relationships with the state. These registered relationships (going under a variety of names including civil unions, domestic partnerships and reciprocal beneficiaries) were originally adopted as a way to allow same-sex couples to achieve some of the benefits of marriage, typically including spousal inheritance rights. The statutory systems differed in their details, but where these statutes existed registered couples were generally treated like married couples for state, but not federal, law purposes.

In 2015, however, the United States Supreme Court issued a landmark decision in *Obergefell v Hodges* granting same-sex couples the right to marry. As Justice Anthony Kennedy stated, 'No union is more profound than marriage, for it embodies the highest ideals of love, fidelity, devotion, sacrifice, and family'. Thus, Justice Kennedy, writing for the majority, concluded that same-sex couples should have the same right as heterosexual couples to 'aspire to the transcendent purposes of marriage and seek fulfillment in its highest meaning'. In virtue of the fundamentality of the right to marry, the court held that all states and the federal government are now required to allow and recognize same-sex marriage, along with all the rights that flow from married status, including inheritance rights.

In light of *Obergefell* the status of statutorily recognized non-marital partnerships are in flux. Some states continue to make civil marriage and spousal equivalent available to couples, giving couples a choice between two formed of committed relationships, but the law is highly state-specific and subject to change.

Beginning in 2005 same-sex couples in England have been allowed to enter into civil partnerships that provide many of the same succession benefits as marriage.[6] Subsequently in 2013 the Marriage (Same Sex Couples) Act recognized same-sex marriage in England, granting same-sex couples all legal benefits of marriage.[7]

Same-sex marriage

Further discussion of marriage rights for same-sex couples is found in Chapters 1.1–1.2 and 1.4 of this book.

6 The Civil Partnership Act 2004 (U.K.).
7 Marriage (Same-Sex Couples) Act 2013 (U.K.).

Cohabiting couples

Neither the US nor England provide intestacy rights for cohabiting couples, i.e. couples who live together in an intimate relationship but are neither married nor registered in a civil partnership. This is unlike the law of many other common law jurisdictions, including New Zealand, Saskatchewan and several territories in Australia, which treat surviving cohabitants the same as surviving spouses for purposes of intestacy.[8]

In the US there are generally no survivorship protections for couples that have not married or entered into civil unions. However, a limited number of states currently recognize common-law marriage: Alabama, Colorado, Iowa, Kansas, New Hampshire, Rhode Island, South Carolina, Texas, Utah and Washington, D.C. In recent years many states have begun to do away common-law marriage, which one court labeled as antiquated and fraught with inconsistencies, ambiguities and vagaries.[9] However, where states have abolished common-law marriage, they generally continue to recognize common-law marriages which occurred prior to repeal.[10]

English law does not recognize common-law marriage and does not provide explicit protection for cohabiting couples under its intestacy statute. However, since 1996 cohabitants who have lived together as spouses can claim family provision from the estate of the deceased partner by virtue of his or her status as cohabitant. Based on the nature of the relationship, the cohabitant may be awarded as much or more as he or she would have received as a spouse under intestacy. However, unlike intestacy, family provision claims require the surviving partner to pursue litigation.[11]

The question of the proper treatment of cohabiting couples has received much attention in England in recent years. In 2011 the Law Commission reconsidered the legal treatment of cohabiting couples and made the recommendation that intestacy protections should be extended to cohabiting couples. Under their proposal a person living as a spouse in the same household as the deceased up until the date of death would have the same entitlement as a spouse under the intestacy rules, provided that the deceased was not married or in a civil partnership at the time of death and provided the couple lived together for five years (or two years if they had a child together who lived with them).[12] This reform proposal was based on sociological studies, including the Nuffield Survey,[13] which found that when people were asked their views about the appropriate division of an estate in a variety of factual scenarios, they generally supported distributing property to the surviving cohabitant.[14] However, the UK Parliament has, to date, failed to adopt this reform proposal.

Who counts as a child?

The determination of who counts as a child matters for a variety of purposes. First, a child is a primary taker under intestacy statutes. Second, the determination of whether someone is a child

8 Council of Europe Family Policy Database, Social Policy and Family Law: Marriage, Divorce, and Parenthood, 2009.

9 *PNC Bank Corp. v W.C.A.B. (Stamos)*, 831 A.2d 1269, 1279 (Pa. Commw. Ct. 2003).

10 Georgia, Idaho, Pennsylvania, Ohio, and Oklahoma.

11 Law Commission, *Intestacy and Family Provision Claims on Death*, 2011, H.C., 331, pp. 8–9 (U.K.).

12 Ibid. section 1.99.

13 'Nuffield survey' refers to research published in National Centre for Social Research, *Inheritance and the Family: Attitudes to Will-Making and Intestacy* (2010). The report was funded by the Nuffield Foundation and conducted in collaboration with Professor Gillian Douglas from Cardiff Law School, Cardiff University. Information on the study can be found at www.natcen.ac.uk/study/inheritance-and-the-family

14 Ibid. section 8.35.

can matter for purposes of determining who takes under a will or trust of either the parent or a more distant relative. Third, in England, a child is entitled to make a claim for family maintenance based on his or her status as the decedent's child. Finally, in the US, the ability to receive social security support payments depends upon whether someone is treated as a child under the state intestacy statutes. With changing mores and changing reproductive technology, the question of who counts as a child is also in the process of changing.

Non-marital children

At common law, a non-marital child was treated as the child of neither parent. In the US, a non-marital child was treated as the child of the mother, but not the father. In 1977 the US Supreme Court ruled that marital and non-marital children must be treated the same for purposes of intestacy. However, states were allowed to provide different rules for establishing parenthood for mothers and fathers. As a result, most states provided that a child was always treated as the child of the mother and treated as a child of the father provided paternity was established during the father's life. The reason for the different treatment of fathers was a concern about the evidentiary problems of proving paternity. However, with the availability of DNA testing, it is no longer difficult to prove paternity. As a result, many states have changed their rules to provide that the marital status of the parents has no effect on whether a child is treated as a child of either parent. The law in England underwent a similar transformation. Since 1987, the marital relationship of the parents has no effect on whether a child is treated as the child of either parent.[15]

One area where the law is changing is in terms of the ability to prove paternity, in particular whether paternity can be proven after death or whether it must be proven during life. Increasingly, states are moving to allow paternity to be proven after the death of the father.[16] Where paternity can be proven after death, this has raised another issue, namely whether courts will require family members of the deceased to facilitate DNA testing by either providing their own DNA sample or allowing exhumation of the body. Courts have taken different approaches to this question. For example, in 2008 in Maine, the Supreme Judicial Court held that probate court had the authority to order the exhumation of testator's body for a DNA test when there is good cause for the exhumation.[17] New York state has also allowed posthumous exhumation of genetic material, but placed additional requirements on the exhumation and subsequent genetic testing. Namely, posthumous exhumation must be reasonable and practicable under the totality of circumstances, and not impose an undue hardship on the decedent's family.[18]

Adopted children

Adopted children are treated the same as natural children of their parents for all purposes. Therefore, if a child is adopted then for succession law purposes the child is treated as a child of the adopting parents and the adopting parents are treated as the parents of the child. However, less clear is the effect of the adoption on other members of the adopting family. Under the stranger-to-the-adoption rule it was traditionally the case that adopted children were only treated as the child of the adopting parents, but not of more distant relatives. Under this rule, if a grandparent's

15 Kerridge and Parry, op. cit., n 3, p. 19.
16 K.S. Knaplund, 'Equal Protection, Postmortem Conception, and Intestacy', U. *Kan.* L. *Rev.* 53, 2005, 627–58.
17 *In re Estate of Kingsbury*, 946 A.2d 389 (Me. 2008).
18 See e.g. *Matter of Poldrugovaz*, 50 A.D.3d 117 (N.Y. App. Div. 2008).

estate was to be distributed among his grandchildren, grandchildren who had been adopted by their parents would not be included in the distribution. As adoption has become more commonly accepted, this differing treatment of adopted children no longer conforms to societal values. Most states of the US (as well as the Uniform Probate Code) have abandoned this distinction and now provide that adopted children are treated the same as biological children for all purposes.[19] Moreover, at least one state has ruled a statute unconstitutional which did not allow an adopted child to inherit from a half-sister by adoption.[20]

Another issue in adoption is the effect of the adoption on the adopted child's relationship to his or her biological family. Some states follow the rule that adoption severs ties with the biological family for all purposes. However, while this rule makes sense in an out-of-family adoption (where court records are often sealed), it does not make sense in the situation where the adoption is by a family member. For example, where a child's father has died and the mother remarries and the new husband adopts the mother's children, the adoption is not intended to sever the children's relationship with the biological father's family. In order to address this situation, some jurisdictions in the US (along with the Uniform Probate Code) have drawn a distinction between in-family and out-of-family adoptions such that in family adoptions do not sever ties with the biological family.[21]

A current issue is in determining what counts as an in-family adoption. In some cases, it is only an in-family adoption if the child is adopted by the spouse of another parent.[22] In other cases, the concept of in-family adoption has been extended to the situation where any family member of a parent of a child adopts the child.[23]

Children of posthumous reproduction

One of the most vexing problems facing succession law today is the proper treatment of posthumously conceived children. The first human pregnancy resulting from frozen sperm occurred in 1953. The first child born from cryopreserved embryo was born in 1984 and the first child conceived from a cryopreserved egg was born in 1986. In 2017 it was estimated that over 68,000 children are born each year in the US from assisted reproductive technology including the use of frozen sperm.[24] The success of cryopreservation means that it is no longer necessary for a genetic parent to be alive in order for a child to be created from the parents' genetic material.[25] The problem of posthumously created children is particularly great in the US where posthumous conception is an entirely private affair. This contrasts with the law of England where there is greater regulatory oversight over artificial conception (see Chapter 3.1 of this book).

19 The one place where the stranger to the adoption rule still has some persuasive authority is when the adoption takes place when the adopted 'child' is an adult.

20 *MacCallum v Saymour*, 686 A. 2d 935 (Vt. 1996). *But see*, *Lutz v Fortune*, 758 N.E. 2nd 77, 84 (Ind. App. 2001). *Discussed in*, W. McGovern, S. Kurtz and D. English, *Wills, Trusts, and Estates: Including Taxation and Future Interests*, 4th edition, St. Paul, MN: West, 2010.

21 See e.g. N.Y. C.L.S. Dom. Rel. § 117.

22 *Duran v Duran*, 900 N.E.2.d 454 (Ind. 2009); *Ellis v West*, 971 S.2d 20 (Al. 2007).

23 American Law Institute, *Restatement 3rd of Property: Wills & Other Donative Transfers*, Philadelphia: American Law Institute, 2011, §2.5(2)(b).

24 Centers for Disease Control and Prevention, American Society for Reproductive Medicine, Society for Assisted Reproductive Technology, *2010 Assisted Reproductive Technology National Summary Report*, Atlanta: U.S. Department of Health and Human Services, 2012.

25 B. Carpenter, 'A Chip Off the Old Iceblock: How Cryopreservation Has Changed Estate Law, Why Attempts to Address the Issue Have Fallen Short, and How to Fix It', *Cornell Journal of Law and Public Policy* 21, 2011–12, 347–430.

There is no consensus regarding the proper treatment of posthumously conceived children for purposes of succession law. Instead there has been a patchwork of legislation and case law addressing this problem. There is a continuum of options for the law in addressing this situation. At one end of the spectrum, the law could have a bright line test requiring conception before a person's death in order for the deceased person to be treated as the parent of any resulting child. The advantage of this position is that at the time of a person's death, he can be certain that his legal status as a parent has been fixed. This is the position of the Uniform Status of Children of Assisted Conception Act, promulgated in 1988.[26] This statute has only been adopted by two jurisdictions: North Dakota and Virginia. Given the fact that this model legislation was proposed so long ago, and the issues it considered have been addressed in a more recent model act (the 2002 Uniform Parentage Act), it is unlikely that many other jurisdictions will enact this particular model statute.

At the other end of the spectrum, the law could have a bright line test that provides that posthumously conceived children always be treated as the child of the genetic parent for inheritance and other purposes, regardless of when they are conceived. This position arguably provides the greatest protection for posthumously conceived children. However, it raises serious practical problems, particularly in its application to the rules of inheritance, since a person's estate cannot be distributed until all possible heirs are identified. Because genetic material can be used many years after being stored, this rule would essentially make it impossible to close an estate for so long as there was stored genetic material. Mindful of this problem, this rule has not been adopted by any court or legislature.

Most courts and legislatures addressing this issue have instead chosen a middle ground, generally providing that a posthumously conceived child will be treated as the child of a deceased genetic parent if (1) the parent intended for his or her genetic material to be used for posthumous reproduction and (2) the child is born within a reasonable time after the parent's death.[27] This is similar to the position adopted in the latest Uniform Act addressing this issue, the 2002 Uniform Parentage Act. This model statute, adopted in seven states, provides a general rule that posthumously conceived children are not treated as children of the deceased parent (similar to the rule provided in the Uniform Status of Assisted Conception Act). Rather than having a bright line test, however, it also provides an exception for cases where the deceased spouse consented in a record that if assisted reproduction were to occur after death, the deceased individual would be a parent of the child.[28]

Most posthumous conceptions use frozen embryos and other reproductive matter. In these cases, the donor (by virtue of having stored gametes or embryos during life) has demonstrated a desire (or at least a willingness) to have his or her genetic material used to create a child. However, recently there has been a new mode of posthumous reproduction that does not involve any level of 'buy-in' by the gamete provider: retrieving sperm from men who are recently deceased, brain dead, comatose or in a persistent vegetative state for use in posthumous procreation. While there is little evidence about how often posthumous sperm retrieval occurs, these requests appear to be increasingly being made and granted. While this

26 Section 4(b) provides: An individual who dies before implantation of an embryo, or before a child is conceived other than through sexual intercourse, using the individual's egg or sperm, is not a parent of the resulting child.

27 See e.g. Cal. Prob. Code § 249.5; Iowa Code Ann. § 633.220A; *Woodward v Comm'r of Soc. Sec.*, 760 N.E.2d 257 (Mass. 2002); *In re Estate of Kolacy*, 753 A.2d 1257 (N.J. Super. Ct. Ch. Div. 2000); *Restatement 3rd*, op. cit., §2.05, Comment 1.

28 Uniform Parentage Act 2002 (UPA), Section 707.

issue has not yet come up for women, because it is not currently technologically feasible to harvest gametes from dead women, it is likely just a matter of time before such a procedure is available.[29]

Who decides whether this posthumous retrieval of reproductive material will occur? In the US there is no statutory law addressing this issue. In many cases, these decisions are being made by emergency room doctors and urologists responding to requests of grieving family members (sometimes, but not always, with the advice of in-house hospital attorneys and hospital protocols). A number of hospitals as well as the American Society for Reproductive Medicine have issued guidelines for when posthumous gamete retrieval should occur. All of these proposals start with the notion that some form of pre-mortem consent should be required, but the difference is whether explicit consent is required or whether there will be a presumption of consent in the absence of evidence to the contrary.[30] In most cases, posthumous sperm retrieval will occur in cases where there is very little evidence as to what the decedent intended, so the presumptions will dictate the outcome.

There have been a limited number of cases in which courts have been brought in to decide whether exhumation of genetic material should occur.[31] Beyond retrieval, those in control of the genetic material may have to jump additional hurdles in its use for reproductive purposes due to potential ethical concerns, such as the potential hesitance of doctors to assist in such procedures.[32] Should children born from exhumed sperm be treated as the child of the deceased parent? The posthumous conception cases have all required some degree of consent by the decedent parent. Based on these standards, children conceived as a result of posthumous gamete retrieval could not be eligible to be treated as the child of the deceased parent. However, if these procedures become more common courts will need to address the equity of preventing children conceived from posthumously exhumed sperm from inheriting from their biological fathers.[33]

Intestacy allocations

The law of intestacy provides a plan of disposition for property that is not disposed of by will or otherwise. Intestacy statutes in common law countries are designed to provide a distribution that approximates what decedents would have done if they had made a will.[34] In common law countries, such as the US and England, intestacy statutes operate largely as default, rather than mandatory, rules. That is, intestacy rules only apply to the extent that a decedent has failed to dispose of his property by will. Nonetheless, intestacy statutes play a significant role in the actual distribution of a decedent's estate since it is widely accepted on both sides of the Atlantic that most people able to write wills fail to do so. A 2009 study estimated that 65 percent of Americans die without wills.[35] A 2010 study estimated that between a half and two-thirds of adults in

29 K. Katz, 'Parenthood from the Grave: Protocols for Retrieving and Utilizing Gametes from the Dead or Dying', *Univ. Chicago Legal Forum* 2006, 289–316.

30 Ibid. p. 300.

31 *Matter of Zhu*, 2019–53327, 2019 N.Y. Misc. LEXIS 2448 (N.Y. Sup. Ct. May 16, 2019).

32 See e.g. Ethics Committee of the American Society for Reproductive Medicine, *Posthumous Retrieval and Use of Gametes or Embryos: An Ethics Committee Opinion*, 2018, pp. 3–5.

33 See further J. Hans, 'Attitudes Towards Posthumous Harvesting and Reproduction', *Death Studies* 32(9), 2008, 837–69.

34 *King v Riffee*, 309 S.El.2d 85, 87–88 (W. Va. 1983). This is in contrast to the role of intestacy statutes in civil law countries where the focus is on distributing a person's property in accordance with societal values.

35 Law Commission, op. cit., n 15, section 1.3.

England and Wales have not made a will.[36] As intestacy statutes are particularly likely to apply to people with less wealth, the plan of disposition provided by intestacy can have a significant effect on those for whom the inheritance would matter most. Because of the broad application of intestacy statutes many current reform efforts have focused on ensuring that these rules comport with people's preferences.

Current policy issues in intestacy focus on how a decedent's property should be allocated between a spouse and blood relatives (including children, parents and more distant relatives). In order to understand these rules it is important to understand the structure of intestacy statutes. There is a common pattern to intestacy statutes that applies in all jurisdictions. First, a share is given to the surviving spouse either outright or in a life-estate. In some cases this share can be as much as 100 percent of the decedent's property. After a share has been set aside for the spouse, the next takers are the decedent's children, grandchildren and great-grandchildren (this line is known as the decedent's 'issue' or 'descendants'). If the decedent is survived by issue, no one other than the spouse and issue will share in the decedent's estate. If the decedent does not have any issue, then any share that does not go to the surviving spouse passes to the decedent's other blood relatives including parents, siblings and cousins. A small number of jurisdictions also include step-children as possible intestate takers in limited situations.[37] Finally, if there is no living relative covered by the intestacy statute, then the decedent's property escheats to the state.

How much to a spouse?

One area that has undergone significant change in recent years is the share afforded the surviving spouse under intestacy law. (For full discussion of the position in Japan, see Chapter 6.4 of this book.) Historically, under English common law (on which both current English law and American law is based), spouses were only entitled to a life estate in the land of their deceased spouse. Limiting spouses to a life interest stemmed from a fear that if the surviving spouse inherited land outright, it could be permanently removed from the decedent's family, particularly if the surviving spouse remarried or had children by another marriage. This common law rule was carried into many early intestacy statutes that limited the share afforded to the surviving spouse to a life estate in a portion of the decedent spouse's estate.

However, over the past 50 years, there were several empirical studies in both the US and England that found that people preferred to leave more to their spouses than that which had previously been provided by intestacy statutes.[38] As a result of these studies, most jurisdictions have revised their laws to (1) provide the spouse with a significantly larger share of the decedent spouse's estate, often as much as the entire estate and (2) abandon the use of life estates in favour of outright distributions of property.

Spouse's share in the absence of children

Under most state statutes in the US, the surviving spouse inherits the entire estate if the decedent leaves no children (or other issue) or parents. This is based on the belief that people would

36 Ibid., section 2.2.

37 McGovern et al., op. cit., n 25, p. 2.2.

38 M. Fellows, R.J. Simons and W. Rau, 'Public Attitudes About Property Distribution at Death and Intestate Succession Laws in the United States', *American Bar Foundation Research Journal* 3, 1978, 319–91; L.W. Waggoner, 'The Multiple-Marriage Society and Spousal Rights under the Revised Uniform Probate Code', *Iowa L. Rev.* 76, 1991, 223–72.

prefer that their property be given to their spouses, rather than to siblings, grandparents or any other collateral relative or ancestor.[39] Prior to 2014, English law took a slightly different approach by providing that the surviving spouse inherits everything only if the decedent is not survived by parents, siblings, nieces or nephews. However, in 2014 the Inheritance and Trustees' Powers Act was passed, which specified that spouses will receive the entire estate in the absence of children or other issue.[40]

In the US, if there are no children or other issue, but the decedent is survived by a spouse and a parent (or other relative entitled to take under intestacy in this situation), the surviving spouse is usually given a statutory amount and then a portion of the excess of the decedent's estate. This gives the decedent's parents a portion of the decedent's estate only in situations where the estate is larger than the statutory share. Under the UPC, the surviving spouse is entitled to the first $300,000 outright and three-quarters of the excess over that amount, leaving the surviving parents with only one-quarter of the decedent's estate in excess of $300,000.[41] In England the Law Commission has recommended that the law in England be revised to provide that in all cases where the decedent is survived by a spouse and parent, that all of the decedent's property be distributed to the surviving spouse.[42] In 2014, Parliament followed the Law Commission's recommendation, and revised the law to provide spouses with the decedent's entire estate.[43]

One of the reasons for giving such a large share to the surviving spouse is out of concern that she is dependent on those resources to live. However, one of the downsides of these large outright transfers in the case where there are no children of the marriage is that resources given to the surviving spouse are unlikely to return to the decedent spouse's family. One state, California, has responded to this problem by providing that if a surviving spouse dies intestate shortly after the first spouse, then the family of the first spouse is entitled to claim a portion of the intestate estate of the surviving spouse.[44] This statute is at best rough justice, and can be somewhat complicated to administer.

Division between spouse and issue

An important current policy issue in succession law is how property should be divided between a person's spouse and children. The modern trend to increase the intestacy share of the surviving spouse is more qualified when there are children in the picture. In that case other factors come into play and different jurisdictions have taken different approaches.

First, if the children are all children of the decedent and the surviving spouse, and if neither spouse has children from outside of the marriage, then it is increasingly common in the US to give the surviving spouse the entire estate. There are several reasons for this. First, if the children were minors, then a guardianship would be required to handle any share going to the children. Guardianships can be expensive and cumbersome. Moreover, a guardianship seems particularly unnecessary in this situation since the surviving spouse is likely to use the inheritance to support the children. Second, regardless of the age of the children, if the surviving spouse is also the parent of the decedent's children, then she is likely to take those children's interests into account during life and also at her death. This is referred to as the conduit theory.[45]

39 McGovern et al., op. cit., n 25, p. 9.

40 Inheritance and Trustees' Powers Act 2014 (U.K.).

41 Uniform Probate Code 2008 (UPC), Sections 2–102(2) and 2–102(2).

42 Ibid., section 1.85.

43 Inheritance and Trustees' Powers Act 2014 (U.K.).

44 California Probate Code 2013, Section 6402.5.

45 Restatement 3rd, op. cit., Section 2.2 Reporter's Note.

If either spouse has children from outside of the marriage, then these statutes typically give less to the surviving spouse out of concern that the conduit theory might not apply to these situations. First, if the decedent spouse has children who are not children of the surviving spouse, property going to the surviving spouse may never get to the decedent spouse's children if the surviving spouse is not close to her stepchildren. Secondly, if the surviving spouse has children of her own who are not children of the decedent, then upon the surviving spouse's death, she is likely to distribute her estate evenly to all of her children, effectively diluting the share that might otherwise go to the decedent's own children. These rules are based on the assumption that people most likely prefer their property to pass to their children over their stepchildren. While this might be the case in many cases, the assumption is less likely to apply when the step-parent came into the stepchild's life at an early age.

Nonetheless, even in situations where there are children from outside the marriage, the surviving spouse will still get the lion's share of the decedent's estate because the surviving spouse is given a large statutory share (between $225,000 and $300,000), and then between 50 and 75 percent of the rest of the decedent's property.[46] Since the vast majority of probate estates will be less than the statutory share, the surviving spouse will still effectively be given the entire estate of the decedent – even when there are children from outside of the marriage.

Similar to the US, in England there has been a shift in recent years to increase the share given to the surviving spouse under intestacy. As of 2014, a surviving spouse is entitled to take the whole estate unless the decedent is also survived by children.[47]

The English Law Commission specifically considered whether it would be appropriate to give all to a spouse when the decedent is survived by a spouse and children, as is common in the US. The Commission recognized several arguments in favour of this view, including (1) that estate planners report that the vast majority of people writing wills provide all to spouse; (2) all to spouse is most likely to meet the financial needs of the family, particularly where there are minor children; and (3) English law has no forced heirship for children, so there is no justification to import that principle through the intestacy statute.[48]

Despite these arguments, the Commission favoured giving a share to the decedent's children under intestacy because of a belief that it was 'unfair' to leave children out of intestacy. This view was also supported by studies of public opinion.[49] Based on this reasoning, the proposal of the Commission was that when a decedent was survived by a spouse and children, the spouse should receive the statutory minimum, plus half of the excess, leaving the children with half of the excess over the statutory minimum. In 2014 England adopted this proposal by English Law Commission, and surviving spouses are now entitled to half of the excess above the statutory minimum.[50] However, since the spouse's statutory minimum is so high (£250,000), this updated rule effectively only provides benefits to children of wealthier decedents.

Limits on testamentary freedom

Succession laws of the US and England start with the principle of freedom of testation. That is, the ability of a person to control the disposition of his or her estate at death. However, freedom of testation is not absolute. In the US, married decedents are limited in their ability to control

46 UPC, op. cit., n 46, Section 2–102.
47 Inheritance and Trustees' Powers Act 2014 (U.K.).
48 UPC, op. cit., n 46, sections 2.28–2.31.
49 Ibid., sections 2.32–2.38.
50 Inheritance and Trustees' Powers Act 2014 (U.K.).

their property at death in some states by elective share statutes, which provide a surviving spouse with a minimum share of a decedent spouse's estate. In England, freedom of testation is limited by family maintenance statutes. These statutes allow certain individuals to claim against a decedent's estate. In recent years there have been changes and considerable discussion regarding the proper scope of protections that should be afforded by elective share and family maintenance statutes.

Elective share statutes

When available, elective share statutes allow a surviving spouse to claim a portion of a decedent spouse's estate, regardless of the terms of the decedent spouse's will.

Elective share statutes can only be fully understood within the context of the two systems of marital property law that exist in the US: community property (followed by nine states) and separate property (followed by 41 states).[51] In community property states, surviving spouses receive some protection against disinheritance under community property rules which grant each spouse a 50 percent ownership interest in all property earned during the marriage. However, there are no such protections in separate property states where marriage has no effect on property ownership. In order to protect spouses in separate property states from disinheritance, all separate property states (with the exception of Georgia) provide protection for the surviving spouse in the form of elective share statutes.

Elective share statutes allow a surviving spouse to claim a minimum portion of a decedent spouse's estate, regardless of the testator's wishes. Thus, if a decedent writes a will that gives everything to his children or favourite charity (or anyone else other than his or her spouse), the surviving spouse is entitled to claim a portion of the decedent's estate. Elective share statutes are written in gender-neutral terms. However, since most wives survive their husband and most husbands have earned more money during the marriage than their wives, these statutes are most likely to apply as protections for wives against disinheritance by their more propertied husbands.

One of the current issues in succession law is whether the goal of elective share statutes should be to provide support for a surviving spouse during her life, or whether elective share statutes should instead try to approximate a fair division of the couple's assets (similar to the result that would be achieved under community property or equitable distribution principles used in divorce). Traditionally, elective share statutes focused on providing support to a surviving spouse. Massachusetts is a good example of a traditional style elective share statute.[52] The surviving spouse is given a life estate in between one-third and one-half of the decedent's probate estate. The problem with this type of statute is that it is easily evaded as people can move their property from being probate property to being non-probate property (by creating trusts or putting the property in a joint tenancy).[53] Moreover, a life estate interest provides only minimal benefit to a surviving spouse since she typically has no ability to force the sale of the underlying property or even require that the property be invested in a way that produces income.

The drafters of the Uniform Probate Code have drafted an elective share statute that abandons the support theory and is instead based on a partnership theory of marriage. The partnership theory of marriage recognizes that the unemployed spouse's non-market efforts, such as childcare and housekeeping, contribute to the family's acquisition of wealth. As a result, the goal of the UPC elective share statute is to give the surviving spouse the right to claim a significant

51 Madoff et al., op. cit., n 1, Section 6.02.

52 MGLA 191 section 15.

53 *Bongaards v Millen*, 793 N.E.2d 335 *Mass. 2003.

portion of the couple's combined assets. The specific portion is based on the length of the marriage, and for couples who have been married at least 15 years, the surviving spouse is entitled to claim 50 percent of the couples' combined property. The UPC elective share statute is similar to principles of equitable division that apply in the divorce context (see Chapter 2.6 of this book). However, the UPC elective share statute has not been widely adopted. Indeed, since first proposed in 1990, this version of the UPC elective share has only been adopted in less than 20 percent of the states.

Family maintenance statutes

An important part of English succession law is the law of family provision that allows certain individuals to apply to the court for a discretionary distribution from the decedent's estate. Family provisions are only available to individuals that fall within certain defined categories: spouses and civil partners, former spouses and former civil partners, cohabitants who have lived together for at least two years, children who the deceased treated as a child of his or her family in relation to a marriage or civil partnership and any other person who was being maintained by the deceased.[54] Note that parents are not included in this list and are therefore not entitled to claim a family provision unless they were being maintained by the decedent.

The family provision statute directs the court to make 'reasonable financial provision' for the applicant, but the phrase has two different meanings depending on the identity of the applicant. If the applicant is a surviving spouse or civil partner, then the standard means 'such financial provision as it would be reasonable in all circumstances of the case for a husband or wife ... or civil partner to receive, *whether or not that provision is required for his or her maintenance* (emphasis added)'.[55] This amount is intended to be at least equal to that which the surviving spouse or partner would be entitled to receive upon divorce.[56] If the applicant is in any of the other categories, then 'reasonable financial provision' is based on the actual maintenance needs of the applicant.[57] The effect of this standard is that a non-spouse or civil partner is unlikely to be able to claim a portion of the decedent's estate if that person is adequately employed or otherwise able to support him or herself.

The Law Commission considered a number of proposals regarding possible modification to the family provision statute. The first was to change the rights of children – specifically the Law Commission considered the question of whether an order for the benefit of a child of the deceased might cease to be limited by the 'maintenance' standard. Under current law, there are many situations where a decedent's property is likely to pass to his or her spouse rather than children (e.g. if the decedent dies intestate and the estate is less than the statutory share). Yet, if the spouse is not a parent of the child, then it is unlikely that the inheritance will ever make its way back to the child. Although a child is able to make a claim for a family provision, current law imposes a significant limitation because the child is limited to a maintenance level of support. If the adult child is adequately employed his claim for a family provision is unlikely to be successful. Some of the consultees favoured reforming the current standard for family provision to remove the maintenance standard on the grounds that it would be fairer for children to be able to claim substantial provision from their parents' estates. However, the majority expressed dislike for a move towards forced heirship and away from testamentary freedom. They recognized

54 The 1975 Act, s.1.
55 The 1975 Act, s.1(2). Discussed at Kerridge and Parry, op. cit., n 3, p. 169.
56 Kerridge and Parry, op. cit., n 3, p. 170.
57 Ibid.

that parents can choose to disinherit their children, and felt that this is right goes to the root of basic English law. As a result of this discussion, no recommendation was ultimately made on this issue.[58]

Another issue that was considered but rejected, was whether parents and/or siblings should be added to the list of individuals entitled to claim a family provision. The arguments in favour of including parents were particularly strong because – as some consultees argued – parents will usually have maintained their child at some point and it is more likely that a parent will become dependent on their child in their later years than other more remote relatives. Nonetheless, there was reluctance to expand the categories, particularly since parents who were truly being supported by the decedent would already be able to file claims as dependents.[59] Finally, the Commission considered whether to expand the list of those eligible to file claims to include caretakers (the English term, carers). The consultees felt that despite the moral claims of caretakers to inherit, it would be too difficult to apply such a rule.[60]

The Law Commission did make some suggestions for changing the Family Provision statute that were adopted in the final proposal. The first recommendation was to reform the standard for cohabitants to require a shorter period of cohabitation if the cohabitant had a child with the deceased. Under this proposal, if the deceased and the cohabitant had a child together, then the cohabitant could make a claim for a family provision against the decedent's estate even if they had not lived together for the full two years.[61] Another recommendation was with respect to the provision that applied to those whom the deceased treated as a child of his or her family in relation to a marriage or civil partnership. The Law Commission felt that it was inappropriate to limit this category to those which arose as a result of a relation to a marriage or civil partnership. That is, if a single person treated someone as his or her child, then that 'child' should be able to make a claim for family provision. While there was some concern that the phrase 'child of the family' might create uncertainty, the Commission received testimony that this was a term that was well understood by the courts.

58 Law Commission, op. cit., n 15, sections 6.2–6.26.
59 Ibid., sections 6.81–6.88.
60 Ibid., sections 6.89–6.94.
61 Ibid., sections 8.144–8.158.

PART 3

Parenting and parenthood

3.1

ASSISTED CONCEPTION AND SURROGACY IN THE UNITED KINGDOM

Emily Jackson

This chapter covers the regulation of assisted conception (such as *in vitro* fertilization (IVF) and donor insemination) and surrogacy in the United Kingdom (for discussion of such regulation in Australia, see Chapter 3.2 of this book). In addition to pioneering IVF, the UK was also one of the first countries to regulate it through a comprehensive licensing regime. In contrast, for the last 30 years, the UK's regulation of surrogacy has been piecemeal and patchy (for further discussions of surrogacy see Chapters 3.2 and 7.1 of this book). This difference is hard to explain and defend, given that surrogacy arrangements raise issues that are at least as complicated as those raised when a couple undergoes IVF with their own sperm and eggs. A consultation launched by the Scottish and English Law Commissions in 2019 may lead to new surrogacy legislation within the next few years.

Assisted conception: the (limited) role of the Human Fertilisation and Embryology Authority (HFEA)

The regulation of assisted conception in the UK consists in a special regime set up by the Human Fertilisation and Embryology Act 1990 (the Act), as amended, and administered by the Human Fertilisation and Embryology Authority (HFEA). The Act provides that the creation, use and storage of embryos, and the storage and use of gametes, can only take place under a licence granted by the HFEA.[1] Carrying out any of these activities without a licence is a criminal offence.[2]

Although the HFEA therefore exercises considerable control over licensed fertility treatment in the UK, its reach is not comprehensive. No licence is required for a doctor to prescribe superovulatory drugs, for example, despite the risks to women and babies from multiple births. Of increasing practical significance, treatment services provided in other countries also inevitably lie outside the HFEA's control. Throughout the world, it is becoming more common for people to travel to receive fertility treatment.[3] There are a number of drivers of cross-border reproductive

1 Human Fertilisation and Embryology Act 1990, ss. 3 and 4.

2 Human Fertilisation and Embryology Act 1990, s. 41.

3 F. Shenfield, J. de Mouzon, G. Pennings, A.P. Ferraretti, A. Nyboe Andersen, G. de Wert and V. Goossens and the ESHRE Taskforce on Cross Border Reproductive Care, 'Cross Border Reproductive Care in Six European Countries', *Human Reproduction* 25, 2010, 1361–8.

care: cost (IVF is cheaper in Eastern Europe and Asia); avoiding long waiting lists (for example, for eggs or for ethnically matched donors); avoiding legal restrictions (although a change in the law is imminent, it has been common for French lesbian couples and single women to travel to Belgium for treatment; British couples might travel to the US for sex selection), and a perception that care abroad will be better or that treatment is more likely to succeed.[4]

Of course, cross-border reproductive treatment is not available to everyone. Even in countries like the Ukraine and India, where treatment is comparatively cheap, the costs are still substantial and for most people, unaffordable. There can also be risks. Women have returned to the UK after IVF in India pregnant with triplets and quads. In addition to the health risks to pregnant women and babies, higher order multiple births impose significant costs on the National Health Service (NHS). As we see later, going abroad for surrogacy treatment can cause additional problems, such as the child not being recognized as a British citizen from birth.

Regulating access to treatment

The only statutory restriction upon access to treatment in the UK is contained in section 13(5) of the Act. In its original version, this instructed clinicians that a woman should not be provided with treatment services unless account had first been taken of the welfare of any child to be born 'including the need of that child for a father'. When it introduced reforming legislation in 2008, the government had assumed that deleting the 'need for a father' from section 13(5) would simply bring the 1990 Act into line with post-1990 family law reforms and with equality legislation. In practice, this amendment proved to be hugely controversial, with the press and parliamentarians claiming that removing 'the need for a father' impugned the importance of fatherhood itself. As a result, the 'need for a father' was replaced by the 'the need for supportive parenting'.

The HFEA's Code of Practice instructs clinicians to consider whether there are any 'factors that are likely to cause a risk of significant harm or neglect to any child who may be born or to any existing child of the family', such as 'previous convictions relating to harming children', or 'child protection measures taken regarding existing children'.[5] It also specifies that, in the absence of any specific risk factors, all parents should be assumed to be supportive.[6] Although section 13(5) has been criticized for placing an unfair burden upon infertile individuals,[7] who are not any more likely to pose a risk to their children than fertile people,[8] in practice, relatively few prospective patients are turned down by clinics as a result of their 'welfare of the child' assessments.[9] Of much more practical importance, as a brake on access to treatment, is the fact that infertility treatment is expensive (one cycle of IVF commonly costs around £5,000) and its availability within the NHS is patchy. Unlike any other routine medical treatment in the UK,

4 L. Culley, 'Crossing Borders for Fertility Treatment: Motivations, Destinations and Outcomes of UK Fertility Travellers', *Human Reproduction* 26, 2011, 2373–81.

5 HFEA, *Code of Practice*, 9th edition, para 8.14.

6 Ibid., para 8.15.

7 See, for example, E. Jackson, 'Conception and the Irrelevance of the Welfare Principle', *Modern Law Review* 65, 2002, 176–203.

8 S. Golombok, E. Ilioi, L. Blake, G. Roman and V. Jadva, 'A Longitudinal Study of Families Formed through Reproductive Donation: Parent-Adolescent Relationships and Adolescent Adjustment at Age 14', *Developmental Psychology* 53, 2017, 1966–77.

9 For discussion, see further E. Lee, S. Sheldon and J. Macvarish, 'After the "Need for … a Father": "The Welfare of the Child" and "Supportive Parenting" in Assisted Conception Clinics in the UK', *Families, Relationships and Societies* 6, 2017, 71–87.

most fertility treatment is provided in the private sector. For many couples, the strain of experiencing fertility problems is exacerbated by the financial burdens of treatment.

The statute does not set an upper age limit for female patients. Instead, age limits (which tend to be in the range of 50–55 years of age) are set by individual clinics.[10] Pregnancy is riskier for older women, and so there may be clinical reasons not to provide treatment beyond a woman's early fifties, but some people have also suggested that there are child welfare reasons to prevent older motherhood. Setting an upper age limit for women, but not men, on child welfare grounds could be said to reinforce traditional assumptions about family life, however. As Büchler and Parizer point out:

> The argument that children born to older parents have a higher risk of becoming orphans before reaching adulthood is much less frequently used when dealing with older fathers; society seems to be more tolerant of older men who bear children, as it is presumed that they are with younger women who will take care of the offspring.[11]

Of course, it might be countered that nature imposes an age limit on female motherhood through the menopause. But to argue that technology should not interfere with 'natural' limits on fertility would be to argue against *any* use of reproductive technologies, all of which are undoubtedly unnatural.

Regulating the use of gametes and embryos

Consent to the use of gametes

Consent to the creation of an embryo, or to the use of one's gametes in the treatment of others must be in writing.[12] This has caused particular difficulties in a handful of cases in which someone has died without giving consent in writing to the posthumous use of their sperm or eggs. Following the cases of *R v Human Fertilisation and Embryology Authority, ex parte Blood*,[13] and *L v Human Fertilisation and Embryology Authority*,[14] women were allowed to export their deceased husbands' sperm in order to be able to use it in the absence of their written consent. The Court of Appeal also decided that export should be permitted in *R (on the application of M) v Human Fertilisation and Embryology Authority*,[15] in which a woman was permitted to export her deceased daughter's eggs, so that she could fulfil her orally expressed wish that she wanted her mother to 'carry my babies'.

In *Y v A Healthcare NHS Trust*,[16] Knowles J adopted a new solution to the problem that a man had not given written consent to the posthumous use of his sperm. Eleven days before Z and his wife Y were due to begin a cycle of IVF treatment, Z had suffered catastrophic injuries in a motorcycle crash. He was not going to recover, and Y wanted sperm samples to be retrieved. Knowles J was satisfied that Z and Y had a settled intention to have another child, and that Z had

10 A. Büchler and K. Parizer, 'Maternal Age in the Regulation of Reproductive Medicine: A Comparative Study', *International Journal of Law, Policy and the Family* 31, 2017, 269–90.
11 Ibid.
12 Schedule 3.
13 [1999] Fam 151.
14 [2008] EWHC 2149 (Fam).
15 [2016] EWCA Civ 611.
16 [2018] EWCOP 18.

told Y that he would want her to be able to use his sperm posthumously. As a result, she declared that the retrieval, storage and use of Z's sperm would be lawful in his best interests, under the Mental Capacity Act 2005, and directed that a relative (other than Y) should be able to sign the written consent to use on his behalf.

Consent to the use of embryos

Of course, it is possible that the gamete contributors will subsequently disagree about the use of their frozen embryos. In the UK the law is clear: the Act allows for the variation or withdrawal of consent to the use or storage of an embryo.[17] This means that once either gamete provider has withdrawn his or her consent to the embryos' use or continued storage, they must be destroyed or allowed to perish. Hence, whichever partner does not want their embryos to be used in treatment effectively has a right of veto.[18] Reforms introduced in 2008 provide for a 12-month 'cooling off period', during which the embryos cannot be used or disposed of without both parties' consent, with the hope that a couple might be able to reach an agreement during this time.[19]

'Social' egg freezing

Until recently, while it was common to freeze sperm and embryos for future use, success rates using frozen eggs were extremely low. A new fast-freezing technique, known as vitrification, has changed this, and, as a result, has created a new option for women concerned about their age-related fertility decline. Of course, although success rates using frozen eggs might be better than they used to be, most IVF cycles do not result in the birth of a child, and so it is important that women are properly informed that what is known as 'social' egg freezing does not guarantee them a baby.

Some commentators have argued that, rather than encouraging women to undergo ovarian stimulation and surgical egg retrieval, we should make it easier for women to combine work and motherhood in their twenties. In practice, however, women do not resort to egg freezing because of family-unfriendly workplaces. Rather, the reason most women give for freezing their eggs is that they have not yet found a partner with whom to start a family.

The average age at which women choose to freeze their eggs is around 37, by which time their fertility is already in decline. This is not clinically ideal, because more cycles of egg retrieval may be necessary in order to retrieve sufficient eggs to give a reasonable chance of pregnancy. It may nevertheless be advisable to freeze eggs in one's late thirties, because the Act places a ten year limit on the storage of gametes and embryos,[20] with an option for extension only for people who are or are likely to become 'prematurely infertile'.[21] If a woman freezes her eggs in her late thirties, she will have until her late forties to use them. In contrast, if a woman freezes her eggs at the age of 25, they will have to be disposed of when she is 35, that is, before she is likely to want to use them. This is not intentional: 'social' egg freezers were simply not within the contemplation of the drafters of the Human Fertilisation and Embryology (Statutory Storage

17 Schedule 3, para 4.
18 *Evans v United Kingdom* (App. No. 6339/05) (2007).
19 Schedule 3(4A).
20 Section 14(3).
21 Human Fertilisation and Embryology (Statutory Storage Period for Embryos and Gametes) Regulations 2009, regulations 3(3) and 4(3).

Period for Embryos and Gametes) Regulations 2009. It is to be hoped that the government will amend these Regulations in order to provide an option for extension for women who have not yet decided whether to use their frozen eggs.

Gamete donation

All egg and sperm donation that takes place in licensed clinics is regulated by the HFEA. But in the case of sperm donation, informal and unregulated donation is also possible. In the past, informal sperm donation tended to happen among friends and acquaintances – a not uncommon scenario might be a male friend helping a lesbian couple to have a baby through self-insemination. In such cases, if the adults subsequently disagree over contact, the courts have been sympathetic to the idea that there should be contact between the child and his or her biological father, even where the mother and her female partner are the child's legal parents.[22]

Informal donation arrangements between strangers are becoming more common as a result of introduction websites, which work like dating websites and enable would-be donors and recipients to make contact with each other. These websites are largely unregulated because they do not involve the 'procurement' of sperm, and hence do not need an HFEA licence. There are risks associated with entering into these arrangements, however. The sperm will not have been subjected to the same tests for quality, as well as for HIV and common genetic disorders, as are routine in a licensed centre. There is no limit on how many families can be born from one donor, and no register of information for donor-conceived individuals. Some men advertise themselves as willing to donate through 'NI (natural insemination) only', i.e. through sexual intercourse. Informal donation arrangements can also go badly wrong, particularly if the parties have different expectations of the arrangement.[23] Nevertheless, there are also positive reasons why some people prefer to find a donor informally, and not just because it might be cheaper than treatment in a licensed clinic. Informal donation can allow the child to get to know the donor during childhood, and some recipients are even looking for a co-parenting arrangement.[24]

Anonymity

Regulations which came into force in April 2005 removed anonymity for all donations after that date. Children born following non-anonymous donation will be able to access identifying information (that is their donor's name, place and date of birth and last known address) once they reach the age of 18. Anonymity was not removed retrospectively, although it is possible for pre-2005 donors to register their willingness to be identified. This means that some children may be able to access identifying information before 2023, when the first children conceived after anonymity was abolished reach the age of 18.

Of course, a child will obviously only be able to apply to the HFEA for identifying information if she knows, or suspects, that she was conceived using donated gametes. Unless a child born to heterosexual parents is told about the circumstances of her conception, she will usually assume that she was conceived naturally, and will not have any reason to make an application to receive information about her donor. Children born to lesbian couples or to single women are

22 *Re G (A Child)* [2013] EWHC 134 (Fam).

23 See, for example, *Re X (No 2: Application for Contact by the Biological Father)* [2015] EWFC 84.

24 V. Jadva, T. Freeman, E. Tranfield and S. Golombok, 'Friendly Allies in Raising a Child': A Survey of Men and Women Seeking Elective Co-Parenting Arrangements Via an Online Connection Website', *Human Reproduction* 30, 2015, 1896–906.

in a different position, since they will realize from a fairly young age that a third party must have played a role in their conception.

Although openness is more common than it used to be, many parents do not tell their children that they were conceived using donated gametes. In one study of 36 donor insemination families and 32 egg donation families, 'about half of the children conceived by egg donation and nearly three-quarters of those conceived by donor insemination remained unaware that the person they know as their mother or father is not, in fact, their genetic parent'.[25] Even among parents who intend to tell their children, many do not, in fact, do so, perhaps because 'parents who wait for "the right moment" are unlikely to ever find such a time'.[26] The right to identifying information may therefore make little difference in practice to the majority of children conceived using donated gametes. Instead, it is hoped that the removal of anonymity will promote a culture of openness, and that parents will be persuaded of the benefits of openness. The HFEA's Code of Practice tells clinics that they should encourage patients to be 'open with their children from an early age about how they were conceived'.[27]

It is noteworthy that in debates over the removal of anonymity of donors, it is often assumed that donor-conceived individuals' interest is in learning the identity of their donor. In practice, it seems clear that donor-conceived people are often more interested in identifying their half-siblings.[28] This may be because people are interested in what John Eekelaar has called 'communal identity', and with learning where and how they 'fit in'.[29] Families created using the same donor may therefore feel as if they have a bond with each other, without needing to meet the donor himself.

Payment

Sperm donors can be given a fixed sum of £35 per clinic visit to cover all of their expenses, and egg donors receive a fixed sum of £750 per cycle of donation, again to include all of the costs associated with the donation. One reason for having a fixed sum is that it means that clinics do not have to require donors to produce receipts for all of their actual out-of-pocket expenses. In practice, however, donors with few or no expenses will obviously receive more 'compensation' than those who have significant travel costs or childcare expenses.

Egg-sharing schemes involve substantial, albeit indirect, payment for egg donation. These are schemes in which a woman who needs IVF treatment agrees to donate half of the eggs retrieved during one cycle in return for a free or cheap cycle of IVF. Given inadequate NHS funding, these schemes are attractive to women who cannot afford IVF. In egg-sharing schemes, donation does not pose any additional risk to the donor's health, because the donor would be undergoing egg retrieval anyway. It has, however, been suggested women might be upset to learn that another woman has had children using their eggs, if their own treatment fails. In

25 J. Readings, L. Blake, P. Casey, V. Jadva and S. Golombok, 'Secrecy, Disclosure and Everything in-between: Decisions of Parents of Children Conceived by Donor Insemination, Egg Donation and Surrogacy', *Reproductive Biomedicine Online* 22, 2011, 485–95.

26 M.A. Tallandini, L. Zanchettin, G. Gronchi and V. Morsan, 'Parental Disclosure of Assisted Reproductive Technology (ART) Conception to Their Children: A Systematic and Meta-Analytic Review', *Human Reproduction* 31, 2016, 1275–87.

27 See, for example, HFEA, *Code of Practice*, 9th edition, para 20.8.

28 V. Jadva, T. Freeman, W. Kramer and S. Golombok, 'Experiences of Offspring Searching for and Contacting Their Donor Siblings and Donor', *Reproductive BioMedicine Online* 20, 2010, 523–32.

29 J. Eekelaar, 'Family Law and Identity', *Oxford Journal of Legal Studies* 38, 2018, 822–40.

practice, however, there is some evidence that egg sharers feel considerable solidarity with other infertile women.[30]

Number of offspring

There is a limit on the number of children that may be produced from the gametes of one donor, which is expressed as 'up to ten families'. Donors are entitled to set a lower limit, and this is usually done in order to donate only to a known recipient, for example, to one's infertile brother. The British Fertility Society has advocated a higher limit, in order to increase the availability of sperm,[31] while others argue that it may be challenging for children to come to terms with having a very large number of half-siblings.[32]

Parentage

Maternity

At common law,[33] and according to the Human Fertilisation and Embryology Acts 1990 and 2008 (the 1990 Act determines the parentage of children born before 1 April 2009, and the 2008 covers children born after this date), the woman (or as we see later, the person) who gives birth to a child is her mother. This is the case regardless of whether she is also the child's genetic mother.

Paternity

If the woman receiving treatment is married to a man, section 35 of the 2008 Act (section 28(2) of the 1990 Act) applies, and the mother's husband will be the father, unless he did not consent to her treatment. Where the woman having treatment is not married or in a civil partnership (see more later), and wishes a man to be the father of a child conceived using donated sperm, the agreed fatherhood conditions apply. Fatherhood can be acquired through the consent of both mother and father. Access is not restricted to the mother's partner. The only limit is that the man cannot be within the prohibited degrees of relationship (for the purposes of incest) with the woman. This means that, with his consent, a woman could agree to a male friend being her child's father, but not her brother.

Same-sex couples

The 2008 Act treats same-sex couples in the same way as opposite-sex couples, with one important linguistic difference, namely that while a mother's male partner can become the child's father from birth, the woman's same-sex partner will be the child's second legal parent. The

30 Z.B. Gürtin, K.K. Ahuja and S. Golombok, 'Emotional and Relational Aspects of Egg-Sharing: Egg-Share Donors' and Recipients' Feelings about Each Other, Each Others' Treatment Outcome, and Any Resulting Children', *Human Reproduction* 27, 2012, 1690–701.

31 British Fertility Society, 'Working Party on Sperm Donation Services in the UK', *Human Fertility* 11, 2008, 147–58.

32 For discussion and a contrary view, see J. Millbank, 'Numerical Limits in Donor Conception Regimes: Genetic Links and "Extended Family" in the Era of Identity Disclosure', *Medical Law Review* 22, 2014, 325–36.

33 *The Ampthill Peerage Case* [1977] AC 547.

mother's same-sex spouse or civil partner will be the child's second legal parent unless she did not consent to her treatment.[34] For women who are not married or in a civil partnership, the agreed female parenthood conditions mirror the agreed fatherhood conditions.[35] Once again, the only restriction on who may become a second legal parent in this way is that she must not be within the prohibited degrees of relationship, so a woman could nominate a friend to be her child's second legal parent, but not her sister. The 2008 Act's parenthood provisions are complex and difficult to read, which may explain why the radical change effected by the 2008 Act, namely that a child can have, in law and from birth, two female parents, was subject to very little discussion, in sharp contrast to the outcry over the proposal to delete the largely symbolic (but easier to understand) reference to the child's 'need for a father'.

Single women

The final category of patients envisaged by the Act is women who do not wish anyone to be their child's second parent. Women whose spouses or civil partners do not consent to their treatment will also fall within this group. In these situations, the child has only one legal parent.

Transgender parents

The statutory scheme does not specifically address the possibility of transgender parenthood. While normally couples who use their own gametes in treatment are self-evidently the child's parents, and not subject to any special rules, this may not be true for people who stored gametes, or embryos created using their gametes, before their gender was reassigned. For example, if a male-to-female trans person wants her female partner to be inseminated with sperm she stored before she became a woman, she could become the child's second legal parent, via the 'agreed parenthood conditions', but not because her sperm was used in treatment. In the past fertility preservation through sperm or egg freezing was not offered routinely to people undergoing gender reassignment. This is now changing, and for the first time, the HFEA's ninth Code of Practice includes guidance on treating trans patients, including giving them advice about fertility preservation.[36]

In addition to the use of previously frozen sperm and eggs, a female-to-male trans person might be able to give birth, if his reproductive organs were not removed as part of a gender reassignment operation. Of course, under UK law, this would mean that the trans man is the child's mother (because the person who gives birth to a child is always her mother). This was challenged in *R (on the application of TT) v Registrar General for England and Wales* by a trans man who had given birth, and who wished to be recorded on his son's birth certificate as his father, or failing that as his parent, rather than as his mother.[37] TT had undergone intrauterine insemination in a licensed clinic. The HFEA can issue licences for the provision of 'treatment services', which are defined in section 2 as services 'for the purpose of assisting *women* to carry children' (my emphasis). As a result, Sir Andrew McFarlane P expressed 'some doubt that the treatment was lawfully provided under the HFEA regime'. It must, he argued, 'be at least questionable whether the provision of treatment services to a man is within the range of activities that the HFEA is permitted to authorise by licence'. Although 'not for determination in the present

34 Human Fertilisation and Embryology Act 2008, s. 42 (1).

35 S. 44.

36 HFEA, *Code of Practice*, 9th edition, paras 4.11–4.17.

37 [2019] EWHC 2384 (Fam).

claim', Sir Andrew McFarlane P 'anticipate[d] that these are matters that will now be considered closely by the Authority and by ministers'. On the substantive issue of whether TT could be registered as the child's father, Sir Andrew McFarlane P held that:

> Being a 'mother', whilst hitherto always associated with being female, is the status afforded to a person who undergoes the physical and biological process of carrying a pregnancy and giving birth. It is now medically and legally possible for an individual, whose gender is recognised in law as male, to become pregnant and give birth to their child. Whilst that person's gender is 'male', their parental status, which derives from their biological role in giving birth, is that of 'mother'.

TT was therefore a male 'mother' for legal purposes, while 'for all other purposes, be they social, psychological or emotional, TT will be a male parent to his child and therefore his "father"'. The government had conceded that registering TT as his son's father interfered with their art. 8 right to private and family life, but Sir Andrew McFarlane P found that this interference was justified by the need for 'a coherent and certain scheme of birth registration', which required 'that the person who gives birth to a child is registered on the occasion of every birth'.

Surrogacy

Surrogacy can involve the surrogate inseminating herself with the intended father's sperm, in which case she will be the genetic as well as the gestational mother. This is known as 'traditional' surrogacy, and it can be accomplished without any professional assistance. In 'gestational' surrogacy, an embryo created using one or both of the intended parents' gametes is transferred to the surrogate's uterus. Since in vitro fertilization is involved, gestational surrogacy arrangements in the UK necessarily involve treatment in a centre licensed under the Act and regulated by the HFEA. It is, however, increasingly common for people to enter into surrogacy arrangements overseas.

The Surrogacy Arrangements Act 1985 was passed in order to prohibit commercial involvement in the initiation and negotiation of surrogacy arrangements. It is not an offence to enter into a surrogacy arrangement, but the agreement itself is not enforceable.[38] Hence, the intended parents cannot sue the surrogate if she refuses to hand over the baby, and nor can she sue them if she does not receive any of the agreed payments, or if they refuse to take the baby after birth. So while it is lawful to enter into a surrogacy contract, none of the parties are bound by its obligations.

Parenthood after surrogacy

The surrogate will always be the child's legal mother from birth. Section 38 of the 2008 Act treats the surrogate's husband (if she has one) as the father of the child, unless it can be shown that he did not consent to her treatment. Where a married surrogate's husband knows of her decision to become a surrogate and does not object, he can be assumed to consent, and will, as a result, be the child's father. If the surrogate is unmarried, it may be possible for her register the intended father as the child's father from birth. Alternatively, as long as she is not a close relative, she could register the intended mother as the child's 'second legal parent' from birth. Even

38 Surrogacy Arrangements Act 1985, s. 1B.

if one of the intended parents is the child's legal parent, because the surrogate will continue to be child's mother, the intended parents can both become the child's legal parents only through a parental order or adoption.

Parental orders

When deciding whether to make a parental order, the child's welfare is the court's paramount consideration.[39] Section 54 of the 2008 Act sets out several conditions that must be satisfied before a parental order can be made. For example, at least one of the applicants must be genetically related to the child (thus ruling out surrogacy for couples who need to use both a sperm and an egg donor, a restriction which is hard to justify both under art. 8 and through its tension with the paramountcy principle); conception must not have been by natural intercourse; the surrogate mother must have given consent to the making of the order, and the child must be living with the applicants at the time of the application. The 2008 Act widened eligibility for parental orders to include unmarried and same-sex couples, but the application still had to come from a couple. This was challenged in *Re Z (A Child) (No 2)*,[40] and following the Secretary of State's concession that the ban on single applicants was incompatible with art. 14, taken in conjunction with art. 8, a remedial order added a new section 54A to the 2008 Act, which enables a single intended parent to apply for a parental order.

Until the judgment in *Re X (A Child) (Surrogacy: Time Limit)*,[41] it was thought that that section 54(3), which specified that 'the applicants must apply for the order during the period of six months beginning with the day on which the child is born' imposed a strict time limit on applications for parental orders. In that case Sir James Munby P decided that this cannot have been Parliament's intention, because 'Slavish submission to such a narrow and pedantic reading would simply not give effect to any result that Parliament can sensibly be taken to have intended'. As a result, the time limit has now effectively disappeared, and parental orders have been made in respect of children as old as 13.[42]

Section 54(8) specifies that 'no money or other benefit (other than for expenses reasonably incurred)' must have been paid, unless authorized by the court. In fact, the court routinely retrospectively authorizes payments greater than 'expenses reasonably incurred'. Because the child's welfare is the court's paramount consideration, there has been no case in which a court has refused to authorize payments retrospectively on the grounds that the sum paid was too large. The UK's prohibition on commercial surrogacy is therefore completely ineffective.

Adoption

If the intended parents are unable to apply for a parental order, perhaps because the surrogate refuses to consent, the intended parents could apply to adopt the child. In practice, adoption following a surrogacy arrangement is rare. More usually, where the intended parents cannot apply for a parental order, the court will employ other family law tools in order to ensure that the child has a settled home. For example, in *Re H (A Child) (Surrogacy Breakdown)*,[43] the surrogate withheld her consent to the making of a parental order. The judge nevertheless concluded

39 Human Fertilisation and Embryology (Parental Orders) Regulations 2010.
40 [2016] EWHC 1191 (Fam).
41 [2014] EWHC 3135 (Fam).
42 *A v C* [2016] EWFC 42.
43 [2017] EWCA Civ 1798.

that it would be better for the child to live with the intended parents, so a residence order was made in favour of the intended parents, with contact every three weeks with the surrogate and her husband.

Conflicts of laws and immigration issues[44]

It is increasingly common for British citizens to enter into surrogacy arrangements overseas, and these arrangements raise further legal difficulties. Even if the intended parents are, in the end, eligible for a parental order, entry to the UK may not be straightforward, because at birth, the child's mother will be the foreign surrogate. In *Re X and Y (Foreign Surrogacy)*,[45] for example, there was a clash between Ukrainian law, which recognized the intended parents as the child's parents from birth, and UK law, which did not. As a result, the child was potentially both stateless and parentless.

Given the increasing number of foreign surrogacy cases which raise immigration issues, the UK Border Agency has issued specific guidance on *Inter-Country Surrogacy and the Immigration Rules*.[46] In bold and partially underlined typeface, paragraph 6 warns:

> **Even if the surrogate mother's home country sees the commissioning couple as the 'parents' and issues documentation to this effect, UK law and the Immigration Rules will not view them as 'parents'. Only where the surrogate mother is single is there a chance of UK law viewing the sperm donor/ commissioning male as the legal 'father'.**

The guidance then sets out different scenarios and explains how the child might be brought into the UK. Matters are simplest if the foreign surrogate is unmarried and the intended father is the genetic father. He will then be considered the child's legal father for immigration purposes, 'so long as he is so identified on official documentation and can prove his connection by way of accredited DNA evidence'. He may then be able to pass British citizenship to his child, or sponsor the child's entry to the United Kingdom under the Immigration Rules. If the foreign surrogate is married, her husband will be the child's legal father. In order to bring the child to the UK, the surrogate and her husband would have to give up their parental responsibility and an application would have to be made for entry clearance to bring the child to the UK outside the Immigration Rules, at the discretion of the Secretary of State.

Surrogacy law reform

In 2018 the Scottish and English Law Commissions embarked upon a joint review of the law relating to surrogacy. They published a lengthy consultation paper in 2019,[47] and after reviewing the responses, they plan to publish a final report, accompanied by a draft bill, in 2021. The 2019 Consultation Paper made a series of proposals for reform, including setting up a comprehensive regulatory system, and enabling some intended parents to be the child's legal parents from birth. The key proposal is the creation of a 'new pathway to legal parenthood' which would be

44 See further Chapters 7.1–7.3 of this book.
45 [2008] EWHC 3030 (Fam)
46 Available at www.ukba.homeoffice.gov.uk/.
47 English and Scottish Law Commissions, *Building Families through Surrogacy: A New Law*, Law Commissions, 2019.

available only to people entering into surrogacy arrangements in the UK, and provided that a number of criteria are satisfied. To be eligible for acquiring parenthood through the new pathway, there would have to be a written agreement between the surrogate and the intended parents and an assessment of the welfare of the child to be born; both the surrogate and the intended parents would have to have received independent legal advice and all parties should have had implications counselling and medical screening and have been subject to an enhanced criminal records check. If after birth the surrogate mother does not object to the intended parents becoming the child's legal parents, this would then happen automatically, and they could register the birth themselves. The Law Commissions suggest that the surrogate should have a window of between two to four weeks in which to object. If she does so, the intended parents would not become the child's legal parents automatically, and they could only become the child's legal parents by applying for a parental order.

Intended parents who are ineligible for the new pathway, including all parents who have had children through international surrogacy arrangements, would therefore continue to be able to acquire parenthood through the 'parental order route'. The Law Commissions have proposed some changes to the rules governing parental orders. For example, they recommend that it should be possible for the court to dispense with the surrogate's consent, where the making of a parental order would be in the child's best interests. They have also proposed that there should be a medical exception to the requirement that at least one of the intended parents is genetically related to the child, so that where the intended parents are unable to use their own gametes, and need to use both a sperm and an egg donor, they could nevertheless be eligible for a parental order.

In addition, the Law Commissions propose that the HFEA should become the regulator for surrogacy and surrogacy organizations, and that there should be a register which would enable children to access information about their origins. They have also recommended unified guidance on nationality and immigration issues for international surrogacy arrangements. On the question of what payments should be allowed, the Law Commissions are of 'the view that the current position cannot be left unchanged' because 'there is too much uncertainty'. But the consultation document does not make a concrete proposal and instead solicits views on whether various types of payments should be permitted – such as essential and/or additional costs related to the surrogate pregnancy, lost earnings and/or lost entitlement to welfare benefits, compensation for pain and inconvenience and 'payment for being a surrogate'. It also asks for consultees' views on how any restrictions on payments could be enforced.

The Consultation does not propose making surrogacy contracts enforceable, but it is worth noting that even in countries where surrogacy arrangements are binding, such as Portugal, Greece and Cyprus, there are limits on their enforceability, as a result of the personal and intimate nature of the agreement.[48] For example, if either party changes their mind before embryo transfer, it would be absurd to force them to go through with the agreement, and no contract can restrict the pregnant woman's right to make decisions about her medical treatment during pregnancy and childbirth.

48 E. Zervogianni, 'Lessons Drawn from the Regulation of Surrogacy in Greece, Cyprus, and Portugal, or a Plea for the Regulation of Commercial Gestational Surrogacy', *International Journal of Law, Policy and the Family* 33, 2019, 160–80.

Conclusion

Taken together, the rules governing assisted conception and surrogacy in the UK present a compelling example of the benefits of clear, prospective regulation. Assisted conception services provided in licensed clinics are carefully regulated. Treatment is generally very safe (the rate of adverse events is lower than that in the rest of the NHS) and disputes are rare. The HFEA's register means that every cycle of treatment is recorded and all gametes and embryos used in treatment are traceable. Clinics and patients may resent the 'burden' of regulation, and the number of forms that have to be filled in, but this is undoubtedly preferable to conceiving children in a regulatory vacuum.

When people enter into surrogacy agreements, there is no prospective scrutiny of the arrangement, and in a growing number of cases, the courts have had to try to safeguard the interests of children *despite* the rules governing surrogacy. Unwanted childlessness can be extremely distressing and the desire for a baby is a powerful one. It should probably not be surprising that people are willing to enter into complex and precarious surrogacy arrangements, both in the UK and overseas. Surrogacy may not be a common way to start a family (there are a few hundred applications for parental orders each year, compared with over 60,000 IVF cycles), but an absence of regulation is not in the best interests of children or of the adults involved in these arrangements. Given the government's statement in 2018 that it 'supports surrogacy as part of the range of assisted conception options',[49] it is to be hoped that within the lifetime of this book, new legislation will bring surrogacy into line with other ways in which people are assisted to have children.

49 Department of Health and Social Care, *The Surrogacy Pathway: Surrogacy and the Legal Process for Intended Parents and Surrogates in England and Wales*, DHSC, 2018.

3.2

REGULATION OF ASSISTED REPRODUCTIVE TECHNOLOGY AND SURROGACY IN AUSTRALIA

Isabel Karpin and Jenni Millbank

The regulation of assisted reproductive technology (ART) and surrogacy in Australia has a very complicated history. There is no single piece of federal law that regulates these fields but, rather, a mixture of federal laws, federal guidelines and state laws governing access to ART, the use of surrogacy, parentage of children born through these means and access to information for offspring and genetic relatives (see also Chapter 3.1 of this book).

Assisted reproductive technology

Federal ethical guidelines on ART derive their enforceability from their link to accreditation requirements and sit alongside the statutory provisions developed in four of the eight Australian states and territories: Victoria, Western Australia (WA), South Australia (SA) and New South Wales (NSW). The net effect of this multi-jurisdictional approach is a patchwork of ART law, policy and practice across Australia.

The Australian government subsidizes ART through the national health system, Medicare. Many (but not all) of the steps in ART treatments are subsidized through partial Medicare rebates, which are not means-tested. For instance, there are Medicare rebates for IVF services such as intra-uterine insemination, frozen embryo transfer and intra-cytoplasmic sperm injection (ICSI). While the amount of the rebate has been reduced since 2009, there is no limit on the number of cycles for which rebates may be obtained and there is no age limit. This means that although private providers in Australia carry out most assisted reproductive treatment, IVF is more affordable and more commonly accessed than in many other comparable countries. By way of comparison, Australia has a much smaller population than the UK, but quite similar numbers of treatment cycles (and comparable proportions of donor cycles).[1] In recent years there has been considerable

1 In the UK there were 75,425 IVF cycles in 2016 of which 13 percent involved donor eggs, embryos or sperm: HFEA, *Fertility Treatment in 2017 Trends and Figures*, 2019. Australia in 2016–17 recorded 77,353 IVF cycles of which 5.9 percent involved donor eggs or embryos: J.E. Newman, O. Fitzgerald, R.C. Paul and G.M. Chambers, *Assisted Reproductive Technology in Australia and New Zealand 2017*, Sydney: National Perinatal Epidemiology and Statistics Unit, the University of New South Wales Sydney, 2019.

controversy over clinics overstating their success rates, providing treatment without highlighting the unlikelihood of success and 'upselling' patients on expensive treatments.[2]

Broad regulatory landscape and history

Federal law

Two major pieces of legislation were introduced at the federal level in Australia in 2002 and substantially amended in 2007. These regulate both embryo research and the use of embryos created outside the body of a woman. These Acts, the Prohibition of Human Cloning for Reproduction Act 2002 (Cth) and the Research Involving Human Embryos Act 2002 (Cth), are mostly silent on the provision of assisted reproductive technologies. However, the Research Involving Human Embryos Act specifically limits the use and development of embryos in the course of a woman's reproductive treatment to ART units that have been accredited by the Fertility Society of Australia's Reproductive Technology Accreditation Committee (RTAC).[3] Consequently, all clinics that create, develop or store embryos, must comply with the RTAC Code of Practice for Assisted Reproductive Technology Units.[4] The RTAC Code in turn requires compliance with the National Health and Medical Research Council Ethical Guidelines on the Use of Assisted Reproductive Technology in Clinical Practice and Research (2017) (NHMRC Ethical Guidelines)[5] – unless a registered ethics body affiliated to the clinic has directed alternate policies. These national guidelines are extensive and cover a range of topics including:

- Requirements for informed consent, including directions regarding the kind of information that should be provided, the provision of counselling and appropriate practices around obtaining consent (paras 4.1–4.7);
- Rules around the use of known and unknown donors of gametes and embryos, including:
  - ensuring a limit on the number of women or families using sperm from a single donor (para 5.3);
  - requiring the use of gametes and embryos from only those donors who agree to the later release of identifying information (para 5.6.1);
  - requiring the provision of non-identifying information about gamete and embryo donors to recipients and donor-conceived people (para 5.7.1);
  - providing for the 'on-donation' of embryos that have been created using donor gametes and donated embryos (para 6.1.3);
  - a requirement that gametes imported from abroad meet Australian standards including those on consent and counselling (para 5.5.1);
  - preventing clinics from accepting potentially discriminatory limitations on the use of donated gametes for particular 'social or ethnic groups' unless the donors is donating to a known individual (paras 5.1.2–5.1.3);

2 See K. Hammarberg et al., 'Quality of Information about Success Rates Provided on Assisted Reproductive Technology Clinic Websites in Australia and New Zealand', *Australian and New Zealand Journal of Obstetrics and Gynaecology* 58, 2018, 330–4.

3 Research Involving Human Embryos Act 2002 (Cth) ss 8, 11.

4 RTAC, *Code of Practice for Assisted Reproductive Technology Units* (revised October 2017) ('RTAC Code of Practice'). Available at www.fertilitysociety.com.au/wp-content/uploads/2017-RTAC-ANZ-COP-FINAL-1.pdf (accessed 17 September 2019).

5 Available at www.nhmrc.gov.au/about-us/publications/ethical-guidelines-use-assisted-reproductive-technology#block-views-block-file-attachments-content-block-1 (accessed 16 September 2019).

- Indicating who is responsible for stored gametes and embryos at each stage of the treatment process and afterwards, and the requirement of mutual consent to use (para 5.11);
- Allowing for the posthumous use of gametes or embryos where there has been clear consent prior to death or where the law permits if there has been a request by a spouse or partner and the gametes were intended for use by surviving partner and there is some evidence that the dying or deceased person would have supported the use (paras 8.20–8.24);
- Providing for disposal of gametes and embryos in a manner that respects the wishes of patients (para 7.6);
- Imposing limits on the use of preimplantation genetic testing (PGT) of embryos to:
    - severe conditions, diseases or abnormalities
    - identify compatible tissue for a parent sibling or other relative, or
    - increase the likelihood of a live birth (para 8.15.1);
- Prohibiting the use of PGT to preferentially select in favour of a severe genetic condition, disease or abnormality (para 8.15.2);
- Prohibiting the use of PGT for non-medical sex selection while raising the issue for further consideration (para 8.14); and
- Prohibiting the practice, promotion or recommendation of commercial surrogacy (para 8.8).

All clinics in Australia must, at a minimum, comply with these National Ethical Guidelines. State legislation may impose additional limits and restrictions and these will be explored later. Treatment services provided in other countries are primarily outside the jurisdiction of federal and state law. However, two states and one territory extend the reach of criminal prohibitions on commercial surrogacy to extraterritorially criminalize people who travel to access paid surrogacy.[6] Since 2017 the national guidelines also provide guidance to Australian practitioners engaged in information giving and advice to patients contemplating treatment abroad.[7]

Regulatory bodies

Although the National Health and Medical Research Council has set down the guidelines for the practice of ART as noted earlier, it has no compliance or monitoring role comparable to the HFEA in the UK (see Chapter 3.1 of this book). At the state level, Victoria, SA and WA all initially had strong regulatory bodies attached to the ART legislative jurisdiction. However, in both Victoria and SA these roles have been significantly reduced.

In 1984, Victoria was the first state in Australia, indeed the first jurisdiction in the world, to enact comprehensive legislation on the provision of ART. Since that first piece of legislation there have been a number of significant amendments. In 1995, Victoria repealed and replaced the 1984 Act. That second Act was then comprehensively reviewed[8] and repealed and replaced in 2008 by the current law which came into effect on 1 January 2010. The Victorian Assisted Reproductive Treatment Authority (VARTA) approves import and export of donor eggs, sperm and embryos and provides information and support for ART users. Victoria is also unique in that it has a Patient Review Panel to approve certain treatments or storage arrangements including surrogacy applications and hear appeals on certain treatment decisions under the Act.

6 A. Stuhmcke, 'Extraterritoriality and Surrogacy: The Problem of State and Territory Moral Sovereignty', in A. Sifris and P. Gerber (eds), *Law in Context*, Sydney and Annandale, NSW: Federation Press, 2013.

7 See J. Millbank, 'What Is the Responsibility of Australian Medical Professionals Whose Patients Travel Abroad for Assisted Reproduction?', *Medical Law Review* 27, 2019, 365–89.

8 See Victorian Law Reform Commission, *Assisted Reproductive Technology & Adoption: Final Report*, 2007.

Table 3.2.1 ART Regulation across Australia: federal accreditation, ethical guidance and licensing conditions established through: Prohibition of Human Cloning for Reproduction Act 2002; Research Involving Human Embryos Act 2002; *NHMRC Ethical Guidelines* (2017); *RTAC Code* (2017)

Australian Capital Territory, Northern Territory, Queensland, Tasmania	No specific ART legislation. For surrogacy: Parentage Act 2004 (ACT); Surrogacy Act 2012 and Surrogacy Regulations 2013 (Tas); Surrogacy Act 2010 (Qld); no legislation in NT.
New South Wales	Assisted Reproductive Technology Act 2007 Assisted Reproductive Technology Regulations 2009 Surrogacy Act 2010 and Surrogacy Regulations 2011
South Australia	Assisted Reproductive Treatment Act 1988 Assisted Reproductive Treatment Regulations 2010 Family Relationships Act 1975
Victoria	Assisted Reproductive Treatment Act 2008 Assisted Reproductive Treatment Regulations 2009 Status of Children Act 1974
Western Australia	Human Reproductive Technology Act 1991 Human Reproductive Technology (Licences and Registers) Regulations 1993 Human Reproductive Technology Act Directions 2004 Surrogacy Act 2008 and Surrogacy Regulations 2009

SA was the second state to introduce comprehensive ART legislation in 1988. This remained relatively unchanged until 2010, when amendments to the Act came into force.[9] These reforms largely deregulated ART within the state, instead requiring compliance with the NHMRC Ethical Guidelines as the primary governance framework. These amendments also abolished the South Australia Reproductive Technology Council which had played a significant regulatory and advice role.

WA passed legislation in 1991 and is the only jurisdiction that has retained a comprehensive regulatory role for its Reproductive Technology Council (RTC). The RTC is administered by the Department of Health; while not an independent body, it has the role of both formulating a Code of Practice and advising the Minister about the suitability of applicants for licenses to conduct ART and their compliance with regulatory controls. The RTC has developed a code of practice that draws heavily on its British counterpart the HFEA.

The most recent jurisdiction to develop specific ART legislation is New South Wales. The current legislation came into force in NSW on 1 January 2010. The NSW legislation does not establish a specialist external regulator or dispute resolution body. Table 3.2.1 sets out the current legislation, codes and guidelines regulating Australian ART services.

Key issues

Access and eligibility for treatment

There is no federal limit on who may access ART services; nor are there specific eligibility requirements. However, the NHMRC Ethical Guidelines require all clinics to have protocols regarding access to and eligibility for treatment in place. State laws may also limit eligibility.

9 See Reproductive Technology (Clinical Practices) (Miscellaneous) Amendment Act 2009 (SA) which replaced the Reproductive Technology (Clinical Practices) Act 1988 (SA) with the Assisted Reproductive Treatment Act 1988 (SA).

Relationship status

While originally all ART laws contained marital status restrictions on eligibility, these have been successively removed, first by sex discrimination challenges brought by heterosexual unmarried couples and single women,[10] and more recently through legislative reform. In 2016 SA was the last state to remove formal exclusions preventing single women and lesbian couples from accessing treatment. Because the legislation in WA is directed towards the treatment of a woman based on her own or her partner's infertility, gay male couples and single men remain unable to access ART services for the purpose of surrogacy arrangements in that state.

Age

The only limit on eligibility for ART prescribed by the NSW legislation is that the person seeking treatment must be at least 18 years old unless married. At the other end of the spectrum, WA expressly excludes treatment for age related infertility, including through the use of egg donation or surrogacy.[11]

Welfare of the child

The NHMRC Ethical guidelines state that 'the interests and wellbeing of the person who may be born as a result of an ART activity must be an important consideration in all decisions about the activity'.[12] In Victoria and WA the (presumptive) welfare of the child who may be born is a ground for refusing treatment. In WA the clinic 'must be satisfied' of the welfare and interests of the child to be born and in SA the Act provides that the welfare of any child to be born 'must be treated as being of paramount importance'.

Criminal records

Earlier SA regulations required that the legislative requirement of the paramount welfare of the potential child be determined through a process whereby patients had to attest in a statutory declaration to their character (including: that they had no outstanding criminal charges, no convictions for sexual or violence-related offences, had never had a child removed from their care and had no diseases or disabilities which would interfere in their ability or capacity to parent a child). This was revoked in 2003. In contrast, in 2008 Victoria introduced a mandatory criminal records and child protection order check prior to treatment. This measure triggers a presumption against treatment where such a check reveals a conviction. In one case a woman was refused access to ART by her clinician on the basis that her husband had been convicted many years earlier of having unlawful sex with a girl of 16 while he was a teacher's aide and the girl was in his care.

10 See e.g. *Pearce v South Australia Health Commission* (1996) 66 SASR 486 and *McBain v Victoria* (2000) 99 FCR 116, discussed respectively, in A. Stuhmcke, 'Lesbian Access to In Vitro Fertilisation', *Australasian Gay & Lesbian Law Journal* 7, 1997, 15–40; K. Walker, '1950s Family Values vs Human Rights: IVF, Donor Insemination and Sexuality in Victoria', *Public Law Review* 11, 2000, 292–307; K. Walker, 'The Bishops, the Doctor, His Patient and the Attorney-General: The Conclusion of the *McBain* Litigation', *Federal Law Review* 30, 2002, 507–34.

11 A recent inquiry recommended review of those provisions so that a woman with 'impending' infertility could access ART services for surrogacy: S. Allen, *The Review of the Western Australian Human Reproductive Technology Act 1991 and the Surrogacy Act 2008 (Report: Part 2)*, 2019.

12 NHMRC Ethical Guidelines, p. 20.

The decision to refuse treatment was appealed and was the subject of four determinations over a three-year period.[13] The Court of Appeal of the Supreme Court of Victoria held that the tribunal was obliged to evaluate 'any identifiable and established risk factors to the child to be born' (per section 15(3) of the ART Act) and the standard required under this principle 'could include the physical, sexual, emotional and developmental well-being of a child'.[14] When the tribunal reheard the entire matter it decided that there was 'no barrier to treatment, and that the carrying out of a treatment procedure is consistent with the best interests of a child who would be born as a result of the treatment procedure'. This decision seems to have been highly influenced by evidence regarding developments since the time of the first decision, which indicated that the husband had made significant changes to his lifestyle and understandings of sexual relationships.[15]

It is the view of the authors that this case amply demonstrates the impracticability and irrationality of these provisions, as clinicians are asked to predict the future well-being of potential children based on a parent's past conduct which is neither static nor necessarily determinative of future conduct. Furthermore, the actions of one parent limit the capacity of both to access ART. A 2019 Review of the Victorian ART system did not recommend any change to this requirement.[16]

Regulating the use of gametes and embryos

Broadly, the use of gametes and embryos can occur where the provider gives express consent to those uses, but the requirements for consent, specifications permitted, timing and the availability of revocation vary, depending upon whether they are generated by the couple or involve donor gametes, and vary slightly across the states.

Consent and withdrawal of consent

The NHMCR Ethical Guidelines require that clinics ensure that before treatment consent is obtained from all participants and their partners and that it is informed, voluntary, competent, specific and documented. In WA and NSW gametes can only be used if the gamete provider has provided effective consent and they are used in accordance with that consent, but there is no specific legislative requirement for partner consent for treatment where the partner is not a gamete provider. In Victoria both gamete providers, or the woman and her partner where her partner is not the gamete provider, must consent to the treatment on a prescribed form. The form must specify the kind of treatment procedure. In SA the legislation is now silent on these

13 The Patient Review Panel decision is not available; this affirmed the original decision of the clinician. On appeal the Victorian Civil and Administrative Tribunal (VCAT) overturned the decision and opted instead to impose conditions on the husband (12 counselling sessions for sex offenders) before his wife could access treatment: *ABY, ABZ v Patient Review Panel* [2011] VCAT 1382. The Court of Appeal overturned the VCAT decision finding that it had erred by limiting its determination to only those facts that related to the offence that triggered the presumption against treatment: *Patient Review Panel v ABY and ABZ* [2012] VSCA 264. The VCAT then reheard the matter and finally authorized treatment: *BY & ABZ v Secretary to the Department of Health & Anor (Human Rights)* [2013] VCAT 625.

14 *Patient Review Panel v ABY and ABZ* [2012] VSCA 264, para 117.

15 *ABY & ABZ v Secretary to the Department of Health & Anor (Human Rights)* [2013] VCAT 625.

16 M. Gorton, *Helping Victorians Create Families with Assisted Reproductive Treatment: Final Report of the Independent Review of Assisted Reproductive Treatment*, Victoria: Department of Health and Human Services, 2019. Available at www2.health.vic.gov.au/about/publications/ResearchAndReports/final-report-independent-review-assisted-reproductive-treatment (accessed 17 September 2019).

matters and so the NHMRC guidelines apply as they do for Tasmania, Queensland, the Northern Territory and the Australian Capital Territory (ACT).

NHMRC Ethical Guidelines and most state laws provide that a gamete donor can only withdraw consent up until the point that an embryo is created or the recipient woman's treatment cycle has begun, whichever is the sooner. Although variously worded, state laws and the NHMRC Ethical Guidelines provide that use of embryos by the woman after divorce or separation from a partner who is a gamete provider is not possible without his consent.

The position of a partner who is not a gamete provider is much less clear. Consent to the conception attempt is routinely required in practice and this consent renders a married partner or a person in a de facto relationship a parent under state parentage laws. If consent were withdrawn this would prevent the partner from being a legal parent but it is less clear whether this would prevent treatment.

Posthumous use

There have been numerous cases in which widows have successfully obtained permission to retrieve the sperm of a deceased or dying partner, despite the restrictive regulation of use of such gametes in the past.[17] If the deceased gamete provider was a member of the couple being treated, most state legislation and the NHMRC Ethical Guidelines permit treatment of the survivor if there is evidence of consent by the deceased to that use and counselling has taken place.[18] Across the states there has been varied interpretation as to whether the deceased's consent needs to be in writing. It is commonplace for gametes to be transferred to less restrictive states for use. In WA the posthumous use of gametes is prohibited although the use of embryos may be possible. In Victoria posthumous use requires the approval of the Patient Review Panel, which has continued to take a restrictive view.[19] The 2019 review of the Victorian scheme recommended that use be permitted in circumstances where the Panel is 'satisfied that the use is not inconsistent with the deceased person's expressed wishes'.[20]

Prolonged embryo storage

While many previous versions of the NHMRC Ethical Guidelines recommended limitation on the duration of the storage of embryos, the current version has removed such restrictions on the basis that suitability of continued storage depends on both personal and clinical considerations. The current guidelines therefore require clinics to have policies in place to support the clinical decisions and to ensure clear patient consent to storage or disposal.[21]

In states with legislation there is less scope for flexibility. In WA the maximum storage period for embryos is ten years; Victoria frames its limits as a period of five years with the option for the clinic to approve extension for another five-year period. A 2019 review of the Victorian

17 See e.g. *Re Section 22 of the Human Tissue and Transplant Act 1982* (WA) [2013] WASC 3; *RE H* [2012] SASC 146 and *(No 2)* [2012] SASC 177; *Re Floyd* [2011] QSC 218 *Re Estate of Mark Edwards* [2011] NSWSC 478; *Bazley v Wesley Monash IVF* [2010] 2 Qd R 207 (the latter two discussed in L. Skene, 'Proprietary Interests in Human Bodily Material', *Medical Law Review* 20, 2012, 227–45.

18 See e.g. *Re Cresswell* [2018] QSC 142. And see evidence of strong patient desire for such use, see A. Stuhmcke, E. Chandler, I. Karpin and J. Millbank, 'Use of Stored Embryos in IVF Following Separation or Death of a Partner', *Journal of Law and Medicine* 20, 2013, 773–88.

19 *XVT v Patient Review Panel* [2018] VCAT 1902.

20 Gorton, op. cit., n 16, p. vii.

21 NHMRC Ethical Guidelines, paras 4.6.3, 4.6.4, 7.0.

regime recommended that there be no limit on the time a patient may store their own gametes or embryos, and that donors should be able to consent for storage of periods up to ten years (and be able to renew such consent). In WA the regulator has discretion to grant further extensions in certain circumstances, but in Victoria currently such power is limited to circumstances prescribed by law. In NSW a clinic must not use a donated gamete or embryo that was provided or created more than 15 years previously except in very limited circumstances.

Disputes

The NHMRC Ethical Guidelines require ART providers to continue to store gametes and embryos in the event that there is a dispute about them, but do not have any provision for how such disputes should be determined. In NSW, while the Act does not directly deal with disputes about treatment, it does require both gamete providers to consent to use, supply and storage of an embryo. This means that where there is a dispute, clinics will most likely do nothing. In WA, once an embryo is formed, the rights to control of and the power to deal with or dispose of that embryo vest jointly in the couple on whose behalf the embryo was developed. In Victoria, where there is a dispute, appeal can be made to the Patient Review Panel which will have regard to guiding principles set down in the Act. A decision must be made within 14 days and can be appealed to the Victorian Civil and Administrative Tribunal and from there to the Victorian Supreme Court.

Genetic testing of embryos

The NHMRC Ethical Guidelines limit the use of pre-implantation genetic testing (PGT) for three purposes:

1. To enable the selection of embryos that do not test positive for a disease or illness that severely limit the quality of life of the person who would be born;
2. To select an embryo with compatible tissue for subsequent stem cell therapy intended for a parent, sibling or other relative; and
3. To increase the likelihood of a live birth.[22]

There is no definition of 'severely limiting the quality of life' in the guidelines so its interpretation is left to clinical geneticists associated with ART clinics in consultation with their patients and counselors.[23] However, the 2017 version of the Guidelines caution that:

- opinions regarding quality of life differ and may change over time as new treatments become available
- there are differing perceptions of genetic conditions, diseases and abnormalities held within the community
- the practice of selecting against some genetic conditions, diseases or abnormalities may threaten the status of, and equality of opportunity for, people who have that condition, disease or abnormality, and lead to stigmatisation and discrimination
- the technology has technical limitations (such as the failure/inability to identify the condition, disease or abnormality of interest) (para 8.16).

22 Ibid., para 8.15.1.
23 I. Karpin and K. Savell, *Perfecting Pregnancy: Law Disability and the Future of Reproduction*, New York: Cambridge University Press, 2012, Ch. 4.

The guidelines also set out the criteria that it recommends clinics consider when determining the ethical acceptability of the use of PGT. These criteria include consideration of the family circumstances, experience with the disability, age of onset, available therapies, stigma associated with the condition and available social support systems (para 8.16.1).

Furthermore, PGT is not funded under Medicare and therefore access to it is limited to those who can afford the very significant cost.

In those rare cases where a parent may wish to use pre-implantation genetic testing to select an embryo that is a tissue match for an existing ill child this practice is now available for a broader range of relatives. However, there must also be approval by an independent body, no evidence the child would not be welcomed and the child's welfare must be considered. Furthermore, the condition must be serious and stem cell treatment the medically recommended option.[24]

Regulatory oversight of these practices under state legislation has been reduced: for example prior to 2008 the regulator in Victoria approved the use of PGT for specific conditions, but now it does not. Instead the determination is left to a doctor with specialist qualifications in human genetics. The only state that still regulates the provision of PGD (now referred to in other legislation and guidelines as PGT) is WA which has a detailed set of criteria developed in 2017 against which a decision to provide PGD must be made.[25] While the views of a clinical geneticist about the seriousness of the condition are key, they are also required to consider the views of the person seeking the testing and their family about how they view the significance of the condition. These requirements are closely aligned with those contained in the 2017 revision of the NHRMC ART Guidelines.

The NHRMC Ethical Guidelines[26] directly prohibit sex selection for non-medical reasons. However, the Committee that develops those guidelines has come to a majority view that 'there may be some circumstances where there is no ethical barrier to the use of sex selection for non-medical purposes'.[27] In particular they have noted

> an ethical difference between a desire to introduce variety to the existing sex ratio of a family and the desire to design the sex of the offspring based on the preferential selection of a particular sex due to an individual's or a couple's cultural or personal bias, influences or desires.[28]

Therefore, although the practice is still prohibited, the Committee has recommended that the matter undergo further community consultation. State laws in Victoria and WA also prohibit embryo diagnostic procedures for non-medical sex selection. Some Australian clinics have actively facilitated international reproductive treatment to enable sex selection for non-medical reasons.[29]

Embryo destruction

The NHMRC Ethical Guidelines include regard for the wishes of patients concerning the manner in which embryos are disposed by requiring clinics to have policies and procedures in place

24 NHMRC Ethical Guidelines, para 8.17.2.
25 Reproductive Technology Council, *Policy on Approval of Diagnostic Procedures Involving Embryos*, 2017.
26 NHMRC Ethical Guidelines, para 8.14.
27 Ibid., p. 72.
28 Ibid., p. 70.
29 Fertility Society of Australia, 'New Data Reveals Growing Trend in Australian Couples Seeking Social Sex Selection in Overseas IVF Units', Media Release, 2 September 2013.

for discarding stored gametes and embryos that 'provide for the responsible party(ies) to determine the means of removal or discard of the embryos from the clinic, including those which are legal, but are not available at the particular clinic'.[30]

Legislation in Victoria and WA restricts the release of embryos from licensed premises until after they have succumbed and are no longer viable. In all the other states the options for self-disposal are broader. Some patients report being able to take their frozen embryos home to succumb, while others report being invited to watch them succumb in the clinic, or are permitted to undertake a non-viable or 'compassionate' transfer, whereby they are placed in the body of the woman at a time when pregnancy is unlikely.[31]

Particular issues with donor gametes

In all jurisdictions in Australia, donation of gametes requires the written consent of the gamete provider and use in accordance with the terms of that consent. In Victoria, regulators have interpreted this to require the contemporaneous consent of the donor to each and every subsequent use after an embryo has been formed, including extensions of storage and decisions regarding destruction and donation for reproduction or research. No other jurisdiction requires this kind of continuing consent from donors, and a 2019 review recommended that these provisions be removed.[32] State laws differ in the many other areas concerning donation, such as identity disclosure regimes and family limits.

Identity disclosure

Since 2004/5 the NHMRC Ethical Guidelines require that all clinics use only donors who consent to being identifiable on request of offspring at the age of majority. While noting that a national identity register is not within its powers, the current NHMRC Ethical Guidelines strongly endorse the creation of such register.[33]

The state laws on identity disclosure are as follows:

- In Victoria, a central government register covered treatment from 1988, originally providing voluntary disclosure for donors between 1988 and 1998, and mandatory identification of donors since 1998;[34]
- In 2017 Victoria controversially introduced retrospective access to identifying information about donors from the pre-1998 era;[35]

30 NHMRC Ethical Guidelines, para 7.6.1.

31 See I. Karpin, J. Millbank, A. Stuhmcke and E. Chandler, 'Analysing IVF Participant Understanding of, Involvement in, and Control over, Embryo Storage and Destruction in Australia', *Journal of Law and Medicine* 20, 2013, 811–30.

32 Gorton, op. cit., n 15, p. viii.

33 NHMRC Ethical Guidelines, p. 129.

34 The recent amendments to the legislation in Victoria have resulted in the relocation of voluntary and mandatory donor registries in place since 1998 from the ITA to the Registry of Births, Deaths and Marriages.

35 See M. Taylor-Sands, 'Removing Donor Anonymity: What Does It Achieve? Revisiting the Welfare of Donor-Conceived Individuals', *UNSW Law Journal* 41, 2018, 555–83; G. Pennings, 'How to Kill Gamete Donation: Retrospective Legislation and Donor Anonymity', *Human Reproduction* 27, 2012, 2881–5; F Kelly et al., 'From Stranger to Family or Something in between: Donor Linking in an Era of Retrospective Access to Anonymous Sperm Donor Records in Victoria, Australia', *Int. Jo. Law, Policy & Fam* 33, 2019, 277–97.

- WA has maintained central government records since 1993 with a voluntary government register introduced in 2002 and mandatory identification of donors since 2004;
- In NSW, a central government register and mandatory donor identification regime has been in operation since 2010, with an additional voluntary register introduced at the same time to cover earlier treatment;
- In SA, legislation was passed in 2009 to enable a voluntary government register – however, by October 2019 this had still not been established.

Mandatory registers and the NHMRC Ethical Guidelines all set an age at which offspring may request identifying information about their donor. In Western Australia this is set at 16, while elsewhere it is 18. There are some provisions enabling earlier access in limited circumstances, which also vary across states.[36] In the states and territories with no legislated donor identity disclosure regimes (Queensland, SA, Tasmania, the ACT and Northern Territory) record keeping and disclosure remains in the hands of clinics. Thus there is a complex mix of government and clinic held records, which differ according to the period of treatment, and result in varied practices of information disclosure.

There is an increasing trend towards State agencies encouraging or compelling parental disclosure of donor conception, for example Victoria introduced, and inquiries in NSW and the Federal Senate recommended, the annotation of birth records for children born through donor conception; a measure rejected by the legislature in the UK during the 2008 reforms and again by the Nuffield Council Report on information sharing in donor conception.[37] The kind of non-identifying information that must be disclosed varies across the states and federally. All except WA require details of past medical history and family medical history while in Victoria the donor's height, build and blood group are specifically required. In NSW the donor's 'physical characteristics' must be provided. Furthermore in NSW and Victoria details of ethnic background are also required and the names of all clinics to which gametes have been donated as well as information about other children born using the donor's gametes.

Family limits

The NHMRC Ethical Guidelines require that clinics take 'all reasonable steps to minimise the number of families created through donated gamete treatment programs'.[38] For many years this was translated into a licensing condition by the federal accrediting body setting a limit of ten families who could use a single donor's gametes in the absence of state law setting a lower limit, but the current Code sets no such numerical limit.[39] Of the three states with statutory limits,

36 See J. Millbank, 'Identity Disclosure and Information Sharing in Donor Conception Regimes: The Unfulfilled Potential of Voluntary Registers', *International Journal of Law, Policy and Family* 28, 2014, 223–56.

37 See Assisted Reproductive Treatment Act 2008 (Vic) s 17B; Senate Legal and Constitutional Affairs References Committee, *Donor Conception Practices in Australia: Report*, 2011 Recommendation 32. These recommendations were not accepted by the current government: See Australian Government, *Government Response to the Senate Legal and Constitutional Affairs References Committee Report, Donor Conception Practices in Australia*, August 2012; Legislative Assembly of New South Wales Committee on Law & Safety, *Inclusion of Donor Details on the Register of Births*, 2012; Nuffield Council on Bioethics, *Donor Conception: Ethical Aspects of Information Sharing*, 2013.

38 NHMRC Ethical Guidelines, para 5.3.1.

39 RTAC, *Code of Practice for Assisted Reproductive Technology Units* (revised October 2010), para 5.10. Available at www.fertilitysociety.com.au/wp-content/uploads/201011201-final-rtac-cop.pdf (accessed

WA set its limit to five families in 2004. NSW set a limit of five *women* in 2010, but this was found to have a discriminatory effect[40] against families involving two female parents, where both women may wish to carry a pregnancy as they were counted as two women not one family.[41] This provision was later amended to make clear that a woman who is the spouse of a child born to another woman did not count as a second woman under the provision. In Victoria the limit of ten was also set by reference to number of *women* rather than families – a 2019 review found that this was discriminatory against lesbian couples and recommended that it be amended to families.

All three Australian states with legislated limits include the donor's own family/ies in the numerical limit, effectively lowering the limit further in those cases where the donor has pre-existing children, and further again if they were from more than one relationship. Clinics in the non-legislated states are free to include or exclude the donor's family in their calculation as they see fit. All state laws and the NHMRC Ethical guidelines provide for the donor, but not the recipient, to set a lower family limit. In NSW and WA legislation expressly provides for 'directed' donation whereby the donor can exclude particular categories of recipient on grounds that could otherwise constitute unlawful discrimination. This is inconsistent with the NHMRC Ethical Guidelines.

Parental status in assisted conception

Parentage laws in every state and territory and in the federal Family Law Act provide that the woman who gives birth to a child is a parent. The de facto or married *partner* of a woman who conceives a child through assisted reproduction is a parent of that child by virtue of their consent to the conception attempt.[42] This covers both formally licensed clinical services and informal home insemination as the means of assisted conception. These parentage laws apply regardless of whether the birth mother or her partner is a gamete provider and also cover a female partner or spouse.

Although gamete donors are not legal parents under all state and territory laws, there was persistent ambiguity in the federal Family Law Act 1975 (Cth) over the status of donors under that Act, with different judges taking contradictory positions over time. Despite legislative reforms to that Act in 2008 this remained unresolved in relation to sperm donors when the mother was a single woman at the time of conception.[43] In 2019 the High Court determined that the court may find, in certain circumstances, that a sperm donor to a single woman is a 'parent' for the purposes of the Family Law Act (which governs disputes about children, including in that case whether the mother could relocate to another country) even though he would not be a parent under state law.[44]

---

17 September 2019); RTAC Code of Practice (2017); It is unclear whether 'advice' that preceded the current guidelines to limit the use of donor sperm to 10 families is still regarded as persuasive: see RTAC, Advice to Units, Technical Bulletin 3, April 2011. Available at www.fertilitysociety.com.au/rtac/technical-bulletins/ (accessed 17 September 2019).

40 See J. Millbank, 'Numerical Limits in Donor Conception Regimes: Genetic Links and "Extended Family" in the Era of Identity Disclosure', *Medical Law Review* 22, 2014, 325–56.

41 Gorton, op. cit., n 16, p. viii.

42 See Status of Children Act 1996 (NSW), s 14; Status of Children Act 1974 (Vic), ss 10A – E; Artificial Conception Act 1985 (WA), ss 5–6A.

43 See discussion in J. Millbank, 'Resolving the Dilemma of Legal Parentage for Australians Engaged in International Surrogacy', *Australian Journal of Family Law* 27, 2013, 135–69.

44 *Masson v Parsons & Ors* [2019] HCA 21.

Intended parents in surrogacy arrangements are not legal parents at birth and must undertake specific transfer processes in order to obtain parental status. This is considered in the discussion of surrogacy next.

Surrogacy

Parentage in surrogacy

The impact of provisions on parentage in assisted reproduction is that children born through surrogacy are registered as the child of the surrogate and her partner (if any). Parentage transfer is therefore required for surrogacy, even if the surrogate is not genetically linked to the child. This is also the case for children born overseas through surrogacy, who may be recognized and registered as the child of the intended parents within that overseas jurisdiction (including through the provision of a birth certificate listing the intended parents) but not within Australia.

Parentage transfer

Between 2004 and 2012 every state and territory in Australia (except the Northern Territory) introduced legislation to enable the transfer of parentage in certain surrogacy arrangements.[45] All of these regimes exclude commercial surrogacy arrangements (defined as those in which payments to the birth mother exceed reasonable expenses or in which there is a paid intermediary) from eligibility. Unlike the UK there is no discretion to retrospectively authorize payments in order to grant transfer of parentage if it is clearly in the child's best interests to make the order in spite of the breach (see Chapter 3.1 of this book).

All of the states have detailed procedural steps for eligibility: agreements must be in writing, be made before conception, involve parties obtaining counselling at one or more points and also obtaining independent legal advice. Very few of these provisions can be waived. Many states also have one or more of the following substantive requirements for eligibility: minimum age requirements for birth mothers and/or intended parents, marital status of intended parents, residence of intended parents within the jurisdiction and/or conception within the jurisdiction, demonstrated clinical need for surrogacy in intended mother, previous children for birth mother, genetic link for intended parent/s, no genetic link for birth mother. Most of these provisions cannot be waived. Broadly speaking the regimes in SA and WA are more restrictive, Victoria, Tasmania and the ACT fall in the middle, while Queensland and NSW are least restrictive in terms of eligibility requirements. Recent attempts to broaden access to ART services and parentage transfer for male couples and single men wishing to utilize surrogacy in WA have stalled,[46] while amendments broadening access in SA to non-genetic intended parents and same-sex couples are expected to pass in 2019.[47]

All of the state regimes are post-birth consent-based systems that entail court oversight and the application of the child's best interests test. Applications can be made when the child is between six weeks and six months of age (with limited discretion to extend beyond that time).

45 Parentage Act 2004 (ACT) divs 2.4–2.5; Surrogacy Act 2010 (NSW) pt. 3; Surrogacy Act 2010 (Qld) Ch. 3 pt. 2; Family Relationships Act 1975 (SA) pt. 2B div. 3; Surrogacy Act 2012 (Tas) pt. 4; Status of Children Act 1974 (Vic) pt. 4; Surrogacy Act 2008 (WA) pt. 3. See J. Millbank, 'The New Surrogacy Parentage Laws in Australia: Cautious Regulation or "25 Brick Walls"?', *Melbourne University Law Review* 35, 2011, 165.

46 Human Reproductive Technology and Surrogacy Legislation Amendment Bill 2018 (WA).

47 Surrogacy Bill 2019 (SA).

Only WA and Victoria require approval of arrangements prior to the conception attempt by the state regulator of fertility treatment in order to access IVF for surrogacy. In WA parentage transfer can *only* be granted if this has been done; whereas in Victoria there is a second pathway to parentage transfer for arrangements that have not been approved for treatment within the state.

Intended parents who are unable to access the state-based parentage transfer regimes for surrogacy can still apply to the federal Family Court for 'parental responsibility' through parenting orders.[48] Such orders authorize intended parents to make educational and medical decisions for the child and allow for the issue of a passport, but do not endure after the child turns 18 and do not grant parental status as such. Thus, parental responsibility orders do not impact on laws that automatically grant vital rights to children, such as inheritance and other compensation laws, nor do they authorize reissue of a birth certificate listing the intended parents. Dozens of applications have been made to the Family Court for parenting orders by intended parents concerning commercial surrogacy arrangements undertaken overseas and in every case parental responsibility has been granted to the intended parents.[49]

International surrogacy and parentage[50]

Like the UK, Australian law dictates that children born overseas through surrogacy require parentage transfer under domestic law. Foreign laws on parentage do not have effect in Australia unless expressly prescribed (and none are). This leads to a complex Catch 22 situation as there must be some recognition of the parent-child relationship to enable the child to be brought on-shore. At present, the federal government grants citizenship by descent in surrogacy as a matter of administrative practice. While the clear wording of the Australian Citizenship Act 2007 (Cth) section 8 is that parent-child relationship in surrogacy will be recognized only through state parentage transfer orders, the relevant government department declared that section inapplicable to overseas arrangements.[51] Instead, the department looks to a genetic link to an Australian parent and 'ordinary meaning' in determining whether children born through surrogacy overseas are the child of an Australian. However an award of citizenship by descent recognizes the parent-child relationship for only that one legal purpose; much to the confusion of parents it does not have effect on other federal or state laws.

As a consequence of the impasse created by state law excluding many arrangements from eligibility for transfer, some Family Court judges took a liberal or 'enlarging' view of definitions of child and parent in order to 'declare' that male genetic parents in surrogacy arrangements *are* legal parents at birth, an approach which was not authoritatively rejected until 2017.[52] Some judges have also recognized overseas court orders from the United States granting parentage in surrogacy as if it were an Australian court order, while others have declined to do so.[53] This created a situation of considerable uncertainty, with single members of the court taking contrary

48 Family Law Act 1975 (Cth) s 33B. Such applications may be brought by those who are not legal parents: at s 65C(c).

49 See e.g. *Haragli & Pasut and Anor* [2018] FamCA 518 and discussion in Millbank, op. cit., n 36 and A. Sifris, 'The Family Courts and Parentage of Children Conceived through Overseas Commercial Surrogacy Arrangements: A Child-Centred Approach', *American Journal of Law and Medicine* 23, 2015, 396–412.

50 See further Chapter 7.1 of this book.

51 *Australian Citizenship Instructions* (2018). Although note that the Federal Court can invalidate such rules if it finds them inconsistent with the legislation: *Minister for Home Affairs v G* [2019] FCAFC 79.

52 *Bernieres & Dhopal* [2017] FamCAFC 180. However see *Overton & Dyson* [2019] FamCA 20 (in the context of relationship breakdown) where such a declaration as made as part of the orders.

53 See *Sigley & Sigley* [2018] FamCA 3; *Allan & Peters* [2018] FamCA 1063; *Rose* [2018] FamCA 978.

views in different cases over time.[54] Despite a number of inquiries, this issue has not yet been resolved.

Conclusion

Assisted reproductive treatment in Australia is a burgeoning industry. Around 16,000 children are born though ART and IVF each year, representing 4.7 percent of births in 2017.[55] The mix of federal and state legislation makes it a difficult task for patients and doctors alike to navigate through the regulatory landscape. This can add to the already fraught and often drawn out process of achieving a pregnancy and creating a family for women and men using these services.

Laws governing the provision of reproductive technology services and surrogacy can and should provide a framework of support for people who are in engaged in complex personal, and clinical, negotiations. We have argued elsewhere for a shift in the role of government towards an explicitly facilitative model of regulation. A dedicated, non-clinic based external body providing information, counselling and facilitating donation of gametes and embryos and mediated communication and donor identity registers would be a highly valuable innovation in Australia. Such a body could guarantee that there was an independent dispute resolution and adjudication forum, as well as ensuring complex legislative frameworks were interpreted clearly and consistently across the Federal system.[56]

54 See e.g. *Mason & Mason and Anor* [2013]; *FamCA 424; Ellison and Anor & Karnchanit* [2012]; *FamCA 602.*

55 Newman et al., op. cit., n 1.

56 J. Millbank, I. Karpin and A. Stuhmcke, 'Towards Facilitative Regulation of Assisted Reproductive Treatment', *Journal of Law and Medicine* 20, 2013, 701–11. In a recent review of the Victorian scheme, Gorton endorsed the creation of such an entity, op. cit., n 16.

3.3

PARENTING ISSUES AFTER SEPARATION

Recent developments in common law countries

*Belinda Fehlberg and Bruce Smyth, with Liz Trinder**

Introduction

In this chapter of the book's First Edition, we sought to answer the question: how do we, as a diverse society, define what parenting arrangements are in a child's 'best interests' (or perhaps more realistically in practice, are the 'least detrimental alternative')[1] if the child's parents separate? How can that vision be fulfilled in practice and how will we know when we have achieved it? Unsurprisingly, six years later these continue to be key challenges for policy regarding parenting after separation. They remain complex challenges given the emotionally and politically charged context in which they arise, 'producing strongly held views, many based on personal experience'.[2] Of course, ensuring that law operates in children's 'best interests' should continue to be at the heart of policy in this area, but the personal impacts of family law and post-separation parenting policy create ongoing difficulty in clarifying beyond that general principle. Unsurprisingly, the 'best interests' principle has long been criticized for its indeterminacy and malleability, with key issues being a lack of clear cut consensus in society about the values to be used when making a determination (including ongoing debate about how much weight should be given to parents' interests or human rights) and the impossibility in most cases of making predictions about the future.[3] Yet as a concept, the 'best interests' principle has the fundamental benefit of re-focusing attention on children, at least in theory, in a context where adult interests can – and often do – so readily prevail. The perennial challenge is to formulate a better alternative.

* We would like to thank Professor Mark Henaghan and Professor Fiona Kelly for their assistance with our questions regarding, respectively, the New Zealand and Canadian positions. Any errors are of course the authors' own.

1 J. Goldstein, A. Freud and A.J. Solnit, *Beyond the Best Interests of the Child*, New York: The Free Press, 1973.

2 UK Justice Committee – Fourth Report, Pre-legislative Scrutiny of the Children and Families Bill, 12 December 2012, para 145.

3 E.g. R.H. Mnookin, 'Child-Custody Adjudication: Judicial Functions in the Face of Indeterminacy', *Law and Contemporary Problems, Children and the Law* 39, 1975, 226–93; J. Eekelaar, 'Beyond the Welfare Principle', *Child and Family Law Quarterly* 14, 2002, 237–50.

In the first half of the twentieth century, child custody law in many western countries moved away from earlier approaches involving paternal preference, followed by 'innocent party' preference, 'maternal' or 'primary carer' preference, and toward an (avowedly) neutral 'best interests' (or 'welfare') standard. Early legislation setting out the principles to be applied in the resolution of parenting disputes typically stated that the best interests of the child were paramount, without further elaboration, leaving interpretation and application to judicial decision-makers.[4] Over time, checklists of factors to guide the exercise of judicial discretion have been added.[5] Most recently, legislatures have increasingly endeavoured to guide outcomes more directly. In Australia, and elsewhere, this has included three (potentially conflicting) considerations:

1 Children must be protected from harm, particularly from domestic abuse[6] (increasingly as a response to (2), and including some increasing attention to the detrimental effect on children of high ongoing parental conflict);
2 That in most cases children will benefit from ongoing involvement of both parents in their lives (increasingly as a political response to the complaint that application of the 'best interests' standard reflected maternal preference);[7] and/or
3 That children need to be protected from poverty, with their parents and the state having a role to play in this (motivated by both child welfare and fiscal concerns within government).

Yet these three ideas, which seem inherently sensible and are now supported by much research evidence do not necessarily sit comfortably together. For example, there is frequently a tension between (1) and (2) (including which should have priority) and questions continue to surround whether (2) affects (3).

Our focus here is on the first two of these three policy concerns (for further consideration of child support, see Chapter 2.7 of this book) as they have been evident in recent years, focusing on the Australian context along with reference to recent proposals and directions in other common law jurisdictions, particularly England and Wales. The intense and ongoing political, policy and research engagement with post-separation parenting policy reform that has characterized Australia, and to a lesser extent England and Wales, makes them particularly useful case studies.

4 See further R. George, *Ideas and Debates in Family Law*, Oxford: Hart Publishing, 2012, Chapter 7, pp. 112–28 (UK) and C. Backhouse, 'The Mother Factor in Australian Child Custody Law, 1900–1950', *Australian Journal of Legal History* 16, 2000, 51–111 (Australia).

5 For example in Australia by the Family Law Amendment Act 1983 (Cth) s. 29 which amended then s. 64 Family Law Act 1975 (Cth) (now ss. 60CC(2), (2A) and (3)); in England & Wales in 1989 with the enactment of the Children Act 1989 (s. 1(3)): George, op. cit., n 4.

6 Throughout this chapter [except in the context of our discussion of Australia, where 'family violence' is used in legislation], we use 'domestic abuse' to describe violent, threatening, coercive or controlling behaviour that occurs in current or past family, domestic or intimate relationships. This includes abuse that is physical, sexual, verbal, emotional, psychological and/or economic control, as well as damage to property, social isolation and other behaviour which causes a person to be fearful. While 'domestic abuse' is the term now preferred in England and Wales (where this book is published), we acknowledge that jurisdictions differ, e.g. 'family violence' in Australia, New Zealand and Canada, and 'domestic violence' in the United States.

7 See further: American Law Institute, *Principles of the Law of Family Dissolution: Analysis and Recommendations*, 2002; K.T. Bartlett, 'Prioritizing Past Caretaking in Child-Custody Decisionmaking', *Law and Contemporary Problems* 77, 2014, 29.

Protection from harm

There is continuing awareness and policy focus on the need to protect children from harm when relationships break down.[8] The complex and difficult circumstances faced by many separating families mean that in many cases, one or more risk factors for children are present. In Australia, for example, a study found that 'family violence and safety concerns are pertinent to a significant proportion of separated parents and may co-occur with other complex issues, including mental ill health and substance misuse'.[9] In that study, comprising 10,000 separated parent participants, 'between 15 percent and 17 percent of parents report[ed] safety concerns for themselves and/or their child as a result of ongoing contact with the other parent' at Waves 2 and 3 of the study, with Wave 3 interviews occurring just over five years after separation.[10] A court file analysis conducted as part of the study found that between July 2012 and November 2014, 41 percent of files involved an allegation of family violence.[11] The pattern is similar in England and Wales, with allegations of domestic abuse being reported consistently in half of litigated child contact cases or more.[12]

Family law and policy in the western world have been increasingly informed by growing awareness that children may be adversely affected by the range of harms to which they may be *directly or indirectly* exposed.[13] This range of potential harms, along with our understanding of their impact on children, began with physical violence and is ever-expanding. Continuing challenges for policy are that the form, severity and risk of harm may vary enormously (from acts of physical violence to emotional abuse and coercive control), the evidence is often unclear and contested, and as a result it is impossible to devise general statements or guidelines about

8 See, for example, Canada's recent Bill-C78, passed by the Canadian Parliament in 2019 and coming into force on 1 July 2020, which includes amendments to the federal Canadian Divorce Act with the result that federal law (which can be used only by married couples) will be more consistent with provincial law (which can be used by married couples and cohabitees). The 2019 changes maintain the existing position that the best interests of the child are the only consideration for parenting decisions under the Divorce Act and make several amendments addressing family violence, including (in addition to inclusion of a non-exhaustive list of best interest criteria that include family violence) the identification of a 'primary consideration' that the child's safety, security and well-being are the most important factors. This extends to the Act's 'maximum contact principle', which will be subject to the 'primary consideration'. See further: Government of Canada, Department of Justice, Legislative Background: An Act to amend the Divorce Act, the Family Orders and Agreements Enforcement Assistance Act and the Garnishment, Attachment and Pension Diversion Act and to make consequential amendments to another Act (Bill C-78 in the 42nd Parliament). Available at www.justice.gc.ca/eng/rp-pr/fl-lf/famil/c78/03.html (undated, accessed 15 November 2019).

9 R. Kaspiew et al., *Evaluation of the 2012 Family Violence Amendments: Synthesis Report*, Australian Institute of Family Studies, October 2015, p. 12.

10 Ibid., p. 15.

11 Ibid., p. 42. See also L. Moloney, B. Smyth, R. Weston, N. Richardson, L. Qu and M. Gray, *Allegations of Family Violence and Child Abuse in Family Law Children's Proceedings: A Pre-Reform Exploratory Study*, Research Report No. 15, Melbourne: Australian Institute of Family Studies, 2007, Table 5.1.

12 The incidence of domestic abuse is reported in 50 percent, 49 percent and 62 percent of litigated cases respectively in J. Hunt and A. McLeod, *Outcomes of Applications to Court for Contact Orders after Parental Separation or Divorce*, London: Ministry of Justice, 2008; M. Harding and A. Newnham, *How Do County Courts Share the Care of Children between Parents?*, Nuffield Foundation, 2015; Cafcass and Women's Aid, *Allegations of Domestic Abuse in Child Contact Cases*, Cafcass/Women's Aid, 2017.

13 See, for example, in the US: J.R. Johnston and N. Ver Steegh, 'Historical Trends in Family Court Response to Intimate Partner Violence: Perspectives of Critics and Proponents of Current Practices', *Family Court Review* 51, 2013, 63–73.

when a particular outcome (such as cessation of a parent – child relationship) should or should not occur.

Where is the 'tipping point' for policy at which, for example, 'domestic abuse' directed by one parent to the other should limit that parent's relationship with the child? Should it depend on the type and severity of the abuse? The motivation of the perpetrator? The impact of the abuse on the victim? Its impact on the child? The likelihood of its continuing? Other contextual factors? The key challenge for policy in this complex arena is to balance the risk of harm to the child arising from exposure to abuse against the harm that might occur by limiting the child's relationship with a parent alleged to be violent. Particularly difficult issues arise in cases involving allegations of child sexual abuse, due to the evidentiary uncertainty that often exists.[14] Increasingly, the approach of the courts in cases of child sexual abuse allegations, as well as domestic abuse perpetrated by a parent,[15] has been to encourage ongoing relationships with (limited) safeguards (such as supervised contact or handover) where risk is identified, with the cessation of parent–child interaction as a last resort.[16] Correspondingly, significant issues have arisen regarding the accessibility and availability of affordable child–parent contact services, related lengthy delays, and lack of regulation of private contact services.[17] A more fundamental limitation is that even where physical handovers or supervised contact is available, it protects largely against possible physical violence, but does not necessarily address the use of child contact and litigation as a mechanism for continued coercive control.

One exception to this approach was the New Zealand Care of Children Act 2004,[18] which provided that if allegations of violence were proven,[19] the Family Court must not make orders allowing that parent to have day-to-day care or contact with this child unless satisfied that the child would be safe. Yet still there was 'a widely held belief in New Zealand that the protection of victims in the Family Court does not go far enough, notwithstanding the legal and judicial schemes'.[20] Legislative amendment in 2014 replaced the then statutory process for dealing with allegations of physical or sexual violence against a child or other party to proceedings with a requirement that the Court consider 'all of the issues impacting on a child's safety holistically when determining a Care of Children Act application'.[21] The principle that 'a child's safety must

14 Ibid.

15 Ibid.

16 See *Re W (Sex Abuse: Standard of Proof)* [2004] FamCA 768 at para 19. Available at www.austlii.edu.au/cgi-bin/sinodisp/au/cases/cth/FamCA/2004/768.html?stem=0&synonyms=0&query=Re%20W%20(se%20abuse) (accessed 30 April 2013).

17 E.g. in Australia, see Australian Institute of Family Studies, Children's Contact Services: Key issues, Child and Family Community Australia Paper No. 35, October 2015.

18 Care of Children Act 2004 (NZ) s. 60 (repealed on 31 March 2014, by section 16 of the Care of Children Amendment Act (No 2) 2013 (2013 No 74).

19 Meaning that there was either:

(a) in force a protection order (available where there is physical, sexual or psychological abuse under the then Domestic Violence Act 1995 (which was repealed and replaced on 1 July 2019 by the Family Violence Act 2018) in favour of or a party to the proceedings, a child who was a subject to the proceedings or a child of the family, or

(b) an allegation that a party had physically or sexually assaulted a party to proceedings, a child who was a subject of the proceedings, or a child of the family: Care of Children Act 2004 (NZ) s. 58 (definition of 'violent party'), (replaced, on 31 March 2014, by section 16 of the Care of Children Amendment Act (No 2) 2013 (2013 No 74)).

20 P. Boshier, 'Family Law: Family Violence', *Family Matters* 88, 2011, 27–30, 30.

21 New Zealand Ministry of Justice, *Te Korowai Ture ā-Whānau: The Final Report of the Independent Panel Examining the 2014 Family Justice Reforms*, May 2019, p. 48.

be protected and, in particular, a child must be protected from all forms of violence'[22] became the first principle in the best interest checklist and 'the only mandatory principle'.[23] Another new section[24] was inserted, requiring the Court, when taking children's safety into account, to have regard to current or previous protection orders, now made under the New Zealand Family Violence Act 2018. That act (which came into effect on 1 July 2019), which allows protection orders to be made in cases of physical, sexual or psychological abuse,[25] also aims to 'strengthen the Family Court's response to family violence'.[26] These continued efforts reflect ongoing evidence and concern that orders continue to be made allowing parents to have day-to-day care or contact with children in circumstances where this is unsafe.[27]

Further complexity surrounds the definition of 'family violence' (see further Chapters 5.1–5.2 of this book). For example, should the definition be subjective (the victim's perception) or include an element of 'reasonableness'? As noted previously, it is now well-established that family violence extends well beyond physical abuse and is about a pattern of controlling behaviour exerted (usually) by men over women, and that (as noted earlier) children are harmed by exposure to this behaviour even when it is not directed at them. Increasingly, these shifts in understanding have been reflected in legal definitions. For example, in 2011 Australia's Family Law Act 1975 (Cth) (which governs parenting and financial disputes on separation) was amended to define 'family violence' as 'violent, threatening or other behaviour by a person that coerces or controls a member of the person's family (the family member), or causes the family member to be fearful',[28] and to include examples of conduct that may constitute family violence, extending from physical and sexual assault to financial abuse, social isolation and pet abuse[29] as well as defining 'exposure' of a child to family violence, once again giving examples and providing that exposure causing serious psychological harm falls within the act's definition of 'child abuse'.[30] In England and Wales, preference for 'domestic abuse' as the descriptor reflects a similar concern to ensure that controlling behaviours beyond physical abuse are captured by the definition (see Chapter 5.2 of this book).

Despite increasing awareness reflected in widening definitions, concern about harm to children has had insufficient traction in the western world in recent years in the context of the push for increased father involvement post-separation (especially equal shared time). In Australia, the 2011 family violence amendments just mentioned occurred in response to research conducted after reforms in 2006 that prioritized both 'meaningful involvement' of parents in their children's lives after separation and the protection of children from physical or psychological harm arising from being subjected or exposed to family violence, neglect and abuse.[31] In essence, the research indicated that the 'meaningful involvement' messages in the legislation were eclipsing the 'protection from harm' messages and that mothers were not encouraged to voice safety concerns for

22 Care of Children Act 2004 (NZ) s. 5(a).
23 New Zealand Ministry of Justice, op. cit., n 21, p. 48.
24 Care of Children Act 2004 (NZ), s. 5A.
25 Family Violence Act 2018 (NZ), ss. 79 and 9.
26 New Zealand Ministry of Justice, op. cit., n 21, p. 48.
27 Ibid., pp. 49–54; *All Eyes on the Family Court*, A Watchdog Report from The Backbone Collective, April 2017. More generally, see Health, Quality & Saefty Commission New Zealand, Family Violence Death Review Committee, *Fifth Annual Report*, 25 February 2016; New Zealand Family Violence Clearing House, University of Auckland, *Violence Against Women*, June 2017.
28 Family Law Act 1975 (Cth) s. 4AB(1).
29 Family Law Act 1975 (Cth) s. 4AB(2).
30 Family Law Act 1975 (Cth) s. 4AB(3) and (4) and s 4 – definition of 'abuse', para (c).
31 Family Law Act 1975 (Cth) ss. 60B(1)(a) and (b), 60CC(2)(a) and (b).

fear of being viewed as discouraging the father's relationship with the child.[32] The Family Law Act (Cth) was therefore amended to, among other things, make clear that protecting children from harm from family violence, neglect and abuse must be given 'greater weight' than 'meaningful relationships' (i.e. that safety trumps contact).[33] Before the changes, research suggested that family violence had no discernible impact on parenting (and property) outcomes unless it was at the severe end of the scale (requiring medical treatment) and corroborated by third parties such as police and medical practitioners.[34]

Subsequent research suggests, however, that the impact of the 2011 amendments has been quite limited. An evaluation of the 2011 amendments published in 2015 found that although awareness and disclosure of family violence had improved, 'courts remained concerned to ensure that, wherever possible, children's relationships with both parents are maintained after separation, except in cases where the evidence was unambiguously in favour of an outcome inconsistent with this approach'.[35] Family law professionals participating in the study were generally of the view that less 'adequate priority' was placed on 'protection from harm' than on the promotion of a 'meaningful relationship' between fathers and their children.[36] Consistent with this ongoing concern, a review of the family law system by the Australian Law Reform Commission recommended in March 2019 that the 'best interests' checklist in the Family Law Act be simplified, with the first consideration being 'what arrangements best promote the safety of the child and the child's carers, including safety from family violence, abuse or other harm to emphasize the importance of arrangements that best promote the safety of children'.[37]

The process in England has closely matched the Australian experience of increasing awareness of domestic abuse being undermined by cultural resistance based on limited understanding of the complex nature of family abuse, a 'contact-at-all-costs' presumption in practice and resource constraints within the family justice system. The approach in relation to domestic abuse has been to attempt to guide judicial practice through non-statutory mechanisms. This started with practice guidelines on domestic violence,[38] to be replaced by a stronger Practice Direction in 2009 (to provide supplemental guidance regarding the operation and interpretation of court rules).[39]

The weaknesses of the 2009 Practice Direction resulted in a further revision in 2017.[40] The new PD12J adopts a broader definition of domestic abuse to include:

32 R. Kaspiew, M. Gray, R. Weston, L. Moloney, K. Hand, L. Qu, and the Family Law Evaluation Team, *Evaluation of the 2006 Family Law Reforms*, Melbourne: Australian Institute of Family Studies, 2009; R. Chisholm, *Family Courts Violence Review*, Canberra: Attorney-General's Department, 2009.

33 Family Law Act 1975 (Cth) s 60CC(2A).

34 R. Kaspiew, 'Violence in Contested Children's Cases: An Empirical Exploration', *Australian Journal of Family Law* 19, 2005, 112–43; Moloney et al., op. cit., n 11.

35 See further Kaspiew et al., op. cit., n 9, p. 79.

36 See further ibid., p. xii.

37 Australian Law Reform Commission, Review of the Family Law System: Final Report (ALRC Report 135, 2019), Recommendation 5. See also: Commonwealth of Australia, Standing Committee on Social Policy and Legal Affairs, *A Better Family Law System to Support and Protect Those Affected by Family Violence*, 2017. The Australian Federal government has not responded to the recommendations in either of these major reports.

38 Lord Chancellor's Advisory Board on Family Law, Children Act Sub-Committee, *A Report to the Lord Chancellor on Contact between Children and Violent Parents*, London: The Stationery Office, 2000.

39 President of the Family Division, *Practice Direction: Residence and Contact Orders: Domestic Violence and Harm*, London: Judicial Office, 2009.

40 President of the Family Division, *Practice Direction 12J Child Arrangements and Contact Orders: Domestic Violence and Harm*, London: Judicial Office, 2017. Available at www.judiciary.uk/wp-content/uploads/2017/09/presidents-circular-domestic-abuse-pd12j-substituted-pd-20170914.pdf

> any incident or pattern of incidents of controlling, coercive or threatening behaviour, violence or abuse between those aged 16 or over who are or have been intimate partners or family members regardless of gender or sexuality. This can encompass, but is not limited to, psychological, physical, sexual, financial, or emotional abuse. Domestic abuse also includes culturally specific forms of abuse including, but not limited to, forced marriage, honour-based violence, dowry-related abuse and transnational marriage abandonment.

Controlling behaviour is defined as

> an act or pattern of acts designed to make a person subordinate and/or dependent by isolating them from sources of support, exploiting their resources and capacities for personal gain, depriving them of the means needed for independence, resistance and escape and regulating their everyday behaviour.

However, it is widely acknowledged that Practice Direction 12J has not been implemented effectively, with courts reluctant to investigate allegations of abuse and ordering arrangements that may put children and parents at risk. Following concerns about high profile cases, in 2019 the Ministry of Justice established a panel of inquiry into how the family courts deal with private family law cases involving allegations of domestic abuse.[41]

A progress report published by the panel noted that evidence gathered for the inquiry pointed to systemic problems with how risk is identified and managed within the family justice system. The report referred to concerns about the experience of the court process, which was reported by some as degrading and re-traumatising. It also pointed to concerns about the outcomes of the court process, and, in particular, a belief that the court prioritized contact with the non-resident parent above the welfare of the child and any risks that the child or other parent may face.[42] Whether the panel will be able to produce workable and acceptable proposals to redesign the system is yet to be seen (see also Chapter 5.2 of this book).

Encouraging parental involvement

In western countries children usually live with their mother when parents separate, largely reflecting highly gendered pre-separation patterns of parenting.[43] A key ongoing policy challenge has been maintaining separated fathers' involvement with their children, given research evidence that children generally benefit from good quality ongoing relationships with both parents.[44] While estimates vary across countries and studies, around one-quarter to one-third of

41 Ministry of Justice, *Assessing risk of harm to children and parents in private law children cases* (August 2019): https://consult.justice.gov.uk/digital-communications/assessing-harm-private-family-law-proceedings/

42 Ministry of Justice, *Assessing Risk of Harm to Children and Parents in Private Law Children Cases: Progress Update*, London, Ministry of Justice, 2019. Available at https://assets.publishing.service.gov.uk/government/uploads/system/uploads/attachment_data/file/841064/assessing-children-harm-progress-update.PDF

43 See B.M. Smyth and R. Chisholm, 'Shared-Time Parenting after Separation in Australia: Precursors, Prevalence and Postreform Patterns', *Family Court Review* 55, 2017, 586 and other articles in this special issue on shared custody internationally.

44 P.R. Amato and J.G. Gilbreth, 'Nonresident Fathers and Children's Well-Being: A Meta-Analysis', *Journal of Marriage and the Family* 1, 1999, 557.

children with a parent living elsewhere see that parent, most often the father, rarely or never.[45] Researchers have suggested a complex range of reasons why this is the case, including the brevity of time the father may have lived with the child,[46] lack of father involvement pre-separation,[47] fathers' perception that mothers are reluctant to allow parent–child contact, mothers' (and sometimes children's) perception that fathers lack commitment to the child,[48] entrenched parental conflict leading fathers to withdraw, new relationships and new children, the passage of time, and the difficulty of maintaining relationships that may be based on brief and superficial 'visits' in which the father's parenting role is minimized and/or feels unclear.[49]

In response to political pressure from fathers' groups, policymakers have attempted to change *laws* in relation to parental responsibility and parenting time, and to change *processes* so that separating parents are encouraged to share the parenting of their children and to discuss and reach agreements about their parenting which are cooperative and child-focused.

At first glance, shared time (definitions range from 35 percent to 50 percent of time with each parent)[50] might seem 'fair' to parents and to children.[51] On the other hand, what seems fair to those fathers who desire shared time may be viewed and experienced as disruptive and even damaging to children by some resident parents (mostly mothers) and by some children themselves. There is also evidence that some fathers find shared time arrangements unsustainable. Children's and parents' lives and preferences are varied, complex and evolving. Each child and family is different and a 'one size fits all' approach ignores these realities. For these sorts of reasons, legislating for shared parenting is more complex than it may first appear.

Parental responsibility

'Parental responsibility', as defined in Australia and England and Wales, includes the power to make major decisions in relation to the child, such as decisions relating to the child's education, medical treatment and religion. For example, 'parental responsibility' is defined in the Australian Family Law Act as 'all the duties, powers, responsibilities and authority which, by law, parents have in relation to children'.[52]

45 See, for example, P.R. Amato, C.E. Meyers and R.E. Emery, 'Changes in Non-Resident Father-Child Contact from 1976 to 2002', *Family Relations* 59, 2009, 41–53; Australian Bureau of Statistics, *Family Characteristics Survey, Australia, 2012–13* (Catalogue No. 4442.0), Canberra: Australian Bureau of Statistics, 2015; M. Hakovirta and M. Rantalaiho, 'Family Policy and Shared Parenting in Nordic Countries', *European Journal of Social Security* 13, 2011, 247; V. Peacey and J. Hunt, *Problematic Contact after Separation and Divorce: A National Survey of Parents*, London: One Parent Families, Gingerbread, 2008.

46 M. Maclean and J. Eekelaar, *The Parental Obligation*, Oxford: Hart Publishing, 1997.

47 T. Haux and L. Platt, *Parenting and Contact before and after Separation*, LSE/University of Kent, 2015.

48 J. Fortin, 'Taking a Longer View of Contact', *Family Law* 2014, 634.

49 J.R. Dudley, 'Increasing Our Understanding of Divorced Fathers Who Have Infrequent Contact with Their Children', *Family Relations* 40, 1991, 279–85; G. Greif, 'When Divorced Fathers Want No Contact with Their Children: A Preliminary Analysis', *Journal of Divorce and Remarriage* 23, 1995, 75–84; E. Kruk, *Divorce and Disengagement: Patterns of Fatherhood within and Beyond Marriage*, Halifax, NS: Fernwood Publications, 1993; Peacey and Hunt, op. cit., n 45.

50 B.M. Smyth, 'Special Issue on Shared-Time Parenting after Separation', *Family Court Review* 2017, 494.

51 W.V. Fabricius, S.L. Braver, P. Diaz and C.E. Velez, 'Custody and Parenting Time: Links to Family Relationships and Wellbeing after Divorce', in M.E. Lamb (ed.), *The Role of the Father in Child Development*, 5th edition, New York: Wiley, 2010, Chapter 7, pp. 201–240; B. Smyth and R. Weston, 'The Attitudes of Separated Mothers and Fathers to Fifty/Fifty Shared Care', *Family Matters* 67, 2004, 8.

52 Family Law Act 1975 (Cth) s. 61B. Section 3(2) of the Children Act 1989 in England & Wales has an identical formulation, other than the addition of 'rights', preceding 'powers and duties'.

In 2006, the Australian legislation was amended to include a presumption of 'equal shared responsibility' which is not applicable where there are reasonable grounds to believe that a person has engaged in family violence or child abuse, and may be rebutted when not in the best interests of the child.[53] When a court proposes to make orders for equal shared parental responsibility, the court must consider whether orders for equal time would be in the child's best interests and reasonably practicable.[54] Unfortunately, the presumption of equal shared parental responsibility has been understood by some (mostly fathers but some mothers and practitioners as well) as a presumption in favour of equal parenting time.[55] Recently, the Australian Law Reform Commission recommended that the Family Law Act 1975 (Cth) should be amended to replace the presumption of 'equal shared parental responsibility' with a presumption of 'joint decision making about major long-term issues', to avoid the ongoing confusion between parenting time and responsibility which this presumption has created[56] (in contrast, 'parental responsibility' is known as 'legal custody' in some states of the United States, as distinct from 'physical custody', which in most US states is the terminology for the child's living arrangements).

In Australia, shared 'parental responsibility' was introduced in 1996 in order to move away from both proprietorial language and thinking in relation to children. The change was made with little fanfare and did not appear to alter the pre-existing position that after separation parents, regardless of marital status, were joint guardians of their child, subject to court order. This lack of controversy may reflect the accepted view (and a right under the US Constitution,[57] art. 8 of the United Nations Convention on the Rights of the Child, art. 8 of the European Convention on Human Rights, and art. 2 of the First Protocol to that Convention) that the authority to make major decisions in relation to the upbringing of one's child is a fundamental aspect of parenting. In 2006, the law was amended again to provide that each parent has '*equal* shared parental responsibility' (emphasis added), due in large part to pressure by fathers' groups who sought recognition of their equal status as parents. This was not viewed as altering the existing legal position, though greater concern surrounded the new legislative requirement that courts making orders for equal shared parental responsibility must consider making orders for shared time[58] (for European examples, see Chapters 3.4–3.5 of this book).

This is not to say, however, that arguments in Australia about shared parental responsibility do not arise or are not important: more the opposite. Although the rate is lower than in the US,[59] the finding in Australia after the 2006 amendments that equal shared parental responsibility was being ordered in 56 percent of judicially determined cases was noteworthy[60] given that adjudicated cases involve parents who are unable to agree on their parenting arrange-

53 Family Law Act 1975 (Cth) s. 61DA.

54 Family Law Act 1975 (Cth) s. 65DAA. In England & Wales, the concept of parental responsibility (decision-making) remains entirely distinct from what is now called 'child arrangements' regarding where children should live and with whom they should spend time (originally 'custody' and 'access' and later 'residence' and 'contact').

55 Kaspiew et al., op. cit., n 32.

56 Australian Law Reform Commission, op. cit., n 28, Recommendation 7.

57 *Troxel v Granville*, 530 US 57 (2000).

58 Family Law Act 1975 (Cth) ss. 61C, 65DAA; C. Banks, B. Batagol, R. Carson, B. Fehlberg, M. Harrison, R. Hunter, R. Kaspiew, M. Maclean, Z. Rathus, H. Rhoades, G. Sheehan and L. Young, 'Review of Exposure Draft of the Family Law Amendment (Shared Parental Responsibility) Bill 2005', *Australian Journal of Family Law* 19, 2005, 79.

59 That said, it is important to acknowledge that the rate of joint legal custody in the US varies considerably by studies and does appear to be steadily increasing; see Fabricius et al., op. cit., n 30, p. 208.

60 Kaspiew et al., op. cit., n 32, p. 188.

ments and where there are likely to be other challenges to parenting capacity. The frequency of orders for equal shared parental responsibility decreased in adjudicated cases following the 2011 family violence reforms mentioned earlier, from 51 percent pre-reform to 40 percent post-reform.[61] While the Australian federal government had said that those changes did not diminish the shared parenting message, it seems that the family violence amendments have played a role in reducing the likelihood of equal parental responsibility orders in adjudicated cases, but not time sharing orders to the same extent.[62] This may reflect judicial perception that it is likely to be harder for high conflict parents to 'consult' and 'make a genuine effort to come to a joint decision' about major long-term issues affecting their child (as they are required to do under FLA section 65DAC) than to parent independently in a shared time high conflict context. However, clinicians generally agree that for children, considerable strain results from navigating 'parallel parenting' arrangements (where separated parents have minimal interaction with each other, including the avoidance of direct handovers) in cases of high parental conflict.[63]

Parenting time

The greater ongoing policy debate internationally since the early 2000s has been about time with children, particularly the extent to which law and policy should support shared time after parental separation.

In many western countries, shared time arrangements slowly but steadily increased from the early 2000s without legal interventions, particularly amongst cooperative separated parents.[64] They appear to be plateauing in recent years (for example, to around 16 percent in Australia over the last decade).[65] The gradual increase reflected social and cultural change, including women's greater workforce participation and greater emphasis on the importance of fathers' involvement in their children's lives.[66] However, plateauing reflects the reality that the pace of change within families is less rapid than some might like to think,[67] that there are likely to be practical limits to the ability of many families to exercise equal (or near-equal) parenting time, and in most countries it is still very much a minority of parents who share care equally – even in 'intact' families

61 Ibid. n 9, p. 49.

62 Ibid.

63 E.g. I. Ricci, *Mom's House, Dad's House: Making Two Homes for Your Child*, New York: Simon and Schuster, 1997, p. 116; E. Seddon, *Creative Parenting after Separation: A Happier Way Forward*, Sydney: Allen and Unwin, 2003; A. Tucker, 'Children and Their Suitcases', *Australian Family Lawyer* 18(6), 2006, 16; R.E. Emery, *The Truth about Children and Divorce: Dealing with the Emotions So You and Your Children Can Thrive*, New York: Penguin, 2006. See also R. Birnbaum and B.J. Fidler, 'Commentary on Epstein and Madsen's "Joint Custody with a Vengeance: The Emergence of Parallel Parenting Orders"', *Canadian Family Law Quarterly* 24, 2005, 337.

64 M.S. Melli and P.R. Brown, 'Exploring a New Family Form: The Shared Time Family', *International Journal of Law, Policy and the Family* 22, 2008, 231–69; H. Juby, C. Le Bourdais and N. Marcil-Gratton, 'Sharing Roles, Sharing Custody? Couples' Characteristics and Children's Living Arrangements at Separation', *Journal of Marriage and Family* 67, 2005, 157–72.

65 Smyth and Chisholm, op. cit., n 43.

66 See, for example, B.D. Allen, J.M. Nunley and A. Seals, 'The Effects of Joint-Child-Custody Legislation on the Child-Support Receipt of Single Mothers', *Journal of Family and Economic Issues* 32, 2011, 124–39; D.W. Shwalb, B. Shwalb and M. Lamb (eds), *Fathers in Cross-Cultural Context*, New York, NY: Routledge, 2013.

67 R. Wilkins, I. Laß, P. Butterworth and E. Vera-Toscano, The Household, Income and Labour Dynamics in Australia Survey: Selected Findings from Waves 1 to 17. Melbourne Institute: Applied Economic & Social Research, University of Melbourne, 2019, Chapter 5.

where parents live together.[68] While mothers continue to have the main responsibility for day-to-day care of children when relationships are intact, on separation there has been increasing challenge to adjust the 'best interests' standard in a way that will support fathers taking on a greater role if they wish to do so.

So far, most jurisdictions have not legislated for shared time. Overall, the policy trend has been towards encouraging both parents to be actively involved in their children's lives post-separation and maximizing parent–child contact within a framework that continues to focus on children's best interests, rather than specifically legislating for shared time. A recent ongoing example is England and Wales, where the Children Act 1989 was amended in 2014 to require the court 'to presume, unless the contrary is shown, that involvement of that parent in the life of the child concerned will further that child's welfare'. However, the government repeatedly assured parliamentarians that the new statutory presumption was not intended to imply shared time or indeed any particular quantity of time. Rather, the purpose was stated to be primarily to counteract a perception, that was not warranted, that the courts were biased against fathers.[69] Indeed the government accepted an amendment to the bill that stated explicitly that '"involvement" means involvement of some kind, either direct or indirect, but not any particular division of a child's time'.[70]

While governments in western countries have remained under some pressure to legislate for shared time among separated parents, mainly due to the influence of fathers' groups, it is fair to say that the policy debates about shared parenting have abated over the past five years. This is a welcome development given research indicating that, relative to the separating parent population as a whole, high-functioning parents are most likely to be able to manage the level of cooperation, communication, flexibility and infrastructure required for workable shared time (meaning that the benefits for children outweigh the drawbacks), and that legislating for shared time results in its use by families that do not have these characteristics.[71] This has become clearer with increased understanding of domestic abuse (see earlier).

There has also been emerging interest in what constitutes 'high conflict' and its various sub-groups and whether – and if so, the extent to which – shared time arrangements are in children's best interests when high ongoing parental conflict exists. Recent work clarifies the risks to children in high conflict shared time arrangements that might otherwise be overlooked, identifying entrenched inter-parental hatred as a key factor.[72] Yet at the same time, and despite considerable work in this area, conflation of 'high conflict' and domestic abuse has continued as a key concern, in the form of a tendency to refer to 'high conflict' to describe what is in reality domestic abuse.[73] This continuance risks euphemizing and mini-

68 Ibid.; T.P. Novales, 'The Equality Rights of Parents and the Protection of the Best Interests of the Child after Partnership Breakdown in Spain', *International Journal of Law, Policy and the Family* 26, 2012, 378–400.

69 Justice Committee, op. cit., n 2, para 153.

70 Enacted as s1(2B) of the Children Act 1989.

71 Kaspiew et al., op. cit. n 9; Kaspiew et al., op. cit. n 32; B. Smyth, J. McIntosh, R. Emery, and S. Higgs Howarth, 'Shared-time parenting: Evaluating the evidence of risks and benefits to children', in L. Drozd, M. Saini, N. Olesen (eds), *Parenting Plan Evaluations: Applied Research for the Family Court*, 2nd edition, Oxford University Press: New York, 2016, pp. 118–69.

72 B. Smyth and L. Moloney, 'Entrenched Postseparation Parenting Disputes: The Role of Interparental Hatred?', *Family Court Review* 55, 2017, 404.

73 E.g. A. Lynch, 'Family Violence and High Conflict: What's the Difference and Does It Really Matter?', *Child Aware*, 2017. Available at https://childaware.org.au/wp-content/uploads/sites/3/2017/06/03-Angela-Lynch.pdf

mizing the significance and risk of domestic abuse, equalizes responsibility for that abuse, and inhibits development of our understanding of the deleterious effects on children and parents of ongoing high parental conflict as a separate issue. Added to this is an apparent increase in claims in Australia and England and Wales that some fathers are prevented from seeing their children because of the behaviour of some mothers (including increasing focus on concepts such as 'parental alienation', 'parental alignment', 'maternal gatekeeping'[74] and claims of false allegations of domestic abuse and child abuse).[75] The push for shared time parenting legislation thus appears to be being replaced by a push for change that will facilitate the discrediting of mothers in order to secure parenting time gains or even sole custody or residence for fathers.

Amid all of this, concerns continue to be raised regarding whether policymakers may also be seeking to allay the concerns of particular groups, especially aggrieved fathers, rather than addressing children's needs. The recent announcement in Australia of a new Joint Parliamentary Inquiry into Family Law and Child Support, before the ink has dried on the last major government-commissioned report,[76] is a good example. A major focus of this Inquiry is the concern of its co-chair, Senator Pauline Hanson, that mothers are making up domestic violence claims in custody battles: 'There are people out there who are nothing but liars and who will use that in the court system',[77] despite consistent research evidence to the contrary.[78]

In England and Wales, there is no evidence that the new presumption of continuing involvement has had any impact on the numbers of children having contact or the amount of contact. However, there is some concern that the presumption has made it harder for parents to argue for and achieve protective measures, including no contact, in cases of domestic abuse.[79] The presumption can be disapplied, but only when involvement would 'put the child at risk of suffering harm *whatever* the form of the involvement' (emphasis added) which can be direct or indirect contact.[80] In consequence, the courts can and do presume contact of some kind is required in all but the most extreme of cases.

Generally, there is ongoing concern that post-separation parenting laws and processes, with their focus on parenting time, typically respond to the interests of adults rather than children. Although the importance of child-responsive approaches and children's meaningful participation in decisions affecting them if their parents separate have been emphasized since the 1980s, they continue to be recognized as unrealized goals by legislators, practitioners, parents and children, despite greater inclusion of children's voices in research, policy and practice.[81] In recent years, family law researchers have increasingly sought to involve children as study

74 E.g. Proposed inclusion of 'parental alienation' as a 'Caregiver-child relationship problem' Code QE52.0 in the International Classification of Diseases 11th Revision (ICD-11). Available at www.learningtoendabuse.ca/docs/WHO-September-24-2019.pdf

75 Concerns around this appear to have driven the announcement of a new Australian parliamentary inquiry into family law and child support: Prime Minister of Australia, Joint Parliamentary Inquiry into Family Law and Child Support, Media Release, 17 September 2019.

76 ALRC, op. cit., n 37.

77 S. Martin, 'Pauline Hanson Sparks Fury with Claim Domestic Violence Victims Are Lying to Family Court', *The Guardian*, Australia edition, 18 September 2019.

78 M. Kaye and J. Wangmann, 'We Don't Teed Another Inquiry into Family Law: We Need Action', *The Conversation*, 20 September 2019.

79 F. Kaganas, 'Parental Involvement: A Discretionary Presumption', *Legal Studies* 38, 2018, 549.

80 Children Act 1989 s.1(6).

81 J. Aldridge, 'Introduction to the Issue: "Promoting Children's Participation in Research, Policy and Practice"', *Social Inclusion* 5, 2017, 89.

participants, as well as co-researchers. Sadly, findings of research involving children underline the ways in which current primary responsiveness to parental needs can stand at odds with the challenges, experiences and needs of children. There is significant disjuncture between adult focus on clock and calendar time, with its emphasis on division of time between parents and dwellings, and the nuances of children's experiences of post-separation parenting arrangements that often require them to move between the physical and emotional terrains of their parents' households.[82]

Conclusion

This brief overview of policy challenges for post-separation parenting has suggested that legislative attempts to articulate how children's 'best interests' will be met fall broadly into three main areas: protecting children from harm, encouraging involvement of both parents (especially fathers) in their children's daily lives and ensuring that parents share the financial responsibility of supporting their children according to parental capacity. These challenges often compete and conflict. The indications continue to be that of the first two of these three main areas, which are our focus in this chapter, encouraging father involvement has continued to be given primacy and that this presents risks for children.

A perennial problem for policy is often that there is pressure to make decisions before research is undertaken to inform policy action.[83] This was very evident in Australia in 2006, where the policy approach was to legislate to encourage shared parenting but to fund research as part of the reform package, allowing detailed consideration of the consequences and leading to further reform in 2011. In contrast, in England and Wales, with the benefit of the Australian experience and research, greater caution has been exercised. However, in the end it is possible that while fathers' interests 'may have limited success in public inquiry processes that rely on research evidence to inform legal change, their justice claims hold significant intuitive appeal for policy-makers'.[84] This observation would seem highly relevant to the recently announced Australian parliamentary inquiry: the research evidence has only recently been thoroughly considered by the Australian Law Reform Commission's review, and there is no doubt the latest inquiry is a political response to fathers who were unhappy with that review's recommendations that would in effect wind back the shared parenting messages resulting from amendments in 2006 (earlier in this chapter). Sadly, Australia continues to be caught in a continuing family law and policy struggle, in which any perceived 'gains' regarding children's safety and ensuring that law and policy operate in children's best interests are likely to be seen by fathers as undermining of their position. The situation is broadly similar in England and Wales, where policy attention on domestic abuse has been followed rapidly by a policy focus addressing the concerns of the fathers' groups,

82 E.g. H. Davies, 'Shared Parenting or Shared Care? Learning from Children's Experiences of a Post-Divorce Shared Care Arrangement', *Children & Society* 1, 2015; S. Kay-Flowers, *Childhood Experiences of Separation and Divorce: Reflections from Young Adults*, Bristol: Policy Press, 2019; U. Zartler and K. Grillenberger, 'Doubled Homes: Doubled Social Ties? Children's Relationships in Post-Divorce Shared Residence Arrangements', *Children & Society* 31, 2017, 144; B. Fehlberg, K. Natalier and B. Smyth, 'Children's Experiences of "Home" after Parental Separation', *Child and Family Law Quarterly* 30, 2018, 3.

83 For a good discussion of this issue see H.R. Schaffer, *Making Decisions about Children*, 2nd edition, Malden, MA: Blackwells Publishers 1998, pp. 1–18.

84 H. Rhoades, 'Yearning for Law: Fathers' Groups and Family Law Reform in Australia', in R. Collier and S. Sheldon (eds), *Fathers' Rights Activism and Law Reform in Comparative Perspective*, Oxford: Hart Publishing, 2006, pp. 125–46.

largely negating any earlier progress. It remains to be seen what impact the current Ministry of Justice inquiry into domestic abuse has on law and practice and whether it might also ignite further calls for action by fathers.

A key conundrum for family policymakers is that, 'while the indeterminate best interest standard may not be good, there is no available alternative that is clearly less detrimental'.[85] On the other hand, 'the very indeterminacy which is criticized enables judges to take into account whatever peculiarities a case throws up'.[86] Moreover, there is now a rapidly growing body of research on post-separation parenting, including in the three areas where legislatures have attempted to guide the 'best interests' principle in recent years mentioned at the start of this chapter and conclusion. Overall, that research suggests that attempting to guide the operation of the 'best interests' (or welfare) principle results in new risks for children. Modifications assume too much about what is in children's best interests and risk taking our attention away from the current needs of the particular child. In the end, '[t]he greatest virtue of the welfare principle is not necessarily that it leads to the best possible outcomes (although of course it aims to do so) but that it makes people think about the child'.[87] Laws that favour maintaining a 'best interests' standard that does not favour particular parenting outcomes, along with resourcing our family law systems to provide professional assistance that encourages child-focused outcomes, remain our best alternative.[88]

85 Mnookin, op. cit., n 3, p. 282.
86 George, op. cit., n 4.
87 Ibid., p. 127.
88 See, for example, Chisholm, op. cit., n 32.

3.4

THE DEVELOPMENT OF 'SHARED CUSTODY' IN SPAIN AND SOUTHERN EUROPE

Teresa Picontó Novales

'Shared custody': expressions and meanings

Given the differences in the practice of 'shared custody' in the family law of different countries (Spain, Portugal, Italy and France, on the one hand, and Anglo-Saxon countries on the other) it is necessary to clarify the meaning of the term and other related terms.

In southern European countries, the tendency of the most recent legal reforms and judicial decisions has been towards establishing that the periods of time that children spend living with each of the parents after separation or divorce should be as equal as possible. More specifically, Resolution 2079 (2015) of the Council of Europe *Equality and Shared Parental Responsibility* states in paragraph 5 that the Assembly calls on member states to

> introduce into their laws the principle of shared residence following a separation, limiting any exceptions to cases of child abuse or neglect, or domestic violence, with the amount of time for which the child lives with each parent being adjusted according to the child's needs and interest.
>
> Once shared custody of the children has been decided, the functions which constitute parental responsibility apply to both parents who will continue to share the titularity (ownership) and exercise of parental responsibility unless a court has suspended it or taken it away permanently.

This section addresses principally Spanish family law but also deals with the characteristics it shares with Italian, Portuguese and French law, together with the differences, particularly in relation to the meaning of 'shared custody' and related terms.

The expression 'shared custody' in Spanish law can be defined in general terms as the way of exercising parental responsibility after partnership breakdown under which the parents actively and equally participate in the personal attention and care of their children, in proportion to their personal circumstances (which may include employment, income, health and so on). This also applies to the material needs of the children. As regards living arrangements, the children can live alternately with each parent for periods of time agreed between themselves or decided by the court.[1]

1 P. Ortuño Muñoz, *El nuevo régimen jurídico de la crisis matrimonial*, Madrid: Civitas, 2006, p. 60.

The separation or divorce of the parents does not deprive them of their obligations towards their children. This includes the payment of *alimentos*,[2] a concept in Spanish law obliging parents to provide for their children in terms of clothing, food, education and due care and attention. The court decides the contribution of each parent in this respect. It is highly advisable for the parents to reach an agreement about the ordinary daily expenses and also other expenses (e.g. medical care) which may otherwise become a source of conflict or dispute between them.

In the national law (the Civil Code) and regional laws covering shared custody, priority is given to the divorce or separation agreements reached between parents. These agreements must include parental planning, setting out the financial contribution each parent must make to the children. If there is no agreement, the criteria followed by the court will be the proportionality of each parent's contribution in relation to their income.[3]

Under shared custody arrangements, each parent is responsible for the ordinary daily expenses of the children when he or she is living with them. The extraordinary expenses are paid in equal parts provided that the financial situation of both parents is similar. If this is not the case, the contribution of each parent must be proportional to his or her resources in relation to both the ordinary and the extraordinary expenses.[4]

The Spanish Supreme Court has noted that if one of the parents is unemployed and has a minimal income, if any, then the other parent is obliged to pay the expenses of the children (art. 146 of the Spanish Code of Civil Law). In a recent case, a father appealed to the Supreme Court on the grounds that shared custody did not oblige him to pay the whole cost of caring for the children merely because the mother did not have a job. The Supreme Court ruled that shared custody does not relieve a parent from the obligation of paying for the care of the children if the other parent does not have a salary or other resources. In any case, the situation of the children cannot depend on the mother being able to find work.[5]

In general terms, the Italian Law (Law 54/2006) establishes the joint exercise of parental responsibility by the parents after divorce or separation. The parents should cooperate in the upbringing and care of their children, and also make joint decisions about the most important aspects of the children's lives (within the framework of co-parenting – *cogenitorialità*).[6] If there is disagreement between the parents about the exercise of parental responsibility, the court makes the decision in the best interest of the child. Then the court also guarantees the rights of the children to maintain contact with both parents (the child has the right to *bigenitorialità*).[7]

Specifically, in Italian law, the concept of *affidamento* regulates, in general terms, the exercise of parental responsibility over the children after the separation of the parents. Unlike Spanish

2 *Alimentos* is understood to mean 'everything which is indispensable for sustenance, nutrition, clothing and medical attention'. It also includes 'education and instruction' (art. 142 of the *Code of Civil Law*).

3 J. Martínez Calvo, 'El "affidamento" y la "collocazione" en el Derecho Italiano: una visión comparada con la guarda y custodia española', en *Revista de Derecho de Familia*, 2018, 78. [Electronic version: https://pjenlinea3.poder-judicial.go.cr/biblioteca/uploads/Archivos/Articulo/El%20affidamento.PDF (Last accessed September 2019)].

4 A-M Pérez Vallejo and M.B. Sainz-Cantero, *Protección de la Infancia y marco jurídico de la coparentalidad tras la crisis familiar*, Valencia: Tirant lo Blanch, 2018, p. 164.

5 FJ° 4, STS 55/2016, 11th February.

6 A. Costanzo, 'I rapporti personali tra genitori e figli nella prospettiva giurisprudenziale', in M. Sesta and A. Arceri (eds), *L'affidamento dei figli nella crisi della famiglia*, Torino: Wolters Kluwer Italia, 2012, pp. 499–500.

7 M. Sesta, 'La nuova disciplina dell'affidamento dei figli nei processi di separazione, divorzio, annullamento matrimoniale e nel procedimento riguardante I figli nati fuori del matrimonio', in M. Sesta and A. Arceri (eds), *L'affidamento dei figli nella crisi della famiglia*, Torino: Wolters Kluwer Italia, 2012, p. 45; Costanzo, op. cit., n 6, p. 517.

law, the decision about the residence of the children with each parent is made by the court at a later stage. First, custody is granted, usually *affidamento condiviso* (shared custody) to both parents. Second, the judge decides the time that the child will live with each parent, which may vary, and the arrangements for contact with the other parent. Shared custody does not imply that the children will live with each parent for a similar period of time. In Italian law, the concept of *collocazione* (placement) identifies the parent with whom the children will live for longer periods of time (art. 337 ter. 2 of the *Italian Code of Civile Law*).[8] Under *affidamento condiviso*, the most important decisions regarding the child are taken jointly by both parents (art. 337 ter. 3). However, the court may decide that for ordinary day-to-day decisions the parents will exercise their parental responsibility separately (art. 337 ter. 3). Both legislation and jurisprudence state that the parents should agree a common approach to the education and upbringing of their children, but on that basis each parent can act separately provided that they do not deviate from the jointly agreed arrangements. However, this does not exclude regular reciprocal consultations between both parents.

As in Spain, under *affidamento condiviso* priority is given to the separation agreement between the parents as regards the financial contribution to the ordinary and extraordinary expenses of maintaining the children. If there is no agreement, the court will decide that each parent should pay in proportion to their income (art. 337 ter. 5 del Code Civile italiano). More specifically, one important criterion courts take into account to determine the contribution of each parent is the period of time that the children will spend with the parent. The parent who has the principal residence (*collocazione*) has to pay the day-to day expenses.[9]

The Portuguese Divorce Law (Law 61/2008) suppressed the concept of 'paternal' responsibility and replaced it with that of 'parental' responsibility. The Portuguese law subsequently established joint parental responsibility (art. 1906.1 Portuguese Civil Law). 'Shared parental responsibility' has become the rule and 'sole parental responsibility' the exception. Then, shared parental responsibility can only be excluded by the decision of the court. In cases of separation or divorce of the parents, the law establishes that the children should have one resident parent and keep a close relationship with both parents, who together should make the major decisions about their upbringing. Shared custody (joint physical custody) does not figure in the law as an explicit option.[10] Specifically, the joint exercise of parental responsibility involves the parents deciding together about the main issues in the lives of their children and about the main residence where the children will live. In this context, for the terms 'joint custody' and 'alternating custody' are not synonymous with 'joint exercise of parental responsibility'.[11] For this reason, it is not correct to use them indiscriminately.[12]

Portuguese law, therefore, establishes the joint exercise of parental responsibility for important issues in the lives of their children after divorce (e.g. education, religion, surgical operations, moving to another city (art. 1906.1 of the Portuguese Civil Code)). At the same time, it establishes that the children will live mainly with one of the parents (main residence) while the other

8 Constanzo, op. cit., n 6, p. 533.

9 See Martínez Calvo, op. cit., n 3.

10 S. Marinho, 'Separate Mothering and Fathering: The Plurality of Parenting within the framework of Postdivorce, Shared Parenting Norms', *Journal of Divorce & Remarriage* 58, 2017, 293. This opinion is not shared by other authors: M.C. Sottomayor, *Regulaçâo das Responsabilidades Parentais nos Casos de Divórcio*, 6th edition, Coimbra: Almedina, 2014, p. 305.

11 M.C. Sottomayor, op. cit., n 10, pp. 304–5. This is a controversial issue: C. Duarte Pinheiro, *O Direito da Família Contemporâneo*, 3rd edition, Lisboa: AAFDL, 2012, pp. 350–1.

12 Sottomayor states that 'in Portuguese law we have 'legal joint custody' without 'physical joint custody': Sottomayor, op. cit., n 10, p. 305.

parent will have visiting rights in the traditional manner. According to Oliveira, this shows that Portuguese law has not established that the time spent with each of the parents should be more or less the same.[13] To summarize, the Portuguese Law 61/2008 replaces the concept of 'custody' in the previous law with the more neutral term 'residence' (art. 1906.3 of the Portuguese Civil Code) to move away from the previous system of 'sole custody' and avoid its associated connotations (custody generally having been granted to the mother).[14] Deciding the residence of the child with one of the parents not only means that the child will live mainly with that parent. It also means that the parent in question will be responsible for the day-to-day care during the time the child is living with him or her.

French law uses the term *l'autorité parentale* which is similar to the Spanish concept of *patria potestad*, which is essentially parental responsibility. This includes the rights and responsibilities of the parents to protect and provide for their children and to educate them (art. 371–1 of the French Civil Code), exercised jointly by both parents, in accordance with the principle of equality between parents. The term *coparentalité*, included in the Law n° 2002–305, means that the two parents exercise the functions of parental authority jointly both when they are together (in a marriage, a *pacte civil de solidarité*, or as a cohabitating couple) and after divorce or separation of the parents.[15] According to this principle of *coparentalité*, the separation or divorce of the parents has no effect on the exercise of parental responsibility (art. 373–2 of the French Civil Code). Therefore, after separation or divorce, the parents have to take decisions jointly about their children (including surgical interventions, religion, hospitalization, etc.). Both parents also have the right to decide on the education of their children.[16]

As regards residence in France, the term *residencé alternée* (similar to shared custody) is based on the idea that the children have a residence with each of their parents, after divorce or separation (art. 373–2–9 of the French Civil Code). The period of time spent with each parent is not necessarily the same. However, the courts have tended to decide that children should spend equal periods of time with each parent, depending on the interest of the child.[17] Despite this tendency, there are often differences in these alternating residence times depending on the age and the development of the children.[18] The legal reforms relating to the *residence alternée* (2002, 2005) retain *l'obligation d'entretien* of the parents to provide support for the children after divorce or separation,[19] which includes maintenance and education (art. 373–2–2 French Civil Code), similar to the arrangements in Spain. This must be included in the agreement of the parents after separation which, if the parents so wish, may be ratified by the court (art. 372–2–7 of the French Civil Code).

Having explained the main features and the terminology relating to shared custody in Spain and in southern Europe, the following section addresses the various types of shared custody and their development at both a legislative and judicial level in recent years.

13 G. Oliveira, 'A ´residência alternada'em Portugal, segundo a Lei n°61/2008', in S. Marinho and S.V. Correia (eds), *Una familia parental, duas casas*, Lisboa: Silabo, 2017, p. 157.

14 This is also open to debate: Oliveira, op. cit., n 13, and Marinho, op. cit., n 10.

15 V. Égéa, *Droit de la famille*, 2nd edition, Paris: LexisNexis, 2018, pp. 596–8.

16 P. Courbe and A. Gouttenoire, *Droit de la famille*, 7th edition, Paris: Sirey, 2017, p. 500.

17 M. Juston, 'La résidence alternée: un droit des parents subordonée à l'intéret de l'enfant', in G. Neyrand and Ch. Zaouche Gaudron (eds), *Le Livre Blanc de la résidence alternée. Penser la complexité*, Toulouse: érès, 2014, p. 36.

18 J. Dahan, 'La résidence alternée: por qui, comment, quand?', in G. Neyrand and Ch. Zaouche Gaudron (eds), *Le Livre Blanc de la résidence alternée. Penser la complexité*, Toulouse: érès, 2014, p. 59.

19 Courbe and Gouttenoire, op. cit., n 16, p. 542.

The development of 'shared custody' in Spain and southern Europe

In Spain, the issue of shared custody being ordered by the courts when there is no agreement between the parents continues to be the subject of debate. In fact, there are even significant differences between the national state law (Law 15/2005) and the laws of five of the country's autonomous regions, Catalonia, Aragon, Valencia, Navarre and Basque Country.

The national law 15/2005 states that, exceptionally, in cases of contested separation or divorce, the court may order shared custody at the request of only one of the parents provided that this is in the best interests of the child (art. 92.8 of the Spanish Civil Code). Aragón was the first Autonomous Region to establish the legal preference of shared custody by order of the court even if there is no agreement between the parents and even if neither parent has applied to the court for custody (art. 80.2, Law 2/2010; STC 192/2016, 16th November). This Aragonese Law (2/2010) was amended after considerable argument in the Regional Parliament and controversy among professionals and the public in general. The legal preference for shared custody in the absence of an agreement between the parents was replaced by a provision in the Law (6/2019) giving the court the competence to decide the kind of custody in accordance with the best interest of the child and certain legal criteria. These criteria include the age of the children, the opinion of the children, the attitude of the parents towards ensuring the stability of their children, the possibilities of combining family life with the work of the parents and the past contribution of each parent to the care of their children during the period of living together (the latter criterion was the most controversial).

The Catalan Civil Code and the Basque Law (7/2015) provide for shared custody in the absence of an agreement between the parents as the priority position, but not as a legal requirement as stated in the previous Aragonese Law (2/2010).[20] Art. 233–10.2 of the Catalan Civil Code states that in the absence of a parental agreement the court should decide on the type of custody of the children as far as possible with joint parental responsibility. However, the court is able to award sole custody if this is in the best interest of the child.

The Basque Law (7/2015) also considers shared custody as the most appropriate arrangement but it must be requested by at least one of the parents and the court must be satisfied that it is not prejudicial to the best interest of the child (art. 9.3). In Navarre, the previous Law (3/2011) and the new Law (21/2019) about custody after the divorce or separation of the parents follow the current Aragonese system of shared custody (Law 6/2019): in the absence of a parental agreement, the court decides taking into consideration the best interest of the child.

At the national level, a Green Paper was presented in the Spanish Parliament in 2014 for the reform of the Civil Law in relation to parental co-responsibility after divorce or separation.[21] To date, this has yet to become a bill. The Green Paper does not propose a legal preference for shared custody when there is no agreement between the parents. In this case, the court is free to decide whether to award shared or sole custody depending on the best interest of the child and following certain legal criteria.[22] Therefore, the court could decide on shared custody even if neither of the parents have applied for it, provided that this is in the best interest of the child (art. 92 bis).

20 I. Domíguez Oliveros, *Custodia compartida preferente o interés del menor?*, Valencia: Tirant lo Blanch, 2018, p. 176.

21 Spanish Ministry of Justice, Green Paper on the reform of the Civil Code in relation to the exercise of co-parental responsibility in cases of annulment, separation or divorce (2014) electronic version www.juecesdemocracia.es/LegislacionActual/Anteproyecto%20de%20Ley%20Custodia%20Compartida%20CM%2019-7-13.pdf.

22 Domínguez Oliveros, op. cit., n 20, p. 71.

In the last six years, Spanish jurisprudence has produced a significant change in relation to shared custody.[23] There has been an increasing tendency in favour of shared custody. The Supreme Court has stated repeatedly that shared custody should be the norm, and not an exception, on the grounds that it preserves the right of the children to maintain relations with both parents, wherever possible from the point of view of the best interest of the child. Specifically, the court has stated, in a decision in July 2014, that shared custody is the arrangement closest to the family life before the divorce or separation, and which guarantees that the parents can continue exercising their parental rights and obligations and participate on equal terms in the upbringing of their children, all of which would be beneficial for the children.[24]

Furthermore, the Supreme Court has referred sometimes to the 'objective goodness' of shared custody.[25] However, the Supreme Court has also pointed out that the main objective of shared custody is not to protect the principle of equality between the parents but to ensure the best interest of the child in the most effective way possible. This is not to say that the interest of the parents should not be taken into account, but that it carries less weight than the best interest of the child.[26] Almost all the Supreme Court decisions since 2015[27] have awarded shared custody. In some cases, it has been argued that this is not an exceptional measure and is applied in the absence of negative circumstances in relation to the best interest of the child.[28]

Moreover, the Supreme Court has also stated[29] that awarding shared custody does not necessarily require a perfect agreement between the parents. A reasonable attitude of the parents towards the upbringing of their children and towards dialogue is sufficient. In this case, the Supreme Court adopts the concept of the best interest of children defined in the Organic Law 8/2015 of 22nd July, on the Protection of Children. According to this law, the best interest of the children requires maintaining their family relationships, satisfying their basic needs, both in material, physical and educational terms and in emotional and affective terms. In any case, we have to ensure that 'the measure adopted in the best interest of the child must not restrict or limit more rights than it gives' (referring to the rights of the parents).[30] Since 2017, the decisions of the Supreme Court have not considered the previous behaviour of the parents towards their children as a determining factor for not granting shared custody. That is to say, unless one of the parents has not spent time with the child nor been concerned with the child before the separation or divorce, shared custody should be granted. Also, a poor relationship between the parents is not in itself a reason for the courts to refuse shared custody, unless the relationship is extremely bad.[31] During the last 15 years, the situation in Spain has changed from one in which the courts almost automatically granted sole custody to the mother with contact and visiting rights for the father to the current situation in which shared custody is

23 Ibid., pp. 74, 110.

24 STS 29th April 2013, STS 2nd July 2014.

25 For example in the following decisions: STS 17th November 2015; STS 3rd May 2016, STS 17th February 2017, STS 22nd September 2017.

26 STS 7th March 2017.

27 STS 15th October 2015

28 STS 194/2016, 29th March, STS 51/2016, 11th February and STS 369/2016, 3rd June, STS 133/2016, 4th March.

29 STS 51/2016, 11th February.

30 Ibid., FJ 3°; STS 680/2015, 26th November, FJ 2°.

31 B. Casado Casado, 'Custodia compartida y corresponsabilidad parental. Evolución, valoraciones sobre el cambio de tendencia jurisprudencial', *Diario La Ley*, 9177, Sección Dossier, 13 de Abril de 2018, Wolters Kluwer, Electronic Document. Available at https://diariolaley.laleynext.es/ (Last accessed October 2019).

the norm. This has been a gradual change since 2008 and 2009 with a marked increase from 2013 and 2014 until today.

Although it has become accepted that over the last decade shared custody has generally become the norm used by the courts and accepted by society in general, above all in the north-eastern regions of the country,[32] a few studies suggest that this may not in fact be the case. For example, recent research carried out by the ATYME Foundation about shared custody 'imposed' by the courts in the absence of an agreement between the parents, in Madrid, Aragón and Málaga, concludes that despite the legal reforms and the recent Supreme Court decisions, shared custody continues to be granted in a minority of cases, whether or not there is an agreement between the parents. However, the same study adds that in Catalonia, the Basque Country and the Balearic Islands, each year the number of court decisions 'imposing' shared custody is increasing.[33]

In general terms, there is a similar tendency in southern European countries towards granting shared custody as opposed to sole custody in judicial practice, especially in France and Italy, and towards making sure both parents spend equal time with their children after separation or divorce. In France, the controversy about *résidence alternée* continues among journalists, jurists, psychologists, psychiatrists and educators. Many meetings and publications have discussed this question with arguments both for and against.[34] For example, *Le libre Blanch de la résidence alternée* (2014) appeared as a response to the *Livre Noir de la garde alternée* (2006). In Hachet's opinion, committed professionals are trying to clarify the issue of *résidence alternée* and inform politicians about what the best solution is in cases of separation or divorce.[35] These experts, basing their arguments on clinical and scientific studies together with their professional experience, feel qualified to judge what is the best arrangement for children after their parents' relationship breakdown. They have been criticized by Hachet for reducing the issue of *résidence alternée* to a psychological problem of childhood.

As we have seen, since 2002 (Law n° 2002–305), when there is no agreement between the parents, the courts in France can award *résidence alternée* provisionally. After this provisional trial period, the court makes a definitive decision on alternating residence with both parents or with only one of them.[36] If there is no agreement between the parents about *résidence alternée*, the courts are reticent about 'imposing' it. However, in general terms there has been an increase in approving *résidence alternée* in judicial decisions.[37]

When courts reject *résidence alternée*, the decision is mainly based on the best interest of the child. Other reasons may include: a bad relationship between the parents, the age of the child, long distances between the parents' homes, or the availability of one of the parents to take care of the child. In cases of *résidence alternée*, the periods of time spent by the child with each parent vary depending on the age and development of the children.[38] The courts have tended to decide

32 L. Flaquer et al., 'A igualdade de género, o bem-estar da criança e a residencia alternada em Espanha', in S. Marinho and S.V. Correia (eds), *Una familia parental, duas casas*, Lisboa: Silabo, 2017, pp. 101–2.

33 Fundación *ATYME, ¿Custodia compartida?* Electronic Document. Available at https://diariolaley.laleynext.es/. https://atymediacion.es/sites/default/files/2019-04/Custodia%20Compartida%20Fundaci%C3%B3n%20ATYME.pdf (Last accessed September 2019).

34 C. Bessière, E. Biland and A. Fillod-Chabaud, 'Résidence alternée: La justice face aux rapports sociaux de sexe et de clase', 2013. Electronic version: https://hal-amu.archives-ouvertes.fr/hal-01547142 (Last accessed October 2019); B. Hachet, 'Résidence alternée. Pratiques polémiques et normes ambivalentes', *Journal des anthropologues*, 2016, 192.

35 Hachet, op. cit., n 34, pp. 203–4.

36 Courbe and Gouttenoire, op. cit., n 16, p. 604.

37 Hachet, op. cit., n 34, p. 205.

38 Dahan, op. cit., n 18, p. 59.

that the children should spend equal periods of time with each parent, depending on the best interest of the child.[39]

In Italy, the courts require the parents to agree on the education and upbringing of their children as a condition for awarding shared custody, but without regard to the level of conflict in the relationship between them unless it is demonstrated that the degree of conflict puts the best interest of the children at risk.[40] During 2019 there has been a fierce controversy in the media and among professionals about two bills modifying the *affidamento condiviso* and there have been calls for the two bills to be withdrawn. The first Bill (DDL nº 735, 1st August 2018) aims to increase the *affidamento condiviso* in judicial practice, while the 'Pillon Bill' (DDL nº 768, 7th August 2018) would make it a legal requirement that the children spend the same periods of time with each parent after separation or divorce (*bigenitorialità perfetta*, art. 11).

In Portugal, there is no consensus among judges as to whether shared custody (physical joint custody) is beneficial for children or even if it is consistent with existing law (Law 61/2008). Consequently, the courts continue to apply the traditional arrangement by which the child resides mainly with the mother while the father has contact and visiting rights.[41] According to Marinho: 'In Portuguese society the father increasingly participates in the upbringing of the children, and there is a growing tendency for the children to spend more similar times with both parents after separation or divorce'.[42] This emphasizes the contradictory situation in which the traditional arrangements about parental roles after separation or divorce continue to co-exist with the new arrangements.

Recent scientific studies[43] which support the idea of 'alternating residence' with each parent being the arrangement which best satisfies the needs of the child and which best guarantees equality between the parents form the basis of the Bill nº 1182/XIII/4ª, 22nd March 2019, which gives preference to this model. The court should give preference to alternating residence whether or not there is an agreement between the parents, provided that it is in the best interest of the child. This bill has been criticized by the *Associaçao Portuguesa de Mulheres Juristas*[44] who consider that imposing whatever custody arrangement without considering the wishes of the parents is an anachronism and represents a backward step in the recognition of the rights of the child. Moreover, this association considers that the promotion of gender equality and insistence on equal periods of time spent by children with both parents from a perspective of 'absolute egalitarianism' poses a risk of 'objectifying' children, limiting their unquestionable right to express themselves.

Conclusion

This chapter addresses the various terms and meanings relating to the shared custody of children after the parents' separation or divorce, and other terms such as parental responsibility (*patria potestad, l'autorité parentale*, etc.), in Spain and other southern European countries (France, Italy and Portugal).

39 Juston, op. cit., n 17, p. 36.

40 Martínez Calvo, op. cit., n 3; Sesta, op. cit., n 7, p. 46; Constanzo, op. cit., n 6, p. 500.

41 S. Marinho and S.V. Correia, 'Notas finais', in S. Marinho and S.V. Correia (eds), *Una familia parental, duas casas*, Lisboa: Silabo, 2017, p. 255.

42 S. Marinho, 'Separate Mothering and Fathering: The Plurality of Parenting within the Framework of Postdivorce, Shared Parenting Norms', *Journal of Divorce & Remarriage* 58, 2017, 293.

43 Marinho and Correia, op. cit., n 41, S. Marinho, op. cit., n 10.

44 Parecer A.P.M.J.-Associação Portuguesa de Mulheres Juristas. Electronic versión: www.apmj.pt/images/noticias/Parecer_APMJ_sobre_RRP.pdf (Last accessed October 2019).

The development of shared custody in these countries has also been discussed, in particular the case of Spain, together with the points of view of experts, professionals, researchers and politicians. The controversy continues between those in favour and those against shared custody as a preferential option by law whether or not there is an agreement between the parents.

While it is true that the application of shared custody has significantly increased, several research studies report that sole custody with the mother and contact and visits by the father remains the most common arrangement. In any case, judges make their decisions case by case depending on what they consider to be the best interests of the children.

The difficulty is whether it is really advisable that the courts award shared custody when neither parent applies nor wants it, or even rejects it.

3.5

PARENTING ISSUES AFTER SEPARATION

A Scandinavian perspective

Anna Singer

Introduction

The law concerning parenting issues after separation has for a long time been a key policy area in the Scandinavian countries.[1] The best interest of the child has been a guiding principle and during the last decades, there have been frequent and sometimes significant legislative initiatives to achieve this. One way of protecting the child's best interest has been the use of joint legal parental responsibility for parents who are not living together. 'Equal parenting' through joint legal responsibility has been seen as an important element to emphasize the child's interest and to give the child an opportunity to have access to both parents even if they are not living together (see also Chapters 3.3–3.4 of this book). At the same time there are ongoing reforms in order to encourage the participation of the child in proceedings concerning parental disputes.

The legislation concerning parental responsibility has developed along the same lines in the Scandinavian countries. There are several reasons for this. In all the countries, the foundation of the current legislation was laid in the beginning of the 1900s, reflecting a common view on parenting. Socio-economic conditions and the development of family patterns are also similar as are views about the best interests of the child. However, there are also some differences in the way post-separation parenting has been heard, regulated and in the pace of change. A change in the legislation in one country is often followed by the other countries; different countries taking the lead at different times and others following.

When divorce rates began to increase at the end of the 1950s, the law stated that only one of the parents could have parental responsibility[2] for a child after the divorce. In practice this was often the mother since she had been the child's primary caretaker. The father's right to contact with the child, by agreement or by court decision, was not sufficient to prevent many fathers losing contact with their children.

With an increasing divorce rate, disputes concerning parental responsibility became more frequent. At the beginning of the 1970s, there was a growing awareness that the regulation of

1 In this chapter Denmark, Norway and Sweden are included in Scandinavian countries, excluding Iceland.

2 The terminology describing parental responsibility varies in the Scandinavian countries. Custody, parental authority and parental responsibility are used. In the following however, the term parental responsibility is used regardless of the term used in the national regulation.

parental responsibility after the parents' separation was not in tune with the times and reform work was initiated, partly as a result of a growing fathers' rights movement. A starting point was that mothers and fathers should be treated equally as parents and that the previous bias resulting in the mother having sole parental responsibility should be abandoned. There was a desire to strengthen the fathers' role in the lives of their children and 'equal parenthood' became the key for the reforms since this was seen as being in the best interests of the child. Joint parental responsibility for separated parents was the means to achieving this, giving the child the opportunity to develop a good and close relationship with both parents.

The promotion of equal parenthood through joint parental responsibility has resulted in far reaching legal solutions for post-separation parenting; including court determined alternating residence for the child against the wishes of one or both parents (see, for southern European countries, Chapter 3.4 of this book). There has also been an increase in the use of alternative methods for dispute resolution, both within and outside the court system, in order to make or help the parents reach an agreement and to keep the conflicts out of court, albeit with limited results. The child's right to be heard in parental disputes has been legislated and encouraged but the implementation is considered unsatisfactory, needing further action. Parenting issues after separation are thus still very much on the political agenda in all Scandinavian countries but the development largely follows previously established lines.

Joint parental responsibility for separated parents

Parents with joint parental responsibility have a right and a duty to decide together in matters concerning the child. Since this can be difficult for parents who are not both living with the child the solution was for a long time to give the parent living with the child sole custody and hence the sole right to make decisions concerning the child. In Sweden joint parental responsibility was first made available to divorced and unmarried parents in 1976 provided the parents jointly requested this.[3] Similar rules were introduced in Norway in 1981[4] and in Denmark 1983.[5] The Norwegian law also created a presumption for joint parental responsibility for married parents after divorce unless challenged by one of them. Similar provisions concerning married parents were introduced in Sweden in 1983[6] and in Denmark in 2002.[7]

Since children still largely lived with their mother even after law reforms in the early 1980s, the joint right to make decisions became a burden for many mothers since the father had to be consulted even if he did not exercise any care regarding the child. Many mothers therefore opposed joint parental responsibility with the result that joint responsibility was ruled out. Equality between mothers and fathers seemed a distant prospect.

However, research indicated that children whose parents had joint responsibility had better contact with both parents than if one of them had sole responsibility. This was taken as an incitement to reform Swedish law at the beginning of the 1990s making it possible for a court to decide on joint parental responsibility even if one parent preferred to exercise this alone but could accept joint responsibility. A further step was taken in 1998 when joint parental responsibility could be decided by the court against the wishes of one of the parents if this was

3 Prop. 1975/76:170 Föräldraskap och vårdnad (Government Bill).
4 Ot.prp. nr. 62 (1979–80); Innst. O. Nr. 30 (1980–81) (Government Bill).
5 Bet. nr. 985/1983 Forældremyndighed og samværsret (Government Report).
6 Prop. 1982/83:168 om vårdnad och umgänge m.m.
7 Lov nr. 461 af 7.juni 2001 om ændring af resplejeloven og forskellige andre love.

considered to be in the best interests of the child.[8] The government declared that the purpose of the provision was to encourage good relations between a child and both parents and that joint responsibility often could contribute to this.[9] A similar provision was introduced in Danish law in 2007.[10] A different path has been taken in Norway. Equal parenthood has been promoted, not by courts ordering joint parental responsibility against the wishes of a parent, but through the use of contact. The greatest possible contact with both parents is considered to be in the best interests of the child.[11] It should be noted that in all Scandinavian countries married parents have joint parental responsibility from the child's birth. Cohabiting unmarried parents can receive joint responsibility through a joint notification to the authorities in Denmark and Sweden. In Norway also unmarried cohabiting parents have joint responsibility ipso jure from the establishment of paternity (or co-motherhood). The joint responsibility is dissolved through court decision if it is considered to be in the best interest of the child.[12] A further step concerning joint parental responsibility was taken from 1 January 2020 giving unmarried non-cohabiting parents joint responsibility ipso jure when the child's second parent has been legally established. Single mothers may obtain sole parental responsibility thorough notification to the National Population Register within a year after the child is born. A father who does not want parental responsibility can in the same way notify the Register.[13]

The option to order joint parental responsibility contrary to the wishes of one parent was interpreted in both in Denmark and Sweden as a presumption in favour of joint responsibility. In several instances the courts decided in favour of joint responsibility where the parents had severe and understandable difficulties cooperating, e.g. when there had been violence in the family, but one of the parents had not succeeded in proving that joint responsibility was not in the interests of the child. A step towards limiting the use of joint parental responsibility against the objections of one parent was taken in Sweden in 2006 when the parents' ability to cooperate became an important factor when deciding on parental responsibility.[14] The same change was made in Denmark in 2012.[15] Joint parental responsibility should not be decided if there are reasons to believe that the parents will not be able to cooperate in matters concerning the child.

One of the problems with joint parental responsibility for parents in conflict is that almost all decisions concerning the child have to be taken jointly. In order to prevent conflicts over

8 Prop. 1997/98:7 Vårdnad, boende och umgänge.

9 Prop. 1997/98:7. p. 49.

10 Lov nr. 499 af 6.juli 2007 Forældreansvarsloven. Bet. 1475/2006.

11 T. Sverdrup, 'Equal Parenthood: Recent Reforms in Child Custody Cases', in B. Atkin (ed.), *The International Survey of Family Law*, 2011 edition, Bristol: Jordan Publishing, 2011, p. 304.

12 § 56 och § 48 barnelova.

13 § 35 barnelova, following res. 13.09.2019 nr. 1121 Delt ikraftsetting av lov 31. mars 2017 om endringer i barnelova mv. (likestilt foreldreskap). T. Sverdrup, 'The Strenghtening of Fathers' Rights in Norwegian Child Law and Other Recent Reforms' in M. Brinig (ed.), *The International Survey of Family Law*, Cambridge: Intersentia, 2018, p. 389.

14 A follow-up of the 2006 reform of the Children and Parent Code in Sweden is reported in the government report SOU 2017:6 Se barnet! (English summary, pp. 41–56) See the government homepage www.regeringen.se/490ab7/contentassets/acc04add4adb4f8fbcb560a4983fdcec/se-barnet-sou-20176. It is suggested that particular importance should be attached to the parents' ability to take joint responsibility in matters concerning the child instead of emphasizing the parents' ability to cooperate. The proposals have not (fall 2019) resulted in legislation.

15 Both these reforms were initiated as a result of evaluations indicating that the possibility to decide on joint responsibility for parents not in agreement was too far reaching and put to use also in cases where a joint responsibility was not in the best interests of the child. For Sweden see SOU 2005:43 *Barnets bästa, föräldrars ansvar* (English summary pp. 41–57) (Government Report); For Denmark see *Familiestyrelsen, Evaluering af forældreansvarsloven*, 2011.

essential questions concerning the child, Swedish courts have the right to determine the child's residence and contact even if the parents have joint responsibility. Other questions concerning the upbringing of the child require both parents' joint decisions unless an immediate decision is necessary in the interest of the child. The Danish law states that important decisions concerning the child have to be made by the parents jointly. The parent with whom the child is living can decide in matters concerning the everyday life of the child, including where the child should live.[16] If the child has alternating residence, decisions concerning everyday life will have to be taken in agreement between the parents. In Norway, where joint parental responsibility cannot be imposed against the wishes of one parent, there is a provision specifying which decisions can be taken solely by the parent with whom the child is living, including where the child should live.[17] The reluctance of the Swedish legislature to regulate the decision-making authority has been justified with reference to the purpose of joint responsibility as being the right of each parent to participate in all decisions concerning the child.

Shared residence for children with separated parents

In all the countries, parents can make agreements concerning with whom a child should live, including shared residence.[18] It is also possible to have residence decided by court. Alternating residence for children with separated parents has become quite widespread. In the majority of cases, the arrangement is the result of an agreement between the parents, but occasionally it follows a court decision. It was estimated that in 2016–2017 around 30 percent of children in Sweden with separated parents have alternating residence.[19] The frequency of shared residence in Denmark and Norway is slightly lower, but rising.[20]

A provision giving the court the option to decide on shared residence against the wishes of one or both parents was first introduced in Sweden in 1998, perhaps as the perceived logical continuation of the possibility to create joint parental responsibility for separated parents even if one objected. The court was also given the authority to decide with whom the child should live. A decision concerning residence can state that the child should live with one of the parents or alternate between the two. Evaluation of the reform indicated that shared residence did not work well for parents who did not agree on this arrangement.[21] The power for the court to order shared residence was kept in the 2006 reform but it was stated that it should be used with caution. The fact that joint parental responsibility should be ordered only when the parents are

16 § 3 forældreansvarsloven.

17 § 37 barnelova.

18 Shared residence is used in the following to describe the arrangement from the parents' perspective. The child is living alternating with both parents.

19 Statistics Sweden, www.scb.se/hitta-statistik/statistik-efter-amne/levnadsforhallanden/levnadsforhallanden/undersokningarna-av-levnadsforhallanden-ulf-silc/pong/statistiknyhet/barns-boende-2016–2017/. Previous statistics from 2012 indicated that 35 percent of children with separated parents had alternating residence, SOU 2011:51 *Fortsatt föräldrar – om ansvar, ekonomi och samarbete för barnets skull*, p. 19. The difference in percentage can at least partly be explained by the use of different methods for collecting information. Around 25 percent of children in Sweden live with one parent.

20 In Norway it was estimated that 25 percent of children with separated parents had alternating residence in 2012, R.H. Kitterød, H. Lidén and K. Aarskaug Wiik, Delt bosted for barna etter samlivsbrudd – en praksis for folk flest in *Sosiologiskt Tidsskift* nr. 1, 2016, 27–50.

21 Socialstyrelsen (The National Board of Health and Welfare) *Växelvis boende. Att bo hos pappa och mamma fast de inte bor tillsammans*, 2004. See also A. Singer, 'Active Parenting or Solomon's Justice? Alternating Residence in Sweden for Children with Separated Parents', *Utrecht Law Review* 4(2), 2008, 35–47, 40–3.

deemed to have the ability to cooperate has also limited decisions on shared residence since joint parental responsibility is a prerequisite.

Since 2010, courts in Norway have also had the option to order shared residence, but only when there are special circumstances and only if the parents have joint parental responsibility.[22] As in Sweden, the legislature has not been willing to rule out the option of deciding on shared residence against the will of a parent, since it is thought that in certain cases it might be in the best interests of the child to have access to both parents in this way. In Norway there have been suggestions to make shared residence a default rule if the parents cannot agree otherwise. This has been considered too radical but in order to encourage shared residence the wording of the relevant provision in the Norwegian law was changed in 2018, now stating in the first sentence that the parents may agree that the child shall reside permanently either with both of them or with one of them. The change was motivated by a wish to make parents aware of shared residence as an option when entering into an agreement on residence.[23] In Denmark there are no explicit provisions concerning shared residence, with one exception. From 1 April 2019 the law states that children, whose parents have been living together with joint parental responsibility, will have shared residence during the first three months following the parents' separation unless the parents reach an agreement on the residence of the child.[24] During that period there can be no court decision concerning the child's residence, only contact.[25] Parents are free to agree between themselves on the child's residence. If no agreement is reached during the three months the matter can be taken to court.

In all the countries, shared residence (or the Danish extensive contact) should only be ordered when it is considered to be in the best interests of the child. Certain conditions must be met, such as that the parents must be living close to one another, and the child must be able to remain in the same school and have access to the same friends and leisure activities independently of residence.

Shared residence requires the parents to cooperate if the arrangement is to be good for the child. In practice, shared residence is in most cases the result of an agreement between the parents, not the result of a court decision. The growing number of children living alternating with both parents indicates that the mere possibility that a court can decide on shared residence may have sent the message to the parents that not only is this kind of arrangement acceptable, it also underlines the importance for the child to have contact with both parents. Current research also indicates that many parents and children are very satisfied with shared residence.[26] There are reasons to believe that shared residence is continuing to increase.

Alternative dispute resolution

With the emergence of the policy of joint parental responsibility for separated parents as a principal rule there has also been a noticeable development of alternative forms of adjudication

22 § 36 Barneloven, Lov 2010-04-09 nr 13: Lov om endringar i barnelova m.v. Ot.prp.nr. 104 (2008–09).

23 Prop. 161 L (2015–2016) Endringer i barnelova mv. (likestilt foreldreskap), p. 64. T. Sverdrup, 'The Strenghtening of Fathers' Rights in Norwegian Child Law and Other Recent Reforms', in M. Brinig (ed.), *The International Survey of Family Law*, Cambridge: Intersentia, 2018, pp. 390–1.

24 § 17 forældreansvarsloven. Lov nr. 1711 af 27. December 2018.

25 In Danish 'deleordningar'. § 21 forældreansvarsloven.

26 See e.g. M. Bergström et al., 'Fifty Moves a Year: Is There an Association between Joint Physical Custody and Psychosomatic Problems in Children?', *Journal of Epidemiology and Community Health* 69, 2015, 8, 769–74; E. Fransson, M. Bergström and A. Hjern, *Barn i växelvis boende – en forskningsöversikt*. Stockholm: Chess: Center for Health Equity Studies, 2015. Available at www.chess.su.se/polopoly_fs/1.261599.1450340833!/menu/standard/file/Barn%20i%20va%CC%88xelvis%20boende%20-%20en%20forskningso%CC%88versikt.pdf

of parental disputes. The shortcomings of court procedures in disputes concerning parental responsibility have long been known. A court procedure often encourages, and indeed requires, the parents to show each other's defects. Future cooperation and joint parental responsibility between them are frequently made impossible. Furthermore, the range of decisions that the court can make is limited; basically only joint or sole parental responsibility or contact arrangements. But these decisions cannot in themselves create the cooperation needed between the parents. Agreements between the parents are considered to provide a better basis for future cooperation. In order to facilitate such agreements, different methods and routines have been developed in the Scandinavian countries.

In Norway, the legal procedure for adjudicating parental conflict was reformed in 2004. The previous administrative route was then abolished and decisions can only be made by a court. However, before a case can be tried, parents, generally, have to attend mediation. The goal of the mediation is to help them reach a written agreement on parental issues. If the mediation does not result in a settlement, the parents can turn to the court. In order to clarify if a settlement is possible, the parents will be called to a preparatory meeting. A child expert can be present at the meeting and can also be at hand for advice and support if the parents try an interim agreement. During the whole procedure in court the judge is obliged to consider the possibility of settlement and should encourage and facilitate this. Lawyers assisting the parents are under a legal obligation to encourage agreements between the parents.[27] One idea underlying the Norwegian model is that the combination of the solemnity of the court and the assistance of professionals can facilitate the process of finding a solution.[28] (See further Chapter 6.5 of this book.)

In contrast to the Norwegian approach, where the court makes decisions concerning parental responsibilities, parental conflicts in Denmark are kept out of court as far as possible. The administrative system for adjudicating parental disputes was reformed from 1 April 2019. A new administrative authority, The Agency for Family Law (*Familieretshuset*, literally the House of Family Law) replaced the Danish State Administration that previously dealt with parental disputes. At the same time a Family Court, a division of the District court, was established.[29] The Agency for Family Law has as a primary task to protect children's interests in family law disputes but also provides a clear and holistic approach to help parents find a solution of their conflict. The Agency has as an overarching and primary task to support children that in any way are affected by a parental conflict. To secure the child's right to well-being and protection is the primary purpose of this new system. Children have independent rights to contact the Agency and ask for assistance.[30]

As a general rule, parents are required to approach the Agency for Family Law through a digital self-service portal. A parent seeking assistance is required to give information about the matter and the circumstances of the family, including information about the conflict and legal situation through a digital form. This information serves as the foundation for a screening of the conflict. Three categories are used to classify the application; the 'green track' which concerns matters that only require information or a decision. The 'yellow track' concerns more complicated matters where the family might have need for help through counselling in order to curb a conflict concerning for example parental responsibility or residence. The 'red track'

27 § 49 barneloven.
28 T. Sverdrup, op. cit., n 11, p. 310.
29 Lov om Familieretshuset. Lov nr. 1702 af 27. December 2018. L. Nielsen and I. Lund-Andersen, *Familieretten*, København: Ex Tuto Publishing A/S, 2019, pp. 44–6.
30 See The Child's Right to Participation.

is for matters where there are clear factors of risk such as neglect, violence, abuse or mental illness.[31] Depending on the matter at hand, the Agency for Family Law can provide a wide range of measures such as counselling and conflict management including multidisciplinary treatment by personnel at the Agency.[32] The goal is to help the parents reach an agreement if appropriate. The Agency for Family Law has the authority to make final decisions in some matters but should bring the case to the Family Court if no agreement is reached and it concerns parental responsibility, residence and contact when the decision will have far-reaching consequences for the child. Decisions of the Agency of Family Law can also be appealed to the Family Court.

In Sweden, disputing parents are encouraged to attend cooperation talks held by the municipal Social Welfare Committee.[33] Talks are voluntary and if no settlement is reached the parents can turn to the court.[34] The judge should, at preliminary hearing, try to clarify if there is any possibility of reaching a settlement. The parents can be requested to (again) attend cooperation talks. Since 2006 a mediator can be appointed by the court. This option is however not used regularly.

The ambition to create equal parenthood through joint parental responsibility for separated parents has necessitated an increased public involvement in the private lives of parents and the family, both in court proceedings and in other ways. One of the aims of recent reforms in all Scandinavian countries has been to help parents reach agreement on parenting issues and to reduce the number of custody cases in court. It is doubtful that this has succeeded to the desired extent.[35] The development of alternative dispute resolution as an alternative to court treatment has clear advantages. An agreement is always better than a decision by the court. But there is a risk that the child becomes a victim of prolonged conflicts between parents. There are also dangers in the judicial system taking on therapeutic tasks such as mediation between parents since in the long run it could undermine the authority of the judiciary. The Danish system could be a move in the right direction.

The child's right to participation

The push towards equal parenthood has throughout been motivated with reference to the best interests of the child. The starting-point is that it is in the child's best interests to have good and close contact with both parents after their separation. This can be achieved through joint parental responsibility, extended contact and even in some cases alternating residence. A focus on the child's best interests calls for, even necessitates, the inclusion of the child as an individual in processes concerning parental conflicts.[36] An important policy question has been how to do this (see further Chapter 4.6 of this book).

31 §§ 5–7 lov om Familieretshuset.

32 §§ 15–23 lov om Familieretshuset.

33 See E. Ryrstedt, 'Mediation Regarding Children: Is the Result Always in the Best Interest of the Child? A View from Sweden', *International Journal of Law, Policy and the Family* 26(2), 2012, 220–41.

34 There is a suggestion that a system similar to the Norwegian mediation be implemented in requiring a certificate of participation in obligatory information meeting as a prerequisite for initiating court proceeding. This suggestion has not (October 2019) resulted in legislation. See SOU 2017:6, pp. 45–6.

35 In SOU 2017:6, p. 44 it is estimated that the increase of parental conflicts in court has increased with 48 percent since the 2006 reform. See also Domstolsverket, Court statistics 2018, table 1.4, p. 13. Available at http://old.domstol.se/upload/Lokala_webbplatser/Domstolsverket/Statistik/court_statistics_2018.pdf.

36 This also follows from art. 12 of the UN Convention on the Rights of the Child. All Scandinavian countries have ratified the convention and it has also been incorporated into Norwegian and Swedish law.

There has been a keen political interest in making provisions concerning the child's right to participation in matters concerning parental issues. However, since joint parental responsibility has been identified as being in the best interests of the child, the purpose of the child's right to participate often becomes unclear. On the one hand, the child should be given the opportunity at least to be heard with his or her views given due weight according to the child's age and maturity. On the other hand, since the best interests of the child has largely been defined in terms of joint parental responsibility, it is not always clear what the child should be heard about and why. This could at least partly explain why there is a feeling that the child's right to be heard has not been implemented to a satisfactory level. However, findings by a Swedish governmental committee indicates that children often are heard but their views, if any, are of no consequence to the final decision and hence not referred to in the judgment.[37]

In all Scandinavian countries, the child has a right to be heard in matters concerning parental responsibility, residence and contact. As early as 1981, the Norwegian law stated that the child should be given an opportunity to put forward his or her views concerning parental issues. The current law states that a child over seven years of age, and younger children able to form their own opinion, should be given information and an opportunity to give their view on personal matters such as parental responsibility, residence and contact before a decision is taken. The views of the child should be given due weight in accordance with the age and maturity of the child. If the child is over 12, the child's views should be given great weight. Since 1996 Swedish law has provisions stating that the views of the child should be given due weight in accordance with the age and maturity of the child, also when deciding on parental responsibility, residence and contact. There is however no legal obligation to inform the child about the matter at hand.[38]

In Denmark, the Parental Authority Act states that the child should be involved in the procedures concerning parental issues through talks, expert investigations or any other way that will shed light on the child's perspective. Furthermore, a child over ten years can request that the Agency for Family Law call the parents for talks concerning parental issues.[39] These provisions are given strength by the law on the Agency for Family Law. The law was introduced in order to strengthen the position of the child when the parents are in conflict. The Agency has as an overarching task to support children that are affected by family law disputes 'in order to ensure the well-being of the child'.[40] The child's right to well-being is of primary importance. In order to ensure that the child's well-being is in focus there is a special Children's Unit where a child can receive individually designed advice and support. The child will also receive a child welfare officer who will serve as a contact person and support for the child. The Children's Unit has a wide variety of support measures,[41] all for the child's well-being and will make sure that the child is informed and involved in the matter in a gentle way. The focus is not necessarily on the views of the child in a family law conflict but rather on the well-being of a child whose parents are not able to fulfil their task as parents.

Concluding remarks

In the Scandinavian countries equality between men and women, between those who are married and unmarried and between mothers and fathers has been an important goal for decades.

37 SOU 2017:6, pp. 277–326.

38 In the government report SOU 2017:6 there is a suggestion that such an obligation be included in the law.

39 § 35 forældreansvarsloven.

40 § 1 lov om Familieretshuset. Lov nr. 1702 af 27. December 2018.

41 §§ 15–20 Lov om Familieretshuset.

The regulation concerning post-separation parenting has been one of the policy areas that has been under constant reform since the end of the 1970s in order to achieve equality between parents, also after their separation. Initially equality in this sense was visualized as being achieved through joint legal parental responsibility for parents not both living together, if necessary against their own will. And it has worked. The idea of equal parenting after separation has gained acceptance in society and against this background it is not surprising that shared residence has come into focus for parents as well as for legislators. Equal parenting calls for equal time with the child!

Equal parenting also requires a certain level of cooperation between the parents. Court procedures are not generally designed to achieve this. Hence a need to develop alternative methods for solving parental conflicts. Society's involvement in parental disputes has increased during the last decade in all Scandinavian countries at the same time as the number of conflicts increase. In parallel, there has been a constant discussion on how to strengthen the child's rights when the parents are in conflict. The child's right to be heard has been confirmed by law in all countries but it is a common view that the implementation of this right has not been as successful as desired. One explanation could be that the joint parental responsibility makes the hearing of the child unnecessary. Another explanation could be that court procedure is not suitable for children's participation. But neither have the existing alternative methods for solving parental dispute been.

The fact that on the one hand equality between parents is a desirable goal, on the other such a solution does not necessarily include the child as a part of or subject in the proceedings creates a dilemma that has occupied and occupies the Scandinavian legislators. In Sweden there has been an evaluation of the previous reform in 2006 and certain suggestions have been made on how to improve the position of the child. Legislation has yet to come as a result of the investigation. In Norway there is currently an investigation at work with the task to formulate a new more modern Children's Act in which the best interest of the child should be the overriding consideration in the procedural handling of parental conflicts as well as in the material decisions according to the law. The new Danish law on the Agency for Family Law stands out as a novel take on how society can handle parental conflicts while at the same time see to the needs of the child on the child's own conditions and not just as a right to be heard. It remains to be seen if the other Scandinavian countries will follow.

PART 4

Child welfare, child protection and children's rights

4.1

CRISIS IN CHILD WELFARE AND PROTECTION IN ENGLAND

Causes, consequences and solutions?

Karen Broadhurst and Judith Harwin

Introduction

Looking back over the past decade, this chapter considers contemporary challenges in child welfare and protection policy and practice in England, resulting from a range of changing social and economic conditions. Organized around the theme of *crisis* – this chapter discusses the continued mismatch between demand for services and their availability, given exceptional cuts to public services following the global financial crisis in 2008–09. The chapter also considers the searching questions prompted by a crisis in service provision, notably the balance between compulsory state intervention and support for family preservation.[1,2] Arguably, austerity has driven children's services further in the direction of late, reactive intervention, resulting in ever-increasing numbers of children entering public care.[3]

As might be expected, England's policy support for forced adoption has continued to be contentious during the past decade. The chapter considers the impact of the Borzova report from the EU Commission in 2015,[4] which raised critical questions about so-called forced adoption and infant removals, as well as new research in the same year which evidenced the scale of women's repeat appearances in care proceeding and repeat removals of children.[5] The chapter also describes the impact of high profile family court judgments, coupled with new research evidence, which have challenged practitioners to consider more thoroughly extended family

1 I. Trowler, C. Webb and J.T. Leigh, *Care Proceedings in England: The Case for Clear Blue Water*, 2018. Available at www.sheffield.ac.uk/polopoly_fs/1.812158!/file/Sheffield_Solutions_Clear_Blue_Water_Full_Report.pdf

2 Lord Justice McFarlane. Holding the risk: The balance between child protection and the right to family life. Bridget Lindley OBE Memorial Lecture. 2017. Available at www.judiciary.uk/wp-content/uploads/2017/03/lecture-by-lj-mcfarlane-20160309.pdf

3 Family Rights Group, *The Care Crisis Review: Summary of Options for Change*, London: The Nuffield Foundation, 2018.

4 O. Borzova, *Social Services in Europe: Legislation and Practice of the Removal of Children from Their Families in Council of Europe Member States*, Council of Europe, 2015. Available at http://assembly.coe.int/nw/xml/XRef/Xref-DocDetails-EN.asp?FileID=21567&lang=EN

5 K. Broadhurst, B. Alrouh, E. Yeend, J. Harwin, M. Shaw, M. Pilling and S. Kershaw, 'Connecting Events in Time to Identify a Hidden Population: Birth Mothers and Their Children in Recurrent Care Proceedings in England', *British Journal of Social Work* 45(8), 2015, 241–60.

resources, firmly positioning adoption as an option of last resort, and which have added to a crisis of confidence regarding the impact of the family courts on family life.

Crisis has also prompted a search for innovation in the delivery of child welfare and protection – can more be done with *less* – through innovative service reform? Thus, the chapter also considers the contribution of the Children's Social Care Innovation Programme[6] launched in 2014 by the Department for Education. This programme succeeded in unlocking the potential of practice pioneers within children's services. However, bright ideas were not always matched by realistic timescales for practice change or durable forms of funding. The case of the Family Drug and Alcohol Court illustrates both these points and is discussed in some detail.

The field of child protection rarely stands still. Changing social conditions change the nature and possibilities of risks to children. Evidence of an increase in the number of older children coming to the attention of child protection services and indeed, entering care, has prompted searching questions about new risks to adolescents. We have witnessed an increasing focus on *extra-familial risks* to older children, which underpins a new model of 'contextual safeguarding'.[7] Again, a sense of crisis pervades the national psyche, given the growing incidence of young people's exposure to knife crime, sexual exploitation, drug and human trafficking.

Finally, this chapter considers whether the growing impetus towards the use of 'bigger' data can bring both insights and balance to debates in child welfare and protection.[8] The increasing digitization of public services records has transformed the possibilities regarding the scale and pace of social research.[9] Studies which are based on full service populations are persuasive[10] and may yet provide a firmer foundation for evidence-informed child welfare and protection policy and practice.

Crisis: a decade of rising demand overwhelms services and the family courts

Children's local authority services in England hold the lead responsibility for the protection of children. Since 2010, these services have faced a 50 percent reduction in their budgets, while demand for services has increased significantly.[11] Successive publications between 2007–08 and 2017–18 from the Association of Directors of Children's Services (ADCS) paint a troubling picture of local authorities stretched far beyond capacity in the context of relentless downward

6 Department for Education, *Overview Report: Department for Education, Children's Services Innovation Programme*, London: Department for Education, 2014. Available at https://assets.publishing.service.gov.uk/government/uploads/system/uploads/attachment_data/file/342051/Overview_of_the_Children_s_Social_Care_Innovation_Programme.pdf

7 C. Firmin, 'Contextual Risk, Individualised Responses: An Assessment of Safeguarding Responses to Nine Cases of Peer-on-Peer Abuse', *Child Abuse Review* 27, 2018, 42–57. doi: 10.1002/car.2449

8 K. Broadhurst and T. Williams, 'Harnessing the Power of Data to Improve Family Justice: A New Nuffield Family Justice Observatory for England and Wales', *Family Court Review* 57(3), 2019, 57, 405–13. https://doi.org/10.1111/fcre.12428

9 M. Jay, J. Woodman, K. Broadhurst and R. Gilbert, *Who Cares for Children? Population Level Data for Family Justice Research*, 2017. Available at http://wp.lancs.ac.uk/observatory-scoping-study/files/2017/10/FJO-NATIONAL-DATA-SCOPING-FINAL.pdf

10 K. Broadhurst, T. Budd and T. Williams, *Towards a Family Justice Observatory: Making It Happen*, Nuffield Foundation, 2018. Available at www.nuffieldfoundation.org/sites/default/files/files/Nuffield_Family_Justice_Observatory_making_it_happen_v_FINAL_13_02_18.pdf

11 National Audit Office, *Financial Sustainability of Local Authorities* HC 834 SESSION 2017–2019, 8 March 2018; National Audit Office: London, 2018.

pressure on their budgets.[12] The overarching message from the ADCS is that funding cuts have prevented early work with families, and increased the risk of crisis-driven reactive interventions.

When we examine the rise in the number of care proceedings being brought before the family courts during the past decade – statistics certainly support the concerns of the ADCS. Authorized by the Children Act 1989, local authorities can apply to the family courts for a care order where significant harm is proven or likely. In 2012–13 the Children and Family Court Advisory and Support Service (Cafcass), which provides independent representation for children within care proceedings through the Children's Guardian, recorded 11,091 applications for England. This was almost double the number of applications received in 2008–09. This upwards trend has continued steadily and in 2016 Sir James Munby (then President of the Family Division) described a crisis in the family courts[13] – with England having no clear strategy for dealing with the crisis. In the most recent year Cafcass records a small decrease in care applications from 2016–17 at 13,573, but a drop of 4.6 percent leaves the total volume of applications persistently high such that the family courts remain overwhelmed.

The latter half of the past decade has therefore been dominated by the search for causes and solutions to both escalating demand and major shortfalls in service provision. The high profile 'Care Crisis Review'[14] funded by the Nuffield Foundation, constituted a wide-ranging exploration of the possible causes of the crisis, and concluded that no single factor could account for the trends just described. The combination of factors implicated in rising demand on both children's services and the courts were seen to result from: increasing family hardship resulting from government austerity measures, decline in preventive services since 2009–10 and a professional culture of 'blame, shame and fear'[15] leading to defensive practices within children's social work. Although the increase in care applications is not uniform across England, there is no doubt that the resources needed to undertake essential assessment work, administer legal proceedings and supervise contact where children are interim placements have depleted budgets for preventative work.[16]

For children subject to care proceedings, many will require placement in foster care. Local authorities are heavily reliant on unrelated foster families to care for the majority of looked after children. However, as demand for foster care has risen, local authorities have not been able to keep pace in terms of recruitment of new carers.[17] Although we are witnessing an increase in the use of kinship care (or special guardianship) this is largely on account of a reduction in decisions to place children for adoption, rather than a reduction in the number of children requiring foster care. Thus, crisis is an apt term to describe the conditions of practice right across the social care and family justice system during the previous decade.

12 The Association of Directors of Children's Services, *Safeguarding Pressures: Phase 6*, Research Report, 2018. Available at https://adcs.org.uk/assets/documentation/ADCS_SAFEGUARDING_PRESSURES_PHASE_6_FINAL-compressed.pdf

13 15th View from the President's Chamber. Available at www.judiciary.uk/wp-content/uploads/2014/08/pfd-view-15-care-cases-looming-crisis.pdf

14 Family Rights Group, *Care Crisis Review: Options for Change*, London: Family Rights Group, 2018.

15 Ibid., p. 4.

16 S. Macleod, R. Hart, J. Jeffes and A. Wilkin, *Local Government Education and Children's Services Research Programme: The Impact of the Baby Peter Case on Applications for Care Orders*, Slough: Local Government Association, 2010.

17 M. Baginsky, S. Gorin and C. Sands, *The Fostering System in England: Evidence Review Research Report*, London: King's College London and Quest Research and Evaluation Ltd, 2018. Available at https://assets.publishing.service.gov.uk/government/uploads/system/uploads/attachment_data/file/629383/The_fostering_system_in_England_Evidence_review.pdf

Crisis: is England's narrow focus on child protection exacerbated in a context of austerity?

The history of child welfare and protection policy in England is of successive, but typically failed, attempts to shift the balance away from reactive child protection responses towards early intervention and prevention. Despite considerable investment in the Early Intervention Foundation[18] – an organization which champions early intervention to improve outcomes for children – all recent evidence points to a reduction in preventative services.[19] Whether we consider family incomes, community level preventative services, childcare provision or local authority early help, all have been eroded in the context of successive government austerity measures.[20] Thus, children's services in England have arguably become increasingly concentrated on child protection – with the consequence that there is little to stem the flow of children into public care. This was certainly the conclusion of the Care Crisis Review of 2018, which concluded that local authorities are *less* able to discharge their duty of care to vulnerable children given considerable cuts to their budgets.

In 2011, Neil Gilbert and colleagues drew a distinction between child welfare systems that take a 'child protection' approach from those that are based on a 'family service' model.[21] The former (dominant in the US, Canada, the United Kingdom – including Scotland[22]) tend to concentrate resources on responding to crises that have occurred, while the latter (dominant in Denmark, Sweden, Finland, Belgium, Germany, the Netherlands) attempt to channel investment into improving conditions for families to reduce the risk of such crises arising. Regarding a child protection orientation – there is little to suggest that countries that favour an investigative, or more intrusive, approach ultimately deliver better outcomes for children. Even in terms of the crude measure of child deaths – the international data on abuse-related deaths provides some support for the view that countries classified as having a stronger family service orientation appear to have lower rates of abuse-related child deaths when compared with countries considered to have a more legally focused, investigation-based system.[23]

Thus, the narrow focus of resources on care proceedings and substitute care which we are currently witnessing in many local authorities in England is unlikely to deliver better outcomes for children – and will certainly do little to strengthen relationships between families and the State. Here it useful to consider the observations drawn by the UN Special Rapporteur on extreme poverty and human rights (Philip Alston) from his recent visit to the UK and Northern Ireland (November, 2018). The Rapporteur concluded that policies of austerity, introduced

18 The Early Intervention Foundation: About EIF. Available at www.eif.org.uk/about/who-is-eif; www.eif.org.uk/why-it-matters

19 Children's Commissioner for England, Evidence Submitted to the Housing, Communities and Local Government Select Committee Inquiry into Funding and Provision of Children's Services, 2019. Available at www.childrenscommissioner.gov.uk/wp-content/uploads/2019/01/evidence-submitted-to-the-hclg-inquiry-into-childrens-services.pdf

20 P. Bywaters, G. Brady, L. Bunting, B. Daniel, B. Featherstone, C. Jones, K. Morris, J. Scourfield, T. Sparks and C. Webb, *Inequalities in English Child Protection Practice under Austerity: A Universal Challenge?*, 2017. Available at https://onlinelibrary.wiley.com/doi/full/10.1111/cfs.12383

21 N. Gilbert, N. Parton and M. Skivenes, *Child Protection Systems: International Trends and Emerging Orientations*, Oxford: Oxford University Press, 2011.

22 A. Stafford and S. Vincent, *Safeguarding and Protecting Children and Young People*, Edinburgh: Dunedin Academic Press, 2008.

23 I. Wallace and L. Bunting, *An Examination of Local, National and International Arrangements for the Mandatory Reporting of Child Abuse: Implications for Northern Ireland*, NSPCC Northern Ireland, 2007. Available at www.nspcc.org.uk/Inform/publications/downloads/mandatoryreportingNI_wdf51133.pdf

in 2010, were continuing largely unabated and delivering 'tragic social consequences'.[24] In particular the Rapporteur noted the decimation of public services budgets, the proliferation of food banks as well as marked increases in homelessness and rough sleeping. In sum, the social safety net for families has been very badly damaged by the political choices made regarding the distribution of resources under austerity.

Turning the tide: differentiated decision-making at the edge of care

So, given little realistic prospect of relief from insufficient budgets to adequately fund children's social care or the family courts, what might be the way forward? One solution, suggested by the Chief Social Worker for England (Isabelle Trowler), has been to divert a proportion of cases from the family court where the likely outcome is that children will be returned home under a supervision order. Trowler's report, which bears the title *Care Proceedings in England: the Case for Clear Blue Water*, is gaining traction in England and there is certainly merit in many of its arguments.[25] The Chief Social Worker and colleagues argue that if children's services reclaimed their primary role and offered intensive support to high-need families, fewer cases would need to come to court. Trowler supports her arguments with reference to increasing use of supervision orders. Supervision orders[26] can be made at the close of care proceedings when a child is returned home and place a duty on the local authority (typically for 12 months) to 'advise, assist and befriend'.

England, as with all European countries, operates within the framework of the European Convention on Human Rights. This framework protects the 'right to respect for family life' for all family members and requires local authorities to strike a fair balance between the interests of the child and those of the parent, in decisions about children's futures. The European court has expressed the view that it is in the child's own best interests that his or her family ties should only be severed in 'very exceptional circumstances'.[27] In this context, the Chief Social Worker's quest for better family support and assessments that differentiate *borderline* from essential family court cases is laudable. However, reference to an increase in the making of supervision orders requires some careful, critical interrogation.

Based on the first ever study to use full-service population level data to examine the cases of children subject to supervision orders,[28] the evidence is that an increase in supervision orders is not uniform across England – rather it is London that demonstrates an increase.[29] This observation is confirmed by the Ministry of Justice, which has also noted variable use of supervision orders across England and very low use of supervision orders in Wales.[30] In addition, an increase in the use of supervision orders cannot simply be attributed to children returning home to par-

24 United Nations General Assembly, *Visit to the United Kingdom and Northern Ireland: Report of the Special Rapporteur on Human Rights and Extreme Poverty*, 2019. A/HRC/41/39/Add.1 United Nations General Assembly; Human Rights Council. Available at https://undocs.org/A/HRC/41/39/Add.1

25 Trowler, n 1.

26 Children Act 1989, s. 35.

27 *YC v United Kingdom* (2012) 55 EHRR 33, para 134.

28 J. Harwin, B. Alrouh., L. Golding, T. McQuarrie and K. Broadhurst, *The Contribution of Supervision Orders and Special Guardianship to Children's Lives and Family Justice: Final Report*, 2019. Available at www.cfj-lancaster.org.uk/app/nuffield/files-module/local/documents/HARWIN_SO_SGO_FinalReport_V2.1_19Mar2019.pdf

29 Ibid., p. 38.

30 B. Alrouh, K. Broadhurst, L. Cusworth, L. Griffiths, R.D. Johnson, A. Akbari and D. Ford, *Born into Care: Newborns and Infants in Care Proceedings in Wales*, 2020. Available at www.cfj-lancaster.org.uk/app/nuffield/files-module/local/documents/Born%20into%20care%20Wales%20-%20main%20report_English_final.pdf

ents; rather the increase in use of supervision orders can be largely attributed to their use *in combination* with special guardianship orders, to bolster family and friends placements. The Children and Families Act 2014 introduced a far shorter statutory timescale for the completion of care proceedings (26 weeks) to prevent delay in decision-making but also as an efficiency measure.[31] There is growing evidence that in some instances final decisions feel hurried, leaving family court practitioners with some doubt about children's futures.[32] One way to counter anxieties is to mandate the local authority to undertake a further period of support/oversight for a kinship placement, by way of a supervision order.

In the context of a crisis in demand on both children's services and the family courts, it is tempting to question compulsory intervention – particularly to try to raise the bar for compulsory intervention in family life. However, child neglect has been consistently linked to poor outcomes across a range of domains in respect of social and emotional development, physical development and academic attainment.[33] Therefore, any policy impetus towards family preservation/diversion of cases from court needs to comprise more than just *rhetoric*. It is difficult to envisage how the conditions for family support can radically or even moderately change in the near future, given the continued context of family poverty and homelessness as just described. The Child Poverty Action Group reports 4.1 million children living in poverty in the UK in 2017–18,[34] and the Institute for Fiscal Studies expects this to rise to 5 million in 2020. When childcare costs are taken into account, more children are pushed into poverty.[35] Recently the Social Metrics Commission estimated that 2.3 million children are living in persistent poverty (i.e. living in poverty for at least two of the previous three years).[36] A critical change is that work is no longer a route out of poverty, with almost three-quarters of the children living in poverty living in households in which at least one adult is working.

The care system struggles to deliver an effective response to children, when children's behavioural and emotional difficulties become too established.[37] This awareness has shifted thinking in respect of the *timing* of care proceedings. Thus, where critics argue for diversion from court, somehow this must be squared with a realistic appraisal of the kinds of support services available to children who remain with their birth families. Research on the impact of neglect and late intervention has a long history. In 2012, conclusions drawn from the Department for Education Safeguarding Research Initiative[38] which documented significant weaknesses in local authority care planning, suggested that social workers were over-optimistic in respect of parents' capacity

31 Children and Families Act 1989 s. 14.

32 J. Simmonds, J. Harwin, R. Brown and K. Broadhurst, *Special Guardianship: A Review of the Evidence: Summary Report*, London: Nuffield Foundation, 2019. Summary report; J. Harwin et al., op. cit., n 28.

33 L.A. Sroufe, B. Coffino and E.A. Carlson, 'Conceptualising the Role of Early Experience: Lessons from the Minnesota Longitudinal Study', *Developmental Review* 30, 2010, 36–51.

34 See Child Poverty Action Group, *Facts and Figures*, n.d. Available at https://cpag.org.uk/child-poverty/child-poverty-facts-and-figures

35 See Institute for Fiscal Studies, *Living Standards, Poverty and Inequality. 2017/18–2021/22*. Available at www.ifs.org.uk/uploads/publications/comms/R136.pdf

36 *Measuring Poverty 2019, A report of the Social Metrics Commission*, 2019. Available at https://socialmetricscommission.org.uk/wp-content/uploads/2019/07/SMC_measuring-poverty-201908_full-report.pdf

37 S.A. Vis, B.H. Handegård, A. Holtan, S. Fossum and R. Thørnblad, 'Social Functioning and Mental Health among Children Who Have Been Living in Kinship and Non-Kinship Foster Care: Results from an 8-Year Follow-Up with a Norwegian Sample', *Child & Family Social Work* 21, 2016. 557–67. doi: 10.1111/cfs.12180

38 C. Davies and H. Ward, *Safeguarding Children across Services: Messages from Research*, London: Jessica Kingsley, 2012.

for change, leaving children too long in situations of harm. This resonates with findings from Brandon and Thoburn's follow-up study of children suffering or deemed likely to suffer significant harm, which concluded that a number of children would have benefited from earlier removal.[39] Thus, it is important to take a long view of the research evidence and ensure *coherence* in policy. Solving the current crisis cannot simply be about devolving responsibility back to families in the absence of adequate support for parenting – which brings us to the next section of this chapter, in which we consider the rise in use of special guardianship placements.

Parity for adoption and special guardianship?

Contemporary adoption in England primarily serves the permanence needs of children removed from their parents on account of child maltreatment or neglect. Since the Blair government's review of adoption,[40] there has been sustained cross-party political support for adoption as an important route out of the care system for young children, in particular. Notable developments include the creation of the Adoption Support Fund in 2015 with a remit to fund therapeutic services that are not provided by local authorities, the removal of ethnicity criteria in the matching process,[41] and the regionalization of adoption agencies to achieve economies in scale.[42] All these measures have one goal in mind. They seek to increase the number of children who find permanent homes with adopters, whether they are single, gay, lesbian or a couple, and to reduce the timescales for placement. However, the figures tell a different story. Over the last four years the number of adoptions has fallen[43] and a more dynamic indicator is the reduction in placement orders.[44] These are the legal orders that entitle local authorities to override parental wishes and start the process of adoption finding. Contributing to the falling numbers, and perhaps a surprising outcome of debates during the past decade, is the emergence of a stronger critique of adoption as the gold standard compared to other placement options (in particular with kinship carers/special guardians). Here wider debates about the non-consensual nature of England's approach to adoption and its place in modern society help to explain why support for adoption has started to *falter*.

The largely non-consensual adoption process in England has much in common with policy in the United States, which is set out in Chapter 4.6 of this book, but stands in strong contrast to that in many European countries. It is not an option in Finland and rarely used in Sweden

39 M. Brandon and J. Thoburn, 'Safeguarding Children in the UK: A Longitudinal Study of Services to Children Suffering or Likely to Suffer Significant Harm', *Child and Family Social Work* 13, 2008, 365–77.

40 Performance and Innovation Unit, *Prime Minister's Review of Adoption: Report from the Performance Unit*, London: HMSO, 2000.

41 Children and Families Act 2014 s. 3.

42 Department for Education, *Regionalising Adoption*, London: Department for Education, 2015; J. Simmonds, *Regionalisation of Adoption Agencies: Ten Views from the Bridge, Briefing Note*, London: CoramBAAF, 2016 J. Simmonds, *Returning to the Bridge: Ten New Views on the Development of Regional Adoption Agencies, Briefing Note*, London: CoramBAAF, 2017. See also www.consultancy.uk/news/16803/government-tasks-ecorys-with-evaluating-regional-adoption-agencies-in-england

43 Department for Education, *Children Looked after in England (Including Adoption), Year Ending December 2019*, 2019. Available at https://assets.publishing.service.gov.uk/government/uploads/system/uploads/attachment_data/file/850306/Children_looked_after_in_England_2019_Text.pdf

44 J. Harwin, B. Alrouh, S. Bedston and K. Broadhurst, *Care Demand and Regional Variability in England (2010/11 to 2016/17)*, 2018. Available at www.cfj-lancaster.org.uk/app/nuffield/files-module/local/documents/Care-Demand-Regional-Variability-Report_2018.02.21_V1.2.pdf

or Germany, but appears to be increasing in Denmark and Norway.[45] As noted by Cooke in Chapter 4.2 of this book, adoption is not favoured in New Zealand or Australia, where issues around the treatment of ethnic minorities have been a particularly sensitive issue. Adoption policy in England has faced considerable challenge from Europe. The Borzova Report (2015)[46] was highly critical of so-called forced adoption and removals of infants at birth, noting England's departure in both respects from other European countries. In the same year, new research reported the scale of birth mothers' repeat appearances in care proceedings in England and repeat removal of children.[47] In drawing attention to the volume of very young babies removed from vulnerable women and heightened risk of repeat family court appearances for women whose babies are adopted,[48] the work of Broadhurst and colleagues also raised fundamental questions about the impact of the family courts on family life.[49]

Disquiet about England's adoption practices is evident, not just from external researchers or policy commentators, but from within the ranks of the family justice system itself. Two high profile Supreme Court and Appeal Court judgments have been instrumental in change. In *Re B (Care Proceedings: Appeal)*[50] the Supreme Court described adoption without parental consent as a decision of last resort – only to be made when all other options had been exhausted. This was followed by *Re B-S (Children)*,[51] in which the final judgment was highly critical of the local authority's failure to consider thoroughly family and friend options. This latter judgment changed practice such that the local authority care plan must indicate that a range of permanency options have been considered and that family options have been exhausted. With early research evidence confirming the positive outcomes of special guardianship as well as the body of professional judgments, the professional lens has shifted back to the resources of the extended family. (See also Chapter 4.6 of this book.)

Special guardianship was introduced with the Adoption and Children Act 2002. This order vests primary parental responsibility in the special guardian for most matters, until the child reaches the age of 18, and to the exclusion of others (i.e. birth parents).[52] However, the basic legal link between the child and his or her birth parents is preserved, as the child remains permanently within the extended family. Special guardianship is often seen as a more palatable option for children unable to live with birth parents, because it preserves family ties and contact, which are seen as beneficial to children's identity and development. During the latter half of the decade, and following the cases of *Re B* and *Re B-S*, a fall in the number of adoptions has been recorded, in tandem with an *increase* in the use of special guardianship – even for the very

45 See Gilbert, Parton and Skivenes, op. cit., n 21, pp. 100, 192, 249.

46 Borzova, op. cit., n 4.

47 K. Broadhurst, B. Alrouh, E. Yeend, J. Harwin, M. Shaw, M. Pilling, C. Mason and S. Kershaw, 'Connecting Events in Time to Identify a Hidden Population: Birth Mothers and Their Children in Recurrent Care Proceedings in England', *The British Journal of Social Work* 45(8), 2015, 2241–2260. https://doi.org/10.1093/bjsw/bcv130

48 K. Broadhurst, C. Mason, S. Bedston, B. Alrouh, L. Morris, T. McQuarrie, M. Palmer, M. Shaw, J. Harwin and S. Kershaw, *Vulnerable Birth Mothers and Recurrent Care Proceedings: Main Findings*, London: Nuffield Foundation, 2017.

49 K. Broadhurst and C. Mason, 'Birth Parents and the Collateral Consequences of Court-Ordered Child Removal: Towards a Comprehensive Framework', *International Journal of Law, Policy and the Family* 31(1), 2017, 41–59. https://doi.org/10.1093/lawfam/ebw013

50 [2013]) UKSC 33.

51 [2013] EWCA Civ 1146.

52 Adoption and Children Act 2002 s. 14. However, birth parents retain very limited rights such as the right to consent or withhold consent to adoption or an adoption placement.

youngest children in the family justice system.[53] This latter shift in practice was not envisaged by the proponents of special guardianship, who saw this option as primarily suiting the needs of older children with established and lengthy relationships with their birth parents, extended family networks and communities.

Adding further weight to arguments in favour of thorough assessment of all potential permanency options for children – in 2019, Harwin et al. reported a low rate of return to court for fresh care proceedings for children subject to special guardianship orders.[54] The findings confirmed earlier studies by Wade and colleagues[55] about the durability of these placements and challenged practitioners to think again about the value of extended family resources. Evidence from Harwin and colleagues was persuasive as it was based on all children in care proceedings, including those made subjects of special guardianship orders, between 2010–11 and 2016–17.[56]

However, as with all parents or carers, adequate support in the face of parenting challenges is vital if children are to flourish. Through special guardianship, over 21,000 children were removed from the care system between 2010–11 and 2016–17. Many are calling for more radical support for special guardians through changes in law and policy as well as practice.[57] Unlike prospective adopters, housing support is not an automatic right and legal aid to ensure special guardians understand the implications of this order is very modest and expenditure varies by local authority. Unlike in adoption, there is no requirement to provide special guardians with any training or preparation so that their consent to the order is fully informed.[58] A highly influential Court of Appeal judgment in 2018[59] highlighted the poor treatment of special guardians in the family court, given difficulties faced in achieving party status in court proceedings accessing legal aid. With only 8 percent of special guardians accessing the Adoption Support Fund and entitlements to support and legal aid highly variable,[60] it would be hard to conclude that special guardianship has achieved parity with adoption.

Older children: contextual safeguarding

The conditions of child protection rarely stand still. A changing trend that warrants particular attention is an increase in older children coming before the family courts in care proceedings. Thus, crisis constitutes not only an increase in volume of children coming before the courts, but also the type of difficulties that public services are now dealing with. Although older children are smaller in number than younger children, often it is the older children who make exceptional demands on services because of placement instability and/or, high cost specialist placements including in secure settings. Rees et al. have suggested that the particular needs of this group

53 Department for Education, *Special Guardianship Review: Report on Findings: Government Consultation Response*, 2015. Available at www.gov.uk/government/consultations/special-guardianship-review

54 Harwin et al., op. cit., n 28.

55 J. Wade, I. Sinclair, L. Stuttard and J. Simmonds, *Investigating Special Guardianship: Experiences, Challenges and Outcomes*, 2014. Available at www.york.ac.uk/inst/spru/research/pdf/SpecialG2014.pdf

56 Harwin et al., op. cit., n 28.

57 The Public Law Working Group (forthcoming 2020) Recommendations to achieve best practice in the child protection and family justice systems.

58 J. Simmonds, J. Harwin, R. Brown and K. Broadhurst, *Special Guardianship: A Review of the Evidence: Summary Report*, Nuffield Family Justice Observatory, 2019. Available at www.nuffieldfjo.org.uk/files/documents/NuffieldFJO-Special-Guardianship-190731-WEB-final.pdf

59 *Re P-S (Children)* [2018] EWCA Civ 1407.

60 Local Government and Social Care Ombudsman, *Firm Foundations: Complaints about Council Support and Advice for Special Guardians*, Coventry, 2018.

are insufficiently understood.[61] The majority of looked after children (in public care) are aged between 10 and 15 years and the care system has a variable track record in respect of improving outcomes for those in long-term foster care.[62] Although adoption has attracted considerable attention in respect of permanency planning, the same cannot be said for older children in long-term foster care or other forms of public care.[63] Those who are 'hardest to help' are, without doubt, children living in residential children's homes, described as 'out of sight and out of mind' by the *All-Party Parliamentary Group Inquiry into Children Missing from Care* (2012). Children in this sector who are placed at a significant distance from their family networks in out-of-area placements are at heightened risk of sexual exploitation, gang related activity and going missing.[64] Thus, local authorities are not only dealing with a larger care population, but, are arguably faced with more complex social problems and are insufficiently resourced to deal with them.

New directions are however emerging in regard to understanding risks to older children as well as the public service response. Academics and practitioners have proposed a greater focus on *extra-familial risks* to older children, and have proposed a new model of 'contextual safeguarding'.[65] Contextual safeguarding recognizes that risks to older children may in fact stem primarily from their neighbourhoods or schools and online, as evidenced by young people's involvement in gang activity and violence, online harms or child trafficking. Contextual safeguarding is a welcome challenge to an overly narrow or individualized concept of risk, which abstracts child from wider environment, and is arguably overdue given the greater influence of peer group and other external influences on contemporary childhood.

Children's services innovation: the Family Drug and Alcohol Court (FDAC)

As stated in the introduction to this chapter, fiscal constraint in public services has also prompted a search for innovation – based on a belief that more can be done with *less*, if the potential of practice pioneers is supported. In 2014, the Department for Education (DfE) launched the Children's Social Care Innovation Programme[66] seeking to unlock this potential. However, funding for practice reform was typically short-term – underestimating the time needed to develop, implement and sustain change. In a number of instances DfE catalyst investment was not followed by mainstream durable funding from local authority budgets. The case of the Family Drug and Alcohol Court (FDAC) illustrates all these points.

61 G. Rees, M. Stein and L. Hicks, *Adolescent Neglect: Research Policy and Practice*, London: Jessica Kingsley, 2011.

62 J. Boddy, *Understanding Permanence for Looked after Children, a Review of Research for the Care Inquiry*, 2013. Available at http://thecareinquiry.files.wordpress.com/2013/04/understanding-permanence-for-lac.pdf

63 G. Schofield, 'Permanence in Foster Care', in G. Schofield and J. Simmonds (eds), *The Child Placement Handbook*, London: BAAF, 2009.

64 House of Commons Home Affairs Committee, *Child sexual exploitation and the response to localized grooming, Second Report of Session 2013–2014*, 2013. Available at www.publications.parliament.uk/pa/cm201314/cmselect/cmhaff/68/68i.pdf

65 C. Firmin, 'Contextual Risk, Individualised Responses: An Assessment of Safeguarding Responses to Nine Cases of Peer-on-Peer Abuse', *Child Abuse Rev.* 27, 2018, 42–57. doi: 10.1002/car.2449

66 Department for Education, *Overview Report: Department for Education, Children's Services Innovation Programme*, London: DfE, 2014. Available at https://assets.publishing.service.gov.uk/government/uploads/system/uploads/attachment_data/file/342051/Overview_of_the_Children_s_Social_Care_Innovation_Programme.pdf

The FDAC court was first piloted in London in 2008, as an innovative treatment alternative to the conventional, adversarial model of public law (care) proceedings.[67] Focused on cases where parental substance misuse is a key concern, FDAC was adapted from a model of problem-solving family drug treatment courts widely used in the United States and which showed promising results.[68] Unlike ordinary care proceedings, parents are provided with a time-limited court-based trial for change. This is facilitated by judges who, in addition to adjudication, play non-traditional roles and by a specialist multidisciplinary team which advises the court, works directly with parents, provides assessment and support, and coordinates inter-agency planning and treatment. Problem-solving court hearings replace traditional hearing because judges and parents communicate directly. The overall aim is to achieve lasting permanency for children, either through reunification or swift out-of-home permanency when reunification is not appropriate. The model draws on the principles of therapeutic jurisprudence and proceedings go beyond adjudication to address the underlying problems through a process that stresses 'voice, validation and respect'.[69]

Although successive evaluations of FDAC[70] reported far higher rates of reduced parental substance misuse, reunification and a better parental experience of court,[71] roll-out was stalled because government funding was not extended beyond 2018. Local authorities were tempted, but ultimately unable to commit to what felt like riskier alternative funding models proposed by the Cabinet Office in the form of social investment bonds. Austerity has ushered in experimental methods of funding public services, which aim to unlock private investment.[72] However, as the Oxford Go Lab[73] determined, there is yet no evidence that alternative sources of commissioning/funding are attractive to public services. Although further time-limited funding has now been reinstated for further roll-out by the Department for Education[74] and a further period of testing is underway, FDAC illustrates ambivalence on the part of central government to support and *sustain* change – even in the face of promising evidence.

Better data for better child welfare and protection policy

This history of child welfare and protection policy is of heated debate and often highly *reactive* swings in policy and practice, following public inquiries into child deaths or exposure of

67 J. Harwin and M. Ryan, 'The Role of the Court in Cases Concerning Parental Substance Misuse and Children at Risk of Harm', *Journal of Social Welfare and Family Law* 29(3), 2007, 277–92.

68 S.D. Worcel, C.J. Furrer, B.L. Green, S.W.M. Burrus and M.W. Finigan, 'Effects of Family Treatment Drug Courts on Substance Abuse and Child Welfare Outcomes', *Child Abuse Review* 17(6), 2008, 427–43.

69 M. King, A. Freiberg, B. Batagol and R. Hyams, *Non-Adversarial Justice*, Alexandria, NSW: Federation Press, 2005, p. 34.

70 J. Harwin, B. Alrouh, K. Broadhurst, T. McQuarrie, L. Golding and M. Ryan, 'Child and Parent Outcomes in the London Family Drug and Alcohol Court Five Years On: Building on International Evidence', *International Journal of Law, Policy and the Family* 32, 2018, 140–69. doi: 10.1093/lawfam/eby006

71 J. Harwin, M. Ryan and K. Broadhurst, 'How Does FDAC Succeed with Parents with Substance Misuse Problems? Exploring Relational Practices within the English Family Drug and Alcohol Court', *Child Abuse Review* 27, 2018, 266–79.

72 D. Neyland, 'On the Transformation of Children at-Risk into an Investment Proposition: A Study of Social Impact Bonds as an Anti-Market Device', *The Sociological Review* 6(3), 2018, 492–510.

73 E. Carter, C. FitzGerald, R. Dixon, C. Economy, T. Hameed and M. Airoldi, *Building the Tools for Public Services to Secure Better Outcomes: Collaboration, Prevention and Innovation*, Government Outcomes Lab., 2018. Available at https://golab.bsg.ox.ac.uk/our-projects/about-evidence-report-2018/

74 UK Government. Available at www.gov.uk/government/news/15-million-investment-to-help-keep-families-safely-together

miscarriages of justice through family court judgments. There has also been a tendency to cherry pick evidence to suit government or organizational policy priorities.[75] In 2011, the Family Justice Review argued that efforts to steer family justice reform were hampered by major deficits in knowledge about how the family justice system is working. However, research to address these deficits is gathering pace, as interdisciplinary teams exploit an increasing volume of electronic data to produce insights *at scale* and over time. A new trend is emerging in the use of large scale administrative data, which holds out the promise of generating robust evidence about both actions and impacts of local authorities and the courts.[76] Research which is based on full-service populations is arguably more persuasive, because accusations of bias or limited generalizability do not apply to carefully executed analysis of total populations over time.

Similarly, the Ministry of Justice is making an increasing wealth of data available via the new PLATO tool, which allows court areas to probe their own statistics regarding care demand and outcomes, and to compare themselves with other courts in England and Wales. Making data available prompts a fresh focus on local decision-making practices and cultures, but also speaks directly to concerns about transparency (or lack of) regarding the black box of family justice.[77] The Nuffield Foundation has funded a new Family Justice Observatory (FJO) for England and Wales, at the heart of which is support for the use of large-scale administrative data. The FJO incorporates a new data partnership between the Centre for Family Justice Research at Lancaster University and the SAIL databank at Swansea University, equipped to produce completely new analyses of single and linked administrative datasets.[78] Already new insights have emerged regarding the marked increasing in care proceedings concerning new-borns and infants in care proceedings in England and Wales, which has catalyzed the development of best practice guidelines when the State intervenes at birth.[79] Building capacity in large-scale, longitudinal research is essential if we are to address the current crisis and reliably understand antecedents and solutions.

Conclusion

In her presidential address to the annual conference of the ADCS in 2012, Debbie Jones urged local authorities to ensure they were on the 'front-foot' in response to major reforms.[80] However, looking back over the past decade, this has been far easier said than done. Neither policy leads nor the courts were able to forecast the upward trend in both demand on frontline children's

75 See n 10.

76 K. Broadhurst, B. Alrouh, C. Mason, L., Holmes, H. Ward, M. Ryan and S. Bowyer, *Born into Care: Newborns in Care Proceedings in England*, Nuffield Family Justice Observatory, 2018. Available at www.nuffieldfjo.org.uk/app/nuffield/files-module/local/documents/Born%20into%20Care_Final%20Report_10%20Oct%202018.pdf

77 K. Broadhurst, L. Robertson, C. Mason, S. Bowyer and J. Wilkinson, *Towards a Family Justice Observatory: A Scoping Study*, London: Nuffield Foundation, 2017. Available at http://wp.lancs.ac.uk/observatory-scoping-study/files/2017/08/National-Stakeholder-Consultation-Main-Findings-Report.pdf; K.E. Broadhurst and T. Williams, 'Harnessing the Power of Data to Improve Family Justice: A New Nuffield Family Justice Observatory For England and Wales', *Family Court Review* 57(3), 2019, 405–13. https://doi.org/10.1111/fcre.12428

78 L. Cusworth, L. Griffiths, A. Akbari, B. Alrouh, S. Bedston, J. Harwin, R. Johnson, K. Jones, J. Smart, S. Thompson, S. Ford and K. Broadhurst, 'The Nuffield Family Justice Observatory Data Partnership', *International Journal of Population Data Science* 4(3), 2019, 3:116.

79 Op. cit., n 68.

80 Association of Directors of Children's Services (ADCS), *Safeguarding Pressures: Phase 3*, 2012. Available at www.adcs.org.uk/download/news/adcs-sg-pressures-p3-report-final.pdf

social care services or the courts, or to anticipate the magnitude of cuts to public sector budgets. As we enter a new decade, a number of clear challenges lie ahead, to which we now turn.

As a priority, further understanding is needed of what can realistically be changed in terms of community infrastructure and preventative services, to reduce the very high rates of care proceedings, particularly in England's most deprived areas. Solutions need to be co-produced with families and consider sustainability from the outset. Although high-profile bursts of government investment may make good headlines, money is not well spent if there is little chance that investment can be sustained. A culture of denial within conservative government also requires evidence informed and concerted challenge, if there is any hope of tackling the current crisis.

Regarding alternative care for children unable to live with birth parents, the latter part of this decade has seen a welcome change in endorsement of the full range of permanency options for children – rather than, a narrow, priority focus on adoption. However, with a new government now in place for the next five years, early signs are that efforts to achieve this balance may be undermined by a return to policy which positions adoption as the gold standard. Thus, it is imperative that robust research evidence is marshalled to challenge regressive trends in policy and myths that have resulted in far too little support for family and friends' carers.[81]

It is equally vital that policymakers understand that the cumulative experience of childhood matters,[82] such that a focus on the early years does not detract from the experience of older children. At present a programme of change for children's homes is underway which is clearly critical and arguably overdue given the vulnerability of this population. However, new and complex risks to older children appear to be growing in number and require a more concerted adolescent strategy. Already, we are seeing investment in understanding gangs' involvement, child sexual exploitation and trafficking.

Finally, positive steps are being made towards evidence informed policy through the greater use of bigger data. The work of the Nuffield Data Partnership team aims to promote step-change in the evidence to underpin policy and practice reform. Over the next five years, it will be important to examine where this programme succeeds and where it fails, in terms of ensuring children social care and family justice reform is firmly underpinned by robust research evidence.

Obviously, there are further challenges head given the UK's exit from the European Union in 2020. At present, the UK will continue to abide by the UNCRC and the Hague Convention on Parental Responsibility and Protection of Children[83] which provide some welcome principles and standards regarding the rights of both children and families. However, in the absence of recourse to the Court of Justice of the European Union, an important balance and check is removed, which is concerning given all the points made in his chapter about family hardship coupled with shortfalls in practice.

81 J. Hunt, 'Grandparents as Substitute Parents in the UK', *Contemporary Social Science* 13(2), 2018, 175–86. https://doi.org/10.1080/21582041.2017.1417629

82 Sroufe et al., op. cit., n 33.

83 For a discussion of UK alignment to international instruments following Brexit, see J. Beaumont, *Interaction of the Brussels IIa and Maintenance Regulations with (Possible) Litigation in Non-EU States: Including Brexit Implications*, Centre for Private International Law, Working Paper 2018/1, 2018. Available at www.abdn.ac.uk/law/documents/EUFam%20book%20-%20Interaction%20of%20EU%20Fam%20Regs%20with%20non-EU%20litigation%20working%20paper%201%202018.pdf.

4.2
CHILD PROTECTION
Promoting permanency without adoption

Allan Cooke

Introduction

This chapter examines how permanency for children is achieved in New Zealand in the child protection context. Since the First Edition of this book, New Zealand law relating to children who enter the care system in New Zealand has undergone major change. First, a new framework, special guardianship, was introduced as from 30 June 2016. Second, the process by which supports are provided for 'permanent caregivers'[1] was substantially amended. And third, changes to the Oranga Tamariki/Children and Young Persons Wellbeing Act 1989 (OTA), as from 1 July 2019, are likely to have a significant effect on permanency outcomes for Māori children in particular. The responsible department of state is the Ministry of Children/Oranga Tamariki (OT).[2]

The 2019 amendments and their impact on permanency

The permanent removal of Māori children from their families and extended family groups, including placement for adoption, has been a profound issue for Māori. Adoption is a legal process quite anathema to Māori because of the legal effect of adoption. Severance of the tie between child and parent removes the child from not only from their familial world – the connection of the child to their *whānau*, *hapū* and *iwi*[3] – but also from ancestors. This is

1 'Permanent caregiver' is defined in the Act as meaning those who have been appointed as special guardians or as guardians of a child under the Care of Children Act 2004 (COCA) and where that order for guardianship was made in substitution for a custody order under the Children, Young Persons, and Their Families (Oranga Tamariki) Legislation Act 2017 (OTA) and who have a parenting order under COCA.

2 *Oranga* means 'welfare' and *tamariki* means 'children'. In addition to the name of the statute changing, so did the name of the agency – from the Department of Child Youth and Family Services to the Ministry of Vulnerable Children/Oranga Tamariki, and then subsequently to the Ministry of Children/Oranga Tamariki.

3 These are the three tiers of groupings within Māori society. The whānau is a group of relatives defined by reference to a recent ancestor, embracing several generations, several nuclear families and several households, and can be characterised by the notion of an 'extended family'. A number of whānau constitute a hapū: all those within the hapū are derived from a common ancestor. Each iwi is made up of related hapū and is associated with a regional territory. See J. Ruru, 'Kua tutū to puehu, kia mau: Māori Aspirations and Family Law Policy', in M. Henaghan and B. Atkin (eds), *Family Law Policy in New Zealand*, 4th edition, Wellington: LexisNexis, 2013.

whakapapa, and is central to Māori life as it ensures the interconnectedness of all living things. This brings about the necessity to maintain a state of balance in all things and at all times. Both departmental policy and judicial reluctance to use adoption in permanency cases has therefore reflected concern at the prospect of children losing those connections. Private law orders under the Care of Children Act 2004 (COCA) which do not have that effect were therefore more 'palatable'. Special guardianship is now also the subject of critique.[4]

That concern reflects what has been called a 'more communitarian approach' than would apply in similar family law jurisdictions.[5] This is of significance, first, because Māori are the indigenous people of New Zealand who have been colonised and who, as a people, still suffer the impact of colonisation[6] and, second, because of the numbers of Māori children who are in the care system.[7] The concern for Māori about the numbers of children being taken into care was a driver for the July 2019 amendments.[8] This is not necessarily in respect of the legal framework used to achieve permanency (but that may be a consequence) but in how the State and its agencies address the question of permanency for Māori children in particular, as opposed to children of other ethnicities.

One of the aspirations of the OTA when first enacted in 1989 was to provide a new approach to the question of Māori children being removed by the state. The act had, as its antecedent, the report *Pūao te Ata Tū* ('Daybreak').[9] The preface of *Pūao te Ata Tū* stated 'At the heart of the issue is a profound misunderstanding or ignorance of the place of the child in Maori society and its relationship with whānau, hapū and iwi structures'. It identified fundamental concerns Māori had about the role they played in society and how they were marginalised in the construction and operation of social policy in respect of children. The report highlighted issues (consequences) arising from the colonisation and the legacy of institutional racism within the then responsible department of state. Children were being placed outside of the kin structure but without any adequate attempt to find foster parents within the *hapū* and without *hapū* being really consulted, 'often as an omission, but more usually through a positive opinion that the hapū had no right to be involved, or because of an exaggerated emphasis on "confidentiality"'.

Those realities continued under the 1989 Act. In describing the lost opportunity of that statute, Judge Sharyn Otene extrajudicially commented:[10]

4 This effect arguably reinforces the impact of colonisation on Māori and the dislocation from family, whānau, hapū and iwi of children taken into care. It is argued that special guardianship framework is the anthesis to the Māori world view. See Radio New Zealand, 23 July 2019. Available at www.rnz.co.nz/news/te-manu-korihi/395036/legality-and-disconnection-between-maori-kids-and-whanau

5 See J. Ruru, op. cit., n 3; B. Atkin, '"Vulnerable" Children, Cultural and Social Realities and Regulation: Moving towards Early Intervention in New Zealand', in C. Rogerson et al. (eds), *Family Law and Family Realities*, The Hague: Eleven Int. Publishing, pp. 403ff.

6 Māori are tangatawhenua – the native or first people of New Zealand.

7 As at 30 June 2017, of the 5,708 children in the custody of OT, 3,518 were Māori. Available at www.msd.govt.nz/about-msd-and-our-work/publications-resources/statistics/cyf/kids-in-care.html. Māori constitute 15 percent of the total population, yet as at July 2017 constituted 61 percent of the children in custody of OT.

8 See Atkin, op. cit., n 5, where he discusses the 'interesting' policy and legislative pathway taken and which influenced by the political/electoral fortunes of the two dominant political parties in New Zealand.

9 J. Rangihau, *Pūao Te-Ata-Tū (Day break): The Report of the Ministerial Advisory Committee on a Maori Perspective for the Department of Social Welfare*, Wellington: New Zealand Government, 1987.

10 *'Care and Protection Past Present and Future'*, prepared for the New Zealand Law Society, Continuing Legal Education Seminar, Oranga Tamariki Act Changes, June 2019, quoting *Re the S Children (No 3)* [1994] NZFLR 971 at 981. See also S. Otene, 'Te Hurihanga Tuarua? Examining Amendments to the Oranga Tamariki Act 1989 That Took Effect on 1 July2019', *NZFLJ* 9, 2019, 139.

But there is, or at least there is perceived, a grand tension between these principles of Māori core and the paramount obligation to the child's welfare and best interests. Judge Inglis QC captured the essence of that tension in the following formulation:

> In stating the various principles which ought to be taken into account, the Act is providing signposts to assist in the search for what is likely to promote the welfare and interests of the child. That search must be conducted on the footing that a choice between options must always be regulated by their impact on the welfare and interests of the child as a member of a family and as an individual, and that where there is a conflict of principles or interests the welfare and interests of the child must be the deciding factor (ss 5(c) and 6). Whatever importance may be attached to the principles in s 13, the Act itself provides that they cannot override the principles in ss 5 and 6.

So, despite the cultural heft of the secion 5 and section 13 principles, they are routinely overpowered when the fact and context-specific inquiry for the particular child assesses the presence of serious harm.

Those themes are reflected in the statistics for Māori children who are removed from their families. This has increased disproportionally, from 100 per 10,000 in 2012 to 132 per 10,000 in 2017. This is also emphasized in the removal of Māori babies: new-born removals were at the rate of 102 per 10,000 births in 2018, compared to the non-Māori rate of 24 per 10,000 birth, a figure that has been stable since 2015.[11] The observation is made that whether this reflects over-exposure of Māori communities to risk factors, or direct bias, or lack of preventative services, needs careful untangling.[12]

The 2019 amendments therefore go beyond the issue of permanency and how that is effected. For present purposes it is sufficient to note that the statutory amendments, through their emphasis on the engagement with Māori that is now essential, will mean that it is unlikely that Māori children will be placed outside of their immediate or extended kin groups.

Importantly, new section 7AA incorporates into the legislation a duty on OT to recognize and provide a practical commitment to the principles of the Treaty of Waitangi.[13] Section 7AA(2)(b) includes the duty to ensure that policies, practices and services have regard to *mana tamaiti* (*tamariki*),[14] and the *whakapapa*[15] of Māori children and the *whanaungatanga*[16] responsibilities of

11 Dr E. Keddell, *Hard to Get into, But Harder to Get Out of: Understanding Recent Trends in Child Protection*, Re-Imagining Social Work, 10 May 2019. Available at www.reimaginingsocialwork.nz/2019/05/hard-to-get-into-but-harder-to-get-out-of-understanding-recent-trends-in-child-protection/ (accessed 1 May 2019).

12 Ibid.

13 New Zealand's founding constitutional document. It was signed on 6 February 1840 between representatives of the British Crown and Māori chiefs. A partnership relationship was created through its signing. Debate has continued since as to the nature and extent of this partnership.

14 This is newly created definition: 'The intrinsic value and inherent dignity derived from a child's or young person's whakapapa (genealogy) and their belonging to a whānau, hapū, iwi, or family group, in accordance with tikanga Māori or its equivalent in the culture of the child or young person'. There is a question mark over whether there can be an equivalent in other cultures.

15 The statutory definition is: 'whakapapa, in relation to a person, means the multi-generational kinship relationships that help to describe who the person is in terms of their mātua (parents), and tūpuna (ancestors), from whom they descend'.

16 Whanaungatanga, in relation to a person, means – (a) the purposeful carrying out of responsibilities based on obligations to whakapapa:(b) the kinship that provides the foundations for reciprocal

their *whānau, hapū* and *iwi*. This is a high-level obligation on OT, and which is now being seen occurring at a local level.[17]

When this duty is seen in conjunction with the new principles, a clear message is being sent: every effort must be made to ensure that Māori children are not removed from their families and where this occurs and return is not possible, any permanent placement must be within *whānau, hapū, iwi*, and if that is not possible, in a Māori placement. Section 5 sets out the principles to be applied in relation to the exercise of powers conferred by the act.[18] Once the decision is made that a child cannot be returned home, then the following factors will fall into play in establishing how the well-being of the child is met: the *mana tamaiti* (*tamariki*) and the child's well-being is to be protected by recognizing the *whakapapa* and the *whanaungatanga* responsibilities of their family, *whānau, hapū, iwi* and family group.[19] There is the obligation on decision-makers to recognize the child's place within their *whānau, hapū, iwi* and family group[20] and, in particular, that the primary responsibility for caring for and nurturing the well-being and development of children lies with those familial groups;[21] consequently, the effect of any decision on the child's relationship with them and their links to *whakapapa* should be considered.[22] The child's sense of belonging, *whakapapa*, and the *whanaungatanga* responsibilities of their family, *whānau, hapū, iwi* and family group should be recognized and respected.[23] Wherever possible the relationship between the child and their family, *whānau, hapū, iwi* and family group should be maintained and strengthened;[24] if possible, a child's family, *whānau, hapū, iwi* and family group should participate in decisions, and regard should be had to their views.[25] Further, the child's place within their community is to be recognized, and, in particular, consideration must be given to how a decision affects the stability of a child or young person (including their education and their connections to community and other contacts). The impact of disruption on that stability should be considered and networks of, and supports for, the child or young person and their family, *whānau, hapū, iwi* and family group that are in place before the power is to be exercised should be acknowledged and, where practicable, utilized.[26]

Where a child is 'permanently' removed, section 13(2)(i) sets out the sequence of desired placements and the factors that are to accompany the placement. The decision must be consistent with the principles set out in sections 4A(1) and 5. It must address the needs of the young person and be guided with preference being given to placing the child with a member of the wider family, *whānau, hapū, iwi*, or family group who can provide a safe, stable and loving home;

---

obligations and responsibilities to be met: (c) the wider kinship ties that need to be protected and maintained to ensure the maintenance and protection of their sense of belonging, identity, and connection.

17 Anecdotal information from practitioners working in the area. Whether this reflects policies that has been formally established and implemented or just local initiatives is unclear.

18 The exercise of ensuring that well-being is at the forefront of decision-making must regard respect and uphold the child's rights set out in UNCROC and the UN Convention on the Rights of Persons with Disabilities [section 5(b)(i)]; address the impact of harm on the child and the steps taken to enable recovery [section 5(b)(ii)] and in addressing the child's needs for a safe, stable and loving home [section 5(b)(iii)].

19 Section 5(1)(b)(iv).

20 Section 5(1)(b)(c).

21 Section 5(1)(b)(c)(i).

22 Section 5(1)(b)(c)(ii).

23 Section 5(1)(b)(c)(iii).

24 Section 5(1)(b)(c)(iv).

25 Section 5(1)(b)(c)(v).

26 Section 5(1)(d).

for the child to live with a family or if that is not possible, in a family-like setting; the importance of *mana tamaiti (tamariki)*, *whakapapa* and *whanaungatanga* being recognized and promoted and, where practicable, a child should be placed with the child's siblings. Lastly, a child should be placed where the child or young person can develop a sense of belonging and attachment.

The revision of section 13 and particularly section 13(2)(i) – which sets out the approach to be taken when a child is at such risk of serious harm within their family, *whānau, hapū, iwi* or family group – will see a greater primacy accorded to Māori children being placed within family, *whānau, hapū* and *iwi* than has previously occurred. When read in conjunction with the obligations imposed on OT to recognize and provide a practical commitment to the Treaty of Waitangi,[27] such placements are likely to be the default position. This is notwithstanding that the law previously used the word 'priority',[28] compared to the new terms 'preferable', 'desirable', 'should be' and 'where practicable'.[29] The wording of section 13(2)(i) and its links back to section 4A(1) and from there to the duties of OT in section 7 and, obligations imposed by section 7AA, will lead to this being the case.

This is also reinforced by section 13(2)(h) of the amended act. This provides that where a child is removed from the care of the member or members of its birth family, *whānau, hapū, iwi*, or family group, then where possible and consistent with best interests, the child is to be returned to the family, *whānau, hapū, iwi* or family group who are the child's usual caregivers. This provision imposes on OT a further duty to look to the child's wider familial group before embarking on a non-kin placement. It also conveys a clear signal that, notwithstanding a child may have been secured within a new non-kin family, if it is consistent with safety and well-being then the child should be placed within his or her familial group. This will raise issues for non-kin caregivers who have had care of a child for a significant period of time and where there is attachment between child and caregiver, and there may be difficult decisions to be taken in individual cases.

Permanency without adoption

Unlike other jurisdictions (such as England and the US), adoption of children in permanency cases has generally not been followed in New Zealand since the passing of the Adoption Act 1955.[30] The rationale was articulated in *Re Adoption 021/001/91*:[31] 'The Courts in New Zealand have tended in such situations to shy away from an adoption process which distorts existing family relationships, preferring to achieve the same object by the adjustment of guardianship rights with the family'. The process since 1989 has seen permanent caregivers obtaining private law orders for day-to-day care[32] and additional guardianship[33] under COCA, which does not

27 Section 7AA.

28 Albeit then qualified by 'should, where practicable. …'

29 In section 13(2)(i)(iii)(A), (B), (C) and (D).

30 Adoption orders in permanency cases do occur but are rare. The number of adoption orders made in New Zealand is low: in 1971 almost 4000 children were adopted, this dropped to fewer than 600 by 1998, see S. Harris, 'Would-Be Parents Left in Limbo as Adoption Numbers Drop', *New Zealand Herald*, online edn, 23 July 2017 In the year ending 30 July 2017 there were 128.

31 (1991) 7 FRNZ 427.

32 A parenting order for day-to-day care expires on the child attaining 16 years of age – unless there are 'special circumstances'.

33 This additional to the child's natural guardians, their mother and father. The guardianship status continues until the child attains the age of 18 years. Guardianship goes beyond and is distinct from day-to-day decision-making in respect of children. Section 16 of COCA requires consultation and joint decision-making between guardians on matters of guardianship.

involve the severing in law of the relationship between child and parent.[34] Permanency cases are 'grafted' onto that framework. The consequence is that the legal connection between the child and their birth parents is maintained. However, it means that those permanent caregivers must negotiate with the other guardians on matters constituting guardianship.[35]

In 2010, the 'Home for Life' policy was introduced to ostensibly better support permanently placed children and their caregivers. This was designed in part to attract new permanent caregivers. In explaining how the preferred legal framework, under COCA, differed from adoption, the policy was ingenuous at best in describing the legal relationship between the caregivers and the birth parents thus:

> What's different from adoption is that while the day-to-day care *responsibility and decision making for the child is held by the 'home for life' parents*, an ongoing legal relationship exists with the birth parents. This might mean the birth parents will seek occasional access visits, *or may wish* to be consulted about the more significant life events that might occur. In those instances social workers liaise and support the parties.[36]

An inherent risk with COCA in securing permanency for children, is of caregivers being challenged on issues of guardianship decision-making (in particular).[37] This has occurred where the child is placed with permanent caregivers and where OT still retains legal status, prior to orders for permanency being made. Once COCA orders are made, if there is a dispute as to guardianship – overseas holidays, haircuts (in some cultural situations), school enrolment, relocation or matters of health – the caregivers must first utilise mandatory out-of-court dispute resolution processes before filing an application with the family court for a determination on the dispute.[38] This places them in the same situation as separated parents of a child who cannot agree on such matters. Similarly, with contact/access or a challenge to care, an application could be filed at any time.[39] It was perceived that greater protections were required to protect children and caregivers from such challenges.

Special guardianship

Special guardianship was enacted as from 30 June 2016 as a vehicle for securing permanency for children in new families. The introductory bill noted that the intention was that in 'Home for Life' placements, guardianship can be 'tailored to meet the child's situation by allowing guardianship rights to be shared between the special guardians and the children's parents or vested solely in the special guardians'.[40] The jurisdiction can be exercised only if the appointment is for the

34 Unless the facts of the case allow for a successful application to be made to deprive a parent of their guardianship under section 29(3) of COCA, which is rare.

35 Section 16(3) of COCA provides that guardianship rights remain extant notwithstanding that a guardian does not care for the child. Subsection (5) requires consultation and joint decision-making between guardians.

36 New Zealand Department for Social Development and Employment, *Why You Should CareYour Care Matters: A Plan for Children in Care*, 2010, p. 17. Available at www.beehive.govt.nz/sites/default/files/CYF_Why_you_should_care.pdf

37 And not overlooking contact/access (COCA uses the expression 'contact': the OTA uses 'access') and day-to-day care.

38 Family Dispute Resolution Act 2013; the requirement is subject to limited exceptions, though a permanent caregiver could come within the exceptions.

39 COCA s 139A prevents a party to a previous proceeding filing any new and substantially similar proceeding within two years of a final order being made, subject to leave from a judge

40 Vulnerable Children Bill, Explanatory Note, p. 8.

purpose of providing the child with a 'long-term, safe, nurturing, stable, and secure environment that enhances the child's interests'.[41] Once appointed, the special guardian becomes a 'permanent caregiver' as defined. Although taking effect as from 2016, there have been relatively few special guardianship orders made.[42] In 2017, there were 39 orders made; in 2018, 48 and as at 16 September 2019, 56.[43] Two reasons may account for the low uptake. First, there has been an issue as to jurisdiction, and in particular the factual and legal circumstances in which the court is empowered to make special guardianship orders.[44] Second, there is a 'concern', expressed mostly informally, that special guardianship is akin to adoption, given that the caregivers so appointed could be a sole guardian or, if an additional guardian, may when appointed as a special guardian, be granted one or more exclusive rights of guardianship.[45]

Removal of orders to support permanency

The second significant statutory change made as from 2016 was the removal from the OTA of the ability of 'permanent caregivers' to obtain orders to support both them and the children in their care.[46]

The legislation now provides for the caregiver to be provided with support from OT as a discretionary exercise.[47] This occurs via an administrative process, involving a contracted agency charged with delivering a range of supports. It requires consultation between the caregiver, the social worker and the agency. An individualized support plan for up to 12 months, based on the needs of the child, 'will be negotiated and agreed to by all parties involved. The plan will be implemented, monitored and reviewed by the Permanent Caregiver Support Service (PCSS) after permanent living arrangements have been formalised'.[48] The PCSS administers two distinct processes – overseeing and reviewing permanent care support plans, and responding to permanent caregiver requests for financial and other assistance which arise in the future. If a new need arises, or an existing support plan is not adequately meeting the needs of the child, caregivers can approach the PCSS directly for financial and other assistance. In some situations, there is a mandatory obligation to provide support.[49] However, this is subject to such stringent

41 Section 113A(1) OTA.

42 In contrast, the COCA figures(orders made) were 2017 (340), 2018 (335) and 2019 (305). The statistics for both COCA and special guardianship were provided by Oranga Tamariki pursuant to a request under the Official Information Act 1982 at as 16 September 2019.

43 The figures provided do not differentiate between the types of special guardianship orders made, ie sole guardianship, additional guardianship or the latter with specific exclusive rights of guardianship being conferred.

44 *Chief Executive of the Ministry for Vulnerable Children v Grant-Shepherd* [2018] NZFLR 718.

45 When an order for sole guardianship is made under the OTA, the rights of all other guardians are suspended and of no effect. Section 114. The legal status of being a guardian remains, unlike an adoption. The Act is silent on what occurs when exclusive rights are conferred on the special guardian. It must, however, be the same.

46 These are services (primarily) and support orders. A services order was used to deliver specific assistance to the caregivers/child in order to address issues arising from the child's care and protection history/journey through care, for example, attachment therapy, therapy to address the consequences of trauma, assessment for foetal alcohol syndrome, teacher aide assistance and funding costs for supervised access.

47 Section 388A(1):

48 https://practice.orangatamariki.govt.nz/previous-practice-centre/policy/noho-ake-oranga/resources/support-and-assistance-for-permanent-caregivers/ This suggests that the permanency support plan is to be finalised after orders have been secured. In practice this process appears reversed. The plan is agreed upon and then orders made.

49 Section 399(2).

threshold criteria that it is unlikely that any permanent caregiver could obtain that support.[50] The act then sets out a process of first, internal review of any decision not to provide assistance that is sought and in accordance with processes established by OT and, second, a right of appeal to the Family Court.

Conclusion

As a consequence of the legislative changes that have occurred since 2016, the New Zealand experience of permanency for children in care is on the cusp of change. There are questions about special guardianship and whether it will become the dominant paradigm for achieving permanency, in contrast to COCA orders. There is (some) resistance to it being utilized, notwithstanding the policy drivers that led to its introduction – around securing certainty of guardianship decision-making when that is required and of preventing birth parents from destabilizing the placement. Those factors are arguably of more importance when children are in a non-kin placement, although in any given instance, there may be issues that may render the special guardianship framework being necessary. The theme of the 2019 amendments, however, whilst primarily (but not exclusively) of significance for Māori children – given the numbers in care – should have the effect of seeing children being far more routinely placed within their immediate/extended familial groups as matter of practice as opposed to being in non-kin care. The amendments will appropriately re-focus what was intended by the OTA when passed in 1989 about Māori children being seen as existing within a *whānau*, *hapū* and *iwi* kin matrix.[51] It will be the challenge for those working in the area – lawyers for parties, lawyers for children, social workers and judges – to address the tension perceived between that re-emphasized legislative expression of intent and the safety of that Māori child within *whānau*, *hapū* and *iwi*. The two are not at all incompatible.

50 Section 38A(2).
51 Dr A. Cooke, *The Black Letter Law Amendments*, New Zealand Law Society, Continuing Legal Education Seminar, Oranga Tamariki Act Changes, June 2019.

4.3

ADOPTION OF CHILDREN IN THE UNITED STATES AND ENGLAND AND WALES

Sanford N. Katz and John Eekelaar

Background

United Nations data show that at the beginning of this century the rate of domestic adoptions (the irrevocable transfer of parental status between individuals) in the United States was one of the highest in the world, three times that in United Kingdom, whose rate itself was about twice that of Germany and four times that of Italy.[1] In many European countries almost all adoptions are intercountry adoptions[2] (on which see Chapter 7.1 of this book). Excluding intercountry adoption, adoption is relatively unusual in most countries compared to the US and the UK, though it is growing in some.[3]

In both countries, adoption has responded to different pressures on families. The earliest US adoption laws provided additional placement options alongside indentured apprenticeships for poor, urban, children placed by their parents in 'orphanages'.[4] Massachusetts enacted the first US law regulating adoption in the US in 1851.[5] The law was unique because it was the first effort to establish judicial supervision over the irrevocable transfer of custody of a child from one adult to another, and because it shifted the focus of adoption policy from the parents to the child. To this end, the law provided for the investigation of prospective adoptive parents

1 UN Department of Economic and Social Affairs, Population Division, *Adoption: Trends and Policies*, New York: United Nations, 2009, p. 69.

2 Ibid., p. 74; J. Sturges and W. Selwyn, *International Overview of Adoption Policy and Practice*, Bristol: University of Bristol, 2001.

3 For example, Australia: see K. Murphy, M. Quartly and D. Cuthbert, '"In the Best Interests of the Child": Mapping the (Re) Emergence of Pro-Adoption Politics in Contemporary Australia', *Australian Journal of Politics and History* 55, 2009, 201–18. And see C Fenton-Glynn, *Adoption without Consent,* Directorate General for Internal Policies of the EU Parliament, Policy Department C: Citizens' Rights and Constitutional Affairs, 2015.

4 See S.L. Porter, 'A Good Home: Indenture and Adoption in Nineteenth Century Orphanages', in E.W. Carp (ed.), *A Historical Overview of American Adoption*, in E.W. Carp (ed.), *Adoption in America: Historical Perspectives*, Ann Arbor: University Michigan Press, 2004, ch. 2, and Introduction.

5 *See* Massachusetts Adoption of Children's Act of 1851, 1851 Mass. Acts, ch. 324 (May 24, 1851). The Supreme Judicial Court of Massachusetts in *Curtis v Curtis*, 71 Mass. (5 Gray) 535, 537 (1856) wrote that '[adoption] is not a question of mere property, … the interests of the minor is the principal thing to be considered'.

to determine their qualifications and fitness for parenthood. The English rejected this radical solution,[6] but allowed poor law authorities to assume parental rights over such children (known as 'poor law adoptions').[7] Legal adoption was introduced for England and Wales only in 1926 (but without inheritance rights until 1949).[8]

Both countries experienced a steady rise in adoptions over the century, with surges after World War II and during the 1960s. A significant goal was to provide for, and mask the origins of, 'illegitimate' children, and also to conceal infertility. This encouraged attempts to 'match' the adoptive parents' bodily features and ethnic background with the child's, so adoption was very often kept secret and generally a taboo subject.[9] In England adoptions peaked in 1968 at 24,831, declining to 4,317 with the virtual disappearance of 'baby' adoptions by 1999 as those stigmas disappeared and abortion became more available.[10] But adoptions from the 'care' system rose gradually, from 2,100 in 1994 to 3,770 in 2005, dropping back to 3,100 in 2011, rising to a high of 5,360 in 2015, thereafter falling by 28.7 percent to 3,820 in 2018.[11] Also in England, it has been suggested that the more recent growth of IVF has contributed significantly to the reduced number of adoptions,[12] although in the US it has been argued that subsidizing IVF has not affected adoption rates.[13]

England and Wales has a reputation for using adoption (mostly involuntary) as a route out of 'care' by the welfare authorities more than other European countries. However, as Lady Hale observed in *In the Matter of N (Children)*,[14] referring to research compiled by the Council of Europe[15] and commissioned by the European Union,[16] other member states do permit adoption without parental consent. However, she added that England and Wales is unusual in permitting parental consent to be dispensed with where the welfare of the child requires[17] rather than on more precise grounds of parental absence or misconduct. That country is also unusual in the speed and frequency with which it resorts to adoption as the way to provide a permanent home

6 N.V. Lowe, 'English Adoption Law: Past, Present and Future', in S.N. Katz, J. Eekelaar and M. Maclean (eds), *Cross Currents: Family Law and Policy in the US and England*, Oxford: Oxford University Press, 2000, ch. 14.
7 Poor Law Amendment Act 1889, s. 1.
8 Adoption of Children Act 1926.
9 See B.P. Gill, 'Adoption Agencies and the Search for the Ideal Family 1918–65', in E.W. Carp (ed.) op. cit., n 4, pp. 160–80.
10 Lowe, op. cit., n 6. J. Lewis, 'Adoption: The Nature of Policy Shifts in England and Wales 1972–2002', *International Journal of Law, Policy and the Family* 18, 2004, 235–55.
11 Department for Education, *Children Looked after in England (Including Adoption)*, Year Ending 31 March 2018, 15 November 2018. Available at https://assets.publishing.service.gov.uk/government/uploads/system/uploads/attachment_data/file/756232/Children_looked_after_in_England_2018_Text.pdf
12 See BBC News, 3 November 2018. Available at www.bbc.co.uk/news/health-46081726. The suggestion was made by the head of the Children and Family Courts Advisory and Support Service (Cafcass).
13 I.G. Cohen and D.L. Chen, 'Trading-Off Reproductive Technology and Adoption: Does Subsidizing IVF Decrease Adoption Rates and Should It Matter?', *Minn. L. Rev.* 95, 2010, 485; S.F. Appleton and R.A. Pollak, 'Exploring the Connections between Adoption and IVF: Twibling Analyses', *Minnesota Law Review Headnotes* 95, 2011, 60 argue that IVF is preferable to adoption owing to problematic aspects of the latter. See also I. Cohen and D.L. Chen, 'Trading-Off Reproductive Technology and Adoption: A Response to Appleton and Pollak', *Minnesota Law Review*, 24 June 2012. Available at https://ssrn.com/abstract=2090021
14 [2016] UKSC 15, para 3.
15 O. Borzova, *Social Services in Europe: Legislation and Practice of the Removal of Children from Their Families in Council of Europe Member States*, Report to the Parliamentary Assembly, 2015, Doc 13730.
16 Fenton-Glynn, op. cit., n 3.
17 Adoption and Children Act 2002, section 52(1)(b).

for children who for one reason or another cannot live with their families. The European Court of Human Rights has, however, held the law to be compatible with the right to respect for private and family life, protected by art. 8 of the European Convention on Human Rights.[18] Scotland, which has similar provisions, does seem to use it less often.[19] (See further Chapter 4.1 of this book.)

In the US, the percentage of children voluntarily relinquished by never-married white women dropped from 19.3 percent before 1973 to 1.7 percent in 1989–95.[20] Nevertheless differences between the countries regarding privately arranged adoptions are to be found with respect to step-parent adoptions and in cases of surrogacy. While the former have become more common in the US with the increase of serial marriage,[21] in England they have been strongly discouraged since 1975 in favour of orders under the divorce jurisdiction.[22] In the US adoption is often the remedy in surrogacy cases where the genetic material of one spouse is used in the reproductive process.[23] For example, where the woman carrying a child has been impregnated by a man married to another woman and that man and woman want the child, the woman who gave birth would have to relinquish the child to the man (the father), and his wife would have to adopt the child. In England, under certain conditions, this could be achieved by a parental order (see Chapters 3.1 and 3.2 of this book).

The countries also differ in the degree of supervision over the adoption process. While each requires judicial sanction for the adoption order, since 1982 in England any placement with a non-relative must be made by an approved agency.[24] Only four US states require this. Others allow individuals (often lawyers) to arrange 'independent' adoptions. The argument in favour is predicated on the notion that children are the property of their birth parents, and those parents should have exclusive authority to make decisions about their children's lives.[25] However independent adoption has assumed the nature of a business

> basically trading in children, even though the sale of children is prohibited, and state statutes limit fees relating to adoption to administrative costs and are often monitored by the courts. Yet questions have been raised about whether such limitations are effective given the broad definition of administrative costs.[26]

The advantage of agency placements is that agencies are staffed by trained social workers who have the skill, experience and understanding to deal with the multifaceted issues that are involved in relinquishing a child for adoption. Further, agencies can provide post-adoption services to the birth parent, adoptive parents and even the child. In placing children in adoptive homes,

18 *YC v United Kingdom* (2012) 55 EHRR 33.

19 In Scotland 1.9 percent of 'looked after' children were adopted in 2015, and 2.1 percent in 2017, compared to about 5.9 percent in England in 2017: Scottish Government, Children's Social Work Statistics, Scotland, 2015–16 (28 March 2017) and Department for Education, Children looked after in England (including adoption), SFR 50/2017, 28 September 2017.

20 U.S. Department of Health and Human Services, *Child Welfare Information Gateway*, March 2005.

21 See S.N. Katz, *Family Law in America*, Oxford: Oxford University Press, 2003, pp. 174–6.

22 Lowe, op. cit., n 6, p. 321.

23 Katz, op. cit., n 21, pp. 161–7.

24 Lowe, op. cit., n 6, p. 325.

25 In *Pierce v Society of Sisters*, 268 US 510, 534 (1925), the US Supreme Court stated: 'It is cardinal with us that the custody, care and nurture of the child reside first in the parents, whose primary function and freedom include preparation for obligations the state can neither supply nor hinder'. See further Katz, op. cit., n 21, pp. 158–61.

26 Katz, op. cit., n 21, pp. 159–60.

however, in the US agencies have discretion in applying the best interests of the particular child and may restrict placement to a heterosexual married couple who reflects traditional cultural values even though as shall be discussed later, the United States Supreme Court has held that same-sex married couples are to be on equal standing with heterosexual married couples and accordingly should be afforded the benefits of marriage.

The post-war surge in adoptions in the US led to a dilution of the idea that adoption is a replication of the natural family. Transracial, intercountry and older-child adoptions increased. The first subsequently encountered resistance on grounds similar to current objections to intercountry adoption (see Chapter 7.1 of this book). Those who considered the continuity of race as a vital concern in the placement of African-American children believed that placing an African-American child with a couple not of that race harmed the child's identity. Others deemed racial considerations to be less important than the value of overall emotional and physical health and immediate placement. This position has been criticized as concealing the societal value of assimilation and integration, placing those values over the preservation and continuity of the African-American culture.[27] These issues have arisen in a different way in England in the context of recent government pressure to promote adoption of children currently in the care system (discussed later).

Types of adoption

Today in the US, adoption may be achieved in three different ways: the formal irrevocable relinquishment of the child by her birth mother and father (if known and available) to the adoptive parent or parents either privately or through a licensed adoption agency (the 'voluntary system'); the ultimate result of a successful termination of parental rights hearing where allegations of child neglect, abuse or abandonment have been proven (the 'involuntary system'); and the outcome of certain surrogacy arrangements or other assisted reproductive techniques. It may not be possible to develop a single family policy that accounts for all three of these methods of family formation unless they are unified under the doctrine of the best interests of the child. In adoption, the best interests of the child should reflect the needs of the child as defined by accepted child development standards, including the need to be raised by an adult or adults who understand the complexities of adoption, genuinely want the child, and have the capacity to provide the child with the appropriate nurturing.[28]

The voluntary system

Standards for placement

In 1972 the US Supreme Court made the fathers of illegitimate children necessary participants in the adoption process.[29] In England, an unmarried father will normally be entitled to be notified of adoption proceedings concerning his child, though his consent is not necessary unless he has 'parental responsibility'.[30] If private (independent) placement is allowed, the birth parents can choose anyone as adoptive parents. In England, the parents' consent must be 'unconditional',

27 R.-A.W. Howe, 'Race Matters in Adoption', *Family Law Quarterly* 42, 2008, 465–80.
28 Katz, op. cit., n 17, pp. 172–4.
29 *Stanley v Illinois*, 405 U.S. 645 (1972).
30 *Re A, B and C (Adoption: Notification of Fathers and Relatives)* [2020] EWCA Civ 41.

though they may restrict it to placement with identified persons.[31] If an agency is used (as required in England), the agency may use the process to promote its own values, though both private and agency adoptions will be subject to judicial approval against statutory standards. In both jurisdictions the expressed standard for decision-making in the adoption context is the best interests of the child.

But agencies have been affected by changes in community values. In the 1950s a statutory requirement to place a child with persons of the same faith as the child 'when practicable' was interpreted strictly in Massachusetts, but less so in New York.[32] US agencies accepting funds from charities that condition their support on non-discriminatory policies cannot place children on a religious basis,[33] and in England, where joint adoption by same-sex couples is permitted,[34] it has been held that a Catholic agency would contravene discrimination law (the Equality Act 2010) by refusing to accept gay couples as prospective adopters.[35] Although this created fears that Catholic adoption agencies would close, it seems that at least some have continued to operate, for example by accepting the new regulations but cutting formal ties with the Catholic Church (which may or may not have affected their funding from that source) like, for example, Catholic Caring Services, which changed its name to Caritas Care on becoming independent from the Diocese of Lancaster, but references its 'Catholic roots' as 'informing its character and mission', at the same time openly accepting gay adopters.[36]

Before 2003 same-sex couples could not marry in any American jurisdiction and therefore it was highly unlikely that they could adopt a child given placement standards of adoption agencies that would prefer traditional married couples over unmarried couples. Second parent adoption, however, provided an opportunity for a partner of a parent to adopt her child if the partner had acted as a *de facto* parent.[37] In *Goodridge v Department of Public Health*[38] the Supreme Judicial Court of Massachusetts, the oldest state supreme court in the United States, allowed a same-sex couple to be married in the state. One of the state's major arguments against this was that heterosexual marriage ensured an optimal setting for child-rearing. The court rejected the argument and stated that adoption was an alternative to procreative heterosexual intercourse. For a state to allow same-sex marriage would seem to support the approval of same-sex couples as parents.

Twelve years later, the United States Supreme Court decided what might be considered the most important family law case in modern American law in that it altered the definition of marriage and thus changed an institution. In *Obergefell v Hodges*,[39] the court held in a 5–4 opinion that the right to marry was a fundamental right inherent in the liberty of the person, and under the Due Process and Equal Protection Clauses of the Fourteenth Amendment same-sex couples may not be deprived the right and that liberty (see further Chapters 1.1 and 1.4 of this book). The majority opinion provides a sweeping history of marriage in the United States, illustrating how important it is to the culture. Absent in the opinion, however, is a discussion on the impact

31 Adoption and Children Act 2002, ss. 19 and 52(5).

32 Katz, op. cit., n 17, pp. 171–2.

33 Ibid., p. 171.

34 Adoption and Children Act 2002, s. 144(4).

35 *Catholic Care (Diocese of Leeds) v Charity Commission* FTC 52/2011 (Upper Tribunal, Tax and Charity Chamber).

36 See W. Oddie, 'How Many Catholic Adoption Societies Have Actually Closed Down; and How Many Are Now Quietly Handing Children over to Gay Adoptive Parents?', *Catholic Herald*, 4 July 2013; Caritas Care website: www.caritascare.org.uk/ and www.caritascare.org.uk/thats-gay-exploration-sex-families/

37 For a discussion of second parent adoption, with case citations, see Katz, op. cit., n 17, pp. 194–5.

38 798 N.E.2d 941 (Mass. 2003).

39 U.S., 135 S.Ct. 2584, 192 L.Ed2d 609 (2015).

on the complex law of marriage. For example, the court omits to state how presumptions, like two people living together are presumed to be married, or a child born during the marriage is presumed to be the product of that relationship, is to be applied, or how informal marriage, like common law marriage is to be evaluated.

More important for this discussion is Justice Kennedy's concluding comment.

> Finally, it must be emphasized that religions, and those who adhere to religious doctrines, may continue to advocate with utmost, sincere conviction that, by divine precepts, same–sex marriage should not be condoned. The First Amendment ensures that religious organizations and persons are given proper protection as they seek to teach the principles that are so fulfilling and so central to their lives and faiths, and to their own deep aspirations to continue the family structure they have long revered.[40]

The question to be asked is to what extent does this statement invite adoption agencies affiliated with a particular religion, like Catholic Charities, to discriminate against same-sex couples as adoption applicants? It should first be noted, that in the United States, if an adoption agency is affiliated with a particular religion, and it seeks to obtain public funds or funds from private charitable organizations, like the United Fund, it cannot discriminate in its placement of children for adoption. In other words, it cannot expressly prefer a couple of the agency's religious affiliation over applicants of a different religion. However, the discrimination may be disguised or hidden in placement decisions, for example, by relegating same-sex couples to the bottom of the list of potential adoptive parents, or by assigning hard to place children, for example, children with medical issues or learning disabilities, older children or children in sibling groups with same-sex couples, a practice known to occur with single male or female applicants.

Two years later, the United States Supreme Court was faced with the issue of identifying same-sex married couples on birth certificates. In *Pavan v Smith*,[41] the court, decided that birth certificates for children born to same-sex married couples should list the same-sex couple as parents of the child. In so holding, the court reversed the decision of the Arkansas Supreme Court, which denied naming the spouse of the same-sex couple as the parent on the child's birth certificate, requiring such a spouse to use adoption in order to be recognized as a parent. In a Per Curiam opinion, the court held that treating the same-sex couple differently from heterosexual married couples infringed on *Obergefell*'s commitment to provide same-sex couples 'the constellation of benefits that the States have linked to marriage'.[42]

Open adoption and access to adoption records

From the 1970s in the US, the secrecy hitherto surrounding adoption diminished and it became more common for birth parents to know the identity of the adoptive parents and even retain some contact with the child.[43] This was partly to encourage more adoptions, but also a recognition of the rights of adopted children.[44] In 1973 the English High Court held that contact

40 135 U.S. at 2607.

41 582 U.S., 137 S.Ct. 2075, 198 L.Ed.2d 636 (2017) (per curiam).

42 135 S. Ct. at 2601.

43 In 1988–89 it was estimated that 55 percent of adoptive families in California had contact with the child's birth family two years after the adoption: Carp (ed.), op. cit., n 4, p. 17.

44 Ibid., pp. 17–18; Katz, op. cit., n 17, pp. 168–70.

between a birth mother and her adopted child was not inconsistent with adoption,[45] and in 1975 adults who had been adopted as children in England and Wales acquired the right to obtain their original birth certificate, allowing an Adoption Contact Register to be created from 1991 which provided a means by which children and birth parents who wish it might be re-united. It seems that more adoptees seek this than birth parents or siblings.[46] However, most contact seems to be by way of annual or biennial correspondence than direct meeting.[47] Although US adoptees may not have a constitutional right of access to their adoption records,[48] a number of US jurisdictions allow adult adoptees access to their birth certificate, and a constitutional challenge to this by birth parents on the ground that this violated their rights to privacy, has failed.[49]

The involuntary system

Because of the decrease in the number of new-born infants made available for adoption by their birth mothers, in both the US and England children who are candidates for adoption are usually products of the child protection system. Most have been abused, neglected or abandoned by their birth parents and have been the subject of termination of parental rights proceedings. The English term for this is 'public law' adoption.

Child abuse and neglect grew into a national social problem in the US in the 1960s. The federal government took the lead in providing the states with model legislation to address it from a legal perspective. The result was the production of the Model Act to Free Children for Permanent Placement and the Model Subsidized Adoption Act.[50] The policy behind the former was to reduce the number of children in temporary foster care and make them available for adoption. Rather than labeling the act a termination of parental rights law, which it essentially was, the drafters wanted to emphasize that the focus was on the child and the child's need for permanence, not on the parent's unfitness. At the same time, the framers recognized that parental rights had to be respected by providing parents a fair judicial process before their rights could be permanently terminated. The aim of the drafters was to achieve a balance between parental rights and the child's interests. The policy behind the Model Subsidized Adoption Act was to facilitate the adoption of hard-to-place children by providing the children, not the adoptive parents, with a subsidy. In that way, prospective adoptive parents, usually the child's foster parents, would not be undertaking a financial burden by adopting their foster child. Linking the two

45 *Re J (a minor)* [1973] Fam 106.

46 Lowe, op. cit., n 6, p. 327; J. Haskey, 'Adoptees and Relatives Who Wish to Contact One Another Using the Adoption Contact Register: Trends, Relationships and Proportions of Records Matched', *Population Trends* 106, 2001, 15–28. Access to such knowledge is protected under art. 8 of the European Convention on Human Rights ('respect for private life'). Although the European Court has held it can be outweighed by a mother's wish for anonymity (*Odièvre v France* (2004) 38 EHRR 43), it seems that the court failed to give sufficient weight to the child's 'right to know': *Godelli v Italy*, App. No. 33783/09, judgment 25 September 2012.

47 C. Jones, 'Openness in Adoption: Challenging the Narrative of Historical Progress', *Child & Family Social Work* 2016, 2; J. Doughty, S. Meakings and K. Shelton, 'Rights and Relationships of Children Who Are Adopted from Care', *International Journal of Law, Policy and the Family* 33, 2019, 1–23.

48 *ALMA Society Inc v Mellon*, 601 F. 2d 1238 (2d Cir.), *cert denied*, 100 S. Ct. 531 (1979).

49 *Doe v Sundquist*, 2 S.W. 3d 919 (Tenn. 1999); Katz, op. cit., n 21, p. 170.

50 The Model Act to Free Children for Permanent Placement is reproduced in S.N. Katz, 'Freeing Children for Permanent Placement Through a Model Act', *Family Law Quarterly* 12, 1978, 203–52. The Model Subsidized Adoption Act is reproduced in S.N. Katz and U.M. Gallagher, 'Subsidized Adoption in America', *Family Law Quarterly* 10, 1976–77, 3–54. Both Acts were developed in part by the first author.

Model Acts was designed to facilitate the removal of foster children from the foster care rolls and provide them with an adoptive home if available. More often than not, the permanent home was that of the children's foster parents.

Concerned at the numbers of older, minority and special needs children in foster care, in 1980 Congress authorized federal government funding to support subsidized adoption provided states made 'reasonable efforts' to prevent the need to remove children from their homes and to return those who had been removed.[51] However, the numbers of children in foster care more than doubled over the following 15 years. The Adoption and Safe Families Act 1997 maintained the requirement to use reasonable efforts to return children, but created exceptions in various circumstances of parental unfitness, sought to hasten the process for severing parental rights and finding 'permanent' solutions, and provided adoption incentive payments for compliant states. There is evidence that, following the act, removed children may have a decreased likelihood of returning home and increased likelihood of being adopted,[52] and that children of substance-abusing parents are as likely to return home, but more likely to spend less time in foster care and be adopted.[53] However, the act has been criticized for perpetuating two contrasting ideals, adoption and family reunification, when intermediate options may be available, such as open adoption and kinship guardianship.[54] (See further Chapter 6.2 of this book.)

In 2000 the UK government announced that 'more can and should be done to promote wider use of adoption for children being "looked after" by social services who cannot return to their birth parents' and announced a goal of increasing the number of public law adoptions in England by 40 percent over the following three years.[55] The Adoption and Children Act 2002 (ACA) therefore sought to facilitate the procedure for achieving this. In essence, it was (and is) still necessary for a court to make a finding that the child is suffering, or is likely to suffer significant harm as a consequence of parental behaviour, but the court could now at the same time make a 'placement' order for the child's adoption (the paramount consideration being the child's welfare throughout their life) either with the parents' consent or without it 'if the welfare of the child requires the consent to be dispensed with'.[56]

As has been noted, this policy was barely successful, adoptions dropping back from 3,770 in 2005 to 3,100 in 2011, and, after a brief rise, beginning to fall again in 2015. In 2013 the Supreme Court had set rigorous conditions for involuntary adoptions (to be a 'last resort')[57] and the decline has been attributed variously to the immediate effects of a Court of Appeal judgment in 2013[58] which criticized existing social work practice and sought to impose strict evidential and procedural standards,[59] and 'austerity' policies introduced in 2010 which reduced local authority resources. Despite this, English policymakers have renewed efforts to encourage

51 Adoption Assistance and Child Welfare Act 1980.

52 R.P. Barth, F. Wulczyn and T. Crea, 'From Anticipation to Evidence: Research on the Adoption and Safe Families Act', *Virginia Journal of Social Policy and Law* 12, 2004–5, 371–99, 387–8.

53 A. Rockhill, 'Is the Adoption and Safe Families Act Influencing Child Welfare Outcomes for Families with Substance Abuse Issues?', *Child Maltreatment* 12, 2007, 7–19.

54 L.S. Adler, 'The Meaning of Permanence: A Critical Analysis of the Adoption and Safe Families Act of 1997', *Harvard Journal on Legislation* 38, 2001, 1–36.

55 Department of Health, *Adoption: A New Approach*, London: The Stationery Office, 2000. In Australia the treatment of 'removed' children had a profound impact on public perceptions of adoption. But from 2007 the adoption of children of substance-abusing parents, and as an alternative to abortion, has been promoted: see Murphy, Quartly and. Cuthbert, op. cit., n 3.

56 Adoption and Children Act 2002, ss. 1, 21, 52.

57 *Re B* [2013] UKSC 33.

58 *re B-S* [2013] EWCA Civ 1146.

59 See J.M. Masson, 'Disruptive Judgments', *Child & Family Law Quarterly* 29, 2017, 401.

the adoption of these children. In the belief that social workers were too concerned with 'racial matching', the Children and Families Act 2014 removed an express requirement that the court give 'due consideration' to the child's racial origin (although it will remain part of the general considerations), and attempted to significantly accelerate the process by requiring decisions to be made within a 26-week framework, extendable only where necessary to decide the matter 'justly'.[60] Indeed, it has been held that an agency's refusal to recruit a couple as potential adopters on the basis of their ethnicity not only contravened equality legislation but also extant regulatory guidance.[61] Other provisions, such enhancing adoption support services, statutory leave and pay entitlement for adopters, advance consideration of arrangements for post-adoption contact had the same objective, though these suffered from 'austerity' financial policies. A model of 'early permanence' whereby, instead of initially placing a child with foster-carers while the adoption processes took place, the prospective adopters were also approved as foster-carers, so the child could be placed directly with them prior to the making of the adoption order, in some cases looking after the child concurrently with the birth parents, has had some success, especially in Northern Ireland.[62]

Despite these measures, the number of children 'looked after' by local authorities who were adopted dropped by 28 percent between 2015 and 2018, despite a 205 percent *increase* in the number of 'looked after' children over that period.[63] So the political pressure to increase the rate of adoptions continues, for example, by ranking local authorities according to their 'scorecards' on the number of adoptions they arrange, leading to concerns about distorting judgments and sidelining alternatives, such as special guardianship (a 'private law' order placing the child in the long-term care of wider family or others known to the parents) (see also Chapter 4.1 of this book). Furthermore, while courts are bound to consider post-adoption contact, it appears that courts are reluctant to impose this against the wishes of the adopters.[64] The most recent survey paints a mixed picture however. Fifty-six percent of responding adoptive parents said they faced 'significant or extreme' challenges, and during 2018, of adopted young people aged 16–18, 39 percent had been involved with mental health services, 27 percent were not in education, employment or training, 25 percent had been excluded from education or fired from employment, 23 percent had alcohol or drug problems and 16 percent had been involved in the criminal justice system. Nevertheless, 79 percent of adoptive parents said they would encourage others to consider adopting.[65]

Conclusion

Both in law and in practice, adoption traditionally has included two basic events: the termination of the birth parents' custodial rights (if not always inheritance rights) and the adoption

60 Children and Families Act 2014, ss. 3, 14. This applies to England only, the matter being devolved in Wales.

61 *Sandeep and Reena Mander v Royal Borough of Windsor and Maidenhead and Adopt Berkshire*, Oxford County Court Case No: C01RG184 (2019).

62 adoptionuk, The Adoption Barometer, July 2019. Available at www.adoptionuk.org/Handlers/Download.ashx?IDMF=fd3d3969-8138-4ede-befd-1018fe629c29

63 Department for Education, *Children Looked after in England (Including Adoption)*, Year Ending, 31 March 2018, 15 November 2018. Available at https://assets.publishing.service.gov.uk/government/uploads/system/uploads/attachment_data/file/756232/Children_looked_after_in_England_2018_Text.pdf

64 See Fenton-Glynn, op. cit., n 3, 3.2.2; *Re B (A Child: Post-Adoption Contact)* [2019] EWCA Civ 29.

65 adoptionuk, *The Adoption Barometer*, July 2019. This was based on an online survey which drew 3500 responses.

procedure resulting in the permanent placement of the child with the adoptive parents.[66] Anything less than that would be foster care, not adoption. However, this is no longer the case. Open adoption is a relatively new concept that provides for the continuity of a limited relationship between birth parents and an adopted child. This might be seen as a victory for parental rights over children's interests. However, it can also be seen as in the interests especially of older children, who will often have experienced relationships with their birth family.[67] Adoption may provide additional security in the child's placement, which other orders may lack, but it may not be necessary to implement a complete transfer of parental status to achieve this. Special guardianship, introduced in England by the Adoption and Children Act 2002, perhaps provides a 'middle way' because, while the special guardian shares parental responsibility with the birth parents (though with the special guardian having the final say), the latter may apply to vary the order with leave of the court, and this can be given only if there has been a 'significant change in circumstances' since making the order. Unlike adoption, special guardianship ceases when the child reaches 18. (See further Chapter 4.1 of this book.)

The institution of adoption in the twenty-first century is totally different from what it was in the nineteenth century and the beginning of the twentieth, when adoption was merely the judicial approval of the irrevocable transfer of a child born to one set of parents to another. Over a century ago, adoption was looked upon as an alternative to the normal biological formation of a family. Children who were the subjects of adoption then were mostly illegitimate, neglected or not wanted by their birth parents for a variety of reasons, including the inability to raise them because of poverty. Adults who adopted children were often thought of as incapable of conceiving a child with all the negative connotations that would carry. It is no wonder, then, that adoption was concealed from everyone, even the child herself, through altered birth records and sealed court records. That changed during the latter half of the twentieth century when litigation over the right to know one's parents made certain information available to adult adopted children.

In general, both biological and adoptive parents have benefited from the changes in adoption laws and processes over the past century. Indeed, it is difficult to overcome the classification of children as parental property. (See further Chapter 4.4 of this book.) The fact that all but four US jurisdictions allow a birth parent the right to place her child for adoption with the person or persons of her choosing is a victory for personal autonomy even though ultimately a judge must approve the placement. However, it is in its use as a child welfare measure for disabled, abused and neglected children that adoption faces its greatest challenges. Governments may have preferred it to long-term fostering not only because they believed it was better for the children (although that is not clear) but because it might be less expensive. But the need for post-placement support can continue for adopted and fostered children. Adoption seems to imply a greater break from the birth family. But even that may not necessarily be the case, though it could signal that return to the birth family is ruled out. Like marriage, adoption is not a static institution with only one definition. The fact that adoption changes with society makes its future unpredictable.

66 Katz, op. cit., n 21, pp. 180–1.

67 See J. Triseliotis, J. Shireman and M. Hundleby, *Adoption: Theory, Policy and Practice*, London: Cassell, 1997, pp. 89–90, and D. Howe, *Patterns of Adoption*, Oxford: Blackwell, 1998, suggesting the potential benefits of open adoption for older children.

4.4

THE MORAL BASIS OF CHILDREN'S RELATIONAL RIGHTS

James G. Dwyer

'Children's rights' connotes to many a plea for special assistance, a claim to sympathy and charity for a vulnerable population. They are positive rights, dependent on adults' choosing to be generous, and thus inherently weaker than the negative liberties that respect for autonomous individuals entails. In addition, when thinking about children's rights many imagine only particular aspects of upbringing that arise after children are embedded in a family, such as schooling, medical care and discipline. Children's coming to be in one particular family rather than another in the first place is generally not thought to be something regarding which they have rights; the family setting is taken for granted, parenting by biological parents assumed as a natural, supra-legal condition.[1]

In fact, however, most of what children need for their healthy development is best viewed as a matter of moral entitlement quite like what autonomous adults demand for themselves, resting on notions of negative liberty, contract and equality. Only modest conceptual modification is necessary to account for children's lack of autonomy – namely, allowing for their rights more routinely to be exercised by a proxy (rather than only occasionally, as with autonomous adults).[2] Moreover, the scope of children's moral rights extends to all aspects of their family life, includ-

1 Many moral and political philosophers have endeavoured – all unsuccessfully, in my view–to justify the common belief that biological parents have a moral right to become legal parents to, and raise, their offspring. Recent examples include M. Chobli, 'How Procreation Generates Parental Rights and Obligations', in J. Ahlberg and M. Chobli (eds), *Procreation, Parenthood, and Educational Rights: Ethical and Philosophical Issues*, New York: Routledge, 2017, pp. 230–45; M. Moschella, *To Whom Do Children Belong? Parental Rights, Civic Education, and Children's Autonomy*, New York: Cambridge University Press, 2016; S.M. Liao, *The Right to Be Loved*, New York: Oxford University Press, 2015; and C. MacLeod, 'Parental Competency and the Right to Parent', in S. Hannan, S. Brennan and R. Vernon (eds), *Permissible Progeny? The Morality of Procreation and Parenting*, New York: Oxford University Press, 2015, pp. 227–46.

2 Even some Will Theorists allow for this. See R. Cruft, 'The Circularity of the Interest and Will Theories of Rights', in M. McBride (ed.), *New Essays on the Nature of Rights*, Oxford: Hart Publishing, 2017, pp. 169–86 (noting theorists who have made this concession and arguing that they have no principled basis for making it). Along with most other rights theorists, I adopt the Interest Theory of rights, under which there is no conceptual difficulty in ascribing rights to beings who are non-autonomous. For defence of the latter theory, see, e.g. M. Kramer, 'Some Doubts about Alternatives to the Interest Theory of Rights', *Ethics* 123, 2013, 245, 246 (2013).

ing formation and termination of family relationships, just as does the scope of adults' rights. From the first moment of a child's life, we should ask not (just) what can we who happen to care about the child do to improve his or her life, but what rights does that child have that prohibit us, individually or collectively, from doing things detrimental to his or her well-being and life prospects, including a poor choice of caretakers.

This chapter schematizes the moral rights of children relevant to their basic welfare and protection from harm. It first addresses formation of children's family relationships, then regulation of particular aspects of their upbringing.

Children's rights to enter or avoid family relationships

A new-born child is a separate human being with needs and interests distinct from those of birth parents. In fact, the child's interests can be in conflict with those of birth parents; the latter typically wish to serve as the child's legal parents and custodians, but they might not be the best choice for that role among available potential caregivers. And it is a choice. Birth parents make a choice, whether they will make themselves available for a family relationship with the child; the state does not force interaction with one's offspring, and it empowers birth parents to relinquish their statutory claim to legal parenthood.[3] The state also makes a choice, reflected in codified or judicially crafted parentage laws, whether it will confer legal parent status on the birth parents or on someone else. With that state-conferred status, legal parents can call on state officials to help them retain possession of the child and exclude others who might wish to take possession of or simply interact with the child. In short, the state creates parent-child relationships, and not only in the adoption context but also when biological parents serve as legal parents and custodians; the state confers legal parenthood status, and that status is the practical foundation of social parenthood.

The state thus takes action in the case of every child that largely determines the child's life course and well-being, given the highly impactful role parents play in any person's life. That particular state actors, such as legislators or judges, might make a particular choice regarding legal parentage based on notions of natural law or moral rights does not mean they are not choosing. State actors play a crucial causal role in formation of children's family life even if they believe they could not morally make a different choice. As a practical matter, they *could* make a different choice, and whatever reasons they have for the choice they do make should be subject to examination.

Choosing family members for someone is an extraordinary thing for the state to do. We adults have a right against the state presuming to do that for us. There is no question of the state's forcing us to be in social relationships with any other human beings. With respect to parent-child relationships, although western states today extract money from some unwilling biological parents (in the form of child support: see Chapters 2.6–2.7, 3.4 and 6.5 of this book), in an effort to privatize the cost of raising children, they do not force those adults to assume a parenting role. And with respect to legal relationships between adults, the state does not force anyone into marriages they have not chosen themselves. For the state to do so would clearly violate negative moral rights, rights embodied in modern constitutions and human rights conventions. This would be so even if the state's aim was just to gratify other individuals' wish to be in a relationship with us or to reward others whom it views as deserving.

3 See, e.g. Mass. Gen. Laws Ann. ch. 210, § 2 (parental consent to adoption).

Children also have this negative moral right against forced intimate association, because they too have tremendous interests at stake in connection with their social relationships, especially family life. Children are also persons under the constitutions and conventions that embody that moral right in law. This would be clear to all in the context of adoption; if the state were to place children in parent-child relationships with adults other than birth parents in an arbitrary fashion or in disregard of children's welfare (e.g. giving them to infertile mentally ill adults as a therapeutic measure), everyone would perceive the violation of children's rights.

There is nothing relevantly different about the state's choice of a child's first caregivers; children have a presumptive right against the state's forcing them into *any* relationship. It is simply the case that children's predicament necessitates the state's nevertheless doing so, such that if done properly the state's infringement of that right is not a violation of it. We might say that placing children into a parent-child relationship with good caregivers is a justified infringement. Or we might impute to children a limited waiver of their right, the crucial limitation being that the state act with the sole aim of benefiting the children and do so competently. The state could not reasonably justify its infringement of this right by saying it is aiming to gratify desires of other individuals or to further collective aims, any more than it could do so to justify infringing the same right of adults. And we could not reasonably impute to children a waiver of their right for the purpose of enabling the state to gratify other persons or to serve state ends.

Regardless of how conceptualized, then, the state's infringing a new-born child's negative right against forced association is justified only if and to the extent that the state aims to serve the child's interests. Thus, parentage laws morally must aim to choose the best available parents for any given child. As a practical matter, we cannot expect the state to do this perfectly, but we can expect it to not knowingly make very bad choices when good choices are available. Yet the state in modern western societies routinely does this; it knows some birth parents have seriously problematic histories of child maltreatment and/or severe dysfunctions such as drug addiction that will prevent them from caring adequately for a child, but it confers legal parent status on them anyway, with permanently damaging consequences for the children. It does this despite the tremendous over-supply of good applicants for adoption of new-borns. The state might reasonably assume it is best for most new-born children to be raised by biological parents, but it is patently false to suppose this true for all children, and it is inexcusable not to exclude birth parents as to whom it is manifestly untrue. Existing parentage laws are morally condemnable and in need of reform.[4]

In sum, we should not overlook the huge role parentage laws play in children's lives, and we should recognize that children have a negative moral right against the state's applying to them parentage laws that force some into family relationships with adults unfit to care for them. Keeping children out of the custody of dysfunctional birth parents is not gratuitous on the part of the state, neither in the context of adoption nor in creating a child's first family, and insisting that the state do so is not a matter of asserting positive rights. In essence, the state stands in a fiduciary role with respect to each new-born child when it makes the parentage decision, and in that role the state must decide based solely on its best judgment of what is in a new-born's

4 Some movement toward reform is reflected in the U.S. in two developments of the past quarter-century – namely, federal law mandating that states require birthing facilities to report any positive toxicology tests of new-borns to the local child protection agency and four states' adoption of 'Birth Match' programs that cross-check new birth records against the state's database for past maltreatment cases. Both of these screening efforts could trigger a process that culminates in placement of the new-born with adoptive parents. See J.G. Dwyer, *Liberal Child Welfare Policy and Its Destruction of Black Lives*, New York: Routledge, 2018, Ch. 4.

child's best interests. A corollary of this view of children's situation is that no adults have a moral right to be in a parent-child with a particular child independently of whether that is in the child's best interests – that is, unless and until the state properly makes a reciprocal choice of that adult on behalf of the child. The right we adults have against forced association does not evaporate when some other person who wishes to initiate an intimate relationship with us has made some extraordinary effort to benefit us; we remain entitled to refuse that partnership on no other grounds than we think it not in our best interests going forward. No plausible moral principle supports a different view of children's right against forced association.[5]

Regulating children's upbringing

To survive and thrive, children need to avoid harmful conduct toward them and to receive several basic goods. Do children have any negative rights to underwrite a demand for these things?

Popular and scholarly discussion of child maltreatment commonly ascribes to children a negative moral right against gratuitous violence, with a corresponding duty on the part of legal parents to refrain from such violence. Many people, however, view the state's position *vis-à-vis* child maltreatment as that of innocent bystander. On this view, it violates no negative right of children to leave them unprotected from parental abuse or neglect, and a demand for state protection amounts to an assertion of positive right against the state, a claim for assistance rather than forbearance, something the Anglo-American legal system is generally loath to ascribe to individuals. The U.S. Supreme Court took this view in *DeShaney v Winnebago County*.[6]

But this is a quite inaccurate perception of the state's situation. As shown earlier, the state plays a crucial role in creating parent-child relationships in the first place. The state also plays a crucial role in children's daily lives after legal and social parent-child relationships are in place, because it establishes the legal rules that govern those relationships, including rules that confer on legal parents extraordinary power over various aspects of children's lives. Negative rights of the child should constrain the state's choices as to the content of that power, just as negative rights of incompetent adults constrain the state's conferral of power over their lives on guardians. The default legal regime in western society is that everyone, including children, possesses a negative right against encroachment on their lives and bodies by other private parties. We all also possess a negative right against others interfering with our efforts to obtain the basic necessities of life in a legal manner, such as employment or soliciting help from others. For certain adults to be legally free to take a child into their home, restrain the child, remove the child's clothing, physically discipline the child and otherwise engage in normal parenting behaviour, and empowered legally to exclude other adults who might wish to help a child, they need the state to confer these profound advantages on them. The state must affirmatively attach various legal privileges and powers to the legal parent role. Someone without legal parent status and such legal advantages who took a child home and confined the child, removed the child's clothing and spanked the child, would be subject to prosecution for serious crimes. As with conferral of legal parent status, the state must be able to justify its bestowal of particular privileges and powers on parents, which is concomitant with a withdrawal of certain rights and immunities from the

5 For fuller treatment of biological parents' moral position in connection with legal parentage, including refutations of arguments based on hypothetical contract or duty of gratitude, see J.G. Dwyer, *The Relationship Rights of Children*, Cambridge: Cambridge University Press, 2006, ch. 7. For description of biological parents' constitutional position, see J.G. Dwyer, 'A Constitutional Birthright: The State, Parentage, and Newborn Persons', *U.C.L.A. Law Rev.* 56, 2009, 755–835, 812–20.

6 489 U.S. 189 (1989).

child, by reference to children's needs. No other legitimate basis exists for giving private parties license to infringe children's negative rights to bodily integrity, privacy and liberty. Children have a negative right against the state's doing this in ways that harm them – for example, by legally authorizing any private parties to inflict violence on them,[7] by empowering parents to waive important statutory rights and benefits the state affords children,[8] or by giving exclusionary powers to adult custodians unprepared to fulfil all a child's developmental needs.[9]

The analogy to adult intimate relationships again helps reinforce this position. As a general matter, adults possess negative rights against physical incursions and forced isolation, and they presumptively carry these with them into marriage. For marrying to limit or eliminate those negative rights would require the state to enact special legal rules authorizing one spouse to do things to the other that would violate a negative right absent the marital relationship. The state in Anglo-American legal culture actually once did this; it authorized husbands to physically chastise, force sex on and confine their wives. If the law gave such authorization today, the legal community and advocates for women would characterize it as a gross violation of women's negative rights *by the state*. This would be so even though women are legally and practically free not to enter into a legal marriage at all if they wish to remain immune to such withdrawal of rights. It is even more clearly an infringement of children's negative rights for the state, after forcing a child to be in a family relationship with particular adults, additionally to give those adults a legal license to hit the child and the power to deny the child important protections and benefits otherwise available to them from the state or from other private parties.

A somewhat different question, though, is whether the state owes any obligation to children or wives to *enforce* any legal prohibitions on violence against them in ongoing family relationships. Are vulnerable persons' negative rights fully respected if the state simply refrains from forcing them into relationships with people known at the time to pose a danger of abuse or neglect and refrains from legally *authorizing* other private parties to harm them? Do vulnerable people have a right to the state's assistance in avoiding private *illegal* harmful behaviour?

One answer rests on the equal protection right all persons possess against the state's arbitrarily treating some group less favourably than other persons. If the state enacts and generally enforces a prohibition against private violence but adopts a policy and practice of enforcing it less or not at all when the victim is the perpetrator's child, there is unequal treatment the state must justify. It certainly could not do so on the grounds that protection from violence is unimportant for or less needed by children. The state should bear the burden of showing that children would somehow be made even worse off if the state enforced child abuse laws more vigorously, and empirical support for such a showing does not exist.

Another way to answer these questions is to emphasize that children, at least young ones, are incapable of exiting from a parent-child relationship. In contrast, spouses are generally are able to leave a marriage if their partner engages in harmful behaviour. Children's inability to exit means

7 See J. Durrant, 'Corporal Punishment and the Law in Global Perspective', in J.G. Dwyer (ed.), *Oxford Handbook of Children and the Law*, Oxford: Oxford University Press, 2020, pp. 293–320.

8 See S. Levin, 'Test of Faith: Haredi Communities and the Right to Education', *Int. J. Law. Policy & Family* 32, 2018, 334–62; J. Shulman, 'Private School Regulation: Individual Rights and Educational Responsibilities', in Dwyer, op. cit., n 7, pp. 699–730; M.A. Hamilton and L.C. Griffin, 'Legislators Should Eliminate Religious Exemptions from Laws Protecting Children', in Dwyer, op. cit., n 7, pp. 731–52.

9 See, e.g. E. Bartholet, 'Contested Child Protection Policies', in Dwyer, op. cit., n 7, pp. 415–36, 419–22 (discussing 'Differential Response' policy that many U.S. states have adopted under which a large percentage of valid child maltreatment reports get channeled to an 'assessment' or 'alternative response' track by which child-protection case workers do nothing but offer the parents assistance and services that the parents are free to refuse).

the state's placing them in a particular family and then declining to remove them from that family despite learning of abuse plays a crucial causal role in their suffering. Conceptually, the state effectively every day renews its decision to place each child in the care of particular adults; it is always either deciding to continue a given child's custody with the same people or deciding to switch custody to other persons. If state actors become aware that existing custodians are abusing a child, to an extent that the child would be better off if permanently removed from those custodians and placed in a different home, children's *negative* rights require the state to do that rather than continuing to confer custodial rights on known abusers.

Lastly, there is question as to the state's obligation to ensure children receive goods conducive to their healthy development, such as shelter, clothing, food, supervision, schooling of a certain character and quality, and medical care (see further Chapters 6.1–6.2 of this book). This is the realm of neglect law. Most political theorizing relating to child rearing has focused narrowly on education and whether the state *may* ensure children receive a secular education promoting autonomy and broad knowledge by imposing compulsory schooling laws and substantive regulation of private school instruction. Theorists fail to recognize that the analysis is the same whether the issue is school curriculum or food. As to either, parents might have reasons, religious or secular, for denying children what the state thinks children ought to receive. As to either, proponents of parents' rights or religious freedom might contend that the state may not force parents either to provide or to allow the state to provide what the parents do not wish children to have.[10] In addition to this question of *permissibility* of state action, though, there is also the question whether the state *must* ensure these things for children – that is, whether children have a right to these goods and to state action that ensures they receive them.

The permissibility question is relatively easy. Just as an adult is entitled to demand certain things as a condition for entering into and then remaining in a marriage, every child has a moral right, which the state would effectuate, to condition acceptance of a family relationship with particular adults (whether birth parents or adoptive parents) on their agreement to abide by certain reasonable conditions. So long as it is consistent with the welfare of children generally (e.g. will not deter too many would-be parents), the state must be free to say to all persons wishing to become legal parents:

> These are the terms, enshrined in law, to which you must agree in exchange for our bestowing on you legal parent status. If you find these terms unacceptable, you are free not to serve as parents to any child; other people can raise this child, on the terms the law has set.

The view that legal parents are entitled to set their own terms of engagement with children is morally groundless and incompatible with our view of other types of caregiving relationships.[11]

The harder question is whether the state could choose *not* to require of parents that they provide certain goods to children. Would it thereby violate any right of children? Again, the analysis should be the same for food and education; both are necessary to positive development, yet some parents might be indifferent or believe their children should receive something radically

10 See J.G. Dwyer and S.F. Peters, *Homeschooling: The History and Philosophy of a Controversial Practice*, Chicago: University of Chicago Press, 2019, describing and refuting the normative claims of parents and organizations who insist the state has no legitimate authority over children's education.

11 For demonstration of how the law governing other relationships rejects the notion of 'other-determining rights', see J.G. Dwyer, 'Parents' Religion and Children's Welfare: Debunking the Doctrine of Parents' Rights', *California Law Review* 82, 1994, 1371–447.

different from what the state values. Could the state confer legal parent status and custody as to a child on particular adults and then remain indifferent as to whether those adults gave the child any food? Or do children have a right to the state's imposing a feeding duty on custodians? If parents' religion tells them children should subsist only on lettuce, is the state permitted to indulge their faith?

The best answer to these questions might rest on a contract rationale and on the concept of fiduciary duty. As explained previously, when the state chooses persons to serve as legal parents and custodians, it effectively acts as a proxy or agent for the child, authorized to make this decision for children solely because they cannot make it themselves, and required to exercise that authority solely to further the child's well-being. The state acts in a fiduciary capacity, bound to choose the best parents from among adults willing to serve; there is no justification for it substituting or adding any other aim in carrying out this function. And it should seek to establish the best possible terms for children in effectively striking a bargain with potential parents. So we should ask what is the best deal, in terms of expectations for provision of goods, that the state, as agent for children, can demand of prospective parents. That could vary depending on social and economic circumstances, but in modern western societies, the expectation could certainly include a parental commitment to provide adequate housing, clothing, nutrition, supervision and protection; to secure the preventive and remedial medical treatment professionals recommend; and to not get in the way of children receiving a liberal education. For the state not to demand these things of parents would violate the right of children correlative to the state's fiduciary duty owed to them, just as a lawyer would breach a fiduciary duty to a client by negotiating a contract in which the client provides goods and services to the other party but gets nothing in return. Enforcing neglect laws against deficient parents amounts in a sense to contract enforcement, holding parents to the terms they implicitly agreed to when they asked to be made legal parents to a child, and the state would also fail in its fiduciary duty to children by failing to monitor and police contract compliance.

Does that leave room for accommodating parental values or ideological beliefs that diverge from the state's secular values and mainstream beliefs? Yes, but less room than current law in most Anglo-American jurisdictions gives. Some differences in values or beliefs are not of great significance to children's well-being, and it would be unwise for the state to refuse to concede parental freedom as to those. For example, medical professionals might not think occasional fasting periods that some religions dictate are optimal for children, but any detriment might be so insignificant that a wise agent for children would indulge that practice, to avoid driving away too many potential parents or making the parental role unnecessarily unpleasant. In addition, the value for children of being raised by biological parents might outweigh the value to children of being raised by people who have no such minor differences of value or belief, so some biological parents will be the best available legal parents for their offspring despite their departure from what the state deems ideal. Further, children learn much from exposure to different values and beliefs and from experiencing particularistic culture within the family.[12] These reasons for accommodation are not sufficiently strong, however, to warrant accommodations that would cause substantial detriment to children. They are insufficient to justify, for example, empowering parents to deny children immunizations, medical care for treatable injuries and illnesses, or a

12 For further exploration of the extent to which the state can appropriately accommodate cultural differences among child rearers, see J.G. Dwyer, 'Regulating Child Rearing in a Culturally Diverse Society', in E. Brake and L. Ferguson (eds), *Philosophical Foundations of Children's and Family Law*, Oxford: Oxford University Press, 2018, pp. 273–92.

liberal education.[13] What we know about child development suggests new-born children would be better off on the whole if the state, as their agent, chose biologically unrelated adults to serve in the parental role rather than birth parents who would deny them these important goods.

Conclusion

Children's moral (and constitutional) rights are stronger in content than is generally supposed. The main obstacle to achieving for them the better parentage decision making and protection from abuse and neglect to which they are entitled is their inability to advocate on their own behalf coupled with lack of substantial adult constituency advocating forcefully in their behalf. The lack of support among adults for reformation of parentage and maltreatment laws in turn reflects a general adult-centric mentality and failure to perceive the negative-rights nature of children's entitlements. The flip-side of misconstruing children's moral position as that of beggars pleading for help is a mistaken view that conferring legal parent status and custody on biological parents, and empowering legal parents to do harmful things to children, is a necessary deference to the negative rights of those adults. In fact, it is the adult members of parent-child relationship who effectively ask the state to give them an extraordinary and gratuitous benefit – namely, possession and control of another human being.

13 See A. Rogers, *The Child Cases: How America's Religious Exemption Laws Harm Children*, Boston: University of Mass Press, 2014 (closely analyzing individual cases in which children suffered grievous harm because of parents' religiously grounded rejection of medical care).

4.5

CHILDREN'S RIGHTS AND PARENTAL AUTHORITY

African perspectives

Julia Sloth-Nielsen

Introduction

Traditionally, children in African societies were raised communally, with extended family members playing a vital role in child rearing and care. The adage 'it takes a village to raise a child' epitomized this communitarian philosophy.[1] Further, the very definition of childhood was affected, as transitions to adulthood under customary systems depended variously on life events such as marriage or forming an independent homestead, and the end of childhood was not linked to chronological age. As regards parental authority, children were subjected to absolute minority status until they attained the requisite of adult status, which could occur well into adult life only.

Until colonial administrations enacted statutory provisions governing children and young persons, children's status and family life were regulated by customary laws. In most parts of sub-Saharan Africa, customary law and civil law continue to co-exist, and therefore customary family law forms an important backdrop to the policy shifts that have been taking place. Under customary law, dispute resolution took place under the auspices of traditional leaders, who administered the affairs of the indigenous peoples in his (almost inevitably) area.[2]

Many African countries have revised their children's laws as well as their family codes in recent times. This has been occasioned by the need to domesticate the UN Convention on the Rights of the Child (UNCRC) and the African Charter on the Rights and Welfare of the Child (ACRWC), the regional child rights treaty. The need to review outdated colonial legislation has also been a driver of law reform, as well as the desire to improve the legislative environment for the most vulnerable children, such as those in need of care and protection and orphans.[3]

Social reality is playing a formative role in relation to family law and policy, including in respect of children's rights. This reality includes rapid urbanization leading to the fragmentation

1 See for instance B. Rwezaura, 'Competing Images of Childhood in Social and Legal Systems of Contemporary Sub-Saharan Africa', *International Law of Law Policy and the Family* 12, 1998, 255–78.

2 C. Himonga, 'African Customary Law and Children's Rights', in J. Sloth-Nielsen (ed.), *Children's Rights in Africa: A Legal Perspective*, Dartmouth: Ashgate Dartmouth, 2008; African Child Policy Forum, 'Spotlighting the Invisible: Access to Justice for Children in Africa' (2018) Addis Ababa.

3 J. Sloth-Nielsen, 'Domestication of Children' Rights in National Legal Systems: Progress and Prospects', in 'African Customary Law and Children's Rights', in J. Sloth-Nielsen (ed.), *Children's Rights in Africa: A Legal Perspective*, Dartmouth: Ashgate Dartmouth, 2008, pp. 53–72.

of the once close knit communal clan structure; HIV/Aids which has wrought havoc on traditional family structures as the disease has had most impact on sexually active persons (including mothers of childbearing age); the rise of the single parent, most often mother, household and the consequent disproportionate burden of childcare upon women; the impact of international children's rights upon law and policy;[4] and the increasing need to introduce measures to regulate aspects of children's welfare and to promote their well-being (such as rules relating to children in institutions). The development goals once formulated as the Millennium Development Goals played a significant role until 2015 (as regards girls' access to education, for example), and the Sustainable Development Goals which followed include significant dimensions pertinent to children's rights and family life, including Goal 5 (achieve gender equality and empower all women and girls everywhere) and Goal 16 which relates to promoting peaceful and inclusive societies, providing access to justice for all, and ending abuse, exploitation, trafficking and all violence against children.

Most African children still grow up under conditions of extreme poverty, which is exacerbated by urbanization, conflict, adverse climatic conditions and economic disparity which leaves large numbers of people unemployed or underemployed.

The African Charter on the Rights and Welfare of the Child

This regional treaty has at the time of writing been ratified by 48 of the 53 member states of the African Union, and universal (continental) ratification is now a distinct possibility. Many states have provided initial and periodic reports to the monitoring body, the African Committee of Experts on the Rights and Welfare of the Child (hereafter ACERWC).[5] Decisions in approximately ten communications brought to the attention of the Committee have been made public, but not one relates to family life.

Given that one causative factor which led to the drafting of the ACRWC in the first place related to the perception that African kinship structure had been insufficiently recognized in the UNCRC,[6] it is not surprising that children's place within the family receives strong emphasis in the ACRWC (referred to below as the 'Charter'). The preamble to the Charter reflects that children in African societies 'occupy a unique and privileged position'. The Charter sets its ambit of protection as all children under the age of 18 years (irrespective of whether majority is attained earlier, e.g. through marriage).

Three main articles lay the foundation for the policy orientation of the Charter concerning family life. First, art. 18 titled 'protection of the family' affirms the family as the natural unit and basis of society, and further requires that states parties are to ensure equality of rights and responsibilities of spouses with regard to marriage and in the event of its dissolution. Art. 18(3) provides that no child may be deprived of maintenance due to the marital status of the parents, ie whether they are married or unmarried. Art. 19 provides that every child shall be entitled to the enjoyment of parental care and protection, with separation from parents to occur only when determined by a judicial authority in accordance with the best interests of the child. Art. 20 on parental responsibilities recognizes that persons other than parents may

4 A. Skelton, 'The Development of a Fledgling Child Rights Jurisprudence in Eastern and Southern Africa Based on International and Regional Instruments', *African Human Rights Law Journal* 9, 2008, 482–501.

5 J. Sloth-Nielsen, 'The African Children's Rights System', in T. Boezaart (ed.), *Introduction to Child Law*, 2nd edition, Cape Town: Juta and Co., 2017.

6 D. Chirwa, 'The Merits and Demits of the African Charter on the Rights and Welfare of the Child', *International Journal on Children's Rights* 10, 2002, 157–78.

have responsibility for the upbringing of the child, as this is referred to more than once in that article. It is this provision in particular which recognizes the prevalence of care arrangements in extended families, and can also be singled out insofar as it spells out in much more detail than the UNCRC that states bear the responsibility 'to assist parents and other persons responsible for the child and in cases of need provide material assistance and support programmes particularly in regard to nutrition, health, education, clothing and housing' (art. 20(2)(a)).

The Charter contains a prohibition on child marriage or the betrothal of girls and boys and requires that it be prohibited. Legislative steps should be taken to set a minimum age of marriage at 18 years, and to make registration of marriages compulsory (art. 21), which depicts child marriage as a harmful social and cultural practice. This is an acknowledgement of the reality of child marriage under customary and religious systems in many parts of the continent – in Malawi for instance, four percent of the population are married before their fifteenth birthday and 24 percent of the population are married before their nineteenth birthday.[7] The ACERWC released a General Comment on Ending Child Marriage (jointly with the African Commission on Human and People's Rights)[8] in 2017. This General Comment does not view child marriage as a form of family life – rather it takes the perspective that child marriage as a harmful manifestation of gender equality and constitutes discrimination based on sex and gender.[9] The prohibition against child marriage is a wide one, extending to betrothal in all forms and to all marriages and unions.[10]

Characteristic of the African human rights conception is a unique provision for the responsibilities of the child (art. 31). These include responsibilities towards the family and, in particular, the responsibility to work towards the cohesion of the family, to respect parents, superiors and elders, and to assist them in times of need. Indeed, under customary law, the duty to maintain parents and elders subsists throughout a child's life. In most recent statutes on the continent, some provision has been made for a statutory incorporation of the responsibilities of children, the obverse side to the provisions for their rights, and again, this article formed the basis of a General Comment that was released by the ACERWC recently.[11] As regards the cited parts of art. 31, the General Comment notes that

> Children are expected to take part in productive activities for the sustenance of the family, such being viewed as an opportunity to learn, grow and develop the capacity to assume greater responsibilities in the larger society. Thus, children taking responsibility for aspects of family and communal life is considered to be an element of the care and protection of children. The family is therefore considered to be an ideal environment for teaching and learning positive values such as respect for adults, respect for the rights

7 See L. Mwambene, 'Recent Legal Responses to Child Marriage in Southern Africa: The Case of Zimbabwe, South Africa and Malawi', *African Human Rights Law Journal* 18, 2018, 527–50.

8 Available at www.acerwc.africa/wp-content/uploads/2018/04/ENGLISH_Joint_GC_ACERWC-ACHPR_Ending_Child_Marriage_14_March_2018.pdf

9 Para 11 of the General Comment. See further F. Banda and J. Eekelaar, 'International Conceptions of the Family', *Int. & Comp. Law Quarterly* 64, 2017, 833–62.

10 Para 16 of the General Comment'. Legislative measures that prohibit child marriage must take precedence over customary, religious, traditional or sub-national laws and States Parties with plural legal systems must take care to ensure that prohibition is not rendered ineffectual by the existence of customary, religious or traditional laws that allow, condone or support child marriage' (para 19).

11 For example, the South African Children's Act 38 of 2008 and the Angolan Holistic Law on the Child of September 2012; Malawi, Botswana and Lesotho all include comparable provisions in their new children's laws (see www.aclr.info for the relevant texts).

of others, and learning to handle responsibilities including actively taking part in the care of younger siblings.[12]

Children's rights, family life and domestic constitutions

Children's rights feature prominently in African constitutions, and commonly include protection for the family, education rights and rights relating to special protection. With the landmark South African constitution of 1996 providing the most extensive basis for justiciable children's rights at the constitutional level initially, children's rights to parental or family care, or to alternative care from the state when deprived of a family environment (section 28(1)(b) of the South African Constitution) has from a constitutional perspective continued to shape family law and policy. The most notable was a Constitutional Court case regarding the emergency removal without a warrant of children accompanying parents who were begging on the street. In the context of the lack of a statutory provision for an automatic court review of the removal intervention by social workers, the Constitutional Court said:

> The coercive removal of a child from his or her home environment is undoubtedly a deeply invasive and disruptive measure. Uninvited intervention by the state into the private sphere of family life threatens to rupture the integrity and continuity of family relations, and even to disgrace the dignity of the family, both parents and children, in their own esteem as well as in the eyes of the community.[13]

Finding the provisions unconstitutional as a violation of children's rights, the Court relied too on the (constitutionalized) principle of the child's best interests. Numerous decisions premised on the primacy of children's best interests as a constitutional standard have been handed down in over 20 years of constitutional democracy, including relating to adoption, intercountry adoption, same-sex parents, surrogacy, the rights of children born out of wedlock, and care and contact.[14]

The most recent Constitutional case affecting family life was *FORSA v Minister of Justice and Constitutional Development.*[15] The matter commenced in 2017 as an appeal of one YG for his criminal convictions of assaulting his teenage child. The appellate judge raised the question as to whether the common law defence of reasonable chastisement available to parents was constitutionally compatible, and invited *FORSA* as well as the Centre for Child Law which engages in children's rights litigation, to enter as *amicus curiae*. Her finding was indeed that the defence was in violation of the Constitution. Whilst YG failed to take the matter further, FORSA appealed this ruling to the Constitutional Court, which delivered it's ruling almost a year after hearing argument on the matter.

The decision of the court did not turn on the best interests of the child, or in fact on any other right explicitly devoted to children, but rather on the general right to freedom and security of the person, and to be free from all forms of violence whether from public or private sources.[16] The wording of the Constitution in fact left the Court little room to manoeuvre, as it is plain that chastisement 'by its very nature entail(s) the use of force or a measure of violence'.[17]

12 Para 28.
13 In *C v Department of Health and Social Development, Gauteng* 2012 [ZACC] 1, [23].
14 For an overview of some landmark children's rights constitutional cases, see J Sloth-Nielsen 'Children's rights jurisprudence in South Africa – a 20 year retrospective' 2019 *De Jure* (forthcoming).
15 2019 CC; FORSA is the abbreviation for the society known as Freedom of Religion South Africa.
16 Section12(1)(c).
17 Para 39 of the judgment.

The Court opined that there cannot be assault (as defined in criminal law) without meeting the requirements of 'all forms of violence'.[18] '"All forms" is so all encompassing that its reach or purpose seems to leave no form of violence or application of force to the body of another person out of the equation'.[19]

The Zimbabwean Constitution[20] is similarly destined to play a role in reshaping family relations, commencing with the landmark decision in *Mudzuru v Minister of Justice and Parliamentary Affairs* in 2015.[21] In *Mudzuru* two young women, aged 18 and 19, brought the case to the Constitutional Court respectively, in terms of section 85(1) of the Constitution of Zimbabwe. The two applicants advocated the protection of children's rights, particularly girl children who are subjected to the challenges of child marriage. The Court had to decide whether the effect of section 78(1) of the Zimbabwean Constitution is to set 18 years as the minimum age of marriage in Zimbabwe. In addition, the Court had to determine whether section 22(1) of the Marriage Act, which prohibited the marriage of a boy under the age of 18 and a girl under the age of 16 years, except with the written permission of the Minister of Justice and the Customary Marriages Act which had no predetermined age of marriage, was constitutional. Finding that child marriage was a harmful traditional and cultural practice which contravened the Constitution, the Court declared that from the date of the judgment (January 2016), no valid marriage under any law may be entered into by a person aged below 18. The Court further declared section 22(1) of the Marriage Act, and any customary and religious practices authorizing any child to be married before the age of 18, to be invalid to the extent of its inconsistency with the Constitution.[22]

Finally, Malawi enacted a constitutional amendment in 2017 to raise the age to which a child was defined in the Constitution from 16 to 18 in accordance with international treaty law. This was a response to an agreement reached in a friendly settlement consequent upon a communication brought against the State Party under the African Charter on the Rights and Welfare of the Child.[23]

Married and unmarried parents

Unlike under most customary law systems[24] where parental authority vested in the male head of the household[25] to the exclusion of both mothers and other males (including potentially a

18 Para 41 of the judgment.

19 Para 42 of the judgment. For further discussion of this case, see Sloth-Nielsen, 'Sideswipes and backhanders: The abolition of the reasonable chastisement defence in South Africa', *International Journal of Law, Policy and the Family* 34(2), 2020 (forthcoming).

20 Kenya's 2010 Constitution also contains a modern and justiciable children's rights provision. The Constitution of Egypt (art. 70) guarantees the rights of a child to a name, family care, basic nutrition, shelter, health services and religious, emotional and cognitive development.

21 *Loveness Mudzuru and Ruvimbo Tsopodzi v Minister of Justice, Legal and Parliamentary Affairs, Minister of Women Affairs, Gender and Community Development*, Attorney-General of Zimbabwe Application 79/14 CC 12/2015.

22 J. Sloth-Nielsen and K. Hove, 'Mudzuru and Another v Minister of Justice, Legal and Parliamentary Affairs & 2 Others: A Review', *African Human Rights Law Journal* 15, 2015, 55 and L Mwambene, 'Recent Legal Responses to Child Marriage in Southern Africa: The Case of Zimbabwe, South Africa and Malawi', *African Human Rights Law Journal* 18, 2018, 527–50.

23 See for a discussion B Mezmur, 'No Second Chance for First Impressions: The First Amicable Settlement under the African Children's Charter', *African Human Rights Law Journal* 19, 2019, 62–84.

24 There are examples of matrilineal customary law systems, but these vested parental authority in the male head of the mother's lineage. Malawi is a case in point.

25 *Bhe* v *Magistrate Khayalitsha (Commission for Gender Equality Intervening)* 2005 (1) SA 80 (CC).

biological father), civil laws have usually awarded mothers automatic parental responsibilities. Married fathers' roles have usually been acknowledged in law, but the position for unmarried fathers has not been consistently regarded as equal to that of mothers. This position is changing in the recent raft of Children's Laws, based both on the prohibition against discrimination on the grounds of birth status contained in the UNCRC and the ACRWC, and on the right of the child to know and be cared for by both parents. Further impetus has been derived from the African Women's Protocol[26] (the Optional Protocol to the African Charter on Human and Peoples' Rights) which, amongst other things, mandates equal treatment of mothers and fathers in relation to child rearing.

In Namibia, the recently promulgated Child Care and Protection Act of 2015 (in force from 2018) grants equal rights to either father or mother to become the custodian parents. Section 99 provides

> (1) Both parents of a child born outside marriage have equal rights to custody of the child born outside marriage. (2) One parent must have custody of the child born outside and both parents may agree on who must have custody.

The section continues to provide that a registered agreement constitutes prima facie proof that the parent named in that agreement has custody of the child and has the legal power to act in that capacity. If there is no agreement as to who must have custody of a child outside marriage, either of the parents may make an application to the children's court to be appointed as the person having custody of the child born outside marriage.

In Kenya, despite a previous ruling in relation to the Children's Act 2001 that the vesting of all parental responsibility on an unmarried mother, to the exclusion of the unmarried biological father, did not unfairly discriminate against children born out of wedlock,[27] the Kenyan constitution now provides that every child has a right to parental care and protection which explicitly includes the equal responsibility of the mother and father to provide for the child, whether married or not. This is likely to lead to revisions to the Kenyan Children's Act.[28]

On 26 May 2016, the Kenyan High Court found unconstitutional a provision in the Birth and Death Registration Act banning the inclusion in an out-of-wedlock child's birth certificate of the name of the child's putative father without his consent. The provision in question stated:

> No person shall be entered in the register as the father of any child except either at the joint request of the father and mother or upon the production to the registrar of such evidence as he may require that the father and mother were married according to law or, in accordance with some recognized custom.[29]

The Court noted that every child has the right to have the name of his or her father added to the birth certificate, regardless of the marital status of the parents. The Court held that the

26 The African Women's Protocol (Protocol to the African Charter on Human Rights Peoples' Rights on the Rights of Women in Africa OAU doc CAB/LEG/66.6 (entered into force 25 November 2005).

27 J. Sloth-Nielsen, L. Wakefield and N. Murungi, 'Does the Differential Criterion for Vesting Parental Rights and Responsibilities of Unmarried Parents Violate International Law? A Legislative and Social study of Three African Countries', *Journal of African Law* 55, 2011, 203–29.

28 Although a 2017 Bill is available on the website of the council for children's services, it does not appear to have been passed yet.

29 Birth and Death Registration Act of 1928, § 12, Cap. 149 (rev. edn, 2014).

above-cited provision, which disallows such a right, is a violation of the equality and freedom from discrimination clause of the Kenyan Constitution.

The Angolan Law of the Child, which was signed in September 2012, contains several notable provisions pertaining to family life and the role of parents. Art. 24 of the act grants men and women equal rights and responsibilities in respect of their children, and it does not appear that there is any distinction based on the marital status of the parents.[30]

Relationships with the extended family

Increasingly family law judgments in the region have begun to recognize the involvement of the extended family in children's lives, bringing civil law concepts closer to both social reality and customary practice. South Africa's Children's Act 38 of 2005 (in force from 1 April 2010) contains the seeds of this development. Section 7, which elaborates a non-exhaustive list of criteria for the determination of the best interests of the child, includes the nature of the personal relationship between the child and any other caregiver or person, and the likely effect upon the child of any separation from 'any brother or sister or other child, or any care-giver or person with whom the child has been living'. Another relevant criterion is the need for the child to remain in the care of *inter alia* his or her extended family, and to maintain a connection with his or her family, extended family, culture or traditions.[31] Parental responsibilities and rights, which replaced the common law concept of parental authority, are not confined to biological or adoptive parents, as any person with an interest in the care well-being and development of the child may apply to court for the award of some or all aspects of parental responsibilities,[32] and parental responsibilities may also be conferred by agreement.[33]

In *LH v LA*, an application by grandparents for the award of contact with the son of their deceased son succeeded. The court stated:

> The Act recognizes that the child is a social being and that members of the extended family, more often than not, play an important part in a child's social and psychological development. Grandparents, more than other relative, usually take a keen interest in the upbringing of their grandchildren and this relationship, provided it is kept within reasonable bounds and does not interfere with parental duties and responsibilities, often assists and complements parental care. There can therefore be little doubt that it is usually in a child's best interests to maintain a close relationship with his or her grandparents.[34]

From Kenya comes the case of *ZAK v MA*, which concerned the liability for maintenance of a stepfather in respect of non-biological children.[35] Judge M. Ngugi said:

> Our society has evolved very rapidly, from the traditional polygamous society to monogamous unions in which parties enter into marriage with children from previous

30 J. Sloth-Nielsen and A. Mandlate, 'A Preliminary Appraisal of the Normative Gains for Children's Rights in the Angolan Children's Act (Act 25/12)', in B. Atkin (ed.), *International Survey of Family Law 2013*, Bristol: Jordan Publishing, 2013.

31 Sections 7(1)(d) and (f).

32 Sections 13 and 24.

33 Section 22.

34 *LH* v *LA* 2012 (6) SA 41 (ECG), [13].

35 *ZAK* v *MA* [2013] eKLR (petition 193 of 2011).

> unions. While the relationship between a couple in a family where there are children from either of the parties' previous relationships is working, the question of parental responsibility for such children may not arise. They are deemed and may be treated as children of the family, entitled to maintenance and all that appertains to the duties of parents to children. It is when the relationship falls apart, as in the present case, that the question of parental responsibility for the children of the other spouse may arise. Looked at through the prism of the Constitution, particularly art. 53(2) which requires that the best interests of the child be the paramount consideration in any matter concerning the child, I believe that a step-parent in such circumstances must be held to have an obligation recognised in law to exercise parental responsibility as defined in Section 23 of the Children Act over his or her step-child. It would be an affront to morality and the values of the Constitution for a party who has had a relationship with a child akin to that of a father or mother to disclaim all responsibility and duty to maintain the child when he or she falls out with the parent of the child. Such responsibility would, however, depend on the circumstances of each case, and the relationship that is shown to have existed between the person in question and the children in respect of whom he or she is sought to be charged with parental responsibility for.

MB v NB,[36] a South African case, decided upon the responsibility of a step-parent to similar effect, and Namibia's Child Care and Protection Act provides separately for kinship care in a dedicated chapter.[37] This relates to the impact of HIV/Aids, which has resulted in a great many children being looked after by extended family members, usually grandmothers. Botswana too has enacted provisions which ensure that a child is almost always associated with a duty bearer, and the 2009 Children's Act provides explicitly for the roles of other relative such as foster parents and step-parents.[38]

Child-headed households

When the impact of HIV Aids on children in sub-Saharan Africa began to emerge during the mid 1990s, the phenomenon of child-headed households was mooted as an area of growing concern. The UNICEF, USAid and UNAIDs Report 'Children on the brink' (2002) predicted a vast number of orphans for whom alternative care would not be available. The Committee on the Rights of the Child in General Comment no 3 (HIV Aids on the Rights of the Child) broached the need for legal recognition of such households, which has led to the inclusion of provisions pertaining to child-headed households in several laws in the region. The legal recognition of households headed by children is intended to promote measures of special protection and assistance, to ensure state support and to make provision for adult supervision and mentoring.[39] At the same time, it heralds a new family form, insofar as the household subsists without an adult at the helm.

36 *MB* v *NB* [2010] (3) SA 220 (GSJ).
37 Chapter 8.
38 J. Sloth-Nielsen, 'A New Children's Law in Botswana: Reshaping Family Relations for the Twenty First Century', in B. Atkin (ed.), *International Survey of Family Law 2012*, Bristol: Jordan Publishing, 2012.
39 M. Couzens and F.N. Zaal, 'Legal Recognition for Child-Headed Households: An Evaluation of the Emerging South African Framework', *International Journal on Children's Rights* 17, 2009, 299–320.

Specialized court services and dispute adjudication

Provisions for specialized children's courts and for enhanced child participation in court processes is an ongoing project on the African continent. In Malawi for instance, justice for children reforms have seen four specialized child justice courts established in the four large towns, and specialized children's courts being rolled out to 28 districts. They adjudicate welfare issues, maintenance of children and juvenile justice matters involving children aged below 18. Judicial officers have received specialized training on children's rights. In Ethiopia, a child-friendly court has been established and in Kenya, specialized children's courts, staffed by dedicated judges, have been set up since the commencement of the Children's Act of 2001. As recently as 2018 it was reported that their numbers were to be extended. Nigeria too has a system of specialized child and family courts. At the same time, child protection studies have shown that for a large number of children, the informal justice system is the only one which is accessible.[40]

Legal representation for children in formal justice systems, provided by state-funded legal aid systems, NGOs and university law clinics has escalated dramatically in the last decade. The wider availability of legal representation for children in many African countries is contributing to children having improved access to justice, including in family law matters, although it is conceded there is a long way to go in many countries.[41]

Child participation

Child participation has been a feature of children's law reform processes: innovative modern technology was used to reach out to children and young people in the lead up to Namibia's Child Care and Protection Bill's formulation,[42] and an extensive consultation process at grassroots level during the drafting of the Law of the Child of Zanzibar (2011) took place.[43] Although felt by some to be alien to African conceptions of children as subservient and dependent beings, a number of statutes have expressed the principle of child participation. The visibility of children's rights has therefore also risen measurably in recent times.

Surrogacy

There have been indications that surrogacy at specific places on the continent is on the rise – including international surrogacy. This may be due to the fact that commercial surrogacy for foreign commissioning parents has been outlawed in erstwhile popular destinations such as India and Thailand.

Whilst South Africa's Children's Act permits altruistic surrogacy if approved by a High Court prior to fertilization, this is restricted to persons domiciled in South Africa. Nevertheless, concerns have been raised that some foreign nationals not domiciled in South Africa have managed

40 African Child Policy Forum, *Spotlighting the Invisible: Justice for Children in Africa*, Addis Ababa, 2018.

41 J. Sloth-Nielsen and B. van Heerden, 'Child Participation and Access to Justice for Children in Africa', paper presented at the conference Gender, Inclusivity and Protecting the 21st Century Family, London, 3–5 July 2019.

42 Legal Assistance Centre, *Public Participation in Law Reform: Revision of Namibia's Draft Child Care and Protection Bill*, Windhoek, 2010.

43 For an early assessment of child participation in law reform processes, see C. Frank and L. Ehlers, 'Child Participation in Africa', in J. Sloth-Nielsen (ed.), *Children's Rights in Africa: A Legal Perspective*, Dartmouth: Ashgate, 2008, pp. 111–29.

to have surrogate motherhood agreements confirmed.[44] In Kenya, there have been at least three reported cases of international surrogacy giving rise to problems once the children were born (an Italian father been unable to secure documentation for otherwise stateless children; a surrogate mother refusing to hand over children to their commissioning father from China; and a court application[45] necessitated by the uncertain legal parentage of a surrogate born child destined to be taken to the United Kingdom). Attention has also been focused in recent times on 'baby factories' in Nigeria,[46] with a recent raid having been carried out to rescue 19 women and four children.[47] International surrogacy is also taking place in Ghana, coinciding with the growth of private IVF clinics.[48] Concern has been expressed that surrogacy may be occurring in an unregulated environment in Africa, as to date only South Africa has legislative provisions governing the legal implications, including those relating to parenthood (see further Chapter 7.1 of this book).

44 J. Sloth-Nielsen, 'Surrogacy in South Africa', in J Scherpe, C. Fenton Glynn and T. Kaan (eds), *Eastern and Western Perspectives on Surrogacy*, Cambridge: Intersentia, 2019, p. 199.

45 *A.M.N and 2 Others v Attorney General of Kenya* [2015] eKLR.

46 O.S. Adelakun 'The Concept of Surrogacy in Nigeria: Issues, Prospects and Challenges' *African Human Rights Law Journal* 18, 2018, 605–24. See also J. Sloth-Nielsen, 'Presentation to the Regional Conference on the Hague Conventions in Africa', South Africa, 3 April 2019 (copy on file with the author).

47 www.news24.com/Africa/News/nigeria-police-rescue-pregnant-women-from-baby-factories-20190930 (accessed 23 October 2019).

48 T. Gerrits, 'Reproductive Travel to Ghana: Testimonies, Transnational Relationships, and Stratified Reproduction', *Medical Anthropology* 37(2), 2018, 131–44,

4.6
CHILDREN'S RIGHTS
The wider context

John Eekelaar and Rob George

The UN Convention on the Rights of the Child (UNCRC)

Although children's rights are now widely accepted as being an important aspect of human rights, they have been opposed for a variety of reasons, including fears that they undermine family life,[1] and the view that they simply reflect adults' views of what children should expect. John Tobin has pointed out that such views rest on one-dimensional concepts of children's rights whereas they represent a multifaceted idea, located within a variety of actual social structures (an important one being the exercise of power), and therefore reflect a 'social interest' in the way children should be treated within them.[2] Similarly, it has been argued that children's rights must be understood within the complex of ideas about rights generally and about human rights in particular, and that they direct the adult world to bring about certain outcomes for children as far as possible from the children's rather than the adults' perspective.[3]

One of the most important manifestations of acceptance of children's rights is the UN Convention on the Rights of the Child of 1989 (UNCRC), which establishes them firmly as an acknowledged source of international obligations on ratifying states. As of 2020, the United States was the only state that had not done this. A number of states have incorporated the Convention in a variety of ways into their domestic legal order.[4] The Convention has been reinforced by Optional Protocol 3 which establishes procedures for reporting violations of the

1 B.C. Hafen and J.O. Hafen, 'Abandoning Children to Their Autonomy: The United Nations Convention on the Rights of the Child', *Harvard International Law Journal* 37, 1996, 449–91.

2 J. Tobin, 'Justifying Children's Rights', *International Journal of Children's Rights* 21, 2013, 395–441.

3 J. Eekelaar, *Family Law and Personal Life*, 2nd edition, Oxford: Oxford University Press, 2017, Ch. 2. In practical terms, this demands what Tobin calls 'participatory research' in order to obtain children's perspectives. It has been called the 'capability approach': see N. Peleg, 'Reconceptualising the Child's Right to Development: Children and the Capability Approach', *International Journal of Children's Rights* 21, 2013, 523, or as promoting 'authenticity' (rather than 'autonomy'): S. Altmann, 'Reinterpreting the Right to an Open Future: From Autonomy to Authenticity', *Law and Philosophy* 37, 2015, 415–36. Contrast L. Ferguson, 'The Jurisprudence of Making Decisions Affecting Children: An Argument to Prefer Duty to Children's Rights and Welfare', in A. Diduck, N. Peleg and H. Reece (eds), *Law and Society: Reflections on Children, Family, Culture and Philosophy: Essays in Honour of Michael Freeman*, Leiden: Brill, 2015, p. 141.

4 L. Lundy, U. Kilkelly and B. Byrne, 'Incorporation of the United Nations Convention on the Rights of the Child in Law: A Comparative Review', *International Journal of Children's Rights* 21(3), 2013, 442–63.

Convention to the UN Committee on the Rights of the Child[5] and by a series of General Comments by the UN Committee on Children's Rights, one of the most important, which was issued too late for reference in the First Edition of this book, being General Comment 14 on the interpretation to be given to art. 3. That article requires states parties to 'undertake to ensure the child such protection and care as is necessary for his or her well-being' and lays down that 'in all actions concerning children, whether undertaken by public or private social welfare institutions, courts of law, administrative authorities or legislative bodies, the best interests of the child shall be a primary consideration'.[6]

Among other things, General Comment 14 points out that the concept of the child's best interests 'is aimed at ensuring the full and effective enjoyment of all the rights recognized in the Convention' which cannot be overridden by an adult's judgment of the child's best interests;[7] that it is a substantive right which demands the child's interests to be 'taken as a primary consideration when different interests are being considered';[8] that if a legal provision is open to more than one interpretation, that which best serves the child's best interests should be chosen;[9] and that, as a rule of procedure, it demands that the impact of any decision on the children affected must be evaluated.[10] The Comment re-iterated[11] the 'inextricable' connection between such evaluation and the child's right to be heard set out in art. 12 that had been observed in General Comment 12 (2009).[12]

Parental responsibilities and the definition and allocation of parenthood

Art. 5 of the UNCRC requires states to

> respect the responsibilities, rights and duties of parents or, where applicable, the members of the extended family or community as provided for by local custom, legal guardians or other persons legally responsible for the child, to provide, in a manner consistent with the evolving capacities of the child, appropriate direction and guidance in the exercise by the child of the rights recognized in the present Convention.

Art. 7 gives children the right to 'be registered immediately after birth' and 'the right from birth to a name, the right to acquire a nationality and. as far as possible, the right to know and be cared for by his or her parents'. In addition, states must 'respect the right of the child to preserve his or her identity, including nationality, name and family relations as recognized by law without unlawful interference' (art. 8).

5 See generally T. Liefaard and J.E. Doek (eds), *Litigating the Rights of the Child: The UN Convention on the Rights of the Child in Domestic and International Jurisprudence*, Dordrecht: Springer, 2015. Uptake of Optional Protocol 3 has been notably slow as compared with the Convention itself.

6 For analyses of art. 3 and its impact, see E.E. Sutherland and L.-A. Barnes Macfarlane (eds), *Implementing Art. 3 of the United Nations Convention on the Rights of the Child: Best Interests, Welfare and Well-Being*, Cambridge: Cambridge University Press, 2016; J. Eekelaar and J. Tobin, 'Article 3: The Best Interests of the Child', in J. Tobin (ed.), *The UN Convention on the Rights of the Child: A Commentary*, Oxford: Oxford University Press, 2019.

7 General Comment No 14, para 4.

8 Ibid., para 6(a).

9 Ibid., para 6(b).

10 Ibid., para 6 (c).

11 Ibid., para 43.

12 General Comment No. 12, paras 70–4.

Consistently with this, it is now becoming common for states to cast parental status primarily in terms of *responsibilities* rather than of rights[13] (see further Chapters 3.3–3.5 of this book). This is true also of the African Charter on the Rights and Welfare of the Child (the 'African Charter') which states in art. 20 that 'Parents or other persons responsible for the child should always act in the best interest of the child' (see Chapter 4.5 of this book). While art. 5 of the UNCRC requires states to 'respect' these responsibilities, art. 18 expressly states that states are under an obligation to ensure that, in exercising those responsibilities '(t)he best interests of the child will be their (the parents') basic concern'. Similarly, while the European Convention on Human Rights protects the parent-child relationship as an aspect of family life, the European Court of Human Rights has stated that, in doing this, the best interests of the child are paramount.[14] It has been stated in the UK Supreme Court that 'it is only as a contributor to the child's welfare that parenthood assumes any significance'.[15]

A hidden problem in these provisions, only recently being exposed, is how 'parent' is to be understood. This is important from the child's perspective because, while being a parent carries responsibilities, it also carries the 'right' to exercise those responsibilities. If it were possible, then, to become the parent of a child by proclamation of intent alone, this might seem to undermine its status, and the accompanying responsibilities, as a right of the child. (See further Chapter 4.4 of this book.) But parenthood can be acquired by intent, as in the case of adoption, and it is now not uncommon for the partner of a 'biological' parent of a child who has no genetic connection with the child to become, by agreement, the 'other' parent of the child,[16] and even for more than two persons to acquire the status.[17] In these cases, the parties' agreement is an element in the allocation of parenthood, but it is not the only one, as the circumstances are defined or regulated by law. It has, however, been argued that

> (p)arental agreements of multiparental families should be *recognized* by the state as long as the family members are in agreement as to each-other's parental status, leaving the power to form a family and determine rights and responsibilities in the hands of individuals.[18]

These developments have produced severe tensions in kinship terminology,[19] and Guillaume Kessler, describing this as 'the parentage disruption', has called for a complete re-construction

13 This was a significant feature of the English Children Act 1989.

14 *YC v United Kingdom* (2012) 55 EHRR 33, para 134. The court's position has not always been so categorical in this regard (see, eg, *Johansen v Norway* (1997) 23 EHRR 33), and some question whether children's best interests should be paramount from an ECHR perspective: see, eg, S. Choudhry and H. Fenwick, 'Taking the Rights of Parents and Children Seriously: Confronting the Welfare Principle Under the Human Rights Act', *Oxford Journal of Legal Studies* 25, 2005, 453.

15 *Re B (A Child)* [2009] UKSC 5, para 37 (Lord Kerr).

16 For example, in England and Wales, if a woman conceives as a result of IVF from a third party at a clinic, her husband or a man with whom there has been a specific agreement, can become the child's parent, as can a woman to whom she is married, or civilly partnered or with whom she is in a relationship: Human Fertilisation and Embryology Act 2008, ss. 35, 37, 427–7; Marriage (Same Sex Couples) Act 2013, sch. 7. By means of a parental order, and the parties' consent, a male same-sex partner of a father can become the second parent of a child conceived through surrogacy: ibid., s. 54.

17 British Columbia, Family Law Act 2011, s. 30. See R. Leckey, 'One Parent, Three Parents: Judges and Ontario's All Families are Equal Act 2016', *International Journal of Law, Policy & the Family* 33, 2019, 298–315.

18 H. Abraham, 'A Family Is What You Make It? Legal Recognition and Regulation of Multiple Parents', *American University Journal of Gender, Social Policy and the Law* 25, 2017, 405–44, 408.

19 N. Cammu, 'How Should We Name the Parents? The Challenges of Plus-Two-Parent Families for Legal Kinship Terminology', *International Journal of Law, Policy & the Family* 31, 2017, 328–43.

of terminology,[20] according to which 'parentage' would designate as 'parents' 'those who have expressed a desire to care for (the child) and who are actually caring for him or her'; 'progenitorship' would refer to individuals who have a genetic link with the child; and 'parenthood' would be used to 'refer to the relationship with third parties who play an important role in the child's life without wanting or being able to claim the status of parent (step-parents, foster families, grandparents ...)'. On this model, 'parentage' could be acquired by means of a 'parental commitment statement', made at any time in the child's life, including before birth. This would exist alongside current ways of acquiring parenthood, such as through intercourse, and, to safeguard children's interests, in some cases there would need to be judicial approval (such as in adoption and surrogacy). Unlike some others, however, Kessler would retain the bi-parental model.

It is perhaps unlikely that universal agreement on such matters will be found soon. Clearly the child's right to receive effective 'parenting' as declared by the UNCRC must be respected, but art. 7 of the Convention also refers to children's right to 'know' their parents, followed by the right to preserve their 'identity' (art. 8). This juxtaposition suggests 'parents' in art. 7 implies a genetic connection since 'identity' can refer to an individual's personal characteristics, which could have inherited genetic components, as well as to a sense of communal belonging.[21] This implies that where possible children should have access to information about their 'progenitors', whether or not they are their caregiving 'parents'.

Protection of private and family life

International instruments protecting the right to 'private' and 'family' life apply to children as much as to adults. A survey of the concept of 'family' in international instruments argues that it consists of both structural and normative elements. The former can consist of actual or fictitious blood relationships, relationships initiated by formal acts (for example, in the case of children, birth within formal marriage, or adoption), or ongoing personal relationships. The latter include anti-discrimination norms (for example against non-marital children) and those protecting children from early marriage.[22]

Where parental status conflicts with the child's best interests, it may be overridden. Indeed, similarly to the UNCRC, the European Court of Human Rights has been clear that the state has positive obligations to protect children from abuse.[23] It is true that it requires a strong case for parents to be deprived of the responsibility (see Chapters 4.1–4.3 of this book), but it is perfectly possible for this to be achieved without waiting for harm to be inflicted on a child: for example,

20 G. Kessler, 'The Parentage Disruption: A Comparative Approach', *International Journal of Law, Policy & the Family* 33, 2019, 316–36.

21 *Mikulić v Croatia* Application 53176/99, Judgment February 2002 (ECtHR); *Jäggi v Switzerland* App. No. 58758/00, final judgment 13 July 2006 (ECtHR). See J. Eekelaar, 'Family Law and Identity', *Oxford Journal of Legal Studies* 38, 2018, 822–40 and S Besson, 'Enforcing the Child's Right to Know Her Origins: Contrasting Approaches Under the Convention on the Rights of the Child and the ECHR', *International Journal of Law, Policy and the Family* 21, 2007, 137. And see, in the context of a transgender parent, *R (on the application of TT) v Registrar General for England and Wales* [2019] EWHC 2384 (Fam).

22 F. Banda and J. Eekelaar, 'International Conceptions of the Family', *International and Comparative Law Quarterly* 66, 2017, 833–62.

23 See, for example, *A v United Kingdom* [1998] 2 FLR 959; *Z v United Kingdom* (2001) 34 EHRR 97. The European Court of Human Rights has frequently referred to the UNCRC, and suggested that it sets out standards 'to which all governments must aspire': *Sahin v Germany* [2003] ECHR 340, para 39.

in England and Wales, the threshold for intervention may be satisfied if significant harm to a child is 'likely'.[24] This may be substantiated, for example, by evidence that a parent has caused harm to other children, thus enabling a child to be removed from the parent at birth.[25]

However, cases arise where there is serious conflict over what constitutes a child's best interests. This often occurs in a medical context, and the study by Alan Rogers of cases in the United States where religious exemption laws prevented medical treatment of sick and dying children because of their parents' religious beliefs provides ample evidence of the problems that can arise.[26] Other jurisdictions take quite a different view of the scope of parental rights in such contexts. In England and Wales, parents who are in agreement with medical opinion about the treatment of a serious medical condition in their child can authorize such treatment without court involvement.[27] However, where there is a dispute between medical professionals and parents, the court has full jurisdiction.[28] The English courts have long established that they make such decisions solely on the basis of their own assessment of the child's welfare, and while the views of parents will be respected as part of the decision-making process, they are not in any sense determinative.[29]

Also, as elaborated particularly in Chapter 3.3 of this book, the possibility that children may be forced into relationships they may not welcome is a real one when their parents are living apart. This can occur not only if parents separate, but where they have never lived together. One of them may be a gamete donor who wishes to commence a relationship with the child, and courts have treated such requests sympathetically[30] (see Chapters 3.1–3.2 of this book). Nevertheless, the mere fact that a person is a biological parent does not establish 'family ties' with a child that demand respect under art. 8 of the European Convention: there must be a 'further legal or factual elements indicating the existence of a close personal relationship'.[31] The fact that a child's parents are married will usually demonstrate such elements, but they can exist without marriage.[32]

24 Children Act 1989, s. 31(2)(a).

25 The issue of the evidence necessary on which a finding of 'likely' harm can be made is, however, controversial: see *re J (Children)* [2013] UKSC 9; M. Hayes, 'The Supreme Court's Failure to Protect Vulnerable Children', *Family Law*, August 2013, 1015–30.

26 A. Rogers, *The Child Cases; How America's Religious Exemption Laws Harm Children*, Amherst and Boston: University of Massachusetts Press, 2014.

27 *Re B (A Minor) (Wardship: Sterilisation)* [1988] AC 199; V. Larcher, F. Craig, K. Bhogal, D. Wilkinson and J. Brierley, 'Making Decisions to Limit Treatment in Life-Limiting and Life-Threatening Conditions in Children: A Framework for Practice', *Archives of Disease in Childhood*, Supp. 2, 100, 2015. Available at http://adc.bmj.com/content/100/Suppl_2

28 *Yates and Gard v Great Ormond Street Hospital for Children NHS Foundation Trust* [2017] EWCA Civ 410, [89]-[115].

29 *Re E (A Minor) (Wardship: Consent to Treatment)* [1992] Fam 11; *Yates and Gard*, ibid. For discussion, see D. Wilkinson and J. Savulescu, 'Alfie Evans and Charlie Gard: Should the Law Change?', *British Medical Journal* 361, 2018, 1891, and various chapters in I. Gould, J. Herring and C. Auckland (eds), *Parental Rights, Best Interests and Significant Harms*, Oxford: Hart Publishing, 2019.

30 See, for example, the English High Court decision in *Re G (A Minor); Re Z (A Minor)* [2013] EWHC 134 (Fam), [2013] 1 FLR 1334.

31 *Lebbink v The Netherlands* (2005) 40 EHRR 18; *Leeds Teaching NHS Trust v A* [2003] 1 FLR 1091; *X, Y and Z v United Kingdom* (1997) 24 EHRR 143; in *Anayo v Germany* [2010] ECHR 2083, the court acknowledged a *potential* relationship between an unmarried father and his child where the lack of an existing relationship was not attributable to the father.

32 J. Liddy, 'The Concept of Family Life under the ECHR', *European Human Rights Law Review* 1, 1998, 15–35; S. Choudhry and J. Herring, *European Human Rights and Family Law*, Oxford: Hart Publishing, 2010, 166–9 and ch. 5.

Children's participation in decisions

While the presence of 'family life' falls within the protection of art. 8 of the European Convention, this is subject to the application of the 'best interests of the child' standard. But this may be compromised by legislative presumptions (see Chapter 3.3 of this book) or neglect of the child's own opinions. The extent to which children's wishes are taken into account in regulating their personal relationships is a rapidly emerging issue. On this the UNCRC is very clear. Art. 12 proclaims that states parties

> shall ensure to the child who is capable of forming his or her own views the right to express those views freely in all matters affecting the child, the views of the child being given due weight in accordance with the age and maturity of the child.[33]

The UN Committee on the Rights of the Child has frequently linked this article with art. 3 of the UNCRC, which requires the child's best interests to be a primary consideration in all actions concerning children. This introduces the child's perspective into understanding the child's interests, and therefore significantly enhances children's rights.

Lady Hale, until 2020 President of the UK Supreme Court, has strongly advocated paying more attention to children's views in court proceedings.[34] However, there is uncertainty how far such views may be treated as evidence in private law proceedings, prompting Lady Hale to ask whether interviewing children was

> more in the nature of a public relations exercise – reassuring the child that she is seen as a real person and enabling her to learn more about what goes on in court – rather than an exercise in helping the judge to make the right decision.

There is a danger that if children are asked their views, but they are then disregarded, they will react badly to the outcome, so the practice is challenging and complex.[35]

Art. 12 is not confined to court proceedings for it extends to 'all matters' affecting children. Following recommendations of the UN Committee on the Rights of the Child, many jurisdictions have established an official body charged with seeking children's views, using, for example, the internet.[36] The child's right to participation is also seen as increasing in Africa (see Chapter 4.5 of this book).

Education

The UNCRC not only recognizes the child's right to education (art. 28), but also sets out criteria for the objectives of that education as being to develop the child's personality, talents and mental

33 See A. Parkes, *Children and International Human Rights Law: The Right of the Child to Be Heard*, Abingdon: Routledge, 2013.

34 L. Hale, 'Are We Nearly There Yet?' Association of Lawyers for Children Annual Conference 2015, Manchester, 20 November 2015. Available at www.supremecourt.uk/docs/speech-151120.pdf. See *re KP* [2014] EWCA Civ 554.

35 See P. Parkinson and J. Cashmore, *The Voice of the Child in Family Disputes*, Oxford: Oxford University Press, 2008; F. Bell, 'Barriers to Empowering Children in Private Family Law Proceedings', *International Journal of Law, Policy & the Family* 30, 2016, 225–47; R. Birnbaum and N. Bala, 'Views of the Child Reports: The Ontario Pilot Project', *International Journal of Law, Policy & the Family* 31, 2017, 344–62.

36 For an analysis of art. 12, see L. Lundy, J. Tobin and A. Parkes, 'Article 12: The Right o Respect for the Views of the Child', in J. Tobin (ed.), *The UN Convention on the Rights of the Child: A Commentary*, Oxford: Oxford University Press, 2019, 397–434.

and physical abilities to their fullest potential; to develop respect for human rights and the principles of the Charter of the United Nations; to develop respect for the child's parents, cultural identity and 'the national values of the country in which the child is living, and from which he or she may originate and for civilizations different from his or her own'; and preparation 'for responsible life in a free society in the spirit of understanding, peace, tolerance, equality of sexes and friendship among all peoples, ethnic, national and religious groups and persons of indigenous origin' (art. 29).

These objectives need to be reconciled with the 'primary responsibility' of children's parents and legal guardians to bring them up (art. 18). The UNCRC does this by describing that responsibility as being 'to provide, in a manner consistent with the evolving capacities of the child, appropriate direction and guidance *in the exercise by the child of the rights recognized in the present Convention*' (art. 5, emphasis supplied). Similarly, art. 2 of the First Protocol to the European Convention on Human Rights, which requires that 'no person shall be denied the right to education' and art. 9 of the Convention, which gives 'everyone' the right to 'freedom of thought, conscience and religion' must be reconciled with the statement in art. 2 of the First Protocol that: 'In the exercise of any functions which it assumes in relation to education and to teaching, the State shall respect the right of parents to ensure such education and teaching in conformity with their own religious and philosophical convictions'. Similarly, while art. 9 of the African Charter proclaims that 'Every child has the right to freedom of thought, conscience and religion', and art. 11 that 'Every child has the right to an education, to develop his or her personality, talents and mental and physical abilities to their fullest potential', that article adds that '(t)his education also includes the preservation and strengthening of positive African morals, traditional values and cultures'. The tensions that can arise between children's rights and parents' rights in this context, particularly in regard to fears over religious extremism have been explored by Rachel Taylor and others.[37] In attempting reconciliation between such conflicts, the European Court of Human Rights has stated that:

> in order to ensure that the restrictions that are imposed do not curtail the (parental) right in question to such an extent as to impair its very essence and deprive it of its effectiveness, the Court must satisfy itself that they are foreseeable for those concerned and pursue a legitimate aim … Furthermore, a limitation will only be compatible with art. 2 of Protocol No. 1 if there is a reasonable relationship of proportionality between the means employed and the aim sought to be achieved [and] [a]lthough the final decision as to the observance of the Convention's requirements rests with the Court, the Contracting States enjoy a certain margin of appreciation in this sphere.[38]

Ritual practices and discipline

The Committee has observed that the parental responsibilities to provide 'appropriate' direction referred to in art. 5 must be read consistently with the whole Convention.[39] Art. 19 of the UNCRC requires states parties to

37 R.E. Taylor, 'Responsibility for the Soul of the Child: The Role of the State and Parents in Determining Religious Upbringing and Education', *International Journal of Law, Policy and the Family* 29, 2015, 15; L. Davies, 'Security, Extremism and Education: Safeguarding or Surveillance?', *British Journal of Educational Studies* 64(1), 2016, 1–19; R. Hill, 'Counter-Extremism in British Schools: Ensuring Respect for Parents' Rights over Their Children's Religious Upbringing', *British Journal of Educational Studies* 65, 2017, 1–15; J. Eekelaar, 'Introduction', in J. Eekelaar (ed.), *Family Rights and Religion*, Abingdon: Routledge, 2017, pp. 7–9.

38 *Catan v Moldova and Russia*, Applications nos 43370/04, 8252/05 and 18454/06, Judgment 19 October 2012.

39 Committee on the Rights of the Child, General Comment No 13, CRC/C/GC/13, 18 April 2011, para 28.

> take all appropriate legislative, administrative, social and educational measures to protect the child from all forms of physical or mental violence, injury or abuse, neglect or negligent treatment, maltreatment or exploitation, including sexual abuse, while in the care of parent(s), legal guardian(s) or any other person who has the care of the child.

This includes 'harmful practices' such as female genital mutilation, forced or early marriage, exorcism and uvulectomy and teeth extraction, which neither the child's 'best interests', nor the parents' or child's rights to cultural identity, can outweigh.[40] There is debate whether a different balance should apply for male circumcision.[41] The African Charter requires governments to 'do what they can to stop harmful social and cultural practices, such as child marriage, that affect the welfare and dignity of children' (art. 21).

The Committee interprets 'violence' strictly, permitting no exceptions,[42] although within a definitional restriction that probably only covers milder forms of physical or other forceful acts if they are inflicted with a punitive purpose.[43] It has recommended to more than 130 states that they should prohibit all corporal punishment in the family and other settings.[44] In an important decision, the South African Constitutional Court has held that the defence of 'reasonable and moderate chastisement' to corporal punishment contravened section 12(1)(a) of the South African Constitution, according to which 'everyone has the right to freedom and security, which includes the right to be free from all forms of violence from either public or private sources', the protection of 'inherent dignity' (section 10) and the child's best interests (section 28(2)). Any attempt to justify such practices on religious or cultural grounds was undermined by 'the availability of less restrictive means to achieve discipline'.[45]

Art. 3 of the European Convention on Human Rights gives everyone, including children, the right to be protected against 'torture or inhuman or degrading treatment or punishment' and any legal provision, such as a parental right to administer reasonable chastisement, that fails to afford such protection, breaches the right.[46] However, it leaves open the possibility that provisions allowing for physical or other chastisement would be compatible with the Convention so long as they restrict such actions to a level not amounting to 'torture or inhuman or degrading treatment or punishment'.[47] But if a state prohibits parents from inflicting any form of corporal punishment, either directly by themselves or by authorizing its use in schools, it would not violate any Convention right of the parents.[48] This does not imply that the Convention *requires*

40 Committee on the Rights of the Child, op. cit., n 7, paras 18–29.

41 See H. Gilbert, 'Time to Reconsider the Lawfulness of Ritual Male Circumcision', *European Human Rights Law Review* 3, 2007, 279–94; H. Askola, 'Cut-Off Point? Regulating Male Circumcision in Finland', *International Journal of Law, Policy and the Family* 25, 2011, 100–19. This became controversial in Germany in 2012: see www.dw.de/circumcision-remains-legal-in-germany/a-16399336

42 Committee on the Rights of the Child, General Comment No 8, CRC/C/GC/8, 2 March 2007, para 17.

43 Ibid., para 15.

44 Ibid. para 5.

45 *Freedom of Religion SA v Minister of Justice and Constitutional Development and others* [2019] ZACC 34. (See further Chapter 4.5 of this book.)

46 *A v United Kingdom* (1997) 27 EHRR 61.

47 The United Kingdom amended the law so as to comply in this way with the Convention. However, it is arguable that it may have failed to do this successfully: Choudhry and Herring, op. cit., n 32, 215. In October 2019 the Children (Equal Protection from Assault) (Scotland) Bill, which would remove the defence of 'justified assault' in cases of corporal punishment inflicted by parents on children, was passed by the Scottish Parliament.

48 *Seven Individuals v Sweden* (1982) European Commission of Human Rights, Admissibility Decision 13 May 1982; *R (Williamson) v Secretary of State for Education and Employment* [2005] 2 AC 246. For South Africa, see *Christian Education South Africa v Minister of Education* (2000) 9 BHRC 53.

states to impose such a prohibition.[49] Nevertheless, the growing influence of the UNCRC on the application of the European Convention might lead to such a result at some time in the future.

Discrimination

Art. 2 of the UNCRC requires states to 'take all appropriate measures to ensure that the child is protected against all forms of discrimination or punishment on the basis of the status, activities, expressed opinions, or beliefs of the child's parents, legal guardians, or family members'. An important English case in 2017 concerned the threat by the ultra-conservative Charedi community to exclude from the community children whose father had left home to live as a transgender person if they had direct contact with her. On the basis of uncontradicted evidence that such exclusion would seriously harm the children, Peter Jackson J had rejected the father's application for direct contact, instead making an order providing for limited indirect contact, with the possibility of gradual restoration of the full relationship.[50] But the Court of Appeal[51] rejected this, asking how the judge could 'properly come to a conclusion dictated by the practices of a community which involve discrimination and victimisation', and suggesting that the court itself might remove the children from the community in order to allow the direct contact it thought would be beneficial to the children. While excluding children on the basis of a parent's transgender status amounts to discrimination *against the child* contrary to the Convention, it is controversial whether this should be overcome by risking the children's welfare in that way.[52]

49 See Chaudhry and Herring, op. cit., n 32, 215–20.

50 *J v B (Ultra-Orthodox Judaism: Transgender)* [2017] EWFC 4.

51 *In the matter of M (Children)* [2017] EWCA Civ 2164.

52 J. Eekelaar, 'Welfare and Discrimination', *Family Law* 48, 2018, 393–7. On the broader question of the right to education of children in such communities, see S. Levin, 'Test of Faith: Haredi Communities and the Right to Education', *International Journal of Law, Policy and the Family* 32, 2018, 334–62.

PART 5

Discrimination and personal safety

5.1
GENDER AND HUMAN RIGHTS

Fareda Banda

Gender is all the rage – rage meaning it is both a focus of attention and also anger. It is at the fault line of inter-generational conversations: 'In our day, there were men and women, none of this gender fluidity business'; heated conversations between feminists – can a transgender woman really know what it is like to be born a woman and to understand the lifetime challenges? Can one reconcile religious prescriptions of the roles of men and women in marriage and the family with developments in science, technology and indeed law? Can there be a universal understanding of gender including within the United Nations family? The evidence which I will explore in this chapter suggests not.

The first part looks at the evolving understanding of gender in the international arena focusing on the work of the United Nations. Thereafter I move on to consider how gender has played out in courts focusing on gender stereotyping and sexual orientation from a family law perspective.

On 'gender': a brief history

Human rights practitioners owe a debt of gratitude to development specialists who elaborated on the significance of gender as a category. For human rights purposes, the term gender can be linked to the intertwining of development with law and policy in the 1970s and specifically the UN Decade for Women from 1975–1985, which had as its goals equality, development and peace.

Cornwall contends that the concept of gender that emerged from the work of mainly western feminists in 1970s was: 'Premised on a set of bounded oppositions, "gender" became shorthand for hierarchical relations of power between "women" and "men". In the process, it came to evoke women battling against all odds on the wrong side of the power differential'.[1] Cornwall also notes that several African writers have identified other differentials including seniority and wealth. She further contends that western feminism failed to 'take account of women's interests as members of generations, families or economic groups. As economic actors in their own

1 A. Cornwall, 'Introduction: Perspectives on Gender in Africa', in A. Cornwall (ed.), *Readings in Gender in Africa*, Martlesham: International Africa Institute and James Currey, 2005, pp. 1–19, 5.

right, women's relationships with other women may in themselves be exploitative or hierarchical as studies of women and slavery illustrate'.[2] Reading from Cornwall's analyses, one can see that whatever the shortcomings of the 'western' construction of gender, it, or varieties closely aligned to it, has/have become the dominant model.

The first robust challenge to the conceptualization of gender in the international arena took place at the 1995 Beijing Conference on Women which marked the tenth anniversary of the ending of the UN Decade for Women.[3] Attempts to broaden the understanding of gender to take on sexual diversity and also to more explicitly acknowledge the disproportionate reproductive burden borne by women, were actively resisted by religious bodies, not least the Holy See. All mention of 'gender' was removed from the Declaration and the Platform for Action which was adopted at the Conference. The appendix attached to the Beijing Conference documentation said:

> the word 'gender' had been commonly used and understood in its ordinary, generally accepted usage in numerous other United Nations forums and conferences;
>
> there was no indication that any new meaning or connotation of the term, different from accepted prior usage, was intended in the Platform for Action.[4]

This meaningless statement suggested that gender could mean whatever you wanted it to mean. In turn, the Holy See prepared a statement to be attached as an addendum to the Beijing Platform, detailing its objections to the use of the term 'gender' and asserting that it only recognized two categories – men and women. In many ways, the binary Holy See version is how many laypeople conceive of the term 'gender'.

In 1997, the UN formally adopted gender mainstreaming as integral to the work of the organization, with UN Secretary-General, Kofi Annan, noting that 'for every human rights violation, there is a gender dimension'.[5] But what did this mean in practice? In her research on gender mainstreaming initiatives in Afghanistan, Kuovo found that there was a superficial understanding of what gender mainstreaming entailed so that often it was interpreted as 'adding women' thus reinforcing the idea of gender as being about women. Indeed Kuovo noted that gender is often used as a synonym for women. She, like others before her, also make the important point that the word 'gender' does not always translate well into other languages, and indeed that there may not be equivalence in understanding what is meant by gender. In the Afghan context, gender was understood as meaning: 'that Afghan women should become like Western women, that they should leave their husbands'.[6]

A more radical interpretation of gender was adopted by the UN Special Rapporteur on Antiterrorism in his 2009 report on gender and anti-terrorist strategies.

2 Ibid., p. 4.

3 Report of the Fourth World Conference on Women, Beijing, 4–15 September 1995, Statement by the President of the Conference on the commonly understood meaning of the term 'gender', 2–3, A/CONF/177/20/Rev.1; see also Rome Statute of the International Criminal Court, 1998, 2187 UNTS 90, art. 7 (3).

4 Beijing-appendix IV.

5 Report of the Secretary-General on the Question of Integrating the Human Rights of Women throughout the United Nations System E/CN.4/1998/49 (25 March 1998) para 9.

6 S. Kuovo, 'Taking Women Seriously? Conflict, State-Building and Gender in Afghanistan', in S. Kuovo and Z. Pearson (eds), *Feminist Perspectives on Contemporary International Law*, Oxford: Hart Publishing, 2011, pp. 159–76, 159.

> Gender is not synonymous with women but rather encompasses the social constructions that underlie how women's and men's roles, functions and responsibilities, including in relation to sexual orientation and gender identity, are defined and understood. ... Consequently, gender is not static; it is changeable over time and across contexts. Understanding gender as a social and shifting construct rather than as a biological and fixed category is important because it helps to identify the complex and inter-related gender-based human rights violations.[7]

UN treaty bodies

While human rights treaties do not include gender as a protected category in their non-discrimination provisions, listing only sex, human rights treaty bodies have broadened the scope of their understanding of gender.[8] In its 2010 General Recommendation No. 28 on State Obligations, the CEDAW Committee sees the two – gender and sex – as interlinked:

> The term 'gender' refers to socially constructed identities, attributes and roles for women and men and society's social and cultural meaning for these biological differences resulting in hierarchical relationships between women and men and in the distribution of power and rights favouring men and disadvantaging women. This social positioning of women and men is affected by political, economic, cultural, social, religious, ideological and environmental factors and can be changed by culture, society and community. The application of the Convention to gender-based discrimination is made clear by the definition of discrimination contained in art. 1.[9]

There are of course other viewpoints, not least that contained within art. 6 of the Cairo Declaration on Human Rights in Islam, 1990 which stipulates that men and women have separate roles and duties to perform though they are equal in human dignity.[10] It very clearly lays out the respective obligations of the husband who has to provide for the family and that of the wife who has the right to keep her own name and manage her money but who is expected to be the homemaker. Although not in force, the Cairo Declaration is echoed in the preamble to the Arab Charter on Human Rights 2004 and in the reservations of States Parties not least Egypt.[11] This complementary view of gender is grounded in what Nzegwu has called a dual sex model.[12] This accepts that men and women are different and sees their different sphere activities as equally

7 UN Special Rapporteur on the Protection of Human Rights and Fundamental Freedoms while Countering Terrorism, A/64/211, 3 August, 2009, para 20. The inclusion of gender identity and sexual orientation met with a great deal of resistance. D. Otto, 'Queering Gender Identity in International Law', *Nordic Journal of Human Rights* 33(4), 2015, 299.

8 UN Special Rapporteur, A/64/211, para 21.

9 CEDAW, *General Recommendation No. 28 on the Core Obligations of States Parties under Art. 2 of the Convention on the Elimination of All Forms of Discrimination against Women*, 16 December 2010, CEDAW/C/GC/28, para 5.

10 Cairo Declaration on Human Rights in Islam. Adopted and proclaimed by Organization of Islamic Conference resolution 217 A (III) of adopted on 5 August 1990.

11 Arab Charter on Human Rights, May 22, 2004, reprinted in 12 Int'l Hum. Rts. Rep. 893 (2005), entered into force March 15, 2008.

12 N. Nzegwu, 'Gender Equality in a Dual Sex System: The Case of Onitsha', *Canadian Journal of Law and Jurisprudence* 7(1), 1994, 73–96.

valued. She critiques what she sees as the inferiority complex embedded in western feminism's wish to 'turn women into men' and which measures women by a male standard rather than on their own terms.

What follows is an examination, through case law, of the push and pull between conservative forces who wish to confine gender to its binary understanding of the roles and responsibilities of men and women, or how society constructs what it means to be a man or a woman, with more radical conceptualizations which seek to problematize the very categories men and women and male and female to take on issues of gender stereotyping, gender identity and sexual orientation.

On gender stereotyping in family law and policy

In their book on *Gender Stereotyping*, Cook and Cusack explain why we stereotype:

> We stereotype to 'script identities', to assign norms and codes by which men and women can be preconceived and expected to live their lives. It is through the understanding of these and other reasons for stereotyping that we can uncover and dismantle the unstated assumptions behind stereotypes. In so doing, we may hope to prevent their perpetuation when that is unjust to those preconceived through stereotypes, and prevent people from making inaccurate and unjust assessments of those seen only through stereotypes.[13]

The European Court of Human Rights has also challenged gender stereotyping in state policy. In *Markin v Russia*[14] the author, who worked as a radio intelligence operator in the Russian military, challenged the refusal to allow him to take time off to look after his children following a divorce. A similarly situated woman would have been permitted to take leave. Markin alleged that the refusal constituted a breach of his art. 8 right to family linked to art. 14 on discrimination. The Russian government acknowledged the distinction in treatment but sought to justify it by arguing that scientific research pointed to the unique bond between mothers and children which necessitated the maternal preference rule. It framed this as 'positive discrimination' for women. Furthermore, the government noted that there were more men serving and allowing men to take time off would impair their battle readiness and thus harm national security. It would be harder to replace men if many were allowed to take parental leave in the same way as women who were mothers. It concluded that the rules did allow for exceptional circumstances where serving male personnel would be permitted to take time off. These special circumstances included severe illness of the mother. The number of men granted exceptional leave was very small. Finally, the State argued that Russian society was 'traditional' and was not ready to accept equality between men and women in the forces.

The Court found for Markin, noting that there was no scientific basis for the maternal preference rule. Rather, women may perform the biological function of giving birth, but caring for the child was something that both parents could, and should, do. The Court ruled that the job undertaken by Markin could be done by others, male or female. Furthermore, the Court noted the evolution of its jurisprudence tackling gender stereotyping and agreed that gender stereotyping was 'disadvantageous both to women's careers and to men's family life'.[15]

13 R. Cook and S. Cusack, *Gender Stereotyping*, Philadelphia: University of Penn Press, 2010. See also S. Cusack, *Gender Stereotyping as a Human Rights Violation*, Geneva: OHCHR, 2013.

14 *Konstantin Markin v Russia* Application no. 30078/06, 22 March 2012 (ECHR).

15 Ibid., para 141; see also para 119; see also Cook and Cusack, n 13, pp. 11–12, 62–3, 69, 127.

In its 2019 report on families, *UN Women* makes the link between women's participation in the paid workforce and their ability to contribute to family income and an increased voice in decisions about how income is to be spent. This has in turn also given women greater economic security and evened out the imbalance of power within the family. Despite these developments *UN Women* also notes that there remains in many places, not least the developed world, a motherhood penalty where the gendered expectation that women will take primary responsibility for looking after children leads to pay gap inequalities between men and women because women living with a male partner will earn less.[16] CEDAW has sought to mitigate this gendered inequality by enjoining states to challenge stereotyped roles for men and women and also to ensure that maternity is seen as a 'social function' with the further requirement of the 'recognition of the common responsibility of men and women in the upbringing and development of their children'.[17]

The *Markin* decision can be contrasted with the majority decision in the South African Constitutional Court case of *Hugo v The President of South Africa*.[18] The President, Nelson Mandela, issued an amnesty permitting the release of mothers of children under the age of 12 from prison. Hugo, a father of a qualifying child (whose mother had died), challenged the amnesty on grounds of discrimination on grounds of sex and gender under section 8 of the Interim Constitution. The majority agreed that there was distinction in treatment but said that it was justified because women were primary caregivers and the President had been motivated by a desire to improve children's lives. In a dissent Justice Kriegler noted that perpetuating gender stereotypes, even if well-intentioned, itself constituted discrimination that was not justifiable:

> In my view the notion relied upon by the President, namely that women are to be regarded as the primary care givers of young children, is a root cause of women's inequality in our society. It is both a result and a cause of prejudice; a societal attitude which relegates women to a subservient, occupationally inferior yet unceasingly onerous role. It is a relic and a feature of the patriarchy which the Constitution so vehemently condemns. Section 8 and the other provisions mentioned above outlawing gender or sex discrimination were designed to undermine and not to perpetuate patterns of discrimination of this kind.

As the *Markin* and *Hugo* cases show, gender stereotyping affects *both* men and women. It is worth noting that men pay a price for a construction of masculinity that forces them to work long hours and thus curtails their ability to spend time nurturing and building bonds with their children and participating fully in family life. The low take up of equal parenting leave by men in the British workforce is testament to the impact of gender stereotypes because men's higher salaries make them less likely to take parental leave if it is paid at the minimal statutory rate; thus continuing work becomes an economic necessity. Even if an employer pays the full rate while the employee is on parental leave, men are still less likely to take time off for fear of being seen as not committed. Moreover, there remains the persistent view that looking after babies is 'women's work' because they were made for it and are better suited – after all men's breasts don't

16 UN Women, *Progress of the World's Women 2019–20: Families in a Changing World Summary*, New York: UN Women, 2019, p. 3.

17 R. Holtmaat, 'Article 5', in M. Freeman, C. Chinkin and B. Rudolph (eds), *The UN Convention on the Elimination of all Forms of Discrimination against Women: A Commentary*, Oxford: Oxford University Press, 2013, pp. 141–67, 141, 142–3, 147–8, 157, 163.

18 *President of the Republic of South Africa v Hugo* 1997 (4) SA 1.

produce milk, to quote one reason that I have heard. This puts pressure on men not to ask for parental leave even if they want to. Men may be right to be fearful, for research has clearly shown that women are more likely to lose their jobs by being made redundant or to be downgraded on their return.[19] Why would men want to face the same discrimination?

Stereotypes based on sexual orientation

In their ten-year review of the Yogyakarta Principles on gender identity and sexual orientation, the drafters added Principle 24 on the right to found a family. The focus is on family formation, emphasizing that states have a duty to: 'Protect children from discrimination, violence or other harm due to the sexual orientation, gender identity, gender expression or sex characteristics of their parents, guardians, or other family members'.[20]

The Inter-American Court of Human Rights case of *Atala Riffo and Daughters v Chile*[21] highlights the challenges that still confront lesbian mothers who want to bring up their children. Atala, a judge in her professional life, was a divorced mother with three daughters. After her divorce she began living with a woman in a lesbian relationship. Her former husband asked for custody of their daughters arguing that it was not in their best interests to be brought up in a lesbian household. The mother had made the 'selfish choice' to place her personal happiness above her maternal responsibilities. This made her unfit to meet her obligations. It was his opinion that children should be brought up in a family comprising a mother and father of different sexes.[22]

The Chilean Supreme Court agreed with him, citing the prejudice and discrimination that the girls would face from the wider society. The court also said that the girls would be confused about their own sexuality. The court held that the child's rights trumped the parent's interests.[23] Atala and her daughters took their case to the Inter-American Court arguing that the allegations against her were libellous and hurtful. There was no foundation in law (the Chilean Civil Code or the law on minors) which stated that 'different sexual choice' was a ground for 'disqualification as a parent'.[24] The Inter-American Commission reinforced that the case was about discrimination and the arbitrary interference in the private life of Ms Atala.[25] It was argued that having ratified the American Convention on Human Rights and agreed to abide by the equal protection and

19 Equality and Human Rights Commission, *Pregnancy and Maternity-Related Discrimination and Disadvantage: Experiences of Mothers*, London: Equality and Human Rights Commission, 2018.

20 Drafted by a combination of civil society advocates, academics and a few UN Special Rapporteurs, these principles seek to incorporate a gender plural reading to human rights. They identify the various ways in which difference impacts the enjoyment of human rights and implore human rights Committees and States to take on a purposive approach to the interpretation of human rights, including within the family. Yogyakarta Principles plus 10, Additional Principles and State Obligations on the Application of International Human Rights Law in Relation to Sexual Orientation, Gender Identity, Gender Expression and Sex Characteristics to Complement the Yogyakarta Principles, 10 November 2017. Available at http://yogyakartaprinciples.org/wp-content/uploads/2017/11/A5_yogyakartaWEB-2.pdf. Site visited 5 November 2019. Principle 24 (H). Principle 24 also provides that surrogacy and other reproductive technologies should be available to all irrespective of gender identity or sexual orientation. See also Principle 2 (m) on equality and non-discrimination.

21 *Karen Atala and Daughters v Chile,* Case 1271–4, Report No. 42/08, Inter-Am. C.H.R., OEA/Ser.L/VII.130 Doc.22, rev. 1 (2008).

22 Ibid., para 39. See also paras 97–8, 105–6, 113.

23 Ibid., paras 54–8.

24 Ibid., para 32.

25 Ibid., para 59. See also paras 72–3.

non-discrimination requirements of the Convention, the State could not now 'claim that their level of social and political development prevents them from understanding that sexual orientation is included as a category for which discrimination is prohibited'.[26] The State countered that it was not the mother's sexual orientation which was on trial. The decision of the Supreme Court merely focused on which parent was best able to meet the children's needs. The State claimed that the father had a good relationship with his daughters and offered 'better conditions for the well-being of the girls' and also noted that the girls had a positive relationship with the father's partner (who was female). It further noted that there was not universal consensus on the issue of sexual orientation and some states were at different stages of recognition than others.

The Court found for Ms Atala and her children. It relied on international and regional jurisprudence to show that there was consensus that the principle of non-discrimination and equality was *jus cogens*.[27] It further noted that there had been several resolutions passed by the Inter-American General Assembly affirming that States should ensure that there was no discrimination on grounds of gender identity and sexual orientation.[28] The court was clear that stereotyping and 'societies not being ready for same-sex relationships' were not justified reasons for allowing prejudice to continue. It held that there had been no proof that the girls had, or would suffer, social ostracization as a result of having a parent who was living in a same-sex relationship. Their best interests had not been adequately weighted and had instead being overtaken by the focus on the mother's conduct which focus was itself discriminatory. It reiterated the UN Children's Rights Committee injunction in its General Comment No 7 on Implementing Child Rights in Early Childhood that children should not be subjected to discrimination because they belonged to 'non-traditional' families.[29]

A different gender stereotype emerged in *González Carreño v Spain*.[30] The complaint was brought to the CEDAW Committee by the mother of a child who had been murdered by her father during a contact visit. The parents had divorced after a turbulent courtship and marriage during which the husband had assaulted and psychologically abused the mother. After the separation she had resisted visitation specifying the ongoing harassment and abuse, but many courts had ordered supervised visits before finally allowing him unsupervised contact with the daughter. During the supervised visits the daughter had also indicated that she did not wish to see her father because he behaved inappropriately (she was frightened) and quizzed her about her mother's private life. He killed the daughter and then himself following an unsupervised visit. The mother brought a complaint to CEDAW arguing a failure of due diligence to protect her child. She also identified a violation of art. 2(f) enjoining the State to eradicate discriminatory practices and customs together with art. 5(a) on modifying cultural patterns and conduct. Specifically, the mother argued that the authorities had ignored her multiple warnings about the man's violence and its detrimental effect on the daughter because they privileged the father's rights to contact over the child's best interest.

Instead, the authorities responsible for providing protection chose to follow the stereotypical view that even the most abusive should enjoy visitation rights and that it is always better for a child to be raised by its father and mother; thus failing to appreciate the rights of the child

26 Ibid., para 73.

27 Ibid., paras 78–82.

28 Ibid., para 86, n 97. For UN General Assembly and Human Rights Council initiatives see para 90.

29 Ibid., para 151 citing CRC General Comment No. 7, CRC/C/GC/7, September 30, 2005 para 12. It also cited ECHR case law and Mexican case law on the same point. Paras 143–4 (Portugal and Austria) and 126–7 (Mexico) On stereotyping see paras 119–20.

30 *González Carreño v Spain* CEDAW/C/58/D/47/2012, Communication No. 47/2012.

and disregarding the fact that she had expressed fear of her father and rejected the contact. The courts took it for granted that it is better to have contact even with a violent father.[31]

The Committee found for Gonzalez, noting that domestic violence should be taken into consideration when making decisions about custody and visitation. The best interests of the child should always prevail.[32] Furthermore, the Committee also found violations of arts 2(f) and 5(a). It ordered the State to provide training for judges and police including on issues pertaining to domestic violence and gender stereotyping.[33] The Committee ordered that damages be awarded to the author of the complaint. These were confirmed by the Spanish Supreme Court which ruled that the findings of human rights treaties bodies and their recommendations were binding on Spain[34] (see also Chapter 5.2 in this book).

On gender-based violence

There have been retrogressive legislative turns on the issue of gender-based violence. Notorious is Russia's dilution of its law on domestic violence and the persistent failures by the State to act to meet its due diligence obligations to prevent, investigate, prosecute and punish perpetrators of gender-based violence.[35] In *Volodina v Russia*,[36] a woman had lived with a man for two years with her son. She fled from the partner leaving him in Ulyanovsk and moved to Moscow to escape persistent violence. He followed her, harassed her, beat her, cut the brakes of her car, stole her handbag removing her two telephones and continually stalked her. The authorities did little to help, either ignoring her, or believing his version, or calling it a domestic dispute or asking for medical evidence months later when it was too late. The law was said to be inadequate to deal with the violence, with the applicant's counsel noting that the de-criminalization of assault in 2017, which now required the bringing of a private prosecution but only if there had been administrative proceedings in the preceding 12 months which had resulted in the offender being found guilty, showed the State's indifference to the suffering of women. There were no protection orders available. The applicant noted that the requirement for private prosecution was unduly onerous leaving the victim open to pressure to reconcile (the preferred option of the authorities) or to further abuse. Statistics were produced to show that:

> About 90% of private prosecution cases were discontinued, either owing to reconciliation or failure to fulfil the legal requirements. In 2015, there had been 2.37 million reports of assault, but only 26,212 cases had resulted in a criminal conviction. In 2017, out of a total of 164,000 instances of assault, only 7,000 had been subject to a criminal investigation.[37]

31 *Gonzalez v Spain*, para 3.8. See also para 3.9.

32 Ibid., para 3.11 (b) (i).

33 Ibid., para 3.11 (b) (iii). See also *K. v Bulgaria*, UN Doc. CEDAW/C/49/D/20/2008 (27 September 2011) and *A.T. v Hungary, A.T. v Hungary*, UN Doc. CEDAW/C/32/D/2/2003 (26 January 2005).

34 See P. Kashyap, '*Gonzalez Carreno v Spain*: What Can Be Expected from the Spanish Supreme Court's Ruling?', *Oxford Human Rights Hub Blog*, 7 November 2018. Available at http://gonzález-carreño-v.-Spain:-what-can-be-expected-from-the-spanish-supreme-court's-ruling (accessed 7 November 2019).

35 J. Stallard, 'The Dark Reality of Russia's Domestic Violence Laws', *BBC*, 7 March 2018. See also Human Rights Watch, *I Could Kill You and Not One Would Stop Me: Weak State Response to Domestic Violence in Russia*, Human Rights Watch, 25 October 2018.

36 Application No. 41261/17,

37 *Volodina v Russia* Application No. 41261 at para 69. Similar observations had been made about the law and its negative effects by the CEDAW Committee in *O.G. v the Russian Federation* (Communication

The applicant made reference to the many instances that Russia had been told by various UN Treaty bodies and Special Procedure Mechanisms to tackle its gender-based violence problem.[38] These included a report by the UN Special Rapporteur on Violence against Women who, in a visit to Russia, had included in her report the cultural justification for gender-based violence:

> the main cause is rooted in patriarchal norms and values. In many meetings held by the Special Rapporteur, authorities referred to an ancient Russian proverb, 'a beating man is a loving man!' Due to strong patriarchal values, husbands in Russia are generally considered superior to their wives with the right to assert control over them, legitimizing the general opinion that domestic violence is a private issue. Women are often blamed for having provoked the violence.[39]

The court reviewed the extensive evidence of the multiple failures of due diligence by the Russian state which included not criminalizing violence but instead relying on a complex administrative-private prosecution model; not having protection orders; not taking seriously multiple reports of violence highlighted in the statistics and exemplified by the applicant's case; not heeding the many recommendations made by international treaty bodies to tackle the violence problem and found that there had been a violation of the applicant's art. 3 right to be free from degrading and inhuman treatment coupled with art. 14 on discrimination. It ordered the State to pay her damages.[40]

Gender and plural family forms

The 'family' and its constitution has again become the site of the resistance in the 'gender wars'. Moves to reintroduce a narrow 'traditional' concept of the family come up against the work of human rights committees which have evolved their definition of family beyond the heteronormative model of two married people to encompass greater diversity. Some states have pushed back on these attempts seeing them as violative of local norms and cultures.[41]

No. 91/2015, 6 November 2017), para 7.7. The Committee had recommended that the State revert the law back to considering domestic violence a criminal act. At para 9 (b)(ii)). This CEDAW opinion was cited in the *Volodina v Russia* at para 65. See also *Jallow v Bulgaria,* Communication No. 32/2011, UN Doc. CEDAW/C/52/D/32/2011 (28 August 2012). In an earlier General Recommendation on Violence (No. 19) the Committee had identified gender-based violence as violence that is 'directed against a woman because she is a woman or that affects women disproportionately'. CEDAW General Recommendation No. 19 on Violence against Women, Doc. A/47/38, 1992, para 6.

38 *Volodina v Russia,* Application No. 41261/17, paras 52–61. The Court also recited the many international interventions at para 125.

39 Ibid., para 61 quoting *Integration of the human rights of women and a gender perspective: violence against women,* a report of the Special Rapporteur on violence against women, its causes and consequences, following her visit to the Russian Federation from 17 to 24 December 2004 (E/CN.4/2006/61/Add.2), para 27. The New York Times notes that an attempt to strengthen the law on domestic violence in 2012 had been resisted by the Orthodox Church's Commission on the Family because it reflected '"the ideas of radical feminism" aimed at victimizing men'. A. Higgins, 'Russia's Police Tolerate Domestic Violence: Where Can Its Victims Turn?', *New York Times,* 11 July 2019, site visited 20 November 2019.

40 Ibid., paras 73–133.

41 See for example Human Rights Committee Concluding Observations Hungary, sixth periodic report, CCPR/C/HUN/CO/6, 9 May 2018, paras 19 and 20 (a-c) on non-recognition of LGBTI rights and paras 25–6 on domestic violence.

In General Recommendation 21 on marriage and family, the CEDAW Committee notes that:

> The form and concept of the family can vary from State to State, and even between regions within a State. Whatever form it takes, and whatever the legal system, religion, custom or tradition within the country, the treatment of women in the family both at law and in private must accord with the principles of equality and justice for all people, as art. 2 of the Convention requires.[42]

In its next General Recommendation on Family and Property, No. 29, CEDAW reiterated that with the UN system, 'the concept of "family" must be understood in a wide sense'.[43] It referenced the Human Rights Committee General Comment 28 on Equality between Men and Women as reflecting that view and quoted the UN Secretary-General's statement marking the observance of the International Year of the Family, that 'families assume diverse forms and functions among and within countries'.[44]

Family formation: on who can't marry – gender normativity and the re-emergence of the 'traditional family'

The right to marry and to found a family is one of the fundamental rights in the Universal Declaration of Human Rights, 1948. In art. 16(3), the UDHR identifies family as the 'the natural and fundamental group unit of society and is entitled to protection by society and the State'. The questions are 'what is natural?' and 'who decides who can marry?' Is the criminalization of same-sex relationships a violation of the right to family life?[45] If your behaviour is criminalized as being 'against the order of nature' and marriage is defined as occurring between a man and a woman only, how real is the right to family life for those who are not heterosexual? The Yogyakarta Principles are clear that there should not be discrimination against people wishing to enter into same-sex relationships.[46] The direction of travel in human rights seems to be in favour of recognizing same-sex relationships and the entitlements to equivalent treatment of couples in these relationships with their opposite sex peers.[47]

42 CEDAW, *General Recommendation No. 21: Equality in Marriage and Family Relations*, 1994, UN A/49/38, para 33.

43 CEDAW General Recommendation No. 29 on art. 16 of CEDAW on Economic Consequences of Marriage and Family, CEDAW/C/GC/29, 26 February 2013, para 17, citing General comment No. 4 of the Committee on Economic, Social and Cultural Rights, on the right to adequate housing (art. 11 (1) of the International Covenant on Economic, Social and Cultural Rights), E/1992/23, para 6.

44 Secretary General Report on the International Year of the Family, A/50/370, para 14.

45 The European court has recognized the right to family life of same-sex couples not eligible to marry. It challenged the exclusion of same-sex couples from a law recognizing and protecting the interests of heterosexual people to enter into civil partnerships as an alternative to marriage holding that there had been a violation of arts 14 (discrimination) and 8 (right to private and family life). *Vallianatos and Others v Greece,* Applications nos 29381/09 and 32684/09, ECtHR, Grand Chamber, 7 November 2013. Available at www.refworld.org/cases,ECHR,5899eafb4.html (accessed 7 November 2019).

46 Yogyakarta Principles. 2007, principle 24. Available at https://yogyakartaprinciples.org/principle-24/ (accessed 7 November 2019). https://yogyakartaprinciples.org/principle-24/

47 See F. Banda and J. Eekelaar, 'International Conceptions of the Family', *International & Comparative Law Quarterly* 66(4), 2017, 833–62. See also Inter American Court of Human Rights Advisory Opinion 24/17, Inter-Am. Ct. H.R. (ser. A) No. 24 (24 November 2017). J. Contesse, 'The Inter-American

However, there has been active resistance to what some States conceive of as the expansion of rights beyond their socially and culturally acceptable limits. At the United Nations some states have argued that the right to marry found in the international bill of rights recognizes only marriage between men and women.[48] They agree with the earlier interpretation of the Human Rights Committee in *Joslin et al. v New Zealand*[49] that marriage was strictly between opposite sex couples. A group of States has therefore pushed for the adoption of resolutions on the 'traditional family'. Significantly there is not a definition provided for 'traditional family' but the resolutions focus on the importance of children having secure family lives.

Other states have used legislation and constitutional law reform to resist recognizing same-sex relationships. In 2014 the Nigerian legislature adopted the Same Sex Marriage Prohibition Act.[50] Meanwhile in 2013 Zimbabwe adopted a new Constitution including a provision which expressly stated that marriage could only be between a man and a woman. Kenya, whose Constitution is considered later in the chapter, also joined its African peers in defining marriage in heteronormative terms. This local resistance seems to be anticipated in General Recommendation No. 29 of the Committee on the Elimination of all Forms of Discrimination against Women, where it provides:

> Certain forms of relationships (namely, same-sex relationships) are not legally, socially or culturally accepted in a considerable number of States parties. However, where they are recognized, whether as a de facto union, registered partnership or marriage, the State party should ensure protection of the economic rights of the women in those relationships.[51]

Gender/sexuality in national courts

In 2019 the Kenyan High Court considered a joint petition challenging the constitutionality of sections 162 and 165 of the Penal Code.[52] Section 162 prohibits carnal knowledge including a man permitting another man to commit acts 'against the order of nature'. The penalty is imprisonment for 14 years. Section 165 prohibits 'gross indecency' between men in public or private. The penalty is a prison sentence of five years. The petitioners challenged the provisions, arguing that they breached the principles of equal protection of the law and the right to equality before the law. Additionally they offended the right to human dignity and unjustifiably encroached on the petitioners' right to privacy. In discriminating on grounds of sexual orientation or gender identity, the Penal Code further impacted the right to access health care. They

Court of Human Rights' Advisory Opinion on Gender Identity and Same-Sex Marriage', *ASIL Insights* 22(9), 26 July 2018.

48 UDHR art. 16, ICCPR art. 23 and ICESCR art. 10.

49 *Joslin et al v New Zealand*, Communication No. 902/1999, U.N. Doc. A/57/40, paras 8.2 and 8.3. Cf. O. Roos and A. Mackay, 'The Evolutionary Interpretation of Treaties and the Right to Marry: Why Article 23(2) of the ICCPR Should Be Re-Interpreted to Encompass Same-Sex Marriage', *George Washington International Law Review* 49(4), 2017. 879. Available at https://ssrn.com/abstract=3039870 (accessed 7 November 2019).

50 Same Sex Marriage Prohibition Act, 2014 (Nigeria). Human Rights Watch, 'Tell me Where I can be Safe: The Impact of Nigeria's Same Sex Marriage (Prohibition) Act', Human Rights Watch Report, 20 October 2016.

51 CEDAW General Recommendation No. 29 on art. 16 of the Convention on the Elimination of all Forms of Discrimination against Women, *Economic Consequences of Marriage, Family Relations and Their Dissolution*, CEDAW/C/GC/29, 26 February 2013, para 24.

52 *EG & 7 others v Attorney General; DKM & 9 others (Interested Parties); Katiba Institute & another (Amicus Curiae)* Petition 150 and 234 of 2016 (Consolidated) Kenya Law.

also argued that the ordinary construction of terms like 'carnal knowledge' were imprecise and could be interpreted, as they were in Black's Law Dictionary, as including both heterosexual and homosexual intercourse.

Denying the petition, the High Court noted that it was tasked with interpreting the statute in line with constitutional provisions. With this in mind the many rules of interpretation required the Court to give meaning to the words as used in the statute – these were clear and had to be given weight. They prohibited certain conduct including same-sex relations. The intent of the legislature was clear and unambiguous. The Court further noted that recognizing same-sex relationships would open the door to the recognition of same-sex marriages or cohabitation (the petitioners had expressly said that they were not asking for the recognition of same-sex marriages). The Court cited art. 45(2) of the Constitution which provides: 'Every adult has the right to marry a person of the opposite sex, based on the free consent of the parties' and noted that this precluded the recognition of same-sex relationships. The Marriage Act 2014 also so provided in section 3(1). The Court argued that there had been public consultations about the content of the Constitution before its promulgation in 2010. The ban on same-sex marriage had come from the people. Their values, now incorporated into the Constitution needed to be respected.[53] The Court went further to say that there was not any scientific proof that LGBTIQ identity was in any way innate. It conceded that there had been an earlier Kenyan Court of Appeal case recognizing LGBTIQ human rights defenders, but this did not mean that the recognition had to apply in every instance.[54] It was on a case by case basis. In this case, recognition would lead to a breach of art. 45(2) of the Kenyan Constitution and was thus not permissible. It acknowledged the wide range of comparative jurisprudence recognizing the rights of LGBTIQ people and striking down laws that criminalized same-sex conduct or 'acts against nature' that had been drawn to its attention. However, it noted that it was not bound to follow these global trends, the absence of consensus in decisions of other courts around the world and that there had not been an example of a country with mirroring provisions to the Kenyan Penal Code.

The Kenyan family law on marriage is more complex than either the Constitution or the Court acknowledge. Specifically, some groups in Kenya and other parts of Africa have personal status laws that recognize woman to woman marriages. Debate has raged over the meaning to be imputed to these marriages. Are they sexual or affective or are they purely functional for the bearing of children (generally) or male heirs (more specifically) or for platonic care and companionship?[55] A woman to woman marriage usually involves an older woman giving bridewealth for a younger one. The younger woman may have relations with a man or men and any children borne of such unions are said to be the progeny of the female couple. Woman to woman marriages are fascinating because they collapse gender stereotypes of 'traditional' roles of husband and wife within the family. This has led to some labelling the bridewealth-giving wife, the 'husband' and the woman for whom bridewealth is given, the 'wife'. In the *Katam* case in Kenya, a 'widow' in a woman to woman marriage sued to receive the inheritance of the older woman who had married her and then subsequently died.[56] The deceased's relatives tried to claim that such marriages did not exist and were not recognized. However, evidence was led on behalf of the widow to show that all the necessary customary formalities had been complied

53 The values argument was also raised by the Orthodox Church and the Minister of Justice, unsuccessfully in the ECHR case of *Vallianatos and Others v Greece,* paras 11 and 14.

54 *Non-Governmental Organizations Coordination Board v EG & amp; 5 others* (2019) eKLR.

55 E.J. Krige, 'Woman to Woman-Marriage, with Special Reference to the Louedu-Its Significance for the Definition of Marriage', *Africa* 44(1), 1975, 11–37.

56 *Monica JesangKatamv Jackson Chepkwony & Another* [2011] eKLR (www.kenyalaw.org).

with so that a valid customary marriage had come into being. This being the case, the widow was entitled to inherit the deceased's estate. The court agreed and found for the widow noting that woman to woman marriages were recognized in customary law and so effect had to be given to them. So on one hand, while same-sex marriage is proscribed, there is a Constitutional guarantee of a respect for culture and customs of the Kenyan people. If customary laws and customs permit woman to woman marriages, surely they cannot be held to be invalid?[57]

In *Letswelestse Motshidiemang v Attorney-General*[58] the petitioner brought a constitutional challenge on the compatibility of the equivalent provisions in the Botswana Penal Code proscribing unnatural acts between men (section 164) and public acts of indecency (section 187) with his enjoyment of human rights.[59] Specifically the petitioner noted that section 164 was vague, violated his right to be free from discrimination, hindered his right to liberty, subjected him to inhuman, degrading and other treatment and violated his right to privacy. Like the Kenyan Court, the Botswana court was provided with comparative jurisprudence by the *amicus curiae* Lesbians, Gays and Bisexuals of Botswana (LEGABIBO) which organization was lavishly praised and thanked by the court.

The High Court in Botswana took an opposite view to the Kenyan Court. An individual, it said, could not be held hostage by the morals and values of a majority. Values changed. The court noted that while the focus and legal protection/recognition of heterosexual sex used to be its link to procreation, that link had long been broken and could not continue to be used to maintain unjust laws. A gay man had no choice in the way he expressed his sexuality. Privacy was a fundamental right which should be respected. The Court pointedly contradicted the Kenyan High Court noting that all the scientific evidence presented pointed to the negative impact on the lives of LGBTIQ individuals. Striking down section 164, the Court said that its time had long passed, people should be free to love whoever they chose without interference or censure. The law was found to have violated all the Constitutional provisions cited. Similarly, the Court chose to sever the part of section 167 that defined and criminalized acts between men in private as indecent. The only part of section 167 left was that criminalizing public acts of indecency.[60]

From these two cases decided in the same year, we learn that there is no 'African' position on issues of sexuality. Writing about the Botswana decision, Viljoen[61] identifies multiple factors that led to this positive result. These include an active civil society that lobbied hard and prepared the ground for the legal challenge and also played an educational role; the importance of influential advocates including former government minister, Judge and equality litigant in her own right, Unity Dow in supporting the cause who was joined by a political elite, including the serving and former president. Viljoen contrasts this political support with the situation in Kenya where politicians have been outwardly antagonistic. There was the additional link to Botswana's high HIV rate

57 This is the view taken in M.W. Kareithi, *A Historical-Legal Analysis of Woman-to-Woman Marriage in Kenya*, LLD Thesis, University of Pretoria, submitted 6 February 2018. Available at www.repositry.up.ac.za (accessed 21 October 2019).

58 *Letsweletse Motshidiemang v Attorney General* MAHG-000591-16.

59 Penal Code (Cap 08:01, Laws of Botswana).

60 The reasoning of the Botswana court, calls to mind the decision of the Indian Supreme Court decision in *Navtel Singh Johar & Ors. v Union of India thr. Secretary Ministry of Law and Justice, W.P.* (Ctrl.) No.76 of 2016 which also struck down the Indian equivalent Penal Code section 377 which outlawed same-sex relationships.

61 F. Viljoen, 'Botswana Court Ruling is a Ray of Hope for LGBT People Across Africa', *The Conversation*, 12 June 2019. Accessed 30 October 2019. For more in-depth analyses of the situation that pertains in different African states, see S. Namwase and A. Jjuko (eds), *Protecting the Human Rights of Sexual Minorities in Contemporary Africa*, Pretoria: Pretoria University Law Press, 2017.

which required an open approach to issues of sexuality. Furthermore, Viljoen cited an Afrobarometer survey which showed that the Tswana public were more accepting of homosexuals.

It is however true to say that while there is a movement towards the removal of criminal penalties on same-sex expression, there remain significant legal barriers to the granting of the full spectrum of human rights to people with the same-sex orientation. In its Resolution 275 the African Commission on Human and Peoples' Rights reiterated that States have a duty to ensure that they address acts of violence against LGBT individuals and also that they take positive measures to eliminate discrimination against this group.[62] The insistence on the sole recognition of heterosexual marriage coupled with the refusal of many states to acknowledge or register changes in gender identity leaves some couples in legal jeopardy. This was most clearly manifested in the Malawian case of *R v Soko and Another*.[63] Here two men purported to enter into a customary engagement, holding a party at the hotel where one worked. Whjile Soko identified as male, the other defendant, Kachepa, identified as a transgender woman. Their assigned birth status was as men meaning that they could never marry each other as marriage was defined in heterosexual terms.[64] Any relationship they had would render them liable to prosecution thus in effect violating their right to marry and to found a family.[65] When the engagement became public, there was outrage. The two were charged with contravening the Penal Code because the two were said to have engaged in conduct which was against the order of nature. After a prurient and humiliating trial where they were asked gender stereotyped intrusive intimate questions including who played the role of the 'woman' in the relationship, the two were convicted of buggery and gross indecency under the Penal Code. The judge said that he had to give the maximum sentence of 14 years in order to scare anyone else who may be tempted to follow their lead.

Emerging trends: the rise of gender identity and its impact on family law and policy

A different liminal state was captured in the Kenyan case of *RM v Attorney General*.[66] This involved an intersex person (RM) who challenged their housing in a male prison where they

62 African Commission Resolution 275 on 'Protection against Violence and other Human Rights Violations against Persons on the basis of their real or imputed Sexual Orientation or Gender Identity' The African Commission on Human and Peoples' Rights (the African Commission), meeting at its 55th Ordinary Session held in Luanda, Angola, from 28 April to 12 May 2014. Available at www.achpr.org/sessions/55th/resolutions/275/. See also African Commission on Human and Peoples' Rights, *General Comment No. 4* on the African Charter on Human and Peoples' Rights: The Right to Redress for Victims of Torture and other Cruel, Inhuman or Degrading Punishment or Treatment (art. 5), Adopted at the 21st Extra-Ordinary Session of the African Commission on Human and Peoples' Rights, held from 23 February to 4 March 2017 in Banjul, The Gambia. Available at www.achpr.org/files/instruments/general-comment-right-to-redress/achpr_general_comment_no._4_english.pdf paras 20 (non-discrimination) and paras 57–61 on Sex and Gender Based Violence.

63 *R. v Soko and Another* (Criminal Case No. 359 of 2009) [2010] MWHC 2.

64 B. Demone, 'LGBTI Rights in Malawi: One Step Back, Two Steps Forward?' The Case of *R v Steven Monjeza Soko and Tiwonge Chimlanaga Kachepa*', *Journal of African Law* 60(3), 2016, 365–87.

65 See also the Kenyan case of *RM v Attorney-General and Others* [2010] eKLR involving an intersex person who had attempted to marry. The marriage had been annulled due to incapacity to consummate. The High Court refused to accept intersex as a status covered by the non-discrimination provision in the Constitution arguing that Kenya was not ready for the recognition of a 'third gender' showing confusion in the meaning of terms and identities.

66 [2010] eKLR.

were subjected to degrading and inhuman searches and mocking by the prison authorities. The Births and Deaths Registration Act only recognized two categories – male and female. RM's parents had registered RM as a male. While the court recognized that RM had been subjected to degrading treatment, it rejected RM's further claim that they had been subjected to discrimination on grounds of sex. It was of the view that an intersex person should be able to decide, or have decided for them, 'on which side of the divide' they fall, male or female and be registered according to one's dominant characteristics.[67] Confusingly, the court also discounted using 'other status' as a category of discrimination because intersexuality was already covered by sex. This shows some confusion on the part of the court as to what intersexuality entailed, with resulting confusion over sex-gender which results in the re-enforcement of the binary. It is noteworthy that RM's attempts to marry had been unsuccessful. Their marriage to a woman was annulled due to incapacity to consummate. One is left wondering what would have happened had RM attempted to contract a woman to woman marriage under customary law. Would that have been recognized? Given the criminalization of same-sex relationships, does this mean that RM could never have a relationship or family life with anyone?

In *Baby A*, a later case involving an intersex child whose birth had not been registered, the RM finding on sex discrimination was upheld.[68] The doctor had initially entered a question mark on the birth records gender category, later recording the child as male on the notification of birth. This was to conform to societal expectations that a child be recorded as male or female. However, the court was more sympathetic to the plight of intersex people than in the *RM* case and noted that the authorities ought to make provision for recognition of this group and also to ascertain their number. Further the rights of the child to an identity were discussed with the amicus citing art. 3 of the Yogyakarta Principles on the right to be regarded as a person before the law. The court agreed that intersex people needed recognition as a class. The court also addressed the issue of consent when discussing confirmatory surgery. It advocated allowing an older child to decide for themselves whether to undergo surgery.[69]

According to the Yogyakarta Principles:

> Gender identity is understood to refer to each person's deeply felt internal and individual experience of gender, which may or may not correspond with the sex assigned at birth, including the personal sense of the body (which may involve, if freely chosen, modification of bodily appearance or function by medical, surgical or other means) and other expressions of gender, including dress, speech and mannerisms.[70]

67 *RM* paras 128–33. See also J. Greenberg, *Intersexuality and the Law*, New York: New York University Press, 2012.

68 *Baby 'A' (suing through her mother, E.A.) and The Cradle the Children Foundation v Attorney General, Kenyatta National Hospital, and the Registrar of Births and Deaths* [2014] eKLR, Petition No. 266 of 2013 (High Court of Kenya at Nairobi, Constitutional and Human Rights Division).

69 In an otherwise wide-ranging General Comment on art. 6 on 'The Right to Birth Registration, Name and Nationality', the African Committee on the Rights and Welfare of the Child does not appear to give consideration to the needs of intersex children. It looks at the importance of registration of birth, upholding the principle of non-discrimination including on grounds of status, maintaining confidentiality of records and privacy, but does not directly address the binaries of most birth registration systems which do not allow for categories other than male and female. ACERWC, General Comment No. 6. Available at www.acerwc.org. See also N. Pikavamenoa, *Intersex Rights: Living between Sexes*, Berlin: Springer, 2019, p. 85.

70 Yogyakarta Principles, 2007, introduction, para 2.

Gender identity is both topical and fraught within western societies.[71] Classed under the T in LGBTIQ, the demand for recognition and respect by transgender persons has generated conflict. The European human rights system has long taken a hands-off approach, allowing states a wide margin of appreciation. However, there has been a notable turn towards requiring States to make provision for people whose gender identity would not hitherto have received recognition, not least following the case of *Goodwin v UK* where the UK was required to ensure that there was scope for the recognition and registration of change in gender in part to remove discrimination and also to guarantee that a person could exercise their art. 12 right to marry.[72] This led to the passage of the Gender Recognition Act 2004.

Surveying the legal, political and social discussions in Europe, Gössl and Völzmann show how, even when recognizing that some people are non-binary or gender fluid, many legal systems still require the recording of a status category, which category choice remains limited to male or female.[73] The debates show that there are different approaches with respect to recognition of a change: does the person have to undergo surgery or can they merely affirm their wish to assume a new gender identity, or indeed their refusal to identify as either male or female? Moreover, does a married person who wishes to transition have to divorce first before transitioning?[74]

Until fairly recently, the option on birth or other identity registration forms of saying neither male or female, or being recorded as 'a third, non-binary gender' was not open. In Germany, intersex people could leave the two choices unmarked opting for a third blank category. In 2017, a Constitutional court challenge brought on grounds of discrimination on grounds of gender was upheld.[75] The court was of the view that limiting registration to two categories privileged heterosexual people and was thus discriminatory. The lack of choice interfered with a right to free and personal development and gender identity. In 2019 a fourth category was added to the registration options – male, female, no entry and finally diverse.

Despite this positive turn in Germany and growing clamour for change in the rest of Europe, Gössl and Völzmann are clear that proof of status linked to registration of sex or gender will continue to throw up challenges in determining entitlements and legal boundaries with regard to a

71 See N. Dethloff, 'Personal Autonomy and Legal Recognition of Sexual and Gender Diversity: The German Perspective' and E. Falletti, 'Protecting Children Affected by Atypical Gender Identity Organization: A Comparative Legal Perspective', in C. Rogerson, M. Antokoloskaia, J. Miles, P. Parkinson and M. Vonk (eds), *Family Law and Family Realities*, The Hague: Eleven International Publishing, pp. 9–18, 435–50; J. Eekelaar, 'Family Law and Identity', *Oxford Journal of Legal Studies* 38, 2018, 822–40.

72 *Goodwin v The United Kingdom* Application No. 28957/95. See further J.M. Scherpe (ed.), *The Legal Status of Transsexual and Transgender Persons* (Cambridge: Intersentia, 2015).

73 S. Gössl and B. Völzmann, 'Legal Gender Beyond the Binary', *International Journal of Law, Policy & the Family* 33(3), 2018, 403–29.

74 Transgender Europe, *Trans Rights Europe Map and Index 2018*, noting that 21 states require divorce before transition: quoted in UN Women, *Progress of the World's Women: Families in a Changing World*, 2019–20, UN Women, 2019, 79. Cf. *G v Australia*, Communication No. 2172/2012 (CCPR/C/119/D/2172/2012) (UN HRC, 15 June 2017) para 7 et seq. See also European Network of Legal Experts in Gender Equality and Non-Discrimination, *Trans and Intersex Equality Rights in Europe*, EU, 2018 (Report written by M. van den Brink and P. Dunne). See also *P v P (Transgender Application for Declaration of a Valid Marriage)* [2019] EWHC 3105.

75 BVERFGE, Case No. 1 BvR 2019/16 (Oct 10, 2017). P. Dunne and J. Mulder, 'Beyond the Binary: Towards a "Third" Sex Category in Germany?', *German Law Journal* 19(3), 2018, 627–48; J.M. Scherpe, A. Dutta and T. Helms (eds), *The Legal Status of Intersex Persons*, Cambridge: Intersentia, 2018.

multitude of issues including birth,[76] marriage,[77] benefit entitlement and also the use of affirmative action programmes targeted at certain underrepresented or disadvantaged groups. They also identify the cross-jurisdictional obligations and problems thrown up by one state having a different gender recognition/registration system to another. In truth, the cross-jurisdictional issue has been dealt with before – when states first started to recognize registration of same-sex marriages or partnerships, some made clear that the status would not always carry the same recognition and entitlements in other jurisdictions as it did in the home jurisdiction.[78] A current example would be a married South African same-sex couple trying to move together to Ethiopia where the Civil Code proclaims that marriages can be annulled on the grounds of behaviour, if one of the heterosexual partners finds that their husband or wife 'has the habit of performing sexual acts with [a] person of the same sex'.[79] If same-sex conduct is considered abhorrent and illegal, then same-sex marriage will not be recognized, wherever it is contracted.

The Inter-American Court and Commission on Human Rights have both taken a positive stance in recognizing gender identity and thus pluralism beyond the male-female binary.[80] In 2015 the Organization of American States (OAS) became the first region to adopt a convention covering older persons which convention also included protection from discrimination on the basis of gender identities and sexual orientation.[81] Meanwhile in 2017 the Inter-American Court issued an advisory opinion to Costa Rica noting that there should be protection from discrimination in both the private and public spheres.[82] Echoing principle 31(c) of the Yogyakarta Principles, it advised States to amend their laws to recognize plural gender identities including their right to have new identity documents; that there should not be any medical or other checks made or required for proof of gender identity and also that States tackle social stigma. Argentina had already enacted a law on gender identity in 2012. Many States have adopted laws recognizing gender identity.[83]

Judges in Nepal and India rejected notions of gender-binary and the criminalization of same-sex conduct grounded in colonial legal transplants in favour of an examination of their own

76 See *R (on the application of TT) v Registrar General for England and Wales* [2019] EWHC 2384 (Fam), where an individual gave birth after having transitioned from female to male, and failed in an attempt to be recorded as the father of the child, discussed in Chapter 3.1 of this book.

77 For example, *P (Transgender Applicant for Declaration of Valid Marriage)* [2019] EWHC 3105 (Fam) where a marriage by an individual who had transitioned from female to male to a woman in England before same-sex marriage was introduced was held void.

78 See *Wilkinson v Kitzinger* [2006] EWHC 2022 (Fam) (Canadian same-sex married couple recognized only as civil partners in England, prior to introduction of same-sex marriage in England); *G v Australia*, CCPR/C/119/D/2172/2012, para 5.15. In Europe, the same-sex marriage would entitle a third national spouse to move and reside with their EU spouse regardless of the status of same-sex marriage within the receiving state: *Coman v Romania*, CASE C-673/16, Judgment of the Court (Grand Chamber) of 5 June 2018, paras 35 and 45.

79 Revised Family Code, 2004, art. 13 (3) (d) (Ethiopia).

80 E. Arrubia, 'The Human Right to Gender Identity: From the International Human Rights Scenario to Latin American Domestic Legislation', *International Journal of Law, Policy & the Family* 33(3), 2019, 360–79.

81 Inter-American Convention on Protecting the Human Rights of Older Persons. Available at www.oas.org/en/sla/dil/docs/inter_american_treaties_A-70_human_rights_older_persons.pdf, art. 5.

82 IACtHR, Advisory Opinion State Obligations Concerning Change of Name, Gender Identity, and Rights Derived from a Relationship Between Same-Sex Couples Advisory Opinion OC-24/17, Inter-Am. Ct. H.R. (ser. A) No. 24 (24 November 2017). See also J. Contesse, 'The Inter-American Court of Human Rights' Advisory Opinion on Gender Identity and Same Sex Marriage' *ASIL Insights* 22(9), 26 July 2018.

83 Arrubia, n 80, 369–75.

socio-cultural frameworks.[84] There they found acceptance for third gender people, called hijras in India and kothis or metis in Nepal.[85] Hijras are a 'distinct transgender and intersex community that has formed a system of shared residence and mutual support'. In the Indian case of *NALSA v Union of India and Others*, the Supreme Court denounced the harassment and discrimination of the hijra and recommended that the State make provision for them to receive socio-economic rights including education and adequate health care. Their right to identify as man, woman or transgender was to be facilitated by the addition of a third gender category on official documents. Furthermore, the government should make an effort to create awareness of 'gender diversity in families' and other institutions including the police and educational establishments.[86]

In the *Sunil Babu Pant* case, the Nepali Supreme Court considered the exclusion of a third category from the definition of sex, including by the Bureau of Statistics. There was not even the option of 'other'.[87] This meant that people of third gender were unrecognized, impacting on their enjoyment of a myriad of other rights, including in education.[88] Further, the court noted that third gender individuals were disrespected by public officials. The court was clear that gender identity and sexual orientation were part of a person's right to self-determination. It was not prepared to countenance societal prejudice as a reason not to recognize the rights of LGBTI people. As natural persons they were as entitled as anyone else to enjoy rights. It recommended that the State make provision for the recognition and enjoyment of the rights of LGBTI people for 'It cannot be construed that "only men" and "women" can enjoy … rights and other people cannot enjoy it only because they have a different gender identity and sexual orientation'.[89] Further, it recommended that in finalizing the Constitution (the interim Constitution was in use and cited in the case), the Constituent Assembly, should, in drafting a new Constitution guarantee, 'non-discrimination on the ground of gender-identity' and the 'sexual orientation' besides 'sex' in line with the Bill of Rights of the Constitution of South Africa.[90]

From this brief overview of global developments in addressing gender identity, the trend in many regions seems to be towards a move from a recognition of only male and female categories to a more plural understanding which takes on gender identity. Less clear are the ways in which these changes will feed into policies on family formation via marriage or civil registration and other status dependent legislation and policy. Also still under consideration are the requirements for recognition of gender identity – self-certification or external validation by a qualified professional.

84 *Navtez Sing Johar and Others v Union of India Ministry of Law and Justice Secretary*, Supreme Court Writ Petition (CRL) No. 76 of 2016 (India-sexual orientation). M.F. Moscati and H. Phuyal, '"The Third Gender Case" Decision of the Supreme Court of Nepal on the Rights of Lesbian, Gay, Bisexual, Transsexual and Intersex People', *The Journal of Comparative Law* 4(2), 2009, 291–7.

85 M. Kumar Sahu, 'National Legal Services Authority v. Union of India and Others (AIR 2014 SC 1863): A Ray of Hope for the LGBT Community', *BRICS Law Journal* 3(2), 2016, 164–75.

86 Human Rights Watch, *India: Enforce Ruling Protecting Transgender People*, HRW, 5 February 2015.

87 *Sunil Babu Pant v Government of Nepal* Writ 917 of 2064 BS [2007 AD] 279.

88 See also the Kenyan case of *Republic v Kenya National Examinations Council and Another* [2014] eKLR, JR Case No. 147 of 2013 requiring the change of name and gender on a high school certificate. See generally A. Jjuko, 'The Protection and Promotion of LGBTI Rights in the African Human Rights System: Opportunities and Challenges', in S. Namwase and A. Jjuko (eds), n 61, pp. 260–300, 296 footnotes 232 and 233.

89 *Sunil Babu* at 284.

90 Ibid.

5.2
DOMESTIC ABUSE
A UK perspective

Rosemary Hunter

Introduction

Although the issue of domestic violence came 'out of the shadows' in western countries in the wake of second wave feminist movements in the 1970s, in the family law arena it continues to struggle for appropriate recognition and responses. Domestic violence is no longer seen as purely a private matter but a matter of state concern. Indeed, the Council of Europe has promulgated a comprehensive Convention on Preventing and Combating Violence against Women and Domestic Violence,[1] and state failures to protect women against domestic violence have been found to constitute human rights violations.[2] In criminal law, many European countries, including the UK, have enacted specific domestic violence offences.[3] Police training and practices in responding to 'domestic incidents' have received sustained attention,[4] and in a number of jurisdictions, again including the UK, specialist domestic violence courts incorporating victim support and advocacy services have been established to deal with criminal prosecutions for domestic violence offences.[5]

In family law, however, concerns to ensure the safety and well-being of women and children constantly contend with competing considerations which tend to minimize the significance and effects of domestic violence. These include limited conceptions of domestic violence and when it is relevant, the courts' pro-contact culture, inattention to the ways in which the family court process may operate as a form of abuse, and the policy push to de-legalize family

1 The Convention came into force on 1 August 2014. It was signed by the UK government in June 2012, but has not yet been ratified. See www.conventions.coe.int/Treaty/Commun/QueVoulezVous.asp?CL=ENG&NT=210

2 *Opuz v Turkey* [2009] ECHR 870; *A v Croatia* [2011] 1 FLR 407; *Hajduova v Slovakia* (2011) 53 EHRR 8.

3 Serious Crime Act 2015 (UK), s. 76 – offence of controlling or coercive behaviour in an intimate or family relationship. See also the criminalization of forced marriage in the Anti-Social Behaviour, Crime and Policing Act 2014 (UK), ss. 121–2.

4 See, most recently, Her Majesty's Inspectorate of Constabulary and Fire and Rescue Services, *The Police Response to Domestic Abuse: An Update Report*, 2019.

5 See, e.g. Centre for Justice Innovation, *Better Courts: A Snapshot of Specialist Domestic Violence Courts in 2013*, 2014.

law (see Chapters 3.3 and 6.5 of this book). Across the whole of family law too, cost-cutting and resource constraints hamper the implementation of those positive policies that exist. This chapter examines these issues in the context of English law and policy, but similar issues will be experienced in other jurisdictions.[6] (See also Chapter 5.1 of this book.)

Understandings of domestic abuse

The traditional conception of domestic violence, encapsulated in the term 'battered wife', focuses on physical violence. Physical violence is prohibited by the criminal law, generally occurs in discrete 'incidents' and generally leaves marks on the body which provide objective evidence that violence has occurred. Domestic violence advocates have, however, developed a broader conception of domestic violence based on women's lived experience of violence, consisting of a range of tactics designed to exercise power and control over the victim and to engender fear of the perpetrator and compliance with his rules. These tactics may include physical abuse, but also sexual, psychological, emotional, verbal and financial abuse, the exercise of male privilege, isolation, threats, coercion and jealous surveillance – what Anne Morris has termed an 'abusive household gender regime'.[7] This form of violence does not occur in discrete incidents but is 'knitted into everyday routines',[8] and by virtue of occurring in the private domain of the home, is often unwitnessed (except by children) and leaves no physical traces.

In recent years the understanding of domestic violence as the exercise of power and control – and specifically Evan Stark's terminology of 'coercive control'[9] – has become pervasive in UK policy and law (for Australia, see Chapter 3.3 of this book). In 2013 the UK government adopted a new cross-government definition of 'domestic violence and abuse' as 'any incident or pattern of incidents of controlling, coercive or threatening behaviour, violence or abuse between those … who are or have been intimate partners or family members'.[10] This can encompass, but is not limited to, psychological, physical, sexual, financial and emotional abuse. The definition goes on to explain 'controlling behaviour' as:

> a range of acts designed to make a person subordinate and/or dependent by isolating them from sources of support, exploiting their resources and capacities for personal gain, depriving them of the means needed for independence, resistance and escape and regulating their everyday behaviour.

'Coercive behaviour' is defined as 'an act or a pattern of acts of assault, threats, humiliation and intimidation or other abuse that is used to harm, punish, or frighten their victim'. In 2015 the criminal offence of 'coercive and controlling behaviour in an intimate or family relationship' was

6 See the special issue on Domestic Violence of the *Journal of Social Welfare and Family Law* 40(4), 2018, 401 ff., which presents the papers from an International Symposium on Contact Disputes and Allegations of Domestic Violence.

7 A. Morris, 'Gendered Dynamics of Abuse and Violence in Families: Considering the Abusive Household Gender Regime', *Child Abuse Review* 18(6), 2009, 414–27.

8 M. Coy, K. Perks, E. Scott and R. Tweedale, *Picking Up the Pieces: Domestic Violence and Child Contact*, London: Rights of Women and CWASU, 2012, p. 23.

9 E. Stark, *Coercive Control: How Men Entrap Women in Personal Life*, New York: Oxford University Press, 2007.

10 See Home Office, *Information for Local Areas on the Change to the Definition of Domestic Violence and Abuse*. Available at https://assets.publishing.service.gov.uk/government/uploads/system/uploads/attachment_data/file/142701/guide-on-definition-of-dv.pdf

enacted.[11] During the same period, the policy language to describe the subject has definitively shifted from 'domestic violence' to 'domestic abuse', reflecting the broader understanding incorporating non-physical forms of abuse.

The Domestic Abuse Bill 2019–21 proposes to introduce a new definition of 'domestic abuse' which refers simply to 'behaviour' rather than 'an incident or pattern of incidents'. Behaviour will be defined as 'abusive' if it consists of physical or sexual abuse; violent or threatening behaviour; coercive or controlling behaviour; economic abuse; or psychological, emotional or other abuse and 'it does not matter whether the behaviour consists of a single incident or a course of conduct'.[12] The Joint Committee appointed to scrutinize the draft bill criticized this proposed definition on the ground (among others) that it failed to recognize the gendered nature of abuse as well as specific forms of abuse experienced in intersectional contexts.[13] While the government rejected the Committee's proposed amendments to the definition, it did amend the bill to provide that statutory guidance to be issued alongside the new act must include guidance about 'particular kinds of behaviour that amount to domestic abuse' and 'must, so far as relevant, take account of the fact that the majority of victims of domestic abuse in England and Wales are female'.[14]

In the family law context, acknowledgement and implementation of the wider definition of domestic abuse has been undermined by other factors. The cross-government definition was incorporated into the Family Procedure Rules in 2014.[15] As discussed later, however, it remains very difficult in practice to establish the existence of a controlling or coercive relationship and to convince the court that this should have an effect on residence and contact orders. In addition, the broad understanding of domestic abuse is not fully reflected in the Regulations enacted under the Legal Aid, Sentencing and Punishment of Offenders (LASPO) Act 2012, which determine eligibility for legal aid in family law proceedings.[16]

The LASPO Act, as part of the Coalition government's austerity cuts to public expenditure, removed eligibility for legal aid for family law proceedings involving divorce, financial remedies and child arrangements following parental separation (see further Chapter 6.5 of this book). As discussed further later, legal aid remains available for mediation in these matters, but not for legal advice, representation or court proceedings, with a narrow exception for victims of domestic abuse. Victims of domestic abuse remain eligible for legal aid for advice, representation and court proceedings, subject to means and evidence tests. As well as falling below the (very low) means threshold, to access legal aid victims are required to produce one of a specified list of forms of documentary evidence to show that they have been subjected to domestic abuse by the other party to the proceedings. The evidence requirement essentially demands that a third party has independently assessed the claimant to be a victim of domestic abuse, whether via previous court proceedings or criminal prosecution, or via the victim having sought assistance from a service provider with regard to domestic abuse.

11 Op. cit., n 3.

12 Domestic Abuse Bill 2019–21 (UK), cl. 1.

13 Joint Committee on the Draft Domestic Abuse Bill, *The Draft Domestic Abuse Bill*, First Report of Session 2017–19, HL Paper 378, HC 2075, 2019, pp. 17–21.

14 Domestic Abuse Bill 002 2019–21 (UK), cl. 66. See also Secretary of State for the Home Department, *The Government Response to the Report from the Joint Committee on the Draft Domestic Abuse Bill*, CP137, 2019, 21.

15 Family Procedure Rules 2010, Practice Direction 12J: Child Arrangements and Contact Orders: Domestic Abuse and Harm, para 3 (the term used in 2014 was 'domestic violence', but this was amended to 'domestic abuse' in 2017).

16 Civil Legal Aid (Procedure) Regulations 2012, reg 33 and Schedule 1.

This requirement not only disadvantages those many victims who have never reported the abuse they are experiencing, but is more likely to be able to be met by victims who have experienced abuse at the more serious – and physical – end of the spectrum, because services are more responsive to such abuse, and hence this is the type of abuse most likely to be reported. Victims experiencing psychological, emotional and financial abuse in coercive and controlling relationships are less likely to be able to produce one of the forms of evidence specified.[17] Moreover, barriers remain to accessing the relevant evidence even if it is theoretically available, for example: the charges imposed by some organizations to provide evidence and the unwillingness of some organizations to do so; data protection difficulties in obtaining evidence from the police;[18] and the general requirement for someone already under considerable stress to jump through another hoop in order to bring proceedings against – or more typically respond to an application made by – an abusive ex-partner. Further, the legal aid means test itself constitutes a particular barrier to those suffering financial abuse who may have no realistic access to the assets which on paper place them above the means threshold.[19] In this way, even the provisions supposedly designed to protect survivors of domestic abuse fail to take into account the practical impacts of coercive and controlling abuse.

Domestic abuse allegations in residence and contact disputes

Court file studies have consistently shown that domestic abuse is raised an issue in 50 to 60 percent of the post-separation parenting cases coming before the family courts in England and Wales.[20] Domestic abuse is relevant in residence and contact disputes as a reason why it may not be in children's best interests to have unrestricted – or any – contact with one of their parents. The adverse impacts on children of witnessing and living with domestic abuse are well established, including trauma, behavioural and emotional problems, effects on social and cognitive development, self-blame, development of inappropriate attitudes towards violence and the damaging effects of their primary carer's parenting capacity being undermined.[21]

17 See, e.g. J. Mant and J. Wallbank, 'The Mysterious Case of Disappearing Family Law and the Shifting Vulnerable Subject: The Shifting Sands of Family Law's Jurisdiction', *Social and Legal Studies* 26(5), 2017, 629–48; S. Choudhry and J. Herring, 'A Human Right to Legal Aid? The Implications of Changes to the Legal Aid Scheme for Victims of Domestic Abuse', *Journal of Social Welfare and Family Law* 39(2), 2017, 152–67; Rights of Women, *Accessible or Beyond Reach? Navigating the Exceptional Case Funding Scheme without a Lawyer*, 2019, p. 50. And for a legal challenge to the original regulations, which resulted in some widening of the forms of evidence allowed, see *R (on the application of Rights of Women) v Lord Chancellor and Secretary of State for Justice* [2016] EWCA Civ 91.

18 See F. Syposz, *Research Investigating the Domestic Violence Evidential Requirements for Legal Aid in Private Family Disputes*, London: Ministry of Justice, 2017. See also Rights of Women, op. cit., n 17, pp. 17, 50, noting the failure of statutory agencies to provide evidence of their own initiative.

19 Ibid.

20 J. Hunt and A. McLeod, *Outcomes of Applications to Court for Contact Orders after Parental Separation or Divorce*, London: Ministry of Justice, 2008; M. Harding and A. Newnham, *How Do County Courts Share the Care of Children between Parents? Full Report*, London: Nuffield Foundation, 2015, both finding domestic abuse alleged in 50 percent of residence and contact cases sampled. Cafcass and Women's Aid, *Allegations of Domestic Abuse in Child Contact Cases*, 2017, finding domestic abuse allegations in 62 percent of contact cases sampled.

21 For recent contributions to and reviews of a large literature, see, e.g. J. Callaghan, J. Alexander, J. Sixsmith and L. Fellin, 'Beyond "Witnessing": Children's Experiences of Coercive Control in Domestic Violence and Abuse', *Journal of Interpersonal Violence* 33, 2018, 1551–81; E. Katz, 'Beyond the Physical Incident Model: How Children Living with Domestic Violence Are Harmed by and Resist Regimes of Coercive Control', *Child Abuse Review* 25, 2016, 46–59; D. McLeod, *Coercive Control: Impacts on*

Practice Direction 12J of the Family Procedure Rules 2014 (PD12J) sets out the procedure courts are required to follow when allegations of domestic abuse are made in residence and contact cases (known in England and Wales since 2014 as 'child arrangement proceedings'). The court must first determine whether the allegations are 'relevant' in that they would, if true, affect any orders the court might make. If so, the court should hear evidence and make specific findings as to the truth of the allegations, and should, in the interim, institute precautionary measures to protect the child and the parent making the allegations from the risk of further harm. If fact-finding establishes that the allegations are true, the court must obtain a risk assessment and consider whether any interventions such as a domestic abuse perpetrator programme are appropriate. Finally, the court must decide what orders will be in the child's best interests and will best protect the child and non-abusive parent from future harm, weighing up the established facts, impacts and ongoing risks of domestic abuse with the other welfare factors in the case. Notably, a finding of domestic abuse is not an automatic bar to (unsupervised) contact.[22] The Practice Direction was first issued in 2008, substantially revised and expanded in 2014 – among other things to incorporate the new cross-government definition of domestic violence just discussed – and further revised in 2017, among other things to reinforce its mandatory nature and to shift to the terminology of 'domestic abuse'.

The research and evidence on PD12J, however, attest to inconsistent implementation, the continuing side-lining and minimization of allegations of domestic abuse in child arrangement cases and continuing failures to protect children from harm,[23] concerns which the successive revisions of the Practice Direction have failed to quell.[24] The reasons for this can be traced to three major sources. Firstly, PD12J's emphasis on securing safety and freedom from abuse for children and non-abusive parents is constantly and fatally undermined by the even stronger commitment throughout the family justice system to the maintenance of relationships between children and both biological parents following parental separation. Secondly, the process of fact-finding has failed to adapt to or accommodate the wider understanding of domestic abuse just discussed. And thirdly, in a situation of significant resource constraints in the family courts, the process of fact-finding and consequent risk assessment and potential behaviour change interventions simply creates too much delay and is likely to be disproportionate to the ultimate outcome

Children and Young People in the Family Environment, Research in Practice, 2018; R.K. Thiara and C. Harrison, *Safe Not Sorry: Supporting the Campaign for Safer Child Contact*, Bristol: Women's Aid, 2016; L. Smith, *Children Experiencing Interparental Coercive Control*, Glasgow: Iriss, 2018.

22 *Re L (A Child) (Contact: Domestic Violence); Re V (A Child); Re M (A Child); Re H (Children)* [2001] Fam 260.

23 See, e.g. Coy et al., op. cit., n 8; R. Hunter and A. Barnett, *Fact-Finding Hearings and the Implementation of the President's Practice Direction: Residence and Contact Orders: Domestic Violence and Harm*, London: Family Justice Council, 2013; A. Barnett, 'Contact at All Costs? Domestic Violence and Children's Welfare', *Child and Family Law Quarterly* 26(4), 2014, 439–62; A. Barnett, '"Like Gold Dust These Days": Domestic Violence Fact-Finding Hearings in Child Contact Cases', *Feminist Legal Studies* 23(1), 2015, 47–78; Thiara and Harrison, op. cit., n 21; R. Hunter, A. Barnett and F. Kaganas, 'Introduction: Contact and Domestic Abuse', *Journal of Social Welfare and Family Law* 40(4), 2018, 401–25.

24 See, e.g. Women's Aid, *Nineteen Child Homicides*, Bristol: Women's Aid, 2016; The Hon. Mr Justice Cobb, 'Review of Practice Direction 12J FPR2010: Child Arrangement and Contact Orders: Domestic Violence and Harm: Report to the President of the Family Division', *Judiciary of England and Wales*, 2017; J. Birchall and S. Choudhry, *'What About My Right Not to Be Abused?' Domestic Abuse, Human Rights and the Family Courts*, Bristol: Women's Aid and London: Queen Mary University of London, 2018; Ministry of Justice, *Assessing Risk of Harm to Children and Parents in Private Law Children Cases: Progress Update*, London: Ministry of Justice Family and Criminal Justice Policy Directorate, 2019.

given that findings of abuse have no specified consequences and some form of contact will almost invariably be ordered.[25] (See also Chapter 3.3 of this book.)

The first two decades of the Children Act 1989 saw a judicial emphasis on the absolute value of contact for children,[26] and the notion that a violent husband could still be a 'good enough' father.[27] Mothers seeking to displace the assumption of contact in order to protect their children's safety faced a high standard of proof, and were often perceived as selfish, obstructive or 'implacably hostile'.[28] Yet the advent of PD12J did not displace the commitment to contact at any cost. Rather, it carved out a narrow and procedurally technical exception to it, which would inevitably be applied minimally. The progress of the Practice Direction has been inexorably accompanied by countervailing reinforcement of the courts' pro-contact culture. For example in *Re C*, the then President of the Family Division, Sir James Munby, set out general principles applying to contact cases, including:

- Contact between parent and child is a fundamental element of family life and is almost always in the interests of the child.
- Contact between parent and child is to be terminated only in exceptional circumstances, where there are cogent reasons for doing so and when there is no alternative. …
- There is a positive obligation on the State … to take measures … to maintain or restore contact … The [court] must grapple with all the available alternatives before abandoning hope of achieving some contact.[29]

It is difficult to reconcile this rhetoric with the competing concerns of PD12J. The only way of doing so found by many courts is to minimize the circumstances in which allegations of domestic abuse are considered 'relevant', for example to circumstances of recent, direct physical abuse of the child, or recent physical abuse of the other parent when the child was present, so that abuse which is 'historic', occurred in the absence of the child, was 'merely' emotional or financial, or where contact has subsequently proceeded apparently without incident, is considered 'not relevant'.[30] Alternatively, domestic abuse may be reframed as (mutual) 'high conflict' and parents expected to put aside their differences in order to co-parent cooperatively.[31]

At the same time as PD12J was expanded and elaborated in 2014, the Children Act 1989 was amended to incorporate a presumption that the ongoing involvement of each parent in the child's life is in the child's best interests.[32] The provision is carefully worded to exclude a parent

25 Harding and Newnham, op. cit., n 20, pp. 75–8; Cafcass and Women's Aid, op. cit., n 20, pp. 14–21; Barnett, 'Contact at All Costs?', op. cit., n 23.

26 E.g. *Re M (Contact: Welfare Test)* [1995] 1 FLR 274; *Re O (Contact: Imposition of Conditions)* [1995] 2 FLR 124.

27 See, e.g. M. Eriksson and M. Hester, 'Violent Men as Good-Enough Fathers? A Look at England and Sweden', *Violence Against Women* 7, 2001, 779–98.

28 E.g. *Re R (A Minor) (Contact: Biological Father)* [1993] 2 FLR 762; *V v V (Contact: Implacable Hostility)* [2004] 2 FLR 851. Cf. *Re D (Contact: Reasons for Refusal)* [1997] 2 FLR 48.

29 *Re C (Direct Contact: Suspension)* [2011] EWCA Civ 521, per Munby P at [47].

30 Hunter and Barnett, op. cit., n 23; Barnett, '"Like Gold Dust These Days"', op. cit., n 23; Hunter et al., op. cit., n 23, pp. 408–9.

31 See L. Trinder, J. Hunt, A. Macleod, J. Pearce and H. Woodward, *Enforcing Contact Orders: Problem-Solving or Punishment?*, London: Nuffield Foundation and Exeter: University of Exeter, 2013, pp. 47, 58, 61–3; B. Archer-Kuhn, 'Domestic Violence and High Conflict Are Not the Same: A Gendered Analysis', *Journal of Social Welfare and Family Law* 40(2), 2018, 216–33.

32 Children and Families Act 2014 (UK), s. 11, inserting new paragraphs (2A), (2B), (6) and (7) into s.1 of the Children Act 1989.

whose involvement would put the child at risk of suffering harm, but this caveat depends on an assessment as to when a parent's involvement would put the child at risk of suffering harm, as against when a lack of contact between the child and the parent would put the child at risk of suffering harm. Arguably, the presumption does no more than codify the pre-existing case law on the importance of ongoing parental involvement, but it reinforces that belief, and makes it even harder for the pro-contact culture to be challenged or dislodged.[33]

Assessments of the risk posed by (allegedly) abusive parents are made not only by the courts but also by Cafcass – the Children and Family Court Advisory and Support Service – which is responsible for writing welfare reports for the court. Research has shown that Cafcass welfare professionals also adhere to the overriding value of a child's ongoing contact with both parents and promote this value through their recommendations on children's welfare.[34] Most recently, the rise of 'parental alienation' discourse in family courts in England and Wales[35] has posed a further challenge, with mothers alleging domestic abuse routinely facing counter-allegations that they are engaged in a campaign of 'parental alienation' by instilling false beliefs in their children that the non-resident parent has been abusive.

In terms of the fact-finding process, the very notion that allegations of domestic abuse must be subject to a separate procedure to determine their veracity appears to stem from and certainly perpetuates a culture of disbelief, whereby allegations are automatically regarded with suspicion (rather than the prevalence of domestic abuse among the population of cases reaching family courts being acknowledged). Moreover, the process throws the burden of proof onto the party making the allegations. Rather than the party seeking contact being required to show why contact will be beneficial, it is the party wishing to limit contact who is required to prove their case, and within the pro-contact culture just outlined, this is a high hurdle to clear. In addition, the fact-finding process is treated as an adversarial, forensic exercise in which individual allegations are required to be itemized and subject to detailed scrutiny. Accordingly, the concept and structure of fact-finding is premised more on an incident-based model of violence than on one based on a pattern of coercive control. The incorporation of the cross-government definition of domestic abuse into PD12J was not accompanied by any substantial adjustments to the fact-finding process or guidance as to how fact-finding should be conducted in relation to allegations of coercive control. The consequence is that patterns of coercive control can be de-materialized in the fact-finding process, resulting in limited and partial findings which fail

33 See, e.g. F. Kaganas, 'Parental Involvement: A Discretionary Presumption', *Legal Studies* 38(4), 2018, 549–70.

34 R.K. Thiara and A. Gill, *Domestic Violence, Child Contact, Post-Separation Violence: Issues for South Asian and African-Caribbean Women and Children*, London: NSPCC, 2012, Section 7; G. Macdonald, 'Domestic Violence and Private Family Court Proceedings: Promoting Child Welfare or Promoting Contact?', *Violence against Women* 22(7), 2016, 832–52; G. Macdonald, 'Hearing Children's Voices? Including Children's Perspectives on Their Experiences of Domestic Violence in Welfare Reports Prepared for the English Courts in Private Family Law Proceedings', *Child Abuse and Neglect* 65, 2017, 1–13.

35 See, e.g. Cafcass, 'Child Impact Assessment Framework'. Available at www.cafcass.gov.uk/grown-ups/professionals/ciaf/; C. Cymru, 'Children's Resistance or Refusal to Spend Time with a Parent: Practice Guidance', 2019. Available at https://gov.wales/sites/default/files/publications/2019-08/cafcass-cymru-childrens-resistance-or-refusal-to-spending-time-with-a-parent-practice-guidance.pdf; Birchall and Choudhry, op. cit., n 24, pp. 32–6; J. Doughty, N. Maxwell and T. Slater, *Review of Research and Case Law on Parental Alienation*, Cardiff: Welsh Government, 2018; A. Barnett, 'A Genealogy of Hostility: Parental Alienation in England and Wales', *Journal of Social Welfare and Family Law*, 42(1), 2020, 18–29. See also L. Nielsen, *Parental Alienation Empirical Analysis: Child Best Interests or Parental Rights?*, Fredericton: Muriel McQueen Fergusson Centre for Family Violence Research and Vancouver: FREDA Centre for Research on Violence Against Women, 2018.

to capture the dynamics of the abusive relationship, the totality of its effects on the children involved and the actual level of ongoing risk.[36] The difficulties of the fact-finding process have been rendered even greater by the LASPO Act, which has resulted in high levels of self-representation in family courts and virtually impossible challenges for litigants in person to navigate its complexity.

Incomplete implementation of PD12J is compounded by severe resource limitations at all levels. The strain on the courts' resources imposed by fact-finding hearings and the delays in listing they entail provide further reasons not to hold them where they can be avoided, or to impose arbitrary limits on the number of 'incidents' that can be put in evidence.[37] Where fact-finding hearings do result in positive findings, courts may be reluctant to allow the time needed for risk assessment and interventions, and insufficient funding available for expert risk assessments and a shortage of domestic violence perpetrator programmes (as well as children's and other victim services) may undermine the possibilities for effectively identifying and addressing risk.[38] The three factors identified mean that orders for no contact remain extremely rare, and while orders for supervised or supported contact may reflect ongoing levels of risk, they are unsustainable in the longer term.[39] Research consistently suggests that children and their non-abusive parents continue to experience abuse – and in the worst cases, serious harm and death – as a result of unsafe contact and residence orders made by family courts.[40]

Ongoing concerns about the family courts' unsatisfactory response to domestic abuse allegations have resulted in a number of further inquiries and reform proposals. Choudhry, for example, has argued that the pro-contact culture could be displaced by considering domestic abuse cases within a human rights framework, in which children's and non-abusive parents' rights to be free from violence would clearly override an abusive parent's qualified rights to family life.[41] The government has promised that statutory guidance to accompany the Domestic Abuse Bill when it is enacted will outline the range of impacts domestic abuse can have on children, will provide that statutory services must recognize these impacts, and will 'consider whether there is a need to amend the definition of harm in the Children Act 1989' in order to ensure that 'children affected by witnessing coercive control receive the protection and support they need'.[42] Most recently, the Ministry of Justice established an expert panel to review the way in which family courts respond to allegations of domestic abuse and protect children and parents from harm in child arrangement proceedings. The Panel

36 A. Barnett, '"Greater Than the Mere Sum of Its Parts": Coercive Control and the Question of Proof', *Child and Family Law Quarterly* 29(4), 2017, 379–400; see also Hunter et al., op. cit., n 23, pp. 410–11; N. Ohana, 'The Archaeology of the Courts' Domestic Violence Discourse: Discourse as a Knowledge-Sustaining System', *feminists@law* 9(2), 2019.

37 Hunter and Barnett, op. cit., n 23, pp. 40–4; Hunter et al., ibid., pp. 409–10.

38 Hunter and Barnett, ibid., pp. 46–54; Hunter et al., ibid., pp. 411–12.

39 Hunter and Barnett, ibid., pp. 54–7; Hunter et al., ibid., pp. 412–13. See also Thiara and Harrison, op. cit., n 21, pp. 23–5; Birchall and Choudhry, op. cit., n 24, pp. 38–40.

40 L. Harne, *Violent Fathering and the Risks to Children*, Bristol: Policy Press, 2011; F. Morrison, '"All over Now?" The Ongoing Relational Consequences of Domestic Abuse through Child Contact Arrangements', *Child Abuse Review* 24, 2015, 274–84; Women's Aid, *Nineteen Child Homicides*, op. cit., n 24; Thiara and Harrison, op. cit., n 21, pp. 14–18; S. Holt, 'Domestic Violence and the Paradox of Post-Separation Mothering', *British Journal of Social Work* 47, 2017, 2049–67; R.K. Thiara and C. Humphreys, 'Absent Presence: The Ongoing Impact of Men's Violence on the Mother-Child Relationship', *Child & Family Social Work* 22(1), 2017, 137–45; Birchall and Choudhry, op. cit., n 24, pp. 44–46; McLeod, op. cit., n 21.

41 See Birchall and Choudhry, ibid.; R. Hunter and S. Choudhry, 'Conclusion: International Best Practices', *Journal of Social Welfare and Family Law* 40(4), 2018, 548–62, 554–60.

42 Secretary of State for the Home Department, op. cit., n 14, paras 53–4.

issued a public call for evidence which received a large number of responses and gathered a range of other evidence. An update on progress issued in October 2019 stated that:

> The evidence gathered highlights systemic issues in relation to how risk is identified and managed which need to be addressed to ensure that victims and children involved in these proceedings are better protected from further harm.[43]

The Panel's final report is due in mid-2020, and will no doubt make further recommendations for reform in this troubled area.

Abuse through the family court process

In addition to concerns about family court decision-making in child arrangement cases involving domestic abuse, concerns have increasingly been expressed about the ways in which the family court process itself may be abusive. This may occur when the abusive partner uses the court process as a means to further control and financially abuse (usually) his former partner through the bringing of repeated applications, or to harass and intimidate her through enforced proximity at court or abusive cross examination. Courts themselves may collude in and exacerbate this abuse by their inbuilt scepticism towards mothers raising objections to unrestricted contact.

Vivienne Elizabeth has coined the term 'custody stalking' to describe the experiences of mothers who, after leaving their abusive partners, have been subjected to prolonged custody and child protection proceedings motivated by the father's desire to continue his coercive control post-separation, cause them distress and weaken their relationships with their children.[44] This phenomenon has increasingly been observed in family courts in England and Wales, and forms part of the Ministry of Justice expert panel's inquiry into harm in the family courts.[45] Likewise, increasing attention has been paid to lack of safety and security at court for victims of domestic abuse.[46] While criminal courts routinely provide for special measures for victims of violence such as screens and video links for giving evidence, and a bar on direct cross-examination in sexual offences cases, practice in family courts lags far behind, both as a result of inadequate court facilities, and by virtue of the fact that the provision of such measures is a matter of judicial discretion. The availability of special measures and 'participation directions' to protect parties in family courts is governed by Practice Direction 3AA of the Family Procedure Rules 2010 (PD3AA) which deals with vulnerable witnesses. The invocation of PD3AA first requires the court to identify a party as 'vulnerable'. However the institutionalized suspicion surrounding domestic abuse allegations tends to militate against understanding an alleged victim of abuse as vulnerable unless and until the allegations have been proved – and will then

43 Ministry of Justice, op. cit., n 24, p. 8. The author is a member of this expert panel.

44 V. Elizabeth, 'Custody Stalking: A Mechanism of Coercively Controlling Mothers Following Separation', *Feminist Legal Studies* 25(2), 2017, 185–201.

45 One of the review's terms of reference relates to the use (or otherwise) of s.91(14) of the Children Act 1989 to restrain repeated harassing applications for the making, variation and enforcement of child arrangement orders.

46 See, e.g. All Party Parliamentary Group on Domestic Violence, *Domestic Abuse, Child Contact and the Family Courts: Parliamentary Briefing*, Bristol: APPG on DV and Women's Aid, 2016; House of Commons Hansard, 'Domestic abuse victims in family law courts', 15 September 2016, Vol 614, Col 1081–1120; Thiara and Harrison, op. cit., n 21, pp. 26–7; Birchall and Choudhry, op. cit., n 24, pp. 26–8.

depend on the nature of the abuse that has been established and the court's assessment of its effects on the victim.

The phenomenon of abusive cross-examination, where an alleged abuser acting as a litigant in person takes the opportunity directly to cross-examine his alleged victim, and/or a victim of abuse is required directly to cross-examine her abuser, has become a pressing issue with the rise of litigants in person following the LASPO Act. This issue is also addressed in PD12J, which provides that at a fact-finding hearing, 'each party can be asked to identify what questions they wish to ask of the other party', and 'the judge should be prepared where necessary and appropriate to conduct the questioning of the witnesses on behalf of the parties, focusing on the key issues in the case'.[47] The option for the judge to take over questioning has caused a great deal of angst in family courts, which on the one hand have recognized the appalling experience of being directly cross-examined by or being required directly to cross-examine one's abuser,[48] but on the other hand have been extremely uncomfortable with the judge assuming this role, with many judges exhibiting great reluctance to do so,[49] and adopting a range of (equally unsatisfactory) strategies to avoid it.[50]

The Domestic Abuse Bill contains provisions which will automatically bar direct cross-examination in family proceedings and allow the court to appoint counsel for the purposes of cross-examination, but only in cases where the existence of domestic abuse has been elsewhere established, or the alleged victim is able to produce 'evidence' of domestic abuse as required to be eligible for legal aid.[51] This not only perpetuates the culture of disbelief, but will also leave a wide area in which judges may exercise discretion whether or not to prohibit direct cross-examination. Given experience to date, it is unclear whether judicial reluctance to recognize vulnerability and allow special measures, or judicial enthusiasm for any form of third party assistance for litigants in person, is most likely to prevail. Further, while the Domestic Abuse Bill will extend the automatic provision for special measures to victims of domestic abuse offences as well as sexual offences in criminal courts, it does not contain any equivalent provisions applying to family courts.[52] The issue of safety and security in court for victims of domestic abuse is another area within the Ministry of Justice panel's terms of reference, and its recommendations in this regard are awaited.

More generally, several studies have identified that mothers seeking to raise issues of domestic abuse in child arrangement proceedings experience the family courts as a 'hostile environment',

47 Practice Direction 12J, para 28.

48 See, e.g. J. Munby, '16th View from the President's Chambers: Children and Vulnerable Witnesses: Where Are We?', *Family Law*, February 2017, 151–62; *Re A (a minor) (Fact-Finding: Unrepresented Party)* [2017] EWHC 1195 (Fam) per Hayden J; *JY v RY* [2018] EWFC B16 per DJ Read.

49 See N. Corbett and A. Summerfield, *Alleged Perpetrators of Abuse as Litigants in Person in Private Family Law: The Cross-Examination of Vulnerable and Intimidated Witnesses*, London: Ministry of Justice, 2017. See also e.g. *Re D (Appeal-Failure of Case Management)* [2017] EWHC 1907 (Fam).

50 There was an Initial attempt to order HMCTS to pay for the provision of representation for cross-examination: *Q v Q* [2014] EWFC 31, but this was ruled out by the Court of Appeal in *Re K and H (Children)* [2015] EWCA Civ 543. Other possible strategies have included appointing a children's guardian and asking them to conduct cross examination: see *PS v BP* [2018] EWHC 1987 (Fam), but cf. *Re D (Appeal-Failure of Case Management)* [2017] EWHC 1907 (Fam); granting rights of audience to a McKenzie Friend to conduct cross-examination: see *Re J* [2018] EWCA Civ 115 per McFarlane LJ at [73]; dispensing with questioning: see *RJ v CM* [2018] EWHC 2509 (Fam); or requiring the parties to cross-examine to the best of their (limited) ability, regardless of the traumatic effects: see Birchall & Choudhry, op. cit., n 24

51 Domestic Abuse Bill 2019–20, cl. 59.

52 See Joint Committee on the Draft Domestic Abuse Bill, op. cit., n 13, pp. 39–41.

in which they are judged and held to account, and their motives for raising concerns questioned, in ways not apparently directed towards fathers.[53] Participants in Burchill and Choudhry's research also reported being addressed disparagingly and in the same demeaning manner as their abusive ex-partners had done, as well as judges and family court professionals minimizing their experiences of abuse, victim-blaming and disregarding their human rights.[54] These studies suggest that in line with the courts' pro-contact approach and culture of disbelief, victims of domestic abuse seeking to restrict contact – who are most often mothers – encounter gender bias in family courts,[55] and often find the court process unsupportive disempowering and re-traumatising.

Other family court proceedings involving domestic abuse

The issue of domestic abuse is not relevant only to child arrangement proceedings, but its relevance in other proceedings has to date received little recognition. Since divorce is a paper-based procedure and a divorce petition may be based on a range of factors without any necessary mention of a respondent's abusive behaviour – or indeed may deliberately omit mention of domestic abuse for fear of repercussions[56] – the issue has tended to remain hidden within the divorce process. Recent research by Trinder et al., however, found that 42 percent of petitions based on the respondent's alleged 'behaviour' included reference to some form of abuse that would meet the cross-government definition just discussed.[57] The research also highlighted how a controlling spouse can use their ability to contest the other spouse's petition to make divorce unnecessarily difficult, which in turn strengthens the argument for divorce reform and the abolition of defended divorce.[58] The recent high-profile case of *Owens v Owens*, an extremely rare case in which a husband pursued his objections to his wife's divorce petition all the way to the UK Supreme Court, and was ultimately successful in obstructing the divorce, arguably illustrates this point.[59]

Domestic abuse in financial proceedings is also just beginning to receive attention in England and Wales. While a party's 'conduct' is a matter to which a court may have regard in determining financial remedies, the legislation specifies that it shall only do so 'if that conduct is such that it would in the opinion of the court be inequitable to disregard it'.[60] This sets a high threshold which has generally excluded reference to domestic abuse in financial proceedings. However there are a number of ways in which domestic abuse may be relevant to such proceedings apart from as an issue of 'conduct'.[61] As with child arrangement proceedings, financial proceedings – or behaviour as a respondent to proceedings – may be used by an abusive spouse as part of an ongoing pattern of coercive control. Similarly, too, a party who has been subjected to domestic abuse by her former spouse may be a vulnerable witness and require special measures

53 Coy et al., op. cit., n 8; Thiara and Gill, op. cit., n 34; Burchill and Choudhry, op. cit., n 24.
54 Burchill and Choudhry, ibid., pp. 19–23, 30–2.
55 Ibid.
56 See L. Trinder, D. Braybrook, C. Bryson, L. Coleman, C. Houlston and M. Sefton, *Finding Fault? Divorce Law and Practice in England and Wales: Full Report*, London: Nuffield Foundation, 2017, p. 50.
57 Ibid., p. 75.
58 L. Trinder and M. Sefton, *No Contest: Defended Divorce in England and Wales*, London: Nuffield Foundation, 2018.
59 *Owens v Owens* [2018] UKSC 41 (per Lady Hale in particular).
60 Matrimonial Causes Act 1973, s 25(2)(g).
61 See J. Crisp and R. Hunter, 'Domestic Abuse in Financial Remedy Applications', *Family Law* 49, 2019, 1440–6.

to protect her safety and security at court, including protection from abusive cross-examination. Finally, the outcome of financial proceedings may serve to perpetuate financial abuse. Australian research has shown that a history of domestic abuse is correlated with poor financial outcomes for victims, resulting often in long-term financial hardship,[62] while Barlow et al.'s research in the UK found that women more than men are subject to gendered expectations about compromising their financial position for the sake of an amicable settlement, and women are far more likely than men to 'give up' on a fair settlement in the interests of pragmatism (just taking what they can get), sacrifice (prioritizing the maintenance of peace and good relations over their longer-term financial well-being) or self-preservation (getting out of an abusive relationship as quickly as possible and trying to limit further abuse).[63] Given courts' traditional avoidance of matters of 'conduct', however, it is likely to take some time to change the culture of financial proceedings so that both lawyers and judges are alert to issues of domestic abuse and the ways in which it might undermine the fairness of both the court process and outcomes.

The final area of family courts' responsibility in relation to domestic abuse is in the making of injunctions – known as non-molestation orders and occupation orders – under the Family Law Act 1996. The Act does not specify any particular form/s of behaviour required to trigger eligibility for a non-molestation order. The applicant and respondent must fall within one of the specified categories of 'associated persons', but these categories are broad, and include current or former spouses, civil partners or heterosexual or same-sex cohabitants, parties who have had an intimate relationship of significant duration without having lived together and parties who have a child together.[64] In deciding an application for a non-molestation order, the court must simply have regard to all the circumstances, including the need to secure the health, safety and well-being of the applicant and of any relevant child.[65] An order may be made for a specified period or indefinitely, although in practice, orders tend to be made for a relatively short duration.[66] Breach of a non-molestation order is a criminal offence.[67]

Applications to County Courts for non-molestation orders saw a long-term decline from 2003–2012, but have since steadily increased, with 20,400 applications and 27,183 orders made in 2018, both higher than the respective numbers in 2003.[68] The increase is likely to be attributable to a combination of the LASPO Act and changes to police procedures. Under the LASPO Act, one of the forms of evidence which can be used to establish eligibility for legal aid for children's or financial proceedings is 'a relevant protective injunction'.[69] It was entirely predictable that this would result in an increase in the number of applications for

62 G. Sheehan and B. Smyth, 'Spousal Violence and Post-Separation Family Law Outcomes', *Australian Journal of Family Law* 14(2), 2000, 102–18; B. Fehlberg and C. Millward, 'Family Violence and Financial Outcomes after Parental Separation', in A. Hayes and D. Higgins (eds), *Families, Policy and the Law: Selected Essays on Contemporary Issues for Australia*, Melbourne: AIFS, 2014, 235–44; R. Kaspiew et al., *Domestic and Family Violence and Parenting: Mixed Method Insights into Impact and Support Needs: Final Report*, Melbourne: AIFS and Sydney, ANROWS, 2017.

63 A. Barlow, R. Hunter, J. Smithson and J. Ewing, *Mapping Paths to Family Justice: Resolving Family Disputes in Neoliberal Times*, Basingstoke: Palgrave Macmillan, 2017, especially Chapter 8.

64 Family Law Act 1996 (UK), s. 62.

65 Ibid., s. 42(5).

66 Ibid., s. 42(7). One domestic abuse charity advises that non-molestation orders are normally granted for six months: www.reducingtherisk.org.uk/cms/content/injunctions#

67 Ibid., s. 42A.

68 Ministry of Justice, Family Court Tables (April-June 2019), Table 17. Available at www.gov.uk/government/statistics/family-court-statistics-quarterly-april-to-june-2019

69 Civil Legal Aid (Procedure) Regulations 2012, Schedule 1, para 7.

non-molestation orders.[70] In addition, changes to the law on police bail which came into force in April 2017 dramatically reduced both the use of bail and the length of time for which bail can be imposed on suspects under police investigation. In the past, a person arrested for a domestic violence offence would generally be released on pre-charge bail subject to conditions which prohibited contact with the victim. Since this no longer routinely occurs and victims are not therefore protected by bail conditions,[71] there is a greater need for non-molestation orders to fill the gap.

While non-molestation orders are designed to prevent further harassment and abusive behaviours, occupation orders remove the perpetrator of abuse from the family home, a vital remedy in a context in which there is a severe shortage of refuge accommodation and alternative housing options. Such orders, have, however, proved to be a much less accessible than non-molestation orders. The law on when an occupation order may be made is more complex and difficult to navigate, with varying entitlements depending on relationship and/or property ownership status.[72] In addition, courts have demonstrated considerable reluctance to interfere with perpetrators' property rights, with the Court of Appeal describing occupation orders as a 'Draconian' remedy, only justified in exceptional circumstances,[73] and 'a last resort in an intolerable situation'.[74] More recent cases indicate a more purposive judicial approach to the granting of occupation orders,[75] but the earlier case law appears to have had a permanent chilling effect. In 2018, only 4,737 applications were made for occupation orders and only 2,259 orders were granted. These numbers have fallen slightly rather than increasing since 2012, and it is notable that many fewer orders are made than the number of applications.[76]

In addition, courts remain reluctant to make occupation orders on an *ex parte* basis, which renders them practically ineffective in the kind of crisis situations which might call for the removal of the perpetrator from the family home.[77] In response to this deficiency, a new form of emergency response was piloted in 2011–12 and rolled out nationally in 2014. This scheme enables a senior police officer to issue a 'domestic violence protection notice' (DVPN, or 'go order') which requires the perpetrator to leave the home and prevents him from entering or approaching it for up to 48 hours. Within that period, the police must make an application to a Magistrates Court for a 'domestic violence protection order' (DVPO), which, if granted, extends the exclusion for a period of 14–28 days.[78] Early evaluations of the pilot scheme and national roll-out indicated that these orders were generally viewed positively by practitioners and victims, although there was also evidence of wide variations in police awareness and implementation, and a need for greater consideration of their use in cases of coercive control as opposed to physical violence, as well as better coordination with services for both victims and perpetrators.[79] Subsequent experience

70 See, e.g. R. Hunter, 'Doing Violence to Family Law', *Journal of Social Welfare and Family Law* 33(4), 2011, 343–59.

71 See, Joint Committee on the Domestic Abuse Bill, op. cit., n 13, pp. 32–5; L. Dearden, 'Bail Changes to Be Reviewed after Suspected Rapists, Murders [sic] and Paedophiles Released without Restrictions', *Independent*, 5 November 2019.

72 Family Law Act 1996, ss. 33–8.

73 *Chalmers v Johns* [1998] EWCA Civ 1452.

74 *Re Y (Children) (Occupation Order)* [2000] 2 FCR 470.

75 See, e.g. *L v L* [2012] EWCA Civ 721; *PF v CF* [2016] EWHC 3117 (Fam).

76 Ministry of Justice, Family Court Tables, op. cit., n 68.

77 See, e.g. M. Seagal, 'The Ouster Dilemma', *Family Law* 39, 2009, 295.

78 Crime and Security Act 2010, ss. 24–33.

79 L. Kelly et al., *Evaluation of the Pilot of Domestic Violence Protection Orders*, London: Home Office, 2013; Home Office, *Domestic Violence Protection Orders (DVPO): One Year On-Home Office Assessment of National Roll-Out*, London: Home Office, 2016.

suggests that the level of usage of DVPOs by police forces has been disappointing, with part of the explanation residing in the fact that police received no additional funding to support applications for DVPOs.[80]

The government has subsequently announced its intention to repeal DVPNs and DVPOs and replace them with a new 'go to' order named 'domestic abuse protection' notices and orders (DAPNs and DAPOs). These new orders are one of the centrepieces of the Domestic Abuse Bill,[81] and will supposedly improve on the existing model by allowing applications by victims and third parties to family courts as well as police applications to Magistrates courts; enabling courts to attach positive conditions to orders such as participation in a domestic abuse perpetrator programme or a requirement for electronic monitoring; enabling courts to make DAPOs for whatever duration the court considers appropriate rather than being limited to 28 days; and making breach of an order a criminal offence.[82] The Joint Committee on the Domestic Abuse Bill expressed considerable reservations about these proposals, including concerns that the need for funding, infrastructure and training to support the imposition of positive conditions had not been sufficiently thought through, the potential for inconsistent approaches between civil and criminal courts, and the fact that police would have to pay a court fee for DAPO applications whereas victims would not. Combined with the ongoing lack of additional funding for the police, this difference in cost could undermine the entire scheme.[83] Despite these criticisms, the government signalled its intention to press on with the provisions, accompanied by necessary infrastructure and guidance, and with their effectiveness to be tested in a limited-scale pilot before any national roll-out.[84] If this does eventuate, it is difficult to see how the existing drawbacks of insufficient funding and courts' reluctance to make longer-term orders interfering with property rights will not be replicated.

Domestic violence and de-legalization

The final area of family justice in which safety concerns collide with competing policy considerations is the area of alternative dispute resolution. Successive UK governments have heavily promoted family mediation in preference to court proceedings, on the basis that mediation reduces conflict, improves parental communication, supports parental autonomy and self-determination and is likely to produce more lasting outcomes (see Chapter 6.5 of this book). As a result, it is said to be better for the parties themselves and especially for their children, and not incidentally for the public purse in reducing demands on court resources and legal

aid funds. While the LASPO Act cut legal aid funding for all family court proceedings, it continued to provide legal aid for family mediation for those meeting the legal aid means test. Furthermore, the Children and Families Act 2014 enshrined in legislation the previously non-statutory 'Pre-Application Protocol' requiring all applicants for child arrangements or financial orders, regardless of funding status, to attend a mediation information and assessment meeting (MIAM) prior to issuing court proceedings.[85] And while legal aid remains available for court proceedings for victims of domestic abuse, with a corresponding exemption from the MIAM

80 See Select Committee on the Domestic Abuse Bill, op. cit., n 13, pp. 24, 31.

81 Domestic Abuse Bill 2019–21, Part 3.

82 HM Government, *Transforming the Response to Domestic Abuse: Consultation Response and Draft Bill CP15*, London: Home Office, 2019, pp. 25–31.

83 Joint Committee on the Domestic Abuse Bill, op. cit., n 13, pp. 32–2.

84 Secretary of State for the Home Department, op. cit., n 14, pp. 22–7.

85 Children and Families Act 2014, s. 10.

requirement for such victims, many victims, as discussed previously, do not meet the evidential requirements for legal aid and MIAM exemption, and so are left with recourse either to mediation or to self-representation in the family court, both of which pose dangers to their physical safety and psychological well-being, and to the safety and fairness of any agreements reached or orders made.

Even if a MIAM exemption is unavailable, matters should be screened out of mediation if there is a history of abuse in the relationship such that one party has the capacity to control or intimidate the other. However research on MIAMs indicates that screening for domestic abuse may be inadequate due to time pressures, inadequate understanding of the dynamics of domestic abuse, or a belief that mediation will always offer a preferable process to court proceedings.[86] The latter belief is belied by the traumatic experiences of mediation – and unsatisfactory outcomes achieved – recounted by some of Barlow et al.'s interviewees who mediated against a background of domestic abuse.[87] But while new training materials for mediators on screening for domestic abuse have been developed based on this research,[88] the invidious options for those unable to afford legal representation remain.

The main adjustment made to the mediation process in England and Wales where there is a background of domestic abuse but the parties have nevertheless 'chosen' to mediate is to place the parties in separate rooms with the mediator shuttling between them, rather than meeting face-to-face. But while shuttle mediation may prevent a physical attack during the course of a meeting, it is a wholly inadequate response to domestic abuse more generally, doing nothing to counter the dynamics of coercive control, the risk of retaliatory action outside the building, or the perpetrator's ability to achieve his desired result. Specialist models for mediating domestic abuse cases which seek to address these wider issues have been developed elsewhere, but they inevitably make the mediation process more costly.[89] Consequently, despite potentially saving the legal aid costs of court proceedings, there is no realistic prospect of a specialist mediation model being developed and funded in England and Wales.

Conclusion

This review of English law and policy relating to domestic violence reveals a mixed picture. On the one hand, the need to respond adequately to safety concerns and to protect both adult and child victims from further abuse has been widely recognized and supported in policy and legislation such as the cross-government definition of domestic abuse, the criminalization of controlling or coercive behaviour in an intimate or family relationship, revisions to PD12J and

86 Barlow et al., op. cit., n 63, pp. 96–104; A. Bloch, R. McLeod and B. Toombs, *Mediation Information and Assessment Meetings (MIAMs) and Mediation in Private Family Law Disputes: Qualitative Findings*, London: Ministry of Justice, 2014, pp. 27–8, 30–1; R. Hunter, 'Exploring the LASPO Gap', *Family Law*, May 2014, 660–3; P. Morris, 'Mediation, the Legal Aid, Sentencing and Punishment of Offenders Act 2012 and the Mediation Information Assessment Meeting', *Journal of Social Welfare and Family Law* 35(4), 2013, 445–57.

87 Barlow et al., ibid., pp. 104–8, 207.

88 The training materials are restricted access, but were developed as part of the follow-on Creating Paths to Family Justice project. Available at https://socialsciences.exeter.ac.uk/law/research/groups/frs/projects/creatingpathstofamilyjustice/

89 See Barlow et al., op. cit., n 63, pp. 207–8; R. Hunter and A. Barlow, 'Reconstruction of Family Mediation in a Post-Justice World', in M.F. Moscati and M. Roberts (eds), *Family Mediation: Contemporary Issues*, London: Bloomsbury Professional, forthcoming 2020; Hunter and Choudhry, op. cit., n 41, pp. 548–54.

the current Domestic Abuse Bill. On the other hand, these policies and provisions have been persistently undermined by other ideologies, agendas, resource limitations and public funding cuts. The prospects of escaping from some of these dilemmas appear slim. While the Ministry of Justice's expert panel has identified a need for structural and systemic change in family courts' responses to allegations of domestic abuse in children's proceedings, the record to date offers little hope for game-changing reform. Continuing incremental efforts at improvement, accompanied by continuing compromises and reversals, seem the most likely scenario for the foreseeable future.

PART 6

The role of the state and its institutions

6.1

STATE SUPPORT FOR FAMILIES IN EUROPE

A comparative overview

Kirsten Scheiwe

Introduction

What is the role of the state and its interrelationship with private obligations in supporting families with children? Traditional family policies emerging as part of welfare state developments, mainly since the 1920s, were widely based on the assumption of a 'male breadwinner' and support for the married couple, but contained also some maternalist elements. Care obligations were widely left to the private domain, and public support was limited. This traditional model is becoming outmoded, ideas and practices about gender equality, employment and parenting have changed.

Welfare state policies face new challenges. Birth rates are declining, falling on average below reproduction rates. Divorce rates are increasing and poverty levels of solo parent families as consequence of divorce or separation are high. Family forms are becoming increasingly diverse (see Chapters 1.1–1.5 and 5.1 of this book). The costs of children are increasing, due to prolonged or expensive schooling, education and training, and the rising opportunity costs of maternal employment. Expectations about parental performance are higher. Globalization, migration and the increasing mobility of workers create new challenges (see Chapter 7.3 of this book). There is a growing demand for services in overburdened families. Changing gender roles and the diversification of family forms, the demands of equality and the democratization of the family challenge the normative models of traditional family policy and require new coordination axes of state support policies.

While the regulation of family benefits is a domain of national legislation, international and supranational law have gained importance. The UN Convention on the Rights of the Child guarantees social rights of children, social security and an adequate standard of living for children (arts 6, 26, 27) which have to be granted without discrimination (art. 2, sec. 1). The European Social Charter, a Council of Europe treaty, grants the right to appropriate social, legal and economic protection (art. 16). EU law that coordinates social security entitlements including family benefits for migrating workers' family members has been the basis of extensive case law of the ECJ. The last years have seen increasing conflicts between EU member states over the possibility of cutting down or indexing family benefits or carers' rights that are 'exported' to the children or partner of the entitled EU migrant worker residing in another country. Transnational families and conflict rules in cross-border cases[1] are a new challenge and have provoked disagreements between EU Member States; the EU Council plans reforms and has reached a provisional compromise with the European Parliament[2] on the amendment of the EU coordination rules of social security systems, including income-replacing cash benefits and other family benefits.

How to compare state support for families?

While comparative family law is a well-established legal academic field, the comparison of state policies supporting families has been largely left to social sciences.[3] There is very little transdisciplinary discourse between legal and social sciences on the law and practice of family benefits and social rights supporting children and families. This is also due to the complexity of the family policy field which encompasses a huge variety of policy measures and instruments, such as family benefits, child allowances and tax credits (targeted to combat family and child poverty), means-tested minimum income benefits and housing allowances, maternity, paternity and parental leaves and benefits and other care-related rights to time-off for parents, as well as family and educational services (from child protection and social work intervention to early childhood education and care services). The three major policy fields of support for families with children – financial support, leaves and services, especially early childhood education and care (ECEC) – will be discussed in depth.

Comparative family policy pursues different research strategies to overcome these difficulties. One approach compares not single policy items, but a range of measures ('family policy packages'[4]) and develops ideal types or family policy 'regime types'.[5] Some draw comparisons based on model calculations, using definitions of rights and entitlements from national reports or comparative tables. Some researchers focus upon institutional change of family policy within a historical and institutionalist sociological framework;[6] and part of this literature draws upon feminist theories and includes gender models in social policy or 'care regimes' into the analytical

1 G. Strban, 'Family Benefits in the EU: Is It Still Possible to Coordinate Them?', *Maastricht Journal of European and Comparative Law* 23, 2016, 775–95.

2 Council of the EU Press Release 371/18 of 21/06/2018; provisional agreement of 25 March 2019 between the Council and the European Parliament, document 7698/19 amending Regulation (EC) No 883/2004 on the coordination of social security systems and Regulation (EC) No 987/2009 laying down the procedure for implementing Regulation (EC) No 883/2004.

3 C. Saraceno, *Family Policies, Concepts, Goals and Instruments*, Turin: Collegio Carlo Alberto, 2011.

4 For examples of this 'package' approach, see S. Kamerman et al., *Social Policies, Family Types, and Child Outcomes in Selected OECD Countries*, OECD Social, Employment, and Migration Working Papers No.6/2003, J. Fagnani and A. Math, 'Family Packages in 11 European Countries: Multiple Approaches', in C. Saraceno and A. Leira (eds), *Childhood: Changing Contexts*, Bingley: Emerald, JAI, 2008, pp. 55–78; N. Van Mechelen and J. Bradshaw, 'Child Poverty as a Government Priority: Child Benefit Packages for Working Families, 1992–2009', in I. Marx and K. Nelson (eds), *Minimum Income Protection in Flux: Reconciling Work and Welfare in Europe*, London: Palgrave Macmillan, 2013, pp. 81–107.

5 M. Daly and E. Ferragina, 'Family Policy in High-Income Countries: Five Decades of Development', *Journal of European Social Policy* 28, 2018, 255–70. For the literature on typologies see C. Saraceno and W. Keck, 'Can We Identify Intergenerational Policy Regimes in Europe', *European Societies* 10, 2010, 675–96.

6 For typologies with a historical-institutional dimension see T. Bahle, 'Family Policy Patterns in the Enlarged Europe', in J. Alber, T. Fahey and C. Saraceno (eds), *Handbook of Quality of Life in the Enlarged European Union*, Abingdon: Routledge, 2008, pp. 100–26. F.-X. Kaufmann, 'Politics and Policies towards the Family in Europe: A Framework and an Inquiry into Their Differences and Convergences', in F.-X. Kaufmann et al. (eds), *Family Life and Family Policies in Europe, Vol. 2: Problems and Issues in Comparative Perspective*, Oxford: Oxford University Press, 2002, pp. 427–500); Saraceno and Keck, op. cit., n 5.

categories of comparison.[7] It is usual to classify certain types of family policy models, distinguishing between the continental European countries, Anglo-Saxon countries, Nordic countries and southern Europe together with the former socialist Eastern European countries. Different 'families of nations of family policy' in Europe[8] are labelled as 'autonomy' (United Kingdom, Netherlands, Ireland), 'universality' (Sweden, Denmark, Norway, partly Finland), 'subsidiarity' (Belgium, France, Luxembourg, Germany, Austria, Switzerland) and 'familism' (Portugal, Spain, Italy, partly Greece) types. Although the typologies differ, one can conclude that 'family policy comes in types and that it is possible to identify signature approaches to family (and gender) policies'.[9]

Besides the classical objective of easing the financial burdens for families, combating poverty and supporting the family as a system *sui generis*, family-related cash benefits serve various ends such as labour market policies, activation (especially for mothers and one-parent families), enhancement of education and others.[10] Since service provision (benefits in kind) can be a functional equivalent to cash benefits, the provision of childcare and early childhood education and care (ECEC) plays a role. Not only are poverty reduction, the functioning of the family and child welfare important purposes of state support, these are supplemented by policy goals related to child development and educational attainment of children (as in the EU 'social investment strategy'). Under the 'activation paradigm', maternal employment is being pushed, and the entitlement conditions for the receipt of income support by (solo) parents hampered by child-rearing responsibilities have been cut down in a number of countries to shorten periods of (maternal) absence from the labour market. In short, the underlying logic of state intervention into the family has changed from the idea of financially stabilizing the family as a separate system *sui generis* (formerly based on the traditional breadwinner model) towards multiple policy goals.[11] The EU 'child investment strategy'[12] and the EU pillars of social rights[13] are examples of this changing family policy mix of transfer- and service-oriented benefits and multilayered policy objectives.

Supporting families to meet the costs of children and family care – financial support

The classic family benefits, developed since the 1920s, were family allowances, child allowances and tax rebates as well as maternity pay; nowadays, the picture has become much more complex.

7 F. Bettio and J. Plantenga, 'Comparing Care Regimes in Europe', *Feminist Economics* 10, 2004, 85–113; J. Lewis, 'Gender and the Development of Welfare Regimes', *Journal of European Social Policy* 2, 1992, 159–73.
8 Bahle, op. cit., n 6.
9 M. Daly and E. Ferragina, op. cit., n 5, p. 257.
10 M. Mätzke and I. Ostner, 'Explaining Recent Shifts in Family Policy', *Special Issue of Journal of European Social Policy* 20, 2010, 387–98; they speak of the 'increasingly instrumental value of family policy and its loss of *sui generis* qualities', at 395.
11 M. Mätzke and I. Ostner, op. cit., n 10.
12 Commission Recommendation 2013/112/EU, *Investing in Children: Breaking the Cycle of Disadvantage, OJ L 59*, 2013, pp. 5–16; H. Frazer and E. Marlier, *Progress across Europe in the Implementation of the 2013 EU Recommendation on 'Investing in Children: Breaking the Cycle of Disadvantage'. A Study of National Policies*, European Social Policy Network (ESPN), Brussels, European Commission, 2017; N. Morel, B. Palier and J. Palme (eds), *Towards a Social Investment Welfare State?*, Bristol: Policy Press, 2011; C. Saraceno, 'A Critical Look to the Social Investment Approach from a Gender Perspective', *Social Politics* 22, 2015, 257–69.
13 Communication from the Commission to the European Parliament, the Council, the European Economic and Social Committee and the Committee of the Regions, *Establishing a European Pillar of Social Rights*, Brussels, 26.4.2017, COM(2017) 250 final.

These benefits are part of different systems (universal, categorical social security and income-tested benefits). Housing benefits or the provision of public housing complete the picture. In most European countries most expenditure in support of families is through cash payments, but expenditure on service provision is growing faster and was in general not cut down during the financial crisis of 2008 and the following period of austerity measures. Family allowances vary greatly in the amount paid and the eligibility criteria, and in some countries, benefit rates vary also by the age and number of children.

Family allowances, child allowances, tax allowances

How has financial support for families developed over the last decades? How have cut-backs and changes, such as increased means-testing or targeting, affected different family forms, inequalities and poverty levels? While *family allowances* in the past were nearly universal in the Eastern European countries, some have introduced means-testing.[14] During and after the financial crisis of 2008 in Europe, cutbacks of cash benefits and tax allowances took place in a number of countries as part of austerity measures, but they displayed considerable variation.[15] Means-testing and targeting of benefits have been strengthened in a number of states, even in those countries (such as France) that used to rely more on universal child and family benefits.

Looking at the '*autonomy group*', serious cutbacks occurred in the UK, a country that is characterized by the importance of and the high spending on means-tested transfers to families.[16] While family transfers and services were extended during the Blair period,[17] they were reduced during austerity policies. In the UK, the former universal child benefit has been made means-tested; the income threshold affects also middle class families negatively. The introduction of a 'benefit cap' in 2013, revised and further reduced by the Welfare Reform and Work Act 2016, on numerous social benefits (including child benefits, child tax credits, housing benefits, maternity allowances and other social benefits) inflicted poverty; the cuts had a disproportionate negative impact upon women, especially single parents and minority women.[18] This led to

14 C. Saraceno, 'De-Familization or Re-Familization? Trends in Income Tested Family Benefits', in T. Knijn and A. Komter (eds), *Solidarity between the Sexes and the Generations: Transformations in Europe*, Cheltenham: Edward Elgar, 2004, pp. 68–88; 76ff.

15 For a comprehensive overview, see Eurofound, *Families in the Economic Crisis: Changes in Policy Measures in the EU*, Luxembourg: Publications Office of the European Union, 2015; S. Bothfeld and S. Rouault, 'Families Facing the Crisis: Is Social Investment a Sustainable Social Policy Strategy?', *Social Politics* 22, 2015, 257–69; Y. Chzhen, 'Unemployment, Social Protection Spending and Child Poverty in the European Union during the Great Recession', *Journal of European Social Policy* 27, 2017, 123–37, Y. Chzhen, B. Nolan, C. Cantillon and S. Handa, 'Impact of the Economic Crisis on Children in Rich Countries', in B. Cantillon, Y. Chzhen, S. Handa and B. Nolan (eds), *Children of Austerity: Impact of the Great Recession on Child Poverty in Rich Countries*, Oxford: Oxford University Press, 2017, pp. 8–29, M. Daly and E. Ferragina, op. cit., n 5; M. Nygård, F. Lindberg, C. Nyqvist and C. Härtull, 'The Role of Cash Benefit and In-Kind Benefit Spending for Child Poverty in Times of Austerity: An Analysis of 22 European Countries 2006–2015', *Social Indicators Research*, 2019, https://doi.org/10.1007/s11205-019-02126-8.

16 Fagnani and Math, op. cit., n 4.

17 M. Daly, 'Shifts in Family Policy in the UK under New Labour', *Journal of European Social Policy* 20, 2010, 5433–43.

18 L. Lammasniemi, 'The Benefit Cap and Infliction of Poverty', *Journal of Social Welfare and Family Law* 41, 2019, 368–71. See also the harsh critique of Philip Alston, special UN rapporteur on extreme poverty and human rights, in his report of the visit to the UK and Northern Ireland of 2018 (A/HRC/41/39/Add.1).

litigation[19] on whether the revised benefit cap discriminates against lone parents and their young children and infringes international law (arts 8 and 14 and art. 1 of Protocol 1 of the ECHR and art. 3 UNCRC). The Supreme Court rejected this claim and held by a majority of 5–2 that the discriminatory effects of the benefit cap were justified. With regard to tax credits, there is a major reform under way in the UK, where gradually a universal credit (UC) is introduced which will eventually replace tax credits, and some other social security benefits between 2020 and 2023. The UK is a major example for a trend towards the fiscalization of family benefits, including childcare costs.[20]

Within the *Nordic countries* (the '*universality group*'), the level of family benefits has mostly been held stable, it was sometimes even increased (Sweden raised the child allowance and housing allowances after 2008 in steps and extended the in-work tax credits to augment household income). But Finland froze the universal child benefit for three years from 2013 onwards and cut the child benefit by 8 percent in 2015, while targeted measures for low-income families were strengthened, especially through an increase of the basic amount of the means-tested social assistance, with a higher uprating for solo parents than for other low-income households.[21]

In *continental European countries* such as France and Germany, family benefits were reduced partially, but not in general or even increased. France, a family policy pioneer with an established and generous benefit system, is an interesting example. After the outbreak of the financial crisis in 2008, at first additional benefits were offered to poorer families. While the level of child and family benefits was kept stable in 2011, a freezing of family benefits followed in 2012, and later various measures were implemented to reduce the deficits of the social security family branch by 2017 which targeted family benefits to a greater extent on lower income households.[22] The cap on tax benefits related to the number of children (*quotient familial*) was lowered, and early childhood benefits were reduced, while the family benefit supplements for low-income families increased.[23] From 2013 to 2018, the benefit for lone parents (*allocation de soutien familial*) increased by 25 percent, and the benefit for poor families with numerous children was raised. The trend in France is to strengthen redistribution towards lower income families within cutbacks, which may affect not only high-income households, but also middle-class families negatively.

Family benefit rates among EU countries were least generous in the *southern European group*, and in most of the former socialist Eastern European EU-member states.[24] Spain and Greece, the countries most severely hit by the crisis, reacted with cutbacks; in Greece former universal and categorical benefits (child allowance and benefit for large families) were abolished and replaced by a 'uniform child support allowance' targeted towards solo parents and low-income families, particularly with three or more children, with a maximum allowance of €40 per month for each child, which reduces support overall for families. Portugal has restricted eligibility criteria and targeted low-income families; benefit amounts as well as tax allowances for families were

19 *R (DA & Others) v Secretary of State for Work and Pensions* [2019] UKSC 21.

20 T. Ferrarini, K. Nelson and H. Höög, *The Fiscalization of Child Benefits in OECD Countries*, GINI Discussion Paper No. 49, Amsterdam: AIOS, 2012.

21 Eurofound, op. cit., n 15, p. 22.

22 In 2015, benefit rates were cut by 50 percent for families with a monthly income above 6,000 euro and by 75 percent above 8,000 euro (augmented by 500 euro per child of the family).

23 O. Thévenon, W. Adema and N. Ali, 'Family Policy in France and Europe: Recent Changes and Effects of the Crisis', *Population and Societies* 2014, 1–4, p. 4.

24 Bahle et al., op. cit., n 6 based on data of 2004; N. Van Mechelen, S. Marchal, T. Goedeme, I. Marx and B. Cantillon, *The CSB-Minimum Income Protection Indicators Dataset*, Antwerp: Herman Deleeck Centre for Social Policy, University of Antwerp, 2011.

reduced, particularly in 2010 and 2011.[25] This led to half a million families losing the entitlement to the main cash benefit for families (*abono de família*). Special benefit increases for children under one year or families with more than one child under three and for solo-parent families were kept in place. Cuts and tightened eligibility criteria for minimum income benefits between 2010 and 2013 led to a 40 percent reduction in state expenditure on this means-tested anti-poverty measure.

In the *former socialist Eastern European countries*, Poland is exceptional in having extended family benefits after 2016. A child benefit '500+' programme was introduced in 2016, granting 500 Polish zloty (about €115) per month per child, universal from the second child on, while low-income families received it from the first child. Poland registered a considerable increase in births in 2017. From 2019 onwards, the benefit was made universal also for the first-born child. While it had some success in reducing child poverty, there is concern about potentially negative impact upon mothers' employment participation.[26] Other Eastern European countries experienced serious cutbacks. Slovenia targeted the formerly universal child benefit at low-income families with less than 64 percent of the national average wage and reduced it for those with less than 42 percent. This led to a serious drop of recipient rates of child benefit to 61 percent of all children under 18 in 2014, compared to over 85 percent in the period before reforms.[27]

Minimum income benefits (MIB) are not an explicit, but an important implicit family benefit,[28] since they guarantee the minimum existence level for families through a means-tested benefit that as well takes maintenance, support and care obligations into account. The European Social Charter grants a right to minimum income (art. 13.1), and income support is one of the three social inclusion pillars. Reductions of MIB, as in Portugal or Slovenia, or the introduction of stricter means tests for the unemployed, as in France and Hungary, affect families strongly. Also age restrictions in access (as in France and Spain) have effects on young unemployed persons and their families.

Solo-parent families are a particularly vulnerable group.[29] Activation policies stress the importance of maternal employment. Countries that used to allow solo parents to be out of the labour market for long periods under income support schemes have reduced this period over time. For example, in the UK the child's age at which mothers were expected to take up work was reduced from 16 to seven in 2010, and then to five in 2012. In Germany, the age limit of three has remained stable under the means-tested scheme, while reforms in 2008 concerning post-divorce maintenance compelled divorced mothers to seek employment earlier on a similar model as means-tested income support.[30] Comparing solo-parents' social rights in France, Germany, Sweden and the UK, it was shown that France provides most choice and a mix of support for solo parents in combining employment and care at an acceptable level of income security,

25 Eurofound, op. cit., n 15, pp. 25ff.

26 A. Bargu and M. Morgandi, Can Mothers Afford to Work in Poland? Labor Supply Incentives of Social Benefits and Childcare Costs, Washington, DC: World Bank, 2018.

27 Eurofound, op. cit., n 15, p. 26.

28 M. Dalli, 'Comparing the Access Conditions for Minimum Income Support in Four EU Member States for National, EU and Non-EU Citizens', *Journal of Social Welfare and Family Law* 41, 2019, 233–51; P. Frericks, R. Och and J. Höppner, 'The Family in Minimum Income Benefits in Europe: An Institutional Analysis', *Social Politics* 2019, https://doi.org/10.1093/sp/jxz003.

29 Y. Chzen and J. Bradshaw, 'Lone Parents, Poverty and Policy in the European Union', *Journal of European Social Policy* 22, 2012, 487–506; J. Van Lancker, J. Ghysels and B. Cantillon, 'The Impact of Child Benefits on Single-Mother Poverty: Exploring the Role of Targeting in 15 European Countries', *International Journal of Social Welfare,* 24, 2015, 210–22.

30 K. Scheiwe, 'The Costs of Caring for Children before and after Divorce: Contradictory Legal Messages and Their Gendered Effects', in D. Mayes and M. Thomson (eds), *The Costs of Children Parenting and Democracy in Contemporary Europe*, Cheltenham: Edward Elgar, pp. 152–70.

while Sweden guarantees a high level of income for solo parents in full-time employment. Support levels are much lower in Germany and the UK.[31] *Activation policies* are an explosive mix of anti-poverty policy, saving state expenditure, family policy and family law reform and are a double-edged sword, promising on the one hand better employment chances and income gains for solo parents, while they risk to overburden solo parents and are not necessarily in the best interest of the child.[32]

For children in solo parent families who receive too little or no child maintenance payments by an absent parent, the provision of *guaranteed child maintenance* schemes is important, less bureaucratic, easier to access and often not means-tested. Austria, Belgium, Denmark, Finland, France, Germany, Latvia, Norway, Poland, Portugal and Sweden have guaranteed child maintenance schemes. Portugal restricted eligibility criteria in 2010, reducing the income threshold of the child, while Latvia after 2012 increased the Subsistence Guarantee Fund for advanced child maintenance payments. Under EU law that coordinates family benefits for EU/EEA migrants, eligibility for guaranteed child maintenance benefits cannot be excluded based on citizenship; therefore Austria had to change its system of advanced maintenance payments after a judgment of the ECJ and extend eligibility to other non-national EU citizens.[33]

Housing benefits or the provision of public housing are another important element of anti-poverty policy for families, but are often underestimated or ignored in comparative research.[34] Only exceptionally are means-tested housing benefits in Europe quantitatively more important than means-tested income support for families, for example in Sweden. In Spain, where impending eviction of families from housing property due to failure to pay mortgages is a serious problem, a law of 2013 provides for the temporary suspension or postponement of evictions for low income families. In the UK, the conditions for entitlement for public housing subsidies in terms of bedroom space per individual of the family were tightened from 2014 onwards. More attention should be paid to housing benefits, public housing provision and to the protection of the family home in case of divorce or separation as an integral part of family policy and infrastructural policy, which is particularly relevant to solo-parents and in general to low-income families.[35]

The time squeeze – leave policies to reconcile employment with parental care obligations

The provision of leave as a right is included in the Charter of Fundamental Rights of the European Union (arts 24 and 33) and in the United Nations CRC (arts 5, 18 and

31 K.J. Bieback, 'Alleinerziehende im Sozialrecht anderer europäischer Länder', *Archiv für Wissenschaft und Praxis der sozialen Arbeit* 42, 2011, 56–67.

32 W. Keck and C. Saraceno, 'The Impact of Different Social-Policy Frameworks on Social Inequalities among Women in the European Union: The Labour-Market Participation of Mothers', *Social Politics* 20, 2013, 297–328.

33 ECJ, *Judgment of 15 March 2001, Offermanns (C-85/99, ECR 2001 p. I-2261)*; ECJ, *Judgment of 5 February 2002, Humer (C-255/99, ECR 2002 p. I-1205)*.

34 H. Domansky, 'Housing Conditions', in Alber, Fahey and Saraceno, op. cit., n 6, pp. 235–53.

35 C. Dewilde, 'Divorce and Housing: A European Comparison of the Housing Consequences of Divorce for Men and Women', in H.-J. Andreß and D. Hummelsheim (eds), *When Marriage Ends: Economic and Social Consequences of Partnership Dissolution*, Cheltenham: Edward Elgar, 2009, 263–85. The protection of the owner-occupied family home for the needier family members through family law is stronger in two of the 'familialist' southern European countries and in the 'autonomy' group countries, the UK and Ireland.

27). The main instruments are maternity, paternity and parental leave and benefits, as well as other care-related rights to time off or working time flexibility. A tendency over the last decade was a stronger linkage of leave policies and leave benefits to labour market and employment policy goals, such as activation of mothers and shorter absence from the labour market (especially of solo parents), and in general towards gender equality and targeting fathers as carers.[36]

Within the *EU*, Directive 2010/18/EU set a minimum standard for parental leave of four months, including one month minimum that is reserved to the 'other parent' ('daddy month') and is not transferable. This was substituted by the new Directive (EU) 2019/1158 on work-life balance for parents and carers, which entered into force on 1 August 2019. It regulates paternity leave, parental leave, caregivers' leave and flexible working arrangements for working parents or caregivers. Member states have three years to adapt the national laws and regulations. The EU Directive 2019/1158 applies to all workers who have employment contracts or other employment relationships, to be defined by Member States. Member States have also the competence to define marital and family status and to establish which persons are to be considered to be a parent, which means that the recognition of different family forms and of parental status under Directive EU 2019/1158 may vary across EU Member States. However, there is a trend to extend leave entitlements to non-traditional families and same-sex partners.[37] Paternity leave of at least ten working days for fathers or equivalent second parents around the time of birth has to be granted, compensated at least at the level of sick pay. The existing right to a four months parental leave is specified by making two months non-transferable between parents; compensation at a level to be set by member states has to be provided. A right to take parental leave in a flexible way is guaranteed, such as part-time leave or splitting the leave in time periods. A right to five days carers' leave per year for workers providing personal care or support to a relative or person living in the same household is granted. The right to request flexible working arrangements (reduced working hours, flexible working hours and flexibility in place of work) is extended to all working parents of children up to eight years old, and all carers. This will unify the right to paternity leave and parental leave within the EU at minimum levels.

Paternity leave, a gender-specific entitlement granted shortly after a child's birth, encompasses in most countries two to ten days, but some are longer.[38] Various measures have also been taken to set incentives for fathers' take-up of parental leave through bonuses or 'quota' and other measures. These measures signify an important shift towards a different role model for fathers as

36 For details on leave regulation see the annual comparative reports and literature at www.leavenetwork.org; A. Koslowski, S. Blum, I. Dobrotić, A. Macht, and P. Moss (eds), *International Review of Leave Policies and Research 2019*. Available at www.leavenetwork.org/lp_and_r_reports/; M. De la Corte-Rodríguez, *EU Law on Maternity and Other Child-Related Leaves: Impact on Gender Equality*, Alphen: Kluwer Law, 2019; I. Dobrotić and S. Blum, 'Inclusiveness of Parental-Leave Benefits in Twenty-One European Countries: Measuring Social and Gender Inequalities in Leave Eligibility', *Social Politics* 23, 2019; C. Castro-García and M. Pazos-Moran, 'Parental Leave Policy and Gender Equality in Europe', *Feminist Economics* 22, 2016, 51–73; P. Moss, A.-Z. Duvander and A. Koslowski (eds), *Parental Leave and Beyond: Recent International Developments, Current Issues and Future Directions*, Bristol: Policy Press, 2019; O. Thévenon, 'Leave Policies for Parents in a Cross-National Perspective: Various Paths along the Same Course?', in B. Eydal and T. Rostgaard (eds), *Handbook of Family Policy*, Cheltenham: Edward Elgar, 2018, pp. 124–38.

37 For details, see Koslowski et al, op. cit., n 36; European Platform for Investing in Children (EPIC), *Leave Policies and Practice for Non-Traditional Families*, Brussels 2019.

38 Koslowski et al., op. cit., n 35, pp. 16–19; M. Karu and D.-G. Tremblay, 'Fathers on Parental Leave: An Analysis of Rights and Take-up in 29 Countries', *Community, Work & Family* 21, 2018, 344–62.

carers, although take-up rates and impact upon the participation of fathers in family work have been somewhat modest,[39] with the highest increase of fathers' participation in the Scandinavian countries.[40]

Parental leave regulation as well as the level of *parental benefits* during leave above the minimum requirements vary considerably with regard to eligibility criteria (universal or employment-related), duration, parts reserved to one parent only and benefit levels. Most European countries provide fewer than 15 months of parental leave, while 'long leave countries' (Czech Republic, Estonia, France, Germany, Hungary, Lithuania, Slovakia and Spain) grant up to three years or more.[41] The level of payments displays great variation between nearly wage replacement rates, 'well-paid parental leave benefits',[42] and higher and low flat-rate benefits. Some countries (Cyprus, Greece, Ireland, Malta, Netherlands, Spain, UK) had no payment during parental leave; the Directive 2019/1158 provides for two months of paid parental leave. In Europe a few countries grant exclusively wage-related benefits (from Denmark paying about 33 months' wages to Italy paying six). Slovakia, Hungary and Poland grant rather high flat-rate benefits. But stronger employment links to entitlements or higher benefits levels may give fewer parents access due to the increasing precariousness of employment or unemployment. An example is Germany where the parental leave benefit level as wage replacement was augmented considerably in 2010, while cuts of the parental benefits (*Elterngeld*) affected the long-term unemployed and families in receipt of means-tested income support who were excluded from this benefit.

EU legislation on *maternity leave* was maintained; Directive 92/85/EEC[43] guarantees a 14-week minimum *maternity leave* around the time of childbirth, of which two weeks are mandatory for the mother. There is a trend towards a short birth-related maternity leave in some countries (e.g. Sweden grants the mandatory two weeks maternity leave and has substituted the other period by gender-neutral parental leave). The length of post-birth maternity leave differs widely, from a few weeks to 12 months or more.[44] In some countries, part of the maternity leave was made transferable from the mother to the father (Bulgaria, Croatia, Czech Republic, Spain, the UK), especially in countries where maternity leave is rather long; this blurs the lines with parental leave. Discrimination is still an ongoing problem (dismissal of pregnant women or of parents taking leave).[45] The ECJ decided in two cases in 2014 that EU law under Directive 92/85/EEC ('the Pregnant Workers Directive') and Directive 2006/54/EC on the implementation of the principle of equal opportunities and equal treatment between men and women does not include women who became a mother using surrogacy and is not discriminatory.[46]

39 A. Smith and A. Koslowski, 'Working Fathers in Europe: Earning and Caring', *European Sociological Review* 27, 2011, 230–45.

40 G. Eydal and T. Rostgaard, 'Policies Promoting Active Fatherhood in Five Nordic Countries', in R. Musumeci and A. Santero (eds), *Fathers, Childcare and Work: Cultures, Practices and Policies*, Bingley: Emerald Publishing Limited, 2018, pp. 257–79.

41 Koslowski et.al., op. cit., n 36, p. 21.

42 For this notion see Koslowski et. al., op. cit., n 36.

43 Maternity leave for EU Member States is regulated by Council Directive 92/85/EEC of 19 October 1992, *OJ L 348*, 28.11.1992, pp. 1–7.

44 Koslowski et. al., op. cit., n 36, pp. 8–12.

45 European Equality Law Network, *Family Leave: Enforcement of the Protection against Dismissal and Unfavourable Treatment*, Luxembourg: Publications Office of the EU, 2018.

46 Cases C-363/12, ECLI:EU:C:2014:159, C 167/12, ECLI:EU:C:2014:169.

Changing services for families, children and young persons

Childcare services and preschool facilities as part of early childhood education and care (ECEC) are long-standing areas of policy which have recently been subject to dynamic change, with increasing involvement of international organizations such as the OECD, the EU, the COE and the World Bank, promoting higher female employment rates and childcare provision under different paradigms.[47] The European Pillar of Social Rights states that children have the right to affordable early childhood education and care of good quality, and a Council Recommendation[48] invites EU member states to make ECEC accessible, affordable and inclusive. However, ECEC services are very heterogeneous in Europe. Frequently, demand is not met, especially for children under the age of three. However, eight European countries (Denmark, Germany, Estonia, Latvia, Slovenia, Finland, Sweden and Norway) guarantee a place in ECEC for each child at an early age of the child, either soon after birth, from one year on (Germany, Norway, Sweden) or from 18 months on (Estonia, Latvia). Of all children aged four or above, 95.3 percent are now in ECEC in the EU-28.[49]

A guarantee to a place in ECEC for a child is granted in two ways, either based on a rights-based approach and a legal guarantee to a place, or by making participation in kindergarten or (pre)school from an early age compulsory. The trend is that the starting age of compulsory school or kindergarten has been lowered in a number of countries; the lowest compulsory starting age is three years in Hungary and in France (since September 2019). The last year of pre-primary education has been made compulsory in 16 European educational systems.[50]

Despite this general tendency, there are still gaps in many countries, and supply does not meet demand, especially for under-threes. There is also concern about the development of quality and the professionalization of staff in ECEC,[51] since expansion has happened sometimes at the expense of quality, e.g. by lowering the staff-child ratios or increasing group size. Tendencies of marketization of childcare in some countries are critically discussed.[52] Affordability and the question of how parents are supported in bearing childcare costs (subsidies for fees, tax credits) are important issues. Where ECEC is compulsory, no costs occur. But all over Europe, most families have to pay fees for ECEC for the youngest group of children, while it is more frequently cost-free for children from age three on, especially during the last year before obligatory

47 R. Mahon, 'After Neo-Liberalism? The OECD, the World Bank and the Child', *Global Social Policy* 10, 2010, 172–92; for the EU social investment strategy, see literature in n 12.

48 Council Recommendation of 22 May 2019 on High Quality Early Childhood Education and Care Systems, OJ C 189, 5.6.2019.

49 European Commission/EACEA/Eurydice/Eurostat, *Key Data on Early Childhood Education and Care in Europe–2019 Edition*, Luxembourg: Publications Office of the European Union, 2019, p. 43.

50 European Commission/EACEA/Eurydice/Eurostat, *Compulsory Education in Europe 2019/20: Facts and Figures*, Luxembourg: Publications Office of the EU, 2019, pp. 5ff; see also P. Moss, 'The Relationship between Early Childhood and Compulsory Education: A Properly Political Question', in P. Moss (ed.), *Early Childhood and Compulsory Education: Reconceptualising the Relationship*, Abingdon: Routledge, 2013, pp. 2–50.

51 European Commission/EACEA/Eurydice/Eurostat, op. cit., n 49; G. Dahlberg, P. Moss and A. Pence, *Beyond Quality in Early Childhood Education and Care: Languages of Evaluation*, 3rd edition, Abingdon: Routledge, 2013; OECD, *Engaging Young Children: Lessons from Research about Quality in Early Childhood Education and Care, Starting Strong*, Paris: OECD Publishing, 2018.

52 D. Brennan, B. Cass, S. Himmelweit and M. Szebehely, 'The Marketisation of Care: Rationales and Consequences in Nordic and Liberal Care Regimes', *Journal of European Social Policy* 22, 2012, 377–91; E. Lloyd and H. Penn (eds), *Childcare Markets: Can They Deliver an Equitable Service?*, Bristol: Policy Press; M.A. Yerkes and J. Javornik, 'Creating Capabilities: Childcare Policies in Comparative Perspective', *Journal of European Social Policy* 29, 2019, 529–44.

schooling in primary education. After-school care for school children[53] is another critical issue of service provision; school time schedules are still a serious impediment to parental employment in a number of countries, and after-school care provision is very uneven.

There is also a growing demand for *domestic services* and support with *housework and care* for children and elderly persons in need of long-term care living at home. What is mainly women's work is often kept in the shadow (economy), but is becoming visible as a form of family support that intersects with employment and migration policy ('global care chains'). New service demands arise due to demographic change, increasing mobility and changing female employment patterns, and inequalities run high along class, gender, race and citizenship lines. Policy responses vary between inactivity and public support through state subsidies or tax deductions for private employment of care workers or the provision of some public services. Different models and mixes of state support related to care and housework in the family home are pursued. Some countries like France, Belgium and the canton of Geneva in Switzerland have developed explicit policies for registering informal household workers and subsidizing the private employment of home helpers and domestic workers through state subsidy of social security contributions, tax benefits or vouchers for the use of agency-supplied care work.[54] A globalized care market is developing with extensive amounts of irregular care work in private households, and often very poor working conditions.[55] While not usually seen as an issue of family policy, this should be brought from the shadow economy into the social policy arena. This is also a transnational family policy issue with regard to migrant workers who often have children in their country of origin, which raises many questions about third-country nationals' right to family reunion and their entitlement to family benefits for family members living abroad.[56]

Conclusions

How have policies towards supporting families in meeting their needs developed at the national and European level, and how have new challenges been met? The three different dimensions and instruments investigated here (financial support, leave and time policies, service provision and ECEC) tend to be interconnected more strongly and are overarched by multiple policy goals. The former dominant goal of supporting families as systems with particular sui generis qualities are superimposed by other policy goals, especially activation and labour market concerns or educational goals. The challenge of combating poverty and social inequalities for families has not been met up to now, putting particular groups at risk. Financial support for families through cash benefits and tax rebates has undergone cuts in many countries in the years following the financial crisis of 2008, especially in the countries most hit by the crisis, contributing to the very uneven picture of generosity of state support packages for families. Leave policies have been an area of expansion, and the EU has set minimum standards for parental leave as well as for paternity leave, combined with incentives for stronger involvement of fathers.

53 J. Plantenga and C. Remery, 'Out-of-School Childcare: Exploring Availability and Quality in EU Member States', *Journal of European Social Policy* 27, 2017, 25–39; Eurofound, *Out-of-School Care: Provision and Public Policy*, 2020 (forthcoming).

54 M. Tomei, 'Decent Work for Domestic Workers: Reflections on Recent Approaches to Tackle Informality', *Canadian Journal of Women and the Law* 23, 2011, 185–211.

55 In 2011, the International Labour Organization adopted the ILO convention 189 'Decent work for domestic workers', ratified by 29 countries in November 2019.

56 See H. Stalford, 'Benefits, Babies and the Insignificance of Being British', *Journal of Social Welfare and Family Law* 40, 2018, 370–5 for the exclusion of third-country national carers from 'better' UK social benefits.

Many countries have introduced compulsory ECEC or lowered the age of compulsory schooling, also with a view to including disadvantaged children and parents who did not use childcare facilities and to tackling social inequalities. The diversification of family forms has not yet been met sufficiently in terms of benefit entitlements and sharing or splitting of benefits and social rights. Although same-sex parents in formalised relationships enjoy mostly the same rights as (married) parents, this does not hold true for all countries or for non-formalized families.[57] The development of leave policies and of services for families, especially of ECEC for children, is characterised by displaying a tendency towards a 'Scandinavization' of policies; nonetheless, the chances of a common European family policy model seem to be faint.[58] The coordination of different policy areas relevant to the support of families and individual family members is therefore important if sustainable family policies are to develop.[59] At the EU-level, the coordination of family benefits is an issue contested by some Member States with regard to the indexation of family benefits and exported care benefits, bringing about the risk of some downgrading of the former coordination rules of family benefits in the EU. Child and family poverty remain a huge challenge for the future. In 2017 an estimated 24.9 percent of children in the EU-28 were at risk of poverty or social exclusion. With regard to household type and family form, single parents with dependent children (46.7 percent) and two adults with three or more dependent children (30.9 percent) had the highest risk rates.[60] Despite the EU 'social investment strategy', child poverty is an ongoing problem – and this is not the only challenge.

57 European Platform for Investing in Children (EPIC), *Leave Policies and Practice for Non-Traditional Families*, Brussels, 2019; C. Waaldijk, *More and More Together: Legal Family Formats for Same-Sex and Different-Sex Couples in European Countries: Comparative Analysis of Data in the Laws and Families Database Families*, Families and Societies Working Paper Series no. 75, Stockholm: Stockholm University, 2017.

58 Bahle et al., op. cit., n 6, p. 120.

59 See the recommendations in Report of the High-Level Task Force, *Social Cohesion for the Council of Europe*, Strasbourg: TFSC, 2007, 31E.

60 Eurostat, *Archive: People at risk of poverty or social exclusion.* Available at https://ec.europa.eu/eurostat/statistics-explained/index.php/People_at_risk_of_poverty_or_social_exclusion.

6.2
STATE SUPPORT FOR FAMILIES IN THE UNITED STATES

Maxine Eichner

Introduction

For much of the twentieth century, the United States had a welfare state premised on the assumption of maternal caretaking, albeit a welfare state that provided scanter support than most other wealthy, industrialized countries. The US model assumed that families' caretaking and human development responsibilities would be performed by wives and mothers, who would generally be supported financially by their husbands. Accordingly, state support for families was not seen as appropriate in the ordinary course of events. It was instead directed to those families who possessed no breadwinner. Financial support to these families by the state substituted for the breadwinner's pay and ensured that the caregiver-mother could stay at home to care for children.[1]

It has been almost half a century since women in the US, as in other western countries, began to move into the workplace in great numbers, and to stay there after having children. Between 1975 and 2018, the percentage of US women in the workforce with children under the age of six years grew from 39 percent to 65 percent.[2] Women with children between the ages of six and 17 increased their participation in the workforce from 55 percent in 1975 to 76 percent in 2018.[3] As a result, 67 percent of families are now headed either by two working parents or by an unmarried working parent.[4]

Although the dominance of the dual-working-parents or single-working-parent pattern of American family life is no longer new, the United States has failed to move to a model of the

1 T. Skocpol, *Protecting Soldiers and Mothers: The Political Origins of Social Policy in the United States*, Cambridge: The Belknap Press of Harvard University Press. The Aid to Dependent Children Act, Pub. L. No. 74–271, 49 Stat. 620 (1935), later renamed the Aid to Families with Dependent Children Act, Pub. L. No. 78–257, 58 Stat. 277 (1944) (AFDC), was the centerpiece of this system. AFDC was repealed by the Personal Responsibility and Work Opportunity Act of 1996, Pub. L. No. 104–93, 110 Stat. 2105 (1996).

2 US Bureau of Labor Statistics, *Women in the Labor Force: A Databook*, US Department of Labor, 15 December 2011; US Bureau of Labor Statistics, *Employment Characteristics of Families–2018*, US Department of Labor, 18 April 2019.

3 US Bureau of Labor Statistics 2011, op. cit., n 2; US Bureau of Labor Statistics 2019, op. cit., n 2.

4 Calculated from US Census Bureau data, *Families with Own Children: Employment Status of Parents by Age of Youngest Child and Family Type, 2017–2018 Annual Averages*, US Department of Commerce, 2019.

welfare state that adequately supports these families. In contrast to its European counterparts (on which, see Chapter 6.1 of this book), the US has instituted few policies that help family members reconcile work with caretaking responsibilities. What is more, it has retracted past government supports for poor women and their families on the theory that women's entry into the workplace means that they should now be able to support their families on their own. In addition, it has moved to a system of child welfare that expects families to care for members on their own, and is quick to remove children from families who fail to live up to this model.

This chapter first describes existing US public policy regarding families' caretaking obligations and other welfare needs. It then discusses the costs of the United States' leaving families to deal with their members' dependency issues largely without state support. Finally, the chapter considers conceptual and political challenges to implementing more supportive policies in the United States.

US support for family obligations

Work and family reconciliation policies

For much of the twentieth century, the US welfare model was premised on women's caretaking, and therefore focused its attention on subsidizing mothers who had inadequate income supports so that they could stay at home and care for their children.[5] Since mothers have moved into the workplace in greater numbers, however, few institutional changes have been made to ensure that families can continue to care adequately for their children and other family members. Although the current workforce includes roughly 96 percent of fathers and 72 percent of mothers with children under 18,[6] US law does little to safeguard workers' caretaking responsibilities when they conflict with work.

The only statutory protection explicitly granted by federal law to protect caretaking when it conflicts with work is the Family and Medical Leave Act of 1993 (FMLA).[7] The 12 weeks of unpaid leave that the FMLA guarantees, however, cover only a fraction of the time necessary to raise children.[8] Furthermore, the FMLA defines the conditions that give rise to leave in a manner that excludes most of the caretaking that family members require. For example, parents may obtain leave to care for children only in circumstances involving the birth or adoption of a child, or in situations involving a severe medical emergency.[9] Parents who need time to deal with more mundane caretaking needs, or to stay at home with a child sick with the flu, are left to fend for themselves.

Moreover, the terms of the FMLA's coverage severely restrict the application of even the minimal guarantees that it does provide. Because the Act applies only to employees who work for companies with 50 or more employees, and employees must satisfy particular prerequisites, roughly 40 percent of the workforce (65 million employees) are not eligible for leave.[10] Furthermore, the FMLA simply guarantees that a worker can return to his or her job after the leave; it provides for no wage replacement during the leave. As a result, the vast majority of covered employees (by one count, 78 percent) cannot afford to make use of the available leave.[11]

5 Skocpol, op. cit., n 1.

6 US Bureau of Labor Statistics 2019, op. cit., n 2.

7 Family Medical Leave Act of 1993, 29 U.S.C. §§ 2601–2654 (2018).

8 Ibid., § 2612(a), (c).

9 Ibid., § 2612(a)(1).

10 Ibid., § 2611(2)(A)–(B); J.A. Klerman et al., *Family and Medical Leave in 2012: Technical Report*, Abt Associates, 2012 (revised 2014), p. 21.

11 D. Cantor et al., *Balancing the Needs of Families and Employers: Family and Medical Leave Surveys*, US Department of Labor, 2001. See also Klerman, op. cit., n 10 (finding 45 percent of surveyed eligible

Eight states and the District of Columbia have recently moved to fill this void by passing paid parental leave and, in some cases, paid family leave for caretaking for medical conditions.[12] California, the first state to pass paid parental leave, currently provides for up to six weeks of benefits (rising to eight weeks in July 2020), paid at approximately 60 to 70 percent of a worker's average weekly earnings.[13] Since then, other states have passed still more generous laws. For example, Washington State's paid parental leave programme, which will take effect in 2020, will offer wage replacement of up to 90 percent of an individual's average weekly earnings for 12 weeks.[14] Connecticut's paid family leave law, scheduled to take effect in 2022, will provide wage replacement of up to 95 percent of weekly earnings for 12 weeks.[15] And Oregon is set to provide the nation's most generous paid leave in 2023, allowing workers to receive up to 100 percent of their average weekly earnings for 12 weeks, up to a weekly limit of $1,215, plus an additional two weeks relating to pregnancy, childbirth, or a related medical condition including lactation.[16] Many of these state laws support paid caretaking leave for seriously ill family members at the same funding levels and durations as paid parental leave.[17]

The United States' family-work reconciliation policies fare poorly when compared against other countries. In fact, the World Policy Center has found that the US is one of only eight countries with no national laws providing some form of paid parental leave; the others are the Marshall Islands, Suriname, Palau, Papua New Guinea, Nauru, Micronesia and Tonga.[18] In contrast to the well-developed reconciliation policies of its wealthy, industrialized European counterparts, the United States not only lacks paid maternity leave, it also has no paid parental leave (again, except for the few states that have partially filled this gap), no protection against parents working long hours, no parity of wages or benefits for workers who work part time in order to accommodate caretaking and no paid vacation.[19]

To add to the caretaking problems of American working families, the American labour that family members enter without any protections for family responsibilities has the highest hour expectations of any wealthy industrialized country. The 1,786 hours that the average American worker works annually amounts to over ten more weeks a year of work than German workers (1,363 hours) and significantly more hours than France (1,520), Sweden (1,474), Canada (1,708 hours) and the United Kingdom (1,538). This means that even in the countries at the higher end of the scale, Canada, full-time employees work roughly the equivalent of two fewer weeks a year than their American counterparts.[20]

---

employees failed to take leave because they could not afford unpaid time off); Diversity Data Kids, *Challenges with Taking FMLA Leave*, Brandies University, n.d. (finding 34 percent of FMLA-eligible employees from 2007–2011 could not afford to take unpaid leave).

12 See generally A Better Balance, *Overview of Paid Family & Medical Leave Laws in the United States*, 22 July 2019.

13 Employment Development Department, *Calculating Paid Family Leave Benefit Payment Amounts*, State of California, 2018.

14 Employment Security Department, *Washington Paid Family & Medical Leave*, Washington State, July 2019.

15 *Governor Lamont Signs Historic Law Enacting Family and Medical Leave in Connecticut*, The Office of Governor Ned Lamont, 25 June 2019.

16 R. Bradbury, 'Oregon Passes 12-Week Paid Family Leave Policy', *HR Dive*, 3 July 2019.

17 Division of Temporary Disability and Family Leave Insurance, op. cit., n 15 (citing New York and New Jersey laws).

18 WORLD Policy Analysis Center Database, *Adult Labor and Working Conditions: Infant Caregiving*, WORLD Policy Analysis Center, 2019.

19 M. Eichner, *The Free-Market Family: How the Market Crushed the American Dream (and How It Can Be Restored)*, New York: Oxford University Press, 2020; B. Woodhouse, *The Ecology of Childhood: How Our Changing World Threatens Children's Rights*, New York: New York University Press, 2020.

20 OECD Data, *Hours Worked*, Organisation for Economic Co-operation and Development, 2018.

The absence of reconciliation policies in combination with the high hours demanded in the workplace means that American parents work substantially longer hours than parents in other countries. American parents in two-earner families together spend a combined average of 83 hours per week at their jobs, compared to 63 hours for dual earners in the Netherlands and 77 hours in Finland and Sweden.[21] Particularly remarkable are the high percentages of American couples working very long hours. Almost two-thirds of American dual-earner couples with children report joint work weeks of 80 hours or more. In most other wealthy industrialized countries, closer to one-third of couples spend this much time in the workplace.[22] When unpaid childcare and household responsibilities are calculated along with labour market responsibilities, American working parents on average spend almost ten hours a day, seven days a week between paid work and non-market work.[23]

Not only does the United States provide no policies to lighten the heavy time demands of the US workplace, it has played little role in ensuring adequate care for children while their parents work. In contrast to many other wealthy nations, the US does not provide public day care or early education for young children.[24] Nor does it generally subsidize private day care for children, even for families who could not otherwise afford it. In 2011 the government provided aid for childcare only for 5.3 percent of children under five, and 4.1 percent of children under 15.[25] In all, about 60 percent of the cost of US childcare is assumed by parents.[26] In addition, the US has no compulsory federal standards for safety, staffing or teaching curricula for privately provided early childhood care or education. In 2011 only 10 percent of all childcare centers and 1 percent of all family childcare homes met voluntary national standards of care and quality education.[27] Individual states have not filled this void. State licensing standards generally regulate issues of health and safety, but do not usually cover quality of care.[28] Many types of caretaking arrangements, including informal babysitters and small family childcare homes, are exempted by state law from meeting even these licensing standards. Because the majority of non-parental care takes place in these settings, most childcare in the United States goes virtually unregulated.[29]

Welfare system/poverty transfers

The US has adopted the same hands-off posture to helping families meet their members' dependency needs in other public policy spheres beyond work-family reconciliation. In the current

21 C. Medalia and J. Jacobs, 'Working Time for Married Couples in 28 Countries', in *The Long Work Hours Culture: Causes, Consequences and Choices*, Bingley: Emerald Group, 2008, Table 3.

22 Ibid.

23 S.M. Bianchi, J.P. Robinson and M.A. Milkie, *Changing Rhythms of American Family Life*, New York: Russell Sage Foundation, 2006, p. 117. Mothers who work full-time average 68 hours per week, while fathers who work full-time average 67 hours per week between market and non-market work. Ibid.

24 Eichner, op. cit., n 19, ch. 5. The main exception is the federal Head Start program, which provides means-tested education for three- and four-year-olds. Yet only 13 percent of three-year-olds and 38 percent of four-year-olds were in state-funded pre-kindergarten programs: W.S. Barnett and A. Friedman-Krauss, *State(s) of Head Start*, National Institute for Early Education Research, 2016, pp. 42–43. Due to underfunding, only four in ten eligible children living in poverty received Head Start services, while only one in 20 eligible children received Early Head Start services. S. Schmit and C. Walker, *Disparate Access: Head Start and CCDBG Data by Race and Ethnicity*, Center for Law and Social Policy (CLASP), February 2016, pp. 8, 10.

25 US Census Bureau, *Who's Minding the Kids? Child Care Arrangements: Spring 2011*, US Department of Commerce, April 2013.

26 Child Care Aware of America, *The US and the High Cost of Child Care: 2018 Report*, 2018, p. 47.

27 Ibid.

28 Eichner, op. cit., n 19, ch. 5.

29 Ibid.

system, it is families, not the state, who are assumed properly responsible for supporting children financially, whether or not parents have the means to do so. As a result, despite being the wealthiest country in the world, the poverty rate among children in the United States is among the highest in the industrialized world. In 2017, 17 percent of all children and 29 percent of African-American children lived below the poverty threshold.[30] In all, 12.8 million children were poor in the United States, and 5.9 million of those children lived in extreme poverty.[31] This is a substantially higher rate than in wealthy, industrialized European countries. For example, all Nordic countries have child poverty rates between 3 and 9 percent.[32] Although some other wealthy nations, such as France, Ireland, New Zealand and the United Kingdom, have higher child poverty rates than the United States before government aid, the United States' government aid policies are much less ambitious than these countries, and its child poverty rates are accordingly substantially higher.[33]

Moreover, the US has rolled back even the scant protections that had been available to needy families in the past on the view that, in the contemporary world, mothers should be expected to work to support their children. In 1996, the US Congress converted the childcare subsidy previously available to stay-at-home mothers to a transitional childcare subsidy intended to move poor mothers into the workplace so that they could support their families on their own.[34]

Child welfare system

The view that families should properly support their members without state assistance also underlies the mandate of the US child welfare system. Although the child welfare system is run by individual states, child welfare policy is dictated by the federal Adoption and Safe Families Act of 1997 (ASFA).[35] Under it, state agencies responsible for children's welfare are not triggered into action unless and until they receive a report of maltreatment. Once abuse or neglect is deemed substantiated, however, coercive state intervention is mandated. ASFA seeks to assure that once the state steps in, its involvement with families will be finite and, preferably, brief. While ASFA declares that states must make efforts to keep the child in the home and to reunify the child if a period of foster care is necessary,[36] in keeping with the United States' general recalcitrance toward ongoing state support for families, federal funding standards make it far more difficult for states to be compensated for providing assistance to preserve families than for providing foster care or adoption for the child.[37] As a consequence, a relatively small proportion of families actually receive any services for family preservation. When they do, the assistance

30 Children's Defense Fund, *Child Poverty in America 2017: National Analysis*, 12 September 2018.

31 Ibid.

32 United Nations Children's Fund, *Innocenti Report Card 13: Fairness for Children*, April 2016.

33 J. Gornick and E. Nell, 'Children, Poverty, and Public Policy: A Cross-National Perspective,' *LIS Working Paper Series*, No. 701, May 2017, Table 2.

34 Personal Responsibility and Work Opportunity Act, Pub. L. No. 104–93, 110 Stat. 2105 (codified as amended in scattered sections of 42 U.S.C.).

35 Adoption and Safe Families Act, Pub. L. No. 105–89, 107 Stat. 649 (codified as amended in scattered sections of 42 U.S.C.).

36 Ibid., § 671(a)(15)(B).

37 C.A. Scarcella, R. Bess, E.S. Zielewski and R. Green, *The Cost of Protecting Vulnerable Children IV*, Washington, DC: The Urban Institute, 2004. Congress allocated $5.3 billion for foster care services during the 2019 fiscal year, but only $790 million for family services, a category that covers family preservation services, community-based family support services, adoption promotion and support services, and reunification services. Congressional Research Service, *Child Welfare: Purposes, Federal Programs, and Funding*, 1 August 2019.

is generally short-term, crisis-oriented, and fails to deal effectively with chronic issues such as poverty, inadequate mental health care and substance abuse that brought these families into the system in the first place.[38]

Under the current approach, a large number of children (approximately 270,000 annually) enter the foster care system.[39] Most remain in care for substantial periods of time. Once a child is placed in foster care, the mean and median length of stay are 20.1 months and 12.9 months respectively, although a full 6 percent of children (24,838) stay five years or longer.[40] Once in care, ASFA limits the state's efforts to reunify the child with parents by mandating that child welfare agencies seek termination of parental rights if a child has been in foster care for 15 of the previous 22 months, with the goal of pursuing adoption of the child by another family.[41] Roughly half of the children taken into care will eventually be returned to their biological families.[42] However, the model of episodic state involvement that characterizes the current child welfare system, in which the state provides little assistance for reunification for relatively short periods of time, does little to solve the deep-seated problems that generally prompt state intervention in the first place. Because of this, many of the children who enter the child welfare system will cycle through it repeatedly.[43]

The half of children who are not eventually returned to their parents also have a tough road ahead of them. Many of these children will have their relationship with their biological parents legally terminated. In 2017 alone, 69,525 children whose parental rights had been terminated waited in foster care.[44] Yet because of the shortage of families willing to adopt from this pool of children, many children, particularly those who are older, who are African-American, or who have disabilities, will have a difficult time finding adoptive homes.[45] As a result, many will linger in foster care until they 'age out' of the system.[46] (Compare Chapter 4.2 in this book.)

Costs of the current approach

The United States' hands-off approach when it comes to supporting families produces a range of negative consequences. Included among these are the serious tolls these policies take on

38 M. Eichner, *The Supportive State: Families, Government, And America's Political Ideals*, New York: Oxford University Press, 2010, pp. 119–25. E. Fernandez, 'Supporting Children and Responding to Their Families: Capturing the Evidence on Family Support', *Children and Youth Services Review* 29, 2007, 1368–94.

39 Administration for Children and Families, *The AFCARS Report: Preliminary FY 2017 Estimates as of August 10, 2018 (25)*, US Department of Health and Human Services, 10 August 2018. In total, 443,000 children were in the foster care system as of 30 September 2017. Ibid.

40 Ibid.

41 42 USC § 675(5)(E) (2006).

42 Administration for Children and Families, op. cit., n 39.

43 Children's Bureau, *Outcome 4.2: Reentries Into Foster Care*, Administration for Children and Families, 2019 (showing that in 2017, by state, up to 14.8 percent of children reentered foster care within 12 months of a prior episode and up to 16.7 percent reentered foster care more than 12 months after a prior episode).

44 Administration for Children and Families, op. cit., n 39.

45 Ibid. (finding that of children waiting to be adopted in 2017, 9 percent had been in care five or more years; an additional 19 percent had been in care three to four years); A. Schmidt-Tieszen and T.P. McDonald, 'Children Who Wait: Long Term Foster Care or Adoption?', *Children and Youth Services Review* 20, 1998, 13–28; M. Freundlich, 'Supply and Demand: The Forces Shaping the Future of Infant Adoption', *Adoption Quarterly* 2, 1998, 13–42.

46 Administration for Children and Families, op. cit., n 39.

important public goods, including children's welfare, gender equality and the health of families – particularly poor families.

The absence of work-family reconciliation policies means that families are left to their own devices to reconcile the spheres of work and family. Some families deal with this issue through putting their children in day care for long hours, while other families have a member step back from complete attachment to the workforce, often moving to part-time or leaving paid work altogether. Each of these private means of resolving these issues has significant costs.

Families in which all parents are in the workplace must put their children in day care, often for long hours. More than three-quarters of preschool-age children are cared for by someone other than their parents; on average, children with working mothers spend 36 hours a week in such care.[47] This is true even for young children: roughly one-half of children under age one are cared for by someone other than the parents; the same is true for one- to two-year-old children.[48] For school-aged children ages six to 12 whose mothers work, almost half spend an average of 12.5 hours a week in non-parental care beyond what they spend in school.[49] These childcare arrangements do not serve most children well. Although children who attend good quality day care generally fare as well as those who are cared for by a parent, most day care in the United States' lightly regulated system has been judged by experts to be poor to mediocre.[50] Fewer than ten percent of childcare arrangements are considered high quality.[51] These daycares are generally more expensive than middle- and low-income parents can afford.[52]

Other families resolve work-family conflicts by leaving children, particularly but not exclusively older children, home alone for periods of time. In 2011, 14 percent of grade-school children (aged five to 15) with working mothers, and 11 percent of all grade-school children living with a single or married mother (4.2 million children), were 'latch-key kids' after school, travelling home alone and having no parent there to look after them on arrival. These ranged from 2 percent among five- and six-year-olds to 29 percent of 14-year-olds.[53] This system endangers the safety not only of younger children, but also of older children, as they are dramatically more likely to engage in juvenile crime, drugs, sex and other risky behaviour during unsupervised

47 J. Redford et al., *The Years before School: Children's Non-Parental Care Arrangements From 2001–2012*, NCES Report No. 2017–096, US Department of Education, National Center for Education Statistics, March 2017, p. 9, Figure 3; L. Laughlin, *Who's Minding the Kids? Child Care Arrangements*, Current Population Report No. P70–135, US Census Bureau, April 2013, p. 6.

48 Redford et al., op. cit., n 47.

49 J. Capizanno, K. Tout and G. Adams, *Child Care Patterns of School-Age Children with Employed Mothers*, The Urban Institute, 1 September 2000.

50 National Institute of Child Health and Human Development, *The NICHD Study of Early Child Care and Youth Development: Findings for Children up to Age 4½ Years*, US Department of Health and Human Services, National Institutes of Health, 2006, p. 11.

51 Ibid.; Eichner, op. cit., n 19, ch. 5.

52 In 2011, the average annual cost of center-based infant care was more than the annual in-state tuition at public four-year colleges in 35 states; for a 4-year-old, average costs exceeded tuition in 19 states: Child Care Aware of America, *Parents and the High Cost of Child Care: 2012 Report*, National Association of Child Care Resource and Referral Agencies, 14 August 2012. Only 3 percent of eligible infants and toddlers are able to secure spots in Early Head Start due to limited funding. Children's Defense Fund, op. cit., n 30. Twenty-two states had waiting lists for childcare assistance in 2011; California had 187,516 children on the waiting list in early 2011: K. Schulman and H. Blank, *State Child Care Assistance Policies 2011: Reduced Support for Families in Challenging Times*, National Women's Law Center, 11 October 2011.

53 US Census Bureau, op. cit., n 25.

afternoon hours.[54] One UNICEF report ranked the United States 23 out of 25 member countries of the Organization for Economic Cooperation and Development (OECD) in terms of the percentage of teens who eat dinner with their parents several times a week, an indicator of parental-child interaction that UNICEF found to be an important determinant in children's well-being. Both this indicator and the United States' high child-poverty rates contributed to the same report ranking the overall well-being of children in the United States as 37th of the 41 wealthy countries ranked, behind only Mexico, Romania, Bulgaria and Chile.[55]

Still other families resolve the work-family conflict by having one parent, generally the mother, step back at least somewhat from the heavy demands of the U.S. workplace. In some families, mothers remain in full-time jobs, but work fewer hours than in the past, or move to a less demanding full-time job. In other families, mothers move to part-time or even detach themselves completely from the workforce. All of these alternatives have significant costs for sex equality.[56] Mothers are significantly penalized in opportunities for career advancement and pay even when they remain in full-time jobs. Moving to part-time produces a still larger penalty, even when hours are held constant.[57] And stepping temporarily out of the workforce to raise children results in a heavy penalty that can rarely be made up in later years. By one count, highly skilled women will give up nearly 21 to 33 percent of earnings by having children;[58] even if they wait until after age 30 to have children, in order to keep the child penalty as small as possible, they will give up nearly $340,000 in earnings.[59] These inequalities in pay cause women to have less decision-making power within marriages, less future earning power in the case of divorce and lower pensions in the case of their husbands' deaths.[60] In addition, research suggests that the absence of reconciliation policies has caused US women's work rates to stagnate since the mid-1990s. In 1990, the United States ranked seventh in female labour participation among OECD nations; by 2017 it had fallen to fifteenth place.[61]

The problems of reconciling work and family are most intense for poor families, generally those headed by poor single mothers, who cannot afford either to step down from the workplace or to pay for good-quality childcare, and whose caretaking responsibilities hinder paid work. The difficulty in combining work and family, as well as the low levels of government support for poor families, has been linked to the feminization of poverty in the US.[62] In a recent

54 M.B. Larner, L. Zippiroli and R.E. Behrman, 'When School Is Out: Analysis and Recommendations', *The Future of Children* 9, 1999, 4–20, 9.

55 United Nations Children's Fund, *Innocenti Report Card 14: Building the Future*, June 2017, 10.

56 E.T. Wilde, L. Batchelder and D.T. Ellwood, 'The Mommy Track Divides: The Impact of Childbearing on Wages of Women of Differing Skill Levels', *NBER Working Paper Series* 16582, 2010, 1–45.

57 Ibid.; M.J. Budig and P. England, 'The Wage Penalty for Motherhood', *American Sociological Review* 66, 2001, 204–25.

58 Ibid. A recent study found that highly skilled women lose approximately 10 percent of their potential earnings per child. P. England et al., 'Do Highly Paid, Highly Skilled Women Experience the Largest Motherhood Penalty?', *American Sociological Review* 81, 2016, 1161–89.

59 Calculated using the Center for American Progress, *The Hidden Cost of a Failing Child Care System*, and referencing the median salary for female workers aged 25–34 in 2019, $40,508. Bureau of Labor Statistics, Table 3. Median usual weekly earnings of full-time wage and salary workers by age, race, Hispanic or Latino ethnicity, and sex, second quarter 2019 averages, not seasonally adjusted, *Economic News Release*, 17 July 2019.

60 A. Crittenden, *The Price of Motherhood*, New York: Metropolitan Books, 2001, p. 88; J.C. Gornick and M.K. Meyers, *Families That Work*, New York: The Russell Sage Foundation, 2003, p. 47.

61 Organisation for Economic Co-operation and Development, *Employment: Labor Force Participation Rate, By Sex and Age Group*, OECD Stat, 2019.

62 S.S. McLanahan and E.L. Kelly, 'The Feminization of Poverty: Past and Future,' in *Handbook of the Sociology of Gender*, New York: Springer Science+Business Media, 2006, pp. 127–45.

comparison, the US had the highest after-tax poverty rate for single-mother families of the 16 wealthy countries compared.[63]

Indeed, there is no doubt that the absence of support for families in the US is most devastating for poor families, and particularly poor children. Chronic poverty for children jeopardizes not only their present well-being but, also, their future prospects. It puts children at risk of lower cognitive development, poor school achievement and early childbearing, and is associated with reduced years of education and employment prospects.[64] The absence of early childhood education also limits poor children's prospects. Clear evidence links early education programmes to a broad variety of benefits for children, including higher levels of education and employment in later years.[65]

The absence of welfare supports in the US also puts poor families at risk of having their children removed to foster care. In contrast to countries with stronger safety nets, many US families cannot meet the basic needs of children simply because they cannot afford to do so. Several studies show that a substantial percentage of children taken into foster care – at least 10 percent by the Department of Health and Human Services' own numbers and in some studies as high as 30 percent – could remain safely in their own homes if their parents had access to decent housing.[66] Further, many children enter the foster care system simply because their parents cannot afford the mental health treatment the children require.[67] Likewise, a sizeable percentage of children in foster care have parents who themselves have mental-health issues or substance-abuse problems and cannot afford adequate treatment.[68]

Most children who enter the child welfare system have already been significantly damaged by the lack of US family support. The majority have been raised in poverty and have suffered its effects.[69] By the time they enter foster care, moreover, the overwhelming majority will have some sort of physical or mental abnormality that requires medical attention, including greatly elevated rates of suicidal and homicidal ideation, as well as a high level of developmental delays.[70] Taking these children into foster care, whether or not these children would fare better than if left in their homes,[71] causes them even further trauma. Regardless of whether they

63 Gornick and Nell, op. cit., n 33, Table 3.

64 J. Pascoe et al., 'Mediators and Adverse Effects of Child Poverty in the United States', *Pediatrics* 137, 2016.

65 H. Yoshikawa et al., *Investing in Our Future: The Evidence Base on Preschool Education*, Society for Research in Child Development and Foundation for Child Development, 2013.

66 Administration for Children and Families, op. cit., n 39; D.S. Harburger and R.A. White, 'Reunifying Families, Cutting Costs: Housing-Child Welfare Partnerships for Permanent Supportive Housing', *Child Welfare* 83, 2004, 500–1.

67 C. Jenkins, 'Mental Illness Sends Many to Foster Care: Medical Costs Overwhelm Va. Parents', *Washington Post*, 29 November 2004.

68 A. Meinhofer and Y. Angleró-Díaz, 'Trends in Foster Care Entry among Children Removed from Their Homes Because of Parental Drug Use, 2000 to 2017', *JAMA Pediatrics*, 15 July 2019.

69 In a study of three different states' foster-care systems, between 68 and 71 percent of children entering foster care came from families that qualified either for federal welfare benefits or Medicaid: Chapin Hall Center for Children at the University of Chicago, et.al., *Dynamics of Children's Movement Among the AFDC, Medicaid, and Foster Care Programs Prior to Welfare Reform: 1995–1996*, 31 March 2001.

70 K. Turney and C. Wildeman, 'Mental and Physical Health of Children in Foster Care', *Pediatrics* 138, November 2016; H. Anderson, 'Suicide Ideation, Depressive Symptoms, and Out-of-Home Placement among Youth in the U.S. Child Welfare System', *Journal of Clinical Child & Adolescent Psychology* 40, November 2011, 790–6.

71 There is substantial debate over whether many of the children in the US system are truly better served by taking them into foster care, rather than leaving them in their homes. Recent data suggests that at least in cases on the margins for removal, many children would be better off if they were left with their

are returned to their biological families, are adopted, or 'age out' of foster care, the eventual outcomes for adults who have been in foster care as youths are problematic. For example, this population suffers posttraumatic stress disorder at twice the rates of combat veterans; more than half (54.4 percent) have at least one diagnosable mental-health disorder, such as depression, social phobia, panic syndrome or anxiety.[72] And those children who linger in foster care until they 'age out' of the system have outcomes that are devastating based on almost any measure of well-being.[73]

Ideological challenges to state support for families

Widespread beliefs concerning the proper role of government impede state support for families in the US. The founding myth of the US is of a people who threw off the yoke of tyranny to create a limited government. The government's legitimate purposes, in this view, are seen as limited to protecting citizens' liberty and security. Pursuit of other purposes is seen to be illegitimate, paternalistic and potentially tyrannical. This view of government, as commentators have observed,[74] is modeled on the image of autonomous citizens who possess developed life plans; such citizens need government only to protect their liberty to pursue their life plans from others who might interfere. Obviously no persons are born as independent, autonomous citizens; the image of such citizens therefore assumes the presence of people (historically, mothers) who have raised these citizens until adulthood. Even then, the image of autonomous citizens is idealized, and at best applies only to people for a limited part of their lives.

To the extent that this cluster of American beliefs recognizes the dependency of the human condition, it considers dependency issues to properly be dealt with solely by families. In this view, families, like citizens, are properly autonomous; the goal of public policy, in this view, is to keep the family as free as possible from state intervention rather than to assist families. Families in the normal course of events, this view has it, should arrange the circumstances that their

---

birth families. J.J. Doyle, Jr., 'Child Protection and Child Outcomes: Measuring the Effects of Foster Care', *American Economic Review* 97, 2007, 1583–610; C.R. Lawrence, E.A. Carlson and B. Egeland, 'The Impact of Foster Care on Development', *Development and Psychopathology* 18, 2006, 57–76. But see J. Mersky and C. Janczewski, 'Adult Well-Being of Foster Care Alumni: Comparisons to Other Child Welfare Recipients and a Non-Child Welfare Sample in a High-Risk, Urban Setting', *Children and Youth Services Review* 35, March 2013, 367–76.

72 Casey Family Programs, Press Release, 'Former Foster Children in Washington and Oregon Suffer Post Traumatic Stress Disorder at Twice the Rate of U.S. War Veterans, According to New Study', 6 April 2005. See also C. Zlotnick, T. Tam and L. Soman, 'Life Course Outcomes on Mental and Physical Health: The Impact of Foster Care on Adulthood', *American Journal of Public Health* March 2012.

73 G. Fryer, E. Jordan and K. DeVooght, *Supporting Young People Transitioning from Foster Care: Findings from a National Survey*, Child Trends, November 2017 (finding less than 3 percent of youths involved with foster care will earn a college degree by age 25, only 46 percent were employed at age 26, 46 percent of women and 68 percent of men were arrested between the ages of 18 and 26, more than 20 percent became homeless after age 18, and 71 percent of women became pregnant by age 21); M.E. Courtney, Testimony before the Subcommittee on Income Security and Family Support of the Committee on Ways and Means, United States House of Representatives, 'Children Who Age Out of the Foster Care System', 12 July 2007 (showing that 12–18 months after leaving foster care, youths had much lower employment rates than other youths; 14 percent had been homeless after leaving foster care; about one-third had mental health issues; nearly half of women became pregnant – twice as many as their peers; 30 percent of young men and 11 percent of young women had been incarcerated).

74 M. Eichner, op. cit., n 38; M.A. Fineman, *The Autonomy Myth: A Theory of Dependency*, New York: New Press, 2004.

members need privately, through the free market.[75] It is not that there is no role for the state at all when it comes to families in the dominant view: certainly the state should step in to protect children who are being abused or neglected by their parents. Instead, this view conceives of the state as limited to playing a 'residual' role when it comes to the welfare of dependent citizens, stepping in only if and when families fail on their own to meet their members' significant needs. In such a case, the family is conceived as being defective for failing to safeguard its members' welfare on its own without assistance from the state.

The view that families can meet the dependency needs of members by themselves and that the state should stand aside while they do so, however, is based on a deeply distorted picture of contemporary society. In truth, families and their members inevitably interact with a host of societal institutions (work, schools, day care centers, the health care system, the market) that profoundly affect their abilities to meet their members' caretaking and human development needs.[76] Given the limits of families in navigating these institutions, as well as the unique ability that the state has to regulate them, there are strong reasons for the state to ensure that societal institutions support citizens' welfare. Doing so would allay the deep and profound costs to children and society's welfare imposed by the current system.

Political difficulties in achieving adequate US family supports

Government support for US families is also impeded on a political level by the US government's unresponsiveness to the policy preferences of middle- and low-income citizens. Studies by political scientists document the extent to which congressional policy responds to the views of the wealthy, and generally ignores the preferences of middle- and working-class citizens.[77] Indeed, one well-regarded study shows that senators were *less* likely to vote for a policy when their low-income constituents supported it than they would have been otherwise.[78]

These studies help explain the failure of federal policy to serve the needs of working families. They also help account for the decreased government assistance provided to poor families. While in the rest of the industrialized world, increased market inequality has been accompanied by a greater government role in combating poverty, in the US the opposite has occurred.[79] Based on market earnings alone, before government programmes and taxes, the US relative poverty rate is 31 percent. That makes our market-income poverty rate higher than most, but not all, other wealthy countries. Ireland's market income poverty rate tops the list of countries at a whopping 42 percent – far higher than the United States. Our country ultimately has so much more poverty than other countries, including Ireland, because our public policies do far less to address the condition than other countries' public policies do. Once government benefits and taxes are factored in, Ireland's relative poverty rate falls to 10 percent – a 32-percentage-point drop as a result of government programmes. In contrast, US programmes ultimately leave us

75 M. Eichner, op. cit., n 19.

76 See further M. Eichner, op. cit., n 38.

77 See M. Gilens and B. Page, 'Testing Theories of American Politics: Elites, Interest Groups, and Average Citizens', *Perspectives on Politics* 12, September 2014, 564–81; L.M. Bartels, *Unequal Democracy: The Political Economy of the New Gilded Age*, New York: Russell Sage Foundation, 2008; M. Gilens, 'Inequality and Democratic Responsiveness', *Public Opinion Quarterly* 69, 2005, 778–96.

78 Ibid.

79 J.S. Hacker and P. Pierson, *Winner-Take-All Politics: How Washington Made the Rich Richer: And Turned Its Back on the Middle Class*, New York: Simon & Schuster, 2010, p. 52 (drawing from T.L. Hungerford, 'Income Inequality, Income Mobility, and Economic Policy', CRS Report for Congress, 4 April 2008).

with a poverty rate of 21 percent – a reduction of only 10 percentage points.[80] So, at the end of the day, Ireland's child poverty rate is less than half of ours because its pro-family policies do a much better job of ensuring that poor kids get the resources they need.

Conclusion

The US has a vast distance to go in implementing public policies that truly support families in meeting members' dependency needs. In the meantime, American families are dealing with these issues privately at considerable cost to important public goods. Reversing this situation will require both deep ideological and political transformation.

80 Gornick and Nell, op. cit., n 33, 20, table 2.

6.3
LAW AND POLICY CONCERNING OLDER PEOPLE

Jonathan Herring

Introduction

This chapter considers the policy challenges facing the state in legal response to older family members. For too many older people, old age is marked by disadvantage, poverty and exclusion. Yet many older people have fulfilling old ages, playing an important role in society and in the family lives. The legal issues raised by older family members have not received adequate attention.[1] However, there is growing recognition that the issue needs more consideration, especially given the notable changes in age demographics around the world.

Demographics

The world is ageing fast. In 2015 one in eight people worldwide were aged 60 or over. It has been estimated that that by 2050 one in five will be.[2] This increase in the proportion of older people within the world population results from a decrease in fertility and an increase in life expectancy.[3] Worldwide, fertility is expected to decline from 2.82 children per woman in 1995–2000 to 2.15 in 2045–2050. Life expectancy is predicted to increase by 11 years. It was 65 in 1995–2000 but is predicted to be 76 by 2045–2050. It is estimated that by 2030, there will be more people over 60 than children under ten.[4] Ageing is a highly gendered. Globally women outlived men by 4.5 years and 61 percent of those aged over 80 are women.[5] It is expected that worldwide the number of people aged 60 or over will grow by 56 percent from 901 million to 1.4 billion by 2030.[6]

One statistic that is worrying some commentators is the 'old age support ratio'. That is the number of people aged 20 to 64, as compared with those aged 65 or over. Rather crudely this is used to estimate the number of those of 'working age' as compared to older people. This

1 J. Herring, *Older People in Law and Society*, Oxford: Oxford University Press, 2009; B. Clough and J. Herring (eds), *Ageing, Gender and Family Law*, Abingdon: Routledge, 2018.
2 United Nations, *World Population Ageing*, Geneva: United Nations, 2015, p. 2.
3 Ibid.
4 Global Age Watch, *Mainstreaming Ageing into the Post-2015 Process*, London: Help Age International, 2012, p. 1.
5 United Nations, op. cit., n 2, p. 2.
6 Ibid.

ratio has been gradually declining for most countries. In 2015 worldwide on average there were seven 'working age' people for every 'older person'. It is predicted by 2035 this will have halved to 3.5.[7] Such statistics are typically cited as indicating a crisis. However, the fact that we are all living longer is great news! Indeed ageist assumptions tend to underlie the claim that the more older people a society has the worse it is for the society. However, the twentieth century saw a massive increase in the proportion of older people and that did not cause undue difficulties.[8]

Finance

It is commonly assumed that old age is associated with poverty. But this depends very much where in the world you are. In most developed countries and in Latin America older people are generally not significantly poorer than the general population. This is largely due to developed social security programmes. By contrast, in most of sub-Saharan Africa, older people are significantly less well off than the general population.[9] Assumptions that older family members are a 'financial drain' on younger members overlook the fact that that in more developed and the majority of developing countries older people are net providers of financial transfers to their children and young people.[10] In Brazil, Costa Rica and Japan, older persons are net contributors to younger generations until well into their seventies. However, all of this is involves generalizations. In most countries older widows are among the poorest and most vulnerable groups.[11]

The financial well-being of older people has become a major political issue in many countries. The Centre for Strategic and International Studies has produced a report entitled *The Global Retirement Crisis*[12] and the World Bank has published documents on 'the Old Age Crisis'.[13] The link between old age and poverty is straightforwardly explained. In most countries old age is marked by a withdrawal from the job market and a corresponding loss of income. Further, old age can be associated with increased costs in terms of health, social care and heating. Societies have responded to poverty in old age on a number of ways. These will be explored further here. There are three primary sources of financial funding which the state might seek to promote or even enforce.

State benefits

Most developed countries have well-established financial state support for older people through the provision of welfare payments. These are often combined with state-support pension schemes into which a person can choose to contribute (to be discussed shortly) and through a system of other benefits targeted at particular needs for older people, such as fuel allowances and subsided transport.

Self-funding old age

A state might seek to promote the model that people should expect to fund their own needs in old age. There are two primary ways a state might seek to do that.

7 Ibid., p. 5.

8 F. Castles, 'Population Ageing and the Public Purse', *Australian Journal of Social Issues* 35, 2000, 301–15.

9 United Nations, op. cit., n 2, p. 3.

10 S. Harper, K. Howse and S. Baxter, *Living Longer and Prospering? Designing an Adequate, Sustainable and Equitable UK State Pension System*, Oxford: Oxford Institute of Ageing, 2009.

11 Global Age Watch, op. cit., n 4.

12 Center for Strategic and International Studies, *The Global Retirement Crisis*, Washington: CSIS, 1996.

13 World Bank, *Averting the Old Age Crisis*, New York: World Bank, 1994.

The first is to challenge the assumption that being older means one is not financially productive. Although the notion of retirement has been a standard part of the working life in the developed world, at least during the twentieth century, it is coming under challenge in the twenty-first. Increasingly, those over 65 will want, and will be expected, to work beyond that age. Indeed the primary response of some developed countries to the concerns over poverty in old age has been to encourage working beyond the standard retirement age. This is reinforced with legislation prohibiting age discrimination.[14] In 2015 worldwide 30 percent of men and 15 percent of women over 65 were active in the labour force.[15]

The second is to encourage people to save, while in employment, in pensions (or other saving products) to make provision for old age. This encouragement may be by way of tax advantages for those who pay into pensions schemes or by providing state-sponsored pensions schemes. In some states the private pension provision is designed to supplement the basic level of benefits provided by older people. Further, many developed countries have employee pensions schemes, which involve contributions from both an employee as well as an employer into a pension fund. The World Bank[16] has recommended a five-pillar structure. The first pillar is a mandated publicly managed system which is not dependent on contributions. The second is a mandated system which is funded, privately managed and depends on contributions. The third is a voluntary system based on an individual's income. To this they have added that two more pillars which must be in place to ensure poverty is avoided: access to health care and housing.

A major theme in the current debate is the interaction of gender and pensions.[17] Two fundamental assumptions have consistently worked against the interests of women in the area of self-funded pension provision. First, in the past the pensions system was premised on the assumption that women in retirement would be provided for through their husband's pensions.[18] This assumption was always flawed because women in most countries have significantly higher life expectancy than men, although some pension plans include provision for a deceased's spouse.[19] A more significant difficulty is that increased rates of divorce have meant that a woman who has no pension provision of her own cannot assume she will still be married to her husband come retirement. Second, pensions are based on a link between paid employment and pension provision. This means that childcare, care work and other unpaid work is not rewarded come retirement. As women still undertake the largest portion of such work they are severely disadvantaged in pension provision.

Filial obligation

A third source of financial support comes from family members. The extent to which family members regard themselves as obliged to support, or do in fact support, older family members varies around the world, reflecting broader cultural and religious assumptions.[20] For example, traditional Chinese culture is heavily influence by Confucian teaching on *Hsiao* (filial piety)

14 J. Herring, 'Age Discrimination and the Law: Forging the Way Ahead', in E. Parry and S. Tyson (eds), *Managing an Age Diverse Workforce*, Basingstoke: Macmillan, 2011.

15 United Nations, op. cit., n 2, p. 6.

16 R. Holzmann and R. Hinz, *Old-Age Income Support in the 21st Century*, New York: World Bank, 2005.

17 P. Marier, 'Affirming, Transforming, or Neglecting Gender? Conceptualizing Gender in the Pension Reform Process', *International Studies in Gender, State & Society* 14, 2007, 182–98.

18 Department of Work and Pensions, *Women and Pensions*, London: DWP, 2005.

19 S. Arber and J. Ginn, 'Ageing and Gender: Diversity and Change', *Social Trends* 34, 2004, 34–49.

20 P. Jones, J. Lee and X. Zhang, 'Clarifying and Measuring Filial Concepts across Five Cultural Groups', *Research in Nursing and Health* 34, 2011, 310–26. R. Khatun, 'What Do Grown Children Owe Their

and *Shu* (reciprocity),[21] which generate strong feeling and practices of familial care for older people. Japan also has a long tradition of reverence towards older members and a strongly felt obligation among families to care for them.[22] However, these societies have experienced a weakening of the obligation and the expectation of older people in recent years.[23] Liu and Huang,[24] looking at Taiwanese culture, note that a decreasing birthrate, a rising number of women in employment, work pressures, tensions between parents and children and weakening in filial piety have impacted on levels of parental care in Taiwan and the expectations of adults. Economic aspirations of adult children and the desire of older parents not to hold back their children affect the traditional norms (for Japan, see Chapter 6.4 of this book). In western societies there has always been less expectation that older people will be cared for by adult children. Independence and self-sufficiency are seen as the goals in old age, rather than becoming 'a drain' on relatives and tri-generation households are not the norm, at least among indigenous cultures.[25]

To what extent should relatives be financially liable to pay for their older relatives? While most countries have a legal mechanism to require parents to offer financial support for their minor children, only a few have systems requiring older children to support their aged parents. However, this is coming under increased scrutiny given the concerns already mentioned about the costs of meeting the financial needs of older people. A lively philosophical argument has arisen over the extent to which there is a moral obligation for children to care for adult parents. While there is a widespread intuition such a moral obligation does exist, it has proved difficult to formulate its basis. A popular argument is that because parents care for their children during their vulnerability, this generates a reciprocal duty on the children to care for their parents when they are in need.[26] However, this argument faces the difficulty that, while it can be taken that parents cause the child to be born and so to consent to undertake the obligation, the same cannot be said for children. Others, such as Jane English, have argued that the obligations flow from the quality of the relationship. So if the parent-child relationship is a good one, obligations flow from it, as they do in any healthy relationship.[27] Such an approach might argue that obligations do not necessarily follow blood relationships, but rather the social relationship.[28] This too might be questioned on the basis that adult children feel a sense of obligation even where there is a bad relationship. Further, the obligations owed to a parent are thought to be even more than a very close friendship. Stephen Kellet, for example, has argued that the child-parent relationship

---

Parents? A Moral Duty and Legal Responsibility in Bangladesh', *Int. Jo. Law, Policy & Fam.* 32, 2018, 363–73.

21 W. Sin, 'Confucianism, Rule Consequentialism, and the Demands of Filial Obligations', *Journal of Religious Ethics* 37, 2019, 377–93.

22 E. Takagi and Y. Saito, 'A Longitudinal Analysis of the Impact of Family Support on the Morale of Older Parents in Japan: Does the Parent's Normative Belief in Filial Responsibilities Make a Difference?', *Ageing and Society* 33, 2013, 1–24.

23 C.-K. Cheung and A. Kwan, 'The Erosion of Filial Piety By Modernisation in Chinese Cities', *Ageing and Society* 29, 2009, 179–98.

24 H. Zhi, 'Family Care for the Elderly and the Importance of Filial Piety', *The Journal of Nursing* 56, 2009, 83–8.

25 G. Leeson, *The Demographics and Economics of UK Health and Social Care for Older Adults*, Oxford: Institute of Ageing, 2004.

26 J. Blustein, *Parents and Children*, New York: Oxford University Press, 1983.

27 J. English, 'What Do Grown Children Owe Their Parents?', in C. Sommers and F. Sommers (eds), *Vice and Virtue in Everyday Life*, Indiana: Harcourt, 1993.

28 C. Fenton, 'Who Counts as a Parent for the Purposes of Filial Obligations?', *Nordic Journal of Applied Ethics* 11, 2017, 17–32.

is 'like nothing else'.[29] He points out that, to many people, their relationships with their parents and/or their children are of great value and cannot be readily replaced. This raises the question of what these 'special goods' in a child-parent relationship are. The difficulty is that these are likely to be the kind of things (a particular kind of love or affection) which the law can enforce.[30] Duties to pay money are readily enforced in filial obligation statutes, but financial payment is unlikely to be a special good. The payment of money is perhaps not a duty which a child is in a unique position to supply. Indeed there is a wider question over what precisely is required by any obligation of filial piety. One recent contribution to the debate has suggested it creates a duty to care *about* one's parents, but not a duty to care *for* them.[31]

It should not be assumed that, even if the case for a moral obligation is made out, the law should enforce it. Indeed where the moral obligation is generally undertaken voluntarily, in this context as has traditionally been done in Eastern Asian countries, there is a strong case for not making the action legally enforceable, so to infect the value of the relationship with a legal formality, rather than letting the giving of assistance occurring naturally. On the other hand it must not be thought that the legal response is either to enforce or ignore moral obligations. The law is far more subtle than that. It can uphold, bolster or reinforce the obligation in other ways, free of direct enforcement. For example, the law could offer benefits or advantages to those who fulfil their obligations without needing to make it legally enforceable.[32] The law could be used to provide encouragements for family members to undertake practical or financial aid for aged dependant members. This could take a number of forms, such as tax advantages, benefits or changing the law on inheritance.[33] These more indirect methods of supporting financial and care assistance are less likely to infect the natural love-based relationship between an adult child and parent.

Examples of countries which currently have filial support legalisation are some states in the United States, Canada, France, Singapore and Japan.[34] In the US, where filial responsibility statutes exist in a surprising number of states (around 30) they are rarely enforced.[35] In fact, in nearly half of those which have them they have never been used. That said, in Singapore, Canada and Malaysia these have been enforced with more vigour.[36] But even there enforcement is hardly a regular occurrence, in part because it is rare for children not to support their parents. Filial responsibility legislation in those countries takes on the role of confirming the moral ideal, rather than being a set of enforced regulations.

Relying on statutory enforcement certainly raises problems. There is the persistent problem of enforcement and anti-avoidance provisions. A further difficulty would be in drafting any filial responsibility legislation. It would need to address a host of questions. At what degree of need

29 S. Kellet, 'Four Theories of Filial Duty', *The Philosophical Quarterly* 56, 2006, 254–74.
30 Fenton, op. cit., n 28.
31 M. Stuifbergen and J. Van Delden, 'Filial Obligations to Elderly Parents: A Duty to Care?', *Medicine, Health Care and Philosophy* 14, 2011, 63–71.
32 M. Collingridge and S. Miller, 'Filial Responsibility and Care of the Aged', *Journal of Applied Philosophy* 14, 1997, 119–32.
33 J. Herring, 'Together Forever? The Rights and Responsibilities of Adult Children and Their Parents', in J. Bridgeman, H. Keating and C. Lind (eds), *Responsibility, Law and the Family*, Aldershot: Ashgate, 2008.
34 For Bangladesh and India, see Khatun, op. cit., n 20.
35 M. Oldham, 'Financial Obligations within the Family: Aspects of Intergenerational Maintenance and Succession in England and France', *Cambridge Law Journal* 60, 2001, 128–77.
36 C. Bracci, 'Ties That Bind: Ontario's Filial Responsibility Act', *Canadian Journal of Family Law* 17, 2000, 455–500.

for the older person does the obligation to support 'kick in'? What level of income does the child have to have before the obligation is imposed? How are the obligations of an individual towards their parents and their children to be balanced? Which relatives would be covered? How can the obligations be shared between different children who could be liable? Will there be exceptions, for example, in respect of abandoned or abused children? How can the law respond to the unequal gender division in care for parents?[37]

Care issues

It is common to imagine old age as a time of ill health and dependency. Of course it can be, but 40 percent of the world's older population live independently.[38] Almost half of older women live independently alone; many fewer men do.[39] It is notable that more older people are involved in the giving of care than are in the receiving of it.[40]

The practice of care is, therefore, of central significance to older people. Susan Dodds states that carers have been undervalued, exploited and expected to offer unrealistic standards of care.[41] Until recently, care work has gone largely unacknowledged by lawyers and politicians.[42] Care work was seen as a private matter of little public significance. Older people giving care and those caring for older people have been received little public support or recognition. This is changing. There is increasing recognition of the importance of care. Robert Goodin and Diane Gibson[43] have written of the 'decasualization' of care of older people. In the past, they suggest, such care was casual, not in the sense of being unloving or unthoughtful, but rather that it was simply integrated into normal everyday life. They see the increased professionalization of care, the increased number of people requiring care and the pressures carers face in their life as putting strain on the kind of care offered. Whether we are moving to a time when care will predominantly be carried out by professional carers remains to be seen. The developed world certainly seems to be seeing a relocation of care from the private to the public, from collective to commercial services.[44]

Considerable debate surrounds the appropriate legal response to care work.[45] The matter is complex, but here are some of the major issues.

Economics

For some, the issue is essentially economic. The care work needs to be done. If it is not done by carers, either it will fall on the state or dependant people will be left in unacceptable conditions.

37 N. Marks and S. Kang, 'Filial Responsibility', in *Encyclopaedia of Family Studies*, London: John Wiley and Sons.

38 United Nations, op. cit., n 2.

39 K. Stalker (ed.), *Reconceptualising Work with Carers*, Bristol: Jessica Kingsley, 2002.

40 J. Powell, J. Robison, H. Roberts and G. Thomas, 'The Single Assessment Process in Primary Care: Older People's Accounts of the Process', *British Journal of Social Work* 37, 2007, 1043–163.

41 S. Dodds, 'Depending on Care: Recognition of Vulnerability and the Social Contribution of Care Provisions', *Bioethics* 21, 2007, 500–24.

42 HM Government, *Carers at the Heart of 21st-Century Families and Communities*, London: The Stationery Office, 2008.

43 R. Goodwin and D. Gibson, 'The Decasualisation of Eldercare', in E. Feder Kittay and E. Feder (eds), *The Subject of Care: Feminist Perspectives on Dependency*, Totowa, NJ: Rowman & Littlefield, 2003.

44 S. Sevenhuijsen, 'The Place of Care: The Relevance of the Feminist Ethic of Care for Social Policy', *Feminist Theory* 4, 2003, 179–94.

45 J. Herring, *Caring and the Law*, Oxford: Hart, 2013.

We need, therefore, to supply state support at a level to encourage and enable care work to be done. Entirely from an economic point of view there is a danger that if state support is too strong it will be providing funds for work that would be done in any event.[46]

Justice

This perspective argues that for too long society has gained from unrecognized, unrewarded, carework, mainly undertaken by women. Through the notion of privacy and the venerated status of the family, women have provided considerable benefits to society for no compensation. Martha Fineman has written:

> dependency is universal and inevitable – the experience of everyone in society and, for that reason, of collective concern, requiring collective response. However, the essential and society-preserving work inevitable dependency demands has been channelled by society in such a way as to make only *some* of its members bear the burdens of this work. As a result, I argue that there is a societal debt owed to caretakers. ... The existence of this debt must be recognized and payment accomplished, through policies and laws that provide both some economic compensation and structural accommodation to caretakers.[47]

State care and support is needed to repay this debt.

It is also possible for this argument to be used to justify payments between individuals. If two family members (A and B) both have an obligation to care for an elderly parent, but only A undertakes the care, at expense to themselves, then B can be said to have an obligation to compensate A for performing B's share of the work.[48]

Should unpaid informal care be encouraged or discouraged?

A case may be made that all care should be provided by public authorities and regulated private companies and that individuals should be discouraged from engaging in unpaid care of family members. Such an argument could be made from two perspectives. One is that we need to encourage everyone to be financially self-sufficient. Care work (childcare and care for infirm relatives) is a major block for many people, especially women, entering the workplace and achieving financial independence. Of course such an argument would be rejected by those who see great value in family care work. A second argument in favour such discouragement may be that we need greater professionalism in care work; institutionalizing, regulating and inspecting care work enhances its quality. But opponents may fear that increased state involvement does the opposite.

Empowerment of the dependant

Much writing from a disability perspective had questioned the power relationships within the classic 'cared-for/carer' division.[49] This has led some western countries to use direct payments so

46 Ibid., ch. 4.
47 M. Fineman, *The Autonomy Myth*, New York: New Press, 2004, p. 263.
48 G. Douglas, *Obligation and Commitment in Family Law*, Oxford: Hart Publishing, 2018, ch 7.
49 J. Herring, 'The Disability Critique of Care', *Elder Law Review*, 2014, 2.

that people with particular needs receive a cash sum, rather than service from the local authority, enabling them to manage their own social care.[50] Countries vary on the extent to which a person can choose their own relatives to provide that care. Many do not allow a person to pay a spouse or cohabitant for care. A common complaint of social service care provision is that it does not meet the needs of the individual and is inflexible.[51] The wider policy issues are hotly debated. Ungerson has argued:

> by allowing for the payment of relatives who previously have been 'classic' unpaid and formally unrecognised informal carers, [these schemes] actually provide a means whereby the work of care-givers is recognised and recompensed, such that they become more and more like care-workers.[52]

On the other hand, there is a concern that the marketization creates the danger that care will be seen as the responsibility of those who chose to take on the job of carers, rather than recognize it is an inevitable and important part of everyone's lives. It can also reduce care to activities that can be measured and valued, whereas the emotional and relational values cannot be reduced to economic value.

Grandparents' rights

As life expectancy increases and many countries experience greater levels of female employment, the role that grandparents play in their children's life is changing. With more dual-earning households and higher lone parent employment, grandparents are being called upon to play an ever-increasing role in childcare. This in turn produces its own stresses for grandparents. Divorce and relationship breakdown can mean that treasured relationships between grandparents and grandchildren end or become highly strained. Of course, the precise roles that grandparents play vary from family to family. They are inevitably tied up with issues around the parent-child relationships. Parents can, in effect, restrict or enable contact between children and grandparents.[53] And indeed grandparents can play a role in strengthening, or indeed undermining, the relationship between a parent and a child. Ethnic and religious backgrounds of families can play a huge role in determining how grandparents are perceived.[54]

Insofar as family law is concerned, there is a question over whether grandparents should have a special legal standing. Legal systems could grant grandparents a special legal status giving them a special position to bring claims in relation to children. This could, for example, include a presumption in favour of contact between a child and grandparent or a presumption that if parents were unable to look after a child, then grandparents would be preferred carers.

50 J. Herring, 'Personal Budgets: Holding onto the Purse Strings for Fear of Something Worse', in T. Feiler, J. Hordern and A. Papanikitas (eds), *Marketisation, Ethics and Healthcare*, Abingdon: Routledge, 2018.

51 R. Clough, J. Manthorpe, B. Green, D. Fox, G. Raymond, P. Wilson, V. Raymond, K. Sumner, L. Bright and J. Hay, *The Support Older People Want and the Services They Need*, York: Joseph Rowntree Foundation, 2007.

52 C. Ungerson, 'Whose Empowerment and Independence?', *Ageing and Society* 29, 2009, 189–203.

53 M. Mueller and G. Elder, 'Family Contingencies across the Generations: Grandparent-Grandchild Relationships in Holistic Perspective', *Journal of Marriage and Family* 65, 2003, 404–21.

54 J. Jackson, E. Brown, T. Antonucci and S.O. Daatland, 'Ethnic Diversity in Ageing, Multicultural Societies', in M. Johnson (ed.), *The Cambridge Handbook of Age and Ageing*, Cambridge: Cambridge University Press, 2005.

An alternative would be to grant grandparents no special legal status, seeing their involvement with the child as a matter for parental discretion.[55] A third approach, adopted by the European Court of Human Rights,[56] is to argue that the legal position of the grandparent depends on the quality of the relationship between a child and grandparent. Where that relationship is close, good reasons will be required to justify interfering in it; where it is weak, then it is entitled to little legal protection.[57]

Gillian Douglas and Neil Ferguson have argued against enhancing the formal legal status of grandparents[58] on the ground that in the clear majority of cases families are able to resolve issues surrounding relationships between grandparents and grandchildren appropriately following a separation. They are concerned that legal intervention is normally used not as a way of asserting grandparental rights, but rather as part of the battle between the mother and father. Rachel Taylor has argued that there is an important difference between cases where grandparents have taken on the primary responsibility for caring for a child, where the relationship should be protected, and cases where the grandparent is a secondary carer and enforcing legal rights may interfere with the care of a primary carer.[59]

Elder abuse

Elder abuse has only relatively recently been recognized by governments as a major social problem. For too long it has been hidden and ignored.[60] Now that it has been accepted as an issue requiring state attention, many countries are still struggling to find the correct legal response. Elder abuse, it has been claimed, has reached the position domestic violence did several decades ago.[61] The problem is caused by broader social attitudes towards older people and a range of societal practices. It is only in tackling these that elder abuse can be effectively challenged. As the Toronto Declaration on the Global Prevention of Elder Abuse puts it: 'Ultimately elder abuse will only be successfully prevented if a culture that nurtures intergenerational solidarity and rejects violence is developed'.[62]

Defining elder abuse

There is no standard definition of elder abuse.[63] The abuse of older people can take many forms. It can involve sexual abuse,[64] financial abuse, misuse of medication, physical abuse, neglect and

55 *Troxel v Granville* 530 U.S. 57 (2000).
56 *X, Y and Z v United Kingdom* (1997) 24 EHRR 143.
57 See F. Kaganas and C. Piper, 'Grandparents and Contact: "Rights v Welfare" Revisited' *International Journal of Law Policy and the Family* 15, 2001, 250–75.
58 G. Douglas and N. Ferguson, 'The Role of Grandparents in Divorced Families', *International Journal of Law Policy and the Family* 17, 2003, 41–67.
59 R. Taylor, 'Grandparents and Grandchildren', in B. Clough and J. Herring (eds), *Ageing, Gender and Family Law*, Abingdon: Routledge, 2018.
60 House of Commons Health Committee, *Elder Abuse*, London: The Stationery Office, 2004, p. 1.
61 District Judge Marilyn Mornington, *Responding to Elder Abuse*, London: Age Concern, 2004.
62 World Health Organization, *The Toronto Declaration on the Prevention of Elder Abuse* Geneva: World Health Organization, 2002.
63 A. Brammer and S. Biggs, 'Defining Elder Abuse', *Journal of Social Welfare and Family Law* 20, 1998, 385–401. M. Shankardass (ed.), *International Handbook of Elder Abuse and Mistreatment*, Amsterdam: Springer, 2020.
64 R. Hawks, 'Grandparent Molesting: Sexual Abuse of Elderly Nursing Home Residents and Its Prevention', *Marquette Elders' Advisor* 8, 2006, 159–73.

humiliating behaviour.[65] It can be carried out by relatives, carers, friends or strangers.[66] The World Health Organization has adopted the following definition: 'a single or repeated act or lack of appropriate action occurring within any relationship where there is an expectation of trust, which causes harm or distress to an older person'.[67]

There are certainly problems with this definition,[68] but it is useful as a broad basis for discussion. It still leaves open the question of at what age a person becomes an 'older person'. In the US, where states have enacted legislation specifically to address elder abuse, they have tended to use 60 or 65.[69] One approach is that an older person is someone subject to the social disadvantages and prejudicial attitudes that can attach to old age.[70] The difficulty with this is that it does not readily transmit into a statutory formulation. One literature review that looked at evidence of elder abuse around the world, concluded that 6 percent of older people had suffered significant abuse in the last month; 5.6 percent of older couples had experienced physical violence in their relationships; 25 percent of older people had suffered significant psychological abuse.[71] The World Health Organization reports that one in six older people worldwide will have experienced abuse in community settings in the past year.[72] There can be no doubt that elder abuse is prevalent and a major blight on the lives of many older people.[73]

A rights-based approach

Where elder abuse has become recognized as a problem, legal responses often draw on human rights. Generally these are seen as imposing a positive duty on the state to protect the rights of life, protection from torture and inhuman and degrading treatment, and private life.[74] While to some extent the standard criminal law does that, more may be required where the acts of abuse do not come to the attention of the state or where the abuse does not fall within a standard criminal offence. There is much overlap here with the legal responses to domestic violence (see Chapters 5.1–5.2 of this book). However, an additional issue arises in relation to elder abuse where the victims cannot themselves be expected to seek legal intervention by notifying the police or applying for a civil order. This has led some to suggest that there is a need for a legal regime imposing obligations on the state to take steps to protect older people, especially those lacking capacity, from abuse, including investigating complaints and areas of concern; and then, where appropriate, instituting legal proceedings. This may take on a form

65 House of Commons Health Committee, op. cit., n 60, p. 1.

66 C. McCreadie, 'A Review of Research Outcomes in Elder Abuse', *Journal of Adult Protection* 4, 2002, 3–31.

67 World Health Organization, op. cit., n 62.

68 There is, for example, no requirement that the act is unjustified.

69 B. Brandl and T. Meuer, 'Domestic Abuse in Later Life', *Elder Law Journal* 8, 2001, 298–321.

70 Herring, op. cit., n 1, ch. 1.

71 C. Cooper, A. Selwood and G. Livingston, 'Prevalence of Elder Abuse and Neglect: A Systematic Review', *Age and Ageing* 37, 2008, 151–64.

72 World Health Organsation, *Elder Abuse*, Geneva: WHO, 2019.

73 R. Acierno, M. Hernandez, A. Amstadter, H. Resnick, K. Steve, W. Muzzy and D. Kilpatrick, 'Prevalence and Correlates of Emotional, Physical, Sexual, and Financial Abuse and Potential Neglect in the United States: The National Elder Mistreatment Study', *Journal of Public Health* 100, 2010, 292–7.

74 J. Herring, 'Elder Abuse: A Human Rights Agenda for the Future', in I. Doran and A. Soden (eds), *Beyond Elder Law*, Amsterdam: Springer, 2012.

similar to the obligations on local authorities in the area of child protection.[75] (See Chapters 4.1–4.3 of this book.)

Any such legal regime raises some difficult issues. First, the intervention of the state to protect individuals, without that person's request, raises issues of autonomy. Here there is a balance between protecting the current autonomous wish of the victim with the increase in autonomy they may experience if they were removed from the abuse. Many victims in these cases have conflicting wishes. They want to remain in the relationship, but they want the abuse to stop. In such a case it is not easy to determine what is promoting their autonomy. It is not possible to respect these two conflicting desires. John Williams[76] discusses a hypothetical case of a son stealing £10 from his mother from time to time. Her autonomy is only slightly infringed by the abuse. However, if the relationship consisted of persistent emotional abuse, the interference in her autonomy in removing her from the relationship may be less than allowing her to remain in it. It must be remembered that being in an abusive relationship itself undermines autonomy. Leaving a person to suffer abuse where that person does not want to be protected is not necessarily justified in the name of autonomy.[77]

Seeking the correct balance between protection of well-being and protection of autonomy is tricky in this area, as any other.[78] History teaches us that in the name of 'protection' great harms have been done. But, it should be remembered too that in the name of 'protecting private choices' great harm has also been done (think of the approach to domestic violence until recent years). The fact that alternative care for the older person outside the abusive relationship may itself be abusive, especially given the low quality of institutional care in many countries, makes the issue more difficult.[79] Elder abuse is not a single phenomenon. It can encompass a complex range of behaviours: long-standing domestic violence; abuse of caregivers by care recipients;[80] community harassment;[81] an inhibiting fear of violence in public spaces;[82] retaliation by adults of abuse they suffered as children;[83] and abuse of grandparents by grandchildren they are caring for.[84]

Conclusion

As life expectancy increases and old age can no longer be seen as a short period of ill health, we all need to rethink what old age can be. As is clear from this chapter there are issues relating to

75 J. Manthorpe, 'Local Responses to Elder Abuse: Building Effective Prevention Strategies', in A. Wahidin and M. Cain (eds), *Ageing, Crime and Society*, Milton, UK: Willan, 2006.

76 J. Williams, 'State Responsibility and the Abuse of Vulnerable Older People: Is There a Case for a Public Law to Protect Vulnerable Older People Form Abuse', in J. Bridgeman, H. Keating and C. Lind (eds), *Responsibility, Law and the Family*, Aldershot: Ashgate, 2008.

77 See Herring, op. cit., n 74.

78 M. Dunn and C. Foster, 'Autonomy and Welfare as Amici Curiae', *Medical Law Review* 18, 2010, 86–95.

79 See Herring, op. cit., n 1.

80 L. Phillips, E. de Torres and G. Briones, 'Abuse of Female Caregivers By Care Recipients: Another Form of Elder Abuse', *Journal of Elder Abuse & Neglect* 12, 2000, 123–41.

81 S. Biggs, 'A Family Concern: Elder Abuse in British Social Policy', *Critical Social Policy* 16, 1996, 63–81.

82 E. Meyer and L. Post, 'Alone at Night: A Feminist Ecology Model of Community Violence', *Feminist Criminology* 1, 2006, 207–21.

83 A. Campbell Reay and K. Browne, 'Risk Factor Characteristics in Carers Who Physically Abuse or Neglect Their Elderly Dependents', *Aging & Mental Health* 5, 2001, 56–62.

84 J. Kosberg and G. MacNeil, 'The Vulnerability to Elder Abuse for Grandparents Raising Their Grandchildren: An Emerging Global Phenomenon', *Journal of Elder Abuse and Neglect* 15, 2005, 33–52.

the vulnerabilities that old age can bring. But it also brings opportunities too. As grandparents take an ever more active role in caring for their grandchildren, their legal position comes into play. We need to find ways of better recognizing and supporting the care work that older people do and indeed is offered to them. Families are likely to draw ever more on the resources that older people have to offer, as well as to respond to the needs they have. Old age present challenges and opportunities and families play a central part in ensuring that old age is a time of flourishing.

6.4

SUPPORT AND CARE AMONG FAMILY MEMBERS AND STATE PROVISION FOR THE ELDERLY IN JAPAN

Emiko Kubono and Harumi Ishiwata[1]

Introduction

The Civil Code of Japan, which prescribes rights and obligations among family members, was revised in 1947 in the aftermath of World War II. At the time of the revision, it was rare for parents to live long after their children reached the age of majority and it was commonly accepted that ageing parents should be supported and cared for at home by their family members. Consequently, this was not an urgent issue for families and the government. However, Japan later experienced the most rapid ageing of its population in the world. As a result, supporting and caring for ageing parents has become a major issue for families as well as society as a whole (for a general discussion, see Chapter 6.3 of this book).

As the society has aged, individual families have found it difficult to know how to care for ageing parents. The government has therefore had to resolve the policy issue how and to what extent to develop state provisions for the elderly. This chapter mainly examines the ways in which support and care is dealt with in the Civil Code. In fact, the Civil Code has no legal provisions that directly govern the issue of support and care for ageing parents. Attention will therefore be focused on the general relationship between children over the age of majority and their parents, including the recent reform of the law of inheritance. After the explanation of the Civil Code, the kinds of state provision for the elderly will be outlined. Finally, the relationship between obligations among family members and the public provisions will be analyzed.[2]

The relationship between children over the age of majority and their parents: the Civil Code

In Japan, the central issue in the relationship between children over the age of majority and their parents is co-residence. Within the Civil Code, *support* and *inheritance* are related to this issue.

1 This article was originally authored by Kubono and then updated by Ishiwata who mainly wrote the last section 'Recent reform and policy change?'.

2 The Japanese government provides translations of the articles of Japanese laws on the website at www.japaneselawtranslation.go.jp/?re=02.

With respect to support, the relevant issues are: who bears the obligation to support, at what level and in what form? 'In what form' refers to the question whether to invite one's parents into one's home or provide financial support without co-residence. With respect to inheritance, important questions emerge when children over the age of majority inherit from their parents. If one of the children lived with the parents and cared for and supported them, the question arises whether this should to be taken into account, and, if so, in what way (see also Chapter 2.8 of this book).

The obligation to support

There are three categories of obligations which vary according to the person on whom they fall. The first is the obligation of a married couple to support one another and their minor children. This is called *seikatsu hozi gimu* (unlimited special responsibility to provide support for the necessities of life). In this case, the bearer of the obligation must ensure that the standard of living is the same for all concerned parties. The second category is the obligation among lineal relatives by blood (between the parents and their child(ren) over the age of majority, between the grandparents and their grandchildren, and so on) and among siblings; this obligation is called *seikatsu huzyo gimu* (limited responsibility to provide support for the necessities of life). In this case, the person who bears the obligation does not have to drop his or her reasonable standard of living in order to support others. In this second category, there is a degree of ambiguity in deciding exactly when and in what cases providing support is necessary because of the partially subjective criterion of 'reasonable standard of living'. The third category deals with cases among relatives in the third degree (for example, between uncles/aunts and nieces/nephews or between the spouse of the child and the child's parents (Civil Code, arts 725 ff.[3])), which do not fall in either the first or second category. In this case, providing support is not naturally inherent in the relationship. However, under certain circumstances, the family court can impose the obligation of providing support on any one of these relatives.

According to the categories just described, there are cases where more than one person bears the same degree of obligation to support. The Civil Code does not provide any guidance regarding the extent to which the responsibility should be borne as between the liable parties and leaves it up to the parties concerned. If negotiation among the parties does not result in an agreement, the family court decides the matter. Furthermore, if more than one person is entitled to receive support, the priority between them will be also determined first by negotiation and only secondly by the family court.

Is co-residence an obligation?

The means of support is not specified under the Civil Code and the details are negotiated by those concerned. If agreement is not reached through negotiation, the family court decides. However, even if the elderly parent who is entitled to receive support desires co-residence, the parent cannot demand to be invited into the other party's home against their will. Furthermore, it is currently widely interpreted that even the family court cannot force children to support their aged parents by means of co-residence. It is understood that the legal obligation of support is limited to financial support. Support by co-residence can only be achieved by an agreement between the parties. Because of this prevailing interpretation, the issue of securing residence for

3 All the articles cited here are those of the Civil Code.

the elderly who find it difficult to live alone and the question of how to secure care and support for their daily lives have become problems for society as a whole.

Inheritance

From inheriting family property to inheriting individual property

In the post-war revision of the Civil Code, there was a shift from family-property-based inheritance to individual inheritance. According to the Civil Code enacted in the Meiji era, most of the property belonged to *ie*, the family, and inheritance was understood to be succession to the status of the administrator of the family property (the head). The law defined the heirs as the relatives by blood, especially male lineal descendants who would succeed the position as the head. There were therefore severe restrictions on the widow's right to inherit when the head of the family died under the Meiji Civil Code. In contrast, the new Civil Code regards property that is subject to inheritance as purely private property that is liberated from the constraints of the *ie*. consequential changes are therefore made to the definition of 'heir'.

In addition to defining children and others as relatives by blood as heirs, the new Civil Code stipulates that the spouse is always an heir. This is revolutionary because it fundamentally transforms the spouse's status under inheritance law from that as defined under the Meiji Code. Several factors contributed to this revision: the weakening of abstract and generational views of the family such as *kakei bandai* (family line for thousands of generations), the gradual disintegration of extended families and their transformation into nuclear families, and the fact that a married couple assumes the central position in such a nuclear family. It can be pointed out that because of these changes in the family, it is now taken for granted that the surviving spouse should be entitled to at least part of the deceased spouse's estate. As regards the children's right to inheritance, the new Code unifies the inheritance system and stipulates that children shall inherit equal shares. The idea that the entire family property should be inherited by a particular child has now disappeared. There was a further revision of the Civil Code in 1980 that expanded a spouse's share of inheritance. The revision was intended to bring about, as far as possible, an increase in the share of inheritance that a spouse could expect by the introduction of joint ownership in cases where one spouse died.

Evaluation of care through co-residence and other factors in regard to inheritance

If the parents wish to favour a child when a child lives with the elderly parents and provides care, or when he or she helps out in running a family business or farm, there are ways to leave property to that particular child through gifts *inter vivos* or via a will. Both methods are valid. However, some parts of the gifts could be invalidated when the estate is divided at the death of the parent. This is because heirs have the right to receive a set proportion of inheritance as the *legally reserved portion* regardless of the wishes of the deceased (art. 1042 ff.).

As regards provision of care or help with a family business, if there was an employment contract and payment was made for the service, the case will be treated as the transfer of property based on a contract that was carried out legally while the deceased was alive. In this case, it is very unlikely that the validity of the transfer would be denied based on the legally reserved portion at the commencement of inheritance.

Even if no transfer of property was carried out by the method just outlined, children who provided care for their ageing parents or helped with the family business, or contributed a large amount of money for the building or refurbishing of the parents' house, may receive a set amount of compensation as persons who contributed to the decedent. The system allows for the heir who contributed to receive a share of the inheritance made up of the legally entitled share and a contributory portion. The type of contribution that can be taken into account is a 'special contribution' that is made for the purpose of 'the maintenance or increase of the decedent's property through the provision of labor or in the form of property relating to the decedent's business, medical treatment or nursing of the decedent, or other means' (art. 904–2). Contributions will not be regarded as special contributions if they are made at a level that is reasonably expected as part of fulfilling the obligation to support or if all other heirs contributed equally. Because of these restrictions, the cases of inheritance in which contributory portion is admitted are said to be rather rare.

The system of contributory portion applies to joint heirs only. This is a system designed to ensure fairness among joint heirs in the procedure of dividing the inherited property. Consider a case where the co-resident child and his or her spouse (for example, the eldest son and his wife) jointly provided care and nursing to their elderly parents and helped with the family business. Let us further assume that the co-resident son died first and the parents died later. In this case, it is impossible to consider the contribution of the co-resident child's wife in the procedure of the division of inherited property from the parents. The child's wife cannot receive anything in inheritance, unless the decedent made a will to give something to her. The decedent may adopt her in order that she could be an heir, or the decedent and the son's wife may enter into a contract. But it is rare they actually do so.

Changes in the family model

This section briefly examines changes in the family model initiated by the introduction of the new Civil Code as a background to legal provisions. A major sociological study on the ideology of the family contends that there was a shift from the *ie* in the Meiji Civil Code to the family in the new Code.[4] From a legal perspective, it has been argued that while the ideology of the *ie* family was strong, the regime stipulated in the Meiji Civil Code as positive law was not as strong as it is made out to be.[5] It has been pointed out that, even under the Meiji Civil Code, the *ie* family regime had become unworkable.[6] On the other hand, the wording of the new Civil Code does not present a clear model of the family. Therefore, it is difficult to describe a linear change in the family model.

However, it is possible to take a view that the representative family assumed in the new Civil Code is a conjugal family (nuclear family) made up of a married couple and their minor children.[7] The competence given to the head of the family in the Meiji Civil Code to determine the residence of children over the age of majority as well as to give permission to marry was abolished by the new Civil Code. Nevertheless, children over the age of majority have an obligation to support their parents (art. 877). However, as discussed earlier, this duty is not very strict. The current Civil Code also contains provisions relating to the obligation among relatives including children over the age of majority and their parents to assist one another (art. 725 ff). It is understood that this provision has limited effectiveness.

4 E. Ochiai, *Towards the Family in the 21st Century*, 4th edition, Tokyo: Yuhikaku, 2019, p. 98.
5 A. Omura, *Family Law*, 3rd edition, Tokyo: Yuhikaku, 2010, p. 18.
6 Ibid., p. 20.
7 Ibid., p. 24.

As an interim conclusion, Japanese family law shifted from the *ie* family regime to a family model with a married couple at the centre as a result of the post-war amendments of 1947. Sociological studies, however, point out that although there are some minor changes, endogenous forces to form a stem family continue to exercise a strong influence in contemporary Japanese society. On the other hand, if we examine the issue from the perspective of positive law, there is no clear family model to be found in the wording of the law. The question of how to regulate the relationship between parents and their children beyond the age of majority demands further investigation separate from the question of interpretation of the revision of the Civil Code, which also requires consideration of the relationship between the state, society and individuals in the provision of care and nursing of the elderly.

State provision for the elderly

There are three areas in which the State provides support – including financial support and care for the elderly.

Regarding financial support, the National Pension Act was introduced in 1959 when the pension system was extended to citizens in all occupations. However, the amount of the pension was not very large and therefore it was difficult for the elderly to maintain themselves on this pension alone. From 1973, the amount has been gradually raised and now most of the elderly are able to provide for the necessities of life through the pension. It means that they usually do not require support from their child or other relatives.

Policy regarding the elderly was significantly affected by the Long Care Insurance Act of 1997. This established a new public insurance system for care and nursing of the elderly as from 2000. Under the system, people over the age of 40 are obliged to pay an insurance premium and the elderly (over 65 years old) are entitled to care designed to complement their physical and intellectual abilities. Although they pay for services to some extent, it is restricted to 10 percent of the full price.

Relationship between state provisions and private support among family members

Traditionally, and even after World War II, the elderly were financially, physically and mentally supported by their family. In most cases, elderly parents lived with their children. For example, the incidence of co-residence of the elderly over 65 with their children was around 80 percent in 1963. This tradition of family support was a reason why the Japanese government had been reluctant to develop a social welfare system. The introduction of the pension system mentioned previously was a key moment in breaking from that tradition. Nowadays, the elderly are expected to support themselves through the pension and it is only when they are unable to do so that they are entitled to financial support from their children and other relatives.

The public system providing care and nursing services for the elderly was started long after the introduction of the pension scheme. The insurance scheme for care and nursing of the elderly established in 2000 was the first indication of the idea that responsibility for caring for the elderly should be exercised not only by family members but also by society. The insurance scheme has led people to believe that they may rely on public services in caring for their elderly parents. At the same time, the number and types of organizations providing the service have been increasing. The incidence of co-residence of the elderly over 65 with their children dropped to about 39 percent in 2015.

Some problems remain, among which is that a rapid increase of expenditure on the public services for the elderly, such as pensions, medical insurance and care results in a heavy burden on the national budget. However, it can be concluded that the trend that responsibility of supporting the elderly has been taken over by the society to a greater degree than by the family members will continue or even be reinforced.[8]

Recent reform and policy change?

Against the preceding background, the inheritance law was reformed in 2018 in the opposite direction, that is, continuing or even reinforcing support and care of the elderly by the family members.

Protection of surviving wives

The inheritance law reform in 2018 was the most significant reform in 40 years. The main purpose was explained to be the protection of the surviving spouse, especially the wife, in an ageing society. Because of this factor, a surviving spouse can be very old, about 80, at the time of succession. The legislator considered the need for a system that helps the surviving spouses to remain living in the same house after the death of their spouse because the legislator considered that it was difficult for surviving spouses to find a new house. Two systems – first, the right of occupation of the decedent's house, and second, an increase of a spouse's statutory share in inheritance – were proposed.

The legislator proposed to increase the spouse's share in inheritance. For example, it was proposed that if a child and a spouse are heirs, the spouse's share would be two-thirds. The problem with this proposal was that the legislator limited the increase in the spouse's share to couples who have been married for a long time, for example, 20 years. This proposition was severely criticized. Firstly, it was argued that there was no need to increase the spouse's statutory share. Secondly, it was argued that there was no reason why only spouses who had been married for a long time should be protected. In the end, the legislator abandoned the idea of increasing the spouse's share in inheritance, but not the need to protect couples who have been married for a long time.

The reform introduced the following new system to protect such spouses. If the couple has been married for more than 20 years and one spouse transfers the house which he or she owned and in which the couple has lived together to the other, by a donation or a testament, that house is excluded from the decedent's property in the division of inherited property (art. 903, clause 4). Consequently, surviving spouses can succeed to the decedent's house in addition to their own statutory share. This reform in reality leads to an increase of the spouse's share if the couple has been married for more than 20 years. The legislator justified this reform by arguing that a surviving spouse who was married to the decedent for a long time helped the decedent to acquire assets.

Surviving spouses who have been married fewer than 20 years are only be protected by the right of occupation. There are two different rights of occupation. The first is the right to

8 Considering the heavy fiscal burden of state provisions for the elderly, promoting private support by themselves not by other family members could be another alternative. Since the 2000s, interest has grown in such financial products as reverse mortgages and their alternatives which enable senior citizens to convert the value in family homes into retirement income while securing housing: see Trevor Ryan, 'A Reverse Mortgage Over the Family Home as a Panacea in an Ageing Society? Comparative Lessons from Japan', *International Journal of Law, Policy and the Family* 31, 2017, 207–29.

short-term occupation. The surviving spouse can remain in the same house free of charge for at least six months after the death of the decedent and until the end of the division of inherited property (art. 1037). The second is the right of occupation for life (art. 1028). In the division of inherited property, the surviving spouse is granted the right to remain in occupation in the same house free of charge. This right is included in the spouse's statutory share. Thanks to these two types of rights, surviving spouses can continue to live in the same house even if they haven't been married a long time.

Relatives' contribution – protection of heirs' wives?

The legislator proposed the following rule concerning contribution. If there are relatives who are not heirs but who have made a special contribution to the maintenance of the decedent or increase of the decedent's property through providing nursing or medical treatment, or by other means, their contribution is valued and they can demand the heirs to pay for this (art. 1050). The legislator assumed that this rule will mainly be used by a decedent's daughter-in-law. As a result of the reform, the son's wife may now be protected in inheritance because she can receive some property.

This is an advantage of this reform. On the other hand, there may be a risk that a member of the family pressures her into nursing because of the expected financial benefit.

There were arguments for and against this provision in the Legislative Council. Some Council members insisted that such a provision would force family members to look after elders free of charge. According to statistics, in 2013 nursing care service providers were the main care providers for the aged in only 15 percent of all households, in contrast to over 70 percent of care provided by family members. It was suggested that this reform might fix the preceding situation. That means some family members would be forced to nurse the aged person without pay because they would stand to be rewarded after the death of the person under the system of relatives' contribution. However, other Council members approved of the proposition, arguing that in an ageing society the number of people in need of care was increasing, and therefore we should reward the efforts of family members. According to statistics in 2013,[9] children's spouses care for a person of advanced age in about 11 percent of households. There are no detailed data, but most of the children's spouses are likely to be women, the wives of the elderly persons.

A long way to go to adjust the law to family diversity

How should we evaluate the inheritance law reform of 2018?

First, the reform solves present problems to some extent, but not fundamentally. As for the protection of surviving spouses, because of their improved status regarding division of inheritance and the right of occupation, most of the surviving spouses will be able to keep living in the same house in which they lived with the decedent. However, the necessity of protecting the surviving spouse also results from the marital property system. This doesn't work well when a spouse dies. The 2018 reform does not solve this problem. Children's spouses will receive a pecuniary reward through the reform concerning relatives' contributions, to some extent solving the problem of family members having to care for the elderly free of charge. But it is imperative to change the system of nursing so that people can choose to use nursing care service providers more easily.

9 Comprehensive Survey of Living Conditions conducted by Ministry of Health, Labour and Welfare in 2013, p. 32, Available at www.mhlw.go.jp/toukei/saikin/hw/k-tyosa/k-tyosa13/dl/05.pdf.

Second, these reforms protect only the married family. They do not protect unmarried cohabiting couples, including same-sex couples. Only relatives are protected financially for their contribution, so even if a cohabiting partner cares for their partner, the system provides no reward. We need to continue to monitor the situation after the introduction of this reform. If there are any problems or changes in society, we should swiftly change the law in order to solve these problems and to keep up with the changes.

6.5
ACCESS TO FAMILY JUSTICE

Mavis Maclean and John Eekelaar

Introduction

The concerns over costs, which it was stated in the First Edition of this book were driving issues regarding the delivery of family justice, have deepened. Jurisdictions that have in the past attempted to develop therapeutic models to supplement or even partially replace 'adversarial legal' models, such as in the family court movement in the US, or the Family Court of Australia, have found that these models require significant resources if they are to be effective and are looking to alternative models.[1] In England and Wales, the desire goes further, not only to remove most intra-family disputes from courts, but also from the legal domain where the provision of legal resources requires public expenditure.[2] In continental Europe, on the other hand, at least in France, Belgium and Germany, there had been less focus on taking family issues away from courts and lawyers, but rather on strategies to get courts to dispose of cases as quickly as possible, a process described by Hartmund Rosa as 'acceleration',[3] though in France it has now become possible to divorce by agreement without obtaining a court order, though lawyers very much remain involved,[4] and (as described later) the Netherlands has experimented with online dispute resolution.

1 In 2015, however, Croatia, instituted a reformed divorce procedure which is based on those models: B. Rešetar, 'The New Divorce Legislation in the Republic of Croatia under the Influence of Psychology, Sociology and International Law', *International Journal of Law, Policy and the Family* 32, 2018, 63–79.

2 J. Eekelaar, '"Not of the Highest Importance": Family Justice under Threat', *Journal of Social Welfare and Family Law* 33, 2011, 311–17.

3 See H. Rosa, *Social Acceleration: A New Theory of Modernity*, New York: Columbia University Press, 2013; H. Rosa, *Beschleunigung: die Veränderung der Zeitstrukturen in der Moderne*, Frankfurt am Main: Suhrkamp Verlag GmbH, 2005.

4 See F. Ferrand, 'Non-Judicial Divorce in France: Progress or a Mess?', in G. Douglas, M. Murch and V. Stephens (eds), *International and National Perspectives on Child and Family Law: Essays in Honour of Nigel Lowe*, Cambridge: Intersentia, pp. 193–204, and Chapter 2.1 of this book.

Lawyers, courts and court-supported services

The United States

In 2008 it was stated that nearly 75 percent of states had some kind of family court[5] in which the judge acts as a manager who directs the members of high-conflict disputes to the mechanisms appropriate for it, and imposes interventions where necessary[6] and where the court 'recognizes that, regardless of legal label, the underlying family problem is the same in each case and should be addressed in a single forum and supervised by a single judge and support team'.[7] They are usually accompanied by a variety of support services.

Earlier concerns over the power judges exercise over families[8] and 'high conflict cases drift(ing) endlessly through the court system as different alternative dispute resolution measures are tried out and expenses and frustrations mount',[9] have since been supplemented by a growing crisis in funding, leading to a sharp increase in self-represented parties in the US, almost entirely for financial reasons.[10] Responding to this, some courts have developed a range of information services, from personal interaction with court staff at reception to workshops, library facilities, websites and explanatory videos,[11] though individuals have expressed frustration by being told by court staff that they can give information only, not advice.[12] Financial strains have led to doubts whether mandatory mediation was feasible,[13] and to suggestions for extensive review of what court-based services could offer,[14] or possibly to move them to locations within the community outside of the court altogether.[15]

One development has emphasized the value of interdisciplinary collaboration (between lawyers, social workers and health professionals) so that family problems can be approached holistically and normally resolved without going to court,[16] and some schemes have been developed where law, social work and psychology students work side-by-side with a supervising licensed

5 B.A. Babb, 'Reevaluating Where We Stand: A Comprehensive Survey of America's Family Justice Systems', *Family Court Review* 46, 2008, 230–57.

6 A. Schepard, 'The Evolving Judicial Role in Child Custody Disputes: From Fault-Finder to Conflict Manager to Differential Case Management', *U. Ark. Little Rock L. Rev.* 22, 2000, 395.

7 A. Schepard, 'Editorial', *Family Court Review* 46, 2008, 217–18.

8 H. Geraghty and W.J. Mlyniec, 'Unified Family Courts: Tempering Enthusiasm with Caution', *Family Court Review* 40, 2002, 435–52; J.M. Spinak, 'Romancing the Court', *Family Court Review* 46, 2008, 258–74.

9 P.G. Jaffe, D. Ashbourne, and A.A. Mamo, 'Early Identification and Prevention of Parent-Child Alienation: A Framework for Balancing Risks and Benefits of Intervention', *Family Court Review* 48, 2010, 136–52, at 139.

10 R. Zorza, 'An Overview of Self-Represented Litigation Innovation, Its Impact, and an Approach for the Future: An Invitation to Dialogue', *Family Law Quarterly* 43, 2009, 519–44, 520; R.W. Painter, 'Pro Se Litigation in Times of Financial Hardship: A Legal Crisis and Its Solutions', *Family Law Quarterly* 45, 2011, 45–94; Institute for Advancement of the American Legal System (IAALS), *Cases without Counsel: Research on the Experience of Self-Representation in US Family Court*, May 2016.

11 R.L. Kourlis and R. Samnani, *Court Compass: Mapping the Future of User Access through Technology*, Denver: IAALS, May 2017 give examples of Online Dispute Resolution initiatives in some US jurisdictions.

12 See IAALS, n 10.

13 P. Salem, 'The Emergence of Triage in Family Court Services: The Beginning of the End for Mandatory Mediation?', *Family Court Review* 47, 2009, 371–88.

14 L. Fieldstone, 'Ensuring a Place fore Family Court Services in the Family Court of the Future: Do or Die', *Family Court Review* 52, 2014, 627–31 (the service would primarily refer cases on to other providers).

15 P. Salem, 'The Challenges of Family Court Service Reform', *Family Court Review* 52, 2014, 670–7.

16 F.S. Mosten and L. Trava, 'Interdisciplinary Teamwork in Family Practice', *Family Court Review* 56(3), 2018, 437–60.

attorney, psychologist and social worker, and at a lower cost than engaging a personal attorney.[17] Such developments, however, can reach only a fraction of those affected by these problems. Another approach has been to re-appraise the training of family lawyers (including the teaching of family law) so that the lawyers do not simply focus on 'legalistic' aspects of a case, but see the problem as a whole, which includes not only practical issues, but also requires taking an empathetic and understanding attitude to the emotional aspects.[18] These schemes maintain the presence of lawyers in the process, but it has now been argued that, at least in disputes over children, the issues are such that the law itself (and therefore the legal profession) has no role.[19]

Australia and New Zealand

The Family Court of Australia was established in 1975 with ideals similar to those of the US unified family courts, and its own counselling and welfare service. For various reasons, including a perceived need to simplify court procedures, this was supplemented in 2000 by the Federal Magistrates' Court (later, the Federal Circuit Court of Australia) which deals with many family cases.[20] In a serious attempt to reduce pressure on courts, in 2006 the federal government established publicly funded Family Relationship Centres (FRCs) which were designed to link families with services through information and referrals, of which there were 65 in 2009. Originally lawyers were not allowed access to the Centres, but it was found that 'about three-quarters of those who nominated counselling, mediation or FDR as their main pathway to resolution [of parenting arrangements] also made use of lawyers'[21] and 65 percent of people who used Family Dispute Resolution DR also used a lawyer.[22] Therefore in 2009 the earlier strategy of keeping lawyers out of Family Relationship Centres was reversed and a Legal Assistance Partnership Programme to ensure that clients of Family Relationship Centres receive accurate legal advice was introduced.

In 2019 the Australian Law Reform Commission, in a wide-ranging review,[23] recommended that the Australian government should consider allowing state family courts (presently

17 A. Schepard and J.H. DiForza, 'Hofstra's Family Law with Skills Course: Implementing FLER', *Family Court Review* 49(4), 2011, 685–91; M. Taylor, S. Harper, L. Jurecko, J. Melowsky and C. Towler, 'The Resource Center for Separating and Divorcing Families: Interdisciplinary Perspectives on a Collaborative and Child-Focused Approach to Alternative Dispute Resolution', *Family Court Review* 53(1), 2015, 7–22; M.K. Pruett, A. Schepard, L. Cornett, C. Gerety and R.L. Kourlu, 'Evaluation of the University of Denver's Center for Separating and Divorcing Families: The First Out-of-Court Divorce Option', *Family Court Review* 55, 2017, 375–89.

18 Barbara A. Babb, 'Another Look at the Need for Family Law Education Reform: One Law School's Innovation', *Family Court Review* 55, 2017, 5–7; Pauline H. Tesler, 'Can the Relationship Be Saved? The Legal Profession and Families in Transition', *Family Court Review* 55, 2017, 38–58; Natalie A. Knowlton, 'From Talk to Action: How the IAALS Summit Recommendations Can Reshape Family Justice', *Family Court Review* 55, 2017, 97–106.

19 J.B. Singer, 'Bargaining in the Shadow of the Best-Interests Standard: The Close Connection between Substance and Process in Resolving Divorce-Related Parenting Disputes', *Law and Contemporary Problems* 77, 2014, 177.

20 See B. Fehlberg et al., *Australian Family Law; The Contemporary Context*, Melbourne, Australia: Oxford University Press, 2015, p. 29.

21 R. Kaspiew, M. Gray, R. Weston, J. Moloney, K. Hand, L. Qu and the Family Law Evaluation Team, *Evaluation of the 2006 Family Law Reform*, Melbourne: Australian Institute of Family Studies, 2009, p. 67.

22 Ibid., p. 109.

23 Australian Government and Australian Law Reform Commission, *Family Law for the Future: An Inquiry into the Family Law System: Final Report*, ALRC Report 135, March 2019.

responsible for child protection and domestic violence laws) to exercise jurisdiction presently exercisable by federal courts (primarily parenting and property matters) concurrently with those courts, whilst also considering the eventual abolition of first instance federal family courts. The Commission also recommended a variety of enhancements to existing services (rather than creating new Families Hubs, as it had originally suggested) including that the Family Advocacy and Support Service (which had been designed to provide integrated duty legal services and support services to families affected by family violence in the family courts) should be expanded to provide case management to clients in the family law system which would maintain contact with the client outside the court assisting them to maintain contact with appropriate services. Similarly, it recommended that the role of Family Relationship Centres should be enhanced beyond that of primarily providing information and referrals to one which also provided 'case management' where the case managers would

> ensure that clients with complex needs receive supported referrals to relevant services ... that sit outside the family law system. ... These services include housing assistance, health services (such as mental health and alcohol and other drug services), and gambling help services.[24]

In New Zealand a 'National Early Intervention Process' was introduced in 2010. This aimed to separate, through triage, 'standard' from 'urgent' cases so that the latter could come rapidly to a judge, and also allowing the standard cases to be processed more quickly. The Family Court Proceedings Reform Act 2014 went further and required parties to attempt 'family dispute resolution' (FDR) outside court (paid for by themselves) before accessing court, and saw the removal of lawyers from the initial stages of applications under the Care of Children Act 2004 (COCA), with lawyers only able to represent parties when applications are made without notice (in urgent cases), there were previous related applications or the application was made concurrent to a different application type. Yet further dissatisfaction followed, and research showed that (1) while there had been a reduction in volume of cases through the Family Court since the reforms have been in place, the number of urgent applications has greatly increased;[25] (2) even for those with all matters resolved (65 percent), one quarter end up requiring court intervention; (3) there is a perception that the Family Court has become less efficient since the reforms and there is reduced access to legal advice and representation for applicants; and (4) in 40 percent of disputes FDR did not take place because the other party would not participate, in 23 percent because the other party could not be found, and in 14 percent because of cost.[26] On 1 August 2018 the government appointed a panel to review the system, citing concerns over lack of assistance and legal representation.[27]

24 Ibid., para 16.34.

25 See www.justice.govt.nz/assets/Documents/Publications/Without-notice-applications-in-the-Family-Court-Final-Report.pdf (accessed 10 February 2020), concluding that:

> Based on what has been said by interviewed applicants, judges, lawyers and Family Court staff, there is a perception that the Family Court is less efficient since the reforms and there is reduced access to legal advice and representation for applicants.

26 New Zealand Law Society, *Ministry releases reviews into Family Court reforms*. Available at www.lawsociety.org.nz/news-and-communications/latest-news/news/ministry-releases-reviews-into-family-court-reforms (accessed 17 January 2020).

27 Hon A. Little, *Panel appointed to re-write 2014 Family Court reforms*. Available at www.beehive.govt.nz/release/panel-appointed-re-write-2014-family-court-reforms (accessed 3 October 2018).

England and Wales

In 2010 a comprehensive review of the family justice system was undertaken.[28] The government accepted the review's call for a 'single family court with a single point of entry', greater judicial continuity, specialization, leadership and control under stronger management by the judiciary.[29] With regard to support services, the Review Panel considered that the court should be a judicial and not a social work body, though it should work closely with non-legal professionals. It recommended the establishment of a Family Justice Service, charged with prioritizing the interests of children, that would have overall responsibility for and budgetary control over, the delivery of *court-related* social work services, mediation, experts and out-of-court resolution services.[30]

The government responded cautiously, agreeing to set up an interim board 'in advance of any wider structural reform'[31] but no serious structural change has occurred. Instead, the Legal Aid, Sentencing and Punishment of Offenders (LASPO) Act 2012 removed, from April 2013, legal aid for advice and court representation in most private law family issues. It was retained where domestic violence was in evidence (the exact criteria changing over the following years: see Chapter 5.2 of this book) in public law cases (where the state was involved), and in cases involving human rights or international aspects, but payments to lawyers were reduced and eligibility to qualify for such aid as was available became more restrictive. By 2016–17 the number of providers of legal advice that are funded by legal aid had reduced by nearly 50 percent since 2007–08. Private family law cases where neither party was legally represented rose from 16 percent in 2013 to 34 percent in 2016, and cases where both were represented fell from 38 percent to 21 percent. People were still using the courts, but many did so without legal assistance or advice.[32] The total expenditure on private family law legal aid dropped by 68 percent between 2012–13 and 2017–18.[33] Various responses have arisen, from legal professionals acting pro bono, volunteer-based help desks at court (who may give information only, not advice) and 'McKenzie friends' (non-legally qualified persons who assist litigants in person and could be permitted by courts to act as advocates). These provisions are limited and availability throughout the country is patchy.[34]

Belgium and France

As part of a larger project, researchers in France[35] observed the work of five courts dealing with family matters, three in France and two in Belgium. The overall policy strategy in both countries was to process cases as rapidly as possible. In Belgium this took the form of simplifying the ground for divorce (now 'irretrievable breakdown') and the researchers described the acquisition

28 *Family Justice Review, Final Report (Chairman: David Norgrove)*, London: Ministry of Justice, 2011.

29 *The Government's response to the Family Justice Review: A System with Children and Families at Its Heart*, Cm 8273, London: Ministry of Justice and Department of Education, 2012, 44. See also Mr. Justice Ryder, *Judicial Proposals for the Modernisation of Family Justice*, Judiciary of England and Wales, 2012.

30 *Family Justice Review*, op. cit., n 28, paras 2.41, 2.49, 2.62.

31 *The Government Response to the Family Justice Review: A System with Children and Families at Its Heart*, op. cit., n 29, p. 37.

32 See generally M. Maclean and J. Eekelaar, *After the Act: Access to Family Justice after LASPO*, Oxford: Hart Publishing, 2019, ch. 1.

33 See Ministry of Justice, *Post-Implementation Review of the Legal Aid, Sentencing and Punishment of Offenders Act 2012 (LASPO)* CP 37, February 2019, Figure 90, and generally.

34 See generally Maclean and Eekelaar, op. cit., n 32.

35 B. Bastard, D. Delvaux, C. Mouahanna and F. Schoenaers, *L'esprit du temps. L'accélération dans l'institution judiciaire en France et en Belgique*, Paris: ISP, 2013.

of divorce as being like a system of supermarket tickets – first-come, first-served. It is likely that the presence of the parties may even become unnecessary. However, this applies only to the acquisition of divorce. Other courts deal with provisional measures, children and property issues, and these matters can still involve protracted proceedings.

In France, where there is no such fragmentation, judges adopted a number of strategies to accelerate the process. They worked long hours, and organized their courts efficiently. But this is vulnerable to specific circumstances (in one court the system was severely compromised by the judge's maternity leave). Above all, they pressed the parties (who are often accompanied by lawyers) to settle matters themselves. There was therefore little oversight over what was agreed.[36] This led to a drastic reform in 2017 under which parties can obtain a divorce from a notary provided they agree essential matters (for example, concerning compensation payments) and have received the independent advice of two lawyers. If children are involved, they can demand that the case goes to a judge, and the parties are required to certify whether they had asked relevant children if they wanted that. The enhancement of the role of lawyers has been welcomed by that profession (but not by notaries).[37] While the presence of the lawyers may give certain protection to the adults' interests, it is arguable how far children's interests are protected as the process is unsupervised, and it is hard to imagine a child easily questioning the parents' arrangements before a judge.[38] (See further Chapter 2.1 of this book.)

Alternative dispute resolution

The movement to promote alternative dispute resolution grew strongly in the US after its promotion in Atlanta, Georgia, by O.J. Coogler in 1974. This was perhaps aided by an adversarial culture among lawyers, although in 1986 Sarat and Felstiner[39] showed that, in family matters, the aggressive lawyer who sought to aggravate conflict was the exception. In England and Wales research has established that the vast bulk of cases dealt with by lawyers result in negotiated settlement, and that a 'settlement culture' among solicitors practising family law in England and Wales has been established since at least the 1980s.[40] The same is true in Australia[41] and Canada.[42]

Nevertheless, belief that use of lawyers was synonymous with contested court hearings, which would be harmful to the parties and their children, and also expensive, has dominated official thinking in many jurisdictions, including in England and Wales, and legislation in 2014 required any party intending to initiate a family proceeding to attend a Mediation Information

36 See Centre Maurice Halbwachs, *Au tribunal des couples: rapport du recherché pour la mission de recherché droit et justice*, 2010.

37 B. Bastard, 'Family Justice in France: Two Dimensions of 'Digitisation', in M. Maclean and B. Dijksterhuis (eds), *Digital Family Justice: From Alternative Dispute Resolution to Online Dispute Resolution?*, Oxford: Hart Publishing, 2019.

38 See Ferrand, op. cit., n 4.

39 A. Sarat and W.L.F. Felstiner, 'Law and Strategy in the Divorce Lawyers Office', *Law and Society Review* 20, 1986, 93–134.

40 See J. Eekelaar and M. Maclean, *Family Justice: The Work of Family Judges in Uncertain Times*, Oxford: Hart Publishing, 2013, especially Chapter 3.

41 J. Howieson, 'The Professional Culture of Australian Family Lawyers: Pathways to Constructive Change', *International Journal of Law, Policy and the Family* 25, 2011, 71–99.

42 *Meaningful Change for Family Justice: Beyond Wise Words*, Report of the Family Justice Working Group of the Action Committee on Access to Justice in Civil and Family Matters, 19 December 2012. Although the report recognizes that 'consensual' dispute resolution processes are 'widely utilized across Canada', it calls for a 'fundamental shift' towards such processes.

and Assessment Meeting (MIAM) before being allowed to access the court.[43] The government even provided public funding for it. This was not an actual mediation, but an advisory session, often attended by only one party. The hope was that it would encourage parties to use mediation instead of the court.

Yet the New Zealand research just referred to showed that in 40 percent of disputes such procedures did not take place because the other party would not participate, in 23 percent because the other party could not be found and in 14 percent because of cost. In England and Wales, the number of publicly funded MIAMs *fell* by 66 percent between 2012–13 and 2017–18.[44] Formal referrals to National Family Mediation for privately funded mediation dropped by 31 percent between 2012–13 and 2014–115. Although the drop in the number of MIAMs partly reflected a drop in actual court applications as a result of LASPO and also that people were seeing solicitors less often, so referrals by solicitors for mediation fell sharply, it was clear that mediation was not *replacing* the role previously performed either by courts or solicitors.[45] And while government sought to attribute this to a lack of public awareness of mediation, research conducted in 2011 and 2012 of people divorcing and separating after 1996 showed that there was higher awareness of mediation than of solicitor negotiation as a means for resolving disputes both among the public generally and people who underwent divorce or separation, but that despite this, people were much more likely to take up lawyer negotiation than mediation.[46] People appreciated the support given by a lawyer (for which legal aid was still available when the research took place) but found mediation difficult, either because the other party would not take part, or they themselves felt unready for it, and were concerned over power imbalances and partiality by the mediator. Another problem may be that mediation is premised on the presence of a dispute, whereas in many cases the parties are not in dispute as such, but are seeking advice and assistance in resolving their common problem. Under most theories of mediation, however, mediators are not expected to offer advice, especially legal advice.[47]

Attempts to measure the 'success' of mediation as against settlement using lawyers have been bedevilled by a variety of factors, including the range of types of mediation, and the difficulty of obtaining randomized samples, thus avoiding selection effects. Thus a survey of nine studies in the US showed that settlements rates of a variety of mediation processes ranged between 50 percent and 90 percent.[48] One project in the US which used randomized allocation showed higher settlements by couples having mediation and also that, as many as 12 years after the divorce, there was greater father-child contact than with couples not having mediation.[49] However the mediation in that study comprised important therapeutic elements, involved two mediators for each session (averaging five hours in all) with follow-up, and concentrated on high-conflict cases.

43 Children and Families Act 2014, s. 10(1).

44 Ministry of Justice, *Post-Implementation Review of the Legal Aid, Sentencing and Punishment of Offenders Act 2012 (LASPO)* CP 37, February 2019, Para 613.

45 Maclean and Eekelaar, op. cit., n 32.

46 A. Barlow, R. Hunter, J. Smithson and J. Ewing, *Mapping Paths to Family Justice: Resolving Family Disputes in Neoliberal Times*, Basingstoke: Palgrave, 2017.

47 See generally M. Maclean and J. Eekelaar, *Lawyers and Mediators: The Brave New World of Service for Separating Families*, Oxford: Hart Publishing, 2016.

48 J.B. Kelly, 'Family Mediation Research: Is there Empirical Support for the Field?', *Conflict Resolution Quarterly* 22, 2004, 3–35. See also C.J.A. Beck and B.D. Sales, 'A Critical Reappraisal of Divorce Mediation Research and Policy', *Psychology, Public Policy and Law* 6, 2000, 989–1056; E. Douglas, *Mending Broken Families: Social Policies for Divorced Families: How Effective Are They?*, Lanham, MD: Rowman & Littlefield Publishers Inc, 2006.

49 R.E. Emery, D. Sbarra and T. Grover, 'Divorce Mediation: Research and Reflections', *Family Court Review* 43, 2000, 22–37.

There is also evidence that mediators tend to marginalize, or even suppress, references to violence during mediations as it may hinder chances of agreement.[50] British Columbia has enacted that only 'family dispute resolution professionals' should *discuss* alternative dispute resolution prior to court application, in the light of a prior assessment as to the presence of violence,[51] but a Family Justice Working Group has proposed 'consensual dispute resolution processes' should be required before courts are accessed.[52]

Evolution of legal practices

The settlement approach was given special prominence, and perhaps a commercial 'brand', in the US in the development of 'collaborative law' during the 1990s. This involves commitment to seeking resolution without resort to court-processes through 'four-way' meetings between the parties and their lawyers, with an undertaking (the 'disqualification agreement') that both lawyers will withdraw should either client abandon the process and proceed to court. This has, however, not proved as popular as many hoped, with concerns over then inherent sharing of information, screening for violence and the impact of the disqualification agreement.[53] A modified version which retains many of the features of collaborative practice, but without the disqualification agreement, has also been employed.[54] In any event, lawyers now appear to be more ready to work with mediators. The 2006 reforms in Australia, just referred to, have encouraged collaboration between lawyers and mediators.[55] Indeed, many lawyers carry out mediation themselves. In England and Wales it has been estimated that about three-quarters of mediators registered with the Family Mediation Council in 2015 were lawyers.[56] It has been suggested that in appropriate cases lawyer-mediators should be permitted to offer legal advice to both parties when conducting a mediation in a way similar to the joint advice often given to parties by notaries in continental Europe.[57]

Another attempt to reduce costs is to allow lawyers to be engaged to advise clients only on certain aspects of the case ('unbundling').[58] Other usages, which can reduce the burden on courts but almost certainly will not save costs, are arbitration and Early Neutral Evaluation

50 L. Trinder, A. Firth and C. Jenks, '"So Presumably Things Have Moved on since Then?" The Management of Risk Allegations in Child Contact Dispute Resolution', *International Journal of Law, Policy and the Family* 24, 2009, 29–44, also citing earlier research. For similar findings in China, see X. He and K.H. Ng, 'In the Name of Harmony: The Erasure of Domestic Violence in China's Judicial Mediation', *International Journal of Law, Policy and the Family* 27, 2013, 97–115, and in Sweden, with respect to social workers involved in overseeing child contact: A.-S. Bergman and M. Eriksson, 'Supported Visitation in Cases of Violence: Political Intentions and Local Practice in Sweden', *International Journal of Law, Policy and the Family* 32, 2018, 374–93.

51 Family Law Act 2011, s. 8 (BC), coming into effect in March 2013.

52 *Meaningful Change*, n 42.

53 See for example J. Lande, 'Possibilities for Collaborative Law: Ethics and Practice of Lawyer Disqualification and Process Control in a New Model of Lawyering', *Ohio State LJ* 64, 2002/3, 1315–84; Luke Salava, 'Collaborative Divorce: The Unexpectedly Underwhelming Advance of a Promising Solution in Marriage Dissolution', *Family Law Quarterly* 48, 2014–15, 179–97.

54 See J. Lande, 'Practical Insights from an Empirical Study of Co-Operative Lawyers in Wisconsin', *Journal of Dispute Resolution* 1, 2008, 203–66.

55 H. Rhoades, 'Mandatory Mediation of Family Disputes: Reflections from Australia', *Journal of Social Welfare and Family Law* 32, 2010, 183–94.

56 See Maclean and Eekelaar, n 47, p. 72.

57 Ibid.

58 F.S. Mosten, 'Lawyer as Peacemaker: Building a Successful Family Law Practice without Ever Going to Court', *Family Law Quarterly* 43, 2009–10, 489–518, 506.

(ENE). The degree to which arbitration is appropriate in family law cases, in which the interests of third parties (in particular, children) may be at stake, and which (in England and Wales) cannot bind the court, is a matter for debate.[59] In ENE, the evaluation by the neutral third party may help to prompt settlement, but equally may either entrench attitudes or precipitate a desire to go to court. Nevertheless, developments of these types are likely to attract increasing interest and discussion among lawyers and policymakers as they attempt to find ways to reduce pressure on courts. In this context, we have argued that, especially for people without the means to meet legal fees, systems might be encouraged to enable people working in the advice sector who are not qualified lawyers, but who have limited but relevant legal training, to offer advice and support (including legal advice) to people experiencing family problems.[60]

Information, advice and online services

The same economic forces that have been among the drivers of the trends just discussed have stimulated the use of new information technologies to assist in, or even bring about, the resolution of family disputes. These have to compete with commercial enterprises seeking the same market, creating regulatory issues. Nevertheless, attention is likely to be focused on such services as traditional legal support may become harder for people to access.

The Netherlands has experimented with an online platform for resolving disputes surrounding divorce (*Rechtwijzer*) with support from government funding. It listed issues, supported communication between the parties, and guided them to completing a mandatory parenting plan which must be submitted in the Netherlands before a divorce can be granted. At a later stage a 'decision' button was added for parties to receive a decision on a particular issue from a 'decision maker'. However, concerns were expressed about the fairness of some of the agreements reached, and its levels of use was disappointing, especially among people on low income; getting both parties to use it proved difficult and the service was suspended. In 2018 a report from members of parliament, officials, and the Ministry of Health with the Ministry of Justice, *Scheiden zonder Schade*, was published recommending moving away from the online approach, and supporting the use of a single lawyer rather than one for each party with the aim of reducing conflict.[61]

Nevertheless, digital services are being developed in various jurisdictions. In the UK, the Child Maintenance Service (CMS), established in 2012 within the Department for Work and Pensions, demands that potential claimants for child support payments first attempt to reach

59 See L. Ferguson, 'Arbitration in Financial Dispute Resolution: The Final Step to Reconstructing the Default(s) and Exceptions(s)', *Journal of Social Welfare and Family Law* 35, 2013, 115–38; W. Kennett, 'It's Arbitration, but Not as We Know It: Reflections on Family Law Dispute Resolution', *International Journal of Law, Policy and the Family* 30, 2016, 1–37.

60 Maclean and Eekelaar, n 32, ch. 11. 'Limited License Legal Technicians' (LLLTs) in Washington State, USA, acquire a qualification after three years of training (which is considerably shorter, and cheaper, than for a full legal qualification) and may give legal advice (presently confined to family law matters) and own law firms: www.wsba.org/for-legal-professionals/join-the-legal-profession-in-wa/limited-license-legal-technicians (accessed 21 August 2018). For discussion in Ontario about the provision of family legal services by persons other than lawyers in family matters, see *Family Legal Services Review, Report submitted to the Attorney General of Ontario by Justice Annemarie Bonkalo*, December 2016. Available at www.attorneygeneral.jus.gov.on.ca/english/about/pubs/family_legal_services_review/ (accessed 12 September 2017).

61 See B. Dijksterhuis, 'The Online Divorce Resolution Tool "rechtwijzer uit elkaar" Examined', in M. Maclean and B. Dijksterhuis (eds), *Digital Family Justice: From Alternative Dispute Resolution to Online Dispute Resolution?*, Oxford: Hart Publishing, 2019, ch. 11.

a 'Family-Based Arrangement' using online calculators. CourtNav is a Citizens' Advice tool, taken over and modified by the Ministry of Justice,[62] part of a wider programme for modernizing the courts.[63] In Ontario a programme of policy-oriented research known as the Ontario Project has been initiated, with a Family Justice Working Group which had an Action Committee on Access to Justice in Civil and Family Matters and an inquiry into National Self Represented Litigants, both of which reported in 2013, followed by the main report.[64] The report stresses the limitations of information whether in print or on the internet. It sets out a series of 'benchmarks' which it recommends must inform a developing strategy in regard to access to justice. These can be summarized as being to provide initial information that is accessible to people in their everyday lives; insofar as it is provided online, to do so through a single 'hub'; to make written information available to those without the internet; to provide assistance (through a 'trusted intermediary') for those who might have difficulty in accessing, reading, understanding or applying the information to their circumstances; to help people to understand whether a dispute is 'really' a legal dispute; to minimize duplication of persons with whom the individual must deal; to respond to diversity and domestic violence; to take into account financial capacity; to recognize the multiple problems that can accompany family problems; and to offer a 'seamless' process to final resolution.[65]

The importance of early advice has long been recognized, but it has been a challenge to make this accessible to those of limited means, especially in the absence of sufficient public funding. Law school clinics have been developed in the United States since the 1960s but their impact has been limited,[66] and, while some law schools in the UK provide this service, which can give useful assistance without charge, this remains a very small contribution to this need. Other sources of advice, including from the publicly funded 'citizens' advice' sector, provide the opportunity for professional advisers, who are not lawyers but have appropriate legal training, to provide appropriate advice, but again their resources are stretched and they tend to concentrate on issues (such as employment or housing) rather than family problems.[67] In this context, the establishment in Denmark of the Agency for Family Law described in Chapter 3.5 of this book provides an ambitious model for holistic early intervention. In its 'Action Plan' for taking things forward after its review of the effects of the 2013 legal aid cutbacks in England and Wales, the UK government has proclaimed its intention to enhance provision for early support (not yet provided in family law) by looking at ways to increase support for not-for-profit organizations (such as Citizens Advice) which provide legal advice, and which had suffered years of reductions in funding, seeking where possible to co-locate services, and, in particular, to further develop web-based products and digitization of court services (such as online divorce documentation).[68]

Other approaches seek none other than extensive education of the public. It is unclear however what the implications of a better legally educated public would be: for example, might it

62 See Maclean and Eekelaar, n 32, pp. 79–80.

63 See UK Government, *New legislation will modernise the courts*. Available at www.gov.uk/government/news/new-legislation-will-modernise-the-courts.

64 Law Commission of Ontario, *Increasing Access to Family Justice through Comprehensive Entry Points and Inclusivity*, Toronto, February 2013.

65 Ibid., p. 11.

66 Deborah Rhode, *In the Interests of Justice: Reforming the Legal Profession*, New York: Oxford University Press, 2000, 205–6.

67 For a full discussion, see Maclean and Eekelaar, n 32.

68 Ministry of Justice, *Legal Support: The Way Ahead–An Action Plan to Deliver Better Support to People Experiencing Legal Problems*, CP 40, February 2019.

lead to even greater calls on courts and other legal services?[69] While easily accessible information, such as that provided on the UK website, AdviceNow, may be able to enable people to resolve their differences fairly on the basis of such information, future evaluations of these schemes need to investigate the extent to which they are able to ensure that the interests of parties who are in conflict, including their children, are protected. The law can be complicated and its application to individual circumstances may not be straightforward. Research into the comparative effectiveness of telephone and face-to-face services obtained from Legal Service Commission data in England and Wales has shown the former worked well when callers needed information to 'plan or manage' their affairs, but much less well when callers wanted to get someone to do something.[70] It must therefore be asked whether online services can overcome the kinds of pressures that arise in circumstances following divorce or separation. Issues such as these are likely to continue to engage the attention of policymakers seeking for the most cost-efficient means of dealing with family disputes.

Other institutions and practices

Finally, we consider how far state law courts should be willing to give legal effect to the decisions of non-state institutions or practices which purport to bind communities within the state: what are sometimes called 'minority legal orders'. These are usually ethnic or religious populations, and the norms they follow may diverge from those of the state in which they live. States may of course expressly legislate for specific bodies of law to be applied to persons fulfilling certain criteria, as in, for example, personal law systems which mandate the application of religious law to persons identified with particular faiths, as in India among other countries, although, as Ahmed has pointed out, this risks 'misrecognizing' people's actual self-identification and imposing on them norms which they do not accept.[71] Issues might even arise concerning the state's compliance with international human rights standards.[72] On the other hand, attempts to prohibit the application of such norms within these populations, such as when a bill introduced into, but not passed by, the UK Parliament in 2011 sought to prohibit Sharia'h Councils from acting in family matters, could deprive individuals of sources that give legitimacy and meaning (in their eyes) to their actions.

A variety of tactics may be employed to overcome, or at least minimize, these problems. One is to provide for the recognition of decisions of such institutions, provided that they apply only state law, or norms compatible with human rights standards.[73] A recent review in England and Wales[74] has suggested they be subject to monitoring and licence by an official body, though

69 Maclean and Eekelaar, n 32, ch. 10.

70 N.G. Balmer, M. Smith, C. Denvir and A. Patel, 'Just a Phone Call Away: Is Telephone Advice Enough?', *Journal of Social Welfare and Family Law* 34, 2012, 63–85.

71 F. Ahmed, 'Remedying Personal Law Systems', *International Journal of Law, Policy & Family* 30, 2016, 248; see generally F. Ahmed, *Religious Freedom under the Personal Law System*, New Delhi: Oxford University Press, 2016. For an imaginative case for fusing personal law systems into a hybrid single system in post-colonial jurisdictions, see E. Bonthuys, 'Pluralist Marriage Laws in a Former Colonial System: Cultural Authenticity or Hybridization?', *International Journal of Law, Policy & Fam.* 34(2), 2020. See also Chapter 1.3 of this book.

72 See Y. Sezgin, *Human Rights under State Enforced Family Laws in Israel, Egypt and India*, Cambridge: Cambridge University Press, 2013.

73 See generally F. Banda and L. Fishbayn Joffe (eds), *Women's Rights and Religious Law: Domestic and International Perspectives*, Abingdon: Routledge, 2016.

74 *The Independent Review into the Application of Sharia Law in England and Wales*, Cm 9560, February 2018: 'Siddiqui Report'.

this was rejected by the government as this might be seen as adding 'legitimacy to the perception of the existence of a parallel legal system'.[75] A more relaxed approach, coined 'cultural voluntarism',[76] would permit the operation of such institutions, subject to compliance with the general law, but legally enforce their decisions only insofar as that could be done within the principles of existing law, such as the law of contract. Such an approach would be much assisted to the extent that members of minority communities had access to state institutions (such as the family jurisdiction), and exercised such access.

This is more difficult if marriages within a community are not legally recognized, as it is estimated is widely the case for Muslim marriages in England and Wales. This is largely because, unless a separate civil ceremony is conducted, in order to be recognized as valid, such marriages must take place in a registered building, yet few mosques are so registered and many of these marriages take place in homes. The review mentioned earlier sought to remedy this by making those officiating at such ceremonies that did not comply with the requirements for validity subject to penalty. Once again, cultural voluntarism sees value in the state accepting that practices that hold strong meaning for their participants as in themselves capable of acquiring legal recognition by the state, as is indeed the case (for historical reasons) for Quakers and Jews in England and Wales, although, as Maleiha Malik pointed out in the First Edition of this book,[77] 'it is possible to apply "severance" to pick and choose those norms of the minority legal order that can be accommodated'. Hence marriages performed in accordance with a group practice could be legally recognized, subject to compliance with basic conditions such as those concerning age and consent, and the need for registration and perhaps preliminary notice. In July 2019 the Law Commission for England and Wales began work on a review of the law of marriage which could enhance legal recognition of marriages in minority groups, and in this way enhance access to state norms for members of those groups, as is the case in Scotland.[78]

75 See generally R. Grillo, 'Comment on the Report of the Siddiqui Review Panel, 2018', *Journal of Muslims in Europe* 7, 2018, 283–308. Availabe at brill.com/jome.

76 See J. Eekelaar, *Family Law and Personal Life*, Oxford: Oxford University Press, 2017, pp. 176–8.

77 At p. 435.

78 Marriage (Scotland) Acts 1977 and 2014. See further K. O'Sullivan and L. Jackson, 'Muslim Marriage (Non)Recognition: Implications and Possible Solutions', *Journal of Social Welfare and Family Law* 39(1), 2017, 22–41.

PART 7

Globalization

7.1

INTERNATIONAL CHILD ABDUCTION, INTERCOUNTRY ADOPTION AND INTERNATIONAL COMMERCIAL SURROGACY

Mark Henaghan and Ruth Ballantyne

Introduction

This chapter analyzes the current policy challenges facing the Hague Convention of 25 October 1980 on the Civil Aspects of International Child Abduction (the 'Abduction Convention') and the Hague Convention of 29 May 1993 on the Protection of Children and Co-operation in Respect of Intercountry Adoption (the 'Adoption Convention'). Current obstacles for the Abduction Convention include the changing profile of the 'abducting parent', family violence and the 'grave risk' exception, the 'child objection' exception, international interpretation inconsistencies and the problem of non-signatory countries. Likewise, the Adoption Convention has to contend with the socio-economic realities of intercountry adoption and the resulting power imbalances; cultural and political differences; the difficulties of deciding what is in the best interests of children; and problems of interpretation, implementation and enforcement. The chapter ultimately highlights the need for international conventions to constantly adapt and improve to meet the realities of international child abduction and intercountry adoption.

The chapter also considers international commercial surrogacy as a potential replacement for intercountry adoption and the possible creation of a new private international law instrument designed to address the current parentage issues raised by commercial surrogacy.

International child abduction

The Abduction Convention was created by the Hague Conference on Private International Law on 25 October 1980. The Abduction Convention is currently ratified or acceded to by 101 countries,[1] and has two interconnecting objects:

1 See Permanent Bureau of the Hague Conference on Private International Law, 'Convention of 25 October 1980 on the Civil Aspects of International Child Abduction: Number of Contracting States to this Convention', 19 July 2019. Available at www.hcch.net/ (accessed 10 January 2020).

1 to secure the prompt return of children wrongfully removed to or retained in any Contracting State; and
2 to ensure that rights of custody and of access under the law of one Contracting State are effectively respected in the other Contracting States.[2]

The Abduction Convention provides a specific remedy for the wrongful removal or retention of children, in that abducted children (under the age of 16) must be promptly returned to the country from which they were wrongfully removed, unless some narrow exceptions are met.[3] The underlying purpose is to 'protect children internationally from the harmful effects of their wrongful removal or retention',[4] together with deterring parents from absconding overseas with their children in breach of the other parent's 'rights of custody'. The Abduction Convention does not resolve the custody dispute itself, but rather returns the child so the original jurisdiction can address the parenting issues between the parents.

The changing profile of the abducting parent

As originally intended, the goal of the Abduction Convention was to prevent parents who (for whatever reason) were non-primary caregivers from stealthily removing their children to another jurisdiction in the hope that a different country would award them primary care.[5] The stereotypical target of the Abduction Convention was therefore a non-custodial parent (usually a father) who had unlawfully relocated their children in an attempt to find a jurisdiction that would be more sympathetic to their arguments for primary care.[6] Such international forum shopping could be used strategically because what is deemed to be in the best interests of children varies significantly across cultures, legal systems and countries.

However, in reality, the majority of Abduction Convention cases actually involve primary or joint-primary caregivers (usually mothers) who remove their children to another jurisdiction.[7] The reasons why primary or joint-primary caregivers abduct their children are profoundly different from those of other parents. Many primary caregivers remove their children to attempt to escape violent and controlling relationships, or to return home to their country of origin to access familial support networks. As Beaumont and McEleavy explain, this fundamental change in 'the typical profile of an abducting parent' also relates to the movement towards a 'more inclusive approach' to parenting in western countries.[8] There is now greater acknowledgement that 'both parents retain

2 Hague Convention of 25 October 1980 on the Civil Aspects of International Child Abduction ('Abduction Convention'), art. 1.
3 Art. 13.
4 Preamble.
5 E. Pérez-Vera, *Explanatory Report on the 1980 Hague Child Abduction Convention*, The Hague: HCCH Publications, 1982, at [13]. See also B. Hale, 'Taking Flight: Domestic Violence and Child Abduction', *Current Legal Problems* 70(1), 2017, 4.
6 During the 1970s and early to mid-1980s familial child abductors were much more likely to be male rather than female. See P.R. Beaumont and P.E. McEleavy, *The Hague Convention on International Child Abduction*, Oxford: Oxford University Press, 1999, pp. 8–9. See also Hale, op. cit., n 5, pp. 3–4.
7 Lowe and Stephens' statistical analysis of Abduction Convention applications in 2015 found that '73% of taking persons were the mothers of the children involved in the application'. Eighty percent of all taking persons were the 'primary or joint-primary carer of the children involved': N. Lowe and V. Stephens, *A Statistical Analysis of Applications Made in 2015 under the Hague Convention of 25 October 1980 on the Civil Aspects of International Child Abduction: Part I–Global Report*, The Hague: HCCH Publications, 2017, pp. 7–8.
8 Beaumont and McEleavy, op. cit., n 6, p. 10.

duties, and responsibilities in relation to their children' after adult relationships have broken down[9] (see Chapters 3.3–3.5 of this book). The increased emphasis on involving both parents makes it more difficult for primary caregivers to relocate, thus more primary caregivers unlawfully abduct their children. The Abduction Convention was never designed to address this situation, and thus the primary remedy of return may not be in the best interests of these children.[10]

Regardless of this changing profile, it is important to note that any form of abduction is likely to have a significant impact on the children involved. Being taken from a familiar place with established routines to a foreign country is disruptive to a child's emotional well-being. The negative effects of parental abduction can also have long-term consequences. Marilyn Freeman's small-scale qualitative research into the long-term effects of parental abduction on adults and young persons abducted as children found that 'abduction can have extremely serious consequences'.[11] These consequences include adverse mental health outcomes, as well as difficulties maintaining relationships.[12] Many of the individuals interviewed by Freeman felt that:

> their adult and intimate relationships have been coloured by the abduction they experienced and they reported finding it difficult to connect with people. Some spoke about not being able to keep friends and relationships going because, when something is taken away so abruptly, and when the most important people in their lives could 'just go', they have found that they cannot fill the hole when they grow up.[13]

Other interviewees 'talked about the significant emotional effects they had suffered from the abduction, for example, psychotic breakdowns, post-traumatic stress, depression, and panic attacks, with some of these effects lasting to the present day'.[14]

However, not all 'abducted' children are affected in the same way, and the motivation behind the abduction may be relevant in some circumstances. For example, children who are removed to a different country by their primary caregiver to escape family violence are likely to have very different experiences of their abduction than children who are removed overseas by a non-custodial parent seeking primary care.[15] If the abductor is the non-custodial parent then the children will have to adjust to living with a different parent with whom they may not have a fully formed relationship. These children will also have a significantly diminished relationship with the parent who used to be their primary caregiver. Where the abductor is the primary or joint-primary caregiving parent, the experience may be easier for children because they are more likely to have a strong, established bond with that parent. However, if the children also have a strong emotional connection with the other parent, then the resulting reduction in contact caused by the abduction will be a significant loss to the children.

9 Ibid.

10 Marilyn Freeman, 'In the Best Interests of Internationally Abducted Children? Plural, Singular, Neither or Both?', *International Family Law* 2002, 82.

11 Marilyn Freeman, 'International Family Mobility: Relocation and Abduction: Links and Lessons', *International Family Law* 2013, 46.

12 Marilyn Freeman, *Parental Child Abduction: The Long-Term Effects*, Watford: International Centre for Family Law, Policy, and Practice, 2014, p. 31.

13 Ibid.

14 Ibid.

15 Beaumont and McEleavy, op. cit., n 6, pp. 7–8.

Family violence and the 'grave risk' exception

Although precise figures are unknown, many primary and joint-primary caregivers who abduct their children are seeking to escape family violence.[16] There are growing concerns that the Abduction Convention's primary principle of return is particularly harsh to these parents, especially as the Abduction Convention does not specifically address family violence.

Courts differ as to whether previous incidences of family violence and the fear of abuse continuing establishes an exception to return because it constitutes a 'grave risk that his or her return would expose the child to physical or psychological harm or otherwise place the child in an intolerable situation'.[17] The traditional view, as expressed by the Family Court of Australia, is that as long as the country of return has domestic laws that protect spouses, partners and children from family violence then the child is to be returned.[18] This is based on judicial comity, whereby it is not for the country to which the child has been abducted to tell other countries how to enforce domestic protection laws, as long as such laws are in place.[19] However, while most countries have laws protecting family members from violence, the realities of how these laws are enforced can vary widely.[20]

Most courts will not accept the 'grave risk' exception to prevent return where there has been no physical violence towards the children involved, even where there has been serious intimate partner violence between the two parents.[21] As Nelson explains:

16 See N. Lowe, M. Everall and M. Nicholls, *International Movement of Children: Law, Practice and Procedure*, Bristol: Jordan Publishing Limited, 2004, p. 335. Greif and Hegar found violence in 54 percent of child abduction cases from a 1993 study of 368 left-behind parents: G. Greif and R. Hegar, *When Parents Kidnap: The Families behind the Headlines*, New York: Free Press, 1993, pp. 18–19. See also M. Weiner, 'International Child Abduction and the Escape from Domestic Violence', *Fordham Law Review* 69, 2000–2001; and M. Weiner, 'The Potential and Challenges of Transnational Litigation for Feminists Concerned about Domestic Violence Here and Abroad', *American Journal of Gender Social Policy and Law* 11, 2003, 765.

17 Abduction Convention, art 13(b). For more examples of how courts have interpreted family violence in relation to the 'grave risk' exception, see Hale, op. cit., n 5 and B. Lubin, 'International Parental Child Abduction: Conceptualizing New Remedies through Application of the Hague Convention', *Washington University Global Studies Law Review* 4, 2005.

18 See *Murray and Tam v Director of Family Services* (ACT) (1993) 16 Fam LR 982. For the position in New Zealand, see *A v A* [1996] 2 NZLR 517 (CA) and *S v S* [1999] NZFLR 625, as discussed by J. Caldwell, 'Child Welfare Defences in Child Abduction Cases: Some Recent Developments', *Child and Family Law Quarterly* 13, 2001, 129. For a Japanese perspective, see S. Yamaguchi and T. Lindhorst, 'Domestic Violence and the Implementation of the Hague Convention on the Civil Aspects of International Child Abduction: Japan and U.S. Policy', *Journal of International Women's Studies* 17(4), 2016. While Japan did not formally ratify the Convention until January 2014, its wide definition of domestic violence, which includes psychological abuse, is notably far-reaching in comparison to the United States (who ratified the Convention in 1988).

19 On the subject of international judicial comity, see S. Nelson, 'Turning Our Backs on the Children: Implications of Recent Decisions Regarding the Hague Convention on International Child Abduction', *University of Illinois Law Review* 2, 2001; and M. Kaye, 'The Hague Convention and the Flight from Domestic Violence: How Women and Children are Being Returned by Coach and Four', *International Journal of Law, Policy and the Family* 13, 1999, 191–212.

20 See L. Silberman, 'The Hague Child Abduction Convention Turns Twenty: Gender Politics and Other Issues', *International Law and Politics* 33, 2000, 239–40; and N. Robertson et al., *Living at the Cutting Edge: Women's Experiences of Protection Orders*, Hamilton: University of Waikato, 2007, p. 3.

21 This may change when the Hague Council on General Affairs and Policy of the Conference formally accepts the long awaited *Guide to Good Practice on Art. 13(1)(b) of the 1980 Convention* (the *Guide*). The *Guide* (due to be approved in March 2020) clearly envisions the possibility of the grave risk exception being successfully invoked in relation to violence solely between parents, stating 'the grave risk to the

> if there is no evidence that *the child* was harmed, courts will likely find no grave risk. Even in cases where there is clear evidence of spousal abuse, sometimes extremely severe, courts have refused to find grave risk because the child himself was not abused.[22]

The reality is that once there is evidence of family violence, regardless of whether it is directed at an adult partner or a child, that partner and child are at risk (see Chapter 5.2 of this book). If courts ignore this real and present danger there can be fatal consequences. Lindhorst and Edleson provide two examples of Abduction Convention cases when returns have ended in death: one involving the death of an adult partner and one involving the death and serious injury of two children.[23] These case studies 'illustrate the gravity of the decisions being made in Hague Convention cases that include domestic violence, and demonstrate why research is urgently needed on the circumstances of these families'.[24]

Courts ruling on Abduction Convention cases need to carefully consider the safety of parents and children before they automatically return children. As Lindhorst and Edleson explain:

> Judges who decide to return a child to a habitual residence … should require that the safety and well-being (both physical and economic) of the child and abused parent be secured *before* ordering the return of a child. Undertakings and mirror orders cannot ensure a child's or mother's safety in the face of a grave risk of physical or psychological harm … and should not be considered an appropriate remedy to such dangers.[25]

Courts must assess the credibility of the evidence of the 'abducting parent' in terms of the wording of the Abduction Convention. If there is clear evidence a parent or child has been physically, sexually or psychologically abused by the contesting parent in the past, there is a grave risk they will be exposed to this violence if returned. In such situations, the 'grave risk' exception should be employed to prevent automatic return.[26] More effective use of this exception does not damage judicial comity principles, or criticize foreign family violence provisions. Rather, it is an application of the Abduction Convention to the realities of the situation and recognizes that even the best family violence laws in any country cannot guarantee safety.

---

child may also be based on potential harm to the taking parent by the left-behind parent upon return'. See Hague Conference on Private International Law, *Revised Draft Guide to Good Practice on art. 13(1)(b) of the 1980 Convention*, The Hague: HCCH Publications, February 2019, p. 23. However, a last minute addition to the *Guide* in November 2019, a sentence that reads 'evidence of the existence of a situation of domestic violence, in and of itself, is therefore not sufficient to establish the existence of a grave risk to the child', could considerably undermine this position. Consequently, Rhona Schuz and Merle Weiner instigated a petition to reword this sentence and ensure that the grave risk defence is applicable to violence directed towards children, as well as solely between parents in relevant circumstances. See R. Schuz and M.H. Weiner, 'A Small Change That Matters: The art. 13(1)(b) Guide to Good Practice', 21 January 2020. Available at www.familylaw.co.uk/ (accessed 12 February 2020).

22 Nelson, op. cit., n 19, 678.

23 T. Lindhorst and J.L. Edleson, *Battered Women, Their Children, and International Law: The Unintended Consequences of the Hague Child Abduction Convention*, Boston: Northeastern University Press, 2012, p. 23.

24 Ibid.

25 Ibid., p. 194.

26 See Schuz and Weiner, op. cit., n 21.

Parents who flee overseas with their children to escape family violence frequently do so out of a sense of desperation, believing there are no other options available.[27] The current over-emphasis on return runs the risks of undermining the best interests of children, especially in family violence cases. Courts should consider the 'grave risk' exception more carefully and, where appropriate, exercise their discretion to refuse to return children more often. This is demonstrated by some cases in the United States which trend towards protecting children and parents escaping family violence.[28]

The 'child objection' exception

A court can currently refuse to order the return of a child if that child objects to being returned. Art. 13 of the Abduction Convention states:

> The judicial or administrative authority may also refuse to order the return of the child if it finds that the child objects to being returned and has attained an age and degree of maturity at which it is appropriate to take account of its views.

Generally, courts have interpreted this 'child objection' exception narrowly.[29] Some judges choose to rely on the 'age and maturity' part of the exception to completely exclude young children's views. However, we should not invalidate children's objections and views simply because they are young Indeed, the Childhood Studies movement is based on the premise that all children, regardless of their age, have valid perspectives of their own world and reality.[30] This does not mean that children's views should be determinative; the court must still exercise judgment as to the weight to be given to the particular children's views. But, at the very least, children should be heard and respected and their objections to being returned should be assessed in the context of their own realities[31] (see Chapter 4.6 of this book).

27 See Weiner, 'International Child Abduction and the Escape from Domestic Violence', op. cit., n 16, 625–6. Whilst a relocation application is the preferred option (see ch. 7.2 in this book), in reality financing such an application can be difficult and the constant fear of violent repercussions make this impractical for many parents.

28 See, for example, *Baran v Beaty* 526 F 3d 1340 (11th Cir 2008). In this case a mother had abducted her child from Australia because the father had been verbally and physically abusive to her. The court refused to return the child to Australia despite the absence of evidence of abuse to the child. The mother was not required to prove that there were insufficient mechanisms in Australia to ameliorate the risk of grave harm to the child.

29 *White v Northumberland* [2006] NZFLR 1105 (CA) illustrates the requirements to be successful under this exception:

- Does the child object to return? If so;
- Has the child attained an age and degree of maturity at which it is appropriate to give weight to the child's views? If so;
- What weight should be given to the child's views? And;
- How should the residual statutory discretion be exercised?

For a detailed analysis of the 'child objection' defence, see Caldwell, op. cit., n 18, 130–3.

30 See M. Henaghan, 'Why Judges Need to Know and Understand Childhood Studies', in M. Freeman (ed.), *Law and Childhood Studies*, Oxford: Oxford University Press, 2012; and A. Robinson and M. Henaghan, 'Children: Heard But Not Listened to? An Analysis of Children's Views Under s 6 of the Care of Children Act 2004', *New Zealand Family Law Journal* 7, 2011, 39.

31 For a New Zealand perspective, see *Hollins v Crozier* [2000] NZFLR 775 (FC); *W v N* [2006] NZFLR 793 (HC); and *SL v SLN* [2013] NZFLR 1000 (FC).

This assessment process is made more difficult by the fact that the Abduction Convention does not specify any mechanisms for actually ascertaining that children object to being returned or what their views are more broadly. This lack of guidance creates significant uncertainty as to the appropriate way to ascertain children's views, leading to inconsistent approaches internationally. For example, in some jurisdictions it may be left to the parent who opposes return to bring the objection to the court's attention. If that parent chooses not to do so, the child's perspective is ignored. In Australia the court relies on reports written by family consultants, who are court-appointed professionals (such as social workers and psychologists) with relevant family law expertise.[32] Some Australian judges have also suggested that a court should make its own inquiries about a child's objections via a judicial interview.[33] Alternatively, in New Zealand, it is now standard practice to appoint an independent lawyer for child to represent children's views in Hague Convention cases and advocate in their best interests.[34]

Once it has been established (by any kind of mechanism) that a child objects to being returned, supplementary difficulties arise in assessing the degree of objection.[35] Courts have been inconsistent as to the degree of objection required,[36] and whether the objection needs to be about returning to the left behind parent, rather than to the state of habitual residence.[37] Such a technical approach undermines the Abduction Convention and does not consider children's objections adequately. Any objection to living with a particular parent is, in reality, also an objection to the place where they live.[38] Greater consistency in dealing with this exception to return is desirable to ensure that all children are properly heard and that any objections they may have are properly considered, especially in light of art. 12 of the UNCROC, which states:

> States Parties shall assure to the child who is capable of forming his or her own views the right to express those views freely in all matters affecting the child, the views of the child being given due weight in accordance with the age and maturity of the child.

32 Some children have expressed dissatisfaction with such reports and are especially unhappy 'about the techniques employed by report writers, the lack of confidentiality, the feeling that their views have not properly been understood or taken seriously, and the filtering and reinterpretation by the report writer of what they have said'. See M. Fernando and N. Ross, 'Stifled Views: Hearing Children's Objections in Hague Child Abduction Cases in Australia', *International Journal of Law, Policy and The Family* 32, 2018, 101. See also M. Fernando, 'How Can We Best Listen to Children in Family Law Proceedings?', *New Zealand Law Review* 3, 2013, 387–407; and P. Parkinson and J. Cashmore, *The Voice of a Child in Family Law Disputes*, New York: Oxford University Press, 2008.

33 For example, in *De L v Director-General NSW Department of Community Services* (1996) 139 ALR 417 Kirby J suggested that it was possible under art. 13 for the judge to interview the child directly to ascertain their views. See also Freeman, op. cit., n 10, 79.

34 See *Piri v Wallace* [2015] NZFC 2665; *Sali v Whitton* [2015] NZFC 3122; *New Zealand Central Authority (on behalf of Ubad) v Hubbard* [2015] NZFC 3205; *MLA v NJD* [2012] NZFC 5567; *SMS v NDL* [2012] NZFC 7106; *AHC v CAC* [2011] 2 NZLR 694 (HC); *SE v WMH* FC Taupō FAM-2010-069-143, 30 July 2010; and *S v S* (2009) 28 FRNZ 99. The appointment of independent legal representation for children in such cases also reflects the fact that children are independent individuals with their own views. See Fernando and Ross, op. cit., n 32, p. 93.

35 Freeman, op. cit., n 10, pp. 79–80.

36 See *Re R (A Minor) (Abduction)* [1992] 1 FLR 105; *Re S (A Minor) (Abduction: Custody Rights)* [1993] Fam 242; *Coates v Bowden* (2007) 26 FRNZ 210 (HC); and *U v D* [2002] NZFLR 529.

37 Freeman, op. cit., n 10, 80. See also *Re M (A Minor) (Child Abduction)* [1994] 1 FLR 390.

38 See *Urness v Minto* 1994 SC 249 where the court

> by creative reasoning, found that where the child preferred living with his mother in Scotland, it implied a rejection of his life with his father in the US and, therefore, amounted to an objection to returning to the state of habitual residence.
>
> *(Freeman, op. cit., n 10, 80)*

Interpretation difficulties

For the Abduction Convention to work as an international instrument it is essential that countries apply its principles uniformly. As Silberman states: 'If Convention cases become subject to varying national approaches and perspectives, neither of the core objectives of the treaty – deterring abductions and directing adjudication of custody cases to the State of the child's habitual residence – will be possible'.[39] However, consistency is difficult to achieve in practice because there is no overarching court or international body responsible for establishing and overseeing different jurisdiction's interpretations of the Abduction Convention.

The Vienna Convention on the Law of Treaties provides specific principles of interpretation for international treaties including the Abduction Convention.[40] Art. 31 of the Convention states that treaties are to 'be interpreted in good faith in accordance with the ordinary meaning to be given to the terms of the treaty in their context and in the light of its object and purpose'. Art. 32 allows 'those interpreting a treaty to look to 'supplementary means of interpretation' to 'confirm the meaning' of the treaty or to 'determine meaning when either the meaning is obscure or it leads to a result which is manifestly absurd or unreasonable'. As the Abduction Convention has international scope, courts can legitimately examine decisions outside their own jurisdiction to ensure the Abduction Convention is interpreted and applied consistently.[41]

The term 'habitual residence' provides a useful example of some of the interpretation difficulties that plague the Abduction Convention. The Convention provides that the removal (or retention) of a child is only unlawful if it

> is in breach of rights of custody attributed to a person, an institution or any other body, either jointly or alone, under the law of the State in which the child was habitually resident immediately before the removal or retention.[42]

Thus, Abduction Convention cases can succeed or fail on the basis of where the judge deems the child's habitual residence to be.

However, the Abduction Convention does not provide a definition of habitual residence, nor do the preparatory reports give any indication as to what the term should mean.[43] This leaves each country (and sometimes each court or authority within each country) to reach its own conclusion as to how to define habitual residence. In 2010 the Court of Justice of the European Union defined a child's habitual residence in terms of a need for the child's residence to have

39 L. Silberman, *Interpreting the Hague Abduction Convention: In Search of a Global Jurisprudence*, New York: New York University Public Law and Legal Theory Working Papers, 2006, p. 10.

40 Ibid., pp. 10–11. See also E. Criddle, 'The Vienna Convention on the Law of Treaties in U.S. Treaty Interpretation', *Virginia Journal of International Law* 44, 2004, 431–500.

41 The increasing advent of online legal databases, including the establishment of the International Child Abduction Database (INCADAT), gives judges greater access to summaries of Abduction Convention cases from around the world. This enhances the potential for more consistent Abduction Convention decisions internationally.

42 Abduction Convention, art. 3.

43 As Silberman illustrates, various countries have defined and applied habitual residence differently. See Silberman, op. cit., n 39, pp. 15–18. See also R. Schuz, 'Habitual Residence of Children Under the Hague Child Abduction Convention: Theory and Practice', *Child and Family Law Quarterly* 13, 2001, 1–24.

'a certain permanence or regularity'.[44] The child's place of habitual residence needs to 'reflect some degree of integration by the child in a social and family environment'.[45] However, the notion of 'permanency' in relation to a child's habitual residence caused judicial concern. In *DL v EL*,[46] Thorpe LJ in the English Court of Appeal considered the English and the French versions of the Court of Justice of the European Union's decision and found that the French version of the case was focused more towards 'stability' than 'permanence'.[47] As Thorpe LJ said '"Stability" has a quite different connotation from permanence'. To establish oneself somewhere with a child is by no means necessarily the same as 'to settle permanently' with the child'.[48] Thorpe LJ viewed the language differences between the English and French versions of the decision as a 'very sound basis for downplaying (if not indeed for eliminating) the implications of permanence as an ingredient of habitual residence'.[49]

In *Re A (Jurisdiction: Return of the Child)*,[50] the UK Supreme Court upheld the approach taken in *DL v EL*,[51] and minimized the utility of using the concept of permanency during a habitual residence consideration.[52] In the leading judgment, Lady Hale distilled a useful summary of the crucial factors in a habitual residence inquiry. She determined that habitual residence is 'a question of fact and not a legal concept' and accepted the European Court's test in that a child's habitual residence is 'the place which reflects some degree of integration by the child in a social and family environment in the country concerned'. Lady Hale also said:

> The social and family environment of an infant or young child is shared with those (whether parents or others) upon whom he is dependent. Hence it is necessary to assess the integration of that person or persons in the social and family environment of the country concerned. ... The essentially factual and individual nature of the inquiry should not be glossed with legal concepts which would produce a different result from that which the factual inquiry would produce.[53]

However, even this approach leaves unanswered questions. What degree of 'integration' in terms of 'social and family environment' is required before a child is habitually resident in a country? At what age does a child need to be individually integrated into the country themselves, rather than merely relying on the integration of their family? The question of habitual residence remains a purely factual and individualistic inquiry, which makes consistency across jurisdictions nigh impossible.[54]

44 Case C-497/10 *Mercredi v Chaffe* [2011] 1 FLR 1293, [44].
45 Ibid., [47].
46 [2013] EWCA Civ 865.
47 Ibid., [71]–[81].
48 Ibid., [77].
49 Ibid., [81].
50 [2013] UKSC 60. The case concerned abduction but involved Pakistan, and was therefore outside the scope of the 1980 Convention.
51 [2013] EWCA Civ 865.
52 [2013] UKSC 60, [51] and [80]. See further *Re C (Children)* [2018] UKSC 8, [2018] 2 WLR 683 at [13] where Lord Hughes emphasizes that habitual residence is a question of fact which requires an examination of integration.
53 Ibid., [54].
54 The New Zealand position on habitual residence is set out in *OEN v TM* [2012] NZFC 5035, and in *O v R* [2018] NZHC 2696.

Even concepts expressly defined by the Abduction Convention lead to similar interpretation difficulties. For example, the concept of 'rights of custody', which are central to the Abduction Convention as it is a breach of them that triggers the remedy of return, is defined.[55] The Abduction Convention defines 'rights of custody' as including 'rights, relating to the care of and the protection of the child, and, in particular, the right to determine the child's place of residence'.[56] The courts have interpreted this concept in a variety of ways to include parents who not only have visitation or access rights, but in some cases, those who have a say on travel restrictions.[57] These differences create interpretative difficulties that need to be resolved.

The significant interpretative inconsistencies created by the Abduction Convention threaten to undermine the entire purpose of having an international instrument. Further steps need to be taken to reduce the major discrepancies in the way different countries apply the Abduction Convention. Establishing more uniform procedures is the only way to truly 'protect children internationally from the harmful effects of their wrongful removal or retention'.[58]

The problem of non-convention countries

Countries who are not signatories to the Abduction Convention can provide safe havens for parents who abduct their own children.[59] Children who are abducted to non-convention countries cannot be returned via the Abduction Convention. As Sattler explains:

> The Convention applies only between contracting states. If a child is detained in a country that is a not a party to the Convention, the parent must seek access to his or her child through the normal legal channels of that country. In many countries, this may mean that one parent is effectively without a remedy to enforce his or her parental rights.[60]

As long as non-convention countries exist, a central tenet of the Abduction Convention is undermined. Until the Abduction Convention is truly universal, an exploitable 'loophole' remains.[61]

Intercountry adoption

Intercountry adoption is not a new occurrence. As Selman states: 'Intercountry adoption is usually accepted as commencing as a global phenomenon in the years following the Second World War'.[62] During this time intercountry adoption has taken several different forms. Initially 'inter-

55 Abduction Convention, art. 3.

56 Art. 5.

57 Different countries have defined and applied 'custody rights' differently. See Silberman, op. cit., n 39, pp. 19–22. See also *Abbott v Abbott* 176 L Ed 2d 789 (2010) where the Supreme Court of the US held that a parent's right to prevent a child from leaving the country is a 'right to custody' under the Abduction Convention.

58 Abduction Convention, Preamble.

59 Latin American and Muslim countries are popular safe havens for parental child abductors, See *Re A (Jurisdiction: Return of Child)* [2013] UKSC 60; and A.G. Hamid et al., 'The Applicability of the 1980 Hague Abduction Convention in Muslim Countries: Particular Reference to the Malaysian Position', *Arab Law Quarterly* 32(2), 2018.

60 M. Sattler, 'The Problem of Parental Relocation: Closing the Loophole in the Law of International Child Abduction', *Washington and Lee Law Review* 67, 2010, 1716.

61 Ibid., 1745–50.

62 P. Selman, 'From Bucharest to Beijing: Changes in Countries Sending Children for International Adoption 1990 to 2006', in G.M. Wrobel and E. Neil (eds), *International Advances in Adoption Research*

national adoption was largely about movement of children from war-torn countries in Europe and Japan to the United States'.[63] Intercountry adoption, as we know it today, originates from the 'aftermath' of the Korean War in the 1950s.[64] Between 1957 and 1969 over 20,000 children from various countries around the world were adopted in the US; over a third of these children were adopted from South Korea alone.[65] These numbers rapidly increased. Intercountry adoptions peaked between 1995 and 2004, reaching a rate of at least 45,000 per year during this time.[66] However, since 2004, intercountry adoptions have been in a steady state of decline. By 2014 there were only 13,504 intercountry adoptions globally.[67]

The Adoption Convention was created by the Hague Conference on Private International Law on 29 May 1993. The Convention is currently ratified or acceded to by 102 countries.[68] It has three primary 'objects':

1 to establish safeguards to ensure that intercountry adoptions take place in the best interests of the child and with respect for his or her fundamental rights as recognized in international law;
2 to establish a system of co-operation amongst Contracting States to ensure that those safeguards are respected and thereby prevent the abduction, the sale of, or traffic in children;
3 to secure the recognition in Contracting States of adoptions made in accordance with the Convention.[69]

The Adoption Convention provides strict requirements that must be met before a child can be permanently adopted from one 'Contracting State' (the State of origin) to another 'Contracting State' (the receiving State).[70] An adoption will only take place if the child's 'State of origin' has 'established that the child is adoptable', that the adoption is in the 'child's best interests' and that the proper consents are obtained from either the parents or the institution where the child lives.[71] The 'receiving State' is obliged to ensure that the parents seeking to adopt the child are 'eligible and suited to adopt' and that the child is or will be 'authorized to enter and reside permanently in that State'.[72]

---

for Practice, West Sussex: Wiley-Blackwell, 2009, p. 43. See also H. Altstein and R. Simon, *Intercountry Adoption: A Multinational Perspective*, New York: Praeger, 1991.

63 Selman, op. cit., n 62, p. 43.

64 Ibid.

65 Ibid.

66 Ibid., p. 44. In 2004, China and Russia together accounted for 51 percent of all adoptions.

67 P. Selman, *Global Statistics for Intercountry Adoption: Receiving States and States of Origin 2004–2015*, The Hague: Permanent Bureau of the Hague Conference on Private International Law, July 2016.

68 See Permanent Bureau of the Hague Conference on Private International Law, 'Convention of 29 May 1993 on Protection of Children and Co-Operation in Respect of Intercountry Adoption: Number of Contracting States to this Convention', 19 December 2019. Available at www.hcch.net/ (accessed 12 January 2020).

69 Hague Convention of 29 May 1993 on Protection of Children and Co-operation in Respect of Intercountry Adoption ('Adoption Convention'), art 1. The Preamble to the Adoption Convention states that 'intercountry adoption may offer the advantage of a permanent family to a child, for whom a suitable family cannot be found in his or her State of origin'. The Adoption Convention is thus aimed primarily at orphaned and abandoned children whose best chance of a permanent family life is through intercountry adoption.

70 Art. 2.

71 Art. 4.

72 Art. 5.

Power imbalances and market forces

One of the primary concerns with intercountry adoption is that the unequal socio-economic positions of the countries that send and receive children is exploitative of some surrogates. On a global scale, intercountry adoption inherently highlights significant power imbalances. As Briggs and Marre state:

> Adoption opens a window onto the relations between nations, inequalities between rich and poor within nations ... transnational adoption has been marked by the geographies of unequal power, as children move from poorer countries and families to wealthier ones – and the forces that make a country rich and powerful are above all historical.[73]

It is telling that, between 2005 and 2018, the countries that most frequently received children through intercountry adoption were the US, Italy, Spain, France and Canada.[74] Conversely, the countries most frequently sending children for intercountry adoption at that time were China, Russia, Ethiopia, Guatemala, Colombia, Ukraine, South Korea, Vietnam, Haiti and India.[75] Gibbons and Rotabi point out that, of the receiving States, the top five are all 'categorized by the World Bank as high-income countries'; by contrast, of the ten major countries of origin for intercountry adoption, only South Korea is considered to be a high-income country.[76]

These socio-economic inequalities increase the likelihood of the involvement of market forces in intercountry adoption.[77] The majority of international adoptees were neither abandoned, nor orphans, but rather placed for adoption as the result of economic necessity.[78] Birth parents may not realistically be able to exercise free choice because a lack of economic alternatives may give these families no other feasible options.[79] Critics of intercountry adoption also point to the inequality in bargaining power between the birth families involved, and wealthier adoptive parents and adoption agencies, especially when the birth families are from third-world countries. This significant financial and power inequality leaves birth families susceptible to exploitation from others who seek to benefit from the arrangement.[80] This may include other family members, adoption agencies and adoptive parents.

Without proper checks and balances, there is a risk that children will suffer significant harm. The negative consequences for children when things go wrong is demonstrated by the high profile case of Alexandra Austin, who was born in Romania but adopted by Canadian

73 L. Briggs and D. Marre, 'Introduction: The Circulation of Children', in D. Marre and L. Briggs (eds), *International Adoption: Global Inequalities and the Circulation of Children*, New York: New York University Press, 2009, pp. 1–2.

74 P. Selman, *Global Statistics for Intercountry Adoption: Receiving States and States of Origin 2005–2018*, The Hague: Permanent Bureau of the Hague Conference on Private International Law, December 2019, p. 2.

75 Ibid., p. 3.

76 J.L. Gibbons and K.S. Rotabi, 'Best Practices in Implementing the Hague Convention', in J.L. Gibbons and K.S. Rotabi (eds), *Intercountry Adoption: Policies, Practices, and Outcomes*, Surrey: Ashgate, 2012, pp. 255–6.

77 Ibid., p. 256. See also D. Smolin, 'Intercountry Adoption as Child Trafficking', *Valparaiso University Law Review* 39, 2004, 281–325.

78 M. Neagu, 'Children by Request: Romania's Children between Rights and International Politics', *International Journal of Law, Policy and the Family* 29(2), 2015, 216.

79 Smolin, op. cit., n 77, 310, questions whether it is ethical to adopt children without first offering financial assistance to the family to stay together.

80 Neagu, op. cit., n 78, 223.

adoptive parents when she was nine years old.[81] Five months after the intercountry adoption had occurred, Alexandra's adoptive parents changed their mind (after adopting a new baby from Romania) and returned Alexandra to Romania. As a result, Alexandra was effectively stateless; she had not been in Canada long enough to acquire Canadian citizenship and she was no longer considered to be a Romanian citizen and was therefore not entitled to state education or health benefits. Consequently, when Alexandra turned 22, she brought a lawsuit against her Canadian adoptive parents saying 'They stole my childhood. They stole my future. They stole my life … I never had a normal life'.[82]

There is also the danger that children may become viewed as commodities to be bought and sold. As Khabibullina states, '[c]hildren in transnational adoption are frequently seen as objects of commodification, available for a price that only wealthy parents can afford'.[83] The Adoption Convention expressly seeks to avoid the creation of a market in children and states that: 'Central Authorities shall take, directly or through public authorities, all appropriate measures to prevent improper financial or other gain in connection with an adoption and to deter all practices contrary to the objects of the Convention'.[84] The Adoption Convention further states:

1 No one shall derive improper financial or other gain from an activity related to an intercountry adoption.
2 Only costs and expenses, including reasonable professional fees of persons involved in the adoption, may be charged or paid.
3 The directors, administrators and employees of bodies involved in an adoption shall not receive remuneration which is unreasonably high in relation to services rendered.[85]

However, some critics argue that the Adoption Convention by itself is not enough to prevent the development of a 'child-selling' market and call for the creation of regulations in this area.[86] As Smolin states:

> adoption can only maintain a principled and enforceable line against child selling and child trafficking when effective systems of enforceable regulation are in place that effectively prevents adoption systems from becoming markets in children. The refusal or failure of the domestic and intercountry adoption systems to put those needed regulations into place speaks volumes regarding the ethics of the domestic and intercountry adoption systems.[87]

It is clear that the ratification of the Hague Convention does not insulate countries from global inequalities and claims of child trafficking.[88] Intercountry adoption policies in the future should

81 Ibid.
82 *Globe and Mail*, 'Adopted, Turned Away, Young Romanian Sues Canadian Pair', Toronto: *Globe and Mail*, 2005.
83 L. Khabibullina, 'International Adoption in Russia: "Market," "Children for Organs," and "Precious" or "Bad" Genes', in D. Marre and L. Briggs (eds), *International Adoption: Global Inequalities and the Circulation of Children*, New York: New York University Press, 2009, p. 174.
84 Adoption Convention, art. 8.
85 Art. 32.
86 Smolin, op. cit., n 77, 323.
87 Ibid.
88 See generally, A. Bainham, 'International Adoption from Romania: Why the Moratorium Should Not be Ended', *Child and Family Law Quarterly* 15, 2003, 223 and D. Smolin, 'Child Laundering as

be underpinned by a stronger drive to more ethically and effectively counter the negative impacts of power imbalances and market forces on the families and children involved.

Cultural and political differences

Intercountry adoptions highlight complex cultural and political factors.[89] Historically, many families were caught up in political and cultural objectives they had no control over. For example, the Ceauşescu regime created a surplus of children in Romania by outlawing birth control and abortion and forcing women to have at least four children 'as a symbol of national pride and power'.[90] Numerous 'impoverished Romanian families' were ultimately unable to support so many children and had no real choice but 'to give them up'.[91] The one child policy in China meant that any so-called extra children had to be aborted, abandoned or adopted.[92] In other countries, poverty and extremely fast-growing populations mean that governments are not able to provide for all their citizens and intercountry adoption is seen as the only way of easing the pressure.[93] These differing political and cultural positions impact the number of intercountry adoptions some countries allow. Thus, intercountry adoption needs to be considered within a range of different cultural and political contexts.

Debating the best interests of children

There remain significant difficulties in determining the best interests of children in this area due to divergent views as to what is actually best for children.[94] Some commentators argue that keeping children in their own country of origin and within their own cultural environment is better for children than allowing them to be adopted internationally,[95] and that children have 'the right to grow to adulthood within the culture and community of their birth'.[96] This aligns with art. 21(b) of the UNCROC, which indicates that domestic measures should be preferred over international adoptions.[97]

Such beliefs lead some countries to severely restrict or place a complete moratorium on intercountry adoption.[98] Once this occurs, such countries must either generate an extensive increase in domestic adoptions, or obtain and provide resources to care for parentless children.

Exploitation: Applying Anti-Trafficking Norms to Intercountry Adoption under the Coming Hague Regime', *Vermont Law Review* 32(1), 2007, 1.

89 See N. Riley, 'American Adoptions of Chinese Girls: The Socio-Political Matrices of Individual Decisions', *Women's Studies International Forum* 20, 1997, 94.

90 J. Ratcliff, 'International Adoption: Improving on the 1993 Hague Convention', *Maryland Journal of International Law* 25, 2010, 336–55. See also I. Iusmen 'The EU and International Adoption from Romania', *International Journal of Law, Policy and the Family* 27, 2013, 1–27.

91 Ratcliff, op. cit., n 90, p. 339.

92 Ibid.

93 Ibid., pp. 339–40.

94 N. Cantwell, *The Best Interests of the Child in Intercountry Adoption*, Florence: UNICEF Office of Research, 2014.

95 See E. Bartholet, 'International Adoption: The Human Rights Position', *Global Policy* 1, 2010, 91–100.

96 S. Dillon, 'Making Legal Regimes for Intercountry Adoption Reflect Human Rights Principles: Transforming the United Nations Convention on the Rights of the Child with the Hague Convention on Intercountry Adoption', *Boston University International Law Journal* 21, 2003, 179–258.

97 Art. 21(b) of the UNCROC recognizes that intercountry adoption may be an appropriate means of care 'if the child cannot be placed in a foster or an adoptive family or cannot in any suitable manner be cared for in the child's country of origin'.

98 See Bainham, op. cit., n 88, 225–8.

However, many countries simply do not have the resources to adequately provide for such children. Consequently, many children are deprived of their rights under the UNCROC. This occurred in Romania when intercountry adoption was banned in 2005 and domestic adoption was restricted to close relatives.[99] This resulted in large numbers of children being institutionalised in domestic orphanages.[100] Given the negative impact this policy had on the children involved, reforms made in 2012 widened the pool of eligible adoptive parents to include 'relatives of the fourth degree of kinship, the spouse of the child's natural parent and, significantly, Romanian citizens who are habitually resident abroad'.[101]

Bartholet, a fierce advocate for intercountry adoption, is deeply concerned about the long-term impact on children of being placed in orphanages and other institutions, stating that:

> child welfare experts know that keeping infants in institutional care for more than a few months puts them at enormous risk of lifelong damage, even if they are ultimately adopted, with the risk increased proportionately with the length of stay.[102]

Bartholet believes that the most fundamental human right children have is the right to a nurturing family, which is often only available to some children through international adoption.[103] Thus, if intercountry adoption is overly restricted because of fears of financial inequalities, societal exploitation or the negative effects of children being removed from their own culture, these children will have no chance of growing up in a family where they are nurtured, loved and provided for.[104]

Others also maintain that intercountry adoption is best for children. In June 2009 an International Adoption Policy Statement (the 'Adoption Statement') was adopted by 130 legal academics and six children's organizations.[105] The Adoption Statement declares that adoption is better than foster and institutional care. It favours a process whereby children who cannot be raised by their own birth parents are placed for adoption as soon as possible, whether overseas or within their own country.

However, not all commentators agree. Smolin argues that the particular best interests of the child premise the Adoption Statement relies on is invalid, saying:

> Of course, it could be argued that the very nature of intercountry adoption, involving a transaction between rich and poor nations, lends itself to abuse, and therefore the choice is ultimately between shutting down intercountry adoption, or allowing it to continue, in the interests of saving children, despite these abuses. This kind of argument implicitly justifies child trafficking in the name of the best interest of the child.[106]

What really is in the best interests of children must be carefully considered in the future and further empirical data regarding the long-term consequences for children who have been adopted

99 Cantwell, op. cit., n 94, p. 36.
100 For details about the 'horrendous' living conditions in some former Romanian orphanages see Bartholet, op. cit., n 95, 92.
101 Cantwell, op. cit., n 94, p. 36.
102 Bartholet, op. cit., n 95, p. 91. For more detailed arguments about intercountry adoption as an alleged exploitative violation of human rights see Bainham, op. cit., n 88, pp. 223–6 and Smolin, op. cit., n 77.
103 Bartholet, op. cit., n 95, pp. 91–2.
104 Ibid., pp. 93–4.
105 Ibid., pp. 98–9.
106 Smolin, op. cit., n 77, p. 325.

internationally would be extremely valuable. However, we must not allow children to 'languish without families' whilst we debate the perfect solution.[107]

Problems of interpretation, implementation and enforcement

Like the Abduction Convention, the Adoption Convention has substantial interpretative problems. A key objective of the Adoption Convention is to determine whether a child is 'adoptable'. However, 'adoptable' is not defined. Nor does the Adoption Convention provide criteria for authorities from the State of origin to follow to ensure that the child is indeed 'adoptable'. This allows countries to develop different practices.[108] Varying interpretations are not an inherent problem, so long as they do not negatively affect the welfare of the child involved.[109] However, some differences in interpretation are fundamentally unacceptable. For example, in some countries birth parents are intentionally misled or deceived into giving up their children for adoption. In Romania, some mothers were reportedly coerced into consenting to adoption, and subjected to physical violence from their partners, as well as threats from adoption facilitators.[110] Adoptive parents and adoption facilitators are 'often accomplices, or at least silent witnesses, to corrupt practices'.[111] However, such children are still deemed to be 'adoptable' because there is no requirement in the Adoption Convention to investigate exactly how children become available for adoption.[112]

Aside from interpretative concerns, there are practical issues to do with implementation. The Adoption Convention requires the setting up of a Central Authority in each country ratifying the Convention to ensure its objects are adhered to.[113] However, the reality is that in under-resourced countries the institutional frameworks the Adoption Convention requires cannot be set up due to a lack of funds. Consequently, children in those countries are not fully protected by the principles of the Adoption Convention.

The Adoption Convention does allow for intermediaries and private agencies to organize intercountry adoptions in some countries. Many of these agencies are corrupt and are motivated by profit, rather than the best interests of the children concerned.[114] There is no easy solution to this dilemma. In an ideal world, the agencies that handle intercountry adoption would be driven purely by the well-being of children. However, this is almost impossible to achieve globally, particularly considering the dire economic needs in many countries.

Rather than unduly restricting intercountry adoptions from such countries, which leaves some children in dismal circumstances with little hope of a future family life, it would be better

107 Dillon, op. cit., n 96, p. 255.

108 Ratcliff, op. cit., n 90, pp. 347–8.

109 See W. Duncan, 'Conflict and Co-Operation: The Approach to Conflicts of Law in the 1993 Hague Convention on Intercountry Adoption', in N. Lowe and G. Douglas (eds), *Families across Frontiers*, The Hague: Kluwer Law International, 1996, pp. 579–80.

110 Neagu, op. cit., n 78, p. 223.

111 Ibid.

112 K.S. Rotabi and J.L. Gibbons, 'Does the Hague Convention on Intercountry Adoption Adequately Protect Orphaned and Vulnerable Child and Their Families?', *Journal of Child and Family Studies* 21, 2012, 106–19.

113 Adoption Convention, Chapter III.

114 See J. Masson, 'Intercountry Adoption: A Global Problem or a Global Solution?', *Journal of International Affairs* 55, 2001, 141–67. See also J.G. Stein, 'An End to Baby Selling: Why the Hague Convention on Intercountry Adoption Should be Modified to Include the Consent Provisions of the Uniform Adoption Act', *Thomas Jefferson Law Review* 24, 2001, 39–82. See also Neagu, op. cit., n 78, 215–36; and J.L. Gibbons and K.S. Rotabi, *Intercountry Adoption: Policies, Practices, and Outcomes*, Surrey: Ashgate, 2012.

for wealthier countries to provide resources for those countries. Such resources could be targeted at creating structures to protect children from exploitation and enable adoption processes that enhance the well-being of children.[115] Dillon believes that the Adoption Convention will never work properly unless there is:

> a global fund to assist in the creation of national adoption departments or official agencies. A genuinely global regime, with the expertise and capacity to respond to national political furors on the subject of adoption, is necessary in order to bring an end to the uncertainty and uneven benefits to children.[116]

Whilst a 'global fund' is a good idea, financial backing for such a fund is unlikely to materialize any time soon. Even if such a regime was implemented, there is no guarantee that such national organizations would interpret, implement and enforce the Adoption Convention consistently across the globe, especially in countries with vastly different political and economic systems.

In addition to issues of implementation, enforcement of the Adoption Convention is a significant problem. Each Central Authority in each country is responsible for determining whether or not children's best interests are being met. If countries diverge from this standard, there is little that the Hague Convention can do in terms of enforcement. This needs to change. The best way to address adoption abuses is to place greater emphasis on enforcement and strengthening misconduct laws.[117]

International commercial surrogacy

The numbers of intercountry adoptions have dramatically reduced in recent years. This decline, caused by a variety of 'complex ethical' reasons, occurred simultaneously with the significant increase in international commercial surrogacy.[118] Commercial surrogacy contracts provide for women who provide pregnancy services (and sometimes their own biological material) to receive money for giving up their parental rights to the child once he or she is born. The legal ramifications of such arrangements are extremely complex. With intercountry adoption, once the State of origin's Central Authority confirms the adoption, it will be accepted by the receiving State. However, when a child is born into an international surrogacy agreement the surrogate mother is deemed to be the legal mother of the child. The commissioning parents have no legal parental relationship with the child, even if the child is the product of the commissioning parents' biological material. The only way commissioning parents can become legal parents is via adoption. However, the Adoption Convention was not designed to deal with this situation. This has been problematic in countries where surrogacy is illegal, such as in India, where some children born via surrogacy have been left stateless and their commissioning parents were unable to leave India with them.[119]

115 Masson, op. cit., n 114, p. 165, takes this one step further and believes that resources should be provided internationally to keep children with their birth families and that intercountry adoption should only be relied upon as a last resort.

116 Dillon, op. cit., n 96, p. 255.

117 Bartholet, op. cit., n 95, p. 98.

118 K.S. Rotabi and N.F. Bromfield, 'The Decline in Intercountry Adoption and New Practices of Global Surrogacy: Global Exploitation and Human Rights Concerns', *Affilia: Journal of Women and Social Work* 27, 2012, 129–41. See also Bartholet, op. cit., n 95, 97.

119 N. Bromfield and K. Rotabi, 'Global Surrogacy, Exploitation, Human Rights and International Private Law: A Pragmatic Stance and Policy Recommendations', *Global Social Welfare* 1, 2014, 123.

The same concerns regarding exploitation and socio-economic inequalities raised in relation to intercountry adoption can equally apply to international commercial surrogacy. On a macro scale, third-world countries may frequently participate in international commercial surrogacy out of financial necessity.[120] Likewise, there is a concern that some surrogate mothers have no real economic choice but to participate.[121] Alarmingly, there is also little research on the long-term health impacts of surrogacy on gestational carriers.

After several international controversies involving surrogacy, many lesser economically developed countries now restrict international commercial surrogacy. For example, India has prohibited foreign applicants from using commercial surrogacy services in an attempt to reduce exploitation.[122] Interviews with surrogates in India prior to the ban reveal the desperation of some surrogate mothers, who undertook the stigmatised role because financially they had little other choice.[123] Thailand, once a popular destination for commercial surrogacy, also prohibited commercial surrogacy in 2015 following several high profile cases. The most notable of which is referred to as the 'Baby Gammy' controversy, which involved a child born with Down Syndrome being abandoned by his Australian commissioning parents and being left in Thailand with his surrogate mother.[124]

In 2015, the Council on General Affairs and Policy of the Hague Conference convened an Experts' Group to explore better ways of addressing international commercial surrogacy.[125] The January/February 2019 meeting of the Experts' Group recommended the development of a general private international law instrument on the recognition of foreign judicial decisions on legal parentage, alongside a separate protocol on the recognition of legal parentage decisions arising from international surrogacy agreements.[126] The Group also suggested that future work in this area needed to consider 'other methods that could enhance the attractiveness and effectiveness of such instruments' such as the creation of uniform legal rules to determine legal parentage.[127]

There are differing opinions on whether the creation of a new private international law instrument would be effective, given the vastly different global approaches to international commercial surrogacy.[128] Any potential international commercial surrogacy legal framework that is developed will face many of the same interpretative, implementation and enforcement challenges as the Adoption Convention, with the added complication that some countries prohibit international commercial surrogacy altogether.[129] Any future framework will need to ensure

120 The countries that allow international commercial surrogacy include Ukraine, Russia and some American states (notably California and Florida). These places have consequently become destinations for couples seeking a child via surrogacy.

121 Rotabi and Bromfield, op. cit., n 118, 136.

122 See the Surrogacy (Regulation) Bill 2016.

123 Bromfield and Rotabi, op. cit., n 119, 123.

124 See *Farnell v Chanbua* [2016] FCWA 17; (2016) 56 Fam LR 84, [56] and [57].

125 Permanent Bureau of the Hague Conference on Private International Law, 'The Parentage/ Surrogacy Project', March 2019. Available at www.hcch.net (accessed 10 January 2020).

126 Permanent Bureau of the Hague Conference on Private International Law, 'Report of the Experts' Group on the Parentage / Surrogacy Project', March 2019 Available at www.hcch.net (accessed 10 January 2020), p. 6.

127 Ibid.

128 C. Fenton-Glynn and J.M. Scherpe, 'Surrogacy in a Globalised World: Comparative Analysis and Thoughts on Regulation', in J.M. Scherpe, C. Fenton-Glynn and T. Kaan (eds), *Eastern and Western Perspectives on Surrogacy*, Cambridge: Intersentia, 2019, p. 572.

129 Several countries, including France, Italy, Germany, China and Japan ban surrogacy arrangements altogether, even if no commercial element is present in the agreement. Other countries such as the United Kingdom, Australia, New Zealand, Israel, and the Netherlands allow altruistic surrogacy only.

surrogates are protected from exploitation, that their health and well-being is protected, and that they receive a fair payment for their services. This is particularly important given the differing standards worldwide on what is deemed exploitative.[130] It is also essential that the child's right to know their identity, particularly their genetic identity, is preserved.[131] Any future framework would also need to clearly address parentage and citizenship issues. Failing to recognize the parentage and citizenship of children born via international surrogacy leaves these children in legal limbo and disconnects them from typically loving and nurturing commissioning parents. Such complexities make it unlikely that a new Convention will be introduced any time in the immediate future, despite a real need for change in this area.

Conclusion

International conventions, such as the Abduction and Adoption Conventions, have a part to play in protecting the best interests of children across the world. However, such Conventions inevitably have limitations that need to be carefully balanced when developing future policies to more effectively address international child abduction and intercountry adoption.

The policy of return at the heart of the Abduction Convention needs careful scrutiny, especially in cases involving family violence, whereby returning children may not always be in their best interests. Children's views are important and should be a respected part of all abduction proceedings, especially if a child objects to being returned. The interpretation difficulties that plague the Abduction Convention need to be better addressed, as does the problem of how best to deal with non-convention countries.

The Adoption Convention does not adequately acknowledge the significant power imbalances and market forces that are involved in intercountry adoptions. The fundamental socio-economic, cultural and political differences between birth parents and adoptive parents need to be carefully measured to ensure that intercountry adoption cannot be aligned in any way with international child trafficking. This needs to be coupled with a detailed examination of how to protect the welfare and best interests of children on a global scale. In the future, Adoption Convention policies must confront classic interpretation, implementation and enforcement problems, and contemplate how to more effectively deal with international commercial surrogacy.

This chapter has demonstrated the ways in which the Abduction and Adoption Conventions are out of step with the realities of many family situations. More empirical research is needed to analyze the effects of international child abduction and intercountry adoption on children. This data should be used to inform much needed future reforms of the Abduction Convention and the Adoption Convention and the creation of a new 'Parentage Convention' for international commercial surrogacy to ensure the best interests of children are really being met.

130 C. Fenton-Glynn, 'Outsourcing Ethical Dilemmas: Regulating International Surrogacy Arrangements', *Medical Law Review* 24(1), 2016, 69.

131 See R. Ballantyne, *Legal Parentage 'By Design': Reimagining Birth Certificates in Aotearoa New Zealand*, LLM Thesis, Wellington: Victoria University of Wellington, 2019, pp. 36–85.

7.2

CHILDREN IN CROSS-BORDER SITUATIONS

Relocation, the 1996 Hague Convention and the Brussels IIa Regulation

Rob George

Introduction

One of the biggest policy challenges for family law in an increasingly globalized society is the creation of effective international legal instruments to protect children who are involved in cross-border situations. The global community has responded to these challenges in a number of ways. Some approaches have focused on particular policy challenges, such as international child abduction or international child adoption (both of which are addressed in Chapter 7.1 of this book),[1] while others have been broader in their scope. This chapter discusses the policy challenges inherent in formulating such international legal instruments and the policy challenges which arise in terms of their interpretation and implementation once in force. To explore these challenges, two case studies are used. The first, which looks at the challenge of agreeing an international approach in the first place, comes from the law of relocation disputes. The second, looking at the challenges arising once an international legal instrument is in place, is the working of the 1996 Hague Convention on Parental Responsibility and Protection of Children[2] and the 2003 Brussels IIa Regulation.[3] The Regulation makes for a particularly interesting example of policymaking: already in its second iteration,[4] the Regulation was 'recast' by the European Union in June 2019,[5] and the new version will enter force in August 2022.[6]

1 See the Hague Convention of 25 October 1980 on the Civil Aspects of International Child Abduction and the Hague Convention of 29 May 1993 on the Protection of Children and Co-operation in Respect of Intercountry Adoption on Intercountry Adoption.
2 The full title is the Convention on jurisdiction, applicable law, recognition, enforcement and co-operation in respect of parental responsibility and measures for the protection of children.
3 Council Regulation (EC) No 2201/2003 of 27 November 2003 concerning jurisdiction and the recognition and enforcement of judgments in matrimonial matters and the matters of parental responsibility.
4 The first version was Council Regulation (EC) 1347/2000.
5 Council Regulation (EU) 2019/1111 of 25 June 2019 on jurisdiction, the recognition and enforcement of decisions in matrimonial matters and the matters of parental responsibility, and on international child abduction.
6 Art. 100.

Relocation: a search for international agreement?

Relocation disputes involve conflict over the question of whether one parent (or other holder of parental responsibility) ought to be allowed to move with their child over a considerable geographic distance, whether to a new country, a new town, or even a new part of the same city. A particular feature of recent years has been the increasing awareness of, and concern about, the different ways in which legal jurisdictions around the world approach relocation cases. Most countries which make use of a version of the welfare principle in child law in general agree that relocation disputes should also be determined based on the outcome that is best for the child. However, given the general indeterminacy of a welfare approach to any child law decision-making,[7] it is unsurprising that in relocation disputes, which revolve almost entirely around predictions about uncertain possible futures, different jurisdictions have adopted different interpretations of what is meant by 'welfare'.

Put at its most basic,[8] these different approaches can be summarized in three main groups.[9] At one end of the spectrum are so-called pro-relocation jurisdictions, where proposals to relocate are thought to be generally favoured. There are two main clusters of jurisdictions in this group. One, typically found in civilian legal systems, have no specific mechanism for preventing a relocation by a parent who is the child's main carer. In France, for instance, although there is a requirement to notify the other parent of a proposed move,[10] the only way to prevent relocation is to transfer the child's residence, and that is not usually a favoured approach.[11] The other cluster of jurisdictions comes from the common law world. A few of these jurisdictions can be identified by express statutory provisions,[12] but most are identified by case law which indicates an important link between the child's welfare and the well-being and happiness of that child's primary carer.[13] These jurisdictions are thought to look favourably on well-planned and bona fides applications to relocate, because they consider that the effect on a primary carer of restricting his or (more commonly) her life choices will impact on the child more adversely in the long term than the reduction of contact with the other parent and the other upheavals of relocation. Examples of this approach include some US states such as New Jersey, Washington and Minnesota. England and Wales was previously seen to be in this cluster, but recent trends suggest that it is no longer appropriate to consider this jurisdiction to be significantly pro-relocation.[14]

At the other end of the relocation spectrum are the so-called anti-relocation jurisdictions. Again, there are both common law and civil law jurisdictions represented here. From the civilian perspective, Sweden offers a good example (on post-separation parenting issues in Sweden and other Scandinavian countries, see Chapter 3.5 in this book). Swedish law favours joint parental

7 See generally R. Mnookin, 'Child-Custody Adjudication: Judicial Functions in the Face of Indeterminacy', *Law and Contemporary Problems* 39, 1975, 226–93.

8 See further R. George, *Relocation Disputes: Law and Practice in England and New Zealand*, Oxford: Hart Publishing, 2014, ch. 1.

9 See T. Foley, *International Child Relocation: Varying Approaches among Member States to the 1980 Hague Convention on Child Abduction*, London: Court of Appeal, 2006.

10 Code Civil, Art 373–2.

11 See H. Baker, J. Hirsch and N. Sauvage, 'International Family Relocation from an English, French and German Perspective', *International Family Law* 2012, 97.

12 See, for example, the US state of Washington, where § 26.09.520 of the Revised Code states that '[t]here is a rebuttable presumption that the intended relocation of the child will be permitted'.

13 See, eg, *Payne v Payne* [2001] EWCA Civ 166, [2001] 1 FLR 1052, or the minority judgment of L'Heureux-Dubé J in *Gordon v Goertz* [1996] 2 SCR 27.

14 See generally R. George, F Judd, D. Garrido and A. Worwood, *Relocation: A Practical Guide*, 2nd edition, Bristol: Jordan Publishing, 2016, chs 1 and 2.

responsibility (PR), and has no mechanism for allowing a relocation if both parents have PR. The only option is for the parent who seeks to move to apply to the court for an order removing the other parent's PR in relation to the child, and courts are reluctant to do so. In the common law world, anti-relocation jurisdictions are identified either by explicit statutory provisions,[15] or by general principles from case law or statutes which highlight the importance to the child's welfare of maintaining a strong and positive relationship with both parents in the event of parental separation.[16] Since relocation, almost by definition, involves a major change, and often a major diminution, in the child's relationship with one parent, these jurisdictions tend not to favour relocation applications. Examples of these jurisdictions are said to include Australia, Sweden, Norway and some US states, such as Pennsylvania, Alabama, Virginia and Connecticut.

In between these two groups we find the so-called neutral jurisdictions, whose legal approaches do not give especial weight to either of these considerations and purport to look at every application with no preconceived ideas about what will be most important to the child or children involved. Jurisdictions which are said to fall within the 'neutral' group include Canada, Belgium and US states such as New York, California and Florida. England and Wales is probably now part of this group.

These variations in approach explain at least some of the reason why international discussions started to consider whether a (more) uniform approach to relocation disputes might be found. However, the policy context of relocation disputes is only indirectly a matter of cross-border concern.

Relocation disputes are often linked in legal thinking with international child abduction cases (as to which, see Chapter 7.1 of this book),[17] but the context is crucially different. By the time a child has been moved across an international border, there is no doubt that there is an international legal problem to be resolved, and this international problem justifies an international response. In the relocation context, however, this matter is less clear, particularly as so-called internal relocation cases (i.e. moves within a country) are now frequently litigated in the same way as international ones.[18] While for some countries with no land borders it might be plausible to adopt different legal approaches to internal and international moves, for countries with numerous land borders a difference of approach may appear wholly artificial in practice.

The Hague Conference on Private International Law has been involved in discussions about whether international relocation ought to be a matter to which it gave attention.[19]

15 See, for example, the US state of Connecticut: Conn Gen Stats § 46b–56d, which specifies that

> the relocating parent shall bear the burden of proving, by a preponderance of the evidence, that (1) the relocation is for a legitimate purpose, (2) the proposed location is reasonable in light of such purpose, and (3) the relocation is in the best interests of the child.

16 Although over-taken by a Supreme Court decision with a different approach, the New Zealand Court of Appeal decision in *Bashir v Kacem* [2010] NZCA 96, [2010] NZFLR 865 is a good example.

17 See, eg, W. Duncan, *Transfrontier Access/Contact and the Hague Convention of 25 October 1980 on the Civil Aspects of International Child Abduction: A Preliminary Report*, Preliminary Document No. 4 of February 2001, The Hague: Hague Conference on Private International Law, 2001; Permanent Bureau, *Preliminary Note on International Family Relocation*, Preliminary Document No. 11 of January 2012, The Hague: Hague Conference on Private International Law, 2012, [12]–[16].

18 See, eg, *Re C (Internal Relocation)* [2015] EWCA Civ 1305, [2016] Fam 253.

19 Permanent Bureau, *Guide To Part II of the Sixth Meeting of the Special Commission and Consideration of the Desirability and Feasibility of Further Work in Connection with the 1980 and 1996 Conventions*, Preliminary Document No. 13 of November 2011, The Hague: Hague Conference on Private International Law, 2011; R. George, 'The International Relocation Debate', *Journal of Social Welfare and Family Law* 34, 2012, 141–52.

In January 2012, two issues received broad agreement from the countries represented at The Hague. The first was that wider ratification of the 1996 Hague Convention on Child Protection and related matters was highly desirable, both in general and especially in the context of assisting with ancillary matters arising after an international relocation.[20] Second, the Conference noted the Washington Declaration on International Family Relocation 2010, which was a statement produced following a conference of mostly judicial delegates and which proposed some guidelines for factors to consider when determining relocation disputes. The Conference found the Declaration to be an interesting and useful document, but there were concerns about parts of its substantive content from some delegates. More generally, the conference was clear that the Declaration was not suitable for implementation into national (or binding international) law, not least because that was not its intended purpose.

However, when it came to the key question of whether the Hague Conference ought to work on relocation itself, there was a lack of consensus. Some states were keen for work to be done with a view to creating an international legal document (whether freestanding or annexed to an existing Convention). Others questioned whether the Hague Conference had any jurisdiction to deal with what was seen as the harmonization of domestic law. Delegates from these states expressed the view that, although international relocation cases have international consequences involving another country, the relocation dispute itself is entirely contained within the country of original residence. Whether the relocation is allowed or refused under domestic law, the case may go on to have an international dimension, but that dimension can be seen as being within the purview of existing international provisions.[21] It is notable that these discussions appear to have come to a close, with little sustained interest in this area over the last few years. While individual states have seen developments in their law and practice regarding relocation, there are few indications that relocation is likely to be the subject of any international legal agreement in the near future.

Applying an international approach

The debates about the potential harmonization of relocation law give insight into the policy challenges that exist in the creation of international legal instruments. The difficulty arises primarily from two issues. One is the seceding of jurisdiction over an issue to an international body as a matter of principle; the other is more practical, in terms of agreeing what the international approach should be. Whereas some areas, like child abduction, have a reasonably clear position which most states adopt, other areas are far more diverse. As explored in this chapter, relocation is one of those areas with a wide range of approaches adopted among states.

A greater degree of success in finding a common approach is seen when it comes to matters of jurisdiction and the recognition and enforcement of orders in relation to children who move internationally. Two legal instruments that adopt this approach will be considered here, namely the 1996 Hague Child Protection Convention and the Brussels IIa Regulation. The relevant

20 For example, the 1996 Convention allows for court orders made in the departure state in relation to the child's ongoing contact and residence arrangements to be automatically recognized and enforced in the new state of residence, if both states have implemented the Convention. See generally N. Lowe and M. Nicholls, *The 1996 Hague Convention on the Protection of Children*, Bristol: Jordan Publishing, 2012.

21 The key provisions are the 1980 Hague Convention on the Civil Aspects of International Child Abduction, the 1996 Hague Convention on the Protection of Children, and (within the European Union) the Brussels IIa Regulation.

parts of the two instruments are based on the same principles,[22] and so can, at the risk of some over-simplification, be considered to be performing the same overall functions. However, the review of the Brussels IIa Regulation, which started in 2016 and culminated with a 'recast' version of the Regulation being approved in 2019, offers an interesting insight into the policy challenges, as well as some of the practical difficulties which international family law can face.

The overarching policy aim of the Convention is 'to improve the protection of children in international situations',[23] and that aim is pursued with five main objectives:[24]

1 to determine the state which has jurisdiction to take measure to protect the child;
2 to determine the law which should be applied by that state in exercising jurisdiction;
3 to determine the law on parental responsibility;
4 to provide for the recognition and enforcement of measures for the protection of children; and
5 to enhance international cooperation between states to achieve these objectives.

In pursuing these aims, 'the best interests of the child are to be a primary consideration'.[25]

Much the same objectives can be found in the Preamble to the Regulation,[26] though the Regulation is also broader in its scope (in particular, it also governs international child abduction within the EU; the 1996 Hague Convention does not address abduction directly, though its provisions can be used to respond to abduction[27]). In cases where either the Regulation or the Convention could apply, the Regulation takes precedence.[28]

While both the Convention and the Regulation are complex legal instruments covering a multitude of family law situations, the focus here is on the mutual recognition and enforcement of orders relating to children in international situations. The idea is simply that orders about residence or contact, say, which are made in State A (which is the child's original country of habitual residence), should be automatically recognized and enforced by a court in State B (to which the child lawfully relocates or visits after the order is made), so long as both states are either signatories to the Convention or are subject to the Regulation.[29] So long as the order is made in the right form, all that needs to be done for it to become effective in State B is for it to be registered there.[30]

One policy challenge in this area is simply in getting states to sign up to the Convention. At time of writing, 56 states had signed the 1996 Convention and it was in force in 52, including all EU countries,[31] compared with the 1980 child abduction Convention's 100 contracting states. It is fair to say that the number of signatory states is increasing fast.

However, the bigger challenge may lie in the effective implementation of the rules. The Brussels IIa Regulation demonstrates this difficulty. While the Regulation in its original and

22 The Regulation is effectively a modified copy of the Convention, applicable between EU States (except Denmark).
23 1996 Hague Convention, Preamble.
24 1996 Hague Convention, art. 1.
25 1996 Hague Convention, Preamble.
26 Brussels IIa, Preamble, especially paras (12), (13), (21), (23) and (25); Brussels IIa recast, Preamble, especially paras (2), (6), (16), (19), (39) and (54).
27 *Re J (1996 Hague Convention: Morocco)* [2015] UKSC 70, [2016] AC 1291.
28 Brussels IIa, art. 61. For intra-EU (except those involving Denmark), the Convention applies only to substantive matters not covered by the Convention. The Convention applies to cases involving children moving from EU to non-EU states which are Convention signatories.
29 Denmark is not covered by the Regulation, but is a signatory to the Convention.
30 Brussels IIa, art. 21.
31 For a list of contracting states, see www.hcch.net/index_en.php?act=conventions.status&cid=70.

2003 versions intended to provide a more effective version of the Convention for use within the EU, significant challenges arose.[32] By 2016, concerns were such that the European Commission proposed reforms, and the 2019 'recast' version of the Regulation is claimed 'to make court proceedings clearer, faster and more efficient'.[33] The 'recast' Regulation aims to: resolve child abduction cases within the EU faster; to ensure that children are heard in all matters governed by the Regulation; to ensure effective enforcement of decisions between Member States; to improve cooperation between states' authorities; and to set out clearer rules on the circulation of authentic legal instruments and agreements.[34] Those claims in themselves offer an interesting insight into the problems that were experienced with the 2003 version of the Regulation.

These are laudable aims, and it is one of the benefits of the EU's legal structure that it is possible to revisit and revise legal provisions so that amendments can be made which incorporate best practice and address problem areas. Beyond the EU, however, such processes are far harder to implement. While the Regulation was originally modelled on the 1996 Convention – and, indeed, still bears much similarity to it after the 2019 revisions – the Regulation is able to adapt and grow. There is no equivalent mechanism for the 1996 Hague Convention, and drafting a new Convention would be an arduous process, both in terms of agreeing to the provisions and in terms of getting states to sign up. While there has been notable progress in increasing the number of signatories to the Convention, it is nearly 25 years old and many states which might have been thought 'obvious' ones to sign up – such as New Zealand – have not yet done so.

Discussion

There are two likely underlying causes of the common policy challenges arising from the debate about the internationalization of relocation law and the debate about the implementation of the 1996 Convention and the EU Regulation. The first comes down to a lack of trust between the courts of different states.[35] It is notable that the 'recast' Brussels IIa Regulation opens by stating that

> [m]utual trust in the administration of justice in the Union justifies the principle that decisions in matrimonial matters and in matters of parental responsibility given in a Member State should be recognised in all Member States without the need for any recognition procedure.[36]

As Peter McEleavy notes regarding the previous version of the Regulation, 'trust' in that context is 'an assertion which is imposed and is strictly policed', but trust loses something of its essential character if it is 'imposed' in this way: as McEleavy says, if trust does not really exist, it may manifest itself as a reluctance to abide by the rules.[37] Until trust is developed 'from the ground up, with practitioners, officials and judges all working in a spirit of openness, collaboration and understanding',[38] these differences in interpretation are unlikely to be resolved.

32 Some of these were discussed in the First Edition of this book.
33 European Commission Press Release, Adoption of new rules to better protect children caught in cross-border parental disputes, MEMO/19/3374 (25 June 2019).
34 Ibid.
35 P. McEleavy, 'The Movement of Children in Europe: Mutual Trust, Distrust and Human Rights', *International Family Law* 2013, 172.
36 Brussels IIa recast, Preamble, para (54).
37 Ibid., p. 172.
38 Ibid., p. 175.

The second and connected likely cause of the difficulty comes from core legal principles applied in national courts around the world. One of those is the welfare principle, whereby the best interests of each child shall be the paramount consideration for a court deciding a case concerning the child's upbringing; another is international human rights instruments such as the European Convention on Human Rights or the United Nations Convention on the Rights of the Child. There is a potential policy tension between these legal principles and some provisions of internationalized family law. In the child abduction context, this tension is highly visible in the debate about whether a court seized in an abduction matter is entitled to order that the child be summarily returned to his or her country of habitual residence, as called for by the 1980 Hague Convention and the Brussels IIa Regulation, or whether the court is required to conduct an in-depth welfare examination to determine whether the child should be returned or not, as demanded by the European Court of Human Rights.[39]

Although less vividly expressed, similar tensions are found in other contexts. If a court in state A has made an order in relation to a child which the court in state B considers to be contrary to the child's best interests, should it enforce that order, or would doing so place the court in breach of its duty to do what it thinks best for the child? Suppose that the order were one which stopped a parent from having any contact with the child, but which the court in state B (being a signatory to the European Convention on Human Rights) doubted was justified; should the court enforce that order, or would doing so place the court in state B in violation of its positive obligations under the European Convention?[40]

In the relocation context, these tensions have so far led to stalemate in terms of proposals to internationalize the legal approach to such cases, but experience in other contexts may give cause to question whether an international agreement would, in practice, lead to more conformity of practice. In child abduction cases and matters falling under the 1996 Convention and the EU Regulation, there is an international situation already in existence; while there is clearly some way to go, the involvement of different states in individual cases (and, within the EU, an overarching judicial body to resolve conflicts) allows for a degree of optimism that greater consistency will come with time. For relocation cases, on the other hand, there is no international element when the national court determines the dispute and so, given the strong influence of national-level family law norms – in particular, the welfare principle with its myriad of interpretations around the world – it seems doubtful that a truly harmonized approach would be achieved even if international agreement were reached.

39 See *Neulinger v Switzerland* (No 41615/07) [2011] 1 FLR 122; *X v Latvia* (No 27853/09) [2012] 2 FLR 860. The UK Supreme Court described this approach as having 'caused wide-spread concern and even consternation' and as being 'entirely inappropriate': *Re S (Abduction: Rights of Custody)* [2012] UKSC 10, [2012] 2 FLR 442, [37]–[38].

40 See, eg, *Elsholz v Germany* (No 25735/94) [2000] 2 FLR 486.

7.3

DIVIDED AND UNITED ACROSS BORDERS

A global overview of family migration

*Jacqueline Bhabha**

Introduction

In her chapter for the First Edition of this Handbook, Helen Stalford notes that UK family migration 'epitomizes the complex challenges associated with asserting personal rights in a public law context'.[1] This statement does not just apply to the UK. With international migration now at nearly 272 million, or 3.5 percent of the global population, very large numbers of families and states across the globe are affected by cross-border mobility, its many social and economic consequences and the legal challenges it presents.[2] And because migration is inherently relational – it impacts the social environment of the person moving, not just his or her individual status – its consequences have repercussions that spill over to relatives who may never have moved, or who moved at very different times from the migrant under consideration. What is more, the consequences of an individual's migration for family are both direct – the impact on the enjoyment of the right to family life – and mediated – the impact on the health or well-being of relatives left behind, the legal and citizenship status of future offspring, the organization of economies of caring and intimacy, the exposure to risk and trauma for family members seeking reunification. It follows that deciding what to include in an overview of family migration requires the exercise of a somewhat arbitrary selection process.

This overview will focus on two key areas. First, it will consider international migration policies relating to the two core aspects of family unity, maintaining unity in the face of legal threats and promoting unity where there has been family separation. Second, the overview will explore how public policies affect individuals who use cross-border migration – typically migration for work or for marriage (or both) – as a family-strengthening or economic-survival strategy, even though the family as a whole does not migrate. Both sets of migration policies affect core public law domains including governments' interests in maintaining border security, promoting political and cultural agendas, enhancing domestic economic development and protecting law and order. But they also impinge on the private interests of immigrant family members in realizing

* I would like to acknowledge the superb research support of Samuel Peisch.

1 J. Eekelaar and R. George (eds), *Routledge Handbook of Family Law and Policy*, Abingdon: Routledge, 2014, p. 691.

2 UN DESA, International Migrant Stock 2019, September 2019. Available at www.unmigration.org.

their aspirations for safety, freedom, self-fulfilment and prosperity. For reasons of space, this overview will not cover internal or seasonal migration, though this type of migration is hugely impactful, especially for the very poorest families, nor will it address executive transfers or corporate family relocations, though this type of migration also has a sizeable economic, cultural and social effect, typically on highly privileged families.

The multifaceted terrain that migration-affected families have to contend with to protect rights taken for granted by those who do not leave their homes spans a vast spectrum. It includes deft navigation of interlocking regimes of law, policy, administrative practice and bureaucratic discretion. These stretch from immigration regulations that probe the authenticity of familial relationships (is this a 'genuine' marriage or a 'marriage of convenience'?) to social policies that determine eligibility for public services ('can undocumented children be enrolled in state school'; 'will using emergency public medical care be considered a public charge that disqualifies the patient from immigration benefits'?), from taxation rules that determine permissible subsidies ('can a male head of household claim child benefits for children from polygamous marriages'?) to nationality regulations that govern transmission of citizenship ('do children born stateless to refugees have a right to the nationality of the host country in which they are born'?). An overarching set of issues concerns the mechanisms used by states to balance the needs and rights of members of migrating families with the needs of states to protect their borders, their economies, their cultural (and often racial) priorities and national security.

Protecting and promoting family unity

Protecting or promoting family unity is a primary focus of families affected by migration. Though national governments differ in their laws and policies in this area – in the income thresholds they require for sponsoring heads of household, in the definitions of family (and in particular of 'child') they apply, in the housing requirements they stipulate for dependents – certain overarching principles, and challenges associated with enforcing them, recur across jurisdictions.[3] A central principle reflects the universal human rights norm, widely codified in international, regional and domestic law, that the family is a fundamental social unit that requires protection against arbitrary or unlawful interference.[4] In the migration context, this principle translates into recognition of a state obligation to respect the enjoyment by migrants of their family life, by according them the right to keep or bring their family with them.[5] However states' obligations to respect immigrants' family unity are not unqualified.[6] Other state obligations, to maintain law and order, or to protect public health and public security, can come into conflict with the immigrants' enjoyment of family unity. A balancing act is thus required between the private interest in the enjoyment of family life, especially the child's

3 M.L. Hawthorne, 'Family Unity in Immigration Law: Broadening the Scope of "Family"', *Lewis and Clark Law Review* 11(3), 2007, 809–33.

4 UDHR art. 16(3); ICCPR art. 23(1); CRC art. 9; ECHR art. 8; American Convention on Human Rights art. 17(1); African Charter on Human and People's Rights art. 18(1).

5 For an overview of the right to family life of refugees and other distress migrants, see Frances Nicholson, 'The Right to Family Life and Family Unity of Refugees and Others in Need of International Protection and the Family Definition Applied', UNHCR Division of International Protection January 2018.

6 H. Lambert, 'Family Unity in Migration Law: The Evolution of a More Unified Approach in Europe', in V. Chétail and C. Bauloz (eds), *Research Handbook on International Law and Migration*, Cheltenham: Edward Elgar Press, 2014, pp. 195–6.

interests in avoiding separation from parents, and the public imperatives dictated by state security and sovereignty.[7]

In terms of protecting already cohabiting families from separation (maintaining family unity), states differ in the balances they strike. At one end of the spectrum are European states, that have tempered the exclusionary impact of deportation proceedings against non-nationals with careful consideration of countervailing factors related to immigrant family well-being. At the other end of the spectrum is the US, which privileges state interest in enforcing the deportation of so-called criminal aliens over all other considerations, except in 'the most extreme and exceptionally compassionate circumstances', a virtually insuperable bar, even for families with US citizen children.[8] As a result, a sharp contrast exists. Family unity in Europe can, in general, be maintained unless a heinous crime or weak familial relationship or an unproblematic family relocation abroad countermands this. By contrast, in the US nothing less than proof of mortal danger is the threshold for discretionary relief from deportation for a non-citizen convicted of a felony, even where affected relatives are US citizens or permanent residents.[9]

Variations in state practice

When it comes to promoting family unity (reunifying separated families), many states have policies that honor the family unity principle for immigrants granted lawful permanent or long-term residence, but not for migrants on short-term or otherwise limited visas.[10] In South Africa, for example, family reunification and permanent residence is allowed for 'certain family members' of permanent residents, including spouses married to citizens or permanent residents for at least five years and, provided the sponsor can demonstrate the ability to maintain them, children and parents too.[11] In South America, growing regional coordination, both within the Mercosur and the Andean Community blocs, has promoted a rights-respecting approach to migration, includ-

7 The importance of family unity for migration affected children is emphasized in the Joint General Comment on this topic prepared by the Committee on the Protection of the Rights of All Migrant Workers and Members of their Families and the Committee on the Rights of the Child, see Joint General Comment No. 3 (2017) of the Committee on the Protection of the Rights of All Migrant Workers and Members of Their Families and No. 22 (2017) of the Committee on the Rights of the Child on the general principles regarding the human rights of children in the context of international migration, CMW/C/GC/3-CRC/C/GC/22, 16 November 2017. Available at www.refworld.org/docid/5a2f9fc34.html, para 29.

8 8 C.F.R. § 1239.2(f). 62 FR 10366, Mar. 6, 1997. Duplicated from part 239 at 68 FR 9838, 28 February, 2003, as amended at 69 FR 44907, July 28, 2004. Available at www.govregs.com/regulations/expand/title8_chapterV_part1239_section1239.1.

9 J. Bhabha, *Child Migration and Human Rights in a Global Age*, Princeton: Princeton University Press, 2014, pp. 88–90.

10 There are exceptions to this general norm however. In the US, unaccompanied migrant children granted 'special immigrant juvenile status', a permanent status for abused, abandoned or neglected minors, are prohibited from ever bringing their parents to join them, even if they become US citizens. V. Thronson, 'The Impact of Special Immigrant Juvenile Status on Access to Protection', in. J. Bhabha, J. Kanics and D. Senovilla-Hernandez (eds), *Research Handbook on Child Migration*, Cheltenham: Edward Elgar, 2018, p. 235. In the UAE, foreign workers are regularly denied the right to bring their families with or to join them, even when they spend decades lawfully working, through the device of limited term, though renewable, visas.

11 Immigration Act 13 of 2002, § 26, 15 Butterworths Statutes of the Republic of South Africa (updated through 2012), available on the University of Pretoria website, at www.lawsofsouthafrica.up.ac.za/index. php/browse/citizens-and-foreigners/immigration-act-13-of-2002/act/13-of-2002-immigration-act-26-may-2014-to-date-pdf/download.

ing family reunification, for nationals of the relevant regional bloc. In Argentina, for example, family reunification is available to spouses, parents, minor unmarried and adult disabled children for both citizens and permanent residents.[12] In addition, the 2002 Mercosur Residence Agreement, in particular, affords migrants generous human rights protections, including the right to live and work in another Mercosur state for two years, to exercise family reunification rights within that time period, and to transform the two-year permit into a right to permanent residency for the whole family. Though the operation of the Agreement has not been without its problems, what emerges is an encouraging approach to the promotion of legal and rights respecting migration opportunity within the South American region. However, recent developments, including electoral shifts and severe economic crises in some key South American states, especially Venezuela, combined with heightened pressure exerted by the United States government on Mexican and Central American countries to curb cross-continental migration, have increased the challenges of delivering on the vision of South American free mobility celebrated at the start of this century.[13]

Some states extend family reunion rights to temporary workers, but discriminate between highly qualified and less qualified workers on term visas, according family unity privileges only to the former. In Russia, for example, only highly skilled foreign workers enjoy the right to bring their families with them.[14] The same is true, on a massive scale, in the states of the Gulf Cooperation Council, the third largest global migration destination (after the United States and the European Union). Whereas migrant workers form a small minority of the population of the US, the EU and Russia, they constitute a sizeable majority of the population residing in the Gulf. In these states, most migrants – the vast majority from South Asia – occupy unskilled or semi-skilled positions, with wage levels below the level required by the GCC states to exercise family reunification. Though they constitute a core driver of the region's economic miracle, these single migrants constitute a de-facto permanent proletarian underclass in the society. Forced to inhabit 'bachelor cities', de facto segregated dormitory spaces on the outskirts of the Gulf cities, the migrant workers pay for their increased earning prospects by trading the enjoyment of family life, of access to social membership or the prospects of integration. In many ways, their circumstances mirror those of African migrant workers in apartheid South Africa and Turkish and Yugoslav guest workers in Western Europe half a century ago.[15] This form of enforced family separation is not chosen but imposed. It is a reflection of dramatic global income inequality. But it also demonstrates the failure of the migrant workers' home governments to instrumentalize the leverage afforded them by their migrating citizens to insist on the enforcement of fundamental human rights.[16]

12 Library of Congress – Family Reunification Law Review, July 2014. At law@loc.gov.

13 D. Acosta, 'Free Movement in South America? The Emergence of an Alternative Model?', *Migration Policy Institute*. Available at www.migrationpolicy.org/article/free-movement-south-america-emergence-alternative-model.

14 O. Chudinovskikh and M. Denisenko, 'Russia: A Migration System with Soviet Roots', *Migration Policy Institute*, May 18, 2017. Available at www.migrationpolicy.org/article/russia-migration-system-soviet-roots.

15 A.M. Gardner, 'Gulf Migration and the Family', *Journal of Arabian Studies* 1(1), 2011, 3–25.

16 The governments of other large labor exporting countries such as the Philippines and Indonesia have done far better than their South Asian counterparts. 'Labour Migration in Asia: Protection of Migrant Workers, Support Services, and Enhancing Development Benefits', *IOM International Organization for Migration*, 2005. Available at https://publications.iom.int/system/files/pdf/labour_migration_asia_2.pdf; 'Labour Migration from Indonesia: An Overview of Indonesian Migration to Selected Destinations in Asia and the Middle East', *IOM International Organization for Migration*, 2010, Available at www.iom.int/jahia/webdav/shared/shared/mainsite/published_docs/Final-LM-Report-English.pdf.

Whereas the ability to initiate family reunification rights was long limited to qualified male heads of household, evidencing the widely diffused, patriarchal assumption that family reunification was about wives and children joining male migrant workers, increasing feminization of migration and concurrent diffusion of non-discrimination human rights norms have generated more inclusive and gender neutral policies.[17] A growing number of states extend family unity rights not only to the male spouses of female migrant workers, but beyond heterosexual married couples and their biological relatives to same-sex couples, to cohabitees, to adopted children and other relatives (in ascending and descending lines) linked by social rather than biological ties.[18] In Australia, for example, homosexual couples can 'reunite' as long as they can prove their relationship has existed for more than a year.[19]

Obstacles to qualification

Closely connected to the wide diffusion of the family unity principle in migration law and policy is a pervasive challenge: establishing the requisite proof that the persons asserting a family relationship are related as claimed. States have long questioned the claims asserted by migrants, whether because documentary proof of the stated relationship is unavailable or deemed inadequate, or because other aspects of the relationship – proof of the requisite financial support, accuracy of answers to probing questions designed to test intimate familial knowledge, DNA matching – fail to satisfy stipulated regulations. As a result, the path to family reunification is often fraught and protracted, exposing migrant families to the heartache of prolonged separation, and to arduous and costly legal procedures to meet documentary and other evidentiary requirements. Even when these challenges are met, stringent entry quotas regularly delay reunion, forcing children to live out significant portions of their childhood separated from parents and to enter new school systems too late to catch up with language or academic skill acquisition.[20]

A particularly challenging obstacle race regularly confronts female migrant workers, forced to leave their children behind in the care of relatives, as they embark on international migration to support them. When economic and legal circumstances enable them to qualify for family reunification, often after years of enforced separation, many have faced unexpected hurdles reflecting bias against female headed households. Long-settled domestic workers have been denied the right to bring their minor children to join them, either because contractual clauses prohibit such reunion or because they do not fulfil stipulated accommodation or income requirements. In other cases, single mothers have encountered legal difficulties proving that they have maintained 'sole responsibility' for or an 'effective family bond' with their children back home, despite evidence of regular remittances and correspondence.[21] In short, the fundamental norm that mandates family protection by the state is often qualified, in the case of migrant families, by policies

17 See J.M. Calvo, 'Spouse-Based Immigration Laws: The Legacies of Coverture', *San Diego L Rev* 28, 1991, 593, 595–600, cited in K. Abrams, 'What Makes the Family Special?', *University of Chicago Law Review* 80(7), 2013, at n 8. See also 1969 American Convention on Human Rights, arts 11 and 17; African Charter of Human and People's Rights, art. 18(1).

18 Library of Congress–Family Reunification Law Review, July 2014. At law@loc.gov.

19 'Comparative Analysis of the Legislation and the Procedures Governing the Immigration of Family Members in Certain OECD Countries', *OECD*. Available at www.oecd.org/els/mig/41563157.pdf (accessed 12 October 2019).

20 Bhabha, op. cit., n 8, pp. 19–59.

21 J. Bhabha and S. Shutter, *Women's Movement: Women under Immigration, Nationality and Refugee Law*, Stoke-on-Trent, UK: Trentham Books, 1994, pp. 129–97; S.K. van Walsum, 'Transnational Mothering, National Immigration Policy and European Law: The Experience of the Netherlands', in S. Benhabib

and practices that generate discriminatory impacts. As a result the ability to sustain family unity or re-establish it after separation is fraught with difficulties despite universal acceptance of the right to respect for family life.

The challenges of state priorities

A challenge to the protection of migrant families arises from the fact that state policies and priorities relating to the family unity principle are, like so much else in the migration context, highly susceptible to political changes in national goals and the priorities related to immigration. A clear example of this phenomenon is the contemporary United States, a country where the celebration of family values and the centrality of family unity to core state missions has long been a fundamental national building block, at least in the post-civil-war era.[22] This pro-family approach has until recently also been a central feature of US immigration policy. 'Prioritizing family-based admissions above all other forms of immigration is a uniquely US phenomenon with deep roots in US immigration history'.[23] Some argue it has also been highly beneficial to US public and economic interests.[24] 'Immediate relatives', namely unmarried children under 21, spouses and parents of US citizens qualify for entry without any numerical restriction. Other relatives, including older unmarried children, spouses and unmarried children of lawful permanent residents, married children of US citizens and siblings of US citizens, can all qualify for 'family-sponsored' reunification, but they may be subject to long delays in effectuating that reunion, because of numerical limits that apply.[25] Nationals of countries with high family reunification demand, such as China, India, Mexico and the Philippines, have very long waiting periods. All sponsors seeking family reunification have to submit a legally enforceable affidavit of support, and prove they can support their relatives at an annual income of no less than 125 percent of the federal poverty level.[26]

The primacy of family-based immigration in the US is born out by the annual allocation of new settlement rights; since it first established quotas limiting immigrant admission in the 1920s, the US has awarded well over half the annual new permanent immigration visas to close family members of citizens and legal residents. In fiscal year 2017 (from April 2016 to March 2017), 66 percent of new permanent residents to the US got their status through family sponsorship compared to only 12 percent through employment-based eligibility.[27] Other countries with annual quotas for family reunification allocate a considerably lower portion of their migration entry to this category. In Australia, for example, 'family stream visas' constituted only 32 percent of the total migration allocation in 2014–2015.[28] This long-established bias in favour of family-based immigration was not only a reflection of the US's commitment to family unity. It was also the

and J. Resnick (eds), *Migrations and Mobilities: Citizenship, Borders and Gender*, New York: NYU Press, 2009, pp. 228–51.

22 Indeed the US's deference to the primacy of families and the importance of curbing state interference with parents' control over their children is a primary reason for the US's non-ratification of the UN Convention on the Rights of the Child. Every other country in the world has ratified this convention.

23 M. Chishti and J. Bolter, 'Merit-Based: Immigration: Trump Proposal Would Dramatically Revamp Immigrant Selection Criteria, but with Modest Effects on Numbers', *Migration Policy Institute*, May 30, 2019, 2. Available at www.migrationpolicy.org. [hereafter Chisti and Bolter]

24 K. Abrams, 'What Makes the Family Special?', *University of Chicago Law Review* 80, 2013, 7–28.

25 Immigration and Nationality Act 1952, as amended (hereafter INA).

26 INA §212(a)(4).

27 Ibid.

28 Law Library of Congress, Family Reunification laws in Selected Jurisdictions, 5.

product of America's long-standing efforts to ensure the predominantly European ethnicity of its immigrants. Because historic national-origin quotas determining the proportion of immigrants to the US (quotas that were only abolished in 1965) ensured the preponderance of West and North Europeans over others, family-based preferences continued for decades to guarantee the continuation of that racial majority among immigrants, as settled immigrants sponsored their family members. In 1960, the largest number of foreign-born nationals in the US were Italians, German and Canadians respectively.

But over time, though the family-based immigration preference continued, political and economic factors altered the racial and national composition of immigrants to the US. By 2017 the US's top three settled foreign-born nationalities were Mexican, Indian and Chinese respectively.[29] If the preference for family-based immigration once ensured a white majority among new settlers in the US, it no longer does. What is more, waiting times have increased enormously for some groups. Whereas the spouse and unmarried child under 21 of a US citizen can apply for entry as soon as their relationship is established, other relatives, including any relatives of lawful permanent residents, and non-immediate relatives of US citizens, are put on a waiting list. The waiting times depend on the sponsor's state (whether the sponsor is a citizen or resident) and on the family member's nationality. Married sons and daughters of US citizens from Mexico or the Philippines, for example, have to wait for 19 years before they can apply for their visas, Filipino brothers and sisters of US citizens have to wait for 23 years to apply. By contrast spouses and young unmarried children of permanent residents only have to wait for three years.[30]

Contemporary US policies

President Trump's government has proposed replacing a substantial proportion of family-based immigration visas with a new high skill employment-based immigration visa. While the spouses and minor children of US citizens and lawful permanent residents would still be eligible for family reunification, the much broader class of relatives that have qualified for family reunification for decades – siblings, parents, grown-up children, other dependent relatives, amounting to almost 40 percent of family-based settlement admissions to date – would, under the new government proposal, be disqualified from applying for a family visa. If enacted, this 'merit-based' immigration reform would reverse historic patterns of US immigration: the annual employment visa settlement quota would rise from 12 percent to 57 percent, and the family sponsorship quota would drop from 66 percent to 33 percent.[31] The most draconian effect of these policies would be on unskilled and low-skilled populations, those who up until now have been able to join already settled relatives in the US as siblings or parents. If enacted these policies will deny the right to lawful family reunification to millions of long-settled immigrants, many of them US citizens. They will also reduce the availability of a flexible and sought after labour force, and one that encourages the integration of already present family members, often by providing valuable unpaid care work within the household;[32] moreover these policies are likely to stimulate yet higher rates of irregular and unsafe migration, forcing

29 Ibid.

30 Scott Garfing, 'A Primer on Family Reunification /Chain Migration', *Georgetown Law*. Available at www.law.georgetown.edu/immigration-law-journal/online/a-primer-on-family-reunification-chain-migration/.

31 Chisti and Bolter, op. cit., n 22, p. 3.

32 Abrams, op. cit., n 23.

many, anxious to enjoy the right to family life, to rely on smugglers and treacherous migration routes.[33]

Family reunification is a primary preoccupation of many migrants. But, as noted previously, so is preventing family separation, particularly where vulnerable family members, such as young children, are concerned. The extreme challenges that can arise in asserting this fundamental private, family right in a public, migration law context have been laid bare by recent developments at the US's southern border. From the start of his presidency, Donald Trump has changed the prevailing official discourse on immigration, the first American head of state to cast immigration as a threat to national security and prosperity, rather than a cornerstone of American identity.[34] Border security, in particular at the south western frontier between the US and Mexico, has been a constant focus of the current administration, most memorably captured by the president's stereotyping of Mexicans as predatory criminals and by his insistence on the need for a continuous, unscalable wall across the approximately 2,000-mile-long border.[35] A central target of the government's border securitization efforts has been the family migration of destitute, distressed Central Americans fleeing extreme violence and lawlessness in their countries of origin.[36]

Whilst cross-border migration between Mexico and the US had long consisted primarily of young single men, overwhelmingly Mexican nationals, migrating for work, often in a cyclical or seasonal manner, recent years have witnessed a radical demographic shift in the composition of the migration.[37] Families, and in particular women and children, have constituted a growing proportion of the human flow, with nationals of the so-called Northern Triangle Countries (Guatemala, El Salvador and Honduras) exceeding Mexicans.[38] The precipitators of this distress migration are multiple – the enduring legacy of colonization, the US's huge demand for drugs, the spillover effects of America's deportation of Latino youth, including gang members, back to their countries of origin, state failure and corruption, and large scale rural to urban migration caused by climate change.[39] The impacts on local populations, particularly children and young people, have been extensive and extreme – very high rates of homicide, pervasive gang recruitment and violence, kidnappings, ransom, rape and other pervasive forms of sexual and gender-based violence.[40] The result has been an experience of overwhelming pressure to migrate as the only available survival and exit strategy. The US government describes this situation as 'a real crisis', even though historic levels of unauthorized migration at the southern border, including

33 Chisti and Bolter, op. cit., n 22, p. 6.

34 Sarah Pierce, *Immigration-Related Policy Changes in the First Two Years of the Trump Administration*, MPI, May 2019, p. 28.

35 M.D. Shea and J.H. Davis, 'Shoot Migrants' Legs, Build Alligator Moat: Behind Trump's Ideas for Border', *New York Times*, October 1, 2019. US Border Patrol, Monthly Apprehensions. Available at www.cbp.gov/sites/default/files/assets/documents/2019-Mar/bp-total-monthly-apps-sector-area-fy2018.pdf.

36 UNHCR, *Children on the Run: Unaccompanied Children leaving Central America and Mexico and the Need for International Protection*. Available at www.unhcr.org/56fc266f4.html.

37 'Under-Age and on the Move', *The Economist*, June 26, 2014. Available at www.nytimes.com/2019/03/05/us/crossing-the-border-statistics.html; www.migrationpolicy.org/research/trends-unaccompanied-child-and-family-migration-central-america (accessed 14 July 2019).

38 Women's Refugee Commission, *Betraying Family Values*, February 2017, 1.

39 For an interesting account focused on El Salvador, see S.B. Coutin, 'Roots of Juvenile Migration from El Salvador', in. J. Bhabha, J. Kanics and D. l Senovilla Hernandez (eds), *Research Handbook on Child Migration*, Cheltenham: Edward Elgar, 2018, pp. 113–26.

40 Kids in Need of Defence & Human Rights Center Fray Matías de Córdova, *Childhood Cut Short: Sexual and Gender-Based Violence against Central American Migrant and Refugee Children*, June 2017.

at the turn of the century, have exceeded recent arrival numbers.[41] Instead of allocating appropriate staffing resources, the U.S. government has initiated extreme anti-migrant measures at its southern border, measures explicitly designed to deter migration, including in particular family migration.

To curb migrant border crossing, the Trump administration announced a 'zero-tolerance' policy in May 2018, criminalizing all undocumented entry.[42] The policy instructed border officials to prosecute all migrants crossing the border without prior authorization, including people fleeing persecution, who under well-established international law, binding on the US, have a right to seek asylum irrespective of prior authorization or documentary confirmation of their claim.[43] The 'zero-tolerance' policy was implemented by border patrol officials, who arrested and detained all unauthorized adult entrants, charging them with the offence of unlawful entry. Large numbers of these entrants were accompanied by children, including in many cases by babies and toddlers. Because these minors could not, by virtue of long-established US law clearly articulated in a landmark Supreme Court case and ensuing settlement, known as 'the Flores settlement', be subject to the prolonged and harsh incarceration envisaged for their parents or guardians arrested on criminal charges relating to their unlawful entry, the children were peremptorily separated from their adult relatives, and handed over by the immigration enforcement authorities to welfare authorities charged with their care and protection.[44]

This 'family separation' policy was introduced on 7 May 2018, without preparation, and without the care and administrative coordination required to ensure basic human rights. Several thousand children, some estimate up to 4,000, including infants and toddlers, were forcibly removed from their parents or guardians and placed in ill-equipped shelter facilities, lacking in the most basic child welfare measures. Babies were handed over to be cared for by unrelated, separated migrant children as young as six or seven who happened to be detained with them; minimal hygiene, nutrition and medical protections were neglected; and basic administrative record keeping, essential to ensure reliable tracking of separated family members – guardians and children – did not take place. The result was one of the most egregious instances of willful official abuse and maltreatment of migrant families in recent history. Only after vigorous litigation and the bipartisan clamor of public outcry, after weeks of dogged insistence on the legality, propriety and necessity of the family separation policy, did the US government partly reverse its course. On 20 June 2018, six weeks after the policy was first instituted, the 'zero tolerance' policy was suspended, the separation of parents or legal guardians from their children at the border was halted, and measures – inefficient and painfully slow – to track and reunite separated children with their traumatized parents or guardians were instituted. The US government's Department of Health and Human Services, responsible for the care of the migrant children,

41 The 'real crisis at our border' argument is forcefully advanced in: Homeland Security Advisory Council, 'Final Emergency Interim Report: CBP Families and Child Care Panel', April 16, 2019, AILA Doc. No. 19041730.

42 Sarah Pierce, *Immigration-Related Policy Changes in the First Two Years of the Trump Administration*, Migration Policy Institute, May 2019, p. 2.

43 Memorandum from Jeff Sessions, Attorney General, to federal prosecutors along the Southwest border, *Zero-Tolerance for Offenses Under 8 U.S.C. § 1325 (a)*, April 6, 2018. Available at www.justice.gov/opa/press-release/file/1049751/download. Cited in Pierce (n 42), p. 11, footnote 65.

44 For an excellent and comprehensive account of the complex 35-year history of the Flores case, and its implications for migrant children's exercise of family reunification rights, see P. Schrag, *Baby Jails*, Oakland: University of California Press, 2020.

identified 2,737 children separated from their parents who were in its care in June 2018.[45] The Department's Inspector General reported in January 2019 'that "thousands" more children may have been separated'.[46] The fallout from the policy continues, with evidence of extreme trauma, including acute mental illness, widely documented.[47]

Though the indiscriminate separation of parents and legal guardians from accompanying children has been halted, the separation of thousands of migrant children, including very young children, from other members of their families (grandparents, older siblings and other relatives), so-called For-Cause separations, continues.[48] The conditions in which these separated children are held by the US authorities have attracted considerable public censure. As an eminent legal expert recently testified before the US House of Representatives Committee on Oversight and Reform:

> In June 2019, a small team of lawyers, a doctor, and I met with nearly 70 immigrant children detained … in Texas. … The children … were dirty and distressed, held for days and weeks without access to soap, showers, toothbrushes, clean clothing, adequate nutrition, or adequate sleep. Over the past year, at least seven children are known to have died in federal immigration custody or shortly after being released. These tragedies occurred after nearly a decade of no reported child deaths. Every day, children are ripped apart from their family members at our borders and detained without access to their loved ones. These separations leave young children isolated for days, weeks and months without their parents, grandparents, aunts, siblings and other familial adult caregivers.[49]

The lawyer's testimony to Congress included searing quotations from some of the children interviewed. A typical excerpt:

> I started taking care of [a five-year-old girl] … after they separated her from her father. I did not know either of them before that. She was very upset. The workers did nothing to try to comfort her. I tried to comfort her and she has been with me ever since. [This five-year-old girl] sleeps on a mat with me on the concrete floor. We spend all day every day in that room. There are no activities, only crying.
>
> *(female aged 15)*[50]

Though the most egregious of the US government's policies undermining the fundamental rights of migrant families, the family separation policy is not the only recent public law measure with a severely deleterious impact on family migration. Shortly after the family separation policy was halted, but with the same migration control and deterrent objective explicitly proffered by way of justification, the US government introduced the so-called Migrant Protection Protocols

45 US Dept of HHS Office of Inspector General, 'Separate Children Placed in Office of Refugee Resettlement Care' (issue brief, HHS, Washington DC, January 2019) cited in Pierce, Immigration-related Policy Changes in the First Two Years of the Trump Administration, p. 2 at n 7.

46 Pierce, op. cit., n 44, p. 2.

47 *Ms L v Immigration and Customs Enforcement*, 310 F. Supp. 3d 1133, 1149–50 (S.D. Cal. 2018).

48 Pierce, n 44, p. 2.

49 Elora Mukherjee, Columbia Law School, 'Regarding a Hearing on The Trump Administration's Child Separation Policy: Substantiated Allegations of Mistreatment', Washington, DC, July 12, 2019, p. 2. Available at https://oversight.house.gov/legislation/hearings/the-trump-administration-s-child-separation-policy-substantiated-allegations-of.

50 Ibid., p. 9.

(MPP) also known as the Remain in Mexico policy. Under this programme, a 'metering' or quota system severely limits the number of asylum applications that are processed by US officials at the border, intentionally generating huge processing backlogs and very long delays before an asylum application can even be lodged. While asylum-seeking families await their turn to formally apply, they are forced back across the US's southern border into a no-man's land on the Mexican side. As US asylum officials, protesting against the new protocols, put it in a recent court petition:

> The MPP, promulgated by the Trump Administration in January 2019, fundamentally changed our Nation's procedures for the processing of asylum applicants who enter the United States through our Nation's Southern Border with Mexico. Prior to the MPP, our country's processing of asylum applicants ensured that people fleeing persecution would not be ... returned to a territory where they may face persecution or threat of torture.[51]

Long known for its lawlessness, its infestation by drug cartels and criminal gangs, and its anarchic lack of state presence, this border area is the site willfully imposed by US authorities on thousands of vulnerable families seeking safety from analogous lawlessness and violence in their home countries.[52] Confirmed reports of shootings, kidnappings, ransoms and brutal sexual violence have not forced a revision of US practice at the border. Rather, this war of attrition exacts its heavy price on those trapped, resulting in reports of gang recruitment and of smuggler-assisted border crossings fraught with hazards at remote sites where border patrol detection is less effective. Far from protecting vulnerable children and their families from the hazards of smuggling and traumatic journeys, the exclusionary policies of the US government seem designed to exacerbate these severe risks. They also increase the proliferation of criminal activity at or near the US border, a development that has spillover effects for national security, for the safety of border communities, and for broader government priorities related to law enforcement, gun and drug policy, and public expenditure.

Another recently implemented policy belies the insistent claim that current US migration deterrent measures are designed to protect Central American children from hazardous migration journeys. To protect unaccompanied children from violence and exploitation en route to the US, the Obama administration had introduced a programme enabling central American children fleeing persecution to apply for refugee status in-country.[53] By helping at-risk children to secure refugee status before they embarked on the perilous journey north, the authorities had been contributing to a safer exit strategy for some, particularly vulnerable children. The Trump government has ended that programme.[54]

Other recent government policies also have noteworthy impacts on the lives of millions of migrant families in the US. With roughly 12 million settled undocumented migrants in the US, approximately 16 million mixed-status families (where some members are citizens or legal residents and others are undocumented) and at least six million US citizen children with an

51 Brief of Amicus Curiae Local 1924 in Support of Plaintiffs-Appellles' Answering Brief and Affirmance of the District Court's Decision, Case 19–15716,06/26/19. 9th Circuit. 2.

52 U.S. Department of State, Mexico 2018 Human Rights Report, March 13, 2019. Available at www.state.gov/wp-content/uploads/2019/03/MEXICO- 2018.pdf. cited in Brief of Amicus Curiae Local 1924 in Support of Plaintiffs-Appellles' Answering Brief and Affirmance of the District Court's Decision, Case 19–15716,06/26/19. 9th Circuit. 22.

53 Pierce, op. cit., n 44, p. 17.

54 Ibid.

undocumented parent, the urgency of providing long settled communities with a path to regularization of their status is evident.[55] The compelling claim to acknowledgement of the de facto social membership of residents, in the main young people with no memory of life outside the US or long settled tax-payers with no criminal record who have spent most of their lives with an irregular migration status, has moved previous US governments to devise amnesty-like policies. One policy in particular, addressed to young people brought to the US as young children, and known as DACA, the Deferred Action for Childhood Arrivals programme, implemented by President Obama, has enjoyed bipartisan support and substantial public uptake. It has so far enabled over 800,000 young people to obtain official recognition of their identity and their eligibility for enrolment as students or workers, and to escape the haunting nightmare of illegal status and deportability. This programme is now in jeopardy; young people becoming eligible under the established criteria can no longer enrol, and it is not clear how long those already enrolled have before their rights to extend their leave are curtailed.[56] A significant measure affording hundreds of thousands of young people and their families a measure of security in the enjoyment of their family life is now in severe jeopardy.

Other attacks on migrant families in the US are numerous: the curtailment of grounds for seeking asylum on the basis of prior domestic violence, a particular attack on migrant women seeking to escape from violence and, often to reunify with relatives in the US;[57] the proposed public charge regulation which would render families who have availed themselves of public services, including welfare benefits and some forms of health service, ineligible to sponsor relatives, a measure that has already had a chilling effect on migrant families uptake of health services;[58] a proposal to DNA test all family members including children attempting to cross the southern border to check the authenticity of claimed family relationships; the termination of a programme encouraging the release of pregnant women from custody; and finally, changed instructions to immigration judges hearing child migrant cases, removing 'the best interest of the child' or the need for a 'child appropriate' hearing environment from the prior guidance given.[59] These changes, both major and minor, constitute a dramatic alteration in the balance between state enforcement interests and family human rights protections in the current US administration of family migration.

Migration for family

Efforts to maintain or create family unity are one of the central preoccupations facing migrating families, a preoccupation that as already noted implicates multiple areas of law and practice, from border control policy to the exercise of discretion in executing deportation orders.

55 Migration Policy Institute: www.migrationpolicy.org/data/unauthorized-immigrant-population/state/US; Center for American Progress: www.americanprogress.org/issues/immigration/reports/2017/03/16/428335/keeping-families-together/; Migration Policy Institute: www.migrationpolicy.org/research/profile-us-children-unauthorized-immigrant-parents.

56 Pierce, op. cit., n 44, p. 31.

57 *Matter of A-B-*, 27 I&N Dec. 316 (Attorney General, March 5, 2018). Available at www.justice.gov/eoir/page/file/1040936/download. Cited in Pierce, op. cit., 19.

58 J. Batalova, M. Fix and M. Greenberg, *Chilling Effects: The Expected Public Charge Rule and Its Impact on Legal Immigrant Families' Public Benefits Use*, MPI June 2018. Kelly Whitener, *How the New Public Charge Rule Impacts Children in Immigrant communities*, Center for Children and Families, Georgetown University Health Policy Institute, August 2019.

59 Pierce, op. cit., n 44, p. 13.

Another central issue facing these families is the integration of family priorities, including financial well-being, political safety and educational opportunity with the migration choices that present themselves – migration for family rather than migration with or to join family. Across the globe, families navigate this integration with the goal of securing advantageous outcomes, for individual members or the family group as a whole. The factors at play implicate a range of relevant personal variables that affect the decisions made, including questions of age, gender and legal status. In practice the outcome is often a complex bargain, with winners and losers distributed across (sometimes unpredictable) vectors of power, authority and capability.

Migration for family has long been a central driver of the labour migration of millions of young single adults. Patterns of such labour migration differ radically over time and geography. South Asian mass labour migration is primarily characterized by the already discussed migration of young single males to the Middle East, typically for limited term contracts that, though renewable, are not convertible into permanent residence. By contrast, the migration of workers from South East Asia has been predominantly female, and has been spread over a much more diverse geography, spanning from East Asia and Australia through the Middle East to Europe and beyond. In the latter case, large numbers of women have chosen, or been selected by their families, to be the primary family breadwinner, often at the cost of enjoyment of family life for years, even decades. While most single male migrant workers return regularly, if infrequently, to their homes, many female migrant workers are encouraged by their families to migrate for the economic benefit of the family even if this entails marriage to unknown individuals abroad, or prolonged periods of absence.[60]

Distinctive patterns of family driven migration occur in particular areas: Afghanistan has, for decades, encouraged the out-migration of very large numbers of its boys, and young men, in part as a protective strategy to avoid enforced recruitment by belligerent forces (including the Taliban); many young Afghans, often eldest sons of large families (including families where the father has been killed or disappeared during the decades long conflict) are sent abroad for reasons of safety and also encouraged to support indigent families back home, even while still in transit or before a secure immigration status is secured.[61] By contrast, some regions in Nigeria have a long history of exporting young girls from certain districts, tied to a flourishing trafficking network that inducts young girls into forced prostitution in known sites across Europe, including Italy, the Netherlands and Eastern Europe.[62] In both cases, migration to support family needs and priorities often exposes the migrating individual to extreme risk and hardship, an exploitative and rights violating strategy rather than a protective one.

South East Asia is the site of long standing and very large-scale family-motivated international migration. Of particular note is the highly gendered nature of this mobility over the last two decades, with women from poor rural communities in Indonesia and the Philippines in particular constituting between 60 and 75 percent of their national migrating workforce. Different sorts of family pressures are at play as drivers of this sizeable flow of girls and young women away from their homes. Most central, perhaps, is the culture of migration that informs the expectations of young women from an early age. Generations of children have experienced the

60 Lan Anh Hoang, 'Young Women as Providers for Households of Origin'. Available at: https://findanexpert.unimelb.edu.au/scholarlywork/1420818-young-women-and-girls-as-providers-for-households-of-origin.

61 UNHCR, Profiling Study of Unaccompanied or Separated Afghan Children Arriving in Sweden in 2015.

62 S. Kara, *Sex Trafficking: Inside the Business of Modern Slavery*, New York: Columbia University Press, 2009, pp. 89–92.

absence of one or both of their parents throughout their childhood. Though available data are incomplete, wide-ranging estimates suggest that between two and nine million children in the Philippines have been left behind by migrating parents.[63] The impact of this enduring separation is complex and far from uniform.[64] Nevertheless, the substantial literature on the topic of 'left behind children' points to some widely confirmed trends, including that mothers send remittances more regularly and generously than fathers, and that the frequency of transnational family communications has increased substantially thanks to the widespread diffusion of information technology.[65]

The literature also highlights the great variability in child-related outcomes in migration-affected families. Maternal out migration tends to have a greater negative impact on left behind child mental health than paternal out migration; and in some, but not all, contexts left behind children drop out of school and associate with gangs or are recruited by traffickers at a higher rate than children of non-migrating parents.[66] On the other hand, in many communities with long-standing patterns of migration, families back home associate female migration with relative prosperity and well-being including enhanced educational opportunity and better employment prospects. In some cases, particularly where the mother overseas is successful, these intergenerationally transmitted migration advantages enable children to elect to 'stay behind', a different perspective to that of 'left behind children'. Some poor rural communities, in Myanmar and Vanuatu, for example, frown on female migration, denying young women keen to participate in overseas guest worker schemes the opportunity to do so. In other contexts, such as Cambodia, traditional familial opposition to female migration is giving way to new development and modernization-fueled family attitudes that strongly encourage female family members to migrate. As a result, Cambodia has witnessed a dramatic growth in female migration, with the number of Cambodian women employed in the garment and sex industries 'unimaginable' even ten years ago.[67] In many situations, the long-standing imperative to service the explicit dependency of both familial and national economic fortunes through one's overseas domestic labour generates a deep-seated migration-oriented culture, often transmitted directly from migrant mother to daughter.[68]

Overall, given the fluidity in migration movements across their communities, many stay or left behind children confront the negotiation of competing pressures – to service family obligations, to conform to social obligations, to fulfil their own personal aspirations. These diverse pressures do not always point in the same direction. Children who have benefited from generous and regular parental remittances can envisage more prosperous futures at home than their parents did. On the other hand, in some regions, family and state priorities have converged to create powerful psychological and social pressures to migrate. Even when young women are seeking personal self-advancement or an escape from oppressive gender norms in the family home, the

63 Cited in Theodora Lam, 'Young Women and Girls Left Behind: Causes and Consequences', in *IOM Supporting Brighter Futures*, 2019, p. 13, n 15. Available at https://publications.iom.int/books/supporting-brighter-futures-young-women-and-girls-and-labour-migration-south-east-asia-and.

64 Ibid., pp. 14–16.

65 H. Beazley, 'Intergenerational Cycles of Migrating for Work: Young Women and Girls Migrating for Work in South-East Asia and the Pacific', in IOM, n 62.

66 H. Beazley, L. Butt and J. Ball, 'Like It, Don't Like It, You Have to Like It': Children's Emotional Responses to the Absence of Transnational Migrant Parents in Lombok, Indonesia', *Children's Geographies*, 16(6), 591–603, DOI: 10.1080/14733285.2017.1407405.

67 Beazley, op. cit., n 64, p. 49.

68 R. Parreñas, 'Long Distance Intimacy: Class, Gender and Intergenerational Relations between Mothers and Children in Filipino Transnational Families', cited in Harriot Beazley, n 64, p. 49.

migration decision is generally embedded within and mediated by the household.[69] In the case of Indonesia, the government has systematically encouraged women from poor communities, celebrated as 'heroes of development', to travel abroad – to reduce domestic unemployment and increase foreign remittances to their families left at home in Indonesia.[70]

In practice, cultural norms vary across communities. In some rural areas, the oldest daughter is expected to migrate at a young age in order to remit funds to support the education of younger siblings. And indeed many of these migrating female workers are very young, frequently under 18. What is more, undocumented female labour migration, in particular to the Middle East, is extremely high – four times greater than official migration.[71] Facilitated by unauthorized agents, these young women are at high risk of exploitation and abuse, isolated from community support, often exposed to predatory male employers within the households in which they work. Cases of extreme rights violations are not infrequent.[72] In others, young girls are encouraged to become brides to men abroad. This is particularly the case in Vietnam, the source of the majority of marriage migrants in South East Asia. Just as migration in general is an economic strategy for families developed at a household rather than individual level, so marriage migration too is a product of collective decision making. And just as the labour migration of young Indonesian and Filipina female domestic workers is mediated by commercial agents, so too is the marriage migration of young Vietnamese girls, on a large scale (approximately 15,000 per year).[73] Here too very young girls can find themselves moved, at the behest of their families, to distant and unfamiliar environments, where their safety and well-being are placed at risk. Migration for family can thus become a migration that generates a new, alien and often exploitative family, but that also fuels transformations in the family of origin – with bride remittances the source of unprecedented income flows and revised gender preferences, daughters replacing sons as the most valued offspring.[74]

Conclusion

Family migration represents a multi-vector site, one in which changing cultural norms about relationships, gender, dependency and obligation intersect with fast moving developments relating to national political priorities, cross-border labour migration, trade, family formation and interpersonal communication. At this juncture of private needs and wishes on the one hand and public priorities and challenges on the other, millions of family members find themselves navigating complex choices, some of which generate outcomes that are life enhancing while others expose them to acute suffering, loss and deprivation. As with other aspects of migration, so too with family migration, border crossing per se is not a predictor of outcomes. The factors in which mobility is embedded determine whether borders end up uniting or dividing families, with all the momentous consequences that flow from that.

69 Ibid., p. 48.
70 Ibid.
71 Ibid., p. 46.
72 '"I Already Bought You" Abuse and Exploitation of Female Migrant Domestic Workers in the United Arab Emirates', *Human Rights Watch*, October 22, 2014. Available at www.hrw.org/report/2014/10/22/i-already-bought-you/abuse-and-exploitation-female-migrant-domestic-workers-united>.
73 Hoang, op. cit., n 59, p. 64.
74 Ibid.

INDEX